RAF Bomber Command Profiles

405 (Vancouver) Squadron RCAF

RAF Bomber Command Profiles

405 (Vancouver) Squadron RCAF

Chris Ward

www.aviationbooks.org

This edition first published 2024 by Aviation Books Ltd., 25 Cromwell Street, Merthyr Tydfil, CF47 8RY.

Copyright 2024 © Chris Ward.

The right of Chris Ward to be identified as Author of this work is asserted by him in accordance with the Copyright, Designs and Patents Act 1988.

The original Operational Record Book of 405 Squadron RCAF and the Bomber Command Night Raid Reports are Crown Copyright and stored in microfiche and digital format by the National Archives. Material is reproduced under Open Licence v. 3.0.

All rights reserved. No part of this publication may be reproduced, stored in a retrieval system, transmitted in any form or by any means, electronic, mechanical, or photocopied, recorded or otherwise, without the written permission of the copyright owners.

This squadron profile has been researched, compiled and written by its author, who has made every effort to ensure the accuracy of the information contained in it. The author will not be liable for any damages caused, or alleged to be caused, by any information contained in this book. E. & O.E.

Every effort is made to trace the copyright holders of photographs and we apologise in advance for any unintentional omissions. These and other errors brought to our attention will be corrected in subsequent editions of this Profile.

Cover design: Topics - The Creative Partnership www.topicsdesign.co.uk

Photos and captions: Clare Bennett

A CIP catalogue reference for this book is available from the British Library.

ISBN 9781915335388

Also by Chris Ward from Bomber Command Books:

Casualty of War: Letters Home from Flight Lieutenant Bill Astell DFC

Dambuster Deering: The Life and Death of an Unsung Hero

Dambusters : The Complete WWII History of 617 Squadron
(with Andy Lee and Andreas Wachtel)

Other RAF Bomber Command Profiles:

IX Squadron
10 Squadron (with Ian MacMillan)
35 (Madras Presidency) Squadron
44 (Rhodesia) Squadron
49 Squadron
50 Squadron
57 Squadron
75(NZ) Squadron (with Chris Newey)
83 Squadron
101 Squadron
102 (Ceylon) Squadron
103 Squadron (with David Fell)
106 Squadron (with Herman Bijlard)
115 Squadron
138 Squadron (with Piotr Hodyra)
207 Squadron (with Raymond Glynne-Owen)
300 Squadron (with Grzegorz Korcz)
301, 304 and 305 Squadrons (with Grzegorz Korcz)
408 (Goose) Squadron RCAF
455, 458, 462, 464 Squadrons RAAF
460 Squadron RAAF
467 Squadron RAAF
514 Squadron (with Simon Hepworth)
619 Squadron

Table of Contents

Introduction 9
Special Acknowledgements. 10
Narrative History 12
June 1941 14
July 1941 18
August 1941 24
September 1941 28
October 1941 32
November 1941 36
December 1941 39
January 1942 42
February 1942 46
March 1942 50
April 1942 54
May 1942 60
June 1942 64
July 1942 70
August 1942 75
September 1942 81
October 1942 88
November and December 1942 93
January 1943 118
February 1943 119
March 1943 123
April 1943 130
May 1943 137
June 1943 143
July 1943 150
August 1943 158
September 1943 168

October 1943	175
November 1943	181
December 1943	187
January 1944	230
February 1944	238
March 1944	243
April 1944	249
May 1944	256
June 1944	264
July 1944	272
August 1944	283
September 1944	295
October 1944	304
November 1944	312
December 1944	318
January 1945	326
February 1945	332
March 1945	340
April 1945	348
Roll of Honour	355
Stations	373
Commanding Officers	373
Aircraft	373
Operational Record	374
Aircraft Histories	376

Introduction

RAF Bomber Command Squadron Profiles first appeared in the late nineties and proved to be very popular with enthusiasts of RAF Bomber Command during the Second World War. They became a useful research tool, particularly for those whose family members had served and were no longer around. The original purpose was to provide a point of reference for all of the gallant men and women who had fought the war, either in the air, or on the ground in a support capacity, and for whom no written history of their unit or station existed. I wanted to provide them with something they could hold up, point to and say, "this was my unit, this is what I did in the war". Many veterans were reticent to talk about their time on bombers, partly because of modesty, but perhaps mostly because the majority of those with whom they came into contact had no notion of what it was to be a "Bomber Boy", to face the prospect of death every time they took to the air, whether during training or on operations. Only those who shared the experience really understood what it was to go to war in bombers, which is why reunions were so important. As they approached the end of their lives, many veterans began to speak openly for the first time about their life in wartime Bomber Command, and most were hurt by the callous treatment they received at the hands of successive governments with regard to the lack of recognition of their contribution to victory. It is sad that this recognition in the form of a national memorial and the granting of a campaign medal came too late for the majority. Now this inspirational, noble generation, the like of which will probably never grace this earth again, has all but departed from us, and the world will be a poorer place as a result.

RAF Bomber Command Squadron Profiles are back. The basic format remains, but, where needed, additional information has been provided. Squadron Profiles do not claim to be comprehensive histories, but rather detailed overviews of the activities of the squadron. There is insufficient space to mention as many names as one would like, but all aircraft losses are accompanied by the name of the pilot. Fundamentally, the narrative section is an account of Bomber Command's war from the perspective of the bomber group under which the individual squadron served, and the deeds of the squadron are interwoven into this story. Information has been drawn from official records, such as group, squadron and station ORBs, and from the many, like me, amateur enthusiasts, who dedicate much of their time to researching individual units and become unrivalled authorities on them. I am grateful for their generous contributions, and their names will appear in the appropriate Profiles. The statistics quoted in this series are taken from The Bomber Command War Diaries, that indispensable tome written by Martin Middlebrook and Chris Everitt, and I am indebted to Martin for his kind permission to use them.

Finally, let me apologise in advance for the inevitable errors, for no matter how hard I and other authors try to write "nothing but the truth", there is no such thing as a definitive account of history, and there will always be room for disagreement and debate. Official records are notoriously unreliable tools, and yet we have little choice but to put our faith in them. It is not my intention to misrepresent any person or RAF unit, and I ask my readers to understand the enormity of the task I have undertaken. It is relatively easy to become an authority on single units or even a bomber group, but I chose to write about them all, idiot that I am, which means 128 squadrons serving operationally in Bomber Command at some time between the 3rd of September 1939 and the 8th of May 1945. I am dealing with eight bomber groups, in which some 120,000 airmen served, and I am juggling around 28,000 aircraft serial numbers, code letters and details of provenance and fate. I ask not for your sympathy, it was, after all, my choice, but rather your understanding if you should find something with which you disagree. My thanks to you, my readers, for making the original series of RAF Bomber Command Squadron Profiles so popular, and I hope you receive this new incarnation equally enthusiastically.

My thanks also to Dave Birrell, a member of the trustees of the Bomber Command Museum of Canada for providing some photos, and as always to my gang members, Andreas Wachtel, Steve Smith, Greg Korcz and Clare Bennett, the last-mentioned my photo editor and caption writer, for their unstinting support, without which my Profiles would be the poorer. Finally, my appreciation to my publisher, Simon Hepworth of Aviation Books Ltd, formerly Mention The War Publications, for his belief in my work, untiring efforts to promote it, and for the stress I put him through to bring it to publication.

Special Acknowledgements.

In writing the original 405 (Vancouver) Squadron Profile in the year 2000, I was given a great deal of assistance, for which I wish to make particular mention. I was indebted to Lorna Hayes, the secretary of the British branch of the 405 (Vancouver) Squadron Association at the time, for not only providing me with information and photographs, but also for putting me in touch with others who could help my research. Lorna was a nineteen-year-old WAAF corporal when she began work in the officers' mess at Gransden Lodge in April 1943. She remembers many of the young men mentioned in these pages, whose lives briefly coincided with hers before ending in some foreign field, in the sea, or even on English soil. She recalls the night in December 1943, when so many fought their way to Berlin and back, only to die tragically at home as fog denied them a safe landing place. She heard aircraft crashing all around, seven of them belonging to 97 (Straits Settlement) Squadron at nearby Bourn and counts this as the worst night of her life. So many young men passed fleetingly through the station at Gransden Lodge, and so few remain today to honour their memory. The living also should be remembered, of course, and Lorna worked hard with others to bring former comrades together for reunions in England.

I was assisted greatly also by Glen Merrifield in Canada, who together with his brother, became a founder member of the squadron's ground staff on the 17th of May 1941. They remained with the squadron until returning to Canada in November 1944. Glen kindly sent me much very useful information, which was included in the original work. Finally, I am grateful to Doreen and Eric Blott, who lived at the time of writing in 2000 in the picturesque village of Great Gransden, which is adjacent to what is left of the wartime RAF station Gransden Lodge. They received me into their home with great kindness and hospitality and allowed me to pore through the copies of the squadron operations book held in the village. Afterwards we drove up to the airfield and stood by the now derelict control tower. On a sunny summer's afternoon in the year 2000, it was difficult to comprehend the tumult surrounding an operational bomber station more than fifty years in the past, but something indefinable remained in the air, and will do so for as long as eye-witnesses to these events remain and thereafter, whenever those who served are called to mind.

I enjoyed writing about 405 (Vancouver) Squadron in 2000 and am grateful to have the opportunity twenty-four years later to expand on the information and provide a more detailed account of this magnificent squadron's wartime history. I hope my modest work rekindles some happy memories among the relatives of those who have passed on and whose own story is part of the history, and most of all I hope they feel that I have done justice to the squadron, and to all those gallant young men who served it in the air and on the ground. We must not forget also the countless men and women who provided vital support as permanent residents on the stations occupied by 405 (Vancouver) Squadron, and by their dedication to the cause contributed to the success of Bomber Command's offensive.

Chris Ward. Skegness May 2024.

Narrative History

On the 31st of October 1939 negotiations began between representatives of the British and Canadian governments on the subject of the British Commonwealth Air Training Plan (BCATP). Both sides approached the talks with entirely different perceptions and goals, and this would lead to protracted discussions and acrimonious relations over the following three years. The "Canadianization" of Royal Canadian Air Force personnel serving with the Royal Air Force was enshrined in Article XV of the BCATP agreement, which originally called for the formation of twenty-five RCAF squadrons overseas. These were to be financed by Canada's contribution to the Plan, still known to this day in the UK as the Empire Air Training Scheme, which was agreed at $350 million. From the outset the talks were dogged by the questions of control of the RCAF contingent and finance, and the Canadian negotiators found themselves being constantly out-maneuvered by their British counterparts.

Canada envisaged an independent air force operating alongside the RAF, much as the American 8th Air Force would from 1942. Britain, however, saw Canada as a source of manpower and intended to integrate Canadian personnel into existing RAF Squadrons, or at least, to place the RCAF squadrons within RAF Groups. Canada expressed itself unwilling to finance RCAF personnel over whom it had no control, and after much wrangling, a compromise was eventually reached, which would allow all RCAF squadrons to operate from stations within close proximity to one-another, and under the same RAF Group. Once sufficient squadrons had been formed, a RCAF Group would come into existence. By the time that negotiations had reached this stage, it was already 1942, and only four RCAF squadrons had thus far been formed, all in 1941. In the event, outside influences caused the programme to be cut back, allowing for just seven new squadrons in 1942, making a total of eleven. However, the number was considered acceptable to constitute an effective Group, and this compromise became a cherished dream in itself, achieving realisation on the 1st of January 1943. This was the best that Canada could achieve, having been backed into a corner by its own negotiators, and thus the RAF acquired the manpower and the control, while Canada footed the bill.

Returning to 1941, the honour of becoming the very first RCAF bomber unit to be formed overseas under Article XV was about to be bestowed. To avoid confusion with other Dominion Air Force units, all Canadian squadrons were to be numbered within the 400-450 range, and thus 405 Squadron was born. It came into existence on the 4 Group station at Driffield on the 23rd of April 1941, under the temporary command of S/L Tomlinson DFC, although it appears, that he was not posted in until the 8th of May. The squadron was to operate the Merlin powered Mk II Wellington, and would, in fact, be only the second squadron in Bomber Command to be entirely equipped with the variant. The first was 104 Squadron, with which 405 Squadron would share Driffield during its brief residency, and which had itself been reformed only three weeks earlier. A few examples of the Mk II had by this time found their way into radial powered Wellington squadrons, where their superior lifting power enabled them to carry a 4,000lb high capacity "cookie" blockbuster into battle.

The first four aircraft, W5487, W5489, W5490 and W5491 were taken on squadron charge on the 6th of May, and within a month a further ten would be added. S/L Tomlinson undertook the squadron's very first flight on the 15th, with a round trip from base to Linton-on-Ouse and

Dishforth, and was accompanied by among others, F/O Wigham, the squadron gunnery leader. On the 20th W/C Gilchrist was posted in from 35 Squadron at Linton-on-Ouse, where he had been a flight commander, and was installed as 405 Squadron's first official commanding officer. 35 Squadron had been given the responsibility of introducing the new Halifax into operational service, and the then S/L Gilchrist, a Canadian serving in the RAF, had taken part in the type's very first operation, against le Havre on the night of the 10/11th of March. On return to England, his Halifax, a type still shrouded in secrecy, was intercepted by an RAF night-fighter and shot down to crash on the Surrey/Hampshire border. Only Gilchrist and one other were able to parachute to safety, and this was an experience he would have to repeat with 405 Squadron.

Over the succeeding three weeks he oversaw the training of the crews as they worked up to operational status, but even when this was achieved, the squadron's initial contribution to the offensive would be modest. It would also take time to build up a strong Canadian presence, and in the meantime, the squadron was a polyglot of nationalities, just like any other in the Command. The 27th saw the arrival of four more Wellingtons, to be followed twenty-four hours later by another four. The 28th was also the day on which S/L Bisset DFC was appointed A Flight commander, and S/L Keddy took over B Flight on the 30th. By the end of its first full month 405 Squadron boasted nine officers, 238 airmen and twelve aircraft, the last mentioned all grounded with a nacelle bearing weakness.

405 Squadron was born into a troubled time for Bomber Command, when frequently changing priorities were distracting it from its strategic bombing role. In March, following an Air Ministry directive, the main emphasis had shifted from attacks on industrial Germany to matters maritime in response to escalating losses of Allied shipping to U-Boots in the Atlantic. This required attacks on the ship-building yards at Kiel, Hamburg, Bremen and Vegesack, the Focke-Wulf aircraft factory at Bremen, where the long-range maritime Kondor reconnaissance/bomber aircraft was produced, and the French ports where U-Boots were based. An additional distraction was the arrival at Brest at the end of March of the German cruisers Scharnhorst and Gneisenau, and their continued presence, along with occasional visits by Prinz Eugen, would result in an eleven-month long campaign against the port and its lodgers.

The performance of the Command was also about to come under scrutiny as powerful voices, particularly in the Admiralty, questioned the need for an independent bomber force, when its aircraft might more effectively be employed by Coastal Command, or to redress reversals in the Middle East. Changing priorities, poor equipment and a lack of bombing and navigation aids placed the C-in-C Bomber Command in a difficult position, and he, Air Marshal Sir Richard Peirse, would ultimately become the scapegoat for a year of disappointing results. In order to provide an assessment of the Command's effectiveness for the War Cabinet, a project was initiated by Churchill's chief scientific advisor, Lord Cherwell, who handed the responsibility to David M Bensusan-Butt, a civil-servant assistant to Cherwell working in the War Cabinet Secretariat. The extent of the Command's failure to date would only be fully appreciated with the publication of this report in August. The grist for his mill was to be provided by bombing photographs taken during night raids over Germany in June and July, and 405 Squadron would become operational in time to participate.

June 1941

Although still under the maritime directive until July, the new month would be dominated by operations against Cologne, Düsseldorf and Bremen, with Kiel and Brest also receiving their share of attention. During the second half of the month Cologne and Düsseldorf would be attacked simultaneously on no fewer than eight nights by forces of varying sizes, and Bremen, including the shipbuilding yards to the north-west at Vegesack, would host six raids. On the 1st, the Hipper Class cruiser Prinz Eugen, which had been acting as consort to Bismarck, arrived at Brest having evaded detection by the Royal Navy following the sinking of the battleship. She would now join Scharnhorst and Gneisenau to form a potential powerful battle group that would continue to be a distraction for Bomber Command for a further eight months.

Düsseldorf was the primary target for 150 aircraft on the night of the 2/3rd, for which 4 Group put up thirty-nine Whitleys from Dishforth, Driffield, Leeming and Linton-on-Ouse. Cloudy conditions ensured a scattered raid by the 107 crews who reported bombing as briefed, but their efforts produced only light damage. Before 405 Squadron undertook its first operation, it suffered its first casualty, when W5487 was destroyed on the ground in a Luftwaffe air-raid on Driffield on the 4th. Small-scale operations held sway for the ensuing week, and it was the 10th before twenty-seven Whitleys from 77 and 102 Squadron headed for the runway prior to taking off for Brest and another shot at its three guests in company with Hampdens and Wellingtons. They negotiated the Channel crossing and flight across the Brest peninsula to reach the target under clear skies to find that a smoke generator had been activated on the sound of the approaching one hundred bombers, and this was effective in screening the target vessels from the eyes of the bomb-aimers, who could only aim at the general area of the docks.

After two months on the side-lines following the grounding of the Halifax, 35 Squadron returned to operations with nine aircraft on the 11th to target Duisburg in company with seventy-one other aircraft including thirty-six Whitleys from Dishforth, Linton-on-Ouse and Middleton-St-George, the last-mentioned now home to the Halifaxes of 76 Squadron. A simultaneous operation by ninety-two Wellingtons and six Stirlings was directed at Düsseldorf, fifteen miles to the south, but no report was forthcoming from either of the main targets, while sources in Cologne, which frequently found itself used as an alternative target, reported damage to 173 houses, the main railway station and dockland buildings.

Pre-empting the new directive a month hence, the night of the 12/13th was devoted largely to attacks on four railway yards on the periphery of the Ruhr, and this was the occasion chosen for the maiden operation not only of 405 Squadron's, but also of the RCAF. A 4 Group force of eighty Whitleys and four 405 Squadron Wellingtons was assigned to the yards at Schwerte, situated at the eastern end of the Ruhr, south-east of Dortmund, for which twelve crews were assigned to fire-raising duties ahead of the main element. At the same time, 5 Group would be attacking yards at Soest, to the north of the one-day-to-be-famous Möhne reservoir, while forces of eighty-two 3 Group and sixty-one 1 Group Wellingtons attended to similar objectives at Hamm and Osnabrück respectively, also north of the Ruhr. Eleven Halifaxes of 35 and 76 Squadrons and seven 3 Group Stirlings, meanwhile, would be attempting to hit the "Buna" synthetic rubber works at Marl-Hüls some ten miles north of Gelsenkirchen.

The crews of Sgts Craig, Dodds and Turner and P/O Fraas departed Driffield between 23.16 and 23.45 each sitting on a 1,000 pounder and four 500 pounders, and after climbing out adopted the now-familiar route across the North Sea and the Frisian Island of Texel before heading south-east across the Ijsselmeer to enter Germany somewhere near the Rhine frontier town of Emmerich. The Turner crew experienced port engine trouble and jettisoned their bombs over Holland, leaving the others to press on and encounter some high cloud and thick industrial haze in the target area, where they delivered their attacks from 7,500 to 10,000 feet between 01.30 and 01.45. A post-raid analysis confirmed that fewer than half of the force had attacked the primary target at a cost of three Whitleys, and it was a similar story at Soest and Hamm, while the local report from Osnabrück described a "lively" attack.

The main operation on the 13th was directed at Brest and its resident warships, for which a force of 110 aircraft was drawn from 1, 3 and 5 Groups, while 4 Group detailed thirty-six Whitleys and six Wellingtons for a return to the railway yards at Schwerte. 405 Squadron was not involved and remained off the order of battle on the night of the 15/16th, when the first of the simultaneous attacks on Cologne and Düsseldorf took place. The latter was directed specifically at the Derendorf marshalling yards and involved thirty-one Whitleys from Topcliffe and Linton-on-Ouse. Ten-tenths cloud persisted all the way to the target area and reduced crews to bombing the approximate area of Düsseldorf, guided by evidence of searchlights and flak.

4 Group detailed a force of thirty-nine Whitleys, sixteen Wellingtons and three Halifaxes for another tilt at Cologne on the 16th, while elements of 1 and 3 Groups were hosted by Düsseldorf. 405 Squadron made ready seven Wellingtons while the crews were briefed to aim for the main railway station located in the shadow of the huge cathedral to the west of the Hohenzollern railway bridge over the Rhine. After one sortie was scrubbed, six Wellingtons departed Driffield between 22.54 and 23.04 with S/L Bisset the senior pilot on duty and bomb loads for four of three 500 pounders, one of 250lbs and six small bomb containers (SBCs) of incendiaries, while two carried a 1,000 pounder, four 500 pounders and two SBCs. They flew out over Orfordness and made landfall on the Belgian coast at Zeebrugge, before bypassing Brussels on their way to the Rhineland capital, where partial cloud cover and industrial haze at both targets led to scattered bombing. The 405 Squadron participants attacked from 1,200 to 10,000 feet between 01.35 and 02.07, the low altitude that of Sgt Farnborough and crew, who were homebound over Overflakkee east of the Ijsselmeer when attacked by a BF110 at 12,000 feet at 02.53. Both engines sustained damage and there were bullet holes in the mainplane, fuselage, rudder, fin and rear turret. W5537 was nursed back across the North Sea to a forced-landing at West Raynham, from which the crew emerged unscathed. They were more fortunate than the crew of Sgt MacGregor in W5522, which was last heard from on W/T in the area of Overflakkee at 03.03 and failed to arrive back with the others to become the first from the squadron to be posted missing from operations. An alaysis of the raid suggested that no damage of significance had occurred.

A raid involving one hundred aircraft was directed at Bremen on the 18th, to which 4 Group contributed twenty-five Whitleys and fifteen Mk II Wellingtons. Low cloud hindered the bombing, and the results were inconclusive and probably disappointing. Small-scale operations against Cologne and Düsseldorf were posted on the 19th, the latter an all-4 Group affair calling upon the services of twenty Whitleys from Topcliffe and Dishforth, whose crews had been briefed to aim for the main railway station. They arrived in the target area to encounter thick haze and moderate heavy flak, through which they bombed from around 8,000 to 12,000 feet and reported a large fire developing behind them as they headed home.

On the 20th the Squadron moved to Pocklington, a new station located some twelve miles east-south-east of York, which had opened as recently as April under the command of G/C Sid Bufton. This former commanding officer of 10 Squadron had been promoted to the post after overseeing the formation of 76 Squadron as the Command's second Halifax unit. That night, a force of 115 aircraft was assembled to send to Kiel in search of the battleship Tirpitz, to which 4 Group contributed twenty Whitleys and eleven Halifaxes from Linton-on-Ouse and Middleton-St-George. Ten-tenths cloud lay across the entire Schleswig-Holstein peninsula with tops at 5,000 feet in the target area, which prevented anything but an area attack from taking place on largely estimated positions.

The Topcliffe and Leeming squadrons were alerted to a return to Düsseldorf on the 21st and learned at briefing that they would be part of a force of twenty-eight Whitleys in company with a similar number of 5 Group Hampdens. They flew out via corridor G to make landfall over the Scheldt estuary, and on arrival in the target area, encountered five to seven-tenths cloud with tops at 5,000 feet and thick haze beneath, which prevented them from identifying any ground features and compelled them to bomb on e.t.a., in the general vicinity of the city. Some observed bursts, while others reported the splash of incendiaries, but it was yet another indeterminate and unsatisfactory raid.

405 Squadron now had sixteen Wellingtons on charge, only half of which were fit for operations along with eight crews, and as the only residents of Pocklington for the time being, the squadron had the honour of launching the station's first offensive foray late on the evening of the 22nd. The target was the naval and shipbuilding port of Wilhelmshaven, situated on the north-western corner of Jade Bay, where the Kriegsmarinewerft had given birth to the pocket battleships Admiral Scheer and Graf Spee, the heavy cruiser Scharnhorst and the battleship Tirpitz along with twenty-seven Type VII U-Boots. W5476 was first away at 23.05 with Sgt Richard at the controls, and it was followed by six others between 23.07 and 23.27, after technical problems grounded a seventh. S/L Keddy was the senior pilot on duty and each Wellington had a bomb load on board of a 1,000 pounder, four and two respectively of 500 and 250lbs and two small bomb containers (SBCs) as they flew out over Whitby heading for a point ten miles north-east of Heligoland, before turning to the south for the run on the target. Sgt McDougal and crew were sixty miles out over the North Sea when the fuel feed to an engine caused a loss of power and persuaded them to turn back, and they were joined on the ground soon afterwards by S/L Keddy and crew, whose intercom had failed. Sgt Thrower's W5521 was hit by shrapnel from a shell fired from a convoy and as the port engine failed the bombs were jettisoned south of Heligoland in order to maintain height. The Wellington sustained further damage from machine-gun fire from a friendly convoy off the Tyne and landed first at Acklington before returning to Pocklington later in the morning. This left just four 405 Squadron crews to deliver an attack from 7,500 to 13,000 feet between 01.40 and 02.10 and like the other twenty-five participating crews failed to land a bomb within four kilometres of the town.

Eighteen Whitleys fared little better when they joined forces with Wellingtons from other groups to hit a special target in Cologne on the following night, while 5 Group was active over Düsseldorf.

Topcliffe was called into action on the 24th to provide twenty-one of thirty-two Whitleys to attack the main railway station in Cologne, while Leeming added a further eleven. Thick haze and five-tenths cloud at 6,000 feet over the sea gave way to a violent thunderstorm at the Belgian coast, while at the target crews found little cloud but thick ground haze and bombed on estimated positions, some observing bursts that could not be plotted and a few developing fires. Local sources reported that only five bombs had hit the city and damaged five houses.

Orders were received at Pocklington and Driffield on the 25th for the two resident squadrons to prepare seventeen Wellingtons between them for an operation against Kiel, where the Germania Werft and Deutsche Werke shipyards were producing U-Boots. They would be sharing the target with thirty Hampdens of 5 Group but almost certainly not scheduled to attack at the same time. Eight 405 Squadron aircraft each received a bomb load of one 1,000-pounder, one 500-pounder, two 250-pounders and two SBCs, before taking off between 22.25 and 22.37 with P/Os Bainbridge and Fraas the senior pilots on duty and flew out over Robin Hood's Bay on course for Rømø Island off Jutland's western coast. Sgt Thrower and crew were thwarted by engine trouble and were back on the ground within two hours, leaving the others to press on over the North Sea, P/O Bainbridge and crew contending with the loss of the port fuel pump, which ultimately prevented them from reaching the target. Crew members had to pump for four hours to keep the fuel flowing and they eventually arrived home only a short time ahead of the others to report that they had bombed Tönning on the Schleswig-Holstein coast from 11,000 feet at 01.00. They were not the only crew to attack an alternative target, as Sgt Craig and crew were unable to locate Kiel through the haze and bombed a flak concentration near Rendsburg, twenty miles short of the primary target, from 9,500 feet at 01.15. Flying with this crew as an observer was a W/C Weir of 6 Group, which at the time was devoted to training and should not be confused with the Canadian 6 Group that would be formed eighteen months hence. The others carried out their attacks from 12,000 to 14,000 feet between 01.00 and 01.40 and had little to report at debriefing, while local sources reported light damage and one fatality.

405 Squadron would take no part in the month's remaining operations and sat out a raid by seventy-three Wellingtons and thirty-five Whitleys on Bremen on the night of the 27/28th, while a force of Hampdens also visited the city to attack the shipbuilding yards at Vegesack further downstream of the Weser. Thirty-eight Whitleys were detailed from Topcliffe, Leeming and Linton-on-Ouse and those reaching the target encountered three to ten-tenths low cloud that prevented them from locating the aiming-point, most simply picking up the River Weser and making timed runs into the heart of the intense and accurate flak that was co-operating with cones of searchlights. It became a disaster for the Whitley element, which lost eleven of its number and there were seven empty dispersal pans at Topcliffe on the following morning that should have been occupied by 77 and 102 squadron aircraft. One of the 77 Squadron Whitleys had ditched a hundred miles off the Yorkshire coast and the crew was eventually rescued, although sadly, not before the pilot had died.

The loss of fourteen aircraft in one night was a new record for the Command, and it is likely, that the Luftwaffe night-fighters were largely responsible. The disproportionately high losses among the Whitley brigade, 31% of those taking part, was a concern, and perhaps pointed to the increasing vulnerability of the type compared with its contemporaries. However, as events were to prove, sporadic losses now belonged to the past as the enemy defences became more organized and adept in the face of greater Bomber Command activity. A steady rate of attrition would afflict all front-line squadrons from now on, and multiple losses from a single operation would become a regular feature.

Linton-on-Ouse and Middleton-St-George took the strain in a return to Bremen on the 29th while Topcliffe and Leeming licked their wounds. The 4 Group ORB frequently referred to "special" targets without providing detail, and the one mentioned for attention in Duisburg on the last night of the month was referred to in the 102 Squadron ORB as an armaments factory. Low cloud and haze over the target completely blotted out all ground features, and it was the searchlight and flak concentrations that confirmed the location of the target area on e.t.a. A number of bomb bursts were observed, but no detail could be gleaned, and it was yet another inconclusive and probably ineffective raid.

During its first month of operations, 405 Squadron took part in four and dispatched twenty-five sorties for the loss of a single Wellington and crew.

July 1941

The main focus of operations during July would be upon manufacturing centres in the Ruhr, including Cologne, and at other locations in the Münsterland between the Ruhr and north-western Germany. The major cities of Bremen, Hamburg and Hannover would continue to attract attention, and it would not be until the final third of the month that targets in southern Germany, principally, Frankfurt and Mannheim, found themselves in the bomb sights of moderately sized forces. An all-4 Group force of thirty-three Whitleys and nine Wellingtons launched the new month's account at Cologne on the 2nd, 405 Squadron contributing nine Wellingtons, each of which received a bomb load of a 1,000-pounder, four 500 and two 250-pounders and two SBCs before departing Pocklington between 23.03 and 23.14 with S/L Keddy the senior pilot on duty. Sgt Gibson and crew turned back after ten minutes when their W/T failed, leaving the others to set course for the Scheldt estuary and traverse Belgium via Liege to enter Germany south of Aachen. A starboard engine issue persuaded Sgt Farnborough and crew to abandon their sortie and jettison their bombs near Eupen, a few miles short of the German frontier, while Sgt Turner and crew bombed what they believed to be Koblenz, located well to the south of their intended destination, from 12,000 feet. The others delivered their attacks through seven-tenths cloud and haze from 6,000 to 11,000 feet between 01.42 and 02.02, contributing to another underwhelming performance that landed only twenty bombs within the city.

The briefing of twenty-nine Whitley crews at Topcliffe and Leeming on the 3rd revealed that the Krupp complex in Essen and its dedicated marshalling yards were to be the night's target for an overall force of ninety aircraft. The Krupp organisation had been the largest manufacturer of weapons in Europe since before the Great War, had a hand in all aspects of German war production from tanks to artillery and ship and U-Boot construction, and was given a controlling share in all major heavy engineering companies in Germany and the occupied countries. It also built manufacturing sites in other parts of Germany, many situated close to concentration camps, and employed vast numbers of forced workers in all of its factories. Once known as "Die Waffenschmiede des Reichs", the weapons-forge of the realm, its manufacturing sites in Essen included the Friedrich Krupp steelworks, the Friedrich Krupp locomotive and general engineering works, the Altenberg zinc works, the Presswerk plastics factory, the Goldschmidt non-ferrous metals smelting plant, six coal mines and ten coke-oven plants, all situated either within or close to the four Borbeck districts, in a segment radiating out from near the city centre to the Rhine-Herne Canal on the north-western boundary on the banks of the Emscher River. The steel and engineering works alone employed in the region of eighty thousand people, and the company's sites covered an area of more than two thousand acres, of which three hundred acres were occupied by factories and workshops. All of that required massive rail and canal access in the form of marshalling yards and its own harbour, and energy from at least four nearby power stations.

The force arrived over the central Ruhr under clear skies to encounter the ever-present curse of impenetrable industrial haze, which forced them to carry out their attacks on e.t.a., and most crews observed bursts and fires but no detail, while local sources reported a light raid, and other Ruhr locations from Duisburg in the west to Dortmund in the east and Wuppertal in the south also recorded bombs falling.

Brest, or more accurately, the cruisers Scharnhorst, Gneisenau and Prinz Eugen were posted as the targets on the 4th and a force of sixty-five Wellingtons and twenty-three Whitleys made ready, nine of the former provided by 405 Squadron. Each was loaded with five 500lb armour-piercing (AP) bombs and six 250lb semi-armour-piercing (SAP), while the crews were briefed to attack a "Hipper" class vessel, which identified it as Prinz Eugen, rather than the two "Scharnhorst" class heavy cruisers. The latter had been dubbed in the British press as Salmon & Gluckstein, in a comic play on the vessels' initials and in reference to the country's largest tobacconist, established in 1873 by a German Jewish émigré and his English partner. They departed Pocklington between 22.37 and 22.56 with S/L Keddy the senior pilot on duty and all reached the target area to find good visibility in which they identified Dock 8 and attacked it from an average of 11,000 feet between 01.20 and 02.04. At debriefing crews claimed to have straddled the dock and the warship with their bombs, and although they were unable to confirm a direct hit, a message of congratulations was received at Pocklington from the 4 Group A-O-C.

On the night of the 5/6th, twenty-nine Whitleys from Leeming, Linton-on-Ouse and Middleton-St-George attacked the garrison city of Münster in the flat agricultural lands north of the Ruhr, while Halifaxes targeted the Braunkohle A G hydrogenation plant, located in the Rothensee district to the north of Magdeburg city centre. Crews returning from Münster reported the town to be in flames, but nothing emerged from local sources to provide details of damage.

Thirty-one Whitleys from Topcliffe and Dishforth and fifteen Wellingtons from Driffield and Pocklington were made ready on the 6th for an all-4 Group operation against a "special" target at Dortmund at the eastern end of the Ruhr, which the 102 Squadron ORB identified as the railway station. The nine 405 Squadron Wellingtons each received a bomb load of a single 1,000-pounder, four of 500lbs and two SBCs before taking off between 22.37 and 22.57 with S/L Keddy the senior pilot on duty. Taking off among them with a similar payload was the crew of P/O Kipp, who were bound for Rotterdam to attack oil storage tanks, a frequent target for freshman crews. The crews of Sgts Farnborough and Scott had to contend with navigational issues and attacked alternative targets at Düsseldorf in the southern Ruhr and Wesel, some thirty-five miles to the north. The others arrived at their destination to find clear skies with industrial haze concealing ground features and carried out their attacks from 10,000 to 12,000 feet between 01.04 and 01.26, some observing bursts between the aiming point and the Rhine docks. W5490 arrived back in the circuit with one dead engine and the other one burst into flames on final approach, causing the Wellington to crash near the airfield, killing the rear gunner, F/Sgt Luckhurst, and severely injuring the other occupants including the pilot, F/O Fraas, who lost his fight for life two days later.

Cologne, and the cities of Münster and Osnabrück were the principal targets posted for attention on the 7th, with the marshalling yards at the last-mentioned assigned to fifty-four Whitleys and eighteen Wellingtons of 4 Group. Located some thirty miles to the north-east of the recently targeted Münster, Osnabrück contained war-production factories in the automotive, steel and paper industries and was a transport hub linking the Ruhr and the northern cities. Nine 405 Squadron Wellingtons each received the same bomb load as for the previous operation and departed Pocklington between 22.40 and 22.58 with W/C Gilchrist leading his men into battle for the first time. The crews of Sgts Gibson and Dodds returned after forty-five and seventy minutes respectively with engine and rear turret failure, while the others pressed on and arrived in the target area to be greeted by near perfect conditions, which they exploited from between 6,000 and 12,000 feet between 01.25 and 01.35, observing many bursts and fires in and around the marshalling yards and in the town. Some returning crews reported that the glow was visible from up to seventy miles away, while local sources mentioned only bombs falling in the south-western suburbs and damaging three buildings.

On the following night, Leeming, Linton-on-Ouse and Middleton-St-George provided twenty-eight Whitleys to attack the marshalling yards at Hamm in company with forty-five Hampdens from 5 Group. Conditions in the target area were favourable, yet only thirty-one returning crews claimed to have attacked the primary target, observing bursts across the yards and the town and reporting fires developing as they withdrew.

A new Air Ministry directive issued on the 9th signalled an end to the maritime diversion, which had been in force since March. It was now assessed that the enemy's transportation system and the morale of its civilian population represented the weakest points, and that Peirse should direct his main effort in these directions. A new list of targets was drawn up, which included all of the main railway centres ringing the industrial Ruhr, the destruction of which would inhibit the import of raw materials and the export of finished products. Railways were relatively precise targets, and were to be attacked during the moon period, while, on moonless nights, the Rhine cities of Cologne, Düsseldorf and Duisburg would be easier to locate for "area" attacks. During periods of less favourable weather conditions, Peirse was to launch operations against more distant objectives in northern, eastern and southern Germany, while still making the occasional concession to the U-Boot campaign and continuing to divert a proportion of the Command's resources to the ongoing situation of the enemy "fleet in being" at Brest.

Aachen, Germany's most westerly city, was posted to host its first major visitation from Bomber Command on the 9th, and the naming of the post office as the aiming point was an indication that this was an assault on the city centre at a time when it was not admitted publicly that population centres were being bombed. A force of eighty-two aircraft included twenty-seven Whitleys and sixteen Wellingtons representing 4 Group, seven of the latter provided by 405 Squadron. They departed Pocklington between 22.56 and 23.03 with P/O Kipp the only commissioned pilot on duty and each crew sitting on the standard bomb load, and all but one made it to the target area, where conditions were favourable and searchlight and flak defences negligible. The squadron scribe did not record the bombing heights and times, but other squadrons bombed from between 8,000 and 13,000 feet and produced widespread destruction, particularly in central districts, where 1,700 dwelling units were destroyed or seriously damaged, de-housing some 3,450 people. Nineteen commercial premises were destroyed and a further seventy damaged, while public buildings were also hit and sixty people killed. One 405 Squadron crew described the target as "one mass of fire", while Sgt Chandos and crew admitted to a navigational error, which resulted in them attacking Cologne in the face of intense searchlight and flak activity. Most were diverted on return because of fog, and all had returned to Pocklington by 16.30 on the following afternoon.

While the other groups took the war to Germany over the ensuing four nights, 4 Group remained inactive and it was the 14th when the teleprinters burst into life to convey the details of that night's operations to Topcliffe, Driffield, Linton-on-Ouse, Middleton-St-George and Pocklington. Nineteen Whitleys from 102 and 77 Squadrons were to join forces with seventy-eight Wellingtons from 1 and 3 Groups to target between them three aiming points in Bremen, the shipyards, the goods station and the Altstadt, while fourteen Halifaxes and twenty Wellingtons from the group went for the Continental Gummiwerke (rubber/tyre works) in Hannover in company with forty-four 5 Group Hampdens and six Stirlings from 3 Group. The eight 405 Squadron Wellingtons each received a bomb load of three 500 and three 250-pounders and six SBCs of 4lb incendiaries and departed Pocklington between 22.30 and 22.43 with P/O Kipp again the senior pilot on duty. They were followed into the air at 22.50 and 22.58 by the freshman crews of P/O Trueman and Sgt Wahlroth, who were bound for Rotterdam to attack the oil storage tanks in the city's docks area. Sgt Chandos and crew aborted their sortie when approaching the Dutch coast after failing to fix a problem with the rear turret, and they returned their bombs to the dump. The others pressed on to find visibility at the target enhanced by illuminator flares, in the light of which streets and buildings stood out, but not the target factory. Bombing was carried out from 10,000 to 15,000 feet between 01.25 and 01.50 and several fires were observed, particularly south of the railway, and an explosion was witnessed on a section of track from a junction to the east of the city. W5534 failed to return with the crew of Sgt Thrower, and news was received eventually via the Red Cross to confirm that all had survived and were in enemy hands. Gunner, Sgt Kirk RCAF, was the first member of the RCAF from a Canadian squadron to be taken into captivity. While the above was in progress, the freshman crews had successfully attacked the oil storage tanks from around 10,000 feet at 01.35 after making a visual identification.

The first large-scale raid of the war on Frankfurt was posted at Pocklington and Driffield on the 21st, when 104 and 405 Squadrons made ready nineteen Wellingtons between them, the eight belonging to 405 Squadron each receiving a bomb load of three 500 and three 250-pounders and six SBCs of incendiaries. The briefing had revealed that they were part of an overall force of thirty-seven Wellingtons and thirty-four Hampdens, which, in keeping with standard practice at the time, would not necessarily be over the target at the same time. The 405 Squadron element took off between 22.53 and 23.16 with S/L Keddy the senior pilot on duty and lost the services of Sgt Gibson and crew to engine trouble and Sgt Dougall and crew to W/T failure, the latter bombing a searchlight concentration at Ostend before turning back. Those reaching the target delivered their attacks from 10,500 to 15,000 feet between 01.41 and 02.11, and on return reported a successful operation in which they believed the railway station and other parts of the city had sustained damage. In fact, according to local sources, few bombs had found the mark and nearby Darmstadt received more than the intended target. Sgt Wahlroth encountered two enemy night-fighters with yellow spotlights in their noses, but the engagement ended with no damage inflicted or sustained. While the above was in progress, eight Halifaxes from 35 and 76 Squadrons were active forty-five miles to the south over Mannheim.

On the 23rd, thirty Whitleys were sent to attack the dry dock at La Pallice, the deep-water port located west of La Rochelle on the Biscay coast between St-Nazaire to the north and Bordeaux to the south. It was home to the 3rd U-Boot Flotilla that was feeding wolfpacks into the Atlantic to savage Allied convoys bringing vital supplies to Britain. However, the objective for this operation was the cruiser Scharnhorst, which had slipped away from Brest unnoticed and was feared to be about to break out into the Atlantic for a campaign of surface raiding. Curiously, the 10 Squadron record described intense searchlight activity, both from the mainland and from the Ile-de-Re on the western approaches to the port, and this was accompanied by moderate flak. In contrast, the 102 Squadron ORB reported clear skies, extreme darkness and very little response from the ground as if to avoid giving away the port's location.

The above operation was actually an unanticipated prelude to Operation Sunrise, a most complex plan that had been developed during the preceding week to target Scharnhorst and Gneisenau at Brest in daylight on the 24th, but the discovery that Scharnhorst had slipped away and was now at berth at La Pallice, some two hundred miles further south, demanded a last-minute alteration. It was decided to send the fifteen-strong 4 Group Halifax element to attend to her, while the original plan went ahead at Brest. This called for 2 Group Blenheims to create a diversion at Cherbourg, and for three Fortress 1s of 2 Group's 90 Squadron to open proceedings at 30,000 feet over Brest to draw up the enemy fighters, while eighteen 5 Group Hampdens acted as further bait at a lower altitude under the umbrella of a Spitfire escort, somewhat in the manner of a 2 Group "circus" operation to allow the RAF fighters to get amongst the BF109s and FW190s. This was intended to leave the way clear for the seventy-nine Wellingtons from 1, 3 and 4 Groups to sneak in, mostly in sections of three, and attack the objectives unescorted.

4 Group contributed eighteen Mk II Wellingtons, nine representing 405 Squadron, which loaded four with a 2,000-pounder and four 500lb SAP bombs and five with eight 500-pounders of the SAP variety, before sending them on their way between 11.26 and 11.53 with W/C Gilchrist and S/Ls Bisset and Keddy the senior pilots on duty. They made their way out over Cornwall in excellent weather conditions under clear skies and approached the target at around 15,000 feet to be greeted by a far more intense flak and fighter response than had been anticipated, suggesting that the feints and diversions had failed in their purpose. A distributor arm in Sgt Farnborough's aircraft had been incorrectly set and the bombs failed to release, but the rear gunner, Sgt Parsons, claimed a BF109 after it closed to one hundred yards and exposed its belly to eighty rounds as it pulled away before going straight down. The other 405 Squadron aircraft are believed to have delivered their attacks from an average of 12,000 feet between 15.32 and 15.40, experiencing a torrid time at the hands of the defences. Sgt Craig and crew were attacked successively by three BF109s and another unidentified fighter, Sgt Higgins in the tail turret claiming one and Sgt Hughes in the nose another, which were observed respectively to dive towards the sea, one with its engine ablaze and the other tail-down. The Wellington's rear turret was knocked out of action and its occupant wounded, and burning fuselage fabric was eventually extinguished by the wireless operator as Sgt Craig and his second pilot struggled to keep the aircraft off the water. The rest of the crew congregated at the back to maintain balance and W5581 was within three hundred yards

of the shore at Torpoint when it ran out of height and ditched at 16.35. The crew scrambled into the dinghy and were picked up by a motorboat, which landed them so that Sgt Higgins could be conveyed to hospital.

Sgt Scott and crew estimated a direct hit by a 500 pounder on Gneisenau and were then attacked from astern by a BF109, the fire from which severely damaged the Wellington and wounded the rear gunner, Sgt Dearnley. They crash-landed at Roborough in Devon, and Sgt Dearnley had to be hacked out of his turret before being delivered to hospital, where he succumbed to his wounds shortly afterwards. Ten of the seventy-nine Wellingtons were shot down by flak and fighters, along with two Hampdens, and among the former were two belonging to 405 Squadron. W5537 was lost without trace with the crew of P/O Trueman after being observed by the Craig crew to come under fighter attack and dive towards the sea, and W5551 was brought down by a fighter to crash at Ploudaniel ten miles north-east of Brest, with fatal consequences for the rear gunner and squadron gunnery leader, F/O Whigham. For the second time in four months, W/C Gilchrist was saved by his parachute, and was initially captured, before escaping and making his way home via Switzerland. Two others evaded capture and made their way to Gibraltar for passage home, leaving just two members of the crew permanently in enemy hands. S/L Bisset and crew returned with excellent photographs of the target and reported Gneiseau to be enveloped in smoke after being straddled by bombs, and in all, six unconfirmed hits were claimed on the vessel.

Meanwhile, the fifteen 35 and 76 Squadron Halifaxes were experiencing a similarly uncomfortable time at the hands of enemy fighters and flak as they attacked Scharnhorst and lost five of their number, while the surviving ten all sustained damage. Five bombs had hit the vessel, causing fairly minor damage, but it was decided to return her to Brest immediately to take advantage of its superior repair facilities.

It would be mid August before a new commanding officer was appointed to replace W/C Gilchrist, and in the meantime, the responsibility for running the squadron fell upon S/L Keddy. Apart from two raids on the 25th involving twenty-five Whitleys from Topcliffe and Leeming and thirty Hampdens of 5 Group at Hannover, and two 35 Squadron Halifaxes on Berlin, 4 Group remained largely inactive until the 30th. The main target on that occasion was Cologne for which a force of 116 aircraft was assembled, seven Halifaxes, eleven Whitleys and six Wellingtons representing 4 Group, all of the Wellingtons belonging to 405 Squadron, and each loaded with a 1,000-pounder, four of 500lbs and two of 250lbs with two SBCs of incendiaries. They took off between 23.26 and 23.55 with S/L Keddy the senior pilot on duty and were followed into the air at 00.30 by the freshman crew of P/O Cox, bound with a similar bomb load for Boulogne to attack the docks and shipping. Sgt Wahlroth and crew turned back within ninety minutes after their a.s.i and gyro failed, leaving the remaining five to reach the target to encounter nine to ten-tenths cloud and severe thunderstorms. They carried out their attacks from around 13,000 feet between 01.46 and 02.35 on largely estimated positions based on evidence of intense flak and searchlight activity and were unable to offer an assessment of the outcome at debriefing. Meanwhile, the Cox crew encountered ten-tenths cloud and icing conditions over the Channel and having been unable to identify Boulogne, jettisoned their bombs into the sea.

During the course of the month the squadron took part in eleven operations and dispatched seventy-seven sorties for the loss of four Wellingtons and three crews.

August 1941

The policy of dispatching small numbers of aircraft to various targets simultaneously rarely produced effective results, but it would continue throughout the remainder of the year, and in fact, until a new Commander-in-Chief arrived in 1942 to provide a different direction. Germany's capital and second cities were posted as the targets for the first night of operations on the 2nd, with aiming points respectively the Friedrichsstrasse railway station and a "special" target, which was probably the battleship Tirpitz at berth. 4 Group supported both endeavours with eight Halifaxes and nineteen Wellingtons at the former in company with elements of 3 Group, and twenty-one Whitleys and a single Mk II Wellington at the latter, while 5 Group attended to Kiel. 405 Squadron loaded seven of its Wellingtons with three 500 and three 250-pounders and six SBCs and dispatched them from Pocklington between 22.10 and 22.16 with the newly promoted deputy flight commander F/L Kipp the senior pilot on duty. At 22.35 the freshman crew of P/O Cox took off for Hamburg carrying a 1,000 pounder, four 500 and two 250-pounders and two SBCs of incendiaries and failed to return after W5527 came down in the North Sea with total loss of life. Meanwhile, the Berlin-bound Sgt Bigglestone and crew were contending with an engine issue and excessive fuel consumption and dropped their bombs on the approximate position of Bremen through ten-tenths cloud before returning to land at Driffield. The others reached Berlin to find clear skies but extreme darkness which cloaked all ground detail and attacks were carried out from 15,500 to 17,500 feet between 01.25 and 02.18. Sgt Gibson's bombs were observed to burst to the east of Tempelhof railway station, while a large explosion in the north highlighted buildings and an extensive fire remained visible for thirty miles into the return journey. F/L Kipp RCAF and crew failed to return in W5483 and were reported by the Red Cross to have survived and to be in enemy hands.

Sunday the 3rd brought orders to Dishforth, Leeming and Topcliffe to prepare thirty-nine Whitleys for an operation that night against the marshalling yards attached to the main goods station in Frankfurt, while seven freshman crews were to attack the docks and shipping at Calais.

Bomber stations were a hive of activity on the 5th as preparations were put in hand for three operations that night against targets in southern Germany. Ninety-eight Wellingtons and Hampdens were assigned to Mannheim, while ninety-seven aircraft, including eleven 4 Group Halifaxes and sixteen Wellingtons attended to railway workshops in Karlsruhe. At the same time, forty-six Whitleys and twenty-two Wellingtons would be targeting an unidentified "special" target at Frankfurt, which was identified in the 102 Squadron ORB as the post office, a euphanism for the bombing of the city centre. Five 405 Squadron Wellingtons each received a bomb load of three 500 and four 250-pounders and six SBCs before departing Pocklington between 22.55 and 23.08 with no senior pilots on duty, and they lost the services of Sgt Chandos and crew almost immediately to generator failure. Sgt Gibson and crew were attacked on two occasions by enemy night-fighters and jettisoned their bombs during evasive action, while Sgt Bigglestone and crew experienced engine trouble and bombed at Aachen, observing a red fire to develop. The remaining two crews of Sgts Turner and Dougall attacked the primary target from 9,000 and 10,000 feet at 01.37 and 01.46 respectively and reported explosions and large fires and even larger fires at Mannheim.

The same three main targets were posted again on the 6th for much reduced forces, 4 Group contributing thirty-four Whitleys and nineteen 1 Group Wellingtons for a return to Frankfurt. Marshalling yards in Dortmund were briefed out as the target for a 4 Group force of twenty Whitleys from Topcliffe and twenty Wellingtons from Driffield and Pocklington on the 7th, while nine Halifaxes joined ninety-seven other aircraft to attack Essen in the night's largest operation. Nine 405 Squadron Wellingtons were loaded with a 1,000-pounder, and two each of 500 and 250-pounders and two SBCs and took off between 22.37 and midnight with P/Os Fleming and McCormack the senior pilots on duty. They adopted the southern route to the eastern Ruhr via corridor G, making landfall over the Scheldt estuary and skirting the southern Ruhr before turning north-east to the target. Sgt Dougall and crew dropped their bombs on the town of Witten, some seven or eight miles short of the primary target, for which no explanation was recorded. Sgt Gibson and crew were attacked on three occasions by enemy night-fighters but evaded them by diving into cloud and continued on to the target to find three-tenths cloud and bright moonlight. The 405 Squadron participants carried out their attacks from 10,000 to 16,000 feet between 01.51 and 02.20, and observed a large fire in the city centre along with bursts close to marshalling yards to the west and east of the aiming point and the Dortmund-Ems Canal and its docks complex north of the city centre.

Forty-two Whitleys were detailed for operations on the 8th, when briefings revealed that they would join forces with fifty Hampdens from 5 Group to attack the Deutsche Werke shipyard at Kiel, where U-Boot construction was under way, and nine Whitleys joined twenty Hampdens at Krefeld on the night of the 11/12th. Berlin, Essen, Hannover and Magdeburg were posted as the destinations for a total of 219 aircraft on the 12th, 4 Group contributing a dozen Halifaxes and twenty-two Wellingtons to an overall force of seventy aircraft assigned to the capital and two Halifaxes to join thirty-three Wellingtons and Stirlings targeting the Krupp complex at Essen.

Nine 405 Squadron crews attended briefing to learn that Berlin's Friedrichstrasse railway station was to be the aiming point, while another source specifies the Air Ministry building in Alexanderplatz, both locations in the city centre, the former on the southern bank of the River Spree near Unter Den Linden and the latter on the northern side. It mattered little, as the intention was to hit the commercial centre of the city and the likelihood of identifying either briefed aiming point was small. The 405 Squadron aircraft each received a load of a 1,000-pounder, four and two 500 and 250-pounders and two SBCs and departed Pocklington between 21.27 and 21.39 with the newly promoted F/L McCormack the senior pilot on duty. Sgt Farnborough and crew turned back during the climb-out because of an unserviceable rear turret and Sgt Gibson and crew returned two hours later after experiencing engine trouble. Sgt Bigglestone and crew were also contending with an engine issue and bombed Bremen from 13,000 feet at 23.48, and seventy-two minutes later, P/O Fleming and crew attacked a flak concentration near the Baltic port of Swinemünde after it became clear that insufficient fuel remained to complete the full sortie. Fewer than half of the original force reached the target, and those from 405 Squadron carried out their attacks from 14,000 to 15,000 feet between 00.28 and 00.50 in the face of a hostile flak defence, observing many bursts and fires. Sgt Scott and crew witnessed a large aircraft ahead blow up "like a rocket" after being hit by a heavy flak shell. Sgt Dougall and crew were lucky to survive when an incorrect altimeter setting caused them to brush a tree as they came in to land at base.

Orders were received across the Command on the 14th to prepare a force of 152 aircraft for an operation against railway installations in Hannover, for which 4 Group detailed fifty-five Whitleys. Other operations on this night against similar targets were to take place at Braunschweig, thirty-five miles east-south-east of Hannover and at Magdeburg a further fifty miles to the south-east. The former was assigned to a 5 Group force of eighty-two Hampdens, while fifty-two assorted aircraft from all groups, including eleven Halifaxes and fourteen Wellingtons representing 4 Group, attended to Magdeburg. Seven 405 Squadron Wellingtons received a similar bomb load to that employed at Berlin and departed Pocklington between 21.55 and 22.25 with F/L McCormack the senior pilot on duty and should have been followed into the air by two freshman crews bound for Rotterdam, but enemy intruder activity prevented them from taking off. Sgt Gibson and crew were the last to take off, possibly delayed by the enemy activity, and with no prospect of reaching the primary target in the allotted window, attack Rotterdam as an alternative. The crews of Sgt Farnborough and F/L McCormack elected not to push on to Magdeburg and muscled in on the attack at Hannover, where they found clear skies and a spirited searchlight and flak response and delivered their bombs from 12,000 and 14,000 feet at 00.54 and 01.15 respectively. At Magdeburg, cloud, searchlight dazzle and ground haze prevented identification of the planned aiming point and the bombing by three 405 Squadron crews took place from 11,000 to 14,000 feet between 00.40 and 00.55. W5496 failed to return with the predominantly RCAF crew of P/O Fleming RCAF, and no clue to their fate ever emerged.

Railway installations in Cologne, Düsseldorf and Duisburg were posted as the targets for operations on the 16th, the Rhineland capital for a predominantly 4 Group force of twenty-nine Whitleys, ten Wellingtons and six Halifaxes, while 5 Group dealt with the second-mentioned and 1 and 3 Group Wellingtons went for Duisburg. 405 Squadron's seven Wellingtons were each loaded with the standard bomb load and departed Pocklington between 23.40 and 23.55 with F/L McCormack the senior pilot on duty. Sgt Sutherland and crew lost their intercom soon after taking off but decided to continue on and reached the target with five of the others to find largely clear skies with patches of cloud and a little ground haze. The bombing was carried out from 10,000 to 16,000 feet between 02.00 and 02.47 and several fires were seen to be spreading, but cloud prevented an assessment, and the only detail was a stick of bombs falling short of the aiming point and hitting the railway station. Sgt Gibson and crew were held in searchlights and attacked by a BF110, which they shook off through evasive action, while P/O Lane and crew joined in the 5 Group attack on Düsseldorf after a navigation error sent them astray. On the way home near Hasselt in Belgium, Sgt Sutherland and crew ran into searchlights and flak and were attacked from astern by a night-fighter, the accurate cannon and machine-gun fire from which mortally wounded the rear gunner, Sgt Payton. Sgt Sutherland pointed the nose at the ground and by the time that the dive was arrested at 1,000 feet, the assailant had been lost. Attention was then turned upon a burning parachute fuelled by oil from the damaged rear turret, and once this had been extinguished flak punctured the starboard tyre, despite which the battered Wellington landed successfully at base. It was a bad night for the Whitley brigade, which lost seven of their number, a massive and unsustainable 24% of those dispatched. Local sources reported a light raid, and the fires may have been at a decoy site.

The new commanding officer, W/C Fenwick-Wilson AFC, another Canadian serving in the RAF, arrived on the 17th from 22 O.T.U., at Wellesbourne Mountford, where he had just converted to the Wellington. He had spent the war to date as an instructor, and his main recent experience had been on Blenheims. It was left to Topcliffe to provide all twenty 4 Group aircraft for a raid on the Focke-Wulf aircraft works in Bremen that night, while thirty-nine Hampdens of 5 Group targeted the city's railway installations. Ten-tenths cloud prevented an assessment of the results, but hits were claimed on the aircraft factory.

It was on the 18th, that the previously-mentioned Butt Report was released, and its disclosures sent shock waves reverberating around the Cabinet Room and the Air Ministry. Having studied more than four thousand bombing photos taken on a hundred night operations during June and July, Mr Butt concluded that only a fraction of the bombs had fallen within miles of their intended targets. This swept away at a stroke any notion that the Command was having an effect on Germany's war effort and demonstrated the claims of the crews to be over-optimistic. This was probably not a revelation to senior figures in the Command and the RAF generally, who had known all along that bombing operations were largely ineffective. Of more concern was the fact that this would provide further ammunition for those calling for the dissolution of an independent bomber force, and the redistribution of its aircraft to other causes, such as the U-Boot campaign in the Atlantic and to counter reversals in the Middle East. The report was a bitter blow to the reputation of C-in-C Sir Richard Peirse, whose period of tenure would be forever unjustly blighted by its criticisms. He would do his best to recover the Command's sullied reputation while he remained at the helm, but the weather would be against him for the remainder of the year.

That night, seventeen Whitleys took part in a raid on Cologne by a largely 5 Group force totalling sixty-two aircraft, which had the West Station as the aiming point. Returning crews claimed many fires, while local sources reported light damage and decoy fire sites again probably lured the bombing away from its intended target. It was another bad night for the Whitley brigade, of which five failed to return, a shocking 29.4% of those dispatched.

The destination for six 4 Group Halifaxes and eleven Wellingtons on the 19th was Kiel, where a "special" target, believed to be railway installations, awaited an overall force of 108 aircraft from all groups. 405 Squadron's six-strong element departed Pocklington between 21.46 and 21.55 with F/L McCormack the senior pilot on duty and had to pass through severe icing conditions over northern Holland and north-western Germany, which prevented many from reaching the primary target. A heavy rainstorm was in progress at Kiel as the remaining bombers arrived overhead, and precisely where the bombs fell is uncertain, but it certainly was not in Kiel. On return, the 405 Squadron crews reported nine to ten-tenths cloud, thunderstorms, lightning and zero visibility and bombing from 4,000 to 15,000 feet between 00.32 and 01.22 based on e,t,a., or evidence of searchlights and flak. F/L McCormack and crew toured the Schleswig-Holstein region for thirty minutes seeking out a target but failed to find one and brought their bombs home.

A force of ninety-seven Wellingtons and Hampdens was assembled on the 22nd to send against three aiming points in Mannheim, for which 4 Group contributed ten Wellingtons, five of them belonging to 405 Squadron. Each received the usual bomb load of a 1,000-pounder and four and two 500 and 250-pounders supplemented by two SBCs of incendiaries, before departing Pocklington between 21.13 and 21.23 with F/L McCormack the senior pilot on duty and W/C Fenwick-Wilson flying as second pilot to Sgt Farnborough. All arrived in the target area to find a patch of cloud that allowed sight of the Rhine, but no other ground detail and bombing was carried out on estimated positions from 11,000 to 15,000 feet between 00.10 and 00.28. The squadron

ORB ventured the claim that the target had been attacked successfully, while local sources reported just six high explosive bombs and serious damage to one house.

Pocklington was not called into action for operations involving 4 Group at Düsseldorf on the 24th, Cologne on the 26th and Mannheim on the 27th, none of which achieved a result commensurate with the numbers committed and the effort expended. On the 28th Duisburg was posted as the target for 118 aircraft, including nine Halifaxes and twenty Wellingtons, eleven of the latter provided by 405 Squadron. Eight were loaded with three 500 and three 250-pounders and six SBCs, while three others for use by freshman crews each received the standard load of a 1,000-pounder, four 500 and two 250-poundes and two SBCs. The crews were briefed to attack railway installations and departed Pocklington between 23.50 and 00.28 with F/L McCormack the senior pilot on duty and W/C Fenwick-Wilson flying as second pilot to Sgt Dougall. They had to run the gauntlet of searchlights and flak between Cologne and Düsseldorf and Sgt Dougall's "F" was peppered and holed, W/C Fenwick-Wilson sustaining a badly-bruised leg. It is believed that they continued on to the target and may have released part of their load but reported attacking Haamstede aerodrome on Schouwen Island in the Schledt estuary from 12,000 feet at 03.45 on the way home. The others were greeted at the target by largely clear skies and extreme darkness and were guided to the mark by numerous searchlights operating in cones and large numbers of illuminating flares. Eight of the 405 Squadron crews delivered an attack from 10,000 to 16,000 feet between 02.04 and 02.35, observing many explosions and fires that offered an impression of a highly effective raid. The freshman crew of Sgt Williams bombed nearby Mülheim-an-der-Ruhr and another of the freshmen, captained by P/O Watts, failed to return in W5488 after coming down in the target area with fatal consequences for all but the second pilot and rear gunner, who fell into enemy hands.

During the course of the monthe the squadron took part in ten operations and dispatched sixty-seven sorties for the loss of four Wellingtons and crews and a rear gunner.

September 1941

On the 1st of September, Sgt Turner was conducting dual control training in W5535 with two pilots on board when the port engine caught fire and it became necessary to crash-land at 21.50 in a field a mile north of the Pocklington airfield. The Wellington was destroyed in the fire but not before the occupants had removed themselves. 4 Group sat out the opening night of the month, while other modest elements of the Command continued the almost-continuous campaign against Cologne. A number of targets were briefed out on the 2nd, until Frankfurt was finally settled upon as the primary target for 126 aircraft, forty-four of them 4 Group Whitleys, while seven Halifaxes joined elements of 3 and 5 Groups to target Berlin. Brest and its lodgers had been left in relative peace since July, and this situation was to be rectified by a force of 140 aircraft from all groups on the 3rd, for which 4 Group contributed nineteen Whitleys and seventeen Wellingtons, including nine of the latter provided by 405 Squadron. Shortly after take-off the elements from 1, 4 and 5 Groups were recalled because of deteriorating weather conditions at base, leaving the 3 Group aircraft and four others who had not picked up the recall to complete the operation. Fifty-three returning crews claimed to have bombed the estimated positions of the warships through an effective smoke screen and no hits were claimed.

77 Squadron moved out of Topcliffe on the 5th and took up residence at Leeming, which was home to 10 Squadron, and they would share the station for the next eight months. A synthetic rubber factory at Marl/Hüls was to be the target for a mixed force of eighty-six aircraft on the night of the 6/7th, with forty-one Whitleys the most populous type. Known locally as the "Buna" works because of the butadiene and natrium chemicals employed in the manufacturing process, the Chemische Werke-Hüls GmbH had been formed in 1938 after its acquisition by the I G Farben company in association with the Bergwerkgesellschaft Hibernia A G. It was located on the northern fringe of the Ruhr, and whether or not it was using slave workers at this time, the I G Farben company would become infamous for drawing its labour force from concentration camps and forcing tens of thousands to toil under the harshest conditions at its many manufacturing sites across Germany. *(In some other of my squadron histories, I have mistakenly placed the Buna works in the Hüls district of Krefeld.)*

A major operation to Berlin was posted on the 7th, for which a force of 197 aircraft was assembled and the crews briefed for one of three aiming-points. 4 Group detailed thirty-one Whitleys, sixteen Wellingtons and six Halifaxes for aiming-point "C", which the 102 Squadron ORB identified as the Schlesischer railway station, situated on the southern bank of the River Spree to the south-east of the city centre. 405 Squadron loaded eight of its Wellingtons with a 1,000 pounder, four 500 and two 250 pounders and two SBCs, and winched the same bomb load into another for the freshman crew of Sgt Suggitt to take to Boulogne to attack the docks and shipping. The latter departed Pocklington first at 20.12, with the main element following on behind between 20.30 and 20.38 with F/L McCormack the senior pilot on duty. The main element set course for the western coast of Schleswig-Holstein on their way to the Baltic, the coastal locations ensuring strong navigation pinpoints to aid them in reaching the target area. Sgt Gibson and crew had to contend with intercom failure and dropped their bombs on the port of Emden before turning back, while the arrival of the others was greeted by clear skies and a hostile flak defence, the searchlights to an extent nullifying the brightness of the moon. They carried out their attacks from 13,000 to 16,000 feet between 22.24 and 00.12 at widely dispersed points from the north-west to the south-eastern suburbs and were among two-thirds of returning crews to report successfully bombing the target. The effectiveness of the attack was partly borne out by local descriptions of damage to a number of war-industry factories, housing, utilities and communications, mostly in the north and east of the city. Fifteen aircraft failed to return, among them 405 Squadron's W5521, and confirmation eventually arrived via the Red Cross that Sgt Saunders RCAF and his crew had survived to fall into enemy hands. Three losses from the night's other operations brought the casualty figure to eighteen aircraft, which represented the highest number of bomber casualties to date in a single night. Six of the missing belonged to 4 Group, but one of these had made it to Sweden, where the crew would be interned for a respectable period. While the above was in progress, the Suggitt crew successfully fulfilled their brief at Boulogne, where they bombed from 12,000 feet at 22.11 and observed five bursts.

The targets on the 8th were a railway workshop and the Henschel tank works in Kassel, for which a force of ninety-seven aircraft was made ready, sixteen Whitleys representing the 4 Group contribution. Four 405 Squadron crews were excited to learn at briefing on the 10th that they would be representing the squadron on its first foray into Italian airspace in company with four other Wellington crews from 104 Squadron and seven in Halifaxes in an overall force of seventy-six aircraft detailed to attack the Fiat steelworks and main railway station. They flew over to the 3

Group station at Stradishall as a forward base and took off between 21.48 and 22.07 with F/L McCormack the senior pilot on duty and a bomb load each of two 1,000 and two 250 pounders. They traversed France over cloud and found the peaks of the Alps standing out, but the northern plains again cloud-covered as they lined up on the target. The head of the bomber stream arrived just before ten-tenths cloud slid across the city and started fires for the benefit of those following on, which included the 405 Squadron quartet, who bombed on the glow from 14,000 to 18,000 feet between 01.00 and 01.25. Returning crews claimed hits on the city centre and Fiat works but no local report emerged to confirm the level of damage.

The destination for a force of 130 aircraft on the 12th was Frankfurt, where the objective was recorded as "special target A", for which 4 Group detailed eighteen Whitleys from Topcliffe and Leeming and ten Wellingtons from Pocklington and Driffield. The seven 405 Squadron participants took off between 20.21 and 20.36 with S/L Bisset the senior pilot on duty and each crew sitting on a bomb load of two 1,000-pounders, two and three respectively 500 and 250-pounders and two SBCs of incendiaries. Having undertaken the entire outward flight over cloud, crews were not surprised to encounter a ten-tenths covering over the target at around 8,000 feet, which completely obscured the ground. They were forced to bomb on estimated positions guided to an extent by accurate flak, and six of the 405 Squadron participants carried out their attacks from 7,000 to 14,000 feet between 23.05 and 23.38, observing flashes and the glow of fires. There was mention of bursts to the west of the docks near the main railway station and on a nearby bridge and local sources reported thirty-eight fires and damage mostly in residential areas, while Mainz, situated some twenty miles to the south-west, also received some bomb loads, among which was the one delivered by Sgt Gibson and crew, whose bombing photo clearly depicted the Allgemeiner Hafen (general harbour) and nearby barracks.

On the 15th, twenty-seven Halifaxes, Wellingtons and Whitleys were to represent 4 Group in a force of 169 aircraft, the crews of which had been briefed to attack railway stations and the Blohm & Voss shipyards in Hamburg. 405 Squadron provided six of the ten 4 Group Wellingtons and loaded each with a 1,000-pounder, four 500 and two 250-pounders and two SBCs, before dispatching them from Pocklington between 20.15 and 20.26 with F/L McCormack the senior pilot on duty. Sgt Suggitt and crew dropped out because of hydraulics and intercom issues, while Sgt Chandos and crew pressed on despite their intercom failure and bombed Wilhelmshaven before turning back. Sgt Gibson and crew ran into heavy flak from the Kiel Canal defences and released their bombs onto one of the offending batteries, and this left just three crews to attack the primary target, for which no details were recorded in the ORB other than an observation of small, red fires.

On the morning of the 18th, Sgt Chandos took off in W5492 with seven others on board for what the ORB recorded as a photographic duty and wireless test at 8,000 feet. Having attained the desired altitude, the dinghy broke loose from its wing stowage and fouled the elevators, sending the Wellington into an uncontrollable spin and dive, which caused it to suffer structural failure at 5,000 feet and crash without survivors at 11.05 two miles north-north-east of Pocklington.

On the 19th, a force of seventy-two aircraft was assembled to target the distant city-port of Stettin, 4 Group supporting the endeavour with nineteen Halifaxes, Wellingtons and Whitleys, five of the Wellingtons belonging to 405 Squadron. A slightly reduced bomb load of three 500 and three 250 pounders and six SBCs was winched into each bomb bay and they departed Pocklington between

22.15 and 22.26 with F/L McCormack the senior pilot on duty. Contending with intercom failure Sgt Gibson and crew unloaded their bombs on Rotterdam docks as the closest target before turning back, while P/O Frizzle and crew never once emerged from cloud and dropped their load somewhere over Schleswig-Holstein. Sgt Sutherland and crew were just some twenty miles west of the primary target when they decided to release their payload over the Brüssow area, leaving just the crews of F/L McCormack and Sgt Dougall to fulfil the brief. The ORB record is confusing and inaccurate but reports that the former caused a large fire to break out near the main railway station, the glow from which remained visible for seventy miles. The latter signalled that they had attacked the target at 02.12 and were on their way home Z8344, but never arrived, the Red Cross ultimately confirming their survival and capture. Sadly, two members of the crew were killed in late April 1945, probably as the result of an Allied strafing attack on a marching column.

On the following afternoon, 4 Group called together eighteen Whitley and two Halifax crews and informed them at briefing that they were to be part of an overall force of seventy-four aircraft to target the Alexander Platz railway station, situated to the east of the River Spree in Berlin's city centre. A further sixteen freshman crews were to join twelve others for a raid on the docks and shipping at Ostend, and it was for the latter that 405 Squadron briefed the crews of Sgts Clark, Hall and Hassan. They departed Pocklington between 19.49 and 19.59, each sitting on the standard bomb load, and found the target area to be concealed beneath a layer of cloud, despite which the Bassin de Chasse was identified as a reference and the bombing carried out from 10,500 to 12,000 feet between 21.36 and 21.45. The Clark crew caused a large fire that remained visible for twenty miles, while the Hall and Hassan crews were saved from blundering into the Harwich barrage balloon by the local searchlight batteries illuminating them. The Berlin-bound force was recalled when over Schleswig-Holstein because of the risk of fog at home at landing time.

The funerals of four of the victims of the accident on the 18th took place with full military honours at Barmby Moor Cemetery at 14.30 on the 22nd. It was on this day that the Canadian High Commissioner paid one of his informal visits to the squadron accompanied by his wife and a new adjutant was appointed, F/L Garneau succeeding F/O Cooper.

Following the Berlin recall, a few minor operations occupied the ensuing five nights, and a hundred aircraft were recalled from various targets on the night of the 26/27th. The largest deployment of Whitleys during the month came on the 29th, when fifty-six were made ready to join eleven Wellingtons and six Halifaxes as 4 Group's contribution to a force of 139 aircraft with Stettin as their destination, while ninety-three other aircraft were assigned to Hamburg. 405 Squadron briefed six crews for the former and two for the latter, those assigned to Stettin each loaded with a 1,000-pounder, three 500 and two 250-pounders and two SBCs, while the Hamburg-bound duo received a standard payload. With further to travel, the six-strong element departed Pocklington first between 18.57 and 19.10 with S/L Bisset the senior pilot on duty, and they were followed into the air at 19.13 and 19.20 by the crews of Sgts Hassan and Clark. They crossed the North Sea over heavy cloud and rain, which began to disperse to some extent as they approached the west coast of Schleswig-Holstein, and clear skies over Hamburg enabled crews to pinpoint on the Elbe and identify the docks and Binnen and Aussen-Alster Lakes. The Hassan crew attacked from 15,000 feet at 21.55 and observed bursts and fires near the river, while Sgt Clark and crew saw their bombs impact between the river and the lakes. The Stettin force had a further 270 miles to travel from Schleswig-Holstein's western coast and arrived in the target area under clear skies at around 22.30

finding that ground haze restricted the vertical visibility. Stettin is separated from the coastal region at Swinemünde by the Stattiner Haff inland sea and Dammscher Lake and lies on the River Oder, all of which provided strong navigational pinpoints for the bombers, five of those from 405 Squadron delivering their attacks from 10,000 to 16,000 feet between 22.35 and 22.42 after picking out the docks. One crew bombed a town to the west, identified in the ORB as possibly Stolzenburg, but as Stettin is now Szczecin in Poland, the name will have been changed.

Both targets were posted for attention again on the following night with a much-reduced force of forty Wellingtons for Stettin and eighty-two assorted aircraft for Hamburg, 4 Group supporting the latter with two Halifaxes, ten Whitleys and five Wellingtons. 405 Squadron briefed the crews of S/L Keddy, F/L McCormack and Sgt Suggitt and sent them on their way from Pocklington between 18.42 and 18.50 each with a standard bomb load. They arrived at the target to find a thin layer of cloud, which combined with ground haze to inhibit identification of ground features and delivered their attacks from 11,000 to 12,500 feet between 21.15 and 22.10. Many bursts were observed along with fires, some near the railway station and there were reports that the Binnen and Aussen-Alster Lakes (Inner and Outer) had been camouflaged, while S/L Keddy brough back a photo of the Blohm and Voss yards. All returned safely home to complete the month's operational activity and the ORB Form 540 was signed off with the flourishing signature of the new adjutant, F/L Jean Garneau.

During the course of the month the squadron took part in eleven operations and dispatched fifty-four sorties for the loss of two Wellingtons, two crews and two additional airmen.

October 1941

The adverse weather conditions that had characterised the second half of September continued into the new month and caused the recall of a modest-sized mainly 5 Group force bound for Karlsruhe on the evening of the 1st. The 4 Group raid on target "A" at Stuttgart was allowed to continue, however, and involved twenty-seven Whitleys and four Wellingtons, while 405 Squadron remained at home and would do so for the first week-and-a-half of the new month. On the 3rd, Sgt Foy and crew were practicing circuits and landings and were about to take off for a second circuit when another Wellington was spotted on finals and in the belief that there may be a collision, Sgt Foy gunned the engines to vacate the runway at the earliest opportunity. Sadly, the brakes were not up to the task and W5518 went through a hedge and required ten days of repair to return it to service.

A few minor operations aside, the Command remained largely dormant until the 10th, when seventy-eight crews were briefed for an operation against the giant Krupp complex at Essen, while sixty-nine others targeted Cologne and twenty-two freshman crews went for the docks and shipping at Ostend. 4 Group contributed twenty-two Whitleys, six Halifaxes and five Wellingtons to the Essen force, and five Wellingtons and four Whitleys for Ostend, all of the Wellingtons for both operations provided by 405 Squadron after 104 Squadron was stood down and posted to Egypt, leaving a small home echelon to rebuild and eventually be renumbered 158 Squadron in the coming February. The freshmen got away early between 18.34 and 18.42 with P/O Frizzle the only commissioned pilot on duty and each crew sitting on a standard bomb load, which three crews delivered from 10,000 to 15,000 feet between 20.05 and 20.43, observing bursts on the eastern bank of the new tidal harbour and the main railway station. The crews of Sgt McNeil and P/O Frizzle were unable to identify the aiming point and jettisoned their bombs.

The crews bound for Essen were each captained by a sergeant pilot, and flying as second pilot to Sgt Williams was the thirty-two-year-old F/L "Johnny" Fauquier, who came from a wealthy family and had been a prewar bush pilot and an instructor in the RCAF since the outbreak of war. This had been a source of great frustration to a natural-born warrior with three thousand hours to his credit, and he was now eager to launch the operational career that would turn him into a Canadian legend. They had to wait until after midnight before departing Pocklington between 00.23 and 00.33, each with a standard bomb load on board, and all reached the target to find eight to ten-tenths cloud, through which they delivered their attacks on largely estimated positions and e.t.a from 12,000 to 15,500 feet between 02.29 and 03.05. Some bursts were observed, and severe icing caused a few bombs to hang up, but it made little difference to the outcome as the adverse weather conditions ultimately rendered the two main operations totally ineffective and a waste of resources. This continuing state of affairs was heaping further pressure on AM Peirse to achieve some kind of success.

A busy night of operations was announced across the Command on the 12th, which would bring the first major raid of the war on Nuremberg, the scene of massive Nazi rallies during and after Hitler's rise to power in the 1930s. A force of 152 aircraft was assembled, of which fifty-four Whitleys, nine Halifaxes and three Wellingtons were provided by 4 Group, whose crews were briefed to aim for the Siemens-Schuckert Werke aero-engine factory. While this operation took place in southern Germany, ninety-nine aircraft were to target Bremen in the north-west, while ninety 5 Group Hampdens and Manchesters tried their hand at the "Buna" synthetic rubber works at Marl-Hüls in the Ruhr. Together with a number of minor operations, this would bring the night's sortie tally to a new record of 373, an improvement of nine on the previous record set in May. Of the seven crews detailed by 405 Squadron only the three captained by S/L Bisset, P/O Frizzle and Sgt Sutherland took off between 19.48 and 19.54, F/L Fauquier flying on this occasion as second pilot to S/L Bisset. Each carried a 1,000-pounder, four 500-pounders, a single 250-pounder and two SBCs and flew out in unusually favourable conditions, Sgt Sutherland and crew contending with an engine issue that persuaded them to jettison their bombs on an unidentified town near Aschaffenburg, thirty miles south-east of Frankfurt and around 120 miles short of the primary target. The crews of S/L Bisset and P/O Frizzle reached their destination and picked out ground features through the haze before delivering their attacks from 6,000 and 14,000 feet at 23.30 and 23.59. They observed huge fires in the vicinity of the railway station and marshalling yards and reported two pillars of smoke rising through 5,000 feet and the glow of fires visible for a hundred miles into the return flight. According to local sources, many outlying communities found themselves under the bombs, one as distant from Nuremburg as sixty-five miles, while the city itself was scarcely touched, and as the succeeding years would show, it would remain a challenging target.

A force of eighty aircraft was assembled for a return to Nuremberg on the 14th and contained a 4 Group contribution of thirteen Whitleys, five Halifaxes and three Wellingtons. The crews were briefed for "special targets A and B", while out on the dispersals the three 405 Squadron Wellingtons each received a bomb load of three 500 and three 250-pounders and six SBCs, before departing Pocklington between 22.53 and 22.57 with S/L Bisset the senior pilot on duty. Cloud accompanied the force all the way across France and into Germany and while flying over Darmstadt at 15,000 feet at 01.45, P/O Lane's aircraft was hit by flak, which damaged the hydraulic feed to the rear turret. They pressed on to reach the target within thirty minutes, flying through snowstorms and generally unpleasant weather conditions to find the target area blanketed by cloud. They established their positions on e.t.a. and evidence of searchlights and flak and bombed with the others from the squadron from 5,000 to 8,000 feet between 02.05 and 02.35. The Pocklington crews landed at Horsham-St-Faith after more than seven hours aloft, and at debriefing it became clear that the majority of crews had failed to reach the target area and had bombed alternatives. Isolated bomb bursts were observed but no crew attacked the briefed aiming points, and no bombing photos were attempted because of the cloud.

Five 405 Squadron crews were called to briefing on the 16th to learn that Duisburg city centre was to be the target that night for a force of eighty-seven aircraft, and that the rest of the 4 Group contribution would be fourteen 102 Squadron Whitleys. The Pocklington quintet took off between 00.49 and 01.11 with S/L Keddy the senior pilot on duty and the same bomb load as for Nuremberg and all of them reached the Ruhr, which they found to be concealed beneath ten-tenths cloud. Bombing was carried out on estimated positions from 10,000 to 16,000 feet between 02.50 and 03.39 based on the volume of flak coming up at them. S/L Keddy and crew withheld their bombs after failing to establish a firm position and attacked the flare path at Gilze-Rijen aerodrome in southern Holland through five-tenths cloud on the way home. At debriefing, Sgt McNeil and crew reported the narrowest possible avoidance of a collision with a BF110 at 10,000 feet, the clearance no more than a foot.

Ports dominated the target list on the 20th, Bremen, Wilhelmshaven and Emden in north-western Germany and Antwerp in Belgium for freshman crews. A force of 153 aircraft drawn from 1, 3 and 5 Groups was assigned to Bremen, while the attack on Wilhelmshaven was to be an all-4 Group show involving thirty-nine Whitleys, three Wellingtons and three Halifaxes. The 405 Squadron trio departed Pocklington between 18.31 and 18.52 bearing aloft the crews of P/O Lane and Sgts Taylor and Warnock and a bomb load each of a 1,000-pounder, four 500 and three 250-pounders and two SBCs. They reached the target area to find three to five-tenths cloud with tops at up to 7,000 feet and haze below, which together with the intense and accurate searchlight and flak defence created challenging conditions for target identification. Bombing was carried out on largely estimated positions from 12,000 and 14,000 feet between 20.31 and 20.51, those arriving later finding increasing amounts of cloud that reduced them basing their attacks on flak and the glow of fires. Inevitably, this resulted in scattered bombing and local sources claimed that only three bomb loads fell within the city, hitting residential areas. While the above was in progress, F/L Fauquier and crew were undertaking their first sortie together and targeting Emden, forty miles away on the eastern side of the Niedersachsen headland. They delivered their standard bomb load from 12,500 feet at 20.25, believing the impact to be south of the River Ems and, therefore, in open country, where the incendiaries were observed to be burning white.

Mannheim was posted as the target for 123 aircraft on the 22nd, and as was common practice, the squadron ORBs recorded the railway station as the aiming point as code for the city centre, while the 4 Group record specified special targets "A" and "C". 4 Group contributed twenty-two Whitleys, six Halifaxes and six Wellingtons, the last-mentioned belonging to 405 Squadron. An unserviceable runway at Pocklington required the main element to launch their sorties from

Linton-on-Ouse, where they each received a standard bomb load of a 1,000-pounder, four 500 and two 250-pounders and two SBCs of incendiaries. They took off between 18.22 and 18.35, having been preceded into the air at Pocklington at 18.15 by the freshman crew of Sgt Hall, who were bound for Le Havre to attack the docks and shipping in company with four other 4 Group aircraft and seventeen from other groups. Those involved in the main event ran into icing conditions over France, which caused some to turn back with frozen instruments, Sgt McNeil and crew among them after around two hours, when they lost their a.s.i to icing and their compass to static electricity arcing off all exposed metal. They jettisoned their load into the sea seven minutes after leaving Zeebrugge, while the others entered Germany north of Luxembourg and ran into nine to ten-tenths cloud in the target area with tops at up to 14,000 feet and a temperature of minus 30 degrees centigrade. Bombing was carried out on estimated positions from between 11,000 and 16,000 feet between 21.19 and 21.35, and apart from the flash of bomb bursts, no results were observed. On return, Sgt Taylor had to crash-land X after the port engine failed on finals, but no injuries were reported, and the Wellington would be returned to service. Sgt Hall RCAF and his predominantly RCAF crew were last heard from on W/T at 21.00, thirty minutes after signalling that they had attacked the target, but Z8419 failed to arrive back at Pocklington and only the remains of one crew member washed ashore near Fécamp, some twenty miles north of the target. An analysis of the Mannheim operation revealed that fewer than half of the force had reached the target area, and local sources confirmed a light and ineffective raid.

405 Squadron took no part in the operation against the Krupp Germania shipyard at Kiel mounted on the night of the 23/24th and supported by 4 Group with twenty-seven Whitleys. Shortly after midday on the 24th the first Halifax II arrived at Leeming to begin 10 Squadron's gradual conversion onto the type. During the course of that afternoon, 405 Squadron made ready five Wellingtons as part of a force of seventy aircraft detailed for a raid on Frankfurt that night. They would carry the 4 Group banner with nine Whitleys of 51 Squadron and took off between 18.21 and 18.41 with P/O Frizzle the senior pilot on duty and a bomb load each of three 500-pounders, a single 250-pounder and six SBCs. Sgt Warnock and crew were traversing The Wash at 19.15 when the compass failed and they decided to attack the nearest alternative target, which turned out to be the docks at Ostend. Ten-tenths cloud over Belgium persuaded P/O Frizzle and crew that it was futile to continue to the primary target and they turned back in search of an alternative. As they approached the Aachen area, W5489 was hit by flak, which punctured a petrol tank and released an alarming smell of leaking petrol to pervade the fuselage. The bombs were dropped on Haamstede aerodrome on Schouwen Island at the mouth of the Scheldt on the way home and a safe landing completed, but while taxiing to its dispersal at 00.10 the Wellington caught fire and was vacated by the crew before becoming totally consumed. Meanwhile, the others attacked the primary target through gaps in the cloud from 12,000 to 15,000 feet between 22.05 and 22.27 and observed yellow fires, but an analysis would reveal that only eight of the original seventy crews had claimed to have reached and bombed Frankfurt.

Pocklington sat out an operation to Hamburg on the 26th, for which 115 aircraft were detailed, seven Halifaxes and sixteen Whitleys provided by 4 Group. The attack was aided by bright moonlight and inflicted a greater degree of damage than was usual for the period but was still not commensurate with the size of the force and the effort expended.

The month ended with another operation against Hamburg on the 31st, for which 4 Group detailed nine Halifaxes, twenty-nine Whitleys and nine 405 Squadron Wellingtons as part of an overall force of 123 aircraft. The 4 Group participants were briefed to attack "special aiming point A", the 405 Squadron element with bomb loads of three 500-pounders, a single 250-pounder and six SBCs of incendiaries. They departed Pocklington between 17.35 and 17.50 with S/L Keddy and F/Ls Fauquier and McCormack the senior pilots on duty and were followed into the air between 17.55 and 18.05 by the freshman crews of P/O Robson and Sgts Frost and McKay, who were bound for the docks at Dunkerque, each with a standard bomb load beneath their feet. The latter element crossed the Channel over six-tenths cloud, which had increased to eight-tenths in the target area, but allowed glimpses of the waterways and docks, which the Robson crew attacked from 12,000 feet at 20.01 and the Frost crew at 20.29. Sgt McKay and crew were hampered by an iced-over windscreen courtesy of an unserviceable de-icer and jettisoned the bombs into the sea after failing to identify the target.

Sgt McLennan and crew were back on the ground within an hour after losing their intercom, while the others in the Hamburg force encountered eight-tenths cloud over the North Sea, which prevented some from identifying their point of landfall and the briefed aiming-point of "Altona A", which is believed to be the location of a power station. The crews of F/Ls Fauquier and McCormack, P/O Frizzle and Sgt Suggitt identified the docks area through gaps in the cloud and delivered their attacks on them, while the crews of Sgt Hassan, Sutherland and Williams bombed the general city area, all between 20.36 and 21.48 from heights of 10,000 to 15,000 feet. Local sources reported fourteen fires, seven of them large, but no significant incidents or damage.

During the course of the month the squadron took part in twelve operations and dispatched fifty sorties for the loss of two Wellingtons and one crew.

November 1941

The Halifax brigade would enjoy a gentle introduction to the new month, while the Whitley and Wellington squadrons represented 4 Group for most of the first week. The Deutsche Werke shipyards at Kiel provided the month's first target for thirty Whitleys on the night of the 1/2nd, while three Wellingtons with freshman crews representing the rebuilding home echelon of 104 Squadron attacked the docks and shipping at Le Havre.

On the 4th, 58 and 405 Squadrons both detailed five freshman crews to attack the docks and shipping at Dunkerque, the latter each receiving the standard bomb load before departing Pocklington between 17.29 and 17.43 for what was the squadron's fortieth operation. They all arrived in the target area to find nine-tenths cloud, through which the crews of P/O Robson and Sgts Guay and Frost caught brief glimpses of the ground, while the crews of Sgts Baltzer and McKay saw nothing and jettisoned their loads. The Robson and Guay crews pinpointed on the docks area and observed their bombs burst across docks 5 and 6, but the Frost crew was forced into violent evasive action and dropped their bombs to the north of the target while in a steep dive.

No doubt still frustrated by his inability to deliver a telling blow on Germany during the extended period of unfavourable weather, and almost certainly eager to rescue the besmirched reputation of the Command after the damning Butt Report, Peirse planned a major night of operations for the night of the 7/8th. The original intention was to send more than two hundred aircraft to Berlin, but continuing doubts about the weather prompted the 5 Group A-O-C, AVM Slessor, to question the wisdom of going ahead, and he was allowed to withdraw his force and send it instead to Cologne. A third operation, involving fifty-three Wellingtons and two Stirlings from 1 and 3 Groups was also to take place with Mannheim as the target. 169 aircraft drawn from 1, 3 and 4 Groups would eventually take off for Berlin, while sixty-one Hampdens and fourteen Manchesters set off for the Rhineland capital. At this stage of the war before the advent of the bomber stream, groups and squadrons decided for themselves the details of their sorties, and the first of the Berlin force took off as early as 17.20, while 4 Group aircraft were departing their stations throughout the evening, culminating with 405 Squadron after 23.00. In addition to the above major endeavours, other small-scale operations would raise the number of sorties to a new record of 392.

At Pocklinton, while ten crews were making the final preparations for the long night ahead, the freshman crews of Sgt Baltzer and F/L Searby took off at 20.07 and 20.14 respectively to attack the docks and shipping at Boulogne and arrived at their destination within ninety minutes to find clear skies and good visibility. They each delivered a standard bomb load from 12,000 and 14,000 feet at 21.40 and observed bursts on the southern edge of docks 4 and 6. After bombing, the Searby crew headed inland to deliver propaganda leaflets (nickels) to the residents of the Montrueil area to the east of Paris, and on the way back over Dover became entangled in the barrage balloon defences, fortunately managing to extricate themselves without mishap.

The Baltzer crew had landed well before the Berlin-bound brigade took off, but that was long gone by the time that the Searby crew touched down at 00.44, almost three hours after the Baltzer crew. The 405 Squadron element had departed Pocklington for Berlin between 23.07 and 23.48 with F/Ls Fauquier and McCormack the senior pilots on duty and a payload in each bomb bay of one 250-pounder less than the standard. As they headed out over the North Sea, they were the last of the 4 Group contribution, which had included forty-two Whitleys and nine Halifaxes. The force had battled the conditions of icing and intense cold, recorded as low as minus 45 degrees, and it became gradually depleted as many crews turned back or sought out alternative targets. On reaching Wilhelmshaven, Sgt McKay and crew estimated that they had insufficient fuel to reach Berlin and return and dropped their bombs, observing bursts, while an engine issue persuaded Sgt Williams and crew to jettison their bombs "safe" in the same area. Those reaching the target found ten-tenths cloud with occasional breaks, through which the crews of Sgts Suggitt and Sutherland caught a momentary glimpse of streets, houses and a bridge, while others bombed on e.t.a. and estimated positions from 14,000 to 17,000 feet between 02.13 and 02.57. F/L Fauquier and crew were unable to establish themselves over the target and bombed the clearly visible port of Kiel on the way home, observing explosions on the western side of the harbour. On landing at Dishforth, Sgt Frost overshot the runway and suffered an undercarriage collapse and F/L Fauquier damaged his Wellington in a collision with a steel obstruction at Sutton Cranswick. A number of 405 Squadron aircraft returned with flak damage, and F/Sgt Hassan RCAF and his crew were absent from debriefing altogether, having last been heard from on W/T at 02.44 on their way home. Their burial in Becklingen War Cemetery some fifty miles south of Hamburg suggests that W5553 came down in that general area of north-western Germany.

Once every aircraft from the night's endeavours had landed, it became clear that a record thirty-seven were missing, more than twice the previous highest loss in a single night. An analysis revealed that only seventy-three aircraft had reached the general area of the capital, and of around forty buildings hit by bombs, just fourteen houses and a gasometer were classed as completely destroyed, this in return for the loss of twenty-one bombers, a dozen of them belonging to 4 Group. The Cologne force came through without loss, but left behind them only the slightest damage, and the Mannheim contingent missed its target altogether while losing seven Wellingtons. This was the final straw for the Air Ministry, and Sir Richard Peirse was summoned to an uncomfortable meeting with Churchill at Chequers on the 8th to make his explanations.

Attention switched to the Ruhr on the following night with the Krupp complex in Essen as the target for fifty-four aircraft including eight Whitleys, which encountered thick industrial haze and an intense searchlight and flak defence. On the 9th, the Blohm & Voss shipyard in Hamburg was posted as the target for 103 aircraft, including a 4 Group contribution of sixteen Halifaxes, Wellingtons and Whitleys. The 405 Squadron quartet consisted of the crews of Sgts Frost, McKay, McLennan and Taylor and departed Pocklington between 17.09 and 17.17, each of them sitting on a standard bomb load. Sgt Frost became unwell during the outward flight and Wilhelmshaven was attacked as an alternative target before he and his crew turned back to report bomb bursts and incendiary fires. The others found favourable conditions over Germany's second city, and while the River Elbe was clearly visible, haze prevented identification of the briefed aiming point and bombs were delivered on the general riverside industrial complex from 15,000 to 16,000 feet between 19.53 and 20.10. It was difficult to assess the outcome and it was left to local sources to confirm three large fires in the city and docks.

On the 13th Peirse was ordered to restrict further operations, while the future of Bomber Command was debated at the highest level, and this edict would remain in force into the coming year. A force of forty-nine aircraft was detailed to attack a "special" unidentified target at Emden on the 15th, possibly a Hipper class cruiser at berth, for which 4 Group detailed eight freshman crews. 405 Squadron briefed the crews of W/C Fenwick-Wilson and Sgt Finn and sent them on their way from Pocklington at 17.28 and 17.53 respectively, each carrying a standard bomb load. They flew out over dense cloud, through which W/C Fenwick-Wilson and crew caught a momentary glimpse of Baltrum Island, which provided a navigation reference sufficient for them to arrive in the general target area and deliver their payload on e.t.a from 14,000 feet at 20.15. The Finn crew bombed on estimated position from 16,000 feet at 20.45 and returned with nothing of value to report.

4 Group was employed sparingly during the remainder of the month, while the other groups conducted modest-scale operations against French ports, and it was the 25th when 4 Group next went to war with an attack on the warships at Brest by eleven Halifaxes in company with seven Stirlings of 3 Group. 1, 3 and 5 Groups took care of business at Emden and Düsseldorf on the 26th and 27th, and it was the last night of the month before 405 Squadron's long lay-off ended with a call to arms for six crews to join a force of 181 targeting Hamburg as part of a 4 Group contribution of twenty-four Whitleys, eleven Halifaxes and the five Wellingtons. In addition, 4 Group detailed ten Whitleys and four Wellingtons, two each from 405 and 104 Squadrons, to join thirty-six other aircraft for a return to the "special" target at Emden and two Whitleys and a single 405 Squadron Wellingtons to attack the docks and shipping at Ostend. The last-mentioned departed Pocklington first at 16.59 with Sgt Swetman at the controls and a standard bomb load on board but turned back in the face of ten-tenths cloud and engine issues when thirty-five minutes from the target.

S/L Bisset was the senior pilot on duty for the main event as the 405 Squadron participants took to the air between 17.05 and 17.21 each with a standard bomb load beneath their feet. Taking off at the same time were the crews of Sgts Suggitt and Sutherland bound for Emden, but both were led astray by navigational errors and bombed alternative targets at Wesermünde and Seestermünde (untraced) respectively from 15,000 feet at 20.35. A message was received from S/L Bisset and crew at 18.35 indicating that they were returning to base, but they failed to arrive, and it must be assumed that W5476 had gone down in the North Sea, taking with it the entire crew. Meanwhile, the others heading for Hamburg mostly made landfall on the Schleswig-Holstein coast to the north of the target and all from 405 Squadron were able to identify the target area aided by moonlight. They delivered their attacks in the face of a hostile searchlight and flak defence from 8,000 to 17,000 feet between 20.25 and 21.12 and observed bursts in the Altona district on the northern bank of the Elbe and in the docks area on the southern bank and general city area. A sea search was mounted on the following day for the Bisset crew, but no trace of the aircraft or a dinghy was found. The loss of S/L Bisset DFC & Bar and crew was a bitter blow to the squadron and station communities, and the presence of such an experienced flight commander would be missed. He was succeeded as A Flight commander by the newly promoted S/L Fauquier.

During the course of the month the squadron took part in eight operations and dispatched thirty-two sorties for the loss of two Wellingtons and crews.

December 1941

The introduction of the Halifax had been a frustrating and painful process, and by the arrival of the final month of 1941, still only 35 and 76 Squadrons were conducting operations with the type, and only then in small numbers, while 10 Squadron was now under training and would soon be joining them. During December, 102 Squadron would also begin to convert from Whitleys, but it would be a slow evolution to operational status that would occupy four months, while the rest of 4 Group persevered with the Wellington and trusty but increasingly obsolete Whitley.

The dominant theme during December would be the continuing presence at Brest of the heavy cruisers Scharnhorst and Gneisenau and sometimes the Hipper class Prinz Eugen, and no fewer than fifteen operations of varying sizes would be mounted against the port and its guests during the month, some by daylight. The weather kept the entire Command on the ground for the first six nights of the new month, and it was not until the 7th that a posted operation would actually go ahead. The target for a force of 130 aircraft was Aachen, Germany's most westerly city, perched on the frontiers of Holland and Belgium. The briefed aiming-point for most was the Nazi Party HQ, which had no special significance other than the fact that it was situated in the city centre, however, the aiming point for twenty-six Whitleys, three Halifaxes and two 104 Squadron Wellingtons was the city's gas works. A second target on this night involved 3 Group Wellingtons and Stirlings against Brest, during which the Stirling element conducted the first operational trials of the Oboe blind bombing device, a system which would not enter service for almost thirteen months. A freshman raid by seventeen Whitleys and five Wellingtons from 4 Group was planned for Dunkerque and the two 405 Squadron participants, the crews of Sgts Swetman and Mather, departed Pocklington at 16.59 and 19.48 respectively, each carrying, it is believed fourteen 250 pounders and two SBCs. Neither located the target and both jettisoned their bombs but dispensed their load of nickels each along the coast at Dunkerque and Ostend and inland at Bruges. The

Aachen operation was compromised by adverse weather conditions and the city escaped serious damage.

4 Group contributed ten Whitleys and five Halifaxes to a raid by sixty aircraft on Cologne on the 11th, which, according to local sources, did not take place, suggesting that the fires reported by returning crews were decoys. On the 14th, 10 Squadron was announced as the latest and third Halifax Squadron after finally completing its conversion, and 102 Squadron received its first example of the type from the factory at Radlett in Hertfordshire. Twenty-five freshman crews were sent to Ostend on the 15th, among them six Whitleys and two Wellingtons provided by 4 Group, the latter belonging to 405 Squadron and containing the crews of Sgts Mather and Frost. They departed Pocklington at 16.51 and 16.53 respectively, their bomb bays filled with fourteen 250 pounders and two SBCs of incendiaries, and both reached the target area, Sgt Frost and crew to encounter ten-tenths cloud, which thwarted their thirty-six-minute-long search and persuaded them to jettison the hardware. In contrast, the Mather crew found five-tenths cloud and observed two of their bombs to impact docks to the north-west of the Bassin-de-Chasse.

A force of eighty-three aircraft was assembled on the 16th for a raid on Wilhelmshaven, which 4 Group supported with a dozen Whitleys from 77 Squadron and ten 405 Squadron Wellingtons and also detailed eight Whitleys and a single 405 Squadron Wellington for freshman crews to employ against the docks and shipping at Dunkerque. Sgt Wigley and crew departed Pocklington first and headed towards the south-east with fourteen 250 pounders in the bomb bay. They arrived at the French coast to find five-tenths cloud, through which the docks were clearly visible and the bombs, delivered from 12,000 feet at 18.25, were observed to straddle docks 4 and 5 and start a large fire in 5. Those assigned to the main event took off between 17.30 and 17.50 with F/L McCormack the senior pilot on duty and a payload of three 500 and three 250-pounders and six SBCs. Sgt Baltzer and crew had to contend with severe icing conditions that caused the a.s.i to freeze, and unable to break free of the cloud, jettisoned their load at 19.40 from 15,000 feet over the Waddenzee between the Frisian Island of Rottumerplaat and the German mainland. For an undisclosed reason, Sgt Taylor and crew bombed Bremen in good visibility aided by the dispensing of three flares and observed a large red fire in the city centre. Meanwhile, the others carried out their attacks at the primary target from 13,000 to 17,000 feet between 19.20 and 20.00, and on return reported large fires throughout the target area. According to local sources, however, the town escaped with only slight damage and no casualties.

On the following night 4 Group sent four Whitleys and three 405 Squadron Wellingtons with freshman crews to attack the docks and shipping at Le Havre, the Canadian trio of Sgts Lefurgey, Wigley and Foy and their crews departing Pocklington between 16.54 and 16.58, each with sixteen 250-pounders beneath their feet. They ran into unanticipated heavy cloud in the target area which defeated the Wigley and Foy crews, who jettisoned thir loads, while the Lefurgey crew were lucky to chance upon a break, through which the docks were visible and turned immediately to carry out a bombing run from east to west at 9,500 feet at 18.43.

A force of 121 aircraft assembled to attack the warships at Brest on the 17th included twenty-four Whitleys and four Wellingtons from the rebuilding 104 Squadron. They found the Brittany coastal area to be protected by nine to ten-tenths cloud and Brest itself by a smoke screen also, but intense searchlight beams streamed through the gaps along with heavy and light flak to provide an indication of the port's location. Two-thirds of returning crews claimed to have bombed the estimated location of the vessels but no hits were claimed. On the following morning 3, 4 and 5 Groups launched Operation Veracity I against Scharnhorst, Gneisenau and Prinz Eugen with a force of eighteen Halifaxes, eighteen Stirlings and eleven Manchesters, 10 Squadron operating Halifaxes for the first time. Accurate bombing was claimed, and black smoke was reported to be rising from Gneisenau, in exchange for which the attackers lost four Stirlings a Halifax and a Manchester.

A small 4 Group return to Wilhelmshaven on the 22/23rd involved twelve Whitleys and ten 405 Squadron Wellingtons, the latter each receiving the standard bomb load before departing Pocklington between 16.55 and 17.12 with W/C Fenwick-Wilson the senior pilot on duty. Sgt Mather and crew aborted their sortie after forty minutes when the starboard engine began to fail and after jettisoning their bombs headed for a landing at Lindholme. As they approached on finals the port engine cut and W5560 was crash-landed short of the runway at 19.55, writing it off with just minor injury to two crew members. Sgt Taylor and crew were defeated by icing conditions and turned back early, while W/C Fenwick-Wilson and crew attacked the seaplane base on the Frisian Island of Borkum. Seven to ten-tenths cloud greeted the others at the German coast and only the crews of Sgt Baltzer and F/O Frizzle positively identified the target, while the rest bombed on estimated positions from 11,000 to 15,000 feet between 18.44 and 19.15, destroying several houses.

The third wartime Christmas was observed in traditional service style, and then it was back to the war for 132 crews who were handed Düsseldorf as their target on the 27th, 4 Group supporting the operation with twenty-nine Whitleys from Leeming, Linton-on-Ouse and Middleton-St-George. An additional fifteen Whitley and five Wellington freshman crews were briefed to carry out attacks on the docks and shipping at Boulogne as part of an overall force of thirty-four aircraft, and among these were the 405 Squadron crews of Sgts Lloyd and Lefurgey. They departed Pocklington at 17.06 and 17.09 respectively with sixteen 250-pounders in each bomb bay and found five to seven-tenths cloud over the target, through which they delivered their attacks and observed bomb bursts across the docks.

The final night of operations for the month and the year was to be a busy one, with operations on the 28th directed at the ports of Wilhelmshaven and Emden by forces of eighty-six 1 and 3 Group Wellingtons and forty assorted aircraft respectively, while 5 Group detailed eighty-one Hampdens for a raid on the "Buna" works at Marl-Hüls in the Ruhr. 4 Group supported the Emden endeavour with fourteen 51 Squadron Whitleys and five 405 Squadron Wellingtons, the latter departing Pocklington between 16.45 and 17.05 with S/L Fauquier and F/L McCormack the senior pilots on duty and a standard load in each bomb bay. They benefitted from perfect conditions and the snow-covered landscape highlighted features to enable crews to establish their positions as they ran in on the aiming point. The attacks were delivered from 12,000 to 16,000 feet between 18.54 and 19.05 and returning crews reported bursts across the docks. Absent from debriefing was the crew of Sgt Williams RNZAF, who had lost their lives when W5561 was brought down to crash in the target area. It was a sad way to end the squadron's first six months of operations.

On the 30th, 4 Group launched Operation Veracity II, a second daylight attack by sixteen Halifaxes against the warships at Brest, from which three failed to return and all of the others sustained flak damage in return for an inconclusive outcome with no confirmed hits.

Since becoming operational, 405 Squadron had taken part in fifty-one operations at a cost of eighteen aircraft and crews, which was about average for the group. It was a satisfactory start to an operational career, which by war's end, would show 405 Squadron to be among the premier units in the Command. For the Command in general, however, it had been a bad year, with little to show by way of improvement over 1940. The three new heavy bombers introduced into service early in the year had all failed to meet expectations, and each had undergone periods of grounding, while essential modifications were put in hand. Their slow rate of production and poor serviceability meant that the Wellington would continue to be the backbone of the bomber offensive for some time to come, although its association with 405 Squadron had only a little over three months to run. The year ended with the stinging criticism of the Butt Report still very much in mind, and with the Command, therefore, in a state of limbo. A year of treading water had cost the Command many of its finest crews for little return, and there had to be some advance in 1942 if the Command were going to survive and become an effective weapon. One bright spot was the delivery during December of the first production Lancasters to 5 Group's 44 Squadron at Waddington, and these would become operational in the spring as the "shining sword" in the hands of a new Commander-in-Chief.

January 1942

The New Year began with the continuing pre-occupation with the German cruisers at Brest, and, following the fifteen raids of varying sizes sent against them during December, there would be no fewer than eleven further operations during January, eight in the first two weeks. 4 Group opened its 1942 account with a small-scale Whitley operation against the docks and shipping at St-Nazaire on the night of the 2/3rd launched from Leeming, Linton-on-Ouse and Middleton-St-George. The first major operation of the year was posted on the 5th and involved a force of 154 aircraft of which Wellingtons were the most populous type, eighty-seven to target Scharnhorst and Gneisenau at Brest and the remainder to aim for the naval docks area. A further thirty-seven crews were briefed to attack the docks and shipping at Cherbourg, and it was for this endeavour that 4 Group contributed eight Halifaxes and seventeen Whitleys. Earlier, Sgt Lefurgey RCAF and his all-RCAF crew had lost their lives in an attempted forced-landing at 10.15 near an artillery range at Strensall, five miles north of York, after W5589 developed a serious engine problem during an air-test. The wireless operator was not on board having failed to catch the transport to the aircraft's dispersal, but Sgt Robson's reprieve would be relatively brief. *(On this day 35 Squadron became 35 (Madras Presidency) Squadron.)*

A modest 1 Group force maintained the pressure on Brest on the 6th, while 4 Group sent eleven Whitleys to bomb Sola aerodrome at Stavanger in Norway, five Wellingtons to attack Cherbourg docks and ten Whitleys and five Wellingtons to deliver leaflets (nickels) to the residents of Paris. 405 Squadron provided all of the Wellingtons for Cherbourg, each bearing aloft a freshman crew and a standard bomb load as they departed Pocklington between 17.19 and 17.32 with P/O Keith Thiele the senior pilot on duty. They were confronted at the French coast by eight-tenths cloud and only the crews of Sgts Graham and Foy chanced upon a gap, through which they observed the docks and delivered their attacks from 3,000 and 14,000 feet at 19.20 and 19.40 respectively, each aided by the light of flares. On return, and landing without lights, P/O Thiele collided with another unlit aircraft and both sustained major damage although no crew casualties.

Continuing the maritime theme, 4 Group prepared twenty-seven Whitleys, Wellingtons and Halifaxes to send to St-Nazaire on the 7th, while the main effort by sixty-eight Wellingtons of 1 and 3 Groups was directed at Brest. While five 405 Squadron crews attended briefing their Wellingtons were each receiving a standard bomb load and take-off was completed without incident between 17.06 and 17.20 with S/L Fauquier the senior pilot on duty. Sgt Taylor and crew turned back early for technical reasons, leaving the others to make landfall over the Brest peninsula in the region of St-Malo and St-Brieuc and arrive at the Biscay coast to find just three-tenths cloud but ground haze that prevented most from identifying ground features. Sgt Allison and crew picked out dock installations and carried out a glide attack to release their bombs from 5,000 feet, while the rear gunner strafed buildings and bursts were observed in the docks followed by a blue explosion. The remaining three crews attacked the general docks area from 5,000 to 15,000 feet, adding to four or five small fires already burning on the western side.

The funerals of all five victims of the training crash took place at Barmby-in-the-Moor cemetery on the 8th during a lengthy break in operations for the squadron. Also on this day, AM Sir Richard Peirse left his post as C-in-C Bomber Command to be succeeded temporarily by AVM Baldwin, the A-O-C 3 Group. In February, Peirse would take up a new appointment as C-in-C Allied Air Forces in India and South-East Asia, but the sense that he had been "sacked" from Bomber Command would linger, and perhaps unjustly tarnish his legacy. That afternoon, briefings were held in preparation for the next round in the campaign against Brest for which a force of 151 aircraft was assembled, 4 Group detailing twenty-eight Whitleys and five Halifaxes to attack the dockyard power station.

4 Group supported an operation against a special target at Wilhelmshaven on the 10th with seventeen Whitleys, and this was followed by operational inactivity until the 15th, when six Halifaxes were detailed to join an overall force of ninety-six aircraft for an attack on Hamburg, following up on the previous night's raid on the same target. A second operation involving fifty aircraft, including thirty-seven Whitleys and eight Wellingtons provided by 4 Group, was to be directed at the port of Emden situated 115 miles to the west. 405 Squadron briefed the three freshman crews of P/O Thiele and Sgts Higginson and Morris (the ORB entry is seriously corrupted) and sent them on their way from Pocklington between 18.31 and 18.44 each with a 1,000-pounder, four 500-pounders and two SBCs in the bomb bay. The ten-tenths cloud over the North Sea dispersed to leave clear skies in the target area with ground haze and a backcloth of snow. The bombing by the 405 Squadron trio was carried out from 12,000 to 13,500 feet, aided by illuminating flares which appeared to be suspended over the target area for minutes, and bursts and fires were observed in the docks area.

Two nights later Bremen was the destination for eighty-three aircraft, of which eleven Wellingtons and two Halifaxes were provided by 4 Group, their crews briefed to attack special aiming point "B", the identity of which is not recorded. However, among regular targets within the city were the Focke-Wulf aircraft factory at Hemelingen, the Korff synthetic oil refinery, the Lloyd Dynamo works and the Deutsche Schiff und Maschinenbau A G shipyards, otherwise known as Deschimag.

This organisation had been formed in the mid-twenties as a co-operation of eight shipyards to compete with the Blohm & Voss and Bremer Vulkan yards. The largest was the A G Weser company, which, after six of the others had fallen by the wayside before the outbreak of war, was partnered only by the Seebeckwerft, now as part of the Krupp empire, after it had been handed a controlling interest in 1941. The eight 405 Squadron crews would be participating in the squadron's fifty-fifth operation of the war, during which the RCAF's first 4,000lb "cookie" was to be delivered by S/L Fauquier in Z8431, which would also be carrying a 1,000-pounder, a 500-pounder, two 250-pounders and two SBCs. The other Wellingtons received a bomb load of two examples each of 1,000, 500 and 250-pounders and SBCs and departed Pocklington between 17.12 and 17.35 with S/L Keddy the other senior pilot on duty. A message was received from S/L Keddy and crew at 18.13 stating that they were returning to base because of engine trouble, and at 18.32 a member of the Royal Observer Corps reported a burning aircraft, believed to be a Wellington, coming down in the sea off the Yorkshire coast at Skipsea. The others, meanwhile, continued on across the North Sea accompanied by unbroken cloud, which persisted over the target and persuaded three crews to bomb Emden as an alternative. The Forms 540 and 541 are contradictory, the former recording that the Fauquier crew's cookie was released by hand over Emden after the bomb-release failed, while the latter specifies Bremen as the location of the impressive detonation. Where-ever it fell, it was the only sighting of an impact and the outcome of the night's activities was, therefore, inconclusive, an analysis revealing that only eight aircraft had reached the primary target, while many attacked Hamburg or joined in at Emden.

S/L Keddy DFC RCAF and three of his crew had perished in the sea, leaving two crew members to endure fourteen hours in a freezing dinghy before being rescued by a Royal Navy destroyer. F/L Scrivens, the squadron bombing leader, and wireless operator/gunner, Sgt Turnbull, were admitted to Sheppey County Hospital suffering from exposure and severe frostbite and Sgt Turnbull had sustained a broken nose. They reported that the starboard engine had caught fire, and while they were preparing to bale out or ditch, they found themselves suddenly emmersed in seawater. They were told that an Air-Sea-Rescue-Launch had been dispatched from Bridlington at 18.40 but returned at 22.25 having found nothing. W/C Fenwick-Wilson led a sea-search, which was also fruitless, and it was the following morning before the news arrived that two crew members had been picked up. The remains of S/L Keddy were recovered from the sea and taken to Hull for cremation, while the other three are commemorated on the Runnymede Memorial. S/L Keddy had been a popular member of the squadron, and his experience and presence would be sorely missed. He was succeeded as flight commander by S/L McCormack.

A force of ninety-nine aircraft was assembled on the 18th to unleash that night against the naval and shipbuilding port of Kiel, 4 Group contributing twenty-five Whitleys from Dishforth and Leeming. The Kiel authorities reported the attack to be the most destructive to date on the port, with damage to the Deutsche Werke U-Boot yards and many town-centre-type buildings. Topcliffe and Linton-on-Ouse provided most of the twenty-one Whitleys made ready to send against the U-Boot pens on Lorient's Keroman peninsula on the 20th, when those arriving over the Brittany coast were greeted by clear skies and only ground haze to muddy the vertical visibility at the target. The bombing was carried out mostly from between 10,000 and 13,000 feet and although a number of bursts were observed across the docks, the results were lost in the kaleidoscope of searchlights and flak. The first phase of the massive construction project on the Keroman peninsula on the southern extremities of Lorient had begun in early 1941 and had only just been completed. The K1, K2 and

K3 structures were capable of sheltering thirty vessels and their crews under cover and the complex boasted a revolutionary lift system, which could raise U-Boots from the water and transport them across the facility to repair and servicing bays. The thickness of the concrete rendered the structure impervious to the bombs available to Bomber Command at the time, and attacks would be directed predominantly at the town and its approaches to prevent access by road and rail, while mining took care of the sea lanes.

A return to Bremen on the 21st involved fifty-four aircraft, 4 Group originally detailing thirteen Wellingtons and six Halifaxes, only for eight to be scrubbed. 405 Squadron loaded six of its eight Wellingtons with a 1,000-pounder and four 500 and four 250-pounders, and the other two for the crews of W/C Fenwick-Wilson and S/L Fauquier with a 4,000lb cookie, before sending them on their way from Pocklington between 17.22 and 17.41. The crews of Sgts Allison and Lloyd and P/O Robson turned back after an hour, the first two-mentioned because of engine issues, leaving the others to run into ten-tenths cloud until reaching 4° East, where it began to disperse to leave relatively clear skies over the target. Searchlights were operating in cones, some of them containing up to fifty beams, and the flak was intense and accurate as Sgt Foy and crew identified the Neustadt Bahnhof (railway station) south of the River Weser and observed their bombs to burst in the vicinity. Sgt Higginson and crew were forced to descend to 8,000 feet after losing their oxygen supply, too low in their estimation to attack Bremen and headed to Emden, where they delivered their bomb load onto the northern end of the docks. P/O Thiele and crew were unable to identify Bremen and bombed a flak concentration somewhere along the bank of the river. Searchlight glare prevented an assessment of the results for most, but the crews of W/C Fenwick-Wilson and S/L Fauquier observed the impressive detonations of their cookies and claimed devastating results and a large, red fire. An assessment revealed that only half of the force claimed to have reached the primary target, and it is unlikely that significant damage was achieved.

Berlin was posted as the target for thirty-two Whitleys on the 23rd, which would be sharing the capital with thirty-five Wellingtons, although, in keeping with the system in place during this period, not necessarily at the same time. In the event, four Whitleys were scrubbed, and the rest encountered patchy low cloud over Berlin city centre, where ground haze added to the challenges of identifying the Alexander Platz railway station aiming point.

Briefing at Pocklington on the 26th informed seven 405 Squadron crews that the northern city of Hannover was to be their target in company with sixty-four other aircraft including three 10 Squadron Halifaxes. Situated midway between the Dutch frontier and Berlin, Hannover was a major contributor to the German war effort and was home among others to the Accumulatoren-Fabrik A G, manufacturers of lead acid batteries for U-Boots and torpedoes, the Continental tyre and rubber factory at Limmer, the Deurag-Nerag synthetic oil refinery at Misburg, the VLW (Volkswagen) metalworks, and the Maschinenfabrik Niedersachsen Hannover and Hanomag factories, which were producing guns and tracked vehicles. The Canadians took off between 17.18 and 17.54 with S/L Fauquier the senior pilot on duty and a cookie in his bomb bay, while the others were loaded with a mix of 1,000, 500 and 250-pounders. The crews of Sgts McLennan and Taylor were on their way home with serviceability issues within ninety minutes, while the others continued on accompanied by ten-tenths cloud over the North Sea, and when this cleared at the Dutch coast, frozen snow-covered waterways hampered navigation. While seeking an alternative target S/L Fauquier and crew recognised Bremen and dropped their cookie onto a built-up area to the north-west of the city, observing a large flash and explosion. The others attacked what they believed to be Hannover, while Sgt Lloyd and crew identified nearby Braunschweig as their alternative target.

4 Group supported freshman operations against Boulogne and Rotterdam on the 28th with five Wellingtons and three Whitleys at the former and twenty-nine Whitleys at the latter. The 405 Squadron crews of Sgts Graham and Morris and P/O Locke departed Pocklington for the French coast between 17.27 and 17.41, each sitting on sixteen 250-pounders, and were greeted by ten-tenth cloud and severe icing conditions. The Morris crew returned to base after failing to identify the primary or suitable alternative target, while the others bombed in the vicinity of Calais and had nothing of value to report at debriefing.

On the 29th a flight of 104 Squadron Wellingtons moved into Pocklington on a temporary basis, as Driffield was unserviceable. As previously stated, most of the squadron had been posted to the Middle East in October for what was intended to be a short period of duty, leaving a small home echelon to continue operating under Bomber Command. This had been building up gradually to squadron strength, and once it was decided in January that 104 would, in fact, remain overseas, it was assumed that the home echelon would retain the coveted 104 Squadron number-plate. In the event this was not to be the case, and on the 14th of February, it would be renumbered 158 Squadron.

The month ended for 405 Squadron with participation in the latest attempt to hit the enemy warships at Brest on the 31st, for which five of its Wellingtons were to join four others from 104 Squadron in departing Pocklington between 17.16 and 17.28 with S/L Fauquier the senior pilot on duty and a W/C McMaster flying with him as second pilot. It is believed that the ORB entry should have read "W/C MacAllister", who would shortly succeed W/C Fenwick-Wilson as commanding officer. P/O Robson and crew turned back early, while the others encountered up to six-tenths cloud at 8,000 feet and were unable to identify the vessels through an effective smoke-screen. S/L Fauquier brought the cookie home in accordance with instructions and Sgt Swetman and crew also returned their bombs to the dump, while the crews of P/O Thiele and Sgt Graham bombed the general docks area through three-tenths cloud from around 10,000 feet.

During the course of the month the squadron took part in eight operations and dispatched forty-four sorties for the loss of two Wellingtons and crews.

February 1942

February was to be a significant month for the Command in a number of ways, and there would also be changes at 405 Squadron. The Duke of Kent visited a snow-bedecked Pocklington on the 1st in his capacity as the principal RAF welfare officer, and he carried out an inspection of crews and aircraft, shaking hands and conversing enthusiastically with personnel, before lunching with the officers. Sadly, he would be killed in a crash in Scotland in August, while flying as a passenger in a Coastal Command Short Sunderland flying boat. The squadron was on stand-by from the 3rd to the 8th, as were a few units from the other groups as intelligence suggested a possible breakout by the enemy fleet from Brest. A further attack on Brest involved sixty aircraft on the 6th, when only a third of the crews claimed to have bombed near the warships, and the results were inconclusive.

There had been no operational activity for 4 Group at the start of the new month, until it stirred from its slumber to send three Whitleys to Emden on the night of the 10/11th. On the following night, six 76 Squadron Halifaxes and twenty-three Whitleys joined twenty other aircraft for a raid on Mannheim, while, among other small-scale operations on this night was a freshman raid on the docks and shipping at Le Havre, which 4 Group supported with six Whitleys and two 405 Squadron Wellingtons. The crews of Sgt Howsan and P/O Durbridge departed Pocklington at 17.36 and 17.38 respectively, each sitting on sixteen 250-pounders, and were able to establish their positions on the River Seine, which was banked by snow but appeared to be free of ice. The Howsan crew released their bombs on their third pass and observed them to straddle the docks area, one flash pinpointed by the rear gunner between the Bassin-du-Maree and the western end of Dock 7. The Durbridge crew was unable to identify ground features through six-tenths cloud and jettisoned the bombs over the Channel fifteen miles off Cherbourg.

Another raid on Brest on this night involved eighteen Wellingtons, the crews of which would have been unaware that they were the last to engage in this seemingly endless saga. As the sound of their engines receded into the eastern cloud-filled skies, Vice-Admiral Otto Cilliax, the Brest Group commander, whose flag was on Scharnhorst, put Operation Cerberus into action at 21.14 with Scharnhorst, Gneisenau and Prinz Eugen slipping anchor, before heading into the English Channel under an escort of destroyers and E-Boats. It was an audacious bid for freedom, covered by bad weather, widespread jamming and meticulously planned support by the Kriegsmarine and the Luftwaffe, all of which had been rehearsed extensively during January. The planning, and a little good fortune, allowed the fleet to make undetected progress until spotted off Le Touquet by two Spitfires piloted by G/C Victor Beamish, the commanding officer of Kenley, and W/C Finlay Boyd, both of whom maintained radio silence, and did not report their find until landing at 10.42 on the morning of the 12th.

The British authorities had prepared a plan in advance for precisely this eventuality under the codename, Operation Fuller, but so secret was it, that few, it seemed, either knew of its full requirements or even of its existence. Once the enemy fleet was spotted in the late morning, frantic efforts were made to get Coastal and Bomber Command aircraft away, and by 21.25 its position was reported off South Foreland. It was 13.30 before the first Bomber Command sorties were launched, the 4 Group stations working frantically to get thirteen Halifaxes and thirteen Wellingtons into the air as part of the largest commitment of aircraft by daylight in the war to date, amounting to 242 sorties. The first six 405 Squadron Wellingtons took to the air between 13.52 and 13.57 with W/C Fenwick-Wilson and S/L Fauquier the senior pilots on duty and a load in each bomb bay of eight 500-pounders. They headed towards The Wash and as soon as they left the Norfolk coast behind, they found themselves in tenth-tenths cloud with tops at 9,000 feet all the way to their search area off the Dutch Frisian islands. Their challenges were exacerbated by rainstorms and squally conditions, which prevented most crews from locating the enemy fleet. With the exception of S/L Fauquier, who descended to 300 feet, none of the 405 Squadron element even caught a glimpse of the sea and the Fauquier crew saw only a BF110 pass from from starboard to port a thousand yards ahead.

They were on their way home with their bombs when the crews of P/O Thiele and Sgt Wigley departed Pocklington at 16.43 and both momentarily sighted one of the heavy cruisers through a break in the cloud. The Wigley crew bombed from 3,500 feet at 18.09, but immediately lost sight of the target and two minutes later inconclusively engaged one of two BF109s at a range of five hundred yards. P/O Thiele and crew spotted a vessel some thirty miles off The Hague but lost it immediately in cloud and failed to relocate it despite descending to 1,500 feet. At debriefing, both crews reported hostile ant-aircraft fire and also noted that the warships were making slow progress, evidenced by the lack of a bow wave and a wake. The few crews that made contact with the fleet did their best to inhibit its progress but, despite the heroic effort and sacrifice by members of Bomber Command, Coastal Command and the Fleet Air Arm, the enemy fleet made good its escape into open sea, although, its own trials and tribulations were not yet over. Scharnhorst struck a mine in the late afternoon and began to fall back, confirming the 405 Squadron testimony, and at 19.55, a magnetic mine detonated close enough to Gneisenau, when off Terschelling, to open a small hole in the starboard side and temporarily, slow her progress also. Later still, at 21.34, when passing through the same stretch of water, Scharnhorst hit another mine which stopped both engines and damaged steering and fire control. The vessel got under way again at 22.23 using its starboard engines and making twelve knots, while carrying an additional one thousand tons of seawater. The day's activities were not yet over for 5 Group, and the crews of twelve Hampdens and nine Manchesters were briefed to lay mines in the Nectarine garden off the Frisians through which the enemy fleet would have to pass to reach safety.

Gneisenau and Prinz Eugen reached the Elbe Estuary at 07.00 on the 13th, and tied up at Brunsbüttel North Locks at 09.30, while Scharnhorst arrived at Wilhelmshaven at 10.00 with three months-worth of damage to repair. The mines had been laid almost certainly by 5 Group Hampdens over the preceding nights and demonstrated the remarkable effectiveness of this war-long campaign against enemy shipping. The entire episode was a major embarrassment to the government and the nation, but, worse still, cost the Command a further fifteen aircraft and crews on top of all of those sacrificed to this endeavour over the past eleven months. 5 Group alone posted missing nine Hampdens and crews, all lost in the North Sea, six of them without trace. On a positive note, this annoying and distracting itch had been scratched for the last time, and the Command could now concentrate its forces against the strategic targets for which it was better suited.

On the 13th, thirty-nine aircraft were sent to Cologne, among them eight Halifaxes from 10 and 76 Squadrons, eighteen 4 Group Whitleys went to Aachen to attack the marshalling yards and twenty-eight freshman crews targeted Le Havre, 4 Group supporting the last-mentioned with seven Whitleys and three 405 Squadron Wellingtons for bombing plus a further Wellington for nickelling duties. The Pocklington element took to the air between 17.28 and 17.43, Sgt Howsan and crew leading and dispensing twenty-two packets of the F11 propaganda leaflets off the French coast from Cap d-Antifer to the mouth of the Seine from 13,000 feet between 19.48 and 20.18. The bombing trio, meanwhile, encountered eight to ten-tenths cloud over the Channel and the crews of P/Os Durbridge, Hemy and Locke all jettisoned their bombs after searching in vain for around thirty minutes.

A new Air Ministry directive issued on the 14th was to change the emphasis of bomber operations from that point until the end of the war. Lengthy consideration having been given to the Butt

Report and the future of an independent bomber force, the new policy authorised the blatant area bombing of Germany's industrial towns and cities in a direct assault on the morale of the civilian population, particularly its workers. This had, of course, been going on since the summer of 1940, but no longer would there be the pretence of claiming to be attacking industrial and military targets. Waiting in the wings, in fact, at this very moment, four days into his voyage from the port of Boston, Massachusetts in the armed merchantman, Alcantara, was a new leader, who not only would pursue this policy with a will, but also possessed the self-belief, arrogance and stubbornness to fight his corner against all-comers on behalf of his beleaguered Bomber Command. Also, on this day, 104 Squadron was renumbered 158 Squadron at Driffield, and would continue to operate the Mk II Wellington alongside 405 Squadron until its conversion to the Halifax in June, two months after 405 Squadron relinquished the Wellington.

Later, on the 14th, 4 Group detailed fourteen Wellingtons and seven Whitleys for an operation to Mannheim, and all but two took off as part of an overall force of ninety-eight aircraft. The five 405 Squadron participants departed Pocklington between 18.03 and 18.36 with F/L Frizzle the senior pilot on duty and three carrying a cookie and two an assortment of 1,000, 500 and 250-pounders. F/L Frizzle and crew ran into severe icing conditions and aborted their sortie as they were unable to maintain altitude, leaving the remaining four crews to reach the target area and drop their loads from estimated positions from 13,000 to 15,000 feet between 21.00 and 21.30. A vivid, purple/blue flash was observed that lasted almost a minute and another flash from the detonation of a cookie left a red glow visible for fifteen minutes after leaving the target.

405 Squadron sat out a freshman operation against St-Nazaire on the 15th and "special" nickelling operations over the ensuing nights over Holland, Belgium, Norway and Paris. A ten-day-long game of musical chairs was enacted at Pocklington as S/L Fauquier assumed temporary command of the squadron on the 17th and F/L Frizzle covered for him as A Flight commander. On the 21st, W/C Fenwick-Wilson assumed temporary command of Pocklington and on the 22nd, ACM Harris took up his appointment as Commander-in-Chief and immediately set about the task of transforming the Command into a war-winning weapon. Harris was a bomber man to the core, who, in the twenties, had developed the theory and practice of precision bombing by both day and night during his stint as a squadron commander in Mesopotamia. Shortly after the outbreak of war he was appointed A-O-C 5 Group, relinquishing the post in November 1940 to become deputy Chief-of-the-Air Staff to Sir Charles Portal. Most recently he had been part of a mission to the United States enlisting support for the European war and had impressed his American counterparts. Harris arrived at the helm with firm ideas already in place on how to win a war by bombing alone, recognising the need to overwhelm a city's defences and emergency services by a concentration of aircraft in time and numbers, and was aware also, that urban areas are most efficiently destroyed by fire rather than blast. It would not be long before the bomb loads carried in his aircraft reflected this thinking and he would also introduce the bomber stream, with strict timings and bombing heights, and sweep away the former less regimented system. This would mean directing the bulk of his strength against a single target, rather than diluting the effectiveness of operations by sending small forces to multiple targets simultaneously. He also set great store by technology and would take a personal interest in the development of electronic aids to navigation and bombing.

During his first week in office Harris contented himself with a continuation of the small-scale raids on German ports and on the night of his appointment sanctioned a raid on the floating dock at

Wilhelmshaven where Scharnhorst was undergoing repair. This was followed on the 25th and 26th by attacks on the floating dock at Kiel that was being employed to repair Gneisenau, the former operation by a force of sixty-one aircraft and not supported by 4 Group, while the following night's endeavour called upon fifteen 4 Group Wellingtons and ten Halifaxes in an overall force of forty-nine aircraft. Two of 405 Squadron's nine Wellingtons had a cookie winched into the bomb bay, and the others each received a bomb load of 1,000, 500 and 250-pounders before departing Pocklington between 18.42 and 18.55 with F/L Robson the senior pilot on duty accompanied as second pilot by W/C MacAllister. Also on board W5516 was F/Sgt Robson, whom fate had spared on the 5th of January, when the rest of his crew had perished in the previously mentioned air-test accident. The crews of P/O Swetmand and F/Sgt Morris turned back early because of icing and Sgt Lloyd and crew jettisoned their load "live" after failing to establish their position at the target. Five crews reached the target area to be greeted by intense searchlight and flak activity, and a stick of bombs was observed to fall just short of the floating dock and result in a large fire that remained visible for fifty miles into the return flight. Red and green explosions were witnessed in the Deutsche Werke U-Boot construction yards and a photograph was snapped of the detonation of a cookie near the town of Schleswig. The operation threw up one of the war's great ironies after a high explosive bomb scored a direct hit on the bows of Gneisenau, now supposedly in safe haven after enduring eleven months of constant bombardment at Brest, and not only did it kill 116 of her crew, it also ended her sea-going career for good. Her main armament was ultimately removed for coastal defence work and her hulk towed to Gdynia, where it would remain for the duration.

405 Squadron's W5516 disappeared without trace with the crew of F/L Robson, and the loss of the commanding officer-elect, W/C MacAllister, set off a second round of musical chairs, which saw W/C Fenwick-Wilson depart Pocklington for pastures new at the Air Ministry on the 27th and leave a vacancy for S/L Fauquier first as temporary station commander, while S/L McCormack sat in the squadron commander's seat, and then as squadron commander, a temporary post that was quickly confirmed as permanent. Thus, the tough and highly experienced former bush pilot "Johnny" Fauquier began the first of his two spells as 405 Squadron's inspirational commanding officer. He would quickly stamp his personality on the squadron, and by war's end would be a legendary figure in both the RAF and RCAF. *(The biography of Air Commodore Fauquier DSO and two Bars, DFC by Dave Birrell is highly recommended.)*

During the course of the month the squadron participated in just five operations and dispatched twenty-eight sorties for the loss of a single Wellington and crew.

March 1942

At the beginning of March, the Halifax squadrons were warned of an imminent screening from operations to allow the delivery of a fresh batch of aircraft equipped with the new navigation device "Gee" or TR1335. For the purpose of this book, the terms Gee and TR are interchangeable. In the meantime, twenty of the type, ten provided by 35 (Madras Presidency) Squadron, were detailed to participate in what would be a template for future operations and a sign of things to come.

Bomber Command's evolution to war-winning capability was to be long, arduous and gradual, but the first signs of a new hand on the tiller came early on in Harris's reign with this meticulously planned attack on the Renault lorry factory, which was located in a loop of the Seine in the district of Billancourt to the south-west of the centre of Paris. The plant was capable of producing 18,000 lorries per year, which was a massive boon to the German war effort, and the attempt to destroy it came in response to an Air Ministry request. The operation would be conducted in three waves, led by experienced crews, and would involve extensive use of flares to provide illumination. Crews were also briefed to attack from as low a level as practicable, both for the sake of accuracy and to try to avoid civilian casualties. In time, such operations would be led by Gee-equipped aircraft, but the 3 Group squadrons already employing the device were forbidden from taking part. A force of 235 aircraft was assembled on the 3rd, a new record for a single target, of which a total of forty-nine Halifaxes, Wellingtons and Whitleys represented 4 Group.

405 Squadron loaded three of its nine Wellingtons with a cookie each and the others with a 1,000-pounder and four each of 500lbs and 250lbs and sent them on their way from Pocklington between 18.25 and 19.03 with S/L McCormack the senior pilot on duty. F/Sgt Baltzer and crew turned back almost immediately with an engine issue, leaving the rest to reach the target and find good visibility beneath the cloud and little opposition. The bombing produced spectacular results with debris flung into the air and the entire site a mass of flames. The operation was a major success for the loss of a single aircraft, and destroyed 40% of the buildings, halting production for a month with the loss of 2,300 vehicles. The success was marred only by the collateral deaths of 367 French civilians in adjacent residential districts, a tragedy that would be repeated in future attacks on urban targets in occupied countries. It was somewhat paradoxical that Harris, as a champion of area bombing, should achieve his first major success via a precision target. On the 5th, 158 Squadron left Pocklington to return to the now serviceable Driffield.

On the 7th 4 Group detailed eleven Whitleys and seven Wellingtons for an attack on the U-Boot pens at St-Nazaire, the four 405 squadron participants departing Pocklington between 01.20 and 01.36 bearing aloft the crews of P/Os Allison, Durbridge, Taylor and Thiele and a bomb load each of one 1,000-pounder and four each of 500lbs and 250lbs. The Taylor crew returned early because of a fuel feed problem, while the others arrived in the target area under clear, moonlit skies and delivered their attacks according to brief, observing bursts, flashes and fires.

As one of Germany's industrial giants and home to the huge Krupp industrial empire, Essen was to feature prominently in Harris's future plans. Many small-scale raids in the past had barely left scratches, and this was not only because of the insignificant weight of bombs employed. The entire urban sprawl of the Ruhr contained around thirty conurbations from cities to small towns, most of which were spewing industrial pollution into the atmosphere. This formed a layer of haze over the region, which even by day, could make the identification of individual built-up areas impossible. Harris would place his faith in the development of electronic eyes, which could penetrate the cloud and haze, and the first of these, Gee, a navigation aid, became available for the opening of a series of operations against Essen on consecutive nights on the 8/9th. 211 aircraft took off over a three-hour period either side of midnight, the leading aircraft of 3 Group equipped with Gee to guide the first wave to the general target area. 4 Group was represented by ten 35 (Madras Presidency) Squadron Halifaxes, and the result was a highly disappointing raid, which destroyed a few houses and other buildings, while missing the Krupp districts altogether. Decoy fire sites in open country south of the target lured away much of the effort, and hundreds of flares igniting at 10,000 to 12,000 feet created a glare, which, together with that from searchlights, rendered aiming-point identification something of a challenge. Local sources described a light raid with some housing damage in southern districts, and this was achieved at a cost to the Command of eight aircraft. It was a disappointing outcome, and it would soon become clear that while a useful aid to navigation, Gee could not be relied upon as a blind-bombing device.

A force of 187 aircraft was made ready to return to Essen on the 9th, 35 (Madras Presidency) Squadron detailing five Halifaxes to join up with a dozen Wellingtons as the 4 Group contribution, while 10 Squadron dispatched seven Halifaxes to a forward base at Lossiemouth with a view to operating against the Tirpitz when conditions allowed. Two of the seven 405 Squadron Wellingtons were loaded with a cookie and the others with two 1,000-pounders, two 500 and four 250-pounders before departing Pocklington between 19.44 and 19.58 with S/L Fauquier the senior pilot on duty. They adopted the northerly route to the Ruhr, which took the force to a point south of Münster, leaving a run of some thirty-five miles in good horizontal visibility to the target. On arrival they encountered five-tenths cloud with tops at around 8,000 feet and found the vertical view onto the target compromised by the usual industrial haze. A large number of incendiaries were reported to be burning in the centre of Essen, five or six large fires were observed on approach and the impression gained was of a highly successful attack, when in fact, the bombing had been scattered over twenty-four other Ruhr towns and cities, with Hamborn and Duisburg the chief beneficiaries. The Essen authorities reported the destruction of two buildings, with seventy-two others damaged, and this was another hugely disappointing outcome.

It was left to seven Wellingtons to represent 4 Group in a force of 126 aircraft bound for Essen on the night of the 10/11th, the 405 Squadron trio consisting of the crews of P/Os Durbridge, McKay and Thiele, who departed Pocklington between 19.38 and 19.44, each with a mix of 1,000, 500 and 250-pounders on board. Unexpected cloud contributed to another dismal performance in which fewer than half of the crews reached the primary target, while thirty-five others bombed alternatives, and the nearest any bombs fell to the Krupp complex was on a railway line serving the general area. On return, the McKay crew reported bombing the primary target from 14,000 feet at 21.56, while Keith Thiele and crew could only claim the belief that they had been over Essen at bomb release. A distress call was received from Z8428 at 23.16, but nothing further was heard from P/O Durbridge and crew, who were duly posted missing, ultimately to be commemorated on the Runnymede Memorial as having no known graves.

Like a dog with a bone, Harris would return to Essen later in the month in a personal war against Krupp that he would win in time, but not before many battles had been lost. On the 11th S/L Fauquier was promoted to wing commander rank, and W/C Fenwick-Wilson was posted to Washington. He would return to the operational scene in March 1944, to take command of 3 Group's 218 Squadron, with which he would complete a seven-month tour of duty. 405 Squadron was not involved in an all-Wellington attack on the Deutsche Werke U-Boot construction yard at Kiel on the 12/13th, while twenty Whitleys represented 4 Group at Emden, but returned to action on the following night, when 4 Group supported a raid on Cologne with eleven 35 (Madras Presidency) Squadron Halifaxes and eight Wellingtons as part of a highly mixed force of 135 aircraft. The five 405 Squadron participants departed Pocklington between 19.13 and 19.23 with P/Os Frost, Locke and Taylor the senior pilots on duty and the usual mix of 1,000, 500 and 250-pounders in each bomb bay. The Frost crew had lost the use of both turrets by the time they made landfall on the Belgian side of the Scheldt estuary and took their bombs home, leaving the others to arrive in the target area and offer the usual diverse opinions as to the cloud conditions. The consensus was that ten-tenths medium cloud hovered to the west and east of the city, while a gap existed right over it in which two to five-tenths cumulus topped out at 11,000 feet. The weather was favourable allowing rivers, bridges and Autobahns to stand out in the partial snow-cover to provide ground features to assist with navigation. Illumination flares were described as of great assistance, and searchlight beams also provided a reference as the Pocklington quartet bombed between 22.16 and 22.30. Returning crews reported fires to the west and north-west of the city centre and local sources confirmed that this had been one of the most destructive raids yet against the Rhineland capital, causing a loss of production at a number of war industry factories, while setting off 260 fires and damaging fifteen hundred houses, albeit the majority only lightly. This was the first Gee led raid to achieve a reasonable degree of success.

A night cross-country exercise by seven of the squadron's crews on the 17/18th wrote off W5497 in a landing accident, and the pilot, Sgt Mitchell, was slightly injured. This occurred during a period of minor operations not involving the squadron, and it was not until the night of the 25/26th that it was next called into action to take part in the latest round in the campaign against Essen. A force of 254 aircraft was assembled, a new record to a single target, and contained a 4 Group contribution of fifteen Wellingtons, of which six belonged to 405 Squadron. They departed Pocklington between 19.38 and 19.53 with P/Os Locke and Taylor the senior pilots on duty, a payload of two 1,000, two 500 and four 250-pounders and S/L Fraser flying as second pilot to P/O Taylor. Sgt Wigley and crew were unable to coax more than 9,500 feet out of "V" and bombed a flare-path to the north of The Hague before turning back, and Sgt Lloyd and crew were unable to establish a pinpoint on the Dutch coast through the haze and after a vain search for a suitable target in the area between Rotterdam and The Hague, returned their bombs to the station dump. The remaining four delivered an attack between 21.33 and 22.05 and were among 181 who claimed at debriefing to have bombed the target area without observing results. Sadly, the massive effort was not rewarded with success, as a decoy fire site at nearby Rheinberg drew off a proportion of the bombing, and only one house in Essen was classed as destroyed, while two others were deemed to be seriously damaged.

Harris was nothing if not persistent and sent a further 104 aircraft back to Essen twenty-four hours later, the five Wellingtons belonging to 405 Squadron departing Pocklington between 19.54 and 20.05 with the newly promoted F/L Thiele the senior pilot on duty and S/L Fraser flying as second pilot to F/Sgt Baltzer. Conditions were favourable and crews were guided to the target by a concentration of flares, although there were complaints that they ignited at too high an altitude. All five 405 Squadron crews reported bombing the primary target between 22.13 and 22.40 in the face of spirited defence, the searchlights ringing the city organised in groups of up to thirty beams. Bomb bursts and fires were observed, and claims were made that the Krupp districts had been hit, but the truth was that this was another dismal failure, which distributed bombs liberally around the Ruhr and destroyed only two houses in Essen.

Thirty-four Halifaxes flew up to forward bases in Scotland at Kinloss, Lossiemouth and Tain on the 27th in preparation for an attack on the battleship Tirpitz in a Norwegian fjord when conditions allowed. This meant that they missed out on the attack on the ancient and historic Hansastadt (free-trade) city of Lübeck on Germany's Baltic coast on Palm Sunday, the 28th. Harris believed that if he could provide his crews with the means to locate a target beyond the range of Gee, they would hit it, and coastlines offered the most distinctive features for the purpose of identification. Hence,

Lübeck, which lies on an island to the east of Kiel and represented the perfect target for destruction by fire because of the narrow streets and half-timbered buildings in its old centre. It was also believed to be lightly defended, which would allow bombing to take place from a lower level than was standard for an urban target. The operation was planned along the same lines as the attack on the Renault factory at the start of the month and involved a force of 234 aircraft attacking in three waves, 4 Group providing seventeen Wellingtons from 405 and 158 Squadrons. The nine-strong Canadian element departed Pocklington over an extended period between 20.47 and 22.03 with S/Ls Fraser and McCormack the senior pilots on duty, four with a cookie in the bomb bay, while the rest carried nine SBCs, each containing ninety 4lb incendiaries. This represented a fire-raising recipe, in which the blast from the light-case blockbusters stripped roofs of their tiles and blew in doors and windows to allow the incendiaries to do their work. P/O Swetman and crew turned back early when their intercom failed, but the others all made it to the target, where cloudless skies and moonlight provided perfect conditions.

Most crews were able to plot the fall of their bombs and observed them detonating on buildings and setting off fires, which quickly spread across the island and left a pall of smoke drifting towards the west. One rear gunner counted ninety-five fires and the glow from the burning city was reported by many to have remained visible on the horizon for a hundred miles into the return flight. S/L McCormack's "L" was engaged by a BF110 and damaged but arrived home safely after more than seven hours aloft. The operation succeeded in destroying almost fifteen hundred houses and seriously damaging almost two thousand more in a 190-acre area of devastation that represented some 30% of the city's built-up area. Twelve aircraft failed to return from what was the first major success for area bombing, and another sign of what was in store for the residents of Germany's towns and cities. There was an outcry following this unexpected attack on Lübeck, which was a vital port for the Red Cross, and an agreement was struck that, in theory, although not entirely in practice, ensured its future protection from bombing.

During the course of the moth the squadron took part in eight operations and dispatched forty-nine sorties for the loss of two Wellingtons and one crew.

April 1942

April would bring to an end 405 Squadron's association with the Wellington, but the final two weeks of operations with the type were to prove expensive. The new month began for 4 Group on the 1st with involvement in operations against the docks and shipping at Le Havre and the Matford (Ford) motor works in Paris's north-western district of Poissy. A force of thirty-four Wellingtons and twenty-two Hampdens was assigned to the former and included eight 4 Group Wellingtons, five belonging to 405 Squadron, which departed Pocklington between 23.10 and 23.21 with S/L Fraser the senior pilot on duty and a bomb load each of sixteen 250-pounders. They were followed into the air between 01.05 and 01.09 by the Paris-bound quartet consisting of the cookie-carrying crews of W/C Fauquier, P/Os Swetman and Taylor and F/Sgt Howsan, who were part of a 4 Group force of twenty-four Whitleys and a dozen Wellingtons. Conditions over the Normandy coast were described by S/L Fraser as "bright as day", which allowed all to identify the target and deliver accurate attacks from 9,000 to 13,800 feet between 01.01 and 01.34. It was difficult to assess the outcome, but several fires had taken hold by the time the bomber retreated to the north. Meanwhile, ninety-five miles away to the south-east, the conditions were equally favourable under bright moonlight and P/O Taylor and crew were approaching at low level when they stumbled into the Paris flak. They pulled away and ran in again, this time at 3,000 feet at 03.00, and after slightly overshooting the aiming point, believed that their cookie had hit a power station. W/C Fauquier's cookie landed in the centre of the designated target area after falling from 4,500 feet at 03.30, while P/O Swetman and crew attacked from 5,000 feet at 03.45 and gained an impression of factory buildings very close to the aiming point lifting into the air. The claims of accurate bombing were not backed up by photo reconnaissance but in truth, it was difficult to assess damage to a specific factory nestling among others in an industrial area. The only casualty was 405 Squadron's Z8527, which crashed near Versailles with fatal consequences for F/Sgt Howsan RAAF and all but his observer, who fell into enemy hands.

While the above operations were in progress, some three hundred miles to the east 3 Group's 57 and 214 Squadrons were losing twelve Wellingtons between them, 34% of those dispatched, in a low-level attack on railway targets at Hanau.

Tragedy struck the squadron on the afternoon of the 4th, when Pocklington's communications aircraft, a Miles Magister, crashed near Barmby Moor, after failing to recover from a slow roll at low altitude during an unofficial aerobatics exercise. On board were S/L McCormack and the senior squadron navigation officer, F/L Featherstone, both of whom were killed instantly. The loss of the B Flight commander in this way was hard-felt, particularly after he had survived twenty-five operations, and at just twenty-one years old was probably the most senior Canadian officer of that tender age.

There was a similar story of failure at a factory target on the 5th when twenty Whitleys went for the Gnome & Rhone aero engine and Goodrich tyre works at Gennevilliers, also located north of Paris city centre. The main event on this night was an attack on the Klöckner-Humboldt aero-engine works in the Deutz district of Cologne on the east bank of the Rhine, for which a new record force of 263 aircraft was assembled. 4 Group contributed sixteen Wellingtons, two of the six representing 405 Squadron loaded with a cookie each and the others with nine SBCs of incendiaries. They departed Pocklington between 22.32 and 22.50 with S/L Fraser the senior pilot on duty and all reached the target area to find largely favourable conditions in which major ground features like the River Rhine could be identified between the patches of low cloud in the light of numerous flares. They were over the target between 01.30 and 02.15 and described fires but no detail and what was clearly a dummy fire site over to the west. A number of crews also reported aircraft falling in flames over the city after being hit by flak. Despite the claims of the crews, the bombing was scattered across the city, destroying or seriously damaging ninety houses and no bombs fell near the factory.

The final 405 Squadron sortie on this night was carried out by the freshman crew of F/Sgt Scott, who took off at 01.43 to attack the docks and shipping at Le Havre with sixteen 250-pounders. Their efforts were hampered by poor visibility, but they bombed from 13,000 feet at 03.50 and suspected that their load had overshot and fallen into the Seine.

Harris's personal battle against Essen continued on the 6th, when a force of 157 aircraft was detailed for the first of a three-raid series in the space of seven nights. 4 Group assigned its two Wellington squadrons to the task and ten aircraft were made ready, two of the four at Pocklington receiving a cookie and the others the usual mix of 1,000, 500 and 250-pounders. They took off between 00.03 and 00.13 and headed into appalling weather conditions of thunderstorms and icing over the North Sea, which persuaded P/O Swetman and crew to turn back with their bombs before reaching the enemy coast. Sgt Higginson and crew pressed on a little further to actually cross the coast before also aborting their sortie and jettisoning the contents of their bomb bay. P/O Allison and crew were unable to identify the primary target through heavy cloud and bombed a flak concentration thought to be at Solingen, situated beyond the southern reaches of the Ruhr. F/Sgt Wigley and crew saw a line of flares as they passed close to Cologne and bombed what they believed to be Essen from 15,000 feet at 03.16 without any conviction of having done so effectively. At debriefings, forty-nine crews claimed to have bombed at Essen, where damage, according to local sources, was insignificant.

On the 8th, the funerals of S/L McCormack RCAF and F/L Featherstone RCAF took place with full military honours, the cortege progressing slowly and respectfully to the small cemetery at Barmby Moor. The main operation that night was to be directed at Hamburg, for which a new record force of 272 aircraft was assembled, 4 Group contributing a dozen Halifaxes and eighteen Wellingtons. 405 Squadron loaded its eight aircraft with either a cookie or nine SBCs of incendiaries and sent them on their way from Pocklington between 21.54 and 22.18 with F/L Thiele the senior pilot on duty. An issue with the port engine ended the interest of Sgt Higginson and crew in proceedings and they landed at 23.16, six minutes before the freshman crew of P/O Toft took off for Brussels bearing twenty-six packages of leaflets, or as Harris described them, "toilet paper", for the edification of the local populace. They would receive their airborne propaganda from 12,500 feet as it fluttered to earth some time after 01.40. Meanwhile, those involved in the main event had to negotiate electrical storms and icing on the way to the target area, where they encountered nine to ten-tenths cloud with tops in places up to 10,000 feet. Although the River Elbe could be identified by some, the city itself was completely obscured, forcing the crews to deliver their mixed high explosive and incendiary loads blindly on e.t.a. and Gee-fix. The crews of Sgt Wigley, F/Sgt Morris and F/L Thiele attacked what they believed to be the primary target from 15,000 to 18,000 feet between 00.27 and 00.52, while the Swetman crew bombed a flak concentration believed to be at Wilhelmshaven, F/Sgt Scott went for Bremen and P/O Allison Wesermünde. Z8358 failed to return with the crew of P/O Locke RCAF, who were reported initially to be safe after a distress message was received to the effect that they were landing on a beach. This proved to be false and the eventual recovery of two bodies, one off the Yorkshire coast and the other off Norfolk, confirmed that the Wellington had gone into the North Sea without survivors. Local sources in Hamburg reported around fourteen bomb loads falling within the city, causing three large fires but no significant damage.

Harris returned to Essen on the 10th, when orders were received across the Command to assemble another large force, this time of 254 aircraft, of which eight Halifaxes and eleven Wellingtons were provided by 4 Group. 405 Squadron made ready six Wellingtons, three for the main event and three for a freshman raid on the docks and shipping at Le Havre, and it was the latter in the form of F/Sgts Chinn and Hill and Sgt MacFarlane and their crews who departed Pocklington first between 20.06 and 20.26 sitting on sixteen 250-pounders each. The Hill crew returned early with a port engine issue, while the Chinn crew identified the French coast and mouth of the Seine but unable to pick out the target, dumped the bombs in the Channel. This left Sgt MacFarlane and crew to fulfil their brief and attack the target from 10,000 feet at 22.26, observing a stick to fall across the docks but produce no visible effect. They crews of F/L Thiele and P/Os Swetman and Toft took off between 22.07 and 22.19 and flew out under starlight with cloud below them to be greeted over the target by up to nine-tenths cloud with tops at 6,000 to 8,000 feet. They were guided to the approximate area of the target by flares, which had burned out by the time they arrived, and all bombed on e.t.a and a Gee-fix. They observing only the glow of incendiaries and on return had nothing of use to pass on to the intelligence sections at debriefing.

Undaunted, Harris ordered another raid on the 12th, for which 251 aircraft were made ready, 4 Group contributing thirteen Halifaxes and seventeen Wellingtons, six of the latter belonging to 405 Squadron. As on the previous occasion, the freshman crews of Sgt MacFarlane and F/Sgt Hill started the night's ball rolling when taking off for Le Havre at 20.40 and 20.43 each sitting on sixteen 250-pounders. Both reached the target where the dazzle from flares created challenging conditions for target identification and bombs were delivered from around 12,000 feet at 23.30 or thereabouts. The Essen-bound crews departed Pocklington between 22.23 and 22.40 with P/Os Swetman and Toft and the newly commissioned P/O Higginson the senior pilots on duty, two carrying a cookie and the others the usual mix of smaller calibre high explosive bombs. P/O Toft and crew turned back early with a starboard engine issue, while F/Sgt Lloyd RAAF and crew were heading towards the Suffolk coast when the port engine burst into flames and defied two attempts to extinguish it. Four members of the crew took to their parachutes, but the RCAF member of the crew, a gunner, was unable to find his and the pilot, F/Sgt Lloyd, in the finest traditions of the service, opted to remain with the aircraft and attempt a forced-landing. Sadly, this gallant gesture cost both men their lives as W5531 crashed at 00.19 three miles east-south-east of Stowmarket.

The Swetman and Higginson crews reached Belgian airspace before overheating engines persuaded them to go no further, and it is not clear at which stage F/Sgt Morris and crew abandoned their sortie. This left just the crews of F/Sgts Wigley and Chinn to reach the target area and find clear skies but fail through the industrial haze to identify ground features. Some crews picked up distinctive bends in the River Ruhr to the south of the city and employed already developing fires as a guide and relied upon Gee to take them through an intense flak barrage to the Krupp complex aiming-point. The 405 Squadron pair attacked the target from 15,000 and 17,000 feet at 01.53 and 02.20 respectively and were among 173 returning crews who claimed to have bombed in that general area. Bombing photos revealed many Ruhr locations, while local sources confirmed a slight improvement in the bombing, reporting some damage in the city, a large fire in the Krupp complex and the destruction of twenty-eight dwelling units. This brought to an end a series of eight heavy raids against the city since the night of the 8/9th of March, during which 1,555 sorties had resulted in fewer than two-thirds of the crews claiming to have bombed in the target area, and just twenty-two bombing photos plotted to within five miles of Essen. In exchange for this, sixty-four aircraft had been lost, industrial damage had been slight, and housing damage modest in the extreme.

When Dortmund was posted as the target on the 14th, six 405 Squadron crews were called to briefing to learn that they would be part of an overall force of 208 aircraft involving nine 4 Group Wellingtons and eight 10 Squadron Halifaxes, while 102 Squadron would launch its first sorties as a Halifax unit on a freshman operation to Le Havre. The main event was the largest by far to be sent against this important industrial city located towards the eastern end of the Ruhr, which was a major centre of synthetic oil production. Two of the 405 Squadron Wellingtons were loaded with a cookie and the others with the usual high explosive mix and departed Pocklington between 22.03 and 22.22 with P/O Toft the only commissioned pilot on duty. F/Sgt Morris and crew turned back early with a number of technical issues, leaving the rest of the force to run the gauntlet of intense searchlight and flak activity as they traversed the most heavily defended region of Germany. Under clear skies they map-read their way by river and railway features to the aiming point, where only the crews of F/Sgts Wigley and Hill delivered an attack from around 14,000 feet shortly after 02.00. On return, F/Sgt Chinn RAAF and crew abandoned a fuel-starved Z8530 near Petersfield in Hampshire at 05.15 and all arrived safely on the ground. The return of W5427 and W5390 was awaited in vain, although a W/T signal had been received from the latter at 05.15 requesting assistance. News eventually reached England that P/O Toft and crew had ditched off the French coast and had been picked up by the enemy, which was better news than that concerning Sgt MacFarlane and crew, who it was learned, had all lost their lives in a crash near Brühl some ten miles south-south-west of Cologne. The operation was a failure that had scattered bombs over a forty-mile stretch of the Ruhr and caused minor damage only at the primary target, while costing the Command sixteen missing aircraft and a further nine compelled by fuel shortage to ditch, force-land or be abandoned by their crews.

A force of 152 aircraft was assembled on the following day to return to Dortmund, this time without a Halifax presence but with seven Wellingtons to represent 4 Group. The four-strong 405 Squadron element departing Pocklington between 23.18 and 23.25 consisted of the crews of W/C Fauquier, F/L Thiele, P/O Higginson and F/Sgt Morris, three loaded with smaller-calibre high explosives and only the Higginson crew sitting on a cookie. The crews had to contend with severe icing conditions on the southern approaches to the Ruhr, and barely half of the force continued on to run into intense searchlight and flak activity over the target, where two-tenths low cloud combined with the industrial haze to muddy the vertical visibility. F/L Thiele and crew found no suitable target over Germany and jettisoned their load, while F/Sgt Morris and crew decided that Aachen was far enough and dropped their bombs in its vicinity from 14,000 feet at 02.29. The crews of W/C Fauquier and P/O Higginson penetrated as far as the Cologne area, where they released their loads from 14,000 and 17,000 feet respectively at 02.47 and 02.42. Debriefings revealed that only about eight crews had reached and bombed the city, local sources confirming the failure of the operation when reporting that only one house had been destroyed and a dozen or so others damaged.

Hamburg was selected as the target on the 17th for a force of 173 aircraft, which included a contribution from 4 Group of eleven Wellingtons, five of them belonging to 405 Squadron on what would be its eighty-sixth operation of the war and final one as a Wellington unit. They departed Pocklington between 23.29 and 23.36 with S/L Fraser the senior pilot on duty, three carrying a cookie and two all-incendiary loads. F/Sgt Hill and crew turned back from the midpoint of the North Sea because of an engine issue, while P/O Higginson and crew had been flying on one engine for some time when they decided to bomb the Frisian Island of Baltrum from 16,000 feet at 01.50. F/Sgt Morris and crew were struggling to climb above 12,000 feet when they came under fire from flak batteries protecting the Kiel Canal and decided to drop their load there at 02.50. S/L Fraser and crew entered Germany south of the recommended track and ran into intense flak from batteries along the Elbe while trying to approach between Cuxhaven and Wesermünde. They were persuaded to seek out a less hostile target and ultimately bombed in the Cuxhaven area from 15,000 feet at 03.05. Only F/L Thiele and crew positively identified Hamburg after pinpointing on the

Elbe under clear skies and following its course into the heart of the city. Haze and searchlight glare left them with the impression of a dark mass representing the built-up area and they dropped their incendiaries about a mile to the west of the briefed aiming point, contributing to seventy-five fires, thirty-three of which were classed as large. Even so, fewer than a third of the bomb loads had actually found the mark and local sources estimated a force of only fifty aircraft.

The squadron was screened from operations on the 18th to prepare to convert to Halifaxes, a process that would keep it away from the operational scene for six weeks. Wellingtons were not removed from Pocklington immediately, as the first Halifaxes had not yet arrived and four crews carried out a sea search following the Hamburg raid, in the hope of finding crews missing from Driffield, but finding nothing. The first five Halifaxes arrived from Middleton-St-George on the 23rd, to be followed by two more from Croft on the 25th, while the actual conversion training was carried out at 1652 Conversion Unit, commanded at the time by S/L Leonard Cheshire at Marston Moor.

A number of significant operations took place in the absence of 405 Squadron, the first of them against Cologne on the 22/23rd, when a Gee-equipped force consisting predominantly of Wellingtons attempted to use the device as a blind bombing aid to overcome the problems of cloud and haze. The result was a marginal improvement on recent performances, but still only a small proportion of the bombs fell within the city. On the following night Harris returned to the formula that had brought him success at Lübeck at the end of March, selecting Rostock as another lightly defended port on the Baltic coast with narrow streets in its old town, and as an added attraction, a Heinkel aircraft factory situated in its southern outskirts. The series of four raids on consecutive nights was to include a 5 Group contingent directed specifically at the factory, while the main element attacked the town with predominantly incendiary bomb loads.

The first operation, which was supported by 4 Group with twenty-five Wellingtons and Whitleys, ended disappointingly, when the Heinkel works escaped damage altogether and most of the bombs intended for the town centre fell two to six miles away. It was a different story twenty-four hours later, however, when the town centre was heavily bombed, although the factory remained unscathed. 4 Group was again lightly represented with just eleven Wellingtons and Whitleys taking part, and this increased to twenty-three when the town was pounded again on the 25/26th, and W/C Guy Gibson led a 106 Squadron element in a successful attack on the Heinkel factory. The final raid took place on the 26/27th, when more than two hundred aircraft were divided equally between the town and the factory and 4 Group chipped in with nine Wellingtons and Whitleys and two 10 Squadron Halifaxes. When the town authorities were able to assess the damage, they recorded over seventeen hundred buildings totally destroyed, five hundred seriously damaged, and an estimated 60% of the main built-up area devastated.

On the 27th, 4 and 5 Groups combined to send thirty-one Halifaxes and a dozen Lancasters to attack the battleship Tirpitz at berth in Trondheim Fjord. No hits were claimed at a cost of four Halifaxes and a Lancaster, and 10 Squadron's commanding officer, W/C Donald Bennett, returned six weeks later after evading capture. The main operation on this night was directed at Cologne, for which 4 Group contributed just two 102 Squadron Halifaxes to an overall force of ninety-seven aircraft. The raid was unusually destructive for the period, although many bomb loads fell outside of the target area.

The Trondheim operation was repeated on the following night employing twenty-three Halifaxes and eleven Lancasters and was again inconclusive at a cost of two Halifaxes. An operation against Kiel involving eighty-eight aircraft on this night included seven Wellingtons and two 102 Squadron Halifaxes and all three shipyards sustained damage. 78 Squadron had now completed its conversion to the Halifax and opened its account with a freshman raid by five crews on the docks and shipping at Ostend on the 29th.

During the course of the month, the squadron took part in fourteen operations and dispatched fifty-nine sorties for the loss of six Wellingtons, four crews and four other airmen, including S/L McCormack in the Magister accident.

May 1942

The new month began with an operation by eighty aircraft on Hamburg on the 3rd, for which 4 Group provided twenty Halifaxes, and although only fifty-four crews reported bombing through cloud on estimated positions, the raid was an outstanding success, which belied both the conditions and the numbers involved. Over a hundred fires were started, half of them classed as large, and one cookie reputedly destroyed eleven apartment blocks. Three raids on Stuttgart on consecutive nights began on the 4th, but this would prove to be an elusive target until much later in the war, largely because of its location in a series of valleys. In an overall force of 121 aircraft, nine 158 Squadron Wellingtons were assigned to the Robert Bosch works located in the north-western suburb of Feuerbach, while six 35 (Madras Presidency) Squadron Halifaxes attended to a "special" target. A clever decoy site near Lauffen, fifteen miles to the north of Stuttgart, was defended by thirty-five searchlights and fifty flak guns and lured away many bomb loads on this night and, indeed, for the remainder of war. 4 Group contributed eleven Halifaxes to a force of seventy-seven aircraft bound for Stuttgart on the following night and seven Wellingtons and seven Halifaxes to a force of ninety-seven aircraft on the 6th, but the nett result of the three operations was little significant damage for the loss of eleven aircraft.

It was at this time that 4 Group's long-serving 51 and 77 Squadrons were sent on attachment to Coastal Command and would remain away from Bomber Command until the end of October. Orders were received at Linton-on-Ouse, Middleton-St-George and Leeming on the 8th to prepare nineteen Halifaxes and ten Wellingtons for a major operation that night against the town of Warnemünde, situated on the Baltic coast at the mouth of the Warnow river north of Rostock. The docks were the site of U-Boot crew training, and also supplied German forces on the Russian front, but, equally important and cited in the ORBs as one of the main aiming points was the Heinkel aircraft factory, the destruction of which was handed to 4 and 5 Groups. The Heinkel factory was possibly the one recently attacked during the series of attacks on Rostock, but the Arado aircraft company also had a manufacturing site at Warnemünde, and this may have been the intended target.

Following the recent successes at Lübeck and Rostock, it offered the prospect of a relatively straightforward target, but would turn out to be not so. The 4 Group plan was to be carried out against the Heinkel works in three phases, beginning with a high-level attack by four Halifaxes and two Wellingtons. This would be followed by a second high-level attack employing thirteen Halifaxes and one Wellington, at the same time as two Halifaxes and a Wellington carried out searchlight suppression from low level, with the intention of creating a clear path for the third phase involving six Wellingtons running in at low level. As this was ongoing, sixty-two 1 Group crews were to drop incendiaries, while others carried out low-level attacks on searchlight and flak batteries. A force of 193 aircraft departed their stations and headed for the North Sea to make landfall on the enemy coast over southern Jutland. Having traversed the peninsula to reach the Baltic coast, crews could see a veritable forest of searchlights seventy miles distant at the target, which they reached soon afterwards under clear skies, only for many to be completely blinded to the actual aiming-points by the glare. The town and River Warnow were identified, but the operation proved more difficult than expected and a shocking nineteen aircraft failed to return from what was an inconclusive outcome. 5 Group lost nine aircraft, including four Lancasters from 44 (Rhodesia) Squadron, while 4 Group posted missing four 158 Squadron Wellingtons and a Halifax each from 10 and 76 Squadrons.

The advent of the four-engine heavy bomber required changes to the make-up of a crew, and this took place on the 11th with the removal of second pilots, second navigators and second wireless operators to create a crew consisting of a pilot (captain), flight engineer (pilot's mate), navigator, bomb-aimer, wireless operator/gunner and mid-upper and rear gunners.

Thereafter, minor operations held sway until the 19th, when Mannheim was posted as the target for 197 aircraft, of which twenty-nine Halifaxes were provided by 4 Group. Nestling on the East Bank of the Rhine, opposite Ludwigshafen, Mannheim was easy to locate by a distinctive bend in the waterway south of the city and was found on this night to be under clear skies but so cloaked in extreme darkness and ground haze, that most carried out their attacks on DR and TR1335 (Gee). At debriefings 155 crews claimed to have reached and bombed the target, while local sources reported an estimated ten bomb loads hitting the city, causing only modest damage, while the rest found open country, and this in return for the loss of eleven aircraft. Another lull ensued as Harris prepared for his masterstroke at the end of the month, and 405 Squadron was by now sufficiently well advanced in its progress towards operational status with Halifaxes to be ready in time to participate.

At the time of the appointment of ACM Sir Arthur Harris as C-in-C, the figure of four thousand bombers had been bandied around as the number required to wrap up the war. Whilst there was not the slightest chance of procuring them, Harris, with a dark cloud still hanging over the existence of an independent bomber force, needed to ensure that those earmarked for him were not spirited away to what he considered to be less-deserving causes. The Command had not yet achieved sufficient success to silence the detractors, and the Admiralty was still calling for bomber aircraft to be diverted to the U-Boot campaign, while others demanded support for the North Africa campaign. Harris was in need of a major victory and perhaps a dose of symbolism to make his point, and out of this was born the Thousand Plan, Operation Millennium, the launching of a thousand aircraft in one night against a major German city, for which Hamburg had been pencilled in. Harris did not have a thousand front-line aircraft and required the support of other Commands to make up the numbers. This was forthcoming from Coastal and Flying Training Commands, and in the case of the former, a letter to Harris on the 22nd promised 250 aircraft. However, following an intervention from the Admiralty the offer was withdrawn, and most of the Flying Training Command aircraft were found to be not up to the task, leaving the Millennium force well short of the magic figure. Undaunted, Harris, or more probably his able deputy, AM Sir Robert Saundby, scraped together every airframe capable of controlled flight or something resembling it, and pulled in the screened crews from their instructional duties. He also pressed into service aircraft and crews from within the Command's own training establishment, 91 Group. Come the night, not only would the thousand mark be achieved, it would be comfortably surpassed.

During the final week of the month, the arrival on bomber stations from County Durham in the north to Cambridgeshire and East Anglia in the south and east of a motley collection of aircraft from training units gave rise to much speculation among crews and ground staff alike, but, as usual, only the NAAFI staff and the local civilians knew what was really afoot. The most pressing remaining question was the weather, and as the days ticked by inexorably towards the end of May, this was showing no signs of complying. Harris was aware of the genuine danger, that the giant force might draw attention to itself and thereby compromise security, and the point was fast approaching when the operation would either have to take place or be abandoned for the time being. Harris released some of the pressure by sanctioning operations on the night of the 29/30th, for which the Gnome & Rhone aero-engine and Goodrich tyre factories at Gennevilliers in Paris were the main targets. A force of seventy-seven aircraft included a contribution from 4 Group of twenty Halifaxes, the crews of which found conditions in the target area to be almost ideal with bright moonlight shining down from clear skies. Despite the advantages, photographic reconnaissance revealed no hits on the Gnome & Rhone factory, but thirty-eight nearby houses had been destroyed and many more damaged.

It was in an atmosphere of frustration and hopeful expectation, that "morning prayers" began at Harris's High Wycombe HQ on the 30th, with all eyes turned upon the civilian chief meteorological adviser, Magnus Spence. After careful deliberation, he was able to give a qualified assurance of clear skies over the Rhineland, while north-western Germany and Hamburg would be concealed under buckets of cloud. Thus, did the fickle fates decree that Cologne would bear the dubious honour of hosting the first one thousand bomber raid in history. At briefings, crews were told that the enormous force was to be pushed across the aiming-point in just ninety minutes, which was unprecedented and gave rise to the question of collisions as hundreds of aircraft funnelled towards the aiming-point. The answer, according to the experts, was to observe timings and flight levels, and they calculated also that just two aircraft would collide over the target. It is said that a wag in every briefing room asked, "do they know which two?"

It was a big day at Pocklington, as 405 Squadron prepared for its maiden operation with Halifaxes and eighty-eighth since becoming operational almost a year earlier. All crews had been recalled from leave on the 25th, and they were addressed by 4 Group's A-O-C, New Zealander, AVM Roddy Carr, on the 26th. With the green light for the operation possible at any moment, ground crews and armourers worked into the night on the 27th to ensure that all sixteen aircraft were on top line, with ammunition belts for the .303s securely installed. 4 Group had 146 aircraft bombed up and ready to go on the 30th, 130 of them Halifaxes, including a dozen from 1652 Conversion Unit at Marston Moor, while nine 158 Squadron Wellingtons and seven Whitleys from training flights made up the numbers. The 4 Group crews had been briefed to attack aiming-point X, one of three areas spanning the city centre from north to south, theirs bordering the western and northern outer ring of the city centre on the western side of the Rhine. Late that evening, the first of an eventual 1,047 aircraft took off to deliver the now familiar three-wave-format attack on the Rhineland capital, the older training hacks struggling somewhat reluctantly into the air, lifted more by the enthusiasm of their crews than by the power of their engines, and some of these, unable to climb to a respectable height, would fall easy prey to the defences or simply drop from the sky through mechanical breakdown. The 405 Squadron element departed Pocklington between 23.31 and 00.27 with W/C Fauquier and S/Ls Fraser and Thiele the senior pilots on duty, the last mentioned having been promoted to succeed S/L McCormack as B Flight commander. Each Halifax carried a bomb load of three 1,000 pounders supplemented by nine SBCs of 90 x 4lb and three of 8 x 30lb incendiaries. They had been given an unrecorded time-on-target and a bombing height, and began the North-Sea crossing at Southwold to make landfall over the Scheldt estuary on a direct course for the target, with a reciprocal return route a little to the south.

F/Sgt Blizard and crew ran into severe icing conditions as they climbed through cloud at 9,000 feet over Cambridgeshire, and the effect on the engine performance was sufficient to persuade them to jettison their load and turn back. The others traversed southern Holland, drawn on for the last seventy miles by the glow of the already burning city, and were greeted at the target by precisely the weather conditions of clear skies and bright, full moon predicted by Magnus Spence. Those arriving early found smoke rising through 8,000 feet and fires confined largely to central and north-western districts and, rather than stoke up existing blazes, sought out undamaged areas. Ten 405 squadron crews delivered their bombs from 13,500 to 14,000 feet between 02.10 and 02.14 and were unable to plot their fall in the glare of fires, but as they turned away, columns of black smoke were drifting up through 10,000 feet, and no one was in any doubt that they had taken part in a successful operation. P/O Swetman and crew had been last to take off after a delay, and bombed Düsseldorf from 14,000 feet at 02.32 after running out of time to attack the primary. P/O Turnbull and crew were in a Conversion Flight Halifax and lost their port-outer engine five miles north-west of Cologne, persuading them to release their bombs immediately from 17,500 feet at 02.39. Nine minutes earlier, they had been fired upon by a BF110 and sustained damage to the tailplane but drove their assailant off with return fire from the rear turret. Once all of the information from returning crews had been collated, it was established that 868 had reached and bombed the primary target and a picture emerged of a city on fire from end to end with never-before-witnessed scenes. Post-raid reconnaissance confirmed that the operation had, by any standards, been an outstanding success, and had destroyed more than 3,300 buildings, while inflicting serious damage on two thousand others. Although the loss of forty-one aircraft represented a new record high, the conditions had favoured both attackers and defenders alike, and in the context of the scale of success and the numbers dispatched, it could not be considered an inordinately high figure. 4 Group registered a remarkably modest loss of six aircraft, three of them Halifaxes, and among them was 405 Squadron's W7707, which disappeared without trace with the crew of Sgt Wadman RCAF. The training units sustained disproportionately heavy casualties amounting to twenty-one aircraft, and this would be a recurring theme whenever they were deployed.

Many senior officers took part in Operation Millennium, including at least one group commander acting strictly against orders, and the majority of the Command's future "shining lights" were also present. Reg "Shady" Lane, a future 405 Squadron commanding officer, was flying with 35 (Madras Presidency) Squadron on this night and won his first DFC.

During the course of the month, the squadron took part in just the above operation involving sixteen sorties and the loss of a single Halifax and crew.

June 1942

While the Millennium force remained assembled, Harris wanted to exploit its potential again immediately, and was no doubt excited about the prospect of visiting upon the old enemy of Essen a similar ordeal to that just experienced by Cologne. Losses and unserviceability meant that 956 aircraft was the best that could be achieved, 4 Group managing 127 Halifaxes, seven Wellingtons and five Whitleys from its front-line and training units, including a dozen Halifaxes belonging to 405 Squadron. Each received a bomb load of three 1,000 pounders and nine and three SBCs respectively of 4lb and 30lbs incendiaries before departing Pocklington between 23.10 and 23.55 with W/C Fauquier and S/Ls Fraser and Thiele the senior pilots on duty. They had been briefed to climb to 3,000 feet on course for Spalding in Lincolnshire, climbing gradually thereafter until crossing the English coast at Southwold at 12,000 feet and benefitted from favourable weather conditions, including the full moon that promised the possibility of actually being able to identify ground detail. There were no early returns from the Pocklington element and the crews reached the target area to find up to ten-tenths low cloud between 3,000 and 8,000 feet, which combined with the industrial haze and smoke still drifting over from Cologne to prevent any meaningful sight of ground features. They were to employ the sprawl of the Borbeck-located Krupp sector as the aiming-point, and a general reference was provided for the 405 Squadron crews by the flak bursting through the cloud. They carried out their attacks from 13,000 to 14,000 feet between 01.23 and 02.05, largely on TR (Gee) supported by occasional visual references on waterways and most could report only a belief that they had bombed Essen. An accurate assessment of results was not possible, and reports of many fires, some identified as dummies, emerged without the detail to give credence. They would have to wait for post-raid reconnaissance to assess what had happened on the ground, and in the meantime, a counting of the cost revealed the loss of thirty-one aircraft. W7713 crashed in the vicinity of Krefeld, located on the western side of the Rhine on the edge of the Ruhr, and there were no survivors from the crew of P/O Baltzer RCAF. Sadly, there would be no major success to mitigate the scale of the loss, local reports confirming that only eleven houses had been destroyed in Essen, with fewer than two hundred others damaged, mostly in southern districts. In fact, more bomb loads had actually fallen on Oberhausen, Duisburg and Mülheim-an-der-Ruhr than on the intended target.

A follow-up raid was planned for twenty-four hours later, and a much-reduced force of 197 aircraft made ready, with 4 Group providing thirty-eight Halifaxes, six of them belonging to 405 Squadron. They departed Pocklington between 23.15 and 23.34 with W/C Fauquier the senior pilot on duty and a similar bomb load each to that of twenty-four hours earlier. They lost the services of Sgt Field and crew soon after take-off because of engine trouble, leaving the others to make their way via the northern route to the Ruhr, crossing the Dutch coast near Egmond and pinpointing on the town of Rheine and stretches of the Dortmund-Ems Canal. They headed south through cloudless skies to reach the Ruhr, where the usual industrial haze impaired the vertical visibility, while a low moon provided some illumination. P/O Morris and crew had just crossed the Rhine when attacked by a BF110, which came up from below and missed with its fire. P/O Morris responded by throwing the Halifax into a dive as the rear gunner returned fire, narrowly missing the assailant, and the bomb load was jettisoned. Most crews would describe the visibility as good, and reported being further aided by flares, which highlighted the Rhine over to the west. Those equipped with Gee confirmed their positions over what they believed to be the Krupp complex aiming-point and the 405 Squadron crews delivered their attacks over the general built-up area from 15,000 feet between 01.39 and 01.46, observing bursts and fires but no detail. Despite the apparent confidence of the crews that they had attacked Essen, local authorities reported just three high explosive bombs and three hundred incendiaries falling in the city to cause only minor damage. Such was the density of the Ruhr, however, with overlapping town and city boundaries, it was difficult not to hit something urban, but concentration was the key to success, and the scattering of bombs over a wide area was never going to achieve a knock-out blow. Fourteen aircraft failed to return, but there were no empty dispersal pans at Pocklington.

By the time that preparations were put in hand on the 3rd to send 170 aircraft against it that night, Bremen had been spared the attentions of a large force since the previous October. Among important targets in the city were the previously attacked Deschimag shipyards and the Focke-Wulf aircraft factory, but the only clue to the briefed aiming point was the reference in the 4 Group ORB to a "special" target. 405 Squadron briefed six crews as part of the 4 Group contribution of thirty-six Halifaxes and they departed Pocklington between 22.54 and 23.00 with S/L Fraser the senior pilot on duty and the standard load in each bomb bay. They flew out under clear skies to the Dutch coast, and for the second operation running lost the services of Sgt Field and crew, this time to excessive fuel consumption. The others pressed on between Amsterdam and Utrecht and entered Germany over the flatlands of the Bentheim region north of the Ruhr. They found the target area to be covered by haze, but the employment of flares enabled the River Weser and the docks to be identified and bombed by the 405 Squadron crews from 16,000 and 18,500 feet between 01.14 and 01.35. Returning crews were not confident that their efforts had been effective, but local reports confirmed the most destructive raid to date on this target, cataloguing damage to the harbour, industrial premises and housing, while claiming damage to the shipyards and the Focke-Wulf aircraft factory in the Hemelingen district to be of no consequence.

Essen was "on" again on the 5th and a force of 180 aircraft made ready, thirty-three of them Halifaxes from Croft, Dalton, Leeming and Middleton-St-George, while 405 Squadron remained at home. The force flew out over Belgium to enter Germany west of Bonn and pick up the River Rhine, some identifying a bend in the River Ruhr to the south-east of Essen, while others relied on a TR-fix, flares or evidence of searchlight and flak concentrations to establish their positions in conditions of poor vertical visibility caused by the ever-present blanket of industrial haze. The operation was another failure that scattered bombs over a wide area, with Oberhausen and Bottrop probably receiving the most.

The first of four attacks during the month on the naval port of Emden was posted on the 6th, and a force of 233 aircraft made ready, 4 Group contributing twenty-seven Halifaxes from Pocklington, Dalton and Linton-on-Ouse, with thirteen this time provided by 405 Squadron. They took off between 23.24 and 23.55 with W/C Fauquier and S/Ls Fraser and Thiele the senior pilots on duty and the standard high explosive and incendiary mix in each bomb bay. Sgt Blizard and crew turned back within an hour after both outer engines lost power and it became necessary for all eight occupants to abandon the fast-sinking W1145 over Lincolnshire and watch as it crashed four miles south-west of Binbrook at 01.45. The others completed the North Sea crossing via the Frisian Islands to find the skies over the coast of north-western Germany to be clear of cloud and the visibility to be good. Sgt West and crew were within thirty miles of the target when engine and rear turret issues ended their interest in proceedings, while the rest of the force benefitted from the dropping of flares to illuminate the Dollart and Ems docks areas. The 405 Squadron crews released their loads from 13,000 to 18,000 feet between 01.21 and 01.55, observing bursts but no detail, but smoke was rising through 8,000 feet as they retreated, and the glow from the port remained visible for up to eighty miles into the return journey. Photographic reconnaissance and local reports confirmed that the raid had been responsible for the destruction of some three hundred houses, with a further two hundred severely damaged in return for the loss of nine aircraft.

The next round of the almost relentless campaign against Essen was posted on the 8th and a force of 170 aircraft assembled, 4 Group putting up forty-two Halifaxes, ten of them belonging to 405 Squadron. They departed Pocklington between 22.52 and 23.00 with S/Ls Fraser and Thiele the senior pilots on duty and the usual load of three 1,000 pounders and twelve SBCs of incendiaries in each bomb bay. F/Sgt Chinn and crew turned back early after the starboard-inner engine cut, leaving the others to fly out in favourable conditions that persisted all the way to the Ruhr, where they were greeted by the expected blanket of ground haze and a hostile searchlight and flak defence. S/L Fraser and crew had approached at 19,000 feet and were forced by the defences down to 8,000 feet, while F/Sgt West and crew went from 20,000 feet down to 900 and neither was able to recover the lost altitude to deliver an attack. This haze combined with the glare from the intense searchlight activity to blind crews to ground features and rendered the attack something of a lottery, the only two recorded attacks by the 405 Squadron crews of P/O Swetman and S/L Thiele taking place from 18,000 feet at 01.19 and 15,000 feet at 01.32. After bombing, Swetman's Halifax was hit in the bomb bay by flak but not seriously damaged.

Returning crews reported bomb bursts but had little or no useful information to pass on at debriefing. Absent from that process at Pocklington were three crews on what was the squadron's blackest night of the war to date. W1111 disappeared without trace with the crew of P/O Morris RCAF, while DG224 crashed some seven miles north-west of Cologne city centre with fatal consequences for P/O Higginson RCAF and all but one of the other seven occupants, the single survivor falling into enemy hands. W7708 was last heard from in a W/T distress signal at 03.40, shortly after which it fell to a night-fighter to crash seven miles west-south-west of the Dutch town of Arnhem. F/L Maclean RCAF and crew all survived, and once on the ground the pilot evaded capture eventually to return home to Canada, where after the war he was to enjoy a distinguished career in politics. The rest of the crew was taken into captivity, and the navigator, P/O Wernham, was one of those murdered by the Gestapo following the "Great Escape" from Sagan III in March 1944. There was shock also at Linton-on-Ouse at the failure to return of four 35 (Madras Presidency) Squadron Halifaxes, and this was relieved a little when a message came through that one had come down in the sea off Great Yarmouth and the crew was in the process of being rescued.

Minor and gardening operations occupied elements of the Command thereafter, and for four nights between the 12th and 15th, no operations at all were mounted. On the 16th, Essen was posted as the target for a modest force of 106 aircraft, which 4 Group supported with thirty-nine Halifaxes, eight of them provided by 405 Squadron, and they departed Pocklington between 22.56 and 23.05 with S/L Fraser and the newly promoted F/L Swetman the senior pilots on duty. They crossed the English coast in the Southwold area and F/Sgt Hill and crew had reached the midpoint of the sea crossing on course for the Scheldt estuary when running into icing conditions that persuaded them to turn back and jettison the contents of their bomb bay. Crews had been briefed to employ TR to locate the target and bomb blindly based on that, which under the conditions of up to eight-tenths cloud on a moonless night with visibility down to three miles, was the best that could be expected. The city of Bonn had been briefed out as the alternative target, and forty-five crews, including most of those from Pocklington, took advantage of the fact that it lay close to the southern route to the Ruhr. Six 405 Squadron crews attacked Bonn from 14,000 to 18,500 feet between 01.20 and 01.54 and only Sgt Knight and crew bombed at Essen from 18,000 feet at 02.11. A post-raid analysis revealed that only sixteen crews had bombed the primary target, while fifty-six others had found alternatives. This concluded a series of five raids on Essen in sixteen nights, during which 1,607 sorties had been dispatched and eighty-four aircraft lost. The city had sustained no industrial damage, and a few wrecked houses was all that Bomber Command had to show for the massive effort expended.

The next three operations would be directed at the port of Emden over four nights, hopefully to build on the success of the attack earlier in the month. A force of 194 aircraft was assembled on the 19th, 4 Group contributing thirty-seven Halifaxes, seven of them made ready by 405 Squadron and given the standard bomb load. They departed Pocklington between 23.34 and 23.40 with S/L Fraser the senior pilot on duty and instructions from the briefing to switch to Osnabrück, eighty miles to the south, if the weather conditions over the coastal region became troublesome. Part of the flare force did, indeed, initiate an attack there by twenty-nine aircraft, among which were the 405 Squadron crews of F/Sgts Allbright and Chinn, who bombed from 17,000 and 12,000 feet at 02.12 and 02.14 respectively. The remaining five from the squadron bombed from 16,000 to 19,000 feet between 01.30 and 02.06 on a TR-fix and were among 127 claiming to have bombed the primary target through eight to ten-tenths thin cloud. Despite the numbers, the Emden authorities reported only a handful of high-explosive bombs falling and a few hundred incendiaries.

A force of 185 aircraft was assembled to return to the port of Emden on the following night, and this time, 4 Group was represented by thirty-eight Halifaxes, nine of them provided by 405 Squadron. They departed Pocklington between 23.46 and 23.55 with S/L Fraser and F/L Swetman the senior pilots on duty and reached the target area, according to some, to find six to eight-tenths cloud between 4,000 and 8,000 feet, while others reported clear skies with ground haze to impair the vertical visibility. The docks were the briefed aiming-point and the town the alternative, and positions were established by TR-fix and glimpses of the coastline. An intense flak barrage accompanied the Pocklington crews as they ran across the aiming point at 12,000 to 17,500 feet, but all made it through between 01.25 and 01.55, and on return reported bomb bursts and fires visible for sixty miles into the return journey. It became clear at debriefings that not all of the force had found the target area and local sources confirmed damage to only a hundred houses, which was a modest improvement on the previous raid, but a poor return for the effort expended.

The Emden series concluded on the 22nd, when a force of 227 aircraft was put together, of which twenty-six Halifaxes represented 4 Group, the ten belonging to 405 Squadron departing Pocklington between 23.38 and 23.47 all captained by NCO pilots. All reached the target area, mostly establishing their approach by identifying the coastline and confirming it via a TR-fix backed up by flak and fires. They ran in on the aiming-point at 12,000 to 18,000 feet between 01.31 and 01.57 and bombed in good visibility under clear skies and moonlight, and some crews were able to distinguish between genuine and decoy fires. F/Sgt Barton and crew suffered the frustration of jammed bomb doors at the moment of bomb release, and they were jettisoned over the sea on the way home. Despite the favourable conditions, the decoy fires succeeded in drawing off many bomb loads, and those finding the target destroyed a modest fifty houses and damaged a hundred more, another disappointing return for the effort expended. At debriefing, F/Sgt Field and crew reported a night-fighter attack seventeen minutes after bombing, in which the airframe and mid-upper turret sustained severe damage and the first and second wireless operator/gunners were slightly wounded.

A new unit, 425 (Allouette) Squadron RCAF, was formed in 4 Group at Dishforth on the 25th, manned predominantly by French Canadians to operate Wellingtons once declared ready later in the summer. This was the day on which the final deployment of the Thousand Force was to take place and bring with it the end of the ill-fated Avro Manchester's operational service. It was an indication of the failure of the Manchester, that the aircraft it had been intended to replace, the Hampden, would continue to serve 5 Group in small numbers until mid-September.

A force of 960 aircraft was assembled, which included 112 Halifaxes provided by 4 Group, bolstered on this night by a contribution from 1652 Conversion Unit and by the return to operations as a Halifax unit of 158 Squadron, now stationed at East Moor. To the above numbers were added five aircraft from Army Co-operation Command and 102 aircraft from Coastal Command, which had been ordered by Churchill to take part, although, its contribution was to be deemed a separate operation. However, the 1,067 aircraft from all sources would represent a larger combined force than that sent to Cologne at the end of May. While some sections of the force had been assigned to specific targets like the Focke-Wulf aircraft factory in the south-eastern district of Hemelingen on the East Bank of the Weser, and the Deschimag shipyards, 4 Group was among those selected to carry out an area attack on the city itself. The 405 Squadron element of seventeen Halifaxes departed Pocklington in two phases, the first of eight aircraft between 23.04 and 23.10 with S/Ls Fraser and Thiele the senior pilots, and the second of nine aircraft between 23.47 and 23.59 with W/C Fauquier leading the way. All were carrying three 1,000 pounders, nine SBCs of 4lb incendiaries and three of 30lbs, but the load carried in W/O Scott's bomb bay in the first wave would not reach the target after the guns in both turrets became unserviceable and could not be fixed by the time the Dutch coast hove into view. F/Sgt Sidney and crew turned back from the second phase element when unable to make the required height and speed, while the others found the target area concealed beneath a blanket of ten-tenths cloud, with excellent visibility above, courtesy of a full moon and the Northern Lights. Bombing was carried out by most on TR-fixes and returning crews could only offer a belief that they had hit the city, the glow of fires providing some evidence. Thirteen 405 Squadron participants delivered their attacks in the general target area from 12,000 to 14,500 feet between 01.11 and 02.35, while the crews of S/L Fraser and F/Sgt Barton bombed at Wilhelmshaven and Hamburg respectively.

A new record loss of forty-eight aircraft represented 5% of those dispatched, and the O.T.Us of 91 Group suffered the highest casualty rate of 11.6%, largely because they were employing tired, old Whitleys, Wellingtons and Hampdens, which were not up to the task. 4 Group posted missing eight Halifaxes, four of them from 102 (Ceylon) Squadron, which represented its heaviest loss from a single operation. Local sources confirmed a number of hits on the Focke-Wulf aircraft factory and some shipyards, along with the destruction of 572 houses, and damage to more than six thousand others, mostly in southern and eastern districts, but estimated the size of the bomber force to be around eighty. The level of success fell well short of that achieved at Cologne but surpassed by far the dismal failure at Essen.

The first of a number of follow-up operations against Bremen was mounted on the night of the 27/28th, and involved 144 aircraft, including thirty-nine Halifaxes from 4 Group, a dozen of them belonging to 405 Squadron. They received an all-incendiary bomb load, four of twelve and three SBCs respectively of 4lb and 30lbs and the remainder fifteen SBCs of 4-pounders. They departed Pocklington between 23.30 and 23.37 with the recently arrived F/L Liversidge the senior pilot on duty and headed for the Dutch coast, on the way losing the services of Sgt Campbell and crew who were struggling to maintain height in icing conditions and returned their bombs to the dump. Weather conditions over north-western Germany were very much as those of two nights earlier, with ten-tenths cloud up to around 4,000 feet and decreasing amounts thereafter as high as 15,000 feet. The sky above was as bright as day under a large moon, even though the Northern Lights, on this occasion, were masked by high cloud. Most located the target area by TR-fix, and the 405 Squadron crews could mostly only estimate that they were over the city as they released their loads from 10,000 to 15,000 feet between 01.35 and 02.07. Shortly before bombing, F/Sgt Barton and crew were approached from below on the starboard quarter astern by a single engine enemy fighter, whose fire missed as the Halifax was thrown into a steep dive to starboard. At the same moment, both turrets were rotating, and this caused the aircraft to flip onto its back and lose five thousand feet before control was regained at 10,000 feet, just in time to drop the incendiaries. Returning crews reported the glow of fires beneath the cloud, and local reports confirmed hits on the previously damaged Atlas Werke shipyard and the Korff refinery, with further details scant and of little value. Absent from debriefing were the crews of W/O Scott RCAF and F/Sgt Field RCAF in W1110 and W1175 respectively, and it was only when three bodies from the former and one from the latter were washed ashore at various points on the Dutch coast that their loss in the North Sea was confirmed. W1110 had been shot down by a night-fighter and crashed at 03.00 some twelve miles south-south-west of Den Helder, while the precise location of W1175 remains unknown.

Reversals in the Middle-East had resulted in a request for heavy bombers to be sent out, and 4 Group's 10 and 76 Squadrons were ordered to prepare a detachment each of sixteen aircraft. As far as both squadrons were concerned this was a to be a sixteen-day sojourn for specific operations, and the first two from 10 Squadron departed for the staging post at Gibraltar on the 29th. The remainder of the overseas detachment would fly out between the 5th and the 14th of July for what would turn out to be considerably more than sixteen days.

Later on the 29th a force of 253 aircraft was assembled, which including thirty-four Halifaxes as the 4 Group contribution, nine of them provided by 405 Squadron on the occasion of its one-hundredth operation. They departed Pocklington between 23.00 and 23.07 bound for Bremen with F/L Liversidge the senior pilot on duty and a bomb load of 1,000-pounders and SBCs and flew out over six to ten-tenths cloud at between 3,000 and 5,000 feet with excellent visibility above. F/Sgt Hill and crew were within sight of the Dutch coast when an issue with the guns in the rear turret forced them to turn back, while F/Sgt Higgins and crew had entered Germany and were eight miles south of Oldenburg with the target just twenty miles ahead when they were thwarted by engine trouble. Those arriving in the target area found around seven to ten-tenths cloud in layers up to 16,000 feet with large gaps that afforded some crews a glimpse of the ground. Four 405 Squadron crews delivered their attacks from 13,000 to 19,000 feet between 01.35 and 01.42, some observing bursts, while most gained only impressions of what was happening beneath the cloud. It was another bad night for the squadron with three empty dispersal pans to contemplate in the cold light of dawn. W1113 was shot down by the night-fighter of Oblt Rudolf Sigmund of II./NJG2 and crashed at 01.48 at Noordwolde in northern Holland with no survivors from the eight-man predominantly RCAF crew captained by F/Sgt Chinn RAAF. W7714 also fell victim to the ever-increasing night-fighter presence over Holland and came down at 02.14 some thirty miles to the north-west of W1113's crash site. They were in sight of the fishing port of Harlingen and the safety of the North Sea, but also only a dozen miles or so from the famed "Wespennest" or wasps' nest Luftwaffe fighter aerodrome at Leeuwarden, and there were no survivors from the mixed RCAF/RAF crew of F/Sgt Sidney RCAF. W7715 crashed in Germany some four miles north-north-west of Nordhorn, close to the Dutch frontier and only the RCAF rear gunner from the crew of F/L Liversidge escaped with his life to be taken into captivity. Local reports spoke of extensive damage to the Focke-Wulf factory, the A G Weser U-Boot construction yard and three other important war-industry premises, along with the local gas works and some limited destruction of housing.

It had been a sobering end to the month for 405 Squadron, during which twelve operations had generated 119 sorties for the loss of ten Halifaxes and nine crews.

July 1942

The 1st of July was celebrated at Pocklington as Canadian Dominion Day, and happily, no operations were planned for that night. A sports meeting was held in the afternoon, which was dominated by the Station HQ team, but W/C Fauquier reputedly won the hundred yards sprint, and prizes were received from the hand of Mrs Carr, wife of the A-O-C, AVM Roddy Carr. A dance took place in the officers' mess that evening and a good time was had by all.

The campaign against Bremen continued on the 2nd, with the preparation of a force of 325 aircraft, more than half of which were Wellingtons. 4 Group squadrons contributed thirty-five Halifaxes, ten of them at Pocklington, and they took off between 23.22 and 23.51 with W/C Fauquier and S/Ls Fraser and Thiele the senior pilots on duty. They set course for the Dutch coast near Alkmaar, and while over the North Sea lost the services of F/Sgt Higgins and crew to intercom and oxygen issues. Rather than waste the sortie or jettison the contents of the bomb bay, they dropped their load on a searchlight and flak position at the western end of Ameland Island before heading home. S/L Fraser and crew ran into a pocket of flak at the Dutch coast and a burst beneath the starboard wing flipped the Halifax onto its back and threw it into a spin, which was halted after the loss of three thousand feet. Pulling back too quickly on the control yoke had the effect of flick-rolling the Halifax to starboard onto an even keel, but the trim tabs were inoperable, and it was decided to seek out an alternative target, for which an aerodrome presented itself. The others reached the target area to find favourable weather conditions, with excellent visibility, no low cloud, high cirrus at around 22,000 feet, a half moon and only a little haze to spoil the view below. Positions were established by TR-fix confirmed by a visual check, but searchlight glare created great difficulty for the bomb-aimers, particularly those assigned to specific aiming-points like the Focke-Wulf aircraft factory and shipyards, and most would settle for estimating the fall of their bombs. The Pocklington crews bombed from 13,000 to 17,500 feet between 01.43 and 01.56, some observing bursts and fires, while others were defeated by searchlight glare and haze. A large fire was reported on the aerodrome attached to the Focke-Wulf factory and another at Delmenhorst to the south-west, and the consensus was of an effective operation. Local reports spoke of a thousand houses damaged, along with four small industrial premises, while three cranes and seven ships were hit in the port, one of the vessels sinking and becoming a danger to navigation. The likelihood is, however, that much of the effort was wasted beyond the city's southern boundary.

4 Group spent the ensuing five nights at home, largely as the result of adverse weather conditions, and committed its squadrons to intensive training. Orders were received across the Command on the 8th to prepare for that night's operation against Wilhelmshaven, for which a force of 285 aircraft was assembled. 4 Group contributed thirty-eight Halifaxes, nine of them provided by 405 Squadron, which took off from Pocklington between 23.43 and 23.56 with S/L Thiele the senior pilot on duty and each crew sitting on three 1,000 pounders and twelve SBCs of 4lb incendiaries. All reached the target to find around three-tenths thin cloud at 10,000 feet and haze below, which for many rendered the identification of ground detail, particularly the docks and shipyard aiming-points, impossible. Positions had to be established on e.t.a. and by TR-fix, some backed up through a brief glimpse of the docks and waterways sparkling in the light of flares. They carried out their attacks from 14,000 to 17,000 feet between 01.35 and 01.55, but F/Sgt Knight and crew suffered a hang-up caused by an electrical fault and by the time that the bombs had been released manually, they fell beyond the aiming point to the east and across the Jade Strait at Eckwarder. A number of bursts and fires were observed in Wilhelmshaven but not the precise point of impact and local sources confirmed some damage, while post-raid reconnaissance revealed that much of the bombing had missed the town to the west.

On the 12th W1097 was written off in a crash-landing at Aberporth airfield in Wales after suffering engine failure, but F/Sgt Slezak and his crew emerged unscathed for what, sadly, would be only a temporary reprieve.

The first of a series of five operations over a four-week period against Duisburg was posted across the Command on the 13th, and a force of 194 aircraft made ready, including thirty-three Halifaxes, eight of them belonging to 405 Squadron. Before they departed Pocklington, the crews of F/L Swetman and P/O Hill set off for the Lyons region of Vichy France at 22.50 to deliver between them 120 packets of four different propaganda leaflets. It took three hours to reach the target area, where the reading matter was dispensed into the slipstream at 12,000 feet between 01.57 and 02.11. Meanwhile, the bombing brigade had taken off between 00.03 and 00.10 each captained by an NCO pilot and the usual 1,000-pounder/incendiary mix in the bomb bays. They flew out through electrical storms and heavy cloud on their way to the Essex coast, and F/Sgt Barton and crew were so badly afflicted by the loss of their TR, IFF and intercom that they were persuaded to turn back. The others continued on over thinning cloud in places until reaching the target area to find a covering of between three and ten-tenths with tops at around 10,000 feet. This allowed some crews to glimpse the ground to establish that they were over the built-up area, while others relied entirely on a TR-fix, which all but guaranteed that the bombing would be widely scattered and largely ineffective. The 405 Squadron crews bombed from 14,000 and 18,500 feet between 02.05 and 02.29, observing nothing other than flashes and had to rely on local sources to confirm an ineffective raid which destroyed eleven houses and seriously damaged a further sixty-eight.

Minor operations and mining occupied the ensuing five nights until the 19th, when orders were received on Halifax, Stirling and Lancaster stations to prepare a force of ninety-nine four-engine types to send that night against the Vulkan U-Boot construction yards at Vegesack, situated on the River Weser a few miles to the north-west of Bremen city centre. 4 Group contributed forty Halifaxes, eleven of them belonging to 405 Squadron, which departed Pocklington between 23.59 and 00.09 with S/L Fraser the senior pilot on duty and seven 1,000 pounders in each bomb bay. They crossed the North Sea over ten-tenths cloud that topped out at 10,000 feet and persisted all the way to the target, where a few gaps were all that crews had to confirm their positions visually. They delivered their attacks unopposed on the basis of a Gee-fix (TR) from 14,000 to 18,000 feet between 02.07 and 02.27 and gained an impression that a lot was going on beneath the cloud, when in reality, the raid had completely missed the target, confirming the fact that the search for an effective blind-bombing system would have to go on. On return to a landing at Elvington, Sgt Langford-Pudney and crew reported that they had searched in vain for forty-five minutes, before bombing a last resort target in the general vicinity. *(This pilot would be recorded in the squadron ORB as Sgt Pudney.)*

A force of 291 aircraft was assembled on the 21st for the second raid of the series on Duisburg, and this number included thirty-nine Halifaxes, eleven of them provided by 405 Squadron, which departed Pocklington between 23.50 and 23.59 with F/L Swetman the senior pilot on duty and four carrying the unusual bomb load of two cookies and the others three 1,000-pounders and a dozen SBCs of 30lb incendiaries. Sgt West and crew turned back because of a h,ydraulics issue shortly after crossing the English coast, leaving the others to reach the target to find clear skies and the usual industrial haze, but sufficiently good vertical visibility aided by flares to confirm their TR-fixed positions visually. The bombing was carried out by the Pocklington crews from 12,000 to 15,000 feet between 01.41 and 02.07 and few saw the results of their efforts, but fires were observed to be taking hold as they withdrew into the moonless skies and the glow remained visible on the horizon for seventy miles. The Duisburg authorities confirmed a moderately successful raid, during which ninety-four buildings had been destroyed and 256 seriously damaged, which represented something of a success and this elusive target, and it is believed that the Thyssen steelworks was among a number of important war industry factories to sustain some damage.

A reduced force of 215 aircraft was made ready to continue the assault on Duisburg on the 23rd, for which thirty-eight Halifaxes were detailed, nine of them representing 405 Squadron, eight of which departed Pocklington between 00.37 and 00.46, leaving the crew of F/Sgt Slezak on the ground until 01.11. Two of the Halifaxes were carrying a pair of cookies and the others three 1,000-pounders and a dozen SBCs of 30lb incendiaries and all crews were captained by an NCO pilot. Sgt West and crew again turned back early after losing their intercom, while the others pressed on across the North Sea over ten-tenths cloud topping out at 5,000 feet. All reached the target area to find that nine-tenths of the white stuff remained beneath them at 8,000 to 12,000 feet, forcing them to establish their positions by Gee-fix. The bombs were delivered from 12,000 to 20,000 feet between 02.24 and 03.03 and disappeared into the cloud in which their detonations and the burgeoning fires were reflected. On return to the Pocklington circuit W7769 circled awaiting its turn to land, but when an engine cut, the Halifax crashed at 04.53 into New Street in Pocklington village, slicing off the corner of a house and smashing into the school before bursting into flames. There were no survivors from among the eight predominantly Canadian occupants captained by the experienced F/Sgt Albright RCAF. It was left to local sources in Duisburg to report housing damage, but it was another unsatisfactory attempt to hit this major centre of war production.

The fourth raid on Duisburg was posted on the 25th, for which the largest force yet of the series was assembled and among the 313 aircraft were 177 Wellingtons and fourteen Hampdens, with the four-engine types making up the numbers. 4 Group contributed forty-one Halifaxes, eight of them provided by 405 Squadron, which departed Pocklington between 23.44 and 00.11 again with no commissioned pilots on duty. Four crews were sitting on two cookies each and the others on three 1,000-pounders and a dozen SBCs of 30lb incendiaries as they flew out over ten-tenths cloud as far as the Dutch coast, where it diminished slightly to seven to nine-tenths with haze below. The crews of F/Sgts Higgins and Slezak turned back at the Dutch coast, the former because of severe icing and the latter after encountering an enemy night-fighter at the same time as an electrical fault rendered the rear turret unserviceable. The others reached the western Ruhr to encounter eight-tenths cloud with thick industrial haze below and established their positions by TR, before aiming their bombs at existing fires from 14,000 and 19,500 feet between 01.42 and 02.11. They could only assume that they were adding to the damage, which, according to local sources, was on a smaller scale than from the previous raids in the series.

A maximum effort was planned on the 26th for the annual last-week-of-July attack on Germany's second city, Hamburg, and 404 aircraft answered the call, among them seventy-three Halifaxes. 405 Squadron made ready thirteen aircraft, which took off between 22.43 and 23.13 with W/C Fauquier and S/Ls Fraser and Thiele the senior pilots on duty, the commanding officer accompanied by the 4 Group Senior Air Staff Officer (SASO), G/C Brook, who had been station commander at Pocklington before the incumbent G/C Corbally. They flew out over the Yorkshire coast to begin the North Sea crossing and attempt to negotiate the frequently met conditions on this route of towering cloud, electrical storms and severe icing, and it was probably at this stage that Sgt Langford-Pudney and crew abandoned their sortie because of port-outer engine trouble. Those reaching the target area were drawn on for the last eight minutes by the sight of fires already burning in the docks area and the southern part of the old town. Apart from a little cloud at 15,000 feet, the skies were now clear and the city basking in bright moonlight as the Pocklington crews carried out their attacks from 12,000 to 18,000 feet between 01.06 and 01.34. S/L Fraser and crew experienced a torrid time after running into searchlights at the Kiel Canal, which held them despite violent evasive action and passed them on from one cone to another for almost an hour. Exhausted, S/L Fraser ordered the bombs to be jettisoned over a built-up area, which they believed may have been Stade located on the western bank of the Elbe to the west of the primary target.

It proved impossible for crews to pick out individual bomb bursts among the many detonations, and the hostility of the searchlight and flak defences dissuaded crews from loitering to make an assessment. Smoke was drifting across the city as the bombers retreated into the clutches of the waiting night-fighters, which played their part in bringing down a massive twenty-nine bombers, or 7.2% of those dispatched. The loss of eight Halifaxes represented an alarming 10.9% and there were two empty dispersal pans at Pocklington to contemplate as daylight arrived over Yorkshire. The remains of W1186 fell onto marshland some seven miles south-east of Stade after apparently exploding in the air, and there were no survivors from among the eight predominantly RCAF occupants captained by F/Sgt Slezak RCAF. On board the brand new W1230, which was flying operationally for the first time, was the crew of Sgt Smith, and only the mid-upper gunner survived to be taken prisoner after the Halifax came down in the Schleswig-Holstein region. Sources in Hamburg confirmed a highly successful operation, which caused widespread damage, particularly in residential and commercial districts, where more than eight hundred houses had been destroyed and a further five thousand damaged, costing 14,000 people their homes. At least eight hundred fires kept the emergency services busy, particularly those dealing with 523 that were classed as large.

The funerals of F/Sgt Albright and four others were held at Barmby Moor Cemetery on the 27th with full military honours. Another maximum effort was called for on the 28th, and a force well in excess of four hundred aircraft was assembled for the return to Hamburg that night. 256 aircraft were provided by 3 Group and the operational training units, which, in the event, would take off alone, after the weather conditions over the 1, 4 and 5 Group stations prompted the withdrawal of their contributions. As conditions worsened over the North Sea, the O.T.U aircraft were recalled, and many of the 3 Group crews turned back also, leaving just sixty-eight to claim to have attacked the primary target, where fifteen large fires and forty smaller ones were reported. This modicum of success was gained at the high cost of twenty-five aircraft, 15% of those dispatched, and four O.T.U Wellingtons also failed to return, while a fifth, a Whitley, ditched, and its crew was picked up safely.

Saarbrücken was posted as the target on the 29th, and a force of 291 aircraft assembled for what would be the largest raid by far on this major industrial and coal-producing Saarland capital city, situated right on the frontier with France in south-western Germany. 4 Group contributed fifty Halifaxes, seven of them made ready by 405 Squadron, which departed Pocklington between 23.10 and 23.16 with no commissioned pilots on duty and three 1,000-pounders and a dozen SBCs of 4lb incendiaries in each bomb bay. They headed for the French coast near Dunkerque to follow a course parallel to the Franco-Belgian border that would lead them directly to the target south of Luxembourg. The cloud that had accompanied them most of the way amounted to seven-tenths in the target area in a band at between 2,000 and 9,000 feet, enabling some crews to confirm their TR positions by visual references on ground features like the River Saar. In the expected absence of a strong searchlight and flak defence, the 4 Group crews had been briefed to bomb their specific aiming-point from a lower level than customary for the period, but not all complied, and the attacks by the 405 Squadron participants were carried out from 4,000 to 18,000 feet between 01.44 and 02.17. Explosions and fires were observed in the northern part of the city around the marshalling yards, some large and emitting black smoke. Returning crews were confident that their bombs had found the mark, and this was confirmed by local reports of severe damage in central and north-western districts, where almost four hundred buildings had been destroyed in return for the loss of nine aircraft.

The month ended with a major assault on the Ruhr city of Düsseldorf, for which a force of 630 aircraft was assembled, the numbers bolstered by a large contribution from the training units. 4 Group supported the operation with seventy Halifaxes, thirteen of them provided by 405 Squadron, which departed Pocklington in two phases between 23.52 and 00.39 with W/C Fauquier and S/Ls Fraser and Thiele the senior pilot on duty. The five first-phase Halifaxes were carrying three 1,000-poundes and a dozen SBCs each, while seven of those in the second phase had two cookies on board and one eight 1,000-pounders. S/L Fraser and crew lost their starboard-inner engine shortly after crossing the Dutch frontier into Germany and were approaching the Rhine when they jettisoned their load "live" in the Kempen area. The others pressed on to the southern Ruhr, where bright moonlight, clear skies and good visibility enabled the crews of the first wave to confirm their TR-fixed positions visually by an S-bend in the River Rhine. They left developing fires for the second wave crews, whose identification of the aiming-point was impeded by the resulting smoke. The 405 Squadron crews carried out their attacks from 8,000 to 15,000 feet between 02.30 and 03.09 in the face of an intense and accurate searchlight and flak defence and reported many explosions and fires and a column of black smoke rising through 10,000 feet as they turned away.

At debriefing, they expressed confidence in the quality of their work, having contributed to the delivery of more than nine hundred tons of bombs, some of which had been wasted in open country, while the remainder had been scattered across all parts of the city and neighbouring Neuss on the opposite bank of the Rhine. Local sources confirmed the destruction of 453 buildings, with varying degrees of damage to fifteen thousand more, and sixty-seven large fires had to be dealt with. The success came at the cost of twenty-nine aircraft, including four Halifaxes, and the O.T.U.s were again hit disproportionately hard, losing fifteen of their number. A sad end to the month for 405 Squadron was manifested by the sight of two empty dispersal pans at Pocklington which should have been occupied by W1109 and W7718. The former crashed nine miles south of Krefeld on the western edge of the Ruhr and there were no survivors from the crew of Sgt Hunter. W7718 went down in flames and crashed at 03.05 on the Belgian side of the frontier some fifteen miles north-east of Genk with the rear gunner still in his turret, while Sgt West and five others escaped by parachute, four to fall into enemy hands and the bomb-aimer, Sgt Pearce RAAF to evade a similar fate. Sadly, the severely wounded wireless operator, P/O Nadeau RCAF, died three days later.

During the course of the month, the squadron participated in eleven operations and dispatched 101 sorties for the loss of five Halifaxes and crews.

August 1942

A gentle start to the new month saw the heavy brigade remain at home because of unfavourable weather on the first two nights, and it was at this time that 419 (Moose) Squadron transferred from 3 Group with its Wellingtons to take up residence at Leeming. 4 Group sent out orders to Middleton-St-George, Pocklington, Topcliffe and Linton-on-Ouse on the 3rd to prepare ten Halifaxes between them for a "moling" operation to Hamburg. Moling operations were unescorted daylight sorties by small numbers of aircraft relying on cloud cover alone for protection and often involved attacking targets in well-defended regions like the Ruhr. The practice cost Bomber Command lives for what could only be considered nuisance raids with the prospect of minimal gains. W/C Fauquier demonstrated excellent leadership qualities by putting himself and S/L Thiele forward as the 405 Squadron representatives on what was a dangerous brief and they and their crews departed Pocklington at 16.07 each sitting on seven 1,000 pounders. The cloud began to diminish at 5.30 ° East over the North Sea and W/C Fauquier stooged up and down the German coast thirty miles out for ninety minutes, progressing as far as 07.49° East before deciding to turn back. The rest of the force made the same decision.

A small-scale operation to Essen was scheduled for the night of the 4/5th and was to involve thirty-eight aircraft, including nine Halifaxes provided by 35 (Madras Presidency) and 405 Squadrons.

The five-strong all-NCO-captained Pocklington element took off between 00.28 and 00.32 with three 1,000-pounders and a dozen SBCs of 30lb incendiaries in each bomb bay and lost the services of Sgt Ferrier and crew to port-outer engine failure at the Dutch coast. Those reaching the central Ruhr had battled their way through towering storm clouds that extended to 20,000 feet, and the remaining 405 Squadron crews of F/Sgts Higgins and Blizard and Sgts Langford-Pudney and Palmer were still in cloud as they bombed on estimated positions from 16,000 to 20,000 feet between 03.02 and 03.11. The Higgins and Palmer crews returned in severely flak-damaged aircraft, the former with a dead port-inner engine and the port side of the fuselage riddled with shrapnel holes, and they were among just eighteen crews claiming to have bombed in the target area.

On the 5th, as his highly successful tour as commanding officer was about to end, W/C Fauquier was awarded a well-deserved DFC. 4 Group added to its strength on the 6th with the arrival of 420 (Snowy Owl) Squadron RCAF on posting from 5 Group, where it had operated Hampdens. It would now convert to Wellingtons at Skipton-on-Swale and would be available for operations in the autumn. Also on this day, W/C Fauquier handed over command of the squadron to the newly promoted W/C Fraser and departed to take up a staff post with the RCAF's Overseas HQ. The fifth and final operation of the three-week campaign against the Ruhr industrial giant of Duisburg was posted later and an overall force of 216 aircraft assembled, to which 4 Group contributed thirty-two Halifaxes. The 405 Squadron element of six departed Pocklington for the final time in anger between 00.37 and 00.46 with S/L Thiele and the recently arrived F/L Bain the senior pilots on duty and the usual Ruhr load of 1,000-pounders and incendiaries. They flew out over the English coast in ten-tenths cloud, by which time F/L Bain and crew had abandoned their sortie because of engine issues and had collided with two parked Wellingtons on landing. The cloud persisted for most of the outward flight, but it was common for the assessment of cloud conditions to vary markedly, and on this occasion, it was reported to be at between zero and ten-tenths over the target with tops at 10,000 feet and barrage balloons tethered as high as 12,000 feet. Positions had to be established by TR-fix confirmed by visual reference aided by fires, flak and flares, and the bombs were delivered blindly by the 405 Squadron crews from 14,000 to 16,000 feet between 02.47 and 02.59.

According to local reports, eighteen buildings were destroyed in Duisburg and sixty-six seriously damaged, and this provided a sad indictment of Bomber Command's performance ove the five-raid series. A total of 1,229 sorties had resulted in the destruction of 212 houses and serious damage to 741 others, and significant industrial damage had resulted from just one raid. In return for this modest gain, Bomber Command had lost forty-three aircraft and crews.

On the 7th, 405 Squadron vacated the station it had occupied for more than a year and moved some thirty miles to the north-west to Topcliffe, situated a few miles to the south-west of Thirsk, while 102 (Ceylon) Squadron moved in the opposite direction.

The process of changing residence was never allowed to interfere with operations, and 405 Squadron had barely settled in at its new home before next appearing on the order of battle on the 9th when Osnabrück was posted as the target for 192 aircraft. 4 Group contributed nineteen Halifaxes, four of them made ready at Topcliffe, from where they took off for the first time operationally between 23.50 and 23.56 with F/L Bain the senior pilot on duty. They flew out over

Withernsea and soon lost the services of Sgt Langford-Pudney and crew who turned back after failing to coax more than 10,000 feet out of their Halifax. The others continued on their way to the Den Helder peninsula on a direct course to the target, situated in the flat agricultural country to the north of the Ruhr and south of Bremen. There were clear skies over the Münster region as they closed on the target, but haze contributed to the poor visibility that awaited them, and they all found that they were unable to establish their positions by TR after it was jammed by the enemy on crossing the Dutch coast. The leading aircraft dropped flares to illuminate the area, and this enabled some crews to pick out railway lines, a canal and the River Hase, but it was mainly the fires, searchlights and flak that pointed the way to the aiming-point. Bombing was carried out by the 405 Squadron crews of Sgts Ferrier and Palmer from 15,000 and 13,300 feet at 02.08 and 02.31 respectively and some bursts and fires were observed. According to some crews at debriefings, the glow from the burning city remained on the horizon for eighty to a hundred miles into the return flight and TR functioned again once the Dutch coast had been crossed. W7709 was homebound over Holland with the crew of F/L Bain, when set upon by a night-fighter and shot down to crash without survivors at 03.42 next to a farmhouse at Oploo. The thatched roof of the farmhouse caught fire, but the occupants were unharmed. Local sources confirmed an effective raid, which destroyed 206 houses and a military building, and damaged a number of industrial premises along with four thousand other buildings, mostly lightly.

The main operation on the night of the 11/12th was the first of two on consecutive nights against the city of Mainz, situated to the south-west of Frankfurt-am-Main, for which 154 aircraft were made ready. The number included a contribution from 4 Group of twenty-five Halifaxes, three representing 405 Squadron, for what would be the first large-scale raid on this target. They set off from Topcliffe between 22.05 and 22.07 with no commissioned pilots on duty and two carrying three 1,000-pounders and twelve SBCs and the other seven 1,000-pounders. As they made their way south to the French coast, F/Sgt Higgins was contending with a serious lack of control, which threated to pitch the Halifax into a stall at the slightest provocation. Five thousand feet were lost in one episode, and it became necessary to jettison the load into the sea and nurse the Halifax home to a safe landing. The others adopted the well-worn route across France that led to this part of Germany, and Sgt Ferrier and crew arrived in the target area having flown out in favourable weather conditions to be greeted by up to eight-tenths cloud with tops at 11,500 feet and a base at around 5,000. They delivered their attack from 17,000 feet at 01.16 and observed bursts and fires, which gave an impression of an effective raid. It was, in fact, highly successful, and caused major destruction in the central districts, where many historic and cultural buildings were damaged or destroyed. In the excellent tome, Bomber Command War Diaries by Martin Middlebrook and Chris Everitt, the losses from this operation are put at six aircraft, but the actual number failing to return was fourteen, while four others were lost in crashes at home. W7748 crashed at Duisburg-Kampen, close to the eastern bank of the Rhine, killing F/Sgt Langford-Pudney and three of his crew, while the flight engineer, navigator and rear gunner escaped by parachute to fall into enemy hands.

Confidence in the Halifax had eroded during the summer in the face of initially unexplained accidents in which aircraft had entered unrecoverable spins and crashed with fatal consequences for the occupants. Sabotage was mooted, but the problem was traced to a number of causes including rudder lock and the "Christmas Tree" effect, the addition of extra items of equipment externally, such as the bulbous dorsal turret, armour plating, exhaust shrouds and even the rough black paint used to prevent searchlight glint. All of this added around 5,000lbs to the all-up weight, without a compensating increase in engine power, which translated into extended take-off runs and a slower rate of climb, and when the maximum load of two 4,000lb cookies was carried, the bomb doors had to be slightly ajar, which added to the drag effect. The rudder-lock issue would be fixed by replacing the triangular tail fins with a larger square design, but it was important to restore confidence in the type and to teach pilots how to avoid and, if possible, manage the flaws while the solutions were being worked on. To that end, 4 Group withdrew from bombing operations from the 13th until the 22nd to focus on intensive training, and it was during this period that a major new innovation was introduced.

Earlier in the month, 35 (Madras Presidency) Squadron had been informed that it was to take on a new role as a founder member of the Path Finder Force as the 4 Group representative, and move to Graveley in Huntingdonshire, a satellite of Wyton and one of 3 Group's principal stations. The new force came into being on the 15th, when all four founder heavy squadrons arrived on their stations in Huntingdonshire and Cambridgeshire, 83 Squadron moving into Wyton, the Path Finder HQ, as the 5 Group representative operating Lancasters, while 156 Squadron retained its Wellingtons for the time-being at Warboys, drawing fresh crews from 1 Group, and 3 Group would be represented by the Stirling-equipped 7 Squadron at Oakington. In addition to the above, 109 Squadron was posted to Wyton, where it would spend the next six months developing the Oboe blind-bombing device and marrying it to the Mosquito under the command of W/C Hal Bufton. The new force would occupy 3 Group stations, falling nominally under 3 Group administrative control and receiving its orders through that group, which was commanded by AVM Baldwin, whose tenure, which had lasted since just before the outbreak of war, was shortly to come to an end. His successor would be AVM Sir Ralph Cochrane, who would be in post a relatively short time before moving on the become A-O-C 5 Group in the coming February.

A "Path Finder" force was the brainchild of the former 10 Squadron commanding officer, G/C Sid Bufton, Hal's brother, and now Director of Bomber Operations at the Air Ministry. He had used his best crews at 10 Squadron to find targets by the light of flares and attract other crews by firing off a coloured Verey light, and it could be said that the concept of target-finding and marking had been born at 10 Squadron. Once at the Air Ministry, Bufton promoted his ideas with vigour and gained support among the other staff officers, culminating with the idea being put to Harris soon after his enthronement as Bomber Command C-in-C. Harris rejected the principle of establishing an elite target-finding and marking force, a view shared by the other group commanders with the exception of 4 Group's AVM Roddy Carr. However, once overruled by higher authority, Harris gave it his unstinting support, and his choice of the former 10 Squadron commanding officer and still somewhat junior, G/C Don Bennett, as its commander, was both controversial and inspired, and ruffled more than a few feathers among more senior officers. Australian, Bennett, was among the most experienced aviators in the RAF, a pilot and a Master Navigator of unparalleled experience, with many thousands of hours to his credit. He was blessed with a brilliant mind, which made him prone to set standards that few others could achieve, and this created a demanding, exacting, but fair leader. It had been he who had been entrusted with setting up the Atlantic Ferry Service earlier in the war, to bring much needed aircraft over from America. He also had the recent and relevant experience as a bomber pilot through his commands of 77 and 10 Squadrons and had demonstrated his strong character when evading capture and returning from Norway after being shot down while attacking the Tirpitz in April. Despite his reserve, total lack of humour and his impatience with those whose brains operated on a lower plane than his, he would inspire in his men great affection and loyalty, along with an enormous pride in being a Path Finder. He would forge the new force into a highly effective weapon, although this would not immediately be apparent.

It had been intended to send the fledgling force into battle for the first time at Osnabrück on the 17th, but the commanding officers declared their squadrons to be unready, and the raid went ahead without them. This was the day on which 419 (Moose) Squadron moved from Leeming to join 405 Squadron at Topcliffe for what would be a brief period of residence. The Path Finders took to the air in anger for the first time on the 18th, when contributing thirty-one aircraft to an overall force of 118 bound for the naval and shipbuilding port of Flensburg, situated on the eastern coast of the Schleswig-Holstein peninsula close to the border with Denmark, where the U-Boot pens were the briefed aiming-point. Over time, Path Finder equipment and tactics would evolve to highly sophisticated levels, but in the early stages, its role was simply to lead the main force crews to a target and establish its position with incendiaries and illumination. To that end on this night, half of the 35 (Madras Presidency) Squadron crews were carrying 30lb incendiaries, while the remainder had loads of 1,000 pounders beneath their feet. They crossed Schleswig-Holstein unaware that the wind forecast guiding their navigation was incorrect, and the entire force was being pushed to the north of the intended track and over southern Denmark. The fact that the ground was largely concealed by haze and extreme darkness added to the difficulties, and what appeared to be Flensburg Fjord was identified and illuminated. In fact, they had strayed over a similar-shaped coastal inlet across the Danish frontier, and this led to a scattering of bombs across territory up to twenty-five miles north of the frontier and into the towns of Abenra and Sønderborg. Flensburg remained untouched by this inauspicious operational debut of a force, which, in time, would become a highly efficient, successful and vital component in Bomber Command's armoury. The operation cost four aircraft, and the doubtful honour of being the first Path Finder crew to be lost fell to that of 35 (Madras Presidency) Squadron's Sgt Smith in W1226.

As part of the shift of 4 Group squadrons to southern Yorkshire, 10 Squadron vacated Leeming on the 18th and took up residence at Melbourne, a satellite of Pocklington. When operations resumed after eight days of settling in, and until late October, its Halifaxes would launch from Pocklington and land at Melbourne while the runways were being brought up to standard. On the 20th, 4 Group detailed five crews to conduct nickelling sorties over four locations in eastern and south-east-central France and then sat out a period of bad weather between the 23rd and 28th.

Mining and minor operations by other groups occupied the five nights between Flensburg and the second Path Finder-led operation, which was against Frankfurt on the 24th and involved a force of 226 aircraft. Forty-three Path Finder aircraft were detailed, among them eight Halifaxes representing 35 (Madras Presidency) Squadron, which headed out across The Wash on course for the Belgian coast and entered Germany over the Eifel region. They encountered five to ten-tenths cloud at between 7,000 and 9,000 feet, with ground haze adding to the difficulties of locating the aiming-point, and it was the flak that guided some Path Finders to the approximate location of the target to deliver their 1,000 pounders and incendiaries. Sixteen aircraft failed to make it home, five of them Path Finders, in return for which local sources confirmed a moderate amount of damage and seventeen large fires.

The first real success for the new force came at Kassel, for which a force of 306 aircraft was assembled on the 27th. 35 (Madras Presidency) Squadron detailed three Halifaxes, which were cancelled, leaving thirty-four other Path Finders to identify and illuminate the target. This they accomplished on a night of little cloud, and the main force crews exploited the opportunity to inflict widespread damage on this important industrial city. Local sources confirmed the destruction of 144 buildings and serious damage to three hundred more, and a number of military establishments were also hit. It was an expensive night for the Command, however, which registered the loss of thirty-one aircraft, three of them Path Finders, all 156 Squadron Wellingtons.

By the time that 405 Squadron was called to action on the 28th, it had been operationally inactive since the 11th and made ready five Halifaxes for a raid that night on Saarbrücken involving 113 aircraft. It was an experimental operation to ascertain the ability of the main force crews to find and bomb a lightly defended target just inside Germany in favourable weather conditions, which on this night included a four-fifths moon. The force consisted of seventy-one Wellingtons with predominantly freshman crews, seventeen Hampdens, a type with fewer than three weeks front-line service ahead of it, and twenty-four Halifaxes, a type with a cloud still hanging over it because of its already-mentioned poor performance and a spate of unexplained crashes. The Halifaxes were provided by the stations at Pocklington, Middleton-St-George, Topcliffe and East Moor along with a brace of 419 (Moose) Squadron Wellingtons, the 405 Squadron element taking off between 19.52 and 19.56 with P/O Shockley the only commissioned pilot on duty and a bomb load of two 1,000-pounders and four SBCs each of 4lb and 30lb incendiaries. This was not the night's main operation, which was to be directed at the city of Nuremberg situated some 180 miles to the east, for which a force of 159 aircraft had been assembled and dispatched.

The Saarbrücken force crossed the Channel under clear skies, losing the services of F/Sgt Fernyhough and crew to a failed a.s.i. on the way, before picking up four to six-tenths cloud between 14,000 and 17,000 feet at the Belgian coast, which then persisted all the way to the target. Visibility was poor, largely because of ground haze, but the River Saar stood out clearly as a reference, and the 405 Squadron crews delivered their attacks from 10,000 to 14,000 feet between 22.59 and 23.16. The raid was a dismal failure that scattered bombs over a wide area and destroyed just fifteen houses, while severely damaging fifty more at a cost of seven aircraft.

At Nuremberg, the Path Finders employed target indicators for the first time in adapted 250lb bomb casings, which were delivered with great accuracy onto the aiming point. The main force crews failed to exploit the opportunity, and according to local sources, only around fifty bomb loads hit the city, while others landed up to ten miles north of the city boundaries. Some damage was achieved and 137 people killed, but this modest success was gained at the cost of twenty-three aircraft, 14.5% of those dispatched and the Wellington element sustained losses of 34%.

During the course of the month, the squadron carried out six operations and dispatched twenty-five sorties for the loss of two Halifaxes and crews.

September 1942

The first half of the new month would distinguish itself through an unprecedented series of effective operations, although, it would begin ignominiously for the Path Finder Force on the night of the 1/2nd, when it marked the wrong target. The city of Saarbrücken, which, as described above, had been attacked ineffectively four nights earlier, had been briefed out as the objective to 231 crews, of which twenty-six were Path Finders and forty-one would be on board 4 Group Halifaxes and Wellingtons. The six 405 Squadron participants departed Topcliffe between 22.56 and 23.03 with P/O Shockley the only commissioned pilot on duty and each Halifax carrying six SBCs each of 4lb and 30lb incendiaries. As BB216 crossed the east coast the port-outer engine caught fire, and although it was extinguished, the port wing was structurally compromised, and the order was given by Sgt MacKenzie RCAF to bale out. The five crew members who had time to comply fell into the sea and two were drowned, while two were picked up and the navigator, P/O Mason, swam for two hours to reach the shore. The Halifax crashed at 23.58 at Chapel-St-Leonards, five miles north of Skegness in Lincolnshire, killing the pilot and the other occupant. The others pressed on across the North Sea over ten-tenths cloud, which began to disperse at the Belgian coast to leave the target basking under clear skies with good visibility, which enabled the Path Finders to confirm their TR-established positions visually using the River Saar as a reference.

The 405 Squadron crews carried out their bombing runs from 10,000 and 14,000 feet between 02.00 and 02.07 and observed bursts and fires, some from other squadrons reporting the entire area of the North Bank of the Saar to be on fire and a very large explosion occurring in the midst of the conflagration. There was no question in the minds of the crews as they retreated to the west, that this had been an outstandingly accurate attack, and some claimed to be able to see the glow of fires from up to 140 miles into the return flight. It was only later that the truth emerged, that the Path Finders had not marked Saarbrücken, but the non-industrial town of Saarlouis, situated thirteen miles to the north-west on a bend in the river similar to that at the intended target. Much to the chagrin of its inhabitants and those in surrounding communities, the main force bombing had been particularly accurate and concentrated, and heavy damage had been inflicted. This could have been an ill-omen for the month's efforts, but, in fact, the Command now embarked on the unprecedented run of effective operations mentioned above.

The accent remained on southern Germany on the following night when Karlsruhe was posted as the primary target for a force of two hundred aircraft, of which twenty-seven Halifaxes and Wellingtons were provided by 4 Group. The city was home among others to a factory belonging to the Deutsche Waffen und Munitionsfabriken A G, better known as DWM, which manufactured all types of firearms from pistols to automatic weapons for infantry and aircraft. The sixe-strong 405 Squadron element was reduced to four when the Halifaxes of Sgt Rea and W/O Ferrier became bogged down on the way to take-off, leaving the crews of the newly appointed B Flight commander, F/L Hillier, F/Sgts Duncan and Palmer and Sgt Campbell to depart Topcliffe between 22.28 and 22.38, again with all-incendiary loads in the bomb bays. They set course for the Belgian coast, before tracking along the Franco-Belgian frontier to the target, which they found to be under clear skies, bathed in moonlight and naked to the eyes of the bomb-aimers high above. The autobahn and the Rhine and its distinctive finger-shaped docks stood out clearly as a guide to the aiming-point and the Topcliffe crews released their incendiaries from 11,000 to 13,000 feet between 01.46 and 02.00. Returning crews reported as many as two hundred fires, the glow from which remained visible for a hundred miles into the homeward journey, post-raid reconnaissance confirming much residential and some industrial damage, while local reports mentioned seventy-three fatalities. Absent from debriefing was the eight-man predominantly RCAF crew of F/L Hillier RCAF in DT487, which was shot down by the night-fighter of Oblt Martinek of I./NJG4 and crashed at 01.46 eight miles south-west of Namur in Belgium. This was at the same time as the bomber force was closing on the target 180 miles to the south-east, which indicates that they had turned back early with some kind of technical problem.

The funerals of two of the victims of the crash of BB216 took place with full military honours at Dishforth Cemetery on the afternoon of the 4th and was attended by the station and squadron commanders, an escort party, a firing party and the Royal Air Force band Topcliffe.

Bremen was posted as the target for that night and a force of 251 aircraft was assembled, while the crews attended briefing to be told that the Path Finders would be rolling out a new three-phase technique, consisting of illumination with white flares, visual marking with coloured flares and backing-up with all-incendiary loads, which if successful, would form the basis of Path Finder operations for the remainder of the war. 4 Group contributed thirty-one Halifaxes and three 419 (Moose) Squadron Wellingtons, five of the former provided by 405 Squadron, which departed Topcliffe between 23.33 and 00.05 with S/L Swetman the senior pilot on duty. P/O Shockley and crew were carrying five 1,000-pounders, while the other crews had a dozen SBCs of incendiaries and a single 1,000-pounder beneath their feet as they flew out in good weather conditions, which persisted all the way into north-western Germany. The crews of Sgt Campbell and F/Sgt Palmer were over enemy territory when technical failures forced them to jettison their loads and turn back, while the others arrived at the target to find only a thin layer of cloud at 5,000 feet between them and the city. A hint of moonlight glinted off the surface of the River Weser and the distinctive shape of the docks and nearby woods enabled the leading crews to establish their positions. The Focke-Wulf aircraft factory in the Hemelingen district was the aiming-point assigned to a 5 Group element, while the bulk of the main force was to target the general city area including the docks. The first Path Finder flares and incendiaries went down at around 01.50 and the 405 Squadron element followed up from 15,000 to 17,000 feet between 01.48 and 02.10. *(The ORB entries are badly corrupted and difficult to read, which may lead to slight errors of times and altitudes.)* There was confidence among returning crews that a successful operation had taken place, and the Focke-Wulf factory was reported to be ablaze. Debriefing claims of fires in the central districts were confirmed by a local assessment, which listed 460 dwelling houses, six large/medium industrial premises and fifteen small ones destroyed, and a further fourteen hundred buildings seriously damaged in exchange for the loss to the Command of twelve aircraft.

On the 6th, two Spitfires and an American Havoc medium bomber arrived at Topcliffe for fighter affiliation exercises with the squadron's Halifaxes, and the Havoc created particular interest among aircrew. Harris couldn't resist another swipe at Duisburg, and a force of 207 aircraft was made ready for that purpose on the 6th, a number that included thirty-four 4 Group aircraft, mostly Halifaxes. 405 Squadron contributed seven Halifaxes, which received a load either of six 1,000-pounders or two 1,000-pounders and a dozen SBCs of incendiaries before departing Topcliffe between 00.32 and 00.45 with P/Os Higgins and Shockley the commissioned pilots on duty. P/O Higgins and crew turned back after an hour when the rear turret became unserviceable, while Sgt Webb and crew lost their port-outer engine and also had to abandon their sortie. The others pressed on to the target, which was partially concealed by cloud and a layer of industrial haze that forced the Path Finders to establish their positions by TR, confirmed as far as possible by visual reference. The searchlight and flak defences provided a firm indication to the main force as to the general whereabouts of the target, but the reflection of the Path Finder flares on the haze combined with the smoke to obliterate ground detail and create the most challenging of conditions. The 405 Squadron crews bombed on e.t.a. from 7,000 to 18,000 feet between 02.45 and 03.10, and immediately after bombing, F/Sgt Fernyhough and crew were hit by flak which caused the starboard-outer engine to cut and flipped the Halifax onto its back. Searchlights and flak followed them down to 7,000 feet as they took violent evasive action until they were able to escape into darkness. The impression of returning crews was that, despite the many fires, the attack had failed to achieve concentration, and some bomb loads had fallen west of the Rhine. They were largely correct, but this was reported locally as the most effective raid on the city to date, which caused the destruction of 114 buildings and serious damage to three hundred more.

On the 7th, RCAF HQ sent a corporal to investigate the shocking pilfering of parcels in the station post office, as a result of which two leading aircraftsmen were taken into custody pending a court martial. On the 8th, Sgt Norman MacKenzie RCAF was laid to rest in Dishforth cemetery alongside his crew mates. An aunt had requested his body be sent for burial to Stornoway on Lewis Island off Scotland's north-western coast, but the authorities considered it to be too far.

There had been no pattern to the choice of targets thus far in the month, southern and north-western Germany and the Ruhr all featuring during the busy first week, and Frankfurt in south-central Germany was posted as the latest target on the 8th, for which a force of 249 aircraft was assembled, twenty-nine of them Path Finders and forty-three, mostly Halifaxes, representing 4 Group. 405 Squadron made ready seven Halifaxes and sent them on their way from Topcliffe between 20.09 and 20.58 with P/O Shockley the only commissioned pilot on duty and a mix of 1,000-pounders and incendiaries in each bomb bay. They set course for the Belgian coast with the intention of following the frontier with France as far as southern Luxembourg before turning east and crossing into Germany, but Sgt Fernyhough and crew had to turn back shortly after crossing the Essex coast when their oxygen system failed. Sgt Murray and crew lost their starboard-outer engine when just twenty minutes from the target but continued on to deliver their payload from 15,000 feet at 00.03. Those reaching the target area offered the usual mixed opinions concerning the conditions, some describing clear skies and good visibility, while others reported up to eight-tenths cloud at between 2,000 feet and 13,500 feet, with poor to moderate visibility made worse by searchlight glare. The intensity of the searchlight and flak activity should, perhaps, have helped to guide the Path Finders to the aiming-point, but surprisingly, they failed to locate the city and most delivered their flares and incendiaries on DR, TR and e.t.a. The remaining 405 Squadron crews carried out their attacks from 13,000 to 18,000 feet between 23.32 and 00.08 and observed bursts and fires but no detail. Returning main force crews reported Path Finder flares to be in evidence, but scattered over a wide area, and it was clear that they were by no means certain of their position in relation to Frankfurt. According to local reports, only a handful of bomb loads hit the intended target, and this halted the run of successes thus far in the month. The majority of bombs appeared to have fallen to the south-west of Frankfurt as far as Rüsselsheim, fifteen miles away. The Rüsselsheim authorities confirmed damage to the Opel tank works and a Michelin tyre factory, which compensated in small measure for the failure to hit the primary target.

The arrival of a USAAF B17E at Topcliffe on return from an operation on the 9th created much interest, and aircrew in particular took the opportunity to inspect it in detail and compare notes with its ten-man crew. On the 10th acting F/L Stone stepped up to succeed the missing F/L Hillier as B Flight commander and attended that night's briefing for an operation to Düsseldorf. The Path Finder Force was constantly evolving in tactics and equipment and had a new weapon in its armoury for this night in the form of the "Pink Pansy", which weighed in at 2,800lbs in a 4,000lb cookie casing, and was the latest attempt to produce a genuine target indicator. A force of 479 aircraft included a contribution from the training units of 91, 92 and 93 Groups, thirty-nine Path Finders and forty-two 4 Group Halifaxes, eight of them provided by 405 Squadron. They departed Topcliffe between 19.54 and 20.28 with S/L Swetman the senior pilot on duty and each loaded with three 1,000-pounders and six SBCs each of 4lb and 30lb incendiaries. They lost the services of Sgt Burton and crew within an hour to port-inner engine failure, while the others pressed on to the target, and those in the vanguard of the Path Finder element found it under clear skies but with the usual industrial haze to impair the vertical visibility. They established their positions on Gee-fix aided by illuminator flares, which highlighted the Rhine and other ground features, and delivered their marker incendiaries either side of 20.30. Other elements of the Path Finders dropped red and green flares to maintain the marking for the main force crews, and by the time of their arrival, fires had taken hold and smoke was becoming a problem. The 405 Squadron crews attacked from 6,000 to 16,000 feet between 22.33 and 22.50 and were largely denied sight of their bursting bombs by searchlight glare. On return, BB212 crashed into a parked 419 (Moose) squadron Wellington, and when the Halifax was evacuated by Sgt Webb and three others, the wireless operator, Sgt Drennan RCAF, was found to be lifeless. At debriefing a dramatic story of survival was told by Sgt Webb and the other three survivors after the port-outer propeller was shot off while over the target, and this sent the Halifax into a spin, which caused the remaining three engines to cut out. Sgt Webb ordered the crew to bale out and both gunners complied before the engines restarted and control was regained. The Halifax was nursed home and landed but could not be stopped in time to avoid the collision, in which the survivors sustained minor injuries and a very short-lived reprieve. It would emerge later that neither gunner had survived after abandoning the aircraft.

It was clear at main force debriefings that the crews were fairly confident about the outcome of the raid, some reporting the glow of the fires to be visible from the Scheldt. Post-raid reconnaissance and local reports confirmed this operation to have been probably the most successful since Operation Millennium at the end of May. Other than the northern districts, all parts of the city and its neighbour across the Rhine, Neuss, had been hit, and 911 houses had been destroyed with a further fifteen hundred seriously damaged. In addition to the destruction also of eight public buildings, fifty-two industrial firms in the two cities sustained damage sufficient to cause a total shut down of production for varying periods. It had been an expensive victory for the Command, however, with thirty-three failures to return, 7.1% of the force, which was a bitter pill to swallow particularly for the training units, to which thirteen of the missing belonged.

For the second time in the month, Bremen was posted as the target on the 13th, and a force of 446 aircraft assembled, again bolstered by aircraft and crews from the training groups. Thirty-one Path Finder crews attended briefings, as did forty-three from 4 Group's squadrons, and at Topcliffe, nine 405 Squadron Halifaxes presented themselves for take-off between 23.36 and 00.07 with W/C Fraser the senior pilot on duty and all-incendiary loads in each bomb bay. They set course for the

Yorkshire coast and the North Sea crossing and were greeted over the Dutch/German frontier region by eight-tenths cloud, which gave way to clear skies by the time the target drew near. At some point on the failure of their port-inner engine, Sgt Burton and crew turned back, while the remainder pushed on to Bremen, where thick haze concealed ground features other than the River Weser and the docks, forcing some of the early Path Finders to release their incendiaries on e.t.a. Fires and searchlight concentrations drew on the remaining Path Finder and main force crews, those from 405 Squadron bombing through haze and smoke from 14,000 to 17,500 feet between 02.25 and 02.33. The 5 Group ORB described the Path Finder performance as unhelpful, but the success of the operation suggested otherwise, and by far exceeded the destruction resulting from June's Thousand Bomber raid. A total of 848 houses was destroyed, and much damage was inflicted on the city's industry, including to the Lloyd Dynamo works, where two weeks production was lost, and parts of the Focke-Wulf factory were put out of action for between two and eight days. Of the twenty-one aircraft lost, fifteen belonged to the training units.

The end of the Hampden era arrived on the following night, when the naval and shipbuilding port of Wilhelmshaven was posted as the target for 202 aircraft, twenty-six of them Path Finders and among the twenty representing 4 Group were five 405 Squadron Halifaxes. The Hampdens were in the hands of 408 (Goose) squadron RCAF, which would shortly transfer from 5 Group to 4 Group to begin conversion to the Halifax. The 405 Squadron element departed Topcliffe between 20.01 and 20.09 with three 1,000-pounders and a dozen SBCs in each bomb bay and the ORB entry too corrupted to identify most of the pilots. They flew out over considerable amounts of cloud, which dispersed in the target area to leave something between clear skies and seven-tenths cloud at 5,000 feet, through which the Path Finders located the target by Gee and confirmed it visually by the shape of the coastline in Jade Bay. However, extreme darkness and ground haze impaired vertical visibility, leaving the waterline and the docks to provide an adequate pinpoint for them to aim at. The main force crews also employed the shape of the coastline and Gee to establish their positions for a bombing run, the 405 Squadron crews delivering their attacks from 13,000 to 16,000 feet between 22.11 and 22.21. It was difficult to assess the outcome, but local reports confirmed this as the most destructive raid yet on this significant port.

After such a run of successes, Harris had to have another go at Essen, and a force of 369 aircraft was assembled on the 16th, which again called upon the training units to supply aircraft and crews. The Path Finders contributed twenty aircraft and 4 Group thirty, of which ten of the Halifaxes belonged to 405 Squadron and departed Topcliffe between 20.31 and 20.53 with the recently promoted F/L Shockley the senior pilot on duty and a bomb load each of three 1,000-pounders and twelve SBCs. The ORB record is badly corrupted, but it can be ascertained that the crews of P/Os Olsen and McIntosh turned back early, the former because of an electrical issue affecting the guns in both turrets and the latter because of excessive fuel consumption. This left eight to carry on to the target area in the central Ruhr, P/O College and crew after enduring a torrid time at the hands of searchlights and flak all the way from Dunkerque, and on arrival crews encountered between three and eight-tenths cloud, but generally good visibility despite the industrial haze. It was possible for some crews to identify ground detail visually by the light of Path Finder flares, but even so, the overlapping boundaries of the Ruhr towns and cities made it difficult to establish positions with absolute certainty, and some of the crews dropping their bombs on e.t.a., including those of 405 Squadron, would find from the evidence of their bombing photos that they had been over Bochum, Oberhausen or some other built-up expanse. Some of the Path Finder flares were estimated to be falling some twenty miles to the east of Essen, which would have put them over Dortmund and Hagen. The 405 Squadron crews bombed from 16,000 to 19,000 feet between 22.27 and 22.44 and all but one returned to report the glow of fires visible for a hundred miles into the return journey.

Local sources would confirm this to be Essen's worst night of the war to date, citing much housing damage, in addition to which more than a hundred medium and large fires had to be dealt with and fifteen high-explosive bombs had found their way into the Krupp complex, as did a crashing bomber loaded with incendiaries. A post-raid analysis revealed that bombs had been scattered across a large part of the Ruhr, with Bochum, Wuppertal and Herne among the hardest hit, and until the advent of Oboe in the coming spring, such inaccuracies remained a fact of life. It was far from a one-sided affair, and cost the Command a massive thirty-nine aircraft, 10.6% of those dispatched, nineteen of them from the training units. 405 Squadron posted missing the crew of F/Sgt Murray RCAF in W7770 and it was not until the wireless operator, P/O Kropf RCAF, returned home after evading capture that the full story emerged. Fifteen minutes before reaching the target a flame damper on the port-inner engine had burned through and during the bombing run the oxygen system failed. The target was bombed, and a course set for home, but a night-fighter attack set the port wing on fire and only two members of the crew had time to escape before it crashed near Maubeuge, close to the Belgian frontier in north-eastern France. The RAF flight engineer was taken into captivity but the rest of the all-RCAF crew lost their lives.

If any period in the Command's gradual evolution to war-winning capability could be seen as a turning point, then perhaps, the first half of September 1942 qualified. It can be no coincidence that the Path Finder Force was emerging from its hesitant start as the crews got to grips with the complexities of their demanding role, and new tactics and aids were being brought to bear against the enemy. It would be no overnight transformation, and failures would still outnumber victories for some time to come, but the encouraging signs were there, that all of the elements of technical and tactical advance were coming together, and with other technological wizardry in the pipeline, it boded ill for Germany's industrial towns and cities.

On the 17th, the 405 Squadron crews of P/O McIntyre and F/Sgt Daggett departed Topcliffe at 01.36 and 01.42 respectively to deliver reading matter to the residents of Paris and fulfilled their briefs from 15,000 and 16,000 feet at around 03.40 before returning safely from uneventful sorties.

Briefings took place for two targets on the 19th, the larger, by a force of 118 aircraft of 1, 3 and 4 Groups and the Path Finders, which had Saarbrücken as its destination, while a simultaneous operation by sixty-eight Lancasters and twenty-one Stirlings of 3 and 5 Groups and the Path Finders targeted Munich. 35 (Madras Presidency) and 156 Squadrons were to provide the marking at Saarbrücken and 83 and 7 Squadrons at Munich, and the two forces would follow a common route as far as Saarbrücken, leaving the Munich element with a further 220 miles to travel to reach the Bavarian capital, the birthplace of Nazism and a city of cultural and industrial significance. 4 Group detailed thirty-three Halifaxes and five Wellingtons, nine of the former made ready by 405 Squadron, which departed Topcliffe between 19.20 and 19.30 with F/L Shockley the senior pilot on duty and two 1,000-pounders and a dozen SBCs in each bomb bay. The Shockley crew was forced to return early after the port-outer engine had to be shut down, and Sgt Duncan and crew were defeated by transmitter/receiver issues. The others made landfall in the Abbeville area and pressed on across France via the familiar route running parallel to the Belgian and Luxembourg frontiers before reaching the target to find good visibility hampered only by ground haze, which caused problems for the Path Finder element. The moonlight on haze produced a kind of glare that added to the difficulties and some Path Finder crews spent forty minutes seeking out the aiming point before admitting defeat, and a study of one crew's bombing photo would reveal that they had attacked the French city of Nancy, some fifty miles south-west of the intended target. The 405 Squadron participants bombed from between 11,000 and 16,000 feet between 22.57 and 23.25 and gained an impression of a scattered raid, about which they had little of use to pass on at debriefing. Local sources reported damage to be superficial and confirmed that the raid had largely missed the city to the west.

Briefings were held on the Halifax stations on the 23rd for an all-4 Group operation that night against the Flensburger Schiffbau AG yards at Flensburg, situated on the Baltic coast of Schleswig-Holstein, which employed almost three thousand workers in the construction of U-Boots. Ten 405 Squadron crews attended briefing, while their Halifaxes were each receiving a bomb load of six 1,000 pounders and two SBCs of incendiaries as part of a force of twenty-eight. They departed Topcliffe between 00.13 and 00.27 with W/C Fraser the senior pilot on duty and encountered severe electrical storms over the North Sea outbound in a bank of cloud at between 15,000 and 20,000 feet. This prevented some crews from establishing a pinpoint on Jutland's western coast while the others pressed on to find five-tenths cloud over the target, which, because of their very low approach height, did not inhibit their view of the ground. Most of the bombers ran in at low level below 3,000 feet, the 405 Squadron participants from 1,200 to 1,500 feet between 03.01 and 03.25, observing a large explosion followed by a red glow and heavy black smoke in the shipyard and another in the town. Sgt Duncan and crew were unable to locate the target and after searching in vain for an alternative, jettisoned their load, while Sgt Campbell and crew attacked a built-up area on the way home and P/O Olsen and crew a searchlight and flak concentration. At debriefings sixteen crews claimed to have reached the target on a night of heavy casualties for the group, which saw five Halifaxes fail to return, 17.8% of those dispatched. The 405 Squadron casualty involved the previously mentioned Sgt Webb RCAF and crew, who had four new members to replace those lost two weeks earlier. Their Halifax, W1274, crashed four miles north of the Danish frontier town of Padborg and all on board lost their lives.

The operation was mounted again on the 26th, for which another force of twenty-eight Halifaxes was detailed, five of them belonging to 405 Squadron, which departed Topcliffe between 20.22 and 20.27 with no senior pilot on duty. The force was recalled from over Denmark at 23.05 after the weather conditions at home deteriorated and most jettisoned their six 1,000-pounders on the way home.

During the course of the month, the squadron took part in thirteen operations and dispatched eighty-six sorties for the loss of five Halifaxes and crews.

October 1942

The new month opened with a further attempt by 4 Group to hit the U-Boot construction yards at Flensburg while elements of 3 and 5 Groups turned their attention upon other Baltic coast objectives at Lübeck and Wismar respectively. Twenty-eight Halifaxes were detailed again, of which eight were made ready by 405 Squadron and loaded with six 1,000-pounders and two SBCs, before departing Topcliffe between 17.50 and 17.56 with no senior pilots on duty. The crews had been briefed to attack from low level, but adverse weather in the target area in the form of three-tenths low cloud and rain showers created challenging conditions, to which was added murderous light flak. P/O College and crew were frustrated by the failure of their bomb doors to open on the first pass but managed to deliver their payload from 1,500 feet on going round again at 21.25. P/O Palmer and crew bombed the primary target from 1,000 feet at 21.35, and although the rear gunner reported bursts, no detail could be gleaned. Other crews observed bursts and a red glow remained visible on the horizon for sixty miles into the return journey, which eight Halifaxes failed to complete, representing a loss rate of 44%. At debriefing, P/O McIntosh and crew reported that they had jettisoned their load at the midpoint of the North Sea crossing for an undisclosed reason, while P/O Higgins and crew had attacked Sylt aerodrome as an alternative target from 6,000 feet at 21.20. The dispersal pans of W7710 LQ-R "Ruhr Valley Express", W7780 and W7802 stood empty and told a tale of a very bruising night for the squadron. The first mentioned crashed four miles north-north-west of Flensburg almost on the Danish frontier, and there were no survivors from the predominantly RCAF crew of P/O Olsen RCAF. W7780 came down in the target area with fatal consequences for the mixed RAF/RCAF crew of P/O Campbell, and W7802 also went down in the target area at Bohlberg on the eastern bank of the fjord, killing P/O Duncan RCAF and the other seven predominantly RCAF occupants.

The Ruhr city of Krefeld was posted as the target for a force of 188 aircraft on the 2nd, for which 4 Group contributed twenty-nine Halifaxes and ten Wellingtons, ten of the former provided by 405 Squadron, each loaded with three 1,000-pounders and twelve SBCs of incendiaries. Located at the western edge of the Ruhr, a few miles to the south-west of Duisburg, Krefeld's industry had been based on silk and velvet textiles but had been given over to war materials production and the presence of a Thyssen-Krupp steelworks was of particular interest to Bomber Command. The 405 Squadron element departed Topcliffe between 18.24 and 18.34 with S/L Stone the senior pilot on duty and all headed for the Suffolk coast to begin the North Sea crossing on course for landfall on the enemy coast over the Scheldt estuary. S/L Stone's compass became unserviceable, and he and his crew were forced to return early, while those arriving in the target area found it to be enveloped in dense industrial haze, which thwarted the Path Finders' best efforts to provide a reference for those following behind. F/L Shockley and crew were a little early and having overshot the target, bombed in the Düsseldorf area from 14,000 feet at 20.43. P/O McIntosh and crew were conducting a shallow-dive approach and were at 11,000 feet when the starboard-inner engine cut out and a flak shell exploded beneath the port wing, sending the Halifax into an uncontrollable fall, which was arrested at 1,000 feet. Full control was regained at 100 feet, by which time the bomb load had been jettisoned and the flight engineer had baled out without seeking permission. They would endure a tense return flight at 500 feet and land safely at Mildenhall, while the others delivered their attacks from 9,000 to 16,000 feet between 20.37 and 21.03 on e.t.a., Gee and whatever target indicators were visible. Returning crews reported some scattered fires, while local sources confirmed that three streets in the northern part of the city had sustained damage, but nothing commensurate with the size of the force and the effort expended. DG228 was homebound over Holland with the mixed RCAF, RAAF and RAF crew of Sgt Murphy RCAF when brought down by flak to crash without survivors nine miles south-south-west of Haarlem and within sight of the North Sea.

On the 4th, W/C Fraser's outstanding service was recognised by the award of a DFC. All heavy groups were alerted on the 5th to an operation that night against the city of Aachen, for which a force of 257 aircraft was assembled, 4 Group contributing thirty-seven Halifaxes and twenty Wellingtons, including some of the latter provided by 420 (Snowy Owl) and 425 (Allouette) Squadrons, which were conducting their maiden operations with 4 Group. The 405 Squadron element of eight departed Topcliffe between 18.20 and 18.28 with F/L Shockley the senior pilot on duty and the standard payload in each bomb bay and climbed away into challenging weather conditions that caused problems particularly in the Path Finder and 3 Group region. Crews were forced to negotiate an electrical storm as they headed for the Essex coast to begin the North Sea crossing to Belgium and over the next two hours 405 Squadron lost the services of Sgt Higgins and crew to icing, P/O McIntosh and crew to port-inner engine failure and F/L Shockley and crew to the loss of their intercom. This left five crews to reach the target, where they encountered eight-tenths cloud at between 8,000 and 14,000 feet and carried out their attacks from 10,000 and 16,500 feet in the absence of a strong marking performance by the Path Finders. On return, W7703 reached the south coast low on fuel and Sgt Hudema RCAF decided to land at the Fighter Command station at West Malling, north-east of Maidstone in Kent. The first attempt failed and while going round again the Halifax stalled and crashed at 00.34 at Wrotham, five miles east-north-east of Sevenoaks, killing the five occupants, the bomb-aimer and rear gunner having taken to their parachutes. Although some damage had occurred at the primary target, much of the effort was scattered far and wide, including onto the Dutch town of Lutterade situated some fifteen miles to the north-north-west, and this would have minor consequences for the Oboe development programme in December.

Osnabrück was posted as the target on the 6th, for which 237 aircraft were made ready, including twenty-two Halifaxes and a similar number of Wellingtons. The seven 405 Squadron participants departed Topcliffe between 18.50 and 18.56 with P/Os College, Hedges and Stewart the commissioned pilots on duty and the standard load in each bomb bay. The Path Finders dropped flares over Makkum in Holland and the Dümmer See to the north-east of the target as route markers, and these proved to be very effective in guiding the main force in, although, inevitably, some bomb loads were released early during the twenty-mile leg between the Dümmer See and the town. Four to eight-tenths cloud lay over the town at 8,000 feet and provided challenging conditions for accurate bombing, although opinions varied as to the quality of the visibility. P/O Hedges and crew had an engine catch fire when two miles south of the Dümmer See and they were forced to jettison their load, leaving the others to attack from 10,000 to 15,000 feet between 21.22 and 21.31 and observe numerous fires as they headed back towards the North Sea. W7763 was racing for the Dutch coast when intercepted and shot down by a night-fighter to crash at 23.55 near Utrecht after the predominantly RCAF crew of P/O Stewart had left it to its fate. Sadly, the parachute of the RAF mid-upper gunner failed to deploy, and he was killed, while his crew mates were taken into captivity. Returning crews described many fires and a glow visible by some from the Dutch coast homebound, and most had confidence in the effectiveness of the raid. According to local reports, 149 houses and six industrial buildings were destroyed, 530 houses seriously damaged and more than 2,700 others slightly damaged.

The naval and shipbuilding port of Kiel was posted as the target for a force of 288 aircraft on the 13th, for which 4 Group weighed in with fifty-four Halifaxes, eleven of them provided by 405 Squadron. The plan called for the Path Finder target-locaters and illuminators to fly out over the Baltic, before turning back onto a westerly heading to drop special markers over the Selenter Lake, the second largest body of water in Schleswig-Holstein, situated some eight miles east of Kiel. The locaters were to lay sticks of flares across the target area at the opening of the attack at 21.09, or, if the aiming-point had definitely been identified, to act as illuminators and drop their flares onto it along with the illuminators, who had a time-on-target between 21.10 and 21.18. This would then leave the way clear, and the aiming-point primed for the main force element to do their job. The 405 Squadron contingent took off between 18.14 and 18.33 with no senior pilot on duty, but the poor serviceability of the Halifax would reduce the numbers reaching the target. Sgt Longley lost a number of flying instruments as he and his crew crossed the Yorkshire coast, and F/Sgt Rea and crew were some seventy miles out from Scarborough when also forced to abort their sortie because of W/T failure. Seventy miles further out still, F/Sgt Daggett's rear turret jammed on the starboard beam and short-circuited, ending this crew's interest in proceedings. Sgt Chretien and crew jettisoned their three 1,000-pounders and twelve SBCs when hit by flak just three miles from the target and the pilot had to contend with a neck wound as he nursed the badly-holed Halifax back to base. The others reached the target area to find almost clear skies and good visibility and the aiming point illuminated and marked by the Path Finders, to which the defenders responded with an effective smoke screen and intense searchlight activity. The 405 Squadron crews carried out their attacks from 15,000 to 17,500 feet between 21.15 and 21.40 and the consensus was of an effective raid. A post-raid analysis and local sources revealed that a decoy fire site had been successful in drawing off half of the attack, and damage in Kiel, although substantial, was less than might otherwise have been.

Three new Wellington squadrons were formed within 4 Group on the 15th, 424 (Tiger) Squadron RCAF at Topcliffe, 426 (Thunderbird) Squadron RCAF at Dishforth and 466 Squadron RAAF at Driffield. Neither Canadian squadron would reach operational status before being posted to the Canadian 6 Group on New Year's Day 1943. Earlier in the month, on the 9th and 27th respectively, 77 Squadron and 51 Squadrons had returned to 4 Group following a six-month period of duty with Coastal Command, and had taken up residence at Elvington and Snaith, where they were now in the process of converting to the Halifax. In another change in organisation, 1658 and 1659 Conversion Units had been formed at Riccall and Leeming to increase training capacity for the expansion of 4 Group.

A force of 289 aircraft was assembled on the 15th to send against Cologne, which had been left in peace for a considerable time, and the operation was supported by 4 Group with fifty Halifaxes and twenty-five Wellingtons. The 405 Squadron element of nine Halifaxes departed Topcliffe between 18.52 and 19.00 with P/Os Atkinson, College and Palmer the senior pilots on duty and each carrying the standard payload. P/O College and crew lost their intercom and turned back early, as did Sgt Waddle and crew when their rear turret failed, while the others headed out over Southwold on course for Goeree island in the Scheldt estuary and encountered stronger-than-forecast winds, which would create difficulties for the Path Finders as they attempted to establish their position. The leading Path Finders found the Rhineland capital to be concealed beneath a layer of five to ten-tenths cloud with visibility so poor that few crews were able to establish a firm position in relation to it. Apart from throwing the operation behind schedule, this ruined the marking sequencing, with the result that there was insufficient of it to attract the main force crews, although the Path Finder flares did illuminate the Rhine to provide something of a reference point. However, the presence of a large decoy fire site was a more powerful lure, and most crews were persuaded by that to waste their effort in open country. The 405 Squadron crews carried out their attacks from 12,000 to 17,500 feet between 20.47 and 21.06 and on return described a scattered and ineffective raid. P/O Palmer and crew handed back their Halifax to the ground crew with eleven flak holes to patch, but they at least made it home, when eighteen others failed to do so, including the 10 Squadron Halifax containing the commanding officer, W/C Wildey. 405 Squadron's W7854 was shot down by the night-fighter of Oblt Rudolf Altendorf of I./NJG4 and crashed at Waterloo in Belgium with no survivors from the all-RCAF crew of F/Sgt Longley RCAF. Local reports mentioned 224 houses sustaining slight damage from the single 4,000 pounder and three other high-explosive bombs and 210 incendiaries that landed within the city, and this was out of a total of seventy-one 4,000 pounders, 231 other high explosive bombs and more than 68,000 incendiaries. This compounded the disappointment caused by the heavy losses and demonstrated that the Command still had a long way to go before becoming truly effective.

Other than an audacious 5 Group attack by daylight against the Schneider armaments works in France on the 17th, the following week brought largely minor operational activity and there were no operations at all involving 4 Group. The lull came to an end on the 22nd, when a new campaign began against Italian cities in support of land operations in North Africa under Operation Torch. The target for the opening round was the city-port of Genoa, home to the Ansaldo shipyard and the naval dockyard, where part of the Italian fleet was sheltering. It was the eve of the opening of the Battle of El Alamein, which, after twelve days' fighting, would see Montgomery push Rommel's forces all the way back to Tunisia and out of the war. Ten 5 Group squadrons mustered between them 101 Lancasters, while 83 Squadron of the Path Finders contributed eleven more to take care of target marking. Some returning crews described the raid as a "miniature-Cologne", and local sources confirmed heavy damage in central and eastern districts, which, because of the need for fuel over bombs, had been achieved with just 180 tons of high-explosives and incendiaries, and remarkably, without loss.

Twenty-four hours later, a force of 122 aircraft consisting of fifty-three Halifaxes, fifty-one Stirlings and eighteen Wellingtons was assembled from 3 and 4 Groups and the Path Finders to attempt to follow up at Genoa. 405 Squadron's element of eleven departed Topcliffe between 17.28 and 17.38 with W/C Fraser the senior pilot on duty and bomb loads of a 1,000-pounder, two 500-pounders and five SBCs containing ninety 4lb incendiaries on what would be the squadron's 137th operation and the final one under Bomber Command for more than four months. They set course for Dungeness on the Kent coast and Berck-sur-Mer on the other side of the Channel, and initially enjoyed good weather conditions under bright moonlight as they traversed France and scaled the Alps and it was only as they passed Turin that they ran into ten-tenths cloud with tops at 4,000 feet, which obscured most ground detail. W/C Fraser and crew searched in vain for the target for thirty minutes, before heading back inland and bombing the town of Asti forty miles north-west of Genoa. The others from the squadron bombed from 10,000 and 17,000 feet between 21.52 and 22.16 and observed bursts and fires, but there was an inkling that the coastal town of

Savona, situated some twenty miles to the west, was also coming under attack. There was no mention at the Topcliffe debriefing that the wrong target may have been bombed, but it soon became clear that the main weight of the attack had fallen on the coastal resort town of Savona, situated some thirty miles to the west of Genoa.

New surroundings and a new role with Coastal Command beckoned for 405 Squadron, and preparations were put in hand to move the squadron from Yorkshire to Beaulieu, on the edge of the New Forest in Hampshire. On the 24th fifteen Halifaxes and crews took part in the move along with five from 158 Squadron at East Moor, and they would consequently miss the rest of the bomber offensive against Italian cities. The campaign continued on this day as 5 Group raided Milan to good effect in daylight, a raid which was followed up by elements of 1 and 3 Groups after dark, and this effectively ended the month's operations.

405 Squadron's service with Coastal Command falls outside the scope of this work, but a brief account of its experiences during the period is appropriate, while still chronicling the events going on in Bomber Command's war. The squadron's duties with Coastal Command were principally anti-U-Boot patrols in the Bay of Biscay, convoy escort, and strikes against enemy shipping both at sea and in ports. The first three sorties were dispatched on the 27th of October into the Bay of Biscay, and such operations were to involve the crews in long hours of high concentration and tedium. One crew came across a U-Boot on the surface on the 2nd of November, but it dived out of sight before an attack could be made. On the 11th, while two of the squadron's Halifaxes were patrolling the Bay of Biscay, one of them encountered a U-Boot being refueled by two surface vessels. P/O Colledge attacked with bombs and machine gun fire from nine hundred feet, and one stick found its target.

On the 19th W/C Fraser was posted from the squadron and was succeeded as commanding officer by W/C Clayton, another of the long serving Canadian officers in the RAF. He had undertaken his first tour with 83 Squadron on Hampdens in 1940/41 and served alongside Guy Gibson of Dambuster fame. On page 105 of his book, Enemy Coast Ahead, Gibson makes reference to Clayton force-landing on a beach in the middle of a mine-field. However, this incident is exactly similar to one experienced by F/L Barker on the 15/16th of October 1940, which is documented, while Clayton's is not. The passage of time has shown a number of inaccuracies in the book, and this appears to be one example. On leaving 83 Squadron Clayton became a founder member and flight commander with the second RCAF unit to form in Bomber Command, 408 (Goose) Squadron, which came into existence in 5 Group on the 24th of June 1941, two months after 405 Squadron's formation. The Geese began Hampden operations in August, and Clayton remained in his post as flight commander until the 26th of March 1942, when he was promoted to wing commander rank and installed as commanding officer. It was a brief appointment lasting just three weeks, by which time he was due a rest from operations.

On the 24th of November F/Sgt Stovel and crew spotted a U-Boot on the surface four miles away, but just failed to close the distance before their quarry crash-dived out of sight. On the 26th Sgt Wober and crew attacked two destroyers and two surface vessels in the face of a spirited anti-aircraft defence, and although missing with their bombs, raked them with machine gun fire. Also, on this day, Sgt Symes and his crew found two U-Boots on the surface, but they also were able to crash-dive before an attack could be mounted. Soon afterwards one of W1094's engines failed and had to be feathered, and a second began to lose power. The aircraft scraped into St Eval, where it bounced on landing and left the runway, coming to a halt with flames beginning to take hold. All but one of the crew managed to scramble away, leaving the mid-upper gunner trapped at his station, upon which Sgt Symes and the flight engineer, Sgt Nichols, returned to the burning aircraft. They eventually freed their comrade by smashing a hole in the fuselage with an axe, and they were clear by the time the Halifax was rent asunder by an explosion.

The squadron's most successful attack on a U-Boot was delivered by F/L Palmer, a future commander of the squadron, and his crew on the 27th. Their depth charges straddled U263, causing extensive damage, but it managed to regain port for repair. A tragic accident on the 29th cost fifteen lives, when DT576 crashed two minutes after taking off from Topcliffe on a ferry flight to Beaulieu. There were no survivors, and the casualty list was made up of W/O Gannon and his crew, and ground staff hitching a ride. The detachment to Coastal command would continue until the end of February 1943, and a number of aircraft were involved in crashes during the period, as itemised in the Aircraft Histories section of this work.

November and December 1942

While the squadron was absent from Bomber Command, the Italian campaign continued with four raids on Genoa during the first half of November, and four on Turin in the second half. The month's only major attacks on German cities were against Hamburg on the 9/10th, and Stuttgart on the 22/23rd, neither of which was outstandingly successful. December began with a failure at Frankfurt on the 2/3rd, and another one at Mannheim on the 6/7th, and these preceded the final three operations to Italy, which were all directed at Turin between the 8/9th and the 11/12th. The most significant operation in December was that mentioned earlier, by six Mosquitos of 109 Squadron against the power station at Lutterade in Holland on the 20th. Led by W/C Hal Bufton, three aircraft bombed successfully, while the other three suffered failure of their Oboe equipment and joined in the main force attack on Duisburg instead. It proved impossible to identify the fall of the Oboe-aimed bombs, because of the craters left by the stray bombs intended for Aachen in October, but further calibration tests would be flown over the succeeding weeks, and the device would be ready in time for the forthcoming Ruhr offensive.

It had been a year of highs and lows for the Command, with a number of spectacular successes punctuated by many failures. There had, though, been a marked improvement on the performance of 1941 as Harris's tactics evolved, and the advent of the Path Finders and the development of electronic bombing aids promised much for the future. As far as the Canadians were concerned, there were now sufficient operational RCAF squadrons to constitute a group, and the official formation of 6 Group would be the first act of the coming year. The year had brought a change of equipment for 405 Squadron, but like all operators of the early versions of the Halifax, it had struggled with serviceability and handling problems. Thirty of the type had been lost by the squadron on operations with Bomber Command between the end of May and mid October, taking with them valuable and gallant crews. Once returned to the bombing war in the coming March, the crews would find it equally testing, and there would be no easing of the rate of attrition.

As the clock ticked towards midnight on New Year's Eve, Canada's government prepared for a moment of significance. They awaited not so much the New Year, but that which came with it, the birth of 6 Group RCAF, a shining symbol of the burgeoning status of the independent Canada. There were many non-British squadrons in Bomber Command, but this was the first foreign organisation to muscle in, and while in public there was harmony between the two high commands, in private it was a different matter. Harris was strongly opposed to the formation of a Canadian Group, and although he valued Canadian airmen and welcomed their presence in the war, he found it difficult to come to terms with their lax attitude in matters of RAF etiquette and discipline. He wanted to distribute them throughout the existing RAF Groups, but Whitehall wanted otherwise, and Whitehall won. Harris also had an intense dislike for Air Marshal Edwards, the Commander-in-Chief of Canada's overseas Air Force, and for the man who would initially be Air-Officer-Commanding 6 Group, AVM Brookes. Both were British born, and neither, as far as Harris was concerned, was worthy of holding a position of authority, particularly anywhere near his Bomber Command. A Headquarters was set up in the baronial Allerton Hall, on the two-thousand-acre estate of Allerton Park, the ancestral home of Lord Mowbray, four miles east of Knaresborough. Its dark, somewhat angular and forbidding aspect soon saw it re-titled by the Canadians as "Castle Dismal".

Above: Construction of infrastructure for the British Commonwealth Air Training Plan in Canada.

Left: S/L Joseph Gutray, Chief Flying Instructor at the Flying School where W/C Fauquier learned to fly.

Below: Canadians embarking for Britain, their happiness suggesting they were not aware of the deprivations they would encounter in wartime England.

W/C P A Gilchrist
405 Squadron Commanding Officer
May 1941 to July 1941

W/C W B Keddy
405 Squadron Commanding Officer
July 1941 to August 1941

405 Squadron Wellington being made ready for the next operation from Pocklington.

MPs visiting No. 554 Anti-Aircraft Battery near Harwich in 1940 watching a demonstration of a searchlight with radar equipment known as ELSIE - 90 cm Searchlight Control Radar (SLC) No 2 Mk VI - which entered service in 1942 and was of immense assistance to anti-aircraft when used against the flying bomb attacks of 1944.

405 Squadron crew prepare to board Wellington, Pocklington 1941

Briefing for 405 Squadron 1941

Ground crew prepare to load a 4000 lb 'Cookie' into the bomb bay of a 405 Squadron Wellington

405 RCAF Squadron Operations Room, Pocklington.

Raid on Brest
405 Squadron Wellingtons joined 35 Squadron Halifaxes to bomb the German battleships Scharnhorst and Gneisenau in Brest docks 24th July 1941.

W/C R M Fenwick-Wilson AFC
405 Squadron Commanding Officer
August 1941 – February 1942

W/C L D G Fraser
405 Squadron Commanding Officer
August 1942 – December 1942

Wellington and Crew in the snow (possibly Sgt L S Mather's Crew)

Aerial photo taken during the 13/14th November 1942 raid on Genoa which included 405 Squadron.

Extensive damage to the Ansaldo fitting out yard on Genoa 23rd and 24th October 1942.

405 Squadron CO W/C J Fauquier (centre) and AVM Don Bennett (right)

F/L Jack McCormack and Crew
L-R: F/L Jack McCormack, P/O W H Fetherston, Sgt N MacLennan, Sgt J Cark, Sgt L E Dodge, Sgt J A Wymark. (Aircrew Remembered)

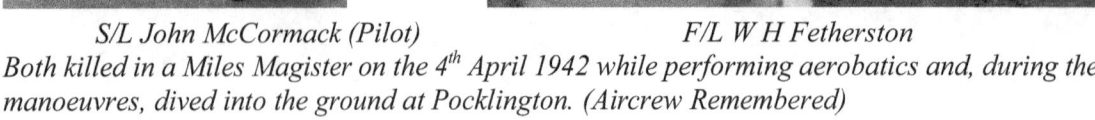

S/L John McCormack (Pilot) *F/L W H Fetherston*
Both killed in a Miles Magister on the 4th April 1942 while performing aerobatics and, during the manoeuvres, dived into the ground at Pocklington. (Aircrew Remembered)

P/O Henry Echin (Chinn) (RAAF) Killed 30th June 1942 on a Bremen operation while with 405 Squadron.

Sgt Moheddeen (Bob) Howsan (RAAF) Lost 1st April 1942 on Poissy operation while with 405 Squadron.

RAAF Servicemen in front of a Wellington, Pocklington. Those in 405 Squadron are: L-R: 1st F/Sgt Echin (Chinn), 4th F/O Durbridge, 6th F/Sgt Howsan, 7th F/O Mitchell, 8th F/Sgt Lloyd, 9th probably F/Sgt Dyson. None of these men served together and all were lost on various bombing operations.

405 Squadron Wellington

405 Squadron Halifax 'Ruhr Valley Express' photo taken from another Halifax. LQ-R failed to return from Flensburg 2nd October 1942.

Above and below: Berlin or Bust Wellington crew and Nose Art

The nose of Handley Page Halifax B Mark II, W7710 LQ-R 'Ruhr Valley Express', of 405 Squadron RCAF, at Pocklington, Yorkshire. An extra truck was added to the nose insignia after each mission. W7710 crashed at Liehuus, Denmark, on the night of 1/2nd October 1942 while returning from a raid on Flensburg, Germany, killing all the crew.

405 Squadron Halifax II W7710 LQ-R in flight.

W/C John Fauquier at his desk July 1942.
Considered Canada's greatest bomber pilot; the most decorated with DSO & two Bars, DFC and MiD. He completed at least 93 operations and apart from two periods of commanding 405 Squadron, was also 617 Squadron's CO 1944-1945.

Fine view of the 'Ruhr Valley Express' Halifax

S/L Bill Swetman. Below: in cockpit of a Halifax MkII

Aerial photograph of Bremen after bombing by a 1000-bomber raid of allied air forces on 25th June 1942. Below: 405 Squadron armourers hard at work..

W/C Johnny Fauquier
Commanding Officer 405 Squadron
February 1942 to August 1942 and April 1943 to January 1944

Sgt Frank Tatro
W/C Fauquier's W/Op/AG on his Wellington operations.

S/L K F Thiele RNZAF DSO, DFC & Two Bars.

F/Sgt Adams, W/C Fauquier's rear gunner

405 Squadron Halifax line-up (a slightly damaged photo taken back to Canada by W/C Fauquier),

Halifax later Mk II series with Perspex nose.

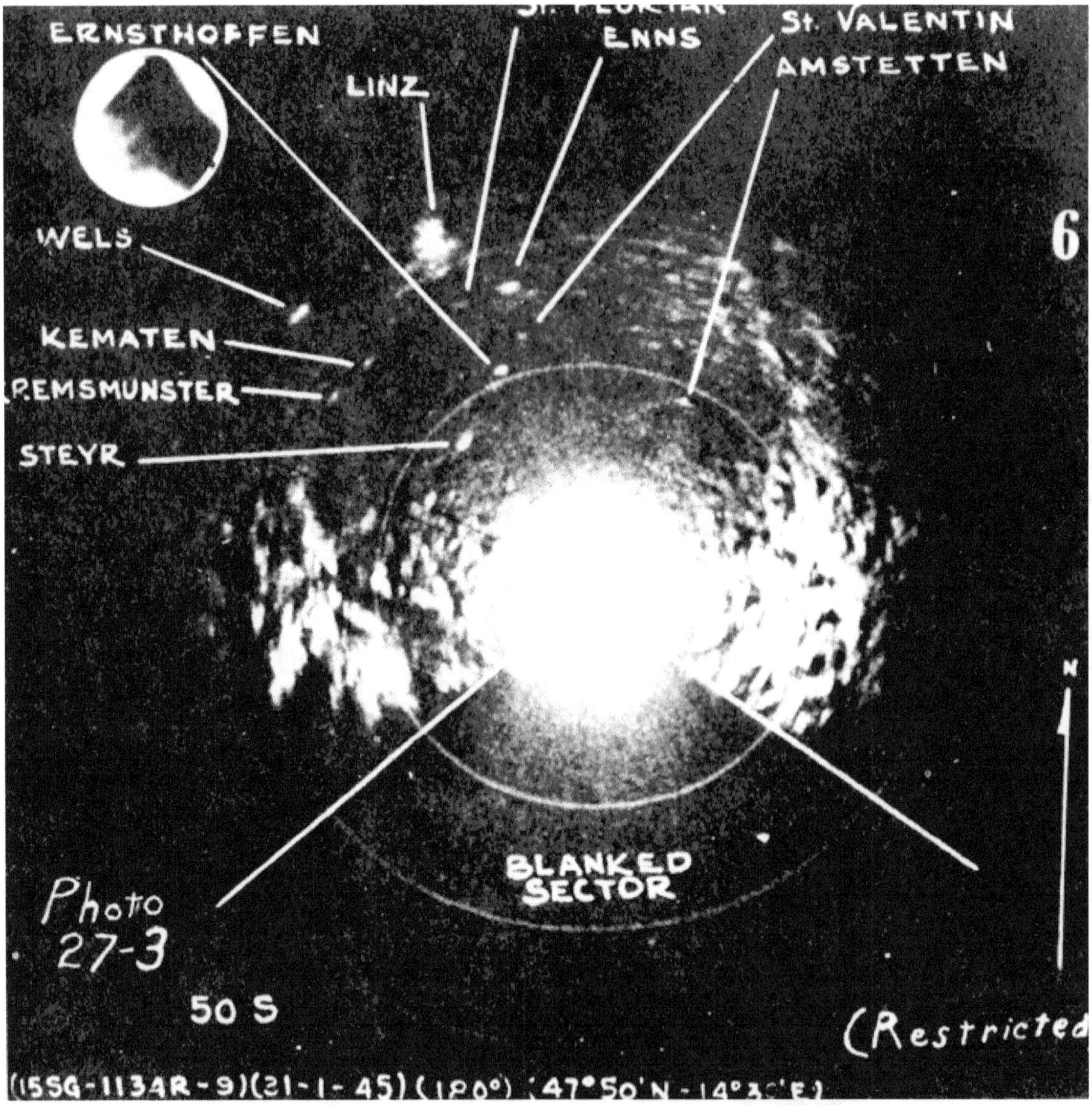

Example of the image from H2S which was the first airborne, ground scanning radar system.

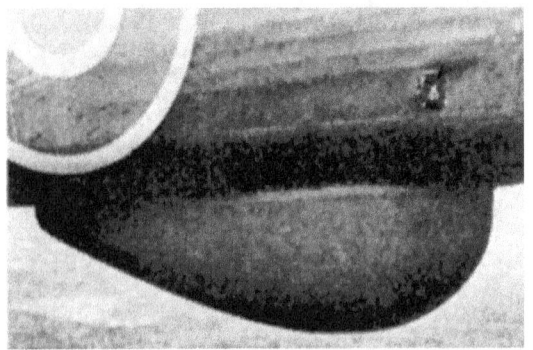 

The H2S radome (left) and its enclosed scanning aerial (right) on a Halifax. The angled plate fixed to the top of the reflector modified the broadcast pattern to make nearby objects less bright on the display.

Bomber Command's first major raid against the Renault Motor Works at Billancourt Paris on 3/4th March 1942.

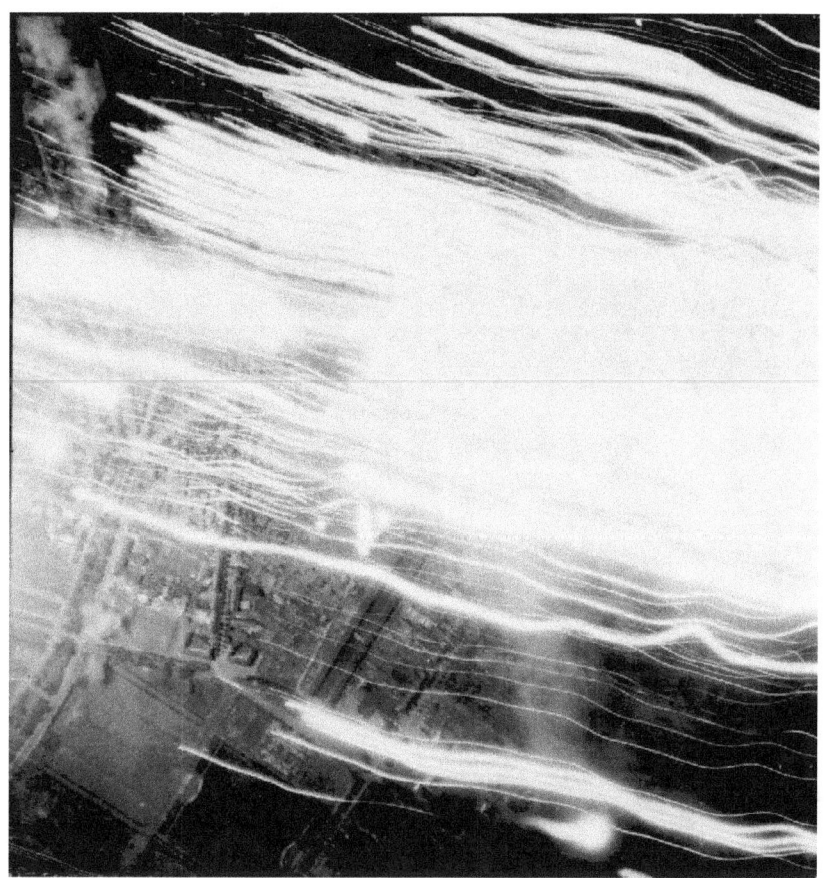
Vertical aerial photograph taken during Operation Millennium, the 'Thousand-bomber' raid on Cologne, Germany 30/31st May 1942. The tracks of a mass of concentrated searchlights and tracer bullets from anti-aircraft fire cover the larger area of the picture as the first bombs explode on the city (lower left).

A Lancaster (not 405 Squadron) dropping Window (the crescent-shaped white cloud on the left of the picture) over Essen during the thousand-bomber raid.

P/O John Horn RAAF was attached to 405 Squadron. He was killed on 2nd August 1941, on a Hamburg operation.

F/Sgt John Dyson, RAAF. was attached to 405 Squadron. He was killed on 26th February 1942 on a Kiel operation.

405 Squadron Crew with Halifax LQ-Q

405 Squadron Halifax Mk II with the distinctive triangular-shaped vertical fins.

Above: Engine fitters worked in precarious positions. Below: Bombing up.

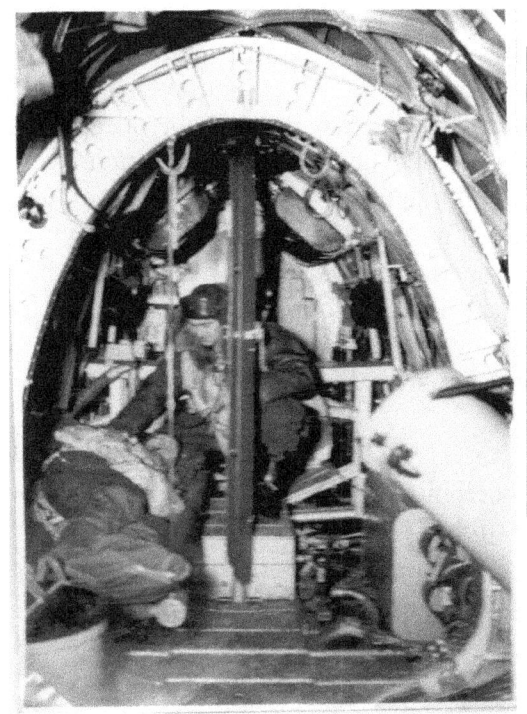

Left and above: Unknown 405 Squadron crew in a Wellington.

405 Squadron members after being seconded to RAF Coastal Command Beaulieu in 1942.

January 1943

At 00.01 on the 1st, 6 Group officially came into being and the 4 Group stations upon which its squadrons had been lodging were officially handed over. Not all RCAF squadrons in Bomber Command were immediately posted to 6 Group, in fact it began life with eight operational squadrons, while a few other units remained in 4 Group for the time being. The founder units were 408 (Goose) and 419 (Moose) Squadrons, each equipped with Halifaxes, and 420 (Snowy Owl), 424 (Tiger), 425 (Allouette), 426 (Thunderbird), 427 (Lion) and 428 (Ghost) Squadrons, which were soldiering on with the trusty Wellington. The Canadian government was demanding Lancasters, and the type would eventually become dominant in the Group, but that would be by war's end, and in the meantime, most of the existing Wellington units and those awaiting posting in or still to form would find themselves converting to the unpopular Halifax.

There was no fanfare to herald the operational debut of the new Group, in fact, it was a damp squib, as the appalling weather conditions forced the cancellation of the intended debut on New Year's Night. For the Command generally, a continuation of the Oboe trials would occupy the first two weeks, during which 109 Squadron Mosquitos marked for small forces of 1 and 5 Group Lancasters at Essen on seven occasions and Duisburg once. For the first time, the cloud cover and ever-present blanket of industrial haze would have no bearing on the outcome of the raid as reliance on e.t.a., DR and Gee was cast aside in favour of Oboe, at least, that is, at targets within the device's range. Until the advent of mobile transmitter stations late in the war, Oboe would be restricted by the curvature of the earth and the altitude at which Mosquitos could fly, but this meant that the entire Ruhr lay within range of Harris's bombers. That said, the success of a raid would still rely on the ability of the Path Finders to back up the initial Oboe markers and maintain a supply of target indicators (TIs) on the aiming point.

It was not until the 3/4th that half a dozen 427 Squadron Wellingtons disappeared into the murk at the end of the runway at Croft on the Group's first operation, to lay mines off the Frisians. Another squadron should have contributed six more to the occasion but was dissuaded by the conditions from taking part. On the 8th, the Path Finder Force was granted group status as 8 Group, and the stations it occupied were transferred from 3 Group. For the purpose of this book, the titles Path Finder and 8 Group are interchangeable.

Inhospitable weather was to characterize January, and there would be no major activity during the first half of the month. 405 Squadron was still embroiled in matters maritime, as a recent resurgence in U-Boot activity continued to take a heavy toll of Allied shipping in the Atlantic. Confirmation of this came with a new Air Ministry directive on the 14th, which authorised the area bombing of those French ports providing bases and support facilities for U-Boots. A target list was drawn up headed by Lorient, and that night, 122 aircraft took off for the first of nine attacks against it over the ensuing month. This was 6 Group's first bombing operation, sixteen aircraft taking part in what was at best only a modestly effective raid.

Lorient was raided for the second time on the 15/16th, and then came two disappointing attacks on Berlin by predominantly Lancaster forces on the 16/17th and 17/18th. The only matters of significance arising out of the former was the complete destruction of the Deutschlandhalle, the largest covered arena in Europe, and the loss of a single Lancaster. The latter raid produced no useful damage but cost twenty-two aircraft. Further attacks on Lorient took place on the 23/24th, 26/27th and 29/30th, and in between, on the 27/28th, the first Oboe ground marking ahead of the heavy aircraft of the Path Finder Force was attempted. This led to an effective raid on Düsseldorf, in which more than 450 houses were destroyed, along with a number of industrial and public buildings. As Harris sought the most effective method of target marking, the first H2S attack of the war was mounted against Hamburg on the 30/31st. It was not an entirely successful debut for the device, but with time and practice it would emerge as a useful addition to the Command's armoury of electronic aids, particularly for use against targets beyond the range of Oboe.

February 1943

It was a time of honing and refining for Bomber Command in preparation for the launching of a major campaign a month hence and February would bring an increase in operations. It opened with the posting of Cologne as the target for an experimental operation by a force of 161 aircraft on the 2nd, for which two marking methods were to be employed. Situated just to the south of the Ruhr, the Rhineland capital city was within range of Oboe Mosquitos, and these were to be supplemented by Path Finder aircraft relying on H2S, a new ground-mapping radar with a scanner housed in a cupola aft of the bomb bay, which produced images of the terrain on a cathode-ray tube. The early model required much practice by the operator to interpret what he was seeing, and the jumble of images over an urban sprawl the size of a major city like Berlin would lead to inaccurate marking, but in time, and with the advent of an improved version, H2S would become an indispensable device that would eventually become standard equipment for main force as well as Path Finder aircraft.

Germany's second city, Hamburg, was posted as the target on the 3rd, for which a force of 263 aircraft was made ready, unusually, with Halifaxes representing the most populous type followed by Stirlings. For what was its first major bombing operation 6 Group contributed twenty-five Halifaxes and twenty-one Wellingtons, which were confronted with one of the frequent massive weather fronts that acted as a gatekeeper for north-western Germany with towering cumulonimbus clouds containing violent electrical storms and icing conditions. Extending to 20,000 feet and beyond and too wide to circumnavigate, this night's front persuaded many crews to turn back, most of them citing frozen guns as the reason. Having arrived at the target the Path Finders were unable to deliver concentrated and sustained marking by H2S, and scattered red and green skymarker flares were all that the main force bomb-aimers had as a reference. No results were observed, but the impression was of an ineffective attack, which was partly confirmed by local reports of forty-five large fires but no concentration or significant damage, and this disappointment was compounded by the loss of sixteen aircraft.

A return to Italy was posted on the 4th with Turin the target for a force of 188 aircraft, while 128 others, mostly Wellingtons, were prepared to continue the assault on Lorient. Turin in northern Italy was home to Fiat's Lingotto and Mirafiori car plants, the Lancia motor works, the Arsenale army munitions factory, the RIV submachine gun works, the Nebioli foundry and plants belonging to the American Westinghouse company. 6 Group contributed fifteen Halifaxes to this endeavour, and sixty Wellingtons to the sixth raid of the series on Lorient. After traversing France and the Alps over cloud, conditions on the Italian side were much improved with clear skies and excellent visibility, which facilitated a visual confirmation of the accuracy of the Path Finder TIs. An estimated one hundred searchlights were active, and the flak defence had also been "beefed-up" but was still inaccurate and in keeping with expectations at an Italian target. *(Following a raid on a German target, a bomb symbol was painted on the forward fuselage below the glasshouse, but after a raid on an Italian target, the symbol would be an ice-cream cone.)* Red TIs were much in evidence in the city centre as the main force crews carried out their attacks and returned with enthusiastic reports of the effectiveness of their work. Local sources confirmed later that serious and widespread damage had resulted.

The seventh raid in the series on Lorient was posted on the 7th and was by far the largest to date, employing 323 aircraft, of which eighteen Halifaxes and fifty-one Wellingtons were provided by 6 Group. The operation was to be conducted in two waves an hour apart, and the first wave arrived in the target area to find clear skies and ideal bombing conditions, which they exploited after making a visual identification of the aiming point confirmed by Path Finder TIs. As they were returning home to report an outstandingly destructive raid, they left behind them a glow in the sky visible from the English coast, which acted as a beacon for the second-phase element to home in on. Despite heavy smoke and haze over the target, they completed what appeared to be a devastating raid.

Before the penultimate raid on Lorient took place, attention was switched to the important naval and shipbuilding port of Wilhelmshaven, situated on the north-western coast of Jade Bay, some sixty miles to the west of Hamburg. Renamed in 1935 from Reichsmarinewerft to the Kriegsmarinewerft, the shipyard had launched the Deutschland class "pocket battleships", Admiral Scheer and Admiral Graf Spee in 1934 and 1936, the Scharnhorst heavy cruiser in 1939 and the mighty Bismarck class Tirpitz in 1941 in addition to twenty-seven type VII U-Boots. A force of 177 aircraft was put together on the 11th from 1, 4, 5 and 8 Groups to carry out an attack, while 6 Group sent twenty-four Wellingtons to conduct mining operations in the Nectarine I and Jellyfish gardens, respectively off the Dutch Frisians and the port of Brest. Ten-tenths cloud over Wilhelmshaven dictated the use of the least reliable marking method, H2S skymarking, although on the credit side, at this more modest and compact urban target with a coastline, it was easier to interpret the images on the cathode-ray screens, and on this night great accuracy was achieved. The red and green flares were right over the aiming point as the force delivered its high explosives and incendiaries, but it was impossible to assess what was happening beneath the cloud until an enormous explosion took place, the glow from which lingered for ten minutes. Many crews commented on this at debriefings across the Command, and there must have been much speculation about the source, which turned out to be the naval ammunition depot at Mariensiel, situated to the south-west of the town. It blew itself into oblivion, devastating 120 acres and causing widespread damage in the dockyard and town.

The penultimate raid on Lorient was to involve the largest force to date of 466 aircraft and a thousand tons of bombs, 6 Group initially detailing twenty-six Halifaxes and seventy-five Wellingtons, all but five of which would take off. As the second wave main force element began the Channel crossing in the Exmouth area, some crews reported observing flares going down over the target two hundred miles away as the first wave attacked. It had been planned to station a number of Path Finder aircraft over the Ile-de-Groix, an island situated some five miles off the mouth of the estuary leading to the port, and illuminate it continuously as a navigation point. The other Path Finder crews followed up over Lorient itself with flares, green TIs and 1,000-pounders in a number of passes from 11,000 to 14,000 feet between 20.35 and 20.56, paving the way for the main force elements to carry out their attacks. The target was located with ease in excellent visibility under clear skies, which, despite drifting smoke, allowed a visual identification of both aiming points, the U-Boot pens on the Keroman peninsula and the town, and returning crews reported massive fires right across the town and the port area.

Orders were received on 1, 5 and 8 Group stations on the 14th to make ready for a return to Italy that night for a crack this time at Milan, for which a force of 142 Lancasters was assembled, while 243 Halifaxes, Stirlings and Wellingtons from 3, 4, 6 and 8 Groups were made ready to try their hand at Cologne, 6 Group providing twenty Halifaxes and thirty-five Wellingtons. They made landfall over the Scheldt estuary, eyes watching out for the green route-marker flares dropped by the Path Finders some twenty miles short of the target. The Path Finders arrived in the target area to encounter ten-tenths cloud with tops at around 7,000 feet and established their positions by H2S and evidence of the accurate flak penetrating the cloud tops. They opened the attack bang on scheduled at 20.15 with red flares with green stars and 1,000-pounders and the main force followed on their heels, mostly to bomb on skymarkers. The cloud prevented an assessment of the results, and the intensity of the flak dissuaded crews from hanging around, but they observed some evidence of burgeoning fires that gave some hope of a successful raid.

An entry in the 405 Squadron Operations Record Book dated the 16th of February 1943 reads; *"Information has been received from British Columbia House, London, England, to the effect that 405 RCAF Squadron has been officially adopted by the city of Vancouver. A cable received from the Honourary Secretary of the Vancouver Women's Canadian Club explained that the city would be delighted to provide for the squadron's needs, and request details concerning what the adoption might truly mean. It is certain that the squadron personnel will receive generous consideration by this organisation, and that every thought and care will be shown towards the welfare of the personnel. To celebrate this adoption, 10,000 cigarettes have been received from B.C. House, London for distribution amongst personnel, which will undoubtedly be the forerunner of a very happy association between this squadron and the Club"*. Preceding these glad tidings is a line and a half stating; *Four a/c carried out Anti-Submarine patrol No 87 and returned safely to base after uneventful trip with nothing unusual to report.* From this point on the squadron would go to war proudly bearing the title of 405 (Vancouver) Squadron. Just two more weeks remained before its return to Bomber Command's fold, and ultimately promotion to a role in which it and the whole of Canada would take particular pride.

Later, that day, the final raid of the series on Lorient was posted and another large force of 377 aircraft assembled, of which twenty-four Halifaxes and fifty-seven Wellingtons were provided by 6 Group. The target was located easily in clear conditions aided by an almost full moon, which enabled a section of the main force element to deliver its bomb loads onto the Keroman peninsula guided by red Path Finder TIs, while the majority of the force dropped incendiaries into the town, which, after nine attacks, 1,926 sorties and four thousand tons of bombs, was now a desolate and deserted ruin.

Preparations were put in hand on the 18th to make ready 195 aircraft for the second of the month's four raids on Wilhelmshaven, for which 6 Group contributed just four Halifaxes. The target area was identified visually in excellent conditions and by red TIs, and bombs were observed to burst and fires to spring up, persuading returning crews that an accurate and concentrated attack had taken place. However, bombing photos revealed that the operation had been a failure, after the main weight of bombs had fallen into open country to the west of the town, and this demonstrated how easy it was to be misled by what the eye saw. Local reports admitted to a number of bombs hitting the town, causing no serious damage or casualties. Twenty-four hours later a force of 338 aircraft set off to return to Wilhelmshaven, with Wellingtons and Halifaxes accounting for 230 of the number and Stirlings and Lancasters the rest. 6 Group dispatched twenty-four Halifaxes and sixty Wellingtons, which again encountered excellent conditions with visibility that enabled them to identify the coastline and line themselves up on the target. The aiming point was marked by green TIs, around which bursts and fires were observed in the docks area and in the town, leaving the crews with the impression that another successful raid had taken place. However, bombing photos told a different story, and revealed that the Path Finder marking had fallen to the north of the built-up area, partly through reliance upon outdated maps, which would now need to be replaced.

The final raid of the series on Wilhelmshaven was posted on the 24th and involved a main force of twenty-seven Halifaxes and seventy-one Wellingtons of 6 Group with seventeen Path Finder Stirlings and Lancasters to provide the marking. They were met over the target by ten-tenths cloud with tops at between 8,000 and 15,000 feet and had to rely on Path Finder skymarkers released on H2S. There was no prospect of assessing the outcome, and local sources would describe the raid as small and causing little damage in the town. On the credit side, no aircraft were lost, and the port would now be left in peace until October 1944.

When Cologne was posted as the target on the 26th, 6 Group responded with twenty-six Halifaxes and sixty-one Wellingtons as part of an overall force of 427 aircraft, those reaching the target area finding good vertical visibility for the bomb-aimers, some of whom were able to identify the bridges over the Rhine. It seems from some comments from other squadrons that a proportion of the force bombed before the Path Finders had a chance to mark, but once the red and green TIs appeared on the ground, the operation appeared to proceed according to plan. Bombing photos showed fire tracks and smoke that suggested an effective raid, when in fact, a large proportion of the effort had fallen to the south-west of the city and perhaps only a quarter had landed in the built-up area, causing much damage to housing, minor industry and public buildings.

Having dealt with Lorient under the January Directive, attention now turned upon St-Nazaire, situated further south along the Biscay coast. The force of 437 aircraft assembled on the 28th included a contribution from 6 Group of twenty-two Halifaxes and fifty-three Wellingtons, and those reaching the target area found clear skies and good visibility with only a little ground haze to contend with. They bombed on red TIs, and it was clear from the many explosions and at least forty fires burning in the docks that the port was undergoing an ordeal of destruction. Post-raid reconnaissance revealed that the marking had been concentrated and the bombing accurate, and local reports confirmed that 60% of the town had been destroyed.

This concluded the month's activity and paved the way for the return to bombing operations of 405 (Vancouver) Squadron, which, earlier, on this day, had concluded its detachment to Coastal Command and begun the process of moving back briefly to Topcliffe, now a 6 Group station, which was home at the time to 424 (Tiger) squadron. During the course of its maritime adventure, the squadron had carried out 349 sorties and filled an important gap, while Coastal Command formed and trained its own Halifax squadrons.

March 1943

March would bring with it the opening rounds of the Ruhr campaign, the first for which the Command was adequately equipped and genuinely prepared, with a predominantly four-engine bomber force at its disposal to carry an increasing weight of bombs and Oboe to provide accuracy. First, however, the crews would have to negotiate operations to Germany's capital and second cities, and it was the "Big City" itself, Berlin, that opened the month's account on the 1st. The crews learned at briefing that six Path Finder Halifaxes and ten Stirlings equipped with H2S were to drop a "landmark" yellow TI each at Butzow, situated some eighty miles north of Berlin, which were to be backed up by seven Halifaxes and sixteen Lancasters. The "special" (H2S-equipped) aircraft were then to release red warning flares twelve miles short of the target followed by red TIs on the aiming-point at the time-on-target of 22.00, which the seven Halifaxes and sixteen Lancasters would back-up with green TIs. As always, the plan was based on a forecast of favourable conditions, in the absence of which, skymarkers would substitute for TIs. A force of 302 aircraft was assembled, made up of 156 Lancasters, eighty-six Halifaxes and sixty Stirlings, 6 Group putting up twenty-one Halifaxes. Those reaching the target found it to be under clear skies with only haze to impair the vertical visibility, however, reliant upon H2S, the Path Finder navigators experienced great difficulty in establishing their positions based on the images on their cathode-ray tubes over such a massive urban sprawl, and this led to scattered marking and the main weight of the attack falling into south-western districts. A post-raid analysis based on bombing photos revealed the attack to have been spread over an area of a hundred square miles, but because of the increasing bomb tonnage now being carried, more damage was inflicted on the city than on any previous raid. 875 buildings, mostly houses, were destroyed and twenty factories seriously damaged, along with railway workshops in the Tempelhof district. It is interesting to analyse the percentage loss rate of each type on this night, as it would be an accurate indicator of their future fortunes. The statistics revealed the loss rate of Lancasters to be 4.5%, and those of the Halifaxes and Stirlings to be 7%.

On the 2nd, 405 (Vancouver) Squadron received a message from AVM "Jack" Slessor, the A-O-C 19 Group Coastal Command, in which he regretted the loss of the squadron to Coastal Command and thanked the crews for their outstanding work. He recognised that convoy duties had not been as interesting as their "proper" job with Bomber Command but wanted the crews to know how important and valuable their work had been. On the following day, a message from the Admiralty expressed similar sentiments, adding that the squadron had contributed greatly to the safety of convoys and had restricted the activities of U-Boots.

While the squadron settled into life at Topcliffe, the bombing war continued with the assembling of a force of 417 aircraft to send against Hamburg on the 3rd, of which eighteen Halifaxes and fifty-seven Wellingtons were provided by 6 Group. Hamburg was found to be nestling under clear skies and in good visibility and some Path Finder and main force crews identified the Hamburg-America landing stage, the Blohm & Voss shipyards, the Binnen-Alster Lake and the main railway station. On return, crews reported numerous fires in the docks area along with black smoke rising to meet them as they turned away and the glow on the horizon visible for up to eighty miles. What was not appreciated, was the fact that a proportion of the markers had fallen onto the town of Wedel, situated some thirteen miles downstream of the Elbe, and had attracted perhaps the bulk of the bombs, while those hitting the primary target had caused a hundred fires that needed to be dealt with before the fire services could go to the aid of their less illustrious neighbour.

The night off for most of the Command on the 4th provided the opportunity for maximum serviceability as the decks were now cleared for the opening of the Ruhr offensive, which over the ensuing months, would change the face of bombing and provide for the enemy an indication of the burgeoning power of the Command. This was a culmination of all that had gone before during three and a half years of Bomber Command operations, the backs-to-the-wall desperation of 1940, the tentative almost token offensives of 1941, the treading water and the gradual metamorphosis under Harris in 1942, when failures still outnumbered successes. It had all been leading to this night, from which point would begin the calculated and systematic dismantling of Germany's industrial and population centres. The only shining light during these dark years had been the quality and spirit of the aircrew, and this had never faltered. The new era would begin on the 5th at Essen, Harris's nemesis thus far and the home of the giant armaments-producing Krupp complex occupying the Borbeck districts, and for the first time since the war began, the Command would have at its disposal a device which would negate the industrial haze protecting this city and its neighbours. The magnificent pioneering work on Oboe by W/C Hal Bufton and his crews at 109 Squadron was about to bear fruit in spectacular fashion, and the towns and cities of Germany's arsenal would suffer destruction on an unprecedented scale.

A force of 442 aircraft included twenty Halifaxes and fifty-eight Wellingtons representing 6 Group, the crews of which attended briefings to learn that the main force element was to bomb in three waves, Halifaxes first, followed by Wellingtons and Stirlings with Lancasters bringing up the rear. Six Path Finder Halifax and fifteen Lancaster crews were briefed to drop a warning yellow TI each when fifteen miles from the target, before backing up the Oboe Mosquitos' red TIs on the aiming-point with greens, and the force was to adopt the southern route to the central Ruhr, making landfall over the Scheldt estuary. An unusually high number of early returns and the bombing of alternative targets, involving thirteen 6 Group aircraft, reduced the size of the force reaching Essen to 362 aircraft. The main force crews employed the Path Finders' yellow route markers as the initial reference point, before exploiting the good visibility to bomb through the industrial haze onto red and green TIs, and the overwhelming impression was of a concentrated attack, which left many fires burning and a glow in the sky reported by some to be visible from the North Sea homebound. At debriefing, crews across the Command reported terrific explosions among fires, which lit up the sky, and a pall of smoke was observed hanging above the dull, red centre of the conflagration. The operation cost the Command an acceptable fourteen aircraft, while post-raid reconnaissance revealed 160 acres of devastation and damage to fifty-three buildings within the Krupp district. The success of the operation was confirmed by local reports of 3,018 houses destroyed and more than two thousand others seriously damaged, and it was a most encouraging start to what would become a five-month-long offensive.

It would be a further week before round two of the Ruhr offensive was mounted, and in the meantime, Harris turned his attention upon southern Germany, beginning with Nuremberg on the 8th. A force of 338 aircraft included nineteen Halifaxes of 6 Group, the crews of which learned at briefing that zero hour was to be 23.15 and that three Path Finder Stirlings and two Halifaxes were to drop illumination flares across the target in two sticks by H2S, to be followed by six Stirlings and three Halifaxes dropping green TIs on the aiming-point, also by H2S, and employing additional flares if necessary. The remaining Path Finder marker crews were to back up with green TIs, unless cloud negated the illuminator flares, in which case red TIs were to be dropped by the H2S-equipped aircraft and backed up by the others with greens, and all Path Finder aircraft were to deliver yellow route markers on the way in and out. Those of the main force reaching the target area had followed the yellow route markers and encountered clear skies with ground haze and extreme darkness. This seemed to impede the Path Finders' ability to locate the city centre blind by H2S, and the main force crews experienced the same difficulty in identifying ground detail, allowing themselves to be guided to the aiming point by a few red and green TIs, which appeared to lack concentration and soon burned out. The initial impression was of a scattered raid, but a greater concentration of fires developed and the glow from these was reported by some to be visible for two hundred miles into the return journey. At debriefing, 83 Squadron's S/L Cooke reported that a cookie and yellow TIs had been jettisoned east of Heilbronn, some forty miles short of the target and accurately backed-up by other Path Finders. Inevitably, this would have drawn off other bomb loads, and local sources confirmed the marking and bombing of Nuremberg to have been spread along a ten-mile stretch, half of it falling short of the city boundaries, while the rest destroyed six hundred buildings and damaged fourteen hundred others, including a number of important war-industry factories.

On the following day, preparations were put in hand to return to southern Germany to attack the city of Munich, situated deep in the Bavarian mountains of south-eastern Germany, a round-trip of more than 1,200 miles. A force of 264 aircraft included a 6 Group contribution of eighteen Halifaxes, the crews of which learned at briefing that white TIs were to be dropped by the Path Finders as route markers to aid the main force crews, and white and green flares over the northern tip of the Ammersee, a large lake situated some twenty miles to the west-south-west of the city centre, which the 5 Group crews, in particular, would use as the starting point for their time-and-distance runs. Nine Stirlings and four Halifaxes were to ground mark by H2S with red TIs at the same time as releasing white flares, and four Lancasters were to drop flares also if required, and then join with eleven Lancasters and four Halifaxes to back up with green TIs. Clear skies and good visibility prevailed at the target and the Path Finder green and white TIs could be seen to have fallen within the built-up area. An enormous orange explosion occurred in a south-western district as crews were carrying out their timed runs to the aiming point from the Ammersee, and another huge explosion at 00.25 lit up the sky for twenty seconds and illuminated an area of ground with a ten-mile radius, described by some as the largest they had experienced. Another particularly large one occurred at 00.43 and fires were taking hold, sending a large pall of smoke rising above the city as the bomber force withdrew to the west, and one 5 Group crew counted eighteen blazes in or close to the city centre. A post-raid analysis concluded that a strong wind had pushed the attack into the western half of the city, where 291 buildings had been destroyed and 660 severely damaged, and this was in exchange for the relatively modest failure to return of eight aircraft. The aero-engine assembly shop at the B.M.W factory was put out of action for six weeks, and many other industrial concerns also lost vital production.

The trio of operations to destinations in southern Germany concluded with the highly industrial city of Stuttgart, a major centre before the war of car production and now home to many war industry companies including Robert Bosch and I G Farben. A force of 314 aircraft was assembled on the 11th, 6 Group contributing thirty-five Halifaxes, the number bolstered by the fifteen provided by 405 (Vancouver) Squadron on its long-awaited return to the fray. Briefings revealed that the Path Finders were to deliver flares and red TIs by H2S across the aiming point, and that these were to be backed up visually with green TIs. At Topcliffe, take-off was accomplished safely between 19.00 and 19.14 with the B Flight commander, the now S/L Palmer, the senior pilot on duty and the new A Flight commander, S/L Logan RCAF, flying as second pilot to P/O Dennison. Each Halifax had six 1,000-pounders and a single 500-pounder in its bomb bay as it crossed the English coast over Eastbourne, heading for the French coast near Dieppe, before pushing on across France to enter Germany in the Strasbourg area with Stuttgart fifty miles straight ahead. P/O Burton and crew ran into severe icing at 8,000 feet and as their Halifax was unable to maintain height, it was decided to abort the sortie and jettison the bomb load. At the same time, F/Sgt McAlpine and crew decided to turn back after failing to fix a wireless equipment problem.

The main force element arrived late at the target because of inaccurately forecast winds and found excellent visibility but the Path Finder TIs already burning out on the ground. This left the way clear for dummy TIs to lure the bombing away from the city centre, and in this endeavour, they were largely successful, although to the bomb-aimers high above, the green TIs appeared to be legitimate and were bombed by the 405 (Vancouver) Squadron crews from 14,600 to 17,500 feet between 22.42 and 23.10. F/O Atkinson and crew landed at Beaulieu, whether out of habit or shortage of fuel is not revealed, but most landed at base or a nearby Yorkshire station, some with flak or night-fighter damage. According to local sources, most of the effort was wasted in open country but the south-western suburbs of Vaihingen and Kaltental were hit and 118 buildings, mostly houses, were destroyed. It was a disappointing outcome, which cost eleven aircraft, five of them belonging to 6 Group and four of those were from 405 (Vancouver) Squadron, three containing eight-man crews.

BB212 was shot down by a BF110 between the Franco/German frontier and the target on the way out and F/Sgt Chretien DFM RCAF and all but his RAF rear gunner survived to fall into enemy hands. It seems that night-fighters were awaiting the returning bombers over north-eastern France, and W7803 fell victim to one to crash some sixteen miles east-south-east of Laon with no survivors from the mixed RCAF/RAF crew of A Flight deputy commander, the long-serving F/L Shockley RCAF. BB250 was homebound at 15,000 feet when crossing paths with a night-fighter, which caused sufficient damage to force the eight RCAF occupants to take to their parachutes and leave their Halifax to crash at 01.00 between Vervins and the Belgian frontier. P/O Dennison, second pilot, the recently posted-in S/L Logan, and three others landed safely and with the aid of the local resistance network retained their freedom, while the rear gunner fell into enemy hands and two crew members lost their lives. P/O Rea's DT745 suffered a similar fate while returning at 15,000 feet and crashed at 23.50 in the Marne region south-east of Reims, all eight occupants surviving, six to evade capture and two to be taken into captivity. It was a sobering return to bombing operations for the squadron, but news that an unusually high number had survived, some of them soon to return home, would be welcomed. In a rather inadequate recompense for these losses, Sgt Daggett's American rear gunner shot down a BF109, and had the satisfaction of seeing the glow as it impacted the ground.

Losses were a fact of life in Bomber Command and could not be allowed to interfere with the process of war, and on each station a team from the Committee of Adjustment would descend upon the billets of the missing men and remove all trace of them to prepare the way for the next occupants. Such was the size of a bomber squadron, and the constant turnover of arrivals and departures, that close friendships beyond one's own crew were discouraged. Perhaps it was different among officers, who were fewer, and were more frequently in each other's company in the officers' mess, but generally, the faces of the missing soon faded from memory, and those returning within a matter of months after evading capture were often shocked to discover how few faces they recognised.

Round two of the Ruhr campaign was posted on the 12th, when 457 crews learned at briefing that Essen was once more to be their destination with a time-on-target for the Path Finders of 21.15. They were to adopt the northern route to the Ruhr, and sixteen Path Finders were to ground mark the town of Dorsten with white TIs as a track guide before backing up the Mosquito-borne Oboe red TIs with greens to provide the main force crews with a solid aiming point. 6 Group detailed twenty-three Halifaxes and sixty-seven Wellingtons, of which seven of the former were provided by 405 (Vancouver) Squadron and took off from Topcliffe for the final time in anger between 19.20 and 19.28 with F/O College the senior pilot on duty and each bomb bay containing three 1,000-pounders and ten SBCs of 4lb and 30lb incendiaries. F/O College and crew were an hour out when two crew members reported the failure of their oxygen supply and forced the sortie to be abandoned, and they landed to find F/Sgt McAlpine and crew already on the ground as a result of intense vibration on both port engines. The others reached the target to find fierce fires already burning beneath clear skies, the smoke from which combined with industrial haze to blot out ground detail. Oboe rendered this of little consequence as the red and green Path Finder TIs identified the aiming point for the 405 (Vancouver) Squadron crews to attack from 13,000 to 20,000 feet between 21.19 and 21.34. P/O Daggett and crew had to take violent evasive action in a vain attempt to avoid the intense flak and landed at Martlesham Heath with an estimated two hundred flak holes to repair. At debriefings crews again expressed confidence in the quality of their work and many reported the glow from the burning city to be visible from the Dutch coast. It was clear that the bombing was accurate and mostly concentrated around the Oboe-laid TIs, and this time, the Krupp complex found itself in the centre of the area of destruction. The defences fought back to claim twenty-three bombers, in return for which, according to post-raid reconnaissance, another highly successful assault on this centre of war production had been achieved. In fact, substantially fewer buildings had been destroyed, but a greater concentration of bombs had inflicted 30% more damage on Krupp than the raid of a week earlier.

During the course of the 13th and 14th, the squadron moved ten miles up the A1 to take up residence at Leeming, which it would share during its brief occupancy with 408 (Goose) squadron. It was the 22nd before orders came through to prepare for the next assault on St-Nazaire, for which a force of 357 aircraft was assembled, including a contribution from 6 Group of thirty-eight Halifaxes, ten of them belonging to 405 (Vancouver) Squadron. Each was loaded with two 1,000-pounders and a selection of indendiaries before taking off between 18.21 and 18.40 with F/L Campbell the senior pilot on duty. At some point, 3 Group sent out a recall signal, to which fifty-five Stirling crews responded, leaving just eight to continue on to the target. F/O Colledge and crew turned back after an hour because of a glycol leak in the port-inner engine, while P/O Symes and crew aborted their sortie after ninety minutes because of a similar leak in their port-outer engine. F/Sgt Stovel and crew were two-and-a-half hours out when the guns in the rear turret became inoperable and they became the squadron's third "boomerang". The bomber stream had flown out over Portland Bill and the remaining seven from 405 (Vancouver) Squadron reached the target area to find clear skies and moonlight that enabled the port and docks to be identified visually aided by the abundance of red and green TIs. They delivered their bombs from 15,000 to 18,000 feet between 21.35 and 21.54 and contributed to an accurate and concentrated attack, which left the town and port areas in flames and massively damaged.

Duisburg was selected as the host for the third operation of the Ruhr offensive, for which a force of 455 aircraft was assembled, 6 Group detailing thirty Halifaxes and eighty-six Wellingtons, although not all would take off. The crews learned at briefing that the Oboe Mosquitos were to drop warning flares five and two-and-a-half minutes before the aiming-point, and then employ the "Musical Wanganui" marking method, the code for Oboe skymarking, releasing red flares with green stars at regular intervals thereafter. Eight 405 (Vancouver) Squadron Halifaxes each received a bomb load of two 1,000-pounders and mix of incendiaries before departing Leeming between 19.14 and 19.24 with F/L Campbell the senior pilot on duty. The somewhat "iffy" serviceability rate continued with two early returns involving the crews of P/O Burton and F/Sgt Stovel because of instrument and compass failures, leaving the others to make their way to the target area, where they found ten-tenths cloud with tops at 10,000 feet and good visibility above. They were greeted by the Oboe release-point parachute flares, which were in the bomb sights as they dropped their loads from 13,500 to 18,000 feet between 21.36 and 21.48, and a large explosion was witnessed at 21.53. What the crews couldn't know, was that five of the Oboe Mosquitos had returned early with equipment failure and a sixth had been shot down, leaving just three to deliver what could be only sparse marking. This was insufficient and led to a scattered and ineffective attack, which, according to local reports, caused only minor damage. Fortunately, the failure cost a modest six aircraft, three of them 6 Group Wellingtons.

One note of concern for 6 Group on this night was a 10% rate of early returns, and this, together with a higher-than-average loss rate over a considerable period would characterise the opening phase of its operational career. In time this would change, and by war's end 6 Group would achieve an impressive record of efficiency and reliability, in the meantime, however, crews saw little prospect of surviving a tour of thirty operations.

Orders were received on stations across the Command on the 27th to prepare for a trip to the "Big City" that night, and a force of 396 aircraft was duly assembled. At briefings, the Path Finder crews were told of their part in the plan, which required eleven Stirlings and eight Halifaxes to drop green route marker flares and yellow warning flares by H2S, before marking the aiming-point with red TIs for two Stirlings, five Halifaxes and twenty-one Lancasters to back up with green TIs. In the event of cloud blotting out the ground, skymarking would be employed. 6 Group contributed thirty-one Halifaxes, nine of them belonging to 405 (Vancouver) Squadron, which each received a bomb load of two 1,000-pounders and mix of 4lb and 30lb incendiaries, before departing Leeming between 19.39 and 20.04 with F/L Campbell the senior pilot on duty. The route took them from the Yorkshire coast across the North Sea to make landfall between the Frisian Islands of Texel and Vlieland and then on a course a little north of Hannover to a point to the south-west of the capital for the run-in to the intended city-centre aiming-point.

An ice-bearing weather front seemed to stretch from the midpoint of the North Sea to north-eastern Germany and a number of crews were unable to continue as a result. P/O Symes and crew were fifty minutes into the outward flight when an electrical fault in the bombing panel ended their interest in proceedings, and shortly afterwards, F/O College and crew were afflicted by a similar fault affecting the guns in the rear turret. P/O Daggett and crew were unable to maintain height due to ice accretion and bombed a built-up area believed to be the port of Emden from 16,000 feet at 21.56, while F/L Campbell and crew were within fifty miles of Berlin when icing persuaded them also to turn back and jettison their bomb load. The Path Finders were reliant upon H2S and established two areas of marking, both well short, and the main force crews had little choice but to aim for them. There was the usual discrepancy in the reported cloud state of zero to nine-tenths as the 405 (Vancouver) Squadron crews tracked in across yellow TIs and carried out their attacks from 15,000 to 17,500 feet between 22.56 and 23.17. From bombing altitude, the attack appeared to be effective but local reports confirmed that the main weight of bombs had fallen between seven and seventeen miles short of the target, and 25% of those hitting the city had failed to detonate. This disappointing outcome cost, what might be considered, a modest nine aircraft.

There would be an opportunity to rectify the failure two nights hence, but in the meantime, St-Nazaire would face its third heavy assault under the January Directive, for which a force of 323 aircraft was made ready on the 28th. 6 Group detailed fifteen Halifaxes and ninety-two Wellingtons, with just five freshman crews representing 405 (Vancouver) Squadron and departing Leeming between 19.30 and 19.36, each sitting on two 1,000-pounders and assortment of 4lb and 30lb incendiaries. They encountered good visibility in the target area and benefitted from red and green Oboe-laid TIs marking out the aiming point as they delivered their attacks from 15,500 and 17,000 feet between 22.24 and 22.30. Returning crews reported concentrated fires, and post-raid reconnaissance confirmed the accuracy and effectiveness of the raid.

The month's final operation was posted on the 29th, when the red tape on the briefing-room wall maps ended again at Berlin. A force of 329 aircraft was made ready, of which twenty-three Halifaxes were provided by 6 Group, four of them representing 405 (Vancouver) Squadron, while 149 Wellingtons, seventy-five belonging to 6 Group, were prepared for an attack on Bochum in the central Ruhr. The plan for the main event required all Path Finder aircraft to drop yellow route markers at predetermined points, and the marker crews to illuminate the Müggelsee to the south-east of Berlin with sticks of white flares and bundles of green flares with red stars by H2S, before they and the backers-up carried out a DR run to the aiming-point to deliver red TIs. The 405 (Vancouver) Squadron contingent departed Leeming between 21.22 and 21.31 with F/L Campbell the senior pilot on duty and crossed the English coast over Flamborough Head on course for Mandø Island off Jutland's western coast. They met bad weather in the form of heavy ice-bearing cloud and static electricity extending from the North Sea to the Baltic, which forced many crews to turn for home, among them fifteen belonging to 6 Group, eighteen from 5 Group and a massive twenty-four from 4 Group. Eight of the 408 (Goose) Squadron crews turned back between 22.24 and 23.15 and they were joined by the 405 (Vancouver) Squadron crews of P/O Symes and Sgt Weber after icing caused engine and turret problems.

The rest of the force, meanwhile, had continued on across Jutland and traversed Kiel Bight and Mecklenburg Bay, before crossing the German coast between Wismar and Rostock on track for the "Big City", where good visibility enabled them to identify the Müggelsee to the south-east of the city as a reference point from which to run in on the aiming-point. The Path Finders were again short with their marking, and the main force arrived late after some of the markers had already burned themselves out. The bombing was carried out by the crews of F/L Campbell and F/O College from 20,000 and 16,000 feet at 00.57 and 01.00 respectively in the face of a heavy searchlight and flak defence, and crews set off for home in the belief that the fires they had left behind, the glow from which was still visible from 150 miles away, indicated that an effective attack had been delivered. In fact, as an analysis of the operation revealed, most of the bombing had been wasted in open country to the south-east of the city, and an accurate figure for damage was not forthcoming. In return for this failure, the Command lost twenty-one aircraft, three belonging to 6 Group, in addition to which, nine 6 Group Wellingtons were missing from the Bochum raid.

During the course of the month, the squadron took part in seven operations and dispatched fifty-eight sorties for the loss of four Halifaxes and crews, but sixteen early returns, almost 30%, put a question mark on the squadron's serviceability record.

April 1943

April would be the least rewarding month during the Ruhr offensive, principally because of the number of operations directed at targets in regions of Germany beyond the range of Oboe. On the 2nd, orders were received to prepare for the final raids on St-Nazaire and Lorient that night, which would bring down the curtain on the January directive. Forces of fifty-five and forty-seven aircraft were made ready with four Halifaxes and five Wellingtons of 6 Group included in the former, the 405 (Vancouver) Squadron crews of Sgt Cooke and P/O Lennox departing Leeming at 19.42 and 19.45 respectively, each sitting on eight 1,000-pounders. Conditions in the target area were favourable with good visibility and a little ground haze, which facilitated a visual identification of the target aided by green Path Finder TIs. The 405 (Vancouver) Squadron duo delivered their attacks from 13,000 and 15,000 feet at 22.23 and 22.26 in the face of heavy and accurate flak and no results were observed. Both St-Nazaire and Lorient had long since been abandoned by the civilian populations and the outcome of the raids was not commented upon by local sources.

The next round of the Ruhr campaign was announced across the Command on the 3rd, when Essen was posted as the target for the third time and a force of 348 aircraft made ready. The heavy brigade consisted of 225 Lancasters and 113 Halifaxes, twenty-two of the former representing 6 Group, and this would be the first occasion on which more than two hundred Lancasters had operated against a single target. The Path Finder contribution amounted to ten Oboe Mosquitos and twenty Lancasters from 83 and 156 Squadrons, the crews of which were to identify the Krupp complex as the aiming-point, and in the event of cloud, skymark it with coloured flares, or if clear skies prevailed, ground mark with red TIs. The five-strong 405 (Vancouver) Squadron element departed Leeming between 19.53 and 19.59 with F/L Campbell the senior pilot on duty and a bomb load of two 1,000-pounders and seven and six SBCs respectively of 4lb and 30lb incendiaries. They joined the bomber stream over the North Sea on their way to make landfall on the Dutch coast near Haarlem and uncomfortably close to the Amsterdam defences. They found almost clear skies over the Ruhr region and that the anticipated industrial haze was negated by the accuracy of the Oboe markers falling around the aiming-point. The attack began slowly, some crews apparently confused by the employment of both sky and ground markers on a clear night, but it built to a crescendo, during which a massive explosion was observed by many crews in the centre of the bombing. The 405 (Vancouver) Squadron crews attacked from 16,400 to 19,000 feet between 21.59 and 22.10, aiming mostly at the TIs burning on the ground and many explosions were witnessed, with fires emitting large volumes of smoke.

Both Leeming Squadrons posted missing two Halifaxes and another belonging to 408 (Goose) Squadron belly-landed on return, happily without crew casualties. The dispersal pans would soon find other occupants as would the twenty-nine beds of the absent crew members, and as the days passed and the war progressed, memory of them would fade. DT808 had been outbound at 15,000 feet when set upon by the night-fighter of Major Werner Streib of I./NJG1 and shot down to crash at 23.20 near Boxmeer in Holland with the German frontier in sight. Both gunners escaped with their lives to fall into enemy hands, but F/Sgt McAlpine and the four other members of this all-RCAF crew lost their lives. F/Sgt McAlpine and one of his gunners, F/Sgt Bradley, had been quite badly injured in a landing crash on return from Kiel in October, while serving with 158 Squadron. In contrast, all but one survived from the eight-man all-RCAF crew captained by P/O Lago, after DT723 fell victim to a night-fighter while homebound at 13,000 feet near Rotterdam, and they were taken into captivity. On return from this operation at 01.15, JB893 collided with the parked JB906 at Leeming, writing the latter off, but no injuries were reported among the crew of F/L Campbell. At debriefings, many crews reported the glow from the burning city to be still visible from the Dutch coast homebound and the consensus was of a successful raid. This was confirmed by bombing photographs and local reports, which spoke of widespread destruction in central and western districts, where 635 buildings had been reduced to rubble and many more seriously damaged. The searchlight and flak defence had been intense, and it became an expensive night for the Command, which registered the loss of a dozen Halifaxes and nine Lancasters. This represented 6% of those dispatched, but it was the respective loss rates of the types that was most telling, with the Halifaxes suffering 10.62% compared with 4% for the Lancasters.

The largest non-1,000 force to date of 577 aircraft was made ready on the 4th for an attack that night on the naval and shipbuilding port of Kiel, for which 6 Group detailed twenty-three Halifaxes and 106 Wellingtons, ten of the former belonging to 405 (Vancouver) Squadron. The crews learned at briefing that the plan of attack called for a time-on-target of 23.00 and for yellow TIs to be dropped by the Path Finders as route markers, before the H2S marker crews in ten Stirlings and six Halifaxes illuminated the aiming-point with flares and marked it with red TIs. Two Stirlings, five Halifaxes and fifteen Lancasters were then to back up with green TIs, leaving two of each type to bomb with the main force. The 405 (Vancouver) Squadron contingent departed Leeming between 20.44 and 20.53 with F/Os College and Weiser the senior pilots on duty and two 1,000-pounders and eight and seven SBCs respectively of 4lb and 30lb incendiaries in each bomb bay. They headed out over Flamborough Head on course for Jutland's western coast, and P/O Symes and crew had reached the Baltic coast by the time that three crew members began to experience oxygen starvation. The bombs were dropped from 18,000 feet at 23.15, and by a process of back-plotting it was determined that would have fallen on or near the Danish town of Haderslev. Meanwhile, the others closed on the target area, where they were guided towards the aiming point by yellow route-marker flares released by the Path Finder heavy brigade either side of 23.00.

Kiel was found to be concealed beneath ten-tenths cloud with good visibility above, and the high explosives and incendiaries were released by the 405 (Vancouver) Squadron participants from estimated positions onto the glow of fires below the cloud from 14,500 to 18,000 feet between 23.25 and 23.37. Among twelve missing aircraft was 405 (Vancouver) Squadron's DT704, which crashed in the target area with no survivors from the predominantly RCAF crew of Sgt Foley RCAF. It was not possible to assess the outcome of the raid, and as bombing photos revealed only cloud, it was left to a post-raid analysis to conclude that decoy fires had been operating and had probably lured away a proportion of the effort, while the strong wind caused the markers to drift, leading the remainder astray and resulting in most of the bombs missing the target altogether. According to local reports, only eleven houses were destroyed, and this was a major disappointment in view of the size of the force involved.

On the 6th, ten crews were briefed at Leeming for a mining operation in the Cinnamon garden off the Biscay ports of La Pallice/La Rochelle, 405 (Vancouver) Squadron providing six of them on what was the squadron's first and only mining operation of the war. All of the Command's main force squadrons could expect to become involved in mining activity on a regular basis, and it was one of the more acceptable ways of introducing freshman crews to operations. This is not to suggest that mining was not a demanding and dangerous undertaking, which of course it was, however, long flights over the sea provided invaluable experience in pinpoint navigation, without the distractions of being over hostile territory, and flak of the lethal light variety would normally only be a problem as the coastal areas for the drop were reached. There was also little chance of a collision, and there was generally less prospect of encountering night-fighters and these long hours of solitude in comparative safety until the target was reached aided the bonding of a crew in the early stages of its tour.

5 Group had carried out the first mine-laying operation of the war on the night of the 13/14th of April 1940, and it was a task to which the Hampden would prove itself eminently suited. This represented the initial tentative steps in a new type of operation for Bomber Command, which would prove to be hugely successful, and by war's end, would have sunk or damaged more enemy vessels than the Royal Navy. The laying of parachute mines by air was given the code-name "gardening" and the entire enemy-held coastline from the Pyrenees in the south-west to the Baltic port of Königsberg in the north-east, and even the northern Italian coast, was divided into gardens, each with a horticultural or marine biological name. The process of delivery was known as planting and the mines themselves were referred to as vegetables, and it would not be long before the other groups joined in to create a spiders' web of mines in chains across all of the sea-lanes employed by the enemy. Ten months after it had begun, an assessment of the efficacy of mining operations revealed that seventeen enemy vessels had been sunk in the Baltic's Great and Little Belts and eighteen damaged. It was believed that a further eighteen had probably been sunk and it was considered safe to estimate that for every known case of a sinking or damage, another would have occurred without news of it reaching England. Among the known sinkings was that of a troopship carrying three thousand men, of whom fewer than four hundred survived.

Take-off from Leeming was accomplished between 20.38 and 20.48 with F/Os Edwards and Weiser the senior pilots on duty and two mines in each bomb bay, and all arrived in the target area to attempt to pinpoint on the Ile-de-Re, before conducting timed runs to the release point. Despite favourable conditions and good visibility, P/O Sattler and crew failed to locate the island and after searching further north abandoned their sortie at 01.07. Four others delivered their stores from 1,000 feet or below between 23.24 and 23.37 and returned safely from uneventful sorties, while the arrival of F/O Edwards RCAF and his predominantly RCAF crew in DT699 was awaited in vain. They were last heard from on W/T at 23.23, and their fate became clear when four bodies washed ashore on the Ile-de-Re and another further north on the mainland at Pornic. This would prove to be the last crew to be lost by the squadron as a main force unit.

On the 8th, 405 (Vancouver) Squadron was notified of its impending transfer to the Path Finder Force, the move to Gransden Lodge in Bedfordshire to be completed by the 19th. In the meantime, the Ruhr offensive continued at Duisburg that night in an operation involving a mixed main force element of 379 Lancasters, Wellingtons, Halifaxes and Stirlings, while ten Oboe Mosquitos would provide the initial marking, backed up by the Path Finder heavy brigade consisting of four Stirlings, twenty Lancasters and eight Halifaxes. 6 Group contributed fifteen Halifaxes and sixty Wellingtons, just four of the former representing 405 (Vancouver) Squadron, which departed Leeming between 21.30 and 21.33, bearing aloft the crews of F/L Campbell, F/O College and P/Os Sattler and Stovel and the same high explosive and incendiary bomb loads as for Kiel. They rendezvoused with the bomber stream after beginning the North Sea crossing at the Norfolk coast and had to climb through ten-tenths ice-bearing cloud before breaking into clear air at 12,000 feet. It was at this stage that most of the 27% of 6 Group participants turned back, among them the crews of F/L Campbell, F/O Colledge and P/O Sattler because of icing and other issues, leaving the Stovel crew to go on alone. They made landfall at Egmond with a time-on-target set for 23.15, before which, the ten Oboe Mosquitos were to drop red warning flares and then greens with red stars and green TIs over the aiming-point. If the weather conditions permitted, one Stirling, seven Halifaxes and fourteen Lancasters would back up with red TIs, while the remaining 8 Group aircraft supported the main force. The bomber stream reached the western Ruhr to encounter ten-tenths cloud with tops in places as high as 20,500 feet, such conditions completely nullifying the Path Finders' attempts to mark either the route or the target, and the bombing had to be carried out on e.t.a., some crews embarking on a time-and-distance run from as far away as the Dutch coast as the last visual reference. The Stovel crew lost a starboard engine shortly before reaching the target at 23.30, but the bombs were dropped from 15,000 feet, immediately after which, a box barrage of flak threw the Halifax into a spin. The remaining three engines cut out and the pilot issued a warning for the crew to prepare to bale out, upon which four, including the second pilot, misunderstood and vacated the aircraft. P/O Stovel regained control at 1,000 feet and three engines came back to life, only to fail again on the way home and cause another spin, which this time was arrested at 6,000 feet. They landed at base at 02.28 after the most tense of sorties and the four crew members had nothing of value to pass on to the intelligence section at debriefing. Absent from that process were nineteen crews, in return for the loss of which, local sources confirmed a widely scattered raid that hit at least fifteen other Ruhr locations and destroyed just forty buildings in Duisburg.

Not content with the outcome, Harris ordered another raid twenty-four hours later, only this time employing a much-reduced force of 104 Lancasters and five Mosquitos. They were guided to the target by red route-marker flares and then red and green skymarkers over the aiming point, which was hidden by ten-tenths cloud with tops at 5,000 to 15,000 feet. Some crews observed a large red glow reflected in the clouds, but local sources confirmed that this was another highly scattered raid, which spread bombs over a wide area of the Ruhr and destroyed only fifty houses in Duisburg.

Frankfurt was posted as the destination on the 10th for 502 aircraft, of which the 144 Wellingtons would represent the most populous type, demonstrating that this trusty old warhorse still had an important part to play in Bomber Command operations. 6 Group provided eighty-eight of the Wellingtons along with twenty-five Halifaxes, just three of the latter belonging to 405 (Vancouver) Squadron and departing Leeming between 23.36 and 23.40 bearing aloft the crews of P/O Sattler and Sgts Crockatt and Phillips. Each was sitting on the same bomb loads as for the previous operations and the plan was standard for a target beyond the range of Oboe. Eleven Stirlings and six Halifaxes were to drop yellow TIs as route markers by H2S, followed by preliminary warning flares, all of which were to be backed up by two Stirlings, ten Halifaxes and seventeen Lancasters. Cloud conditions permitting, the aiming-point was then to be marked by red TIs on H2S, and if not, by green flares with red stars and a white flare, with appropriate backing up with green TIs or coloured flares. The bomber stream adopted the usual course to this region of Germany, following the line of the Franco/Belgian frontier to cross into Germany on an east-north-easterly heading north of Saarbrücken. The H2S marker crews arrived in the target area to be confronted by ten-tenths cloud with tops at between 8,000 and 12,000 feet but found that their red TIs were visible and opted not to sky mark. This was fine in the early stages, until it became impossible to distinguish the genuine TIs from decoys, incendiaries and searchlights, and the backer-up crews experienced great difficulty in establishing an aiming-point. The 405 (Vancouver) Squadron crews went in at 14,500 to 16,500 feet between 02.51 and 03.11, having been guided by preliminary warning flares, and some bombed at whatever was glowing beneath the cloud or on e.t.a., without being able to assess the outcome. Bombing photos revealed nothing but cloud, and local sources confirmed that only a few bombs had fallen into the southern suburbs, a disappointing return for the effort of mounting such a large-scale operation and the loss of twenty-one aircraft.

During a training flight on the afternoon of the 13th, and while attempting to land at Leeming in a crosswind, JB914 came to grief, fortunately without casualties among the crew of Sgt Phillips. That night, 208 Lancaster and three Halifax crews of 1, 5 and 8 Groups were notified of a change of scenery for their next operation, which was to be against the docks at La Spezia on Italy's northern coast some forty miles south-east of Genoa.

The busy round of non-Ruhr operations continued with the posting of Stuttgart as the target on the 14th, for which a force of 462 aircraft was made ready, 6 Group providing twenty-eight Halifaxes and eighty-five Wellingtons, five of the former made ready by 405 (Vancouver) Squadron and given the standard bomb load. At briefing, the crews took in the details of the plan, which involved Path Finder aircraft dropping yellow TIs as route markers at two locations, while at the target, nine Stirlings and eight Halifaxes were to ground mark the aiming-point with red TIs on H2S, at the same time as releasing a short stick of flares. One Stirling and four Lancasters were then to identify the aiming-point visually, and mark it with green TIs for three Stirlings, six Halifaxes and eleven Lancasters to back up also with greens. This would leave three Stirlings, three Halifaxes and five Lancasters to bolster the efforts of the main force. The 405 (Vancouver) Squadron participants departed Leeming for the final time in anger and as a 6 Group unit between 21.23 and 21.27 with F/O Weiser the senior pilot on duty and rendezvoused with the bomber stream on the passage south to begin the sea crossing. The Franco/Belgian frontier was followed to a point beyond Luxembourg, where the force turned towards the east to enter Germany in the Strasbourg area and approach the target from the north-east under clear skies. The Path Finder ground marker crews established their positions by H2S confirmed by visual reference, but as evidence of the shortcomings of H2S in its early form, they were actually short of the city centre when they delivered bundles of white flares, red TIs and 1,000-pounders between 00.47 and 00.56. The backers-up were carrying four green TIs, one of them of the long-burning variety, four 1,000-pounders and a single 500-pounder each, which they dropped between 00.50 and 01.14, also to the north-east of the planned aiming-point.

The main force crews were greeted by plentiful red and green TIs concentrated in a built-up area, and some would claim later to have picked out ground details such as marshalling yards, the railway station, the River Neckar and the Bosch factory through the copious volumes of smoke rising through 8,000 feet. This reinforced their belief that they were over the briefed aiming-point, where the TIs had mostly burned out by the time that the 405 (Vancouver) Squadron crews delivered their attacks on concentrations of fire from around 16,000 feet between 01.20 and 01.30. Twenty-three aircraft failed to return, eight of them belonging to 6 Group, and bombing photos and post-raid reconnaissance confirmed that the Path Finders had not marked the centre of the city, and that a "creep-back" had developed, which had spread along the line of approach. Creep-back was a feature of many large raids and was caused by crews bombing the first fires they came upon, rather than pushing through to the planned aiming-point. It could work for or against the effectiveness of an attack, and on this night worked in the Command's favour by falling across the industrial district of Bad-Canstatt, situated to the north-east of the city centre on the East Bank of the River Neckar. The bombing continued to spread further back along the line of approach onto the residential suburbs of Münster and Mühlhausen, and it was here that the majority of the 393 buildings were destroyed and more than nine hundred others severely damaged.

The squadron was stood down from operations pending its move to 8 Group, which meant that it was absent from a night of heavy operational activity on the 16/17th, when Harris sent over three hundred Lancasters and Halifaxes to distant Pilsen in Czechoslovakia to bomb the Skoda armaments works, and a diversionary force of predominantly Stirlings and Wellingtons to Mannheim. The plan at Pilsen had called for the Path Finders to lay route markers at the start of the run-up to the target, which was to be identified visually, but confusion reigned, and the main force crews bombed the route markers seven miles short of the Skoda works. Beneath the bombs lay an asylum, and it sustained the damage meant for the factory. Thirty-six aircraft failed to return, eighteen of each type, and the Mannheim force also lost eighteen aircraft, making this the highest loss in a single night to date.

The move to Gransden Lodge took place between the 17th and 19th, and involved eighteen Halifaxes, thirty-two officers and ninety-three senior NCOs, and it was at this point that the popular W/C Clayton was posted to Topcliffe to take up a senior staff position with 6 Group. Brought back to succeed him as commanding officer W/C "Johnny" Fauquier, who, after serving his time at RCAF Overseas HQ, had spent a brief period on 6 Group's HQ staff at "Castle Dismal." The squadron's new home bordered the picturesque village of Great Gransden, which now lies just inside Cambridgeshire, although its postal address remains Bedfordshire. During the war, however, it was across the county line in Huntingdonshire, which now exists only as a district after being swallowed up by boundary changes. The squadron would be granted a short bedding-in period to learn the topography and Path Finder ways, and during this week, the port of Stettin, located at the midpoint of Germany's Baltic coast, hosted a successful attack by three hundred aircraft on the 20/21st. Stettin was perhaps the only urban target in Germany never to escape lightly at the hands of the Command. On this night it suffered the destruction of thirteen industrial premises and 380 houses in an area of devastation in its central districts estimated at a hundred acres.

405 (Vancouver) Squadron was declared ready to make its Path Finder debut when Harris returned to the Ruhr at Duisburg on the 26th, along with another new addition to the force, 97 (Straits Settlement) Squadron, which had been posted in from 5 Group and was now stationed at nearby Bourn. New crews acted as supporters, and carried only bombs, while "beefing-up" the Path Finder presence. In time they would graduate to the role of backer-up, in which they maintained the aiming point with fresh target indicators thoughout the course of the raid. Experienced crews became adept in a whole range of blind and visual illuminating and marking roles as techniques evolved, if, that is, they were able to survive and reach the required standard.

A force of 561 aircraft was assembled, the numbers bolstered by the inclusion of 135 Wellingtons, while 215 Lancasters represented the largest contribution by type. The plan called for eight Oboe Mosquitos to drop yellow route markers and red TIs on the aiming-point, the yellows to be backed up by others of the same colour delivered by a dozen Lancasters, while three Stirlings, five 35 (Madras Presidency) Squadron Halifaxes and seven Lancasters backed up at the aiming-point with green TIs. This would leave three 35 (Madras Presidency) Squadron Halifaxes with eleven of 405 (Vancouver) Squadron and eighteen Lancasters, including those from 97 Squadron, to bomb with the main force. The Gransden Lodge element consisting of the crews of F/L Atkinson, F/L Colledge, F/O Weiser, P/Os Gowan, Grant, Harty, Lennox and Symes and Sgts Crockatt, Kirkham and McSorley took off between 00.15 and 00.27 with a 2,000-pounder and seven 1,000-pounders in each bomb bay, before setting course for the Dutch coast on the northern approach to the Ruhr. There were no early returns among the 8 Group Halifax debutants, which crossed the Dutch coast and headed for the final turning point to the north-east of the target to find largely clear skies and good visibility. The 405 (Vancouver) Squadron crews bombed from 8,000 to 18,000 feet between 02.18 and 02.28, and by the end of the raid many fires were evident, although opinions were divided as to the degree of concentration achieved. A large orange explosion was witnessed to the east of the aiming-point at 02.34, and, although fires had not gained a hold by the time of withdrawal, black smoke was rising through 7,000 feet. Seventeen aircraft failed to return, including one each from the Path Finders' 156 and 405 (Vancouver) Squadrons, the latter, JB920, crashing at 02.16 at Walsum on the bank of the Rhine some eight miles north-north-west of Duisburg, killing Sgt Crockatt RCAF and the other seven predominantly RCAF occupants. Post-raid reconnaissance revealed that the attack had fallen short of the city centre and had been focused on the north-eastern districts under the line of approach, thus sparing Duisburg yet again from the full weight of a Bomber Command heavy raid. Even so, local reports confirmed the destruction of more than three hundred buildings, which represented something of a telling blow upon this target.

Large mining operations were mounted on the consecutive nights of the 27/28th and 28/29th, involving 160 and 207 aircraft respectively. The latter resulted in the loss of twenty-two aircraft, the largest-ever loss to result in a single night from mining, but on the credit side, the number of mines delivered, 593, was also a record for one night, and would not be surpassed.

Essen was posted as the target on the 30th, as attention swung once more towards the Ruhr, and would remain upon it almost exclusively now until well into July. A force of 305 aircraft was assembled that included an 8 Group contribution of ten Oboe Mosquitos, four 35 (Madras

Presidency) Squadron Halifaxes, six of 405 (Vancouver) Squadron and sixteen Lancasters of 83, 97 and 156 Squadrons, the heavy brigade all assigned to bomb with the main force. A minor operation by sixteen H2S crews, a dozen from 7 and four of 35 (Madras Presidency) Squadron, was also scheduled for this night as a training exercise, and would be directed at Bocholt, a town situated some twenty miles north of Duisburg almost on the Dutch frontier. The six 405 (Vancouver) Squadron crews departed Gransden Lodge between 00.08 and 00.25 with F/Ls Atkinson and College the senior pilots on duty and a 2,000-pounder, three 1,000 and eight 500-pounders in each bomb bay. After climbing out and setting a course for the Dutch coast, they soon found themselves in the grip of ice-bearing cloud, which persuaded F/Sgt Maddock and crew to turn back and dump their load, while it was Gee failure that ended the Colledge crew's sortie shortly afterwards.

The majority of crews negotiated the conditions to reach the central Ruhr and find ten-tenths cloud with tops in places as high as 21,000 feet. Red and green Oboe-laid Wanganui flares (skymarkers) identified the aiming-point, and three Gransden Lodge crews delivered their attacks from 18,000 and 18,500 feet between 02.47 and 03.04. Returning crews reported the glow of fires beneath the cloud and a number of large explosions, but it was impossible to determine whether or not concentration had been achieved, particularly as bombing photos would show only cloud. DT741 failed to return to Gransden Lodge having been shot down by the night-fighter of Oblt August Geiger of II./NJG1 and crashed at 03.21 on the northern bank of the River Waal, some six miles north-north-west of Nijmegen in Holland. It was an eight-man crew captained by F/L Atkinson, the only member of the RAF, and he lost his life along with the navigator, while the six survivors were taken into captivity. Post-raid reconnaissance and local reports confirmed a lack of concentration and the liberal distribution of bombs onto ten other Ruhr locations, particularly Bottrop to the north, but 189 buildings were destroyed and 237 severely damaged in Essen, and importantly, Krupp sites sustained further damage. The Bocholt element had encountered cloud tops at between 15,000 and 23,000 feet, and some bomb bursts were observed, but no assessment was possible, and crews returned satisfied that they had done their best in challenging conditions.

During the course of the month, the squadron took part in nine operations and dispatched fifty-two sorties for the loss of seven Halifaxes and six complete crews and four additional crew members.

May 1943

May would bring a return to winning ways, with a number of outstanding successes and new records as the Ruhr offensive expanded its horizons to include targets other than Essen and Duisburg. It was, in fact, Duisburg that was posted as the target for each of the first three nights of the new month, before each operation was cancelled. The first of the "new" targets was Dortmund, which had been attacked many times before, but not on the scale planned for it on the 4th, when the force of 596 aircraft represented the largest non-1,000 effort to date. 8 Group made available ten Mosquitos, forty Lancasters, seventeen Halifaxes and six Stirlings, and while they were being prepared by the ground crews and armourers, their crews were in the briefing rooms to be appraised of their part in proceedings. The Mosquitos were to drop yellow track markers, before eight of them ground-marked the aiming-point with green TIs, leaving two in reserve to bomb with the main force if not required for marking duties. Twenty-two Lancasters and two Halifaxes were to back up with red TIs, and all remaining Path Finder aircraft were to bomb with the main force.

While this operation was in progress, six Stirlings and two 35 (Madras Presidency) Squadron Halifaxes were to carry out another H2S training operation, this time against the town of Rheine, situated in the Münsterland to the north of the Ruhr.

At Gransden Lodge the ten 405 (Vancouver) Squadron Halifaxes each had a single 2,000-pounder in the bomb bay supplemented with a selection of 1,000 and 500-pounders and took off between 21.40 and 22.07 with W/C Fauquier and the recently arrived S/L Harris the senior pilots on duty. They joined the bomber stream as it crossed the North Sea before pushing on across Holland to enter Germany to the north of the Ruhr and make its way to the eastern end, where crews found clear skies, good visibility and only industrial and smoke haze to spoil the vertical view. P/O Weber and crew lost their oxygen supply when ninety minutes out and turned back, while P/O Harty and crew ran into flak and JB957 sustained sufficient damage to warrant releasing the bombs early from 13,500 feet at 00.54 when some twenty-seven miles short of the target. Ahead, the initial green Oboe markers were released two minutes early at 00.58 and fell into the city centre, but some of the backing-up fell short and a decoy site was also successful in luring away a proportion of the bombing. The 405 (Vancouver) Squadron crews aimed at red and green target indicators (TIs) from 16,000 to 18,000 feet between 01.03 and 01.33 in the face of intense searchlight and flak activity, and all but one returned safely to home airspace, where weather conditions had become an issue and diversions necessary.

On return to land at Graveley, JB957 crash-landed short of the airfield at 03.15 and was damaged beyond repair, but P/O Harty and crew walked away unscathed. F/O Weiser and crew were running short of fuel as they approached Wyton in JB897 in misty conditions and crash-landed in a field after clipping trees. The Halifax was another write-off, but the crew escaped with a few bruises. At debriefings crews reported many sizeable explosions, including a particularly large one at 01.12, which threw flame to a height of 2,000 feet and burned for ten seconds. They also described developing fires, the glow from which could be seen from 150 miles into the return flight. Post-raid reconnaissance revealed that approximately half of the force had bombed within three miles of the aiming-point, destroying 1,218 buildings and seriously damaging more than two thousand others. Local reports confirmed a death toll of 693 people, which was a record from a Bomber Command attack. It was not a one-sided affair, however, and the loss of thirty-one aircraft was a foretaste of what was in store for the bomber crews operating over "Happy Valley". 405 (Vancouver) Squadron's JB904 was homebound when shot down by a night-fighter to crash close to the Dutch frontier some three miles north-east of Bad Bentheim at 04.35. It was a predominantly RAF crew captained by P/O Lennox RCAF, who, along with the rear gunner, lost his life, while the rest of the crew fell into enemy hands.

A week-long break from major operations ended on the 12th with the posting of Duisburg as the target for a heavy force of 562 aircraft with ten Oboe Mosquitos to take care of the initial marking. In addition to the Mosquitos, 8 Group was responsible for forty-four Lancasters, twenty-five Halifaxes and nineteen Stirlings, the crews of which attended briefings to learn of their part in proceedings. They were told that nine Mosquitos would drop yellow TIs on track as a preliminary warning and red TIs on the aiming-point, which would be backed up with green TIs by five Stirlings, five Halifaxes and twenty Lancasters. The majority of the 405 (Vancouver) Squadron crews were at the PFF Navigation Training Unit, which had been established at Gransden Lodge in April but would shortly move to Upwood. This allowed for five Halifaxes to depart Gransden

Lodge between 23.53 and 23.57 with no senior pilots on duty and a bomb load in each of fifteen SBCs of 4lb incendiaries. They were to bomb again with the main force and after climbing out over the station, headed for the coast to cross the North Sea and make landfall on the Dutch coast in the area of Castricum-aan-Zee. P/O Cowan and cew had been outbound for almost an hour when the bomb-aimer was discovered to be unconscious, and they were forced to turn back. The others reached the target area guided by the yellow tracking flares and found ideal bombing conditions with no cloud and good visibility, which helped the Oboe and H2S crews to mark with great accuracy and focus. The main force crews were able to identify ground features and exploit the opportunity to produce a display of unusually concentrated bombing, the 405 (Vancouver) Squadron element releasing their loads onto red and green TIs from 15,500 to 18,000 feet between 02.13 and 02.21. For, perhaps, the first time at this target, the attack proceeded according to plan, and Duisburg finally succumbed to a devastating assault.

Returning crews described a large explosion at 02.30, streets outlined by fire and a highly successful outcome, the best yet witnessed by some, and their impressions were confirmed by photo-reconnaissance, which revealed extensive damage in the city centre and the Ruhrort Rhine docks, the largest inland port in Germany. 1,596 buildings were totally destroyed and the Thyssen steelworks was hit, while dozens of barges and ships were sunk or damaged. However, many crews were absent from debriefing at stations across the Command, and it soon became clear that the success had been gained at the high cost of thirty-four aircraft. The loss rates by type again made interesting reading and confirmed the established food chain, the Lancasters sustaining a 4.2% loss, compared with 8.9% for Wellingtons, 7.1% for Stirlings and 6.3% for Halifaxes. Such was the level of destruction that Duisburg would now be left in peace for a year.

On the following day, 124 Lancasters of 5 Group were detailed to join forces with thirty-two other Lancasters and twelve Halifaxes of 8 Group, for an attempt to rectify the recent failure at the Skoda armaments works at Pilsen. A simultaneous raid on the Ruhr city of Bochum, home to the Bochumer Verein steel works and situated some three hundred miles to the north-west, would involve a contribution from 8 Group of nineteen Stirlings, three Lancasters and thirteen Halifaxes in an overall force of 442 aircraft, which might, perhaps, split the defences. 405 (Vancouver) Squadron loaded five of its Halifaxes with one 2,000-pounder, two 1,000-pounders and ten 500-pounders and sent them on their way from Gransden Lodge between 23.50 and 23.54 with no senior pilots on duty. Sgt Martin and crew lost the use of their compasses within the first hour and had to turn back, leaving the other four largely inexperienced crews to join the sixteen Path Finders from other squadrons assigned to support the main force. They followed Oboe-laid yellow track markers to the target, a city situated about a dozen miles east of Essen, and found clear skies, but the usual industrial haze to blot out ground detail. The first Oboe Mosquitos dropped red TIs onto the aiming point, but then a gap developed, and although the 7 Squadron Stirling backers-up kept it marked with green TIs throughout, the bombing lacked a degree of concentration, possibly as a result of decoy markers. The 405 (Vancouver) Squadron participants carried out their bombing runs from 13,000 to 18,000 feet between 02.03 and 02.19 and three returned safely having observed the bursts of high explosives and fires beginning to take hold as they turned away. F/O Beattie RCAF and crew were homebound in JB966 and approaching the Ijsselmeer when shot down by a night-fighter to crash near Balkbrug with fatal consequences for the pilot and two others, while the four survivors were taken into captivity. Returning crews reported the target to be a mass of flames by the end of the attack and rocked by many explosions. Photo-reconnaissance revealed the raid to have been moderately effective, and local sources admitted to the destruction of 394 buildings, with more than seven hundred others seriously damaged.

A nine-day break in main force operations allowed the squadrons to rest and replenish, and it was during this period, that 5 Group's 617 squadron entered bomber folklore on the night of the 16/17th with Operation Chastise, the epic attack on the Ruhr Dams, in which many RCAF airmen participated and eleven lost their lives. By the time that the next major operation was posted on the 23rd, the main force squadrons had undergone an expansion with the addition to many units of a third or C Flight, which, in most cases, would eventually be hived off to form the nucleus of a brand-new squadron. The giant force of 826 aircraft was the largest non-1,000 force to date and surpassed the previous record set three weeks earlier by a clear 230 aircraft. The number of available Lancasters had leapt by eighty-eight, Halifaxes by forty-eight, Stirlings by forty and Wellingtons by forty-one, and their destination for the second time in the month was to be Dortmund. The Command had been restored to full health and vigour, and activity on all participating stations was hectic as preparations were put in hand to resume the Ruhr offensive. The ground crews and armourers at Gransden Lodge worked tirelessly to make ready fourteen Halifaxes and provide them with a variety of bomb loads. Nine had five 1,000 and seven 500-pounders winched into their bomb bays, while two had one fewer 1,000-pounder and three had five 1,000 and four 500-pounders and four green TIs as the squadron embarked on its target-marking career. At briefing, the crews learned that they were part of an 8 Group force of thirteen Oboe Mosquitos, twenty Stirlings, thirty-five Halifaxes and fifty-one Lancasters, of which seventy-three of the heavy brigade were to support the main force. Eleven Mosquitos were to drop yellow preliminary warning TIs on track, before marking the aiming-point with Oboe-laid red TIs, which eight Stirlings, eleven Halifaxes and fourteen Lancasters were to back up with green TIs.

The first twelve 405 (Vancouver) Squadron aircraft took off between 22.40 and 23.16 and the last two at 23.37 and 23.40 with W/C Fauquier and the newly-arrived S/L Wolfe the senior pilots on duty. They set course under cloudless skies for the Castricum region of the Dutch coast for the northern approach to the eastern Ruhr and all reached the target area to find a continuation of the clear skies but considerable industrial haze, which, before the advent of Oboe, would have rendered the attack a lottery. The 109 Squadron Mosquitos marked the centre of the city accurately, after which the backers-up, including the 405 (Vancouver) Squadron crews of W/C Fauquier, P/O Cowan and Sgt McSorley, fulfilled their briefs in company with others to ensure that the aiming-point was maintained throughout the raid. Main force crews reported the red TIs to be visible from twenty miles away on approach, and among them the 405 (Vancouver) Squadron participants carried out their runs from 15,000 to 19,000 feet between 01.07 and 01.54. Many explosions were observed, along with fires, which merged into a large area of conflagration that sent thick columns of black smoke rising up through 18,000 feet as the bombers turned away. Returning crews reported fierce night-fighter activity over the target and on the way home, and this was reflected in the high casualty rate of thirty-eight aircraft, the largest loss of the campaign to date. Almost half of these were Halifaxes and eight were Lancasters, and among the former was 405 (Vancouver) Squadron's JB896, which disappeared without trace with the crew of Sgt Martin RCAF. Post-raid reconnaissance revealed the operation to have been an outstanding success, which had hit mainly central, northern and eastern districts, where almost two thousand buildings had been destroyed, and some important war industry factories had suffered severe damage and loss of production. The scale of the success was such that, like Duisburg, this city would remain unmolested by the heavy brigade for a year.

The Ruhr offensive continued with the posting of Düsseldorf as the target on the 25th, for which a force of 759 aircraft was assembled. 8 Group detailed a dozen Mosquitos, nineteen Stirlings, thirty-five Halifaxes and fifty-one Lancasters, 405 (Vancouver) Squadron again contributing fourteen of its Halifaxes. The plan called for the standard procedure of Mosquito-laid yellow preliminary warning TIs on track, and red TIs delivered by Oboe onto the aiming-point. Eight Stirlings, twelve Halifaxes and twenty-three Lancasters were to back these up with green TIs, leaving five Stirlings, fourteen Halifaxes and twenty-five Lancasters to bomb with the main force. The 405 (Vancouver) Squadron element departed Gransden Lodge between 23.20 and 23.48 with S/L Wolfe the senior pilot on duty and ten carrying a 2,000-pounder, one 1,000-pounder and eleven 500-pounders, while four had seven 1,000-pounders in their bomb bays and green TIs. HR806 failed to lift off after engine failure and was written-off in the ensuing crash, from which P/O McMemeny and crew emerged with minor injuries. After climbing out, the others set course for the Scheldt estuary for the southern approach to the Ruhr, in the expectation of finding favourable conditions over the target, for which a ground-marking plan had been prepared. However, when the Oboe Mosquitos arrived in the target area, they were greeted by two layers of cloud with tops at 18,500 feet, and although they delivered their TIs with great accuracy, they could not be seen by the backers-up, and the marking became scattered. The 405 (Vancouver) Squadron backers-up and main force supporters carried out their assigned tasks by H2S from 15,000 to 20,000 feet between 01.34 and 02.12, some after carrying out a timed run from the yellow warning TIs. Some main force crews arriving at the Dutch coast towards the rear of the bomber stream were able to observe feverish activity at the target, still some one hundred miles and thirty minutes flying time away. Post-raid reconnaissance and local reports confirmed that the raid had failed to achieve concentration, possibly as the result of the deployment of decoy markers and dummy fire sites and had developed into an "old-style" scattering of bombs across a wide area. Düsseldorf suffered the destruction of fewer than a hundred buildings, in return for which, twenty-seven aircraft failed to return.

On the 26th, W/C Fauquier and twenty-five representatives of air and ground crew and a Halifax captained by P/O Cowan RCAF proceeded to Path Finder HQ at Wyton to meet with His Majesty King George VI and Queen Elizabeth, who were paying an official visit. On the following day 5 Group would receive them as they undertook a tour of its stations, calling in for lunch at Scampton, where they would meet the "Dambusters".

Harris was not yet done with Essen, and the fifth visitation by the bomber force during the campaign was notified to stations on the 27th, and 518 aircraft made ready. 8 Group prepared two plans of attack, one for ground marking and an alternative for skymarking in the event of cloud cover. In the event, the latter would be employed, involving a dozen Oboe Mosquitos to drop red flares nineteen miles short of the target and green ones ten-and-a-half miles short as a preliminary warning. Continuing on to the target, they were to skymark the aiming-point with red flares with green stars and two white flares for the rest of the group to bomb with the main force. The six-strong 405 (Vancouver) Squadron element departed Gransden Lodge between 22.45 and 22.50 with relatively inexperienced crews on duty, and a bomb load in each Halifax of three 1,000 and a dozen 500-pounders. All reached the target to be greeted by six to eight-tenths cloud with tops at between 12,000 and 20,000 feet and followed the tracking flares until reaching the "Wanganui" skymarkers gently descending into the cloud tops over the aiming-point. The bombing was carried out from 18,000 to 19,000 feet between 01.19 and 01.23, and whether or not Sgt Lebihan RCAF and crew had released their load before HR807 was shot down by flak is unknown. The pilot and three others lost their lives and the three survivors fell into enemy hands. Post-raid reconnaissance revealed that much of the bombing had fallen short, but 488 buildings had been destroyed, mostly in central and northern districts, and ten nearby towns reported themselves to be victims of collateral damage. Twenty-three aircraft failed to return, and the Halifaxes again represented almost half of the casualties.

A force of 719 aircraft was assembled on the 29th, to pitch against a new Ruhr target, the conurbation known as Wuppertal, perched on the southern rim of the Ruhr Valley east of Düsseldorf. It consisted of the towns of Barmen and Elberfeld, which grew wealthy on the proceeds of the rich coal deposits. The aiming-point for this night's attack was to be the Barmen half at the eastern end, for which 8 Group detailed eleven Mosquitos, nineteen Stirlings, thirty-six Halifaxes and fifty-one Lancasters. On this occasion, the route markers were to be dropped by two Stirlings and two Halifaxes, while ahead, the Oboe Mosquitos took care of ground marking with red TIs. These would be backed up by four Stirlings, eleven Halifaxes and twenty-three Lancasters with reds and greens, at the same time as thirteen Stirlings, twenty Halifaxes and twenty-one Lancasters acted as fire raisers by dropping incendiaries. This would leave two Stirlings, five Halifaxes and seven Lancasters to bomb with the main force. The fourteen 405 (Vancouver) Squadron participants departed Gransden Lodge between 22.27 and 22.44 with W/C Fauquier and S/L Wolfe the senior pilots on duty and a mix of high explosives and incendiaries in each bomb bay. Five backers-up were also carrying green TIs as they headed for the Suffolk coast to begin the sea crossing to the Scheldt estuary. P/O Manning and crew lost their port-outer engine soon after taking off and proceeded directly to the jettison area off the coast, while the others negotiated the southern approach to the Ruhr, running the gauntlet of searchlights and flak in the Cologne and Düsseldorf corridor. They were greeted by clear skies in the target area, with the usual industrial haze extending up to 10,000 feet, but the yellow tracking flares clearly identified the final turning-point and the five 405 (Vancouver) Squadron backers-up and eight main force supporters went in at 17,000 to 18,500 feet between 00.51 and 01.07. Meanwhile, the fire-raisers had attacked with a 2,000 pounder and 1,164 x 4lb incendiaries each and the whole town seemed to become a sea of flames rent by many explosions, some flinging debris into the air. It was clear to all that something extraordinary was taking place as the streets below were delineated in a criss-cross pattern and smoke was rising very quickly through 15,000 feet.

Post-raid reconnaissance revealed this to be the most awesomely destructive raid of the campaign thus far, which devastated by fire a thousand acres, or around 80% of the built-up area and destroyed almost four thousand houses, five of the six largest factories and more than two hundred other industrial buildings. It would be some time before the human cost could be established, but it is now accepted that 3,400 people lost their lives during this savage Saturday night. As already described, the defenders had their say also, and fought back to claim a total of thirty-three bombers, ten of them Halifaxes.

On the 31st, 2 Group carried out its final operations as part of Bomber Command. Since the outbreak of war, it had carried the fight to the enemy predominantly by daylight, and in generally outdated and outclassed aircraft. Only with the advent of the Boston, Mitchell and, most crucially, the Mosquito, had its crews been blessed with equipment up to the task. The raw "courage by daylight" displayed by its crews in the finest traditions of the Service, particularly during 1940 and 1941, remains unsurpassed. 2 Group no longer fitted comfortably into an organization committed to transporting the maximum tonnage of bombs to Germany by night, and on the 1st of June it became the nucleus of the 2nd Tactical Air Force, with which its outstanding tradition would continue.

During the course of the month, the squadron carried out seven operations and dispatched sixty-eight sorties for the loss of seven Halifaxes and four crews.

June 1943

The new month began for 8 Group with the arrival of two Mosquito squadrons from 2 Group, 105 and 139 Squadrons having illustrious careers behind them, initially as part of the AASF during the battle for France, and thereafter had served 2 Group with distinction, flying Blenheims until the advent of the Mosquito. Unlike the Mosquitos of 109 Squadron, which operated at maximum altitude for the purpose of Oboe reception, 2 Group Mosquitos had been employed mostly in a low-level strike role against shipping and precision land targets, where speed was their greatest asset. 105 Squadron was to become the second Oboe unit, while 139 Squadron's initial role would be to drop cookies in nuisance raids on German cities as a forerunner of the Light Night Striking Force (LNSF), which would form in 8 Group with the addition of further Mosquito units in 1944. For the time being, both squadrons remained at Marham in Norfolk, which was transferred to 8 Group control, and 109 Squadron would join them there in the following month.

There were no major operations at the start of June because of the weather and other considerations, and although stations across the Command were alerted on most of the first ten days, nothing came of it. 8 Group HQ moved out of Wyton on the 10th to Castle Hill House in Huntingdon, where it would remain for the rest of the war. Despite the fact that bomber crews had one of the most dangerous jobs in military service, they became bored and listless during extended periods of operational inactivity, and most preferred the dangers to the alternatives, like lectures and PT. Many cricket matches were played while the crews kicked their heels on the ground, and there was, no doubt relief, when the operations against Düsseldorf and Münster planned for the 11th actually resulted in briefings taking place. 783 crews learned of their part in the former, 8 Group responsible for forty-seven of them, who would man a dozen Mosquitos, eleven Halifaxes and twenty-four Lancasters. The latter endeavour was to be an 8 Group show, which was, in effect, a mass H2S trial involving seventy-two aircraft. 8 Group's H2S-equipped Stirlings and Halifaxes had thus far been referred to as "special aircraft" in operational plans, but now that 83 Squadron had begun to take on H2S-equipped Lancasters, they would be referred to as "Y" aircraft.

The plan for Düsseldorf would follow the standard pattern in which Mosquito yellow preliminary warning flares were backed up by the other 8 Group aircraft, and the Oboe-laid red TIs on the aiming-point backed up with greens. However, uncertainty concerning the weather conditions resulted in the Mosquitos also carrying target-marking red flares with green stars. 405 (Vancouver) Squadron's six backer-up Halifaxes each received a load of four 1,000 and four 500 pounders and four green TIs, while the six main force supporters had a 2,000-pounder, two 1,000-pounders and eight SBCs of 30lb incendiaries in their bomb bays before departing Gransden Lodge between

23.00 and 23.11 with S/L Wolfe the senior pilot on duty. P/O Tomczak and crew turned back for an undisclosed reason before reaching the English coast, leaving the rest to adopt the southern approach to the Ruhr via the Scheldt estuary and contend with static and lightning conditions in towering ten-tenths cloud with tops at 23,500 feet as they made their way across the North Sea. P/O Harty RCAF and his predominantly RCAF crew ran into flak in the Amsterdam defence zone and sustained damage that left HR797 unable to maintain height, at which point the wireless operator took to his parachute and was never heard of again. The bombs were jettisoned, and a course set for home, and they were around twenty-five minutes flying time from the English coast when the battle to remain airborne was lost. After a successful ditching six of the remaining seven occupants made it into the dinghy, only for the current and wind to take them back towards the enemy coast, where they were picked up by the enemy and taken into captivity. While in captivity, the second pilot, W/O Somerville RCAF, received medical attention, which included the amputation of a foot, and he was ultimately repatriated.

Meanwhile, the cloud had largely dissipated to leave just small amounts at 2,000, 5,000 and 10,000 feet over the southern Ruhr, dependent upon the time of arrival on final approach. Those in the vanguard of the main force were drawn on by yellow tracking flares from 01.05, and red skymarkers with green stars at 01.16, while those a little further back in the bomber stream were guided on by red and green skymarkers. The 405 (Vancouver) Squadron aircraft were spread throughout the bomber stream and carried out their assigned tasks from 14,000 to 19,000 feet between 01.39 and 02.07. The Paramatta marking (ground-marking TIs) did not seem to appear until the first-phase crews were turning away, but they were clearly visible to the crews in the rearguard, who described a sea of flames covering a massive area and columns of smoke rising through 21,000 feet. When all aircraft had been accounted for, thirty-eight were found to be missing, a figure that equalled the heaviest loss of the offensive to date. Post-raid reconnaissance revealed an area of fire across central districts measuring eight by five kilometres, and local reports confirmed 8,882 individual fire incidents. More than seventy war-industry factories suffered a complete or partial loss of production, eight ships were either sunk or damaged in the inland port, while 140,000 people were bombed out of their homes and 1,292 lost their lives. Had it not been for an errant Oboe marker attracting a proportion of the bombing onto open country some fourteen miles to the north-east, the destruction would have been greater.

Bochum was posted to face its second heavy visitation of the campaign on the 12th, and a force of 503 aircraft was made ready for the purpose, 8 Group contributing eleven Mosquitos, a dozen Halifaxes and forty-three Lancasters, six of the Halifaxes representing 405 (Vancouver) Squadron. Crews learned at briefing that two Mosquitos were to drop yellow preliminary warning TIs, before joining seven others to mark the aiming-point with red TIs, which twenty-five Lancasters would back up with greens. That would leave eighteen Lancasters and all of the Halifaxes to bomb with the main force, for which each of the 405 (Vancouver) Squadron aircraft had been loaded with one 2,000 pounder, three 1,000 pounders and ten SBCs of 30lb incendiaries before departing Gransden Lodge between 22.55 and 23.00 with F/L Lawson the senior pilot on duty. They set a course that would take them over central Holland to enter Germany to the west of Münster, before turning south for a direct run on Bochum, situated between Essen to the west and Dortmund to the east. It is believed that night-fighters were waiting over Dutch airspace and the frontier region, and a number of bombers fell victim at this stage of the operation. According to Bomber Command War Diaries, by Martin Middlebrook and Chris Everitt, Bochum was completely covered by ten-

tenths cloud, but, according to many 5 Group crew reports, they encountered three to six-tenths patchy cloud, and many described almost clear skies and good visibility. It was not unusual for opinions on cloud conditions to range from zero to complete cover and depended largely on time of arrival. The 405 (Vancouver) Squadron crews reported between four and eight-tenths stratocumulus over the city with tops at 10,000 feet and clear skies all around and good visibility, while those in the spearhead were greeted by clear skies but a threat of cloud drifting across during the course of the raid. The 405 (Vancouver) Squadron crews bombed on red and green TIs from 18,000 to 19,500 feet between 01.25 and 01.38 and at debriefing reported concentrated fires, the glow from which was visible for up to a hundred miles into the return flight. Photo-reconnaissance revealed 130 acres of devastation, backed up by local reports that 449 buildings had been destroyed and more than nine hundred severely damaged at a cost to the Command of twenty-four aircraft, at least nine of which had fallen victim to night-fighters.

Following a night's rest, the Ruhr offensive continued at Oberhausen, a major centre of oil production situated between Duisburg to the west and Essen to the east. An all-Lancaster heavy force numbering 197 aircraft was made ready, along with six Oboe Mosquitos to provide the skymarking. The raid was carried out in the face of intense heavy flak, which continued to chase the bombers out of the target area into the guns of night-fighters, and between them, they accounted for seventeen Lancasters, 8.4% of the force. Returning crews were confident that a successful blow had been delivered, and this was confirmed by local sources, which reported that the Wanganui flares had been right over the city centre, where 267 buildings had been destroyed and 584 seriously damaged.

During the late afternoon of the 16th, and while engaged in a routine cross-country exercise in HR832, F/L Lawson and his crew encountered a violent electrical storm over Norfolk and following a lightning strike, the Halifax began to break up, before plunging into fenland two miles west of King's Lynn at 19.05. The sole survivor of the impact was the American mid-upper gunner, Sgt Pudney RCAF, who despite injuries which were to prove fatal, pulled his colleagues from the wreckage and walked two miles to get help. (Bomber Command Losses. Vol 4. W.R.Chorley.)

Earlier in the day, 1, 5 and 8 Group stations had been notified that Cologne was to be the target for that night, for which a force of 202 Lancasters and ten Halifaxes was made ready. They learned at briefings that there would be no Oboe Mosquitos on hand to mark the target, as that role was to be undertaken by ten 35 (Madras Presidency) Squadron Halifaxes and six 83 Squadron Lancasters employing H2S. They were also to drop green preliminary warning flares on track, before delivering red flares with green stars and white flares over the aiming-point along with green TI ground markers for the main force element that included the remaining forty-two 8 Group Lancasters. Returning crews confirmed that a proportion of the bombing appeared to have been concentrated where intended, but that a large part had been lured away by dummy markers. This was backed up by local reports, which suggested that only around a hundred aircraft had been involved in the attack. Residential districts bore the brunt of the raid, and 401 houses were destroyed, with 13,000 others sustaining damage to some extent, mostly lightly, while sixteen industrial premises and nine railway stations were hit, along with public and utility buildings.

A second training crash occurred at dawn on the 18th, when HR808 landed at Gransden Lodge with jammed rudder controls and was written off after swinging off the runway, fortunately without injury to P/O Smith and his crew.

Back in October, 5 Group had launched an audacious daylight attack on the Schneider armaments factory at Le Creusot in east-central France, and the Henri Paul transformer station at Montchanin, situated five miles to the south-east that provided its power. Schneider was the French "Krupp" and was the family that sponsored the interwar bi-annual speed competition for float planes from Britain, France, Italy and the USA for which the Schneider Trophy was the glittering prize. Britain won it outright with the Supermarine S6B in 1931 after successive victories in 1927 and 1929. Despite the confidence of returning 5 Group crews, and the leadership of W/C Guy Gibson at the latter, neither target had been dealt with effectively, and it was decided to try again on the night of the 19/20th, for which a force of 290 aircraft, consisting of 181 Halifaxes, 107 Stirlings and two Lancasters, was drawn from 3, 4, 6 and 8 Groups. The Lancasters were the first to be operated by 7 Squadron, which was in the process of converting from Stirlings under a plan to make the Path Finders an all-Lancaster/Mosquito group. The Halifaxes of 405 (Vancouver) Squadron would be phased out in August, but it would be March 1944 before 35 (Madras Presidency) Squadron followed suit.

The plan called for fourteen Stirlings and ten Halifaxes to drop green flares and yellow TIs as route markers by H2S, and for four Stirlings and two Lancasters to illuminate the aiming-point blindly with long sticks of flares. These and the remaining illuminators would keep the aiming-point highlighted, while the main force, including eight Stirlings and fifteen Halifaxes, went about their business, before flying on to Montchanin to repeat the process with twenty-six 8 Group Lancasters acting as the main force. 405 (Vancouver) Squadron loaded nine Halifaxes with fourteen 500 pounders and two with six 1,000-pounders and nine bundles of four white flares, before sending them on their way from Gransden Lodge between 22.30 and 22.40 with W/C Fauquier the senior pilot on duty. Time-on-target was scheduled for 01.45, and there were no early returns among the Gransden Lodge element during the 450-mile outward flight. On arrival in the target area, the weather conditions were found to be excellent, enabling the crews to identify landmarks, such as nearby lakes, with ease. There was no opposition, which was fortunate, as crews would have to make up to five passes over the aiming-points, not counting dummy runs, depending upon their respective roles. The 405 (Vancouver) Squadron crews carried out their briefs from between 6,000 and 8,500 feet between 01.48 and 01.59 and all returned safely to make their reports. Fires and blue electrical flashes were observed, and the consensus was of a successful operation, and although bombing photos would reveal the attack to have fallen within three miles of the aiming-point, very few bombs had hit the target. It was established later, that the Breuil steelworks had been mistaken for the intended target and had attracted most of the bombs, while the transformer station had escaped damage altogether. The problem was partly that main force crews had been trained to aim at TIs from medium to high level and were unused to identifying targets visually from medium to low level.

A hectic round of four major operations to the Ruhr in the space of five nights began with the notification of Krefeld as the target on the 21st, for which a force of 705 aircraft was assembled. At briefings, the 8 Group crews were told that ten Mosquitos would ground mark the aiming-point with red TIs, and if they proved not to be not visible, nine Stirlings, thirteen Halifaxes and eight

Lancasters were to ground mark with yellow TIs by H2S. Twenty-five Lancasters, six Stirlings and six Halifaxes were to back up the reds with green TIs, leaving thirteen Lancasters, thirteen Halifaxes and five Stirlings to bomb with the main force. 405 (Vancouver) Squadron loaded eight of its Halifaxes with three 1,000-pounders and a dozen SBCs of 30lb incendiaries each to deliver as part of the main force, while five backers-up had three 1,000 and seven 500-pounders and green TIs and one had three 1,000 and eight 500 pounders and yellow TIs. They departed Gransden Lodge between 23.29 and 23.43 with W/C Fauquier and S/L Wolfe the senior pilots on duty and all reached the target, situated a short distance to the south-west of Duisburg, but on the western side of the Rhine. Conditions in the target area were ideal, with small amounts of thin cloud between 6,000 and 10,000 feet and bright moonlight, which would preclude the need for the yellow TIs. The 405 (Vancouver) Squadron crews performed their assigned roles from 17,000 to 20,100 feet between 01.40 and 02.10 and all but one returned to attend debriefing. Absent was the all-RCAF crew of F/L Murrell RCAF DFC, who all lost their lives when JD124 went down near Mönchengladbach.

Returning crews described a sea of red fire giving off masses of smoke, with one particular jet-black column of smoke rising through 18,000 feet as they turned away. All were convinced of the success of the operation, and one crew likened it to the Wuppertal-Barmen raid. There was no hint of troublesome flak or night-fighters, and yet, forty-four aircraft failed to return, the heaviest casualties of the campaign to date, and many of these were lost to the Nachtjagd. 35 (Madras Presidency) Squadron, the only other Path Finder unit equipped with Halifaxes, posted missing six crews on a disastrous night for Graveley. A post-raid analysis would conclude that the Path Finders had delivered a near-perfect marking performance, delivering red TIs in concentrated fashion to clearly identify the city centre aiming-point for the main force element. Three-quarters of the bombing photos were plotted within three miles of the aiming-point, where 2,306 tons of bombs wiped out by fire an estimated 47% of the built-up area, destroying 5,517 houses, the largest number to date at a single target, while more than a thousand people lost their lives.

The medium-sized town of Mülheim-an-der-Ruhr, a close neighbour of Duisburg, Oberhausen and Essen, lies around a dozen miles to the north-east of Krefeld, and it was here that the red ribbon terminated on the target maps at briefings across the Command on the 22nd. A force of 557 aircraft was prepared, along with a plan that called for eight Oboe Mosquitos plus two in reserve to drop yellow preliminary warning TIs on track, before marking the aiming-point with red TIs for twenty-nine Path Finder Lancasters to back up with greens. Twelve further Lancasters, five Stirlings and seven Halifaxes were to bomb with the main force, and when the attack was over, two Mosquito crews would bomb as a training exercise. 405 (Vancouver) Squadron was called upon to provide just five Halifaxes, which each received a bomb load of three 1,000-pounders and a dozen SBCs of 4lb incendiaries before departing Gransden Lodge between 23.19 and 23.23 with no senior pilot on duty. The aiming point was marked out under clear skies by red TIs, upon which the payloads were delivered from 17,500 and 19,500 feet between 01.32 and 01.51, by which time the town had already become an inferno. Returning crews reported the glow to be visible from the Dutch coast homebound and commented on the intense searchlight and flak response, the number of night-fighters, and the fact that Krefeld was still burning from the night before. Local reports confirmed that the town had suffered severe damage, particularly in the northern districts, where 1,135 houses had been destroyed and more than 12,000 others damaged to some extent. A post-war British bombing survey would estimate that 64% of the built-up area had been wiped out in this single raid. The road and telephone communications to Oberhausen had been cut, preventing any passage out of the town other than on foot. In fact, some of the bombing had spilled into the eastern districts of Oberhausen, which was linked to Mülheim for air-raid purposes. It was another expensive night for the Command, however, which registered the loss of thirty-five aircraft, with the Halifaxes and Stirlings representing two-thirds of them and suffering a respective loss rate of 7.7% and 11.8%.

Having destroyed the Barmen half of Wuppertal at the end of May in one of the most devastating attacks to date, it was time to visit the same catastrophe on the western half, Elberfeld, for which a force of 630 aircraft was made ready on the 24th. On this occasion, six Lancasters, three Stirlings and three Halifaxes were to deliver the yellow route markers on H2S, while seven Oboe Mosquitos, with two in reserve, marked the aiming-point with red TIs. Eighteen Lancasters, seven Halifaxes and three Stirlings were to back these up with green TIs, leaving fifteen Lancasters, seven Halifaxes and five Stirlings to bomb with the main force. The six Halifaxes at Gransden Lodge assigned to the backing-up role each received a load of six 1,000-pounders and green TIs, while the five main force supporters had three 1,000-pounders and a dozen SBCs of 4lb incendiaries in their bomb bays before taking off between 22.43 and 22.53 with S/L Wolfe the senior pilot on duty. They ran the usual gauntlet of searchlights and flak from the Cologne and Düsseldorf defence zones, the crews of which were aided by the formation of condensation trails at between 18,000 and 21,000 feet to advertise the presence of the bomber stream. There seemed to be fewer guns firing at them over the target, where small amounts of cloud with tops at 17,000 feet were insufficient to obscure the ground. The 405 (Vancouver) Squadron crews carried out their respective tasks from 15,600 to 20,000 feet between 01.03 and 01.27, those arriving at the tail end of the attack, when the built-up area was well-alight, describing thick columns of smoke already passing through 19,000 feet and the glow of fires visible from the Dutch coast.

Post-raid reconnaissance revealed another massively concentrated and accurate attack, which had reduced to rubble an estimated 90% of Elberfeld's built-up area, including three thousand houses and 171 industrial premises. It had also severely damaged 2,500 houses and dozens of important factory buildings, and the fact that more buildings were destroyed than damaged, provided a telling commentary on the conditions on the ground. The number of fatalities stood at around eighteen hundred, and some of the survivors might have been cheered to know that thirty-four bombers, containing 240 of their tormentors, would not be returning to England that night. Among them was the mixed RAF/RCAF crew of Sgt Andrews in HR816, which was sent crashing to earth by a night-fighter in the general target area, with fatal consequences for the Canadian flight engineer and rear gunner, who may have been killed during the engagement. The others escaped by parachute and fell into enemy hands to spend the rest of the war as unwilling guests of the Reich.

The German synthetic oil industry relied on two main production methods, the Bergius process, which involved the hydrogenation of highly volatile bituminous coal to manufacture high-grade petroleum products like aviation fuel, and the Fischer-Tropsch process, which produced lower-grade diesel-type fuels for vehicle, Tank, U-Boot and shipping requirements. Instructions were received across the Command, but not at Gransden Lodge, on the 25th to prepare for the first major attack on the Ruhr city of Gelsenkirchen since 1941, when it had been a regular destination under the Oil Directive. A force of 473 aircraft was assembled, and the crews briefed to focus on the Nordstern synthetic oil plant (Gelsenberg A.G.), which was a Bergius-process manufacturer particularly of aviation fuel. 8 Group was to provide seven Oboe Mosquitos plus two in reserve to drop route markers and skymark the aiming-point, and two to bomb after the main force, but none of its heavy aircraft was to be involved. Ten-tenths stratus lay over the eastern Ruhr with tops at 10,000 to 15,000 feet, which would not have been a problem for Oboe, had five of the Oboe Mosquitos not suffered equipment failures. This caused tracking flares to be late and to drop in the wrong order in a somewhat scattered manner, at a time when the crews were contending with an intense flak barrage. Searchlights illuminated the cloud as the bombing took place on red flares with green stars, and returning crews reported a large explosion at 01.43, and the glow from the target to be visible from the Dutch coast. They had been chased to the sea by a large deployment of enemy night-fighters, which, together with flak, would bring down thirty bombers. Post-raid reconnaissance and local reports confirmed that the operation had failed to achieve accuracy and concentration, and, in an echo of the past, had sprayed bombs all over the Ruhr, leaving Gelsenkirchen largely untouched.

On the 27th a message was received at Gransden Lodge confirming the award of a DFC to S/L Logan and P/O Jennings, who had been posted missing from Stuttgart in March but had evaded capture to return to the UK on the 20th of April and were currently enjoying leave in Canada.

A series of three operations against Cologne spanning the turn of the month began on the 28th, for which a force of 608 aircraft was assembled. At briefings, crews took in the details, which, for those of 8 Group involved nine plus two Mosquitos dropping green flares as route markers sixteen miles short of the target, and then red TIs and red flares with green stars on the aiming-point. Four Stirlings, ten Halifaxes and eighteen Lancasters were to back up with green TIs, leaving four Stirlings, eight Halifaxes and seventeen Lancasters to bomb with the main force. 405 (Vancouver) Squadron briefed a dozen crews, while out on the dispersals seven backer-up Halifaxes were being loaded with a 2,000-pounder, nine 500-pounders and green TIs and five others with a 2,000-pounder and thirteen SBCs of 4lb incendiaries to drop as part of the main force. They departed Gransden Lodge between 23.04 and 23.15 with S/L Wolfe the senior pilot on duty, and all reached the target area, where they encountered ten-tenths cloud below them at 8,000 to 10,000 feet, with good visibility above. They carried out their assigned tasks from 18,000 to 21,000 feet between 01.53 and 02.11 with skymarkers in their sights to aim at, unaware that five of the Oboe Mosquitos had turned back and a sixth was unable to drop its skymarkers. This left just three Oboe Mosquitos to carry out the marking and they were behind schedule by seven minutes and could manage only intermittent flares, as a result which, the omens for a successful attack were not good, particularly as skymarking was the least reliable method because of drift. Returning crews reported the glow of fires beneath the cloud and the presence of smoke rising through them, but in view of the sparse marking, were pessimistic about the likely outcome.

Despite all of the unfavourable elements of thick cloud and sparse and late marking, this proved to be the most devastating raid yet visited upon the Rhineland capital. Post-raid reconnaissance and local reports provided details of forty-three industrial buildings and 6,374 others completely destroyed, and a further fifteen thousand sustaining damage to some extent, which dwarfed the destruction achieved in the highly successful first thousand bomber raid of thirteen months earlier. The death toll was put at 4,377, the greatest by far from a Bomber Command attack, and 230,000 others had lost their homes for varying periods. By recent standards, the figure of twenty-five missing aircraft could be considered moderate, although that was no consolation to the squadrons and stations affected.

During the course of the month, the squadron operated on seven occasions and dispatched seventy-one sorties for the loss of five Halifaxes and four crews.

July 1943

The first two days of the new month were beset by poor weather conditions, which kept all but a few miners and Mosquitos on the ground. The second attack of the current campaign against Cologne was scheduled for the night of the 3/4th, and crews were called to briefings on all operational stations during the late afternoon as a force of 653 aircraft was assembled. The Path Finder crews listened with interest as they were told that ten Mosquitos would drop green flares four-and-a-half miles from the target as a preliminary warning, and red, green and white flares and red TIs on the aiming-point. On this night, the aiming-point was on the East Bank of the Rhine in the industrial Deutz district, where the Klöckner-Humboldt-Deutz works manufactured aero-engines and heavy and tracked vehicles for the Wehrmacht and was served by the nearby Kalk and Gremberg marshalling yards. Nine Halifaxes and twenty-four Lancasters were to back up the red TIs with greens, but in the event that cloud concealed the TIs, they were to bomb on H2S with the main force, along with the remaining nine Halifaxes and seventeen Lancasters. 405 (Vancouver) Squadron made ready eleven Halifaxes, seven to carry three 1,000 and eight 500-pounders plus green TIs, and four loaded with three 1,000-pounders and a dozen SBCs of 30lb incendiaries. They departed Gransden Lodge between 22.45 and 22.55 with no pilots above flying officer rank on duty and headed for the Essex coast to begin the North Sea crossing to the Scheldt estuary.

The meteorological briefing led to an expectation of nine-tenths cloud from the English coast all the way to the target, but what the Path Finder crews in the vanguard encountered was a clear, starlit sky and red Oboe-laid TIs in the bomb sights, which they backed up with greens. There was a certain amount of haze, but this did not interfere with the accuracy of the attack, which developed in concentrated form in the face, initially, of an intense flak defence. Sgt Phillips and crew had been set upon by a single-engine fighter when fifteen miles south-west of the target, and their Halifax sustained severe damage to the tailplance and fuselage, despite which they pressed on, only to find that diminished hydraulics pressure prevented the bomb doors from opening. They would manage to dump the load during the tense and difficult flight home. The remaining 405 (Vancouver) Squadron crews carried out their assigned tasks from 18,100 to 22,000 feet between 01.32 and 01.45 and by the time the raid reached its crescendo, nine-tenths smoke rather than cloud hung over the city. Returning crews described a highly successful raid, which left the city a mass of flames, with smoke rising to 10,000 feet and blotting out ground detail. Some noticed a tendency to creep-back, but the overall impression was of another operation more successful than the Thousand raid against this city at the end of May 1942. Post-raid reconnaissance and local reports confirmed another stunningly accurate and concentrated attack, in which twenty industrial premises and 2,200 houses had been destroyed, and 72,000 people bombed out of their homes at a cost to the Command of thirty aircraft. Among the missing Halifaxes was 405 (Vancouver) Squadron's HR813, which came down near Wavre in Belgium, which suggests that P/O Smith DFC RCAF and his all-RCAF crew were outbound at the time. The rear gunner failed to survive, while the rest of the crew soon found themselves in enemy hands.

Some crews commented on the presence of day fighters over the target, and this was clear evidence of a new tactic being employed by the Luftwaffe. The newly formed JG300 was operating for the first time, employing the Wilde Sau (Wild Boar) tactics, which was the brainchild of former bomber pilot, Major Hans-Joachim (Hajo) Herrmann. The unit had been formed in June with borrowed standard BF109 and FW190 single-engine day fighters to operate directly over a target, seeking out bombers silhouetted against the fires and TIs. On this night, the unit would claim twelve victories, but would have to share them with the flak batteries, which claimed them also. Unaccustomed to being pursued by fighters over a target, it would take time for the bomber crews to work out what was happening, and until they did, friendly fire would often be blamed for damage incurred by unseen causes.

The series against Cologne was brought to an end on the 8th by an all-Lancaster heavy force of 282 aircraft drawn from 1, 5 and 8 Groups, with six Oboe Mosquitos to carry out the initial marking. The city was found to be concealed beneath ten-tenths cloud in two layers, with tops at 8,000 and 20,000 feet, but the Oboe Mosquitos, despite being late in opening the attack, delivered accurate skymarkers for the backers-up and main force element to aim at. The operation was another outstanding success, which hit mainly northern and south-western districts, and destroyed 2,381 domestic buildings and nineteen of an industrial nature. When the dust had settled sufficiently for the local authorities to assess the three-raid series, they reported that it had killed around 5,500 people, rendered a further 350,000 homeless, and destroyed eleven thousand buildings. The cost to the Command was sixty-two aircraft and crews.

The Ruhr campaign was winding down by the time that Gelsenkirchen was posted across Lancaster and Halifax stations on the 9th as the target for that night, for which a heavy force of 408 aircraft was made ready. At briefings, the crews learned of the plan, which required seven Oboe Mosquitos to drop red flares twenty miles short of the target and green flares nine miles further on, before marking the aiming-point with white flares and reds with green stars. The remaining twelve Path Finder Halifaxes and nine Lancasters were to bomb with the main force, leaving four Mosquitos to bomb when the raid was over. The 405 (Vancouver) Squadron crews of F/Os Lefroy and St Louis and P/Os Jensen and Tomczak departed Gransden Lodge between 22.40 and 22.43 with two 1,000-pounders and a dozen SBCs of 30lb incendiaries beneath their feet and made their way to the target above ten-tenths cloud, which stretched over the Ruhr at around 16,000 feet and topped out in places at 20,000 feet. The Oboe skymarkers were several minutes late, partly as a result of a 50% failure rate of the Oboe equipment, while a sixth Mosquito dropped its markers ten miles to the north. The 405 (Vancouver) Squadron crews delivered their attacks from 17,000 to 21,500 feet between 01.24 and 01.28, but in the case of the St Louis crew it was more of a "live" jettisoning. A number of flak detonations rocked the Halifax during the bombing run, and after reporting flares ahead at 01.23, the bomb-aimer, P/O Law RCAF, failed to respond to a call from the navigator a minute later. On investigation he was found lifeless with a head wound caused by flak splinters that had penetrated the nose cone. Large explosions were witnessed at 01.22, 01.38 and 01.41, the last one lighting up the sky like day for ten seconds. A red glow beneath the cloud suggested that an extensive fire was developing, but returning crews could offer only impressions at debriefing, and none was certain as to the outcome. According to local reports, it had appeared that the attack had been meant for Bochum and Wattenscheid, which received more bombs than Gelsenkirchen, where limited damage occurred in southern districts.

Although two more operations to the region would be launched late in the month, Harris was already planning his next attempt to shorten the war by bombing alone and was buoyed by the success of the spring offensive. He could look back on the past four and a half months with genuine satisfaction at the performance of his squadrons, and as a champion of technological innovation, take particular pride in the performance of Oboe, which had been the decisive factor. Although losses had been grievously high, and the Ruhr's reputation as "Happy Valley" well earned, its most important towns and cities had suffered catastrophic destruction. In Britain, the aircraft factories had more than kept pace with the rate of attrition, while the training units both at home and overseas were pouring eager new crews into the fray to fill the gaps. With confidence high in the ability of his Command to destroy almost any target at will, Harris prepared for his next major campaign, the erasure from the map of a prominent German city in a short, sharp series of maximum effort raids to be launched during the final week of the month.

In the meantime, 1, 5 and 8 Groups were alerted to prepare for a trip to Italy to attack the city of Turin, for which 295 Lancasters were made ready on the 12th. Despite poor weather conditions over France, which included icing, the crews were greeted at the target by clear skies and good visibility, and defences up to their usual poor standard, characterised by ineffective searchlights and inaccurate light flak rising to 15,000 feet. The marking was punctual, accurate and concentrated, inviting the main force crews to exploit the opportunity, and a column of black smoke was observed rising through 12,000 feet as they withdrew. The return route involved a low-level circumnavigation of the Brest peninsular, and many of the thirteen missing Lancasters disappeared without trace into the sea after running into enemy night-fighters in this area. Reconnaissance showed the main weight of the attack to have fallen just north of the city centre, and a local report stated that 792 people had lost their lives, the largest number of fatalities from a Bomber Command attack on Italy.

Aachen, Germany's most westerly city and an important railway hub between Germany and the occupied countries, was posted as the target on the 13th and a force of 374 aircraft made ready, which consisted largely of Halifaxes, Wellingtons and Stirlings, with just eighteen Lancasters among the 8 Group contribution. Ten Halifaxes were to drop yellow TIs as route markers, and six Oboe Mosquitos ground mark the aiming-point with red TIs, backed up with green TIs by nineteen Halifaxes. Eleven Halifaxes, six Stirlings and a single Lancaster were to bomb with the main force, which included participants from all but 5 Group. The nine 405 (Vancouver) Squadron backer-up Halifaxes each received a load of one 2,000-pounder, four 1,000-pounders and green TIs, while the three main force supporters had the usual 3 x 1,000-pounder and twelve SBC mix in their bomb bays. They departed Gransden Lodge between 23.15 and 23.26 with S/L Wolfe the senior pilot on duty and lost the services of F/O Lefroy and crew to starboard-outer engine failure within ninety minutes. The others pressed on across Holland and Belgium to find seven to nine-tenths cloud lying predominantly over the eastern half of the city with tops at around 9,000 feet. A strong tail wind had driven the main force crews to the target ahead of schedule, and, as soon as the red TIs went down, so did much of the bombing, giving rise to a sudden proliferation of fires. The 405 (Vancouver) Squadron crews carried out their respective tasks from 18,500 to 20,300 feet between 01.45 and 02.07 and observed what appeared to be a concentrated raid until cloud slid across the area to obscure ground detail. Twenty aircraft failed to return, fifteen of them Halifaxes, and among them was HR905, which was shot down by a night-fighter and fell in pieces some six miles south-east of Helmond in southern Holland. S/L Wolfe DFC was a Canadian who had joined the RAF before the war, and his crew, which on this night included a RNZAF second pilot, contained two other holders of the DFC and two of the DFM. The second pilot and mid-upper gunner were the only survivors, and they were taken into captivity. It was left to local sources to confirm the severity of the damage left behind in Aachen, which amounted to 2,927 buildings completely destroyed, with many industrial, public and cultural buildings seriously damaged.

The tannoys called the faithful to prayer on the afternoon of the 15th, where they learned of that night's operation involving a force of 165 Halifaxes from 4 and 8 Groups directed at the Peugeot motor works in the Montbeliard suburb of Sochaux, situated near France's border with Switzerland. At some 450 miles distance as the crow flies from the 8 Group stations, the target was well beyond the range of Oboe, and it would be up to nine Halifax crews to employ H2S to mark and illuminate the target area with yellow TIs and a stick of white flares. Six Halifaxes were then to drop red TIs onto the aiming-point if it could be positively identified, leaving eight Halifaxes to back up with green TIs and nine to bomb with the main force. 405 (Vancouver) Squadron loaded each of twelve Halifaxes with three 1,000-pounders and between two and five 500-pounders, dependent upon their role, in addition to which four had green TIs, three had yellows and white flares and two had reds and yellows in their bomb bays. They departed Gransden Lodge between 22.05 and 22.35 with W/C Fauquier the senior pilot on duty and S/L Lambert, a bomb-aimer and B Flight commander, flying as usual with F/L Foy. They made landfall on the Normandy coast for the flight across France and according to the 4 Group ORB, a Path Finder aircraft crashed and caused some TIs to ignite near the town of Besançon, some thirty-five miles south-west of the target, and a number of bombing photos were apparently plotted at this location.

Whatever this was, the majority of crews ignored the distraction and pushed on to the intended target, where the visibility was found to be excellent under bright moonlight, which enabled the factory to be identified visually and by the red and green TIs. Zero hour was set for 01.50, and the 405 (Vancouver) Squadron crews presented themselves over the target to carry out their respective roles from 5,000 to 8,000 feet between 01.50 and 02.10. The impression was of a successful attack, and there was confidence that the factory buildings had been hit, but a thick pall of smoke obliterated ground detail towards the end of proceedings, and it would be left to bombing and reconnaissance photos to provide the evidence. These showed that the main marking effort had fallen seven hundred yards to the east of the factory, which sustained only minor damage, and the bombing had hit the town, where 123 civilians were killed. The only Path Finder aircraft to be lost was 405 (Vancouver) Squadron's HR854, which was shot down by a night-fighter while homebound over France and crashed at around 02.25 near Tonnerre. F/L Foy DFC RCAF and his crew all survived, and with the exception of the rear gunner, evaded capture. F/O Sattler and crew landed at Middle Wallop in a badly shot-up Halifax courtesy of a Dornier 217, at which, despite sustaining four separate wounds to his left arm, the mid-upper gunner continued to fire and had the satisfaction of observing the assailant to impact the ground.

Hamburg had been a regular target for the Command throughout the war to date, and had been attacked, amongst other occasions, during the final week of July in 1940, 1941 and 1942. It had been spared by the weather from hosting the first "One Thousand" bomber raid at the end of May 1942, but Harris now identified it as the ideal candidate for destruction under Operation Gomorrah, the intention of which was to cause the maximum impact to the enemy's morale in a short, sharp campaign, employing ten thousand tons of bombs. Hamburg's political status was second only to

Berlin's, and its value to the war effort in terms of ship and U-Boot construction and other war production was undeniable, but it suited Harris's criteria also in other respects. Its location close to a coastline aided navigation and made it accessible from the North Sea without the need to spend time over hostile territory, and its relatively short distance from the bomber stations enabled a force to approach and retreat during the few hours of darkness afforded by mid-summer. Finally, lying beyond the range of Oboe, which had proved so decisive at the Ruhr, Hamburg had the wide River Elbe to provide a solid H2S signature for the navigators high above.

There had been no operations for most squadrons for nine days, despite a number being posted, and by the time that 791 crews trooped into their respective briefing rooms on the 24th, they probably expected the day to end with yet another scrub. Instead, they were read a special message from the commander-in-chief, to announce the beginning of the Battle of Hamburg. They listened intently to the revelation that they would be aided by the first operational use of "window", tinfoil-backed strips of paper of precise length, which, when released in bundles into the airstream at a predetermined point, would drift down slowly in vast clouds to swamp the enemy night-fighter, searchlight and gun-laying radar with false returns and render it blind. The device had actually been available for a year, but its use had been vetoed in case the enemy copied it for use against Britain. It was not realized that Germany had, in fact, already developed its own version called Düppel, which it had withheld for the same reason.

The plan of attack called for eleven Lancasters and nine Halifaxes to drop yellow TIs as route markers, before continuing on to mark the aiming-point with yellow TIs, and if conditions permitted, illuminator flares. The route markers were to be backed up by six Stirlings, thirteen Lancasters and nine Halifaxes, and six Lancasters and two Halifaxes were to use the yellow TIs as a guide, and with the aid of flares, mark the aiming-point with red TIs, which would be backed up with green TIs by the remaining marker crews. This would leave eighteen Lancasters, fourteen Halifaxes and three Stirlings to bomb with the main force. 405 (Vancouver) Squadron loaded fifteen Halifaxes with a variety of combinations of ordnance mostly involving four 1,000-pounders and TIs of various colours and illuminating flares and dispatched them from Gransden Lodge between 22.01 and 22.44 with W/C Fauquier the senior pilot on duty having recently lost both of his flight commanders. F/O McIntyre and crew lost their port-outer engine shortly after take-off and proceeded directly to the jettison area, leaving the others to set course to cross the North Sea, where, at the predetermined point, they began to dispense "window", beginning shortly after 00.30, and the effects appeared to be immediate as few fighters rose to meet the approaching bombers. A number of aircraft were shot down over the sea during the outward flight, two of them 103 Squadron Lancasters, but these were off course and outside of the protection of the bomber stream and may well have been among those returning early with technical difficulties. The efficacy of Window was made more apparent in the target area, where the crews noticed an absence of the usually efficient co-ordination between the searchlights and flak batteries, and defence appeared random and sporadic.

This offered the Path Finders the opportunity to mark the target by visual reference and H2S virtually unmolested, and although the red and green TIs were a little misplaced and scattered, they landed in sufficient numbers close to the city centre to provide the main force crews with ample opportunity to deliver a massive blow. It rarely happened that aircraft arrived in strict bands according to their task, and main force crews were among markers from the opening of the raid at

01.00. In fact, the first 405 (Vancouver) Squadron crew, that of W/C Fauquier, was on scene at 00.57, and the squadron maintained a presence right through until 01.37, carrying out their assigned tasks from 15,000 to 20,000 feet. P/O Cowan and crew picked up the target on H2S some ninety-seconds from bombing, but a flak hit before reaching the release point knocked out the electrical system and severely wounded the mid-upper gunner, leaving them with no option but to jettison the load, which they did twenty miles south-south-west of the target at 21.07. Sadly, Sgt McLellan RCAF would lose his fight for life on the 2nd of August. Returning crews reported a successful operation that had left part of the city ablaze with a column of smoke rising through 20,000 feet. Post-raid reconnaissance revealed that a six-mile-long creep-back had developed, which cut a swathe of destruction from the city centre along the line of approach, out across the north-western districts, and into open country, where a proportion of the bombing had been wasted. In fact, less than half of the force had bombed within three miles of the city centre during the fifty-minute-long raid, in which 2,284 tons of bombs had been delivered, despite which, the city had suffered a telling blow, and fifteen hundred of its inhabitants lay dead. For the Command it was an encouraging start to the campaign, particularly in the light of just twelve missing aircraft, for which "window" was largely responsible.

On the following night, and in the expectation that Hamburg would be covered by smoke, Harris switched his force to Essen, where he could take advantage of the body blow dealt to the enemy defensive system by "window". A force of 705 aircraft was made ready and a plan prepared, which called for Halifaxes and Lancasters of 35 (Madras Presidency) and 156 Squadrons to drop preliminary yellow warning TIs on track by H2S, which would be backed up by elements of 7 and 156 Squadron. Ahead, fourteen Oboe Mosquitos would mark the aiming-point with red TIs, which nineteen Lancasters, nine Halifaxes and five Stirlings would back up with greens, leaving the remaining Path Finder element to bomb with the main force. 405 (Vancouver) Squadron made ready eleven Halifaxes, three assigned to backing up duties and the rest to support the main force, and they departed Gransden Lodge between 21.45 and 21.55 with no senior pilot on duty and a variety of ordnance in each bomb bay. P/O Maddock and crew turned back from the southern tip of Terschelling when the port-inner engine failed, and F/O Tomzcak RCAF and his predominantly RCAF crew were also outbound when HR864 was shot down by a night-fighter to crash at Ten Boer, eight miles north-east of Groningen in northern Holland, thirty miles east of the Luftwaffe's "Wasps' Nest" fighter aerodrome at Leeuwarden. Quite why they had strayed so far north is a mystery, and all but the bomb-aimer, who was captured, took the answer to the grave.

The others arrived in the target area to find four to five-tenths cloud to the west, but clear skies over the aiming-point, with just the usual ground haze to spoil the vertical visibility. Before having the opportunity to bomb, F/O Sattler and crew found themselves coned by searchlights and under attack from flak, which punctured the aircraft's skin and set the starboard-inner engine on fire, leaving them with no option but to jettison the load "live" and head for home. Their squadron colleagues carried out their respective briefs from 18,000 to 20,500 feet between 00.31 and 01.00, and watched a highly concentrated attack develop, which left the ground enveloped in smoke from the many fires and explosions. Returning crews reported concentrated fires around the aiming-point in a one-and-a-half-square-mile area of the city, two large, red explosions at 00.36 and 00.39, and a column of smoke rising through 20,000 feet as they withdrew to the west, the glow remaining visible as far away as the Dutch coast. Twenty-six aircraft failed to return, three of them Path Finders, in exchange for which post-raid reconnaissance confirmed the raid to have been another outstanding success against this important war materials producing city. More than 2,800 houses were destroyed, while the complex of Krupp manufacturing sites suffered its heaviest damage of the war to date.

After a night's rest, a force of 787 aircraft was assembled for round two of Operation Gomorrah, and the crews informed at briefing that yellow route markers would be dropped by H2S on the enemy coast and backed up, and that "Y" aircraft (blind markers) were to deliver red TIs and a stick of flares over the aiming-point, for visual markers to confirm and back up with green TIs. Eleven 405 (Vancouver) Squadron Halifaxes received a bomb load of a 1,000-pounder and six 500-pounders, seven to act as route markers and visual backers-up and four as route markers, and a further three were loaded with a dozen 500 pounders each to deliver as part of the main force. They departed Gransden Lodge between 21.49 and 22.29 with no senior pilots on duty and lost the services F/O Weiser and crew at the midpoint of the North Sea crossing because of port-inner engine and rear turret issues. The remainder pushed on towards Hansastadt Hamburg, crossing the Schleswig-Holstein coast well to the north, none of them having any concept of the events that were to follow their arrival.

A previously unknown and terrible phenomenon was about to present itself to the world and introduce a new word "firestorm" into the English language. A number of factors would conspire on this night to seal the fate of this great city and its hapless inhabitants in an orgy of destruction quite unprecedented in air warfare. An uncharacteristically hot and dry spell of weather had left the city a tinderbox, and the spark to ignite it came with the Path Finders' H2S-laid yellow and green TIs, which fell with almost total concentration some two miles to the east of the intended city-centre aiming-point, and into the densely populated working-class residential districts of Hamm, Hammerbrook and Borgfeld. To compound this, the main force, which had been drawn on to the target by yellow release-point flares, bombed with rare precision and almost no creep-back, and deposited much of its 2,300 tons of bombs into this relatively compact area. The 405 (Vancouver) Squadron crews performed their respective roles from 18,000 to 20,000 feet between 00.55 and 01.26 and observed many explosions and a sea of flames developing below. Those bombing towards the later stages of the raid observed a pall of smoke rising through 20,000 feet, and the glow of fires was reported to remain visible for up to two hundred miles into the return journey.

On the ground, individual fires began to join together to form one giant conflagration, which sucked in oxygen from surrounding areas at hurricane speeds to feed its voracious appetite. Trees were uprooted and flung bodily into the inferno, along with debris and people, and temperatures at the seat of the flames exceeded one thousand degrees Celcius. The defences were overwhelmed, and the fire service unable to pass through the rubble-strewn streets to gain access to the worst-affected areas. Even had they done so, they could not have entered the firestorm area, and, only after all of the combustible material had been consumed, did the flames subside. By this time, there was no-one alive to rescue, and an estimated forty thousand people died on this one night alone. A mass exodus from the city, which would ultimately exceed one million people, began on the following morning, and this undoubtedly saved many from the ravages of the next raid, which would come two nights later. Seventeen aircraft failed to return, reflecting the enemy's developing response to the advantage gained by the Command through "window". No gain was ever permanent, and the balance of power would continue to shift from one side to the other for the next year. For a change, it was the Lancaster brigade that sustained the highest numerical casualties on this night, accounting for eleven of the failures to return.

Bomber Command's heavy brigade stayed at home on the following night, while four Mosquitos carried out a nuisance raid on Hamburg, to ensure that the residents' sleep was disturbed. A force of 777 aircraft was put together to continue Hamburg's torment on the 29th, fourteen of the Halifaxes made ready at Gransden Lodge, while the crews attended briefing to learn of their part in the proceedings. Red TIs and flares were to be employed as route markers, before seventeen Lancasters and eight Halifaxes marked the aiming-point with yellow TIs by H2S to be backed up by thirty-four Lancasters, six Stirlings and nine Halifaxes with greens. Seven 405 (Vancouver) Squadron crews were assigned to backing-up duties and would be sitting on green TIs in addition to their single 1,000-pounder and six 500-pounders, while two others were to act as route markers and the remaining five would have a dozen 500-pounders beneath their feet as part of the main force. They took off between 21.49 and 22.31 again with crews captained by junior officers and NCOs and lost the services of F/O Sattler to Gee failure when some thirty-five miles off Sheringham and P/O Clinton and crew to port-outer engine failure further out over the North Sea. The plan on this moonless night with clear skies was to approach from due north to hit the northern and north-eastern districts, which, thus far, had escaped serious damage, but the Path Finders strayed two miles to the east of the intended track, and dropped their markers just to the south of the already devastated firestorm area. A four-mile creep-back rescued the situation for the Command, by spreading along the line of approach into the residential districts of Wandsbek and Barmbek, and parts of Uhlenhorst and Winterhude. The 405 (Vancouver) Squadron crews carried out their respective briefs from 18,000 to 19,700 feet between 00.38 and 01.17 and reported smoke rising through 17,000 feet and fires visible for two hundred miles into the return journey. It was another massive blow against this proud city, but, as the defenders began to recover from the effects of "window", so the bomber losses began to creep up, and twenty-eight aircraft failed to return home on this night.

Before the final round of Operation Gomorrah took place, the curtain on the Ruhr offensive was brought down finally with a raid on the town of Remscheid, situated on the southern edge of the region, about six miles south of Wuppertal, where the main industries were mechanical engineering and tool-making. Up until this point, only twenty-six people had lost their lives in this town as a result of stray bombs, but it was now to face a modest force of 273 aircraft consisting of roughly equal numbers of Lancasters, Halifaxes and Stirlings with six Oboe Mosquitos and three in reserve to mark out the aiming-point with red TIs. In the absence of 405 (Vancouver) Squadron, 35 (Madras Presidency) Squadron provided the five Halifaxes supporting eight Lancasters in backing up with green TIs, to leave five Lancasters to bomb with the 1, 3, 4 and 6 Group main force. They found clear skies and good visibility and observed many bomb bursts and smoke rising through 5,000 feet as they turned away. A red glow in the sky behind them remained visible as they crossed the enemy coast homebound and gave promise of another Ruhr town left devastated. It would be a post-war bombing survey that established that a mere 871 tons of bombs had laid waste to around 83% of Remscheid's built-up area, destroying 107 industrial buildings and 3,117 houses. Three months war production was lost, and the town's industry never recovered fully. Fifteen aircraft failed to return, and the Stirling brigade suffered 10% casualties.

During the course of the month the squadron participated in eight operations and dispatched ninety-three sorties for the loss of three Halifaxes and crews and a bomb-aimer.

August 1943

Briefings for the final act of Operation Gomorrah took place on the 2nd, and a force of 740 aircraft was assembled, 114 of them provided by 8 Group. 405 (Vancouver) Squadron made ready sixteen Halifaxes, loading them with the appropriate hardware for their respective tasks, which meant that the three H2S blind markers would carry a long-delay-fused (LD) 1,000 pounder and six 500 pounders plus red TIs, the one visual marker a 1,000-pounder (LD) and seven 500 pounders with yellow TIs, four bundles of white flares and one of red with green stars, the four backers-up one 1,000 pounder (LD) and nine 500 pounders and green TIs, and finally, the eight attached to the main force a 1,000-pounder (LD) and ten 500-pounders. They departed Gransden Lodge between 22.54 and 23.29 with the recently posted-in F/L Dare the senior pilot on duty and headed for the coast to begin the North Sea crossing and rendezvous with the bomber stream. F/O St Louis and crew turned back early after losing an engine, while the bomber stream continued on, the spearhead coming into contact with a towering bank of ice-bearing cumulonimbus cloud some 120 miles out at 7° East. It was not an unusual feature of this regular route into north-western Germany, but it was a particularly imposing one, which could not be circumnavigated, and stretched upwards to 20,000 feet and beyond. Upon entering it, aircraft were thrown around by violent electrical storms, and it was a hugely terrifying experience beyond anything that most crews had ever experienced, with enormous flashes of lightning, thunder and electrical discharges that sent instruments haywire. The crews of P/Os Clinton, Gowan and Wood, F/Os McIntyre and Weiser and Sgt Nielsen abandoned their sorties, mostly over north-western Germany between Bremen and Hamburg, and the Wood crew turned their attention on what they believed was Bremervörde aerodrome as an alternative.

Those battling through the conditions to reach the target area found seven to ten-tenths cloud, and while some caught a glimpse of the Elbe and isolated yellow and green Path Finder flares, which might have been jettisoned rather than placed, the majority bombed on e.t.a., on the glow of fires beneath the cloud and the smoke rising through it without any idea of their precise location. Just six 405 (Vancouver) Squadron crews reached the target to carry out their assigned tasks from 15,000 to 19,300 feet between 01.59 and 02.19. No marking took place and bombs were spread over a hundred miles of the Schleswig-Holstein region, the town of Elmshorn, some fifteen miles to the north-west of Hamburg, seeming to attract the most attention, and 254 houses were destroyed. Returning crews were shaken by their experience and were unanimous in their conviction that the operation had been a total failure. The outcome was of little consequence in view of what had gone before, but the Command suffered the relatively heavy loss of thirty aircraft, some of them having fallen victim to the weather conditions. Three empty dispersal pans at Gransden Lodge told of a sad night for 405 (Vancouver) Squadron, which posted missing the crews of F/L Dare, Sgt Phillips DFM and Sgt Gregory. The first mentioned disappeared without trace into the sea in HR917, possibly having fallen victim to the Do217 of Hptm Schönert of II./NJG5 while on their first sortie since joining the squadron. The last mentioned were in HR849, which was brought down by flak over Bremen without survivors on what was the crew's fifth sortie. HR871 was badly damaged by flak and was abandoned over Swedish territory at 02.00, delivering the crew into a token period of internment, which in Sweden, was generally a pleasant experience. They were a mixed RCAF/RAF crew and had been on their twenty-first sortie and while they were absent, the London Gazette published details of Sgt Phillips's DFM, awarded to him for bringing home his badly damaged aircraft from Cologne in early July. Remarkably, fifteen of the missing men were RAF and only six RCAF. During the course of the four raids of Operation Gomorrah, the squadron dispatched fifty-nine sorties, forty-five of which bombed as briefed at a cost of three Halifaxes and crews. (The Battle of Hamburg. Martin Middlebrook).

There were no further operations during the first week of August, but something of future significance for 405 (Vancouver) Squadron took place in Canada on the 6th. This was the day selected for the naming ceremony of the very first Canadian built Lancaster, KB700. The occasion was turned into a massive media event with live coverage on the radio, and a commentary provided by the actor Lorne Greene. The minister for munitions and supply declared the Lancaster the "greatest weapon of destruction that Canada had produced during the war." The name, Ruhr Express, was bestowed upon the aircraft by Mrs C G Power, wife of the minister for National Defence for Air, and the impression was given by the general hype, that it would immediately take-off for England and war against tyranny. Ruhr Express did, indeed, take off, with S/L Reg Lane at the controls, he having returned to Canada at the completion of his second tour of operations and term as flight commander with 35 (Madras Presidency) Squadron. Far from flying to England, however, KB700 was barely able to fly anywhere. She was short of vital instruments and equipment, but in a country seeking to demonstrate its industrial prowess, and in view of the publicity, a postponement of the show was unthinkable. Lane flew the Lancaster to Dorval, Quebec, where the outfitting was completed, and he would indeed, in time, fly KB700 to England.

Italy was now teetering on the brink of capitulation, and Bomber Command was invited to help nudge it over the edge with a short offensive against its major cities. It began with elements of 1, 5 and 8 Groups making ready for all-Lancaster attacks on Genoa, Milan and Turin on the 7th, and with preparations already in hand for, perhaps, the most important operation of the war to date to be launched in ten days' time, the Turin raid was to be used to test the merits of employing a raid controller, or Master of Ceremonies, in the manner of W/C Gibson during Operation Chastise. The man selected for the job was Group Captain John Searby, currently serving as commanding officer of the Path Finders' 83 Squadron, and before that, Gibson's successor as commanding officer of 106 Squadron. 8 Group detailed forty-seven Lancasters from 7, 83 and 156 Squadrons, twenty-three for Milan and twenty-four for Turin, twenty-two of the latter then to continue on to Genoa. It is believed that all 197 aircraft reached their respective targets after flying out in excellent weather conditions, and although the Master Bomber experiment at Turin was not entirely successful, experience was gained which would prove useful for the forthcoming Operation Hydra.

With the squadron about to begin the process of converting to Lancasters, the flight engineers attended lectures on the 7th as the first of a series over the ensuing weeks to familiarise them with engines, fuel systems and everything else thay had know about their new charges. On the 8th, a Dance was held by the aircrew in a show of appreciation for the ground crews, the music provided by the RCAF Overseas Dance Orchestra.

Following a week's operational inactivity after Hamburg, nine 405 (Vancouver) Squadron crews were called to briefing on the 9th to learn of their part in a raid on Mannheim that night for which 8 Group was to provide fifty-four aircraft in an overall force of 457 drawn from all but 3 Group. Red TIs were to be released as route markers, before "Y" aircraft marked the aiming-point with red TIs and a string of flares, while the visual markers followed with yellows and the backers-up with greens. Four of the 405 (Vancouver) Squadron crews were assigned to blind marking duties, each with a load of four 1,000-pounders, red TIs and four bundles of white flares, three were designated as visual markers with five 1,000-pounders and yellow TIs and three to backing-up with ten 500-pounders and green TIs. They took off between 22.50 and 22.58 with F/L Gray the senior pilot on duty, and after climbing out, headed for the rendezvous point over Reading, before exiting England via Beachy Head on course for the French coast at Boulogne. They tracked along the Franco/Belgian frontier and were greeted at the target by a five-tenths layer of broken cloud at 4,000 feet and eight-tenths at 10,000 feet. Despite this, the visibility was fair, and the conditions were irrelevant as far as the H2S-equipped crews were concerned anyway, and those from 405 (Vancouver) Squadron performed their briefed tasks from 17,000 to 19,000 feet between 01.26 and 01.47, and all but one returned home to report a number of very large fires but a generally scattered raid. In fact, according to local reports, 1,316 buildings had been destroyed, forty-two industrial concerns had lost production, and more than fifteen hundred fires of varying sizes had required attention. Six Halifaxes and three Lancasters failed to return, and among the former was HR872 containing the crew of F/L Gray RCAF, which was shot down outbound by the night-fighter of Lt Norbert Pietrek of II./NJG4 and crashed at 01.00 at Awenne in Luxembourg, close to the Belgian frontier.

Nuremberg was posted as the target on the 10th, for which a force of 653 aircraft was assembled, 103 of them representing 8 Group. At briefing, the fourteen 405 (Vancouver) Squadron crews learned that two of them would act as blind markers, one as a visual marker and four as backers-up, while seven would bomb with the main force. They departed Gransden Lodge between 21.30 and 22.05 with W/C Fauquier and the newly posted-in S/L Schneider the senior pilots on duty, the commanding officer, in Lancaster JA920 to launch the squadron's new era. After climbing out and forming up with a 1,300-mile round-trip ahead of them, they set course for Beachy Head on the Sussex coast to follow a route similar to that of the previous night. There were no early returns, and all from the squadron arrived in the target area to find conditions that also reflected those of twenty-four hours earlier with eight to ten-tenths cloud at 12,000 feet. This would impact to an extent on the ground-marking plan, which called for illuminator flares and red TIs to be dropped by H2S on the aiming-point, to be confirmed by the visual markers with yellow TIs and backed up by greens.

The 405 (Vancouver) Squadron contingent carried out their assigned tasks from 16,000 to 19,000 feet between 00.50 and 01.22 and found that the TIs remained visible for a short period only because of the cloud, forcing those of the main force arriving later to bomb on the glow of TIs and fires coming through the cloud. Most were unable to provide details of their precise location in relation to the briefed aiming-point, and an air of pessimism attended some debriefings, while at others, crews reported a good concentration of fires, the glow from which remained visible for 150 miles into the return journey. Post-raid reconnaissance and local reports confirmed that the city had sustained much housing and industrial damage in mostly central and southern districts, and a death toll of 577 people was evidence of the intensity of the bombing. Sixteen aircraft were reported missing, but all returned safely to Gransden Lodge, where W/C Fauquier taxied JA920 into a ditch, causing damage beyond economical repair. One wonders how he explained that away to his aircrews and to the ground crew who had so proudly and diligently prepared the squadron's forst Lancaster for action.

During the course of the 12th, two forces were prepared for a return to Italy that night, one of 504 Lancasters and Halifaxes to attack Milan, which was home to many war factories, including the Isotta Fraschini luxury car works, which had been converted to military vehicle and aero engine manufacture, the Pirelli rubber works, Alfa Romeo, the Caproni aircraft plant, the Breda locomotive, armaments and aircraft works and the Innocenti machinery and vehicle factory. The second force was made up of 152 Stirlings, Halifaxes and Lancasters of 3 and 8 Groups to target the city of Turin situated some ninety miles to the south-west of Milan. 8 Group assigned sixty-seven aircraft to the former and forty to the latter, and it was for their part in the attack on Turin that fourteen 405 (Vancouver) Squadron crews listened intently at Gransden Lodge. Three of them were assigned to blind marking duties, two to visual marking, two to backing-up and seven to bombing with the main force, and they took off between 21.12 and 21.25 with W/C Fauquier and S/L Schneider the senior pilots on duty, the former presumably having to resort to his old Halifax "J". The route would take the bomber stream via Selsey Bill to Cabourg on the Normandy coast, and then south-east in a straight leg across central France to the northern tip of Lake Bourget, to cross the Alps and skirt southern Switzerland before the final run-in on the target. Again, there were no early returns and all arrived in the target area to encounter up to three-tenths thin, low cloud, through which ground features, like the bridges over the River Po, could be identified, aided by moonlight. The "Y" aircraft were to mark with red TIs and strings of illuminator flares, the visual markers with yellow TIs and the backers-up with greens, leaving the way clear for the 3 Group main force and 8 Group supporters to bomb, the latter with nine 500 pounders each. The 405 (Vancouver) Squadron crews carried out their respective tasks from 14,000 to 18,400 feet between 01.10 and 01.20, and observed fires beginning to spread across the city as they retreated back towards the Alps. Both operations were considered successful, but further attacks on Milan by all-Lancaster forces were carried out on the 14/15th and 15/16th, as intensive conversion training began for 405 (Vancouver) Squadron.

The final Bomber Command raid on Italy was to be a modest affair against Turin involving 117 aircraft of 3 Group and thirty-seven 8 Group Halifaxes, fifteen of the latter provided by 405 (Vancouver) Squadron. They departed Gransden Lodge between 20.07 and 20.21 with S/L Schneider the senior pilot on duty and flew out across France in favourable weather conditions, which were helpful also to the Luftwaffe Nachtjagd. A standard marking plan had been briefed out, with route markers over Lake Bourget and red, yellow and green TIs on the aiming-point, and clear skies under bright moonlight should have afforded ideal bombing conditions. In the event, thick haze up to 9,000 feet marred the vertical visibility as the 405 (Vancouver) Squadron participants carried out their respective tasks from 15,000 to 18,000 feet between 00.10 and 00.19 and were confident that they had hit the centre of the city. Only four aircraft failed to return, but among them was the squadron's HR856, which disappeared without trace with the crew of P/O Manning DFC. A proportion of the Stirling contingent was diverted on return from this operation, and many of them were unable to return to their stations on the 17th in time to be made ready for that night's highly important undertaking. This would deplete the available number of Stirlings by sixty and heap an even greater responsibility upon the rest of the force to complete the job at the first time of asking.

Since the very beginning of the war, intelligence had suggested that Germany was researching into and developing rocket technology, and, although scant regard was given to the reports, photographic reconnaissance had confirmed the existence of an establishment at Peenemünde at the northern tip of the island of Usedom on the Baltic coast. The activities there were monitored through Ultra intercepts and surreptitious reconnaissance flights, and the V-1, known to the photographic interpreters at Medmenham because of its wingspan as the "Peenemünde 20", was captured on a photograph. The brilliant scientist, Dr R V Jones, had been able to gain vital information concerning the V-1's range, which would ultimately be used to feed disinformation to the enemy, largely through the double agent "Zigzag", otherwise known as Eddie Chapman. Unfortunately, Churchill's chief scientific adviser, Professor Lindemann, or Lord Cherwell as he became, steadfastly refused to give credence to the existence and feasibility of rocket weapons and held stubbornly to his viewpoint even when presented with a photograph of a V-2 on a trailer, taken by a PRU Mosquito as recently as June. It required the combined urgings of Duncan Sandys and Dr Jones to persuade Churchill of the urgency to act, and Operation Hydra was planned for the first available opportunity, which occurred on the night of the 17/18th. Earlier in the day, the USAAF 8th Air Force had carried out its first deep-penetration raids into Germany to attack ball-bearing production at Schweinfurt and the Messerschmitt aircraft plant at Regensburg, and to the shock of its leaders, had learned the harsh lesson that unescorted daylight raids in 1943 were not viable. The folks at home would not be told that sixty B17s had failed to return. It was vital that the Peenemünde installation be destroyed, ideally, at the first attempt, and a force of 596 aircraft was assembled made up of 324 Lancasters, 218 Halifaxes and fifty-four Stirlings, ninety-four aircraft provided by 8 Group.

The operation had been meticulously planned to account for the three vital components of Peenemünde, the housing estate, where the scientific and technical staff lived, the factory buildings and the experimental site. Each was assigned to a specific wave of aircraft, which would attack from medium level, with the Path Finders bearing the huge responsibility of re-directing the point of aim accordingly, for which each squadron was to provide one crew as a "shifter". That apart, once route markers had been dropped on Rügen island, the Path Finder markers and backers-up were to follow the standard routine of red, yellow and green TIs. After last minute alterations, 3 and 4 Groups were given the residential complex, 1 Group the construction sheds and 5 and 6 Groups the experimental site the whole operation to be overseen by a Master of Ceremonies (referred to hereafter as Master Bomber), and the officer selected for this hazardous and demanding role was G/C Searby of 83 Squadron, who, as already mentioned, had stepped into Gibson's shoes at 106 Squadron after Gibson was posted out to form 617 Squadron. Searby's role was to direct the marking and bombing by VHF, and to encourage the crews to press on to the aiming-point, a task requiring him to remain in the target area and within range of the defences throughout the attack. He would be assisted by two Deputy Master Bombers, W/C Fauquier and W/C John White, the latter a highly experience Path Finder and flight commander with 156 Squadron. W/C Fauquier would be in a Lancaster, which cannot be identified as the squadron ORB referred to aircraft by their code letter rather than serial number.

In an attempt to protect the bombers from the attentions of enemy night-fighters for as long as possible, eight Mosquitos of 139 Squadron were to carry out a spoof raid on Berlin beginning at 23.00, seventy-five minutes before the opening of the main event, and would be led by the highly experienced, and former 49 Squadron commander, G/C Len Slee. In the expectation of encountering drifting smoke as the last wave on target, the 5 Group crews were instructed to employ their oft-used time-and-distance approach to the aiming-point and had practiced this over a stretch of coast near the Wainfleet bombing range at the mouth of the Wash in Lincolnshire, progressively cutting the margin of error from one thousand to three hundred yards.

The eleven Halifaxes departed Gransden Lodge between 21.34 and 20.57 and were followed into the air at 21.14 by W/C Fauquier and crew, and none turned back on a night when the overall early-return rate was lower than normal, suggesting that crews had taken to heart the importance of the operation. The various groups made their way individually to a rendezvous point some ninety minutes flying time or three hundred miles from the English coast and sixty miles from Denmark's western coast, where they formed into a stream. Darkness had fallen as they crossed the North Sea, and twenty miles short of landfall over the southern tip of Fanø island, south of Esbjerg, "windowing" began, in order to simulate a standard raid on a northern or north-eastern city. Southern Denmark was traversed at 18,000 feet, twice the altitude required for the attack, but worryingly, in a band of cloudless sky under a bright moon. The first casualty occurred when 405 (Vancouver) Squadron's HR817 was brought down by the Flensburg flak after straying south of the intended track and there were no survivors from the mixed RCAF/RAF crew of F/O McIntyre. Once at the Baltic coast, the bombers adopted an east-south-easterly course and began to shed altitude gradually during the 240-mile run to the target a little over an hour away, and at the rear of the stream, the 5 Group crews focused on the island of Rügen, the ideal starting point for their timed run to Peenemünde, which lay some fifteen miles beyond it to the south-east.

The skies over the target area were clear and the visibility good despite the deployment of a smoke screen, but even so, the initial marking of the housing estate went awry, and some target indicators fell onto the forced workers camp at Trassenheide, more than a mile south of the intended aiming-point. Inevitably, many of the 3 and 4 Group bombs fell here, inflicting grievous casualties on friendly foreign nationals, who were trapped inside their wooden barracks. Once rectified, however, the attack proceeded according to plan, and a number of important members of the technical staff were killed. The 1 Group second-wave crews encountered strong crosswinds over the narrow section of the island where the construction sheds were located, but this phase of the operation largely achieved its aims, and they were on their way home before the night-fighters arrived from Berlin, having been attracted by the glow of fires well to the north. On arrival at Rügen, the 5 Group crews began their timed run, and reached the experimental site to encounter the expected smoke, before bombing on green TIs between 00.36 and 00.52. They and the 6 Group Halifaxes and Lancasters then ran into the night-fighters, which proceeded to take a heavy toll, both in the skies over the target, and on the route home towards Denmark. Twenty-nine of the forty missing aircraft came from this third wave, seventeen of them belonging to 5 Group and twelve to 6 Group, which represented a loss rate for the Canadians of 19.7%.

On return to Gransden Lodge, W/C Fauquier and crew reported that they had been over the target from 00.11 until 00.55, delivering their load from 8,000 feet as they turned for home. The other ten returning crews reported their presence over the target at 11,000 to 14,000 feet at some time between 00.10 and 00.38, and the consensus was of a successful endeavour. On the main force stations there was praise for the work of the Path Finders and the Master Bomber, and post-raid reconnaissance revealed the raid to have been sufficiently effective to delay the V-2 development programme by a number of months, and ultimately to force the manufacture of secret weapons beneath the Kohnstein Hill at Nordhausen in the Harz mountains. The flight testing of the V-2 was eventually withdrawn eastwards into Poland, beyond the range of Harris's bombers, and thus Peenemünde had been nullified as a threat at the first attempt.

Before the next campaign began, Leverkusen was posted on the 22nd as the target for a heavy force of 449 Lancasters and Halifaxes with Oboe-Mosquitos of 105 and 109 Squadrons to provide the initial marking. The main target was a factory belonging to the infamous I G Farben chemicals and pharmaceuticals company, or to give it its full name, Interessen-Gemeinschaft Farbenindustrie, in English, Common Interest Conglomerate of chemical dye-making corporations. Formed in 1925, it was a merger between BASF, Bayer, Hoechst, Agfa, Chemische Fabrik Griesheim-Elektron and Chemische Fabrik vorm. Weiler Ter Meer and was heavily involved in the development and production of synthetic oil. It employed slave labour at all of its factories across Germany, including 30,000 from the Auschwitz concentration camp, where it had built a plant. One of the company's subsidiaries manufactured the Zyklon B gas used during the Holocaust to murder millions of Jewish victims. The aiming-point for the forty-nine Path Finder Lancasters was the Bayer A G plant, but ten-tenths cloud with tops at 18,000 feet and problems with Oboe-equipment rendered the raid a failure reminiscent of the pre-Oboe era. Local reports would reveal that up to a dozen neighbouring towns had been hit, Düsseldorf suffering the destruction of 132 buildings.

Harris had long believed that the key to ultimate victory lay in the destruction of Berlin, the seat of the Nazi government and the symbol of its power. On the 23rd, orders were received on stations across the Command to prepare for a maximum effort that night against Germany's capital city, which had not been visited by the heavy brigade since the end of March. The crews, of course, could not know that this was to be the first of an eventual nineteen raids on the "Big City", in a campaign which, with an autumn break, would drag on until the following spring. It was a campaign that would test the resolve of the crews to the absolute limit, whilst also sealing the fate of the Stirlings and the Mk II and V Halifaxes as front-line bombers. There are varying opinions concerning the true start date of what became known as the Berlin offensive or the Battle of Berlin, some commentators believing these first three operations in August and September to be the start, while others point to the sixteen raids from mid-November. However, there was little doubt in Bomber Command circles that this was it, a fact demonstrated by the comments in numerous squadron ORBs, which speak of the "long-awaited Berlin campaign" and similar sentiments. The success of the Master Bomber role at Peenemünde sealed the concept for all future major operations, and the officer chosen for this occasion was 405 (Vancouver) Squadron's W/C "Johnny" Fauquier. The route had been planned to take the bomber stream to a rendezvous point over the North Sea, before crossing the Dutch coast near Haarlem and entering Germany between Meppen to the north and Osnabrück to the south. It would then pass between Bremen and Hannover to bypass the southern rim of Berlin, before turning back sharply on a north-westerly course across the city centre, and after bombing, pass out over the Baltic coast and make for the Schleswig-Holstein peninsula. Finally, seventeen Mosquitos were to precede the Path Finder and main force elements to drop route markers at key points in an attempt to keep the bomber stream on track.

A force of 727 aircraft was assembled, of which 134 represented 8 Group, in addition to which, ten 139 Squadron Mosquitos were to provide a "window" screen in advance of the bomber stream. The Oboe Mosquitos were to mark the route with red and green TIs, backed up by H2S Lancasters, but as Berlin was beyond the range of Oboe, the aiming-point was to be marked with red TIs by

H2S, backed up by greens. The ORB does not reveal the make-up of the 405 (Vancouver) Squadron contribution, but we know that W/C Fauquier and crew were in a Lancaster with a light load of green TIs and 120 x 20lb incendiaries to enable them to remain over the target for the duration of the raid, and the fact that three aircraft received a load that included a 4,000lb cookie, a bomb normally associated with a Lancaster rather than Halifax, suggests that four Lancasters and eleven Halifaxes departed Gransden Lodge between 20.14 and 21.12. The crews of Sgts Nielsen and Phillips and F/O St Louis suffered engine failure within minutes of each other early on, while Sgt Larson and crew must have been approaching the western coast of Jutland when the oxygen system failed and forced them also to turn back. Those reaching the target area found clear skies and moonlight, but the Path Finders were unable to identify the aiming-point in the centre of the city, a result of the inherent difficulties of interpreting the H2S images over such a massive urban sprawl and marked the southern outskirts instead. The 405 (Vancouver) Squadron crews carried out their respective tasks from 18,000 to 21,500 feet between 23.42 and 00.18 in the face of intense searchlight activity and moderate flak. It would be established later, that many main force crews had cut the corner to approach the city from the south-west rather than south-east, and this would result in the wastage of many bomb loads in open country and on outlying communities. Returning crews reported large explosions and many fires, the glow from which remained visible for at least 140 miles, and a pall of smoke had already risen to meet them as they turned towards the north-west. Curiously, only a few crews commented on hearing the Master Bomber, and finding his instructions helpful.

A new record of fifty-six aircraft failed to return, and this was made up of twenty-three Halifaxes, seventeen Lancasters and sixteen Stirlings, representing a percentage loss rate respectively of 9.1, 5.1 and 12.9, which perfectly reflected the food chain when all three types operated together. It was a sad night for 405 (Vancouver) Squadron, which posted missing the crews of F/O Harman RCAF and W/O Smith RCAF in HR918 and HR923, the former crashing in the target area without survivors. The sadness was tempered when news came through from Sweden that the Smith crew was safe and enjoying token internment after their Halifax had been badly shot up by a BF109 as they left the target area and had been abandoned by them to crash close to the southern tip at Sandhammaren. Berlin reported a scattered raid, but because of the numbers attacking, extensive damage was caused, a little in or near the centre, but mostly in south-western residential districts and industrialized areas a little further east. Local sources provided a figure of 2,611 buildings destroyed or seriously damaged, and a surprisingly high death toll of 854 people, caused largely, perhaps, by a failure to heed the alarms and go to the assigned shelters.

Orders were received on the 27th to prepare for an operation that night against Nuremberg, for which a force of 674 aircraft was assembled, eighty-five Lancasters and twenty-seven Halifaxes representing 8 Group. 405 (Vancouver) Squadron made ready a dozen Lancasters and Halifaxes, and based on the assumption that those with a cookie as part of their bomb/TI/Flare load were Lancasters identified as E, C, Z and T, with respectively the crews of P/O Cowan, F/O Lefroy, S/L Schneider and F/O Sattler on board, the remaining eight aircraft must have been Halifaxes. At briefing, the crews were assigned to their specific roles as blind markers, visual markers, recentrers and backers-up, five of the Halifaxes to carry eight 500-pounders in addition to their TIs and flares and three with ten 500-pounders as part of the main force. They departed Gransden Lodge between 20.45 and 21.18 and after climbing out, headed for the French coast to follow the line of the frontier with Belgium until crossing into Germany south of Luxembourg on a direct easterly course to the target. There were no "boomerangs" among the Gransden gang, who, along with the rest of the Path Finders, had been briefed to check their H2S equipment by dropping a 1,000 pounder on Heilbronn. There is no mention of compliance in the squadron ORB, and they pressed on towards the target guided by red TIs as route markers, while at the target, "Y" aircraft delivered red TIs and white flares for the visual markers to use as a reference to mark the aiming-point with yellow and green TIs. The backers-up would maintain the aiming-point with green TIs, while the re-centrers, spread throughout the stream, would employ their H2S to keep the bombing on track, also with green TIs. The blind markers reached the target to find clear skies and intense darkness and established their position on H2S to set up initially accurate marking. However, a creep-back developed, which the backers-up and the Master Bomber could not correct, and this resulted in many bomb loads falling into open country, while others hit Nuremberg's south-eastern and eastern districts. The 405 (Vancouver) Squadron crews carried out their respective tasks from 17,000 to 21,000 feet between 00.25 and 01.06 and gained an impression of a fairly concentrated and accurate attack, which produced many fires. At debriefing they described searchlights and night-fighters as numerous, and this seemed to be backed up by the failure to return of thirty-three aircraft, eleven of each type, which again confirmed the vulnerability of the Stirlings and Halifaxes when operating alongside Lancasters. The loss rate on this night was 3.1% for the Lancaster, 5% for the Halifax and 10.6% for the Stirlings.

The main event on the night of the 30/31st was a two-phase attack on the twin towns of Mönchengladbach and Rheydt, the first time that either would experience a major Bomber Command assault. Situated some ten miles west of the centre of Düsseldorf in the south-western Ruhr, they would face an initial force of 660 aircraft of four types, in what, for the crews, was a short-penetration trip across the Dutch frontier, which would be a welcome change from the recent long slogs to eastern and southern Germany. 8 Group detailed fourteen Mosquitos, thirty-one Lancasters and seventeen Halifaxes, seven of the last-mentioned provided by 405 (Vancouver) Squadron. Before this operation was launched, however, six Oboe Mosquitos and six Path Finder Halifaxes were detailed to take part in the first of a series of small-scale operations against ammunition dumps in north-eastern France. On this night the target was situated in the Forét d'Eperlecques near St-Omer and would be attacked by a main force of thirty-three O.T.U Wellingtons of 91, 92 and 93 Groups. The crews of F/O Clinton and P/Os South and Wood took off between 20.49 and 20.51, each carrying green TIs with which to back-up the reds delivered by Oboe Mosquitos, and nine 1,000 and four 500 pounders each for the dump. They arrived in the target area to find clear skies, good visibility and the red TIs clearly visible, onto which they unloaded their hardware from 13,000 to 15,500 feet between 22.01 and 22.09, observing no results.

They were at debriefing by the time that the Ruhr-bound force took to the air, seven Halifaxes at Gransden Lodge between 00.10 and 00.16 with F/O St Louis the senior pilot on duty, five loaded with six 1,000 and six 500-pounders and two with two 1,000 and three 500-pounders with green TIs to back up the aiming point. P/O Campbell and crew abandoned their sortie because of an engine issue during the climb-out, leaving the others to cross the Essex coast on course for Ostend. The plan called for the first wave to hit Mönchengladbach, where the Mosquitos were to ground mark with red TIs for the heavy brigade to back up with greens. They encountered eight to ten-tenths cloud at the opening of the attack with tops at around 10,000 feet, but this would diminish as the raid progressed. The 405 (Vancouver) Squadron participants carried out their respective roles from 14,500 to 19,000 feet between 02.10 and 02.26 and were on their way home by the time that a two-minute pause in the bombing allowed the remaining Path Finders to head south to mark Rheydt. Returning crews reported a near-perfect display of target-marking, which the main force crews exploited with scarcely any creep-back, and the glow from the burning towns could be seen from the Dutch coast homebound. Photo-reconnaissance confirmed a highly accurate and concentrated attack, which destroyed more than 2,300 buildings in the two towns, 171 of them of an industrial nature, along with 869 residential properties. Twenty-five aircraft failed to return, and Halifaxes narrowly sustained the highest numerical casualties.

The month ended with preparations for the second of the Berlin operations on the night of the 31st, for which 622 aircraft were made ready, more than half of them Lancasters. 8 Group detailed 109 aircraft, nine of them Mosquitos, which would join in the route-marking with green TIs and also dispense "window". 405 (Vancouver) Squadron made ready nine aircraft, it is believed four of them Lancasters, which each received a bomb load of a cookie and up to eight 500-pounders dependent upon their role and four Halifaxes with loads of nine 500 pounders to deliver as part of the main force. In addition to these, three Halifaxes were each given a bomb load of nine 1,000 and four 500-pounders and green TIs to join two others from 35 (Madras Presidency) Squadron to mark an ammunition dump in the Forêt-de-Hesdin near Valenciennes for thirty O.T.U Wellingtons.

The plan for Berlin involved blind markers delivering red TIs by H2S onto the aiming-point, which backers-up and recentrers would maintain throughout the raid with green TIs. Four of the 405 (Vancouver) Squadron crews were assigned to blind marking duties, leaving five to bomb with the main force, and they departed Gransden Lodge together with the France-bound trio between 19.56 and 20.53 with no pilots on duty above flying officer rank. They were still climbing out over the station when Sgt Nielsen and crew dropped out with an unserviceable a.s.i, while Sgt Phillips and crew had reached the midpoint of the North Sea before the failure of their starboard-inner engine forced them also to turn back. The crews of P/Os McMenemy, South and Wood, meanwhile, pointed their snouts towards the south with a time-on-target of 22.00, a full ninety minutes before the Berlin raid commenced, and on reaching the target area close to the frontier with Belgium, found eight-tenths cloud with tops at around 2,000 feet. They identified the target by the red TIs dropped by the Oboe Mosquito element, onto which they released their loads from 15,000 to 16,400 feet between 21.53 and 22.09.

The route to the "Big City" on this night took the bomber stream on an east-south-easterly heading across Texel to a position between Hannover and Leipzig, before turning to pass to the south-east of Berlin and approach the city-centre aiming-point on a north-westerly track. The return leg would involve a south-westerly course to a position south of Cologne for an exit over the French coast, but despite the attempts to outwit the enemy night-fighter controller, he would be able to predict to some extent where to concentrate his fighters. The Bomber stream made its way across Holland and northern Germany, where, for the first time, the Germans deployed "fighter flares" to mark out the path of the bombers to and from the target. The Path Finders encountered five to six-tenths cloud in the target area, and this combined with H2S equipment failure and a spirited night-fighter response to cause the markers to be dropped well to the south of the planned aiming-point. The 405 (Vancouver) Squadron crews performed their respective roles from 17,000 to 20,000 feet between 23.27 and 00.08, the main force element becoming involved in an extensive creep-back, which would stretch some thirty miles into open country and outlying communities. Many fires were observed over a wide area, and it was noted by some that two groups of green TIs were ten miles apart, each attracting attention from the main force. The outcome of the raid was a major disappointment, brought about by woefully short marking and the pronounced creep-back, and resulted in the destruction of just eighty-five houses, a figure in no way commensurate with the effort expended and the loss of forty-seven heavy bombers. The percentage loss rates made alarming reading at Bomber Command HQ, the Lancasters with an acceptable and sustainable 3%, the Halifaxes with 11.3% and the Stirlings with 16%. Among the missing was 405 (Vancouver) Squadron's HR915, which was shot down by a night-fighter in the target area delivering P/O Maddock and four of his mixed RAF/RCAF crew into enemy hands, while the wireless operator and rear gunner lost their lives. Two weeks hence, notification of the award of a DFC to P/O Maddock would appear in the London Gazette.

During the course of the month, the squadron took part in a dozen operations and dispatched 129 sorties for the loss of ten Halifaxes and their crews and one Lancaster without casualties to a taxying accident.

September 1943

On the 1st news came through that W/C Fauquier was to be awarded a DSO in recognition of his inspirational leadership of the squadron. On the 2nd, Halifax HR809 crashed at 15.20 on return to Gransden Lodge during a training sortie in the hands of P/O McMenemy and crew, and on the following day, Lancaster ED911 was crash-landed by F/L Moore RNZAF in a field close to the airfield. Both aircraft were damaged beyond repair, while the crews walked away apparently none the worse for their experiences.

Probably as a result of the heavy losses recently incurred by the Halifaxes and Stirlings, an all-Lancaster force was assembled on the 3rd to conclude the current series of operations against the "Big City". The Path Finders contributed eighty-three Lancasters to the overall force of 316 aircraft, of which six belonged to 405 (Vancouver) Squadron, each receiving a payload of a cookie and a combination of 1,000 and 500-pounders along with a selection of red, green and yellow TIs according to their briefed role. They departed Gransden Lodge between 20.13 and 20.25 with W/C Fauquier and S/L Schneider the senior pilots on duty and after rendezvousing with the rest of the force over the North Sea, crossed the Dutch coast over the Den Helder peninsular and adopted a direct course of 350 miles, which took them north of Hannover to Brandenburg, some thirty-five miles short of the target. Long, straight legs were rarely employed because of the risk of interception by the Luftwaffe, but the forecast heavy cloud with tops at 18,000 feet accompanied the stream all the way from the Dutch coast to the target area and helped to keep the enemy at bay.

The Path Finders had been briefed to use H2S to navigate their way via the region's lakes and the town of Brandenburg to the city centre aiming-point, and although the cloud would disperse miraculously in time to leave clear skies, it did not happen before F/O Lefroy and crew had mistaken Genthin on their cathode-ray screen for Brandenburg and Brandenburg for Berlin and dropped their bombs from 20,000 feet at 23.24. Immediately afterwards they realised their error but continued on to pass over Berlin before returning safely. The now clear skies allowed the Path Finders to deliver ground-marking TIs rather than the less reliable skymarkers and the first batch fell right over the aiming-point, before others crept back for between two and five miles along the line of approach from the west. The remaining 405 (Vancouver) Squadron participants carried out their respective tasks from 19,000 to 21,000 feet between 23.13 and 23.25, and the backers-up maintained the marking as the main force Lancasters came in in a single wave. Despite much of the bombing falling short of the city centre, most of it landed within its boundaries and many fires were observed, which appeared to be merging as the bombers turned towards the north for a return route that would intentionally violate Swedish airspace. The glow of fires was visible from the Baltic coast, and as they flew out over Sweden, they were treated to the rare sight of unblacked-out communities below. The Swedish flak batteries offered a token response to the incursion of their airspace, but the shells were set to explode well below the bombers, and as the Lancasters turned to port to skirt the northern tip of Denmark, the Swedes laid their searchlights horizontally in a friendly gesture to point the way. Four Mosquitos laid spoof route marker flares well away from the actual track to mislead the night-fighters, but in the absence of the poorer performing Halifaxes and Stirlings, twenty-two Lancasters failed to return, almost 7% of those dispatched. Local sources confirmed severe damage, principally in the largely residential districts of Tiergarten, Wedding, Moabit and Charlottenburg, but also in the industrial Siemensstadt, which resulted in a significant loss of war production.

Whether by design, or as a result of the loss of 125 aircraft, Berlin was now shelved for the next ten weeks, while Harris sought other suitable targets, of which there were many. He would shortly begin a four-raid series against Hannover stretching over a four-week period, but he focused first on southern Germany, beginning on the 5th with the twin cities of Mannheim and Ludwigshafen, which face each other from the eastern and western banks respectively of the River Rhine. The plan was to exploit the creep-back phenomenon that attended most large operations, by approaching the target from the west, and marking the eastern half of Mannheim, with the expectation that the bombing would spread back along the line of approach across western Mannheim and into Ludwigshafen. A force of 605 aircraft was assembled, which included 103 representing 8 Group, the crews learning at briefing that the blind markers were to mark the target area with red TIs and flares, by means of which the visual markers would confirm the aiming-point with yellow and green TIs.

405 (Vancouver) Squadron made ready fourteen aircraft, eight Lancasters and six Halifaxes, the former with a load consisting of a cookie and six 500-pounders plus TIs and flares and the latter with either two 1,000 and three 500-pounders and selection of TIs or nine 500-pounders. They departed Gransden Lodge between 19.27 and 19.49 with S/L Schneider the senior pilot on duty, and during the climb-out lost the services of Sgt Phillips and crew to an engine issue, leaving the others to set course for Beachy Head and the Channel crossing. They crossed the French coast at Fecamp, before tracking across France to a point five miles south of Luxembourg, where route markers established the final turning point for a direct run on the target. The path Finders were routed in over Kaiserslautern some thirty miles due west of Mannheim, from where they were to carry out a timed run to the aiming-point. They benefitted from almost clear skies and excellent visibility, which was of no consequence to the blind markers but useful to the visual markers, recenterers, backers-up and those bombing with the main force. The 405 (Vancouver) Squadron crews went about their business from 16,900 to 20,100 feet between 22.56 and 23.27 and those arriving towards the later stages of the raid were drawn on by the burgeoning fires fifty miles ahead. A number of large, red explosions were observed at 23.12, 23.23 and 23.27, the last of

which was followed by a purplish-red mushroom of fire. Searchlights were numerous but the flak negligible, and it was the abundance of night-fighters that posed the greatest risk to life and limb.

Black smoke was rising through 15,000 feet as the bombers withdrew to the west, and the glow from the burning cities was visible for 150 miles into the return journey, which thirty-four aircraft would fail to complete. Thirteen Lancasters, an equal number of Halifaxes and eight Stirlings were missing, and the percentage loss rates continued to tell the same story. The one absentee from the returning ranks of 405 (Vancouver) Squadron was Halifax HR810, which crashed six miles south-south-east of the university city of Heidelberg after bombing, killing Sgt Brunton and two of his crew, including the only member of the RCAF on board. This would prove to be the final loss of a Halifax in 405 (Vancouver) Squadron service. Local reports confirmed that both Mannheim and Ludwigshafen had suffered catastrophic destruction, with almost two thousand fires in the latter alone, 986 of them classed as large. Mannheim's reporting system broke down completely, and little detail emerged of this raid, although it would recover in time for the next assault in less than three weeks' time. What is known, is that the main railway station in Mannheim and three suburban stations were destroyed, the important I G Farben-owned Rashig & Sulzer chemicals plant, which was engaged in synthetic oil production and using slave labour, was severely damaged, as were the tank and military tractor factories belonging to Heinrich Lanz and Josef Vogele.

It was sometime during early September that S/L Lane ferried KB700 to England, with the assistance of a ferry pilot. Lane had volunteered for a third tour of operations, despite having already completed fifty-one sorties up to returning to Canada in July, and he would be joining 405 (Vancouver) Squadron in October.

Munich was posted as the target on the 6th, for which 8 Group made ready sixty-nine Lancasters as part of an overall force of 257 Lancasters and 147 Halifaxes, the Stirling brigade made conspicuous by its absence. The plan called for the blind marker element to make an H2S-guided timed run from the Ammersee and deliver illuminating flares and red TIs and for the visual markers to identify and mark the precise aiming point with yellows for backing-up throughout the raid with greens. The 405 (Vancouver) Squadron element of eight Lancasters departed Gransden Lodge between 20.00 and 20.24 with S/L Schneider the senior pilot on duty and a bomb load in each aircraft of a cookie and two 1,000-pounders in addition to their marking ordnance. Those reaching the Bavarian Capital City found conditions to be less than ideal with cloud varying between five and nine-tenths, although some ground features, like the River Isar, could be identified and the red, yellow and green TIs observed. The 405 (Vancouver) Squadron crews carried out their assigned tasks from 18,300 to 20,900 feet between 23.25 and 23.42 and reported a large number of fires grouped around the markers. They were unable to make an accurate assessment, but local reports suggested that the attack had been scattered across southern and western districts. The searchlights were ineffective because of the cloud, but large numbers of night-fighters were again evident, and sixteen aircraft failed to return, thirteen of them Halifaxes, a percentage loss rate of 8.8, compared with 1.2 for the Lancasters.

A series of operations against French targets began on the night of the 8/9th, with the bombing of heavy gun emplacements near the small coastal resort town of Le Portel. This was the final phase of Operation Starkey, a rehearsal for invasion which had begun on the 16th of August, and which was intended to deceive the enemy into believing that the invasion was imminent. Harris was less than enthusiastic about allowing his squadrons to participate in what he considered to be "play-acting" and managed to restrict Bomber Command's involvement to token gestures as on this night. The marking of the batteries, codenamed Religion and Andante, was to be conducted by sixteen Oboe Mosquitos of 105 and 109 Squadrons, with Halifaxes from 35 (Madras Presidency) Squadron and 405 (Vancouver) Squadron backing-up for a main force consisting of 112 Stirlings of 3 Group and 119 Wellingtons from the training units of 91 and 93 Groups. In the 405 (Vancouver) Squadron ORB the operation was referred to as "Pongo" for which the crews of P/O McMenemy and Sgts Larson and Nielsen departed Gransden Lodge between 20.41 and 20.43, each with five 1,000 and six 500-pounders beneath their feet. All reached the target area, where good visibility enabled Boulogne to be identified visually, while the position of the batteries was established by either red or green TIs. Phase 1 began with green Oboe TIs cascading at 22.05, onto which the 405 (Vancouver) Squadron participants released their loads from 16,400 to 17,000 feet between 22.05 and 22.11, and phase 2 began some forty minutes later. Sadly, the Oboe Mosquito element experienced equipment problems, and their markers were consequently either non-existent or late. This created a dilemma for the heavy marker crews, who had to decide whether to carry on with their part in the attack or go round again. In the general confusion the operation was a failure, and neither battery was damaged, while Le Portel suffered grievously and around five hundred of its inhabitants lost their lives. (For a detailed analysis of this operation, see the excellent book, The Starkey Sacrifice, by Michael Cumming, published by Sutton).

On the 15th the teleprinters on 3, 4, 6 and 8 Group stations burst into life to churn out the orders for an operation that night against the Dunlop rubber factory at Montluçon in central France. A force of 369 aircraft was assembled, of which sixty-five represented 8 Group, eight Lancasters and four Halifaxes provided by 405 (Vancouver) Squadron, whose crews learned at briefing that the plan called for the blind markers to mark the target area with red TIs and flares by H2S, and for visual markers to identify the aiming-point and mark it with green TIs for the backers-up to maintain throughout the raid with yellow and green TIs. The 405 (Vancouver) Squadron element departed Gransden Lodge between 20.36 and 20.47 with S/L Schneider and F/Ls Bennett and Weiser the senior pilots on duty and a cookie and mix of 1,000 and 500-pounders supplemented by TIs and flares in each Lancaster bomb bay and three 1,000 and nine 500-pounders in the Halifaxes. Not on duty on this occasion was F/L Weber, who had learned earlier in the day that he had been awarded a DFC. F/L Bennett and crew had been outbound for less than an hour when the port-outer engine failed and ended their interest in proceedings, while the others pressed on across the Channel to make landfall on the French coast, eventually to arrive at the target to find ten-tenths cloud at 12,000 feet and eight to nine-tenths at 4,000 feet. The blind and visual markers went in between 23.27 and 23.59 and enjoyed a clear view of the ground and the buildings forming the target, the 405 (Vancouver) Squadron crews preforming their assigned tasks from 4,000 to 12,600 feet between 23.27 and 23.44. The master Bomber, W/C "Dixie" Dean of 35 (Madras presidency) Squadron directed the attack, which took place in bright moonlight, and it wasn't long before black smoke was seen to rise through 10,000 feet from the developing fires. It was clear to all that the factory complex had been severely damaged in the face of negligible opposition, and just two Halifaxes and a Stirling failed to return.

On the following day, the same groups were alerted to an operation that night against the important and extensive railway yards at Modane, situated on the main line between France and Italy in the foothills of the Alps in south-eastern France. A force of 340 aircraft was assembled, which included sixty-four provided by 8 Group, 405 (Vancouver) Squadron making ready a Lancaster at Gransden Lodge for F/L Bennett and crew and a Halifax each for P/O Campbell and Sgt Borrowes and their crews, the former loaded with a cookie and ten 500-pounders and the latter with five 1,000 pounders each. The RAF contingent would be accompanied for the first time by five B17s of the USAAF Eighth Air Force, who had decided to flirt with night operations after sustaining massive and unsustainable casualties on their daylight forays over Germany. The marking was to be dependent upon a visual reference, but in case the conditions in the target area proved to be unfavourable, red spotfires were to be dropped on Grenoble. A careful timed run from there would culminate in the delivery of red TIs on e.t.a., followed by backing-up throughout the raid with green TIs. The 405 (Vancouver) Squadron trio took to the air between 19.57 and 19.59, crossing the Normandy coast in the bomber stream with more than 230 miles still to negotiate, and all reached the target area to find between zero and two-tenths cloud at 10,000 feet with good visibility and moonlight. Zero hour was set for 00.01, but a patch of cloud right over the aiming-point delayed the start for a brief period. Most of those arriving early were able to visually identify the target, situated in a steep valley, and the red TIs forming a good concentration were backed up by greens. The 405 (Vancouver) Squadron crews bombed with the main force from 12,500 to 15,000 feet between 00,09 and 00.12 and turned for home confident that the target had been dealt with. However, post-raid reconnaissance revealed that the marking had missed the mark and the yards had escaped damage.

On the 20th W/C Fauquier was promoted to Group Captain, and in recognition of his part in the Peenemünde operation, was awarded the DSO, the citation reading; *"This officer is a first class leader whose skilful and courageous example has proved most inspiring. His sterling qualities were well illustrated during an operation against Peenemünde one night in August and again a few nights later in an attack on Berlin. Group Captain Fauquier has displayed boundless energy and great drive, and has contributed in large measure to the high standard of operational efficiency of the squadron he commands."*

When the tannoys called the faithful to prayer on the 22nd, crews learned that they were to be part of a force of 711 aircraft to attack the ancient city of Hannover, situated in northern Germany midway between the Dutch frontier and Berlin. They were told that it was home to much war industry, and although it was probably not known at the time among the Allies, it was also the location of seven Nazi concentration camps. According to Martin Middlebrook and Chris Everitt in Bomber Command War Diaries, the first two operations against Hannover produced concentrated bombing, but mostly outside of the target, while only the third one succeeded in causing extensive damage, which, if the figures are to be believed, seem to be massively out of proportion. The author contends that the reports of the crews after the first two operations suggest strongly that the damage to Hannover was accumulative over the first three raids and did not result from just one, as will be explained in the following narrative. The telling feature is, perhaps, that no reports came out of Hannover to corroborate the testimony of the crews on the first two raids, although post-raid reconnaissance by the RAF after the second one did show that some of the bombing had fallen into open country, and the Path Finders did admit to at least one poor performance.

8 Group prepared eighty-one aircraft for the main event and twenty-nine for a diversionary raid on the town of Oldenburg situated to the west of Bremen and some eighty miles north-west of

Hannover. 405 (Vancouver) Squadron committed nine Lancasters to Hannover, each loaded with a cookie and six 500 pounders in addition to their marker ordnance, while the four assigned to the "spoof" raid each received a cookie and SBCs of incendiaries to attract as much attention as possible. At briefing for the main event, crews learned that the blind markers were to use their H2S to mark the general target area with red TIs and illuminator flares, and that the visual markers would confirm the exact aiming-point with yellow TIs, which the backers-up were to maintain throughout the attack with green TIs. The two Gransden Lodge elements took off together between 18.36 and 19.01 with S/L Logan the senior pilot on duty heading for Hannover and F/L Bennett leading the "spoofers". S/L Logan had recently rejoined the squadron after a spell of leave in Canada following his evasion from France during the Stuttgart raid of the 11/12th of March. The bomber stream came together over the North Sea with a 430-mile outward leg for the main-eventers to negotiate, which not all would complete, but there were no "boomerangs" from Gransden Lodge.

The diversionary force reached their target area first and the 405 (Vancouver) Squadron participants played their part in the deception from 19,500 to 20,000 feet between 21.00 and 21.06, reporting clear conditions and a little ground haze and negligible opposition. Some twenty minutes later the Path Finder spearhead arrived at Hannover, where clear skies and good visibility prevailed, but stronger-than-forecast winds would play their part in pushing the marking and bombing towards the south-east. The attack was scheduled to begin at 21.30, and the first red TIs were observed to go down from the blind marker crews at 21.23, after they had carried out a timed run from Lake Steinhude, north-west of the city. As the visual marker crews ran in on the target, they observed a red TI cascade over the city, but estimated it to have overshot by some four miles, and this was followed by others overshooting by one to four miles with many green TIs falling among them. However, the yellow TIs seemed to be undershooting the reds by two miles and were closer to the city centre aiming-point. Bundles of white flares were added to the kaleidoscope, and it was into this somewhat confused arena that the 405 (Vancouver) Squadron participants delivered their respective ordnance from 15,000 to 21,000 feet between 21.26 and 21.46 in the face of intense searchlights and heavy flak, which was bursting at around 18,000 feet. As they left the target behind them, crews observed a considerable number of fires spreading out over a wide area, the glow from which was still visible from the Dutch coast two hundred miles away. Some main force crews reported a line of fires developing from west to east, with smoke rising through 14,000 feet, while others claimed that fires ran from the aiming-point in a north-north-westerly direction across the city, but all were unanimous, that the raid had been highly successful. Twenty-six aircraft failed to return, twelve of them Halifaxes, which again sustained the highest numerical losses, and this time, at 5.3%, even exceeded the Stirlings' loss rate.

Let us now examine the claim that the main weight of bombs fell two to five miles south-south-east from the city centre, and that the operation largely failed. Firstly, two to five miles in any city means that the bombing fell within the boundaries, and, therefore, within the built-up area. Secondly, the majority of crews, if not all, reported a highly successful raid with fires right across the city, smoke rising to 14,000 feet as they left the scene and the glow visible from the Dutch coast. It is true that crews were very frequently mistaken in their belief that an attack had been successful, but the evidence on this occasion would seem to confirm their testimony. Decoy fire-sites did not produce a glow visible from a distance of two hundred miles, or sufficient volumes of smoke to reach bombing height during the short duration of a raid in a density visible at night.

In fact, fifty-six factories had sustained damaged, railway installations had been severely disrupted, the line to Hildesheim cut and a four-track railway bridge brought down as the result of a direct hit.

On the 23rd, and for the second time in the month, Mannheim was posted as the target, for which a force of 628 aircraft was assembled, seventy-eight of them belonging to 8 Group. At Gransden Lodge, while fourteen Lancasters were being prepared, the crews were being briefed for their part in the proceedings, nine to be part of the main event and five to participate in a diversionary raid on the university city of Darmstadt, located some thirty miles to the north. They learned that Mosquitos were to drop red and green route markers at Mannheim, before the blind marker element delivered flares and red TIs over the target by H2S to guide the visual markers to the precise aiming-point. That was located in the less-severely afflicted northern districts, which they would mark with yellows, followed by the backers-up with greens. The main event Lancasters received a bomb load of a cookie, supplemented by up to six 1,000-pounders in addition to their marker ordnance, while the "spoofers" carried a cookie and incendiaries, and all took off together between 19.09 and 19.24 with S/L Schneider leading the Mannheim element and S/L Logan the "spoofers". The bomber stream pushed on across France and into southern Germany, where they encountered largely clear skies and good visibility.

Zero hour at Mannheim had been set for 21.45, but the head of the bomber stream arrived a little early, a few minutes after the attack on Darmstadt had seen the 405 (Vancouver) Squadron crews attack from 18,500 to 20,000 feet between 21.33 and 21.34. To the south, their squadron colleagues performed their assigned tasks from 16,500 to 20,000 feet between 21.36 and and 21.48 before returning safely. At debriefing, the Mannheim crews reported that smoke had reached around 6,000 feet as they turned away, and that the glow of fires remained visible for 150 miles into the return journey. Thirty-two crews were absent from debriefing, and this time, eighteen of them were in Lancasters, compared with seven each for the Halifaxes and Stirlings, which provided a somewhat topsy-turvy and unusual loss-rate of 5.7%, 3.6% and 6% respectively. Post-raid reconnaissance and local reports revealed that the marking had been accurate and concentrated, although later bombing had spilled over into the northern fringe of Ludwigshafen and out into the nearby towns of Oppau and Frankenthal, where much damage resulted. A total of 927 houses and twenty industrial premises had been destroyed in Mannheim, and the I G Farben factory in Ludwigshafen had been brought to a standstill.

Hannover was posted as the target again on the 27th and a force of 678 aircraft made ready, which included eighty-four Path Finder aircraft, nine Lancasters provided by 405 (Vancouver) Squadron, each loaded with a cookie and six 1,000-pounders. The plan called for the Steinhude Lake to be employed again by the blind (H2S) marker crews as the starting point for a timed run to the target, which would be marked with yellow TIs and the aiming-point identified visually and marked with reds backed up by greens. A diversionary raid on the city of Braunschweig (Brunswick) by twenty-one Lancasters and six Mosquitos of 8 Group involved the 405 (Vancouver) Squadron crews of S/L Logan and F/O Trilsbach, each sitting on a cookie and twelve SBCs of 4lb incendiaries, and it was they who departed Gransden Lodge first at 19.20 and 19.21 respectively. Those participating in the main event followed them into the air between 19.40 and 20.12 with F/Ls Bennett, Weber and Weiser the senior pilots on duty and climbed out through ice-bearing cloud before setting course towards poor weather conditions over the North Sea. There were no early returns, and the bomber stream pressed on behind the Path Finder spearhead, who were unaware that the weather forecasts on which their performance would be based, were incorrect.

The "spoofers" arrived over Braunschweig, thirty-five miles to the south-east of Hannover, to encounter clear skies and F/O Trilsbach and crew carried out their attack on red TIs from 20,000 feet at 21.49 and observed bursts. Whether or not S/L Logan DFC RCAF and his crew attacked the target is unknown as they failed to return in LM345 to make a report. It was learned eventually that the pilot and five others had been taken into captivity, while the bomb-aimer evaded a similar fate, suggesting that the Lancaster had come down in occupied territory rather than Germany. It will be recalled that S/L Logan had evaded capture in March and had recently rejoined the squadron. The result of the inaccurately forecast wind strength and direction was to push the marking some five miles from the city centre towards the north of the city, but at least the weather improved markedly over northern Germany to present the crews with clear skies at the target. The Gransden Lodge element carried out their respective briefs from 20,000 to 21,000 feet between 21.53 and 22.20 and observed many fires with smoke rising to 15,000 feet. Returning crews again reported the glow of fires visible from the Dutch coast, and confidence in the success of the operation was unanimous across the Command, giving lie to the claim that little damage resulted. Post-raid photos did reveal many bomb craters in open country, but also that the main force crews had performed with distinction to hit fifteen square miles and achieve 130 tons of bombs per square mile. Again, the fire and smoke evidence did not support decoy fire-sites, and no local report was forthcoming to shed further light. The loss of thirty-eight aircraft was probably something of a shock, but at least, common sense returned to the statistics to re-establish the status-quo after the topsy-turvy outcome of the Mannheim raid. Seventeen Halifaxes, ten Lancasters, ten Stirlings and one Wellington failed to return, giving loss-rates for the four-engine types of 9% for the Stirling, 7.3% for the Halifax and 3.2% for the Lancaster. A second empty dispersal pan at Gransden Lodge should have been occupied by JB120, which disappeared without trace with the experienced mixed RCAF, RAF and RAAF crew of F/O St Louis RCAF.

The month ended with an operation to Bochum in the central Ruhr on the 29th, for which a heavy force of 343 aircraft and nine Mosquitos was assembled, forty-four of them representing 8 Group. The attack was carried out from cloudless skies in the absence of a 405 Vancouver) Squadron presence and in the face of a strong searchlight and moderate flak defence, some returning crews describing the target as a mass of flames with smoke rising rapidly to meet them, while local reports confirmed the destruction of 527 houses with 742 others seriously damaged.

During the course of the month, the squadron took part in twelve operations, including three "spoofs" and dispatched sixty-nine Lancaster and fifteen Halifax sorties for the loss of three Lancasters and two crews and three Halifaxes and two crews.

October 1943

The start of October was a busy time for the Lancaster squadrons, which would be called upon to participate in six major operations in the first eight nights. The month's account was opened at Hagen, at the eastern end of the Ruhr on the 1st, for which a moderately sized heavy force of 243 Lancasters and eight Mosquitos was drawn from 1, 5 and 8 Groups. Among the twenty-eight Path Finder Lancasters were five representing 405 Vancouver) Squadron, three of which received a bomb load of a cookie and six 1,000-pounders, while the other two had six 2,000-pounders winched into their bomb bays. They departed Gransden Lodge between 18.50 and 18.54 with no senior pilots on duty, and made landfall near Egmond on the Dutch coast, to then skirt the northern edge of the Ruhr as far as Werl, to the north of the now famous Möhne reservoir, from where they would turn sharply to the south-west to run in on the target. They arrived to find ten-tenths cloud with tops at 8,000 feet and red and green Oboe-laid skymarkers to aim at, and carried out a highly effective attack, the 405 (Vancouver) Squadron crews from 16,000 to 20,000 feet between 20.59 and 21.06. The glow of fires beneath the cloud and black smoke rising through it gave promise of a successful operation, local sources reporting the usual housing damage and confirming the destruction of forty-six industrial firms. Among these was a manufacturer of accumulator batteries for U-Boots, and this would have an impact on U-Boot production.

A force of 294 aircraft was assembled from 1, 5 and 8 Groups on the 2nd, the crews learning at briefings that Munich, the Bavarian capital and birthplace of Nazism was to be their target for that night. At Gransden Lodge, fourteen Lancasters were made ready as part of the Path Finder contribution of eighty-eight, and each received a bomb load commensurate with their assigned role, a cookie and three 1,000-pounders for the marker aircraft and an additional two 1,000 pounders for those supporting the main force. They took off between 18.46 and 19.20 with F/Ls Bennett, Weber and Weiser the senior pilots on duty and set a course to the south coast to begin the Channel crossing to the Dunkerque region, before traversing France to enter Germany south of Strasbourg. They reached the target area after an outward flight of some three-and-a-half hours, and encountered cloud over the Wörthsee, situated some fifteen miles west-south-west of the centre of Munich, the starting point for the 5 Group time-and-distance run. The skies over the city were clear of cloud, but the marking was scattered and led to most of the early bombing falling into southern and south-eastern districts. The 405 (Vancouver) Squadron participants performed their respective roles from 16,500 to 20,000 feet between 22.11 and 22.45 and on return suggested that the raid appeared to be concentrated on the eastern side of the city, local sources reporting that 339 buildings had been destroyed.

It was not until the 3rd that the Halifax operators of 4, 6 and 8 Groups were called into action, the crews learning at briefings that they would be part of an overall force of 547 aircraft, consisting of 223 Halifaxes, 204 Lancasters, 113 Stirlings and seven Mosquitos. For Kassel, the industrial city located some eighty miles to the east of the Ruhr, this night's visit would be the first of two during the month, which forever after, would leave their mark on the city. As home among other war industry concerns to the Henschel and Fieseler aircraft factories and the Henschel tank works where the much-feared Tiger Tank was in production, it was a target that needed the command's attention. 8 Group was represented by fifty-five Lancasters, a dozen provided by 405 (Vancouver) Squadron, and twenty-one 35 (Madras Presidency) Squadron Halifaxes in a plan that called for the Mosquitos to provide route markers and for the H2S crews to mark the target blind with yellow TIs and flares. Following up, the visual markers were to identify the aiming point and mark it with red TIs for the backers-up to maintain with greens. The 405 (Vancouver) Squadron element departed Gransden Lodge between 18.32 and 19.02 with S/L Schneider the senior pilot on duty and a cookie and four 1,000 pounders in each bomb bay along with the respective marker ordnance, and there were no early returns as they traversed Holland and the Münsterland to reach the target area. They were met by largely clear skies but thick ground haze, which should not have caused the Path Finder blind markers to overshoot the planned aiming-point, but this they did, and because the light from the flares reflected off the haze, the visual marker crews were unable to determine the location of the aiming-point and withheld their red TIs.

The Germans were operating decoy markers, which, together with the absence of red TIs conspired to lead a quarter of the main force crews astray and waste their bombs outside of the built-up area. The 405 (Vancouver) Squadron crews carried out their respective tasks from 15,000 to 20,000 feet between 21.10 and 21.34, reporting on their return what appeared to be a good concentration of fires and a pall of smoke rising to meet them. In fact, the main weight of the attack had fallen onto the western suburbs, where the Henschel aircraft and tank factories and the Fieseler aircraft plant were hit, but also onto woodland beyond. However, a stray bomb load had fallen onto one of the largest ammunition dumps in Germany, situated three miles north-east of the aiming-point at Ihringshausen, close to the suburb of Wolfsanger, and the resulting explosion at 22.06 devastated the area and attracted more bomb loads. A second explosion ten minutes after the first added to the destruction and left eighty-four buildings flattened and the ground pockmarked by craters, one of which was three hundred feet in diameter. Twenty-four aircraft failed to return, fourteen Halifaxes, six Stirlings and four Lancasters, which gave a loss-rate of 6.3%, 3.2% and 2.9% respectively.

The busy schedule of operations continued on the 4th when Frankfurt was posted as the target and a force of 406 aircraft assembled. This would be the last of six operations in which small numbers of USAAF Eighth Air Force B17s took part, but the Americans could not be convinced to become nocturnal, and October would turn into their blackest month of the war. Between the 8th and 14th alone, 152 bombers would be lost on daylight operations, 11.3%, and in the month as a whole, 214 B17s and B24s, almost 10% of those dispatched, with many more sustaining severe damage. It was a hammer blow to American morale and would result in restricted operations until they were able to provide adequate protection. 8 Group detailed twenty Halifaxes, fifty-two Lancasters and four Mosquitos, the five 405 (Vancouver) Squadron crews learning at briefing that they would be part of the main force and deliver a cookie and five 1,000-pounders each. They departed Gransden Lodge between 18.33 and 18.37 with no senior pilot on duty, and had to follow a somewhat circuitous route, which departed England over the Sussex coast and tracked across France as if heading for southern Germany, before swinging to the north-east and passing to the west of Frankfurt for the final run-in of around eighty miles. This added significantly to the mileage but avoided the flak hotspots from the Dutch coast and north of the Ruhr. They reached the target after a four-hour outward flight, up to an hour of which was accounted for in climbing-out and gaining height before setting course. Frankfurt was found to be clear of cloud, and the H2S-laid TIs and illuminator flares all fell within three miles of the aiming-point and those dropped by the visual markers within a mile-and-a-half, leaving the city at the mercy of the main force, which bombed on red and green TIs. The main weight of the attack fell into the eastern half of the city, which, together with the docks area, became a sea of flames as the 405 (Vancouver) Squadron delivered their payloads from 17,500 to 20,000 feet between 21.26 to 21.38. A large red explosion was observed at 21.37, which threw flames up to 3,000 feet, and smoke was rising through 8,000 feet as the bombers turned away, some crews reporting the glow from the burning city to be visible for 120 miles into the homeward leg. The success was gained at the modest cost of ten aircraft, half of which were Halifaxes.

The busy first week of the month concluded with a main event against Stuttgart, for which a force of 343 Lancasters was drawn from 1, 3, 5, 6 and 8 Groups on the 7th, sixty-seven of them provided by 8 Group, while sixteen other Path Finder Lancasters created a diversion at Friedrichshafen, a hundred miles to the south on the shores of Lake Constance (Bodensee) where the giant former Zeppelin construction shed was now in use to manufacture the Würzburg radar device. A new weapon in the Command's armoury was introduced for the first time in numbers on this night with the participation of a night-fighter-communications-jamming device called "Jostle" in the hands of 1 Group's 101 Squadron. It required a specialist operator in addition to the standard crew of seven, who though not necessarily a German speaker, could recognise the language, and on hearing it jam the signals on up to three frequencies by broadcasting engine noise over them. At 101 Squadron the device was referred to as ABC or Airborne Cigar, and once proved to be effective, ABC Lancasters would be spread through the bomber stream for all major operations, whether or not 1 Group was otherwise involved. The Lancaster would also carry a full bomb load reduced by 1,000lbs to compensate for the weight of the equipment and its operator.

The crews of F/L Bennett, P/O Wood and F/Sgt Larson departed Gransden Lodge between 20.41 and 20.43 bound for the "spoof" target with four 2,000-pounders and marker ordnance beneath their feet, and they were followed into the air immediately by the eleven-strong main element between 20.44 and 20.54 with F/Ls Gowan, Weber and Weiser the senior pilots on duty. The marker element's flares and TIs were supplemented by a cookie and two 1,000-pounders, while those supporting the main force carried a cookie and ten 500-pounders each and reached the target area to encounter ten-tenths cloud at 10,000 feet, which concealed the ground from view. The Path Finder H2S blind markers established two areas of focus for the visual markers and backers-up, which led to bombs falling in many parts of the city from the centre to the south-west. The 405 (Vancouver) Squadron crews carried out their briefed assignments from 17,000 to 20,500 feet between 23.59 and 00.16, while to the south the "spoofers" attacked from 17,500 to 20,000 feet between 23.58 and 00.05, claiming hits on the Zeppelin shed. Returning crews reported their impressions of a scattered attack at Stuttgart, which cost a remarkably modest four aircraft. Whether or not the presence of the radio-countermeasures Lancasters was responsible could not be proved, but it was a promising start, and would lead, ultimately, to the formation of a dedicated RCM group, 100 Group, in November.

The third raid of the series on Hannover was posted on the 8th, and a force of 504 aircraft duly assembled. A large diversionary raid was planned for Bremen to begin at 01.15, five minutes ahead of zero-hour at the main event and would involve seventeen 35 (Madras Presidency) Squadron Halifaxes and seven Lancasters of 8 Group marking for a main force of ninety-five Stirlings. At Gransden Lodge 405 (Vancouver) Squadron made ready fourteen Lancasters for the main event, loading each with a cookie and up to six 1,000-pounders plus marker ordnance appropriate to their assigned roles and sent them on their way between 22.46 and 23.15 with S/L Schneider the senior pilot on duty. After climbing out they set course for the northern tip of Texel to join the bomber stream and traverse northern Holland to enter Germany north of Meppen. All reached the target area to find largely clear skies and red and green TIs marking out the city-centre aiming point, the 405 (Vancouver) Squadron crews performing their respective roles from 15,000 to 20,000 feet between 01.25 and 01.44. Those over the target in the early stages of the attack observed fires just beginning to take hold and it became clear as they retreated westwards, that the fires were developing into a serious conflagration. Curiously, despite the claim by some commentators that this was the one successful raid of the series, there was no mention of the glow remaining visible from a considerable distance, as had been the case with the first two operations. This time a local report did emerge, which described heavy damage in all districts except for those in the west, with a large area of fire engulfing the central districts. A total of 3,932 buildings was destroyed, while thirty thousand others were damaged to some extent and the death toll amounted to 1,200 people. These statistics seem somewhat excessive for a single operation by fewer than five hundred aircraft, particularly in the absence of the kind of crew reports common to the first two raids, and this adds weight to the author's contention, that the above-catalogued damage was accumulative over the three operations. Twenty-seven aircraft failed to return, leaving a question mark over the effectiveness of the diversion at Bremen, and there was a single empty dispersal at Gransden Lodge, which earlier in the evening had been occupied by JA980. S/L Schneider RCAF and his crew had been homebound at 18,000 feet when crossing paths with a night-fighter, which shot it down to crash at 02.20 near Rinteln, midway between Hannover and Osnabrück, killing all but the flight engineer and wireless operator, who fell into enemy hands. The survivors testified after the war that twenty-two-year-old Murray Schneider had remained at the controls to try to give his mixed RCAF, RAF and RNZAF crew time to escape.

The Path Finder and main force squadrons would effectively stand down now for a period of ten days, while Mosquitos of 8 Group took the war to Germany. The crews were, no doubt, relieved when the lull in operations came to an end on the 18th with a call on Lancaster stations to attend briefings. The wall map revealed Hannover as the target for the fourth and last time in this series, and the crews learned that this was to be an all-Lancaster affair involving 360 aircraft, of which sixty-nine were provided by 8 Group, fifteen by 405 (Vancouver) Squadron. The armourers at Gransden Lodge loaded each of the five marker Lancasters with a cookie and up to six 1,000-pounders in addition to their marker ordnance and the remaining ten with six 2,000-pounders before dispatching them between 17.25 and 17.48 with F/L Sattler the senior pilot on duty. They made landfall over Texel and continued on an easterly track across Holland aiming for Cloppenburg, and thence Nienburg and Celle, before turning to the south-west to run in on the target close to the Deurag-Nerag oil refinery at Misburg. They remained unmolested by the defences until encountering a nest of night-fighters on crossing the frontier into Germany, and at least thirteen aircraft were brought down during the ensuing forty-five minutes that encompassed the approach and withdrawal phases. A layer of eight to ten-tenths cloud hung over Hannover with tops at 12,000 to 15,000 feet, and these conditions made it difficult for the Path Finders to establish the aiming-point. It resulted in them dropping both sky and ground markers that lacked concentration, which would lead to a scattering of the effort. The aircraft of the crews of P/O Wood and F/O South were hit by flak during the approach to bomb and the former jettisoned their load some four miles short of the aiming point. The latter's Lancaster was sent into a vertical dive, during which F/O South retained his load, including the markers, in order to not lead the attack astray and despite having sustained a wound to his left arm, refused medical attention until the contents of the bomb bay had been deposited on the aiming point from a lowly 12,000 feet. The others fulfilled their briefs from 18,500 to 20,000 feet between 20.10 and 20.26 and the strong presence of night-fighters dissuaded crews from hanging around to assess the outcome further. On the way home the South crew was engaged by a night-fighter, which was driven off, and they landed safely to report an impression of a scattered attack. It was established later that most of the bombs had fallen into open country, a disappointment compounded by the loss of eighteen Lancasters. The four raids on Hannover had cost the Command 110 aircraft from 2,253 sorties, a loss rate of 4.9%, but much of the city now lay in ruins. The city would receive no further attention for a year, until the oil offensive and the close proximity of the Misburg synthetic oil plant to the east, would ensure that the region remained in the firing line.

The first major attack of the war on the eastern city of Leipzig was planned for the 20th, for which an all-Lancaster force of 358 aircraft was assembled from 1, 5, 6 and 8 Groups. 8 Group was responsible for seventy-three Lancasters, fourteen of them belonging to 405 (Vancouver) Squadron, which took off from Gransden Lodge between 17.36 and 17.51 with F/Ls Bennett and Sattler the senior pilots on duty. Each had a mix of a cookie and 1,000 or 500-pounders in addition to their marker ordnance appropriate to their respective roles, but not all would find its way to the target. F/L Bennett and crew were on their way home within an hour after the oxygen feed to the rear turret rendered the occupant unable to function and avoided the atrocious weather conditions encountered by the others outbound, with a towering front of ice-bearing cumulonimbus east of Hannover extending beyond 20,000 feet. Many crews were persuaded to turn back as engines began to falter and ice-accretion destroyed lift and among these were F/O Clark and crew, whose starboard-inner engine failed. There was an attempt by some to climb into clear air and a crew from a 5 Group squadron had reached 26,500 feet before accepting defeat when still some one hundred miles north of Leipzig. Those pushing on through the front reached the target after a three-and-a-half-hour outward flight, only to then encounter seven to ten-tenths cloud with tops as high as 14,000 feet. The Path Finders had been unable in the conditions to establish and mark the aiming point, leaving crews to bomb on e.t.a., on fires glimpsed through the cloud or on scattered skymarkers. F/O Lefroy and crew suffered a hang-up over the target after circling for ten minutes and dumped their bombs manually shortly after turning away. The remaining 405 (Vancouver) Squadron crews performed their respective roles from 12,000 to 21,000 feet between 20.36 and 21.11 and were unable at debriefing to offer any useful details. Sixteen Lancasters failed to return, six of them belonging to 8 Group, and among these was JB348, which crashed near Werlte in north-western Germany within twenty miles of the Dutch frontier. P/O Wood RAAF and five of his mixed RAF/RCAF crew lost their lives and only the mid-upper gunner survived to fall into enemy hands.

The final major operation of the month was the second one against Kassel, for which preparations were put in hand on the 22nd. A force of 569 aircraft ultimately stood ready to take off in the early evening, twenty-two Halifaxes and fifty-six Lancasters representing 8 Group. At Gransden Lodge, seven crews learned that they would be involved in the main event, while five others were to participate in a diversionary raid on Frankfurt ninety miles to the south as part of a force of twenty-eight Path Finder Lancasters and eight Mosquitos. The latter took off first between 18.00 and 18.07, each carrying a cookie and two 1,000-pounders in addition to the marker ordnance and arrived in the target area to attack from clear skies in good visibility from 17,000 to 20,000 feet between 20.31 and 20.54. Meanwhile, those bound for Kassel took off between 18.18 and 18.38 with F/Ls Bennett and Sattler the senior pilots on duty, the marker crews with a cookie and mix of high explosives and marker ordnance in each bomb bay and the main force supporters with a cookie and six 1,000-pounders each. Part of the bomber stream encountered an electrical storm over the North Sea, which affected P4 and DR compasses and persuaded some crews to turn back, and severe icing became another issue, which put an end to the sortie of F/Sgt Bronikowsky and crew. The others pressed on across Belgium in continuing unfavourable weather conditions, which miraculously improved in the target area to leave clear skies between the bombers and the target, but ten-tenths cloud above them at 24,000 feet.

At the opening of the raid, the illuminator/blind marker crews identified the target by H2S and others by a visual recognition of ground features and some of these overshot the planned aiming-point, leaving the success of the operation reliant upon the visual marker crews backing up. Those from Gransden Lodge carried out their respective briefs from 15,000 to 20,000 feet between 20.47 and 21.10 and observed the bombing to be accurate and concentrated with scarcely any creep-back. Fires were just beginning to take hold as the bombers turned away and it was after the sound of their engines had receded that they joined together to engulf the city in what, in some areas, developed into a firestorm, though not one as fierce as that experienced in Hamburg. The shell-shocked inhabitants emerged from their shelters in the morning to find their city devastated and unrecognisable, and after 3,600 fires had been dealt with, it would be established eventually that more than 4,300 apartment blocks containing 53,000 dwelling units had been destroyed or damaged. This rendered up to 120,000 people homeless, in addition to which 155 industrial buildings had also been destroyed or severely damaged, along with numerous schools, hospitals, churches and public buildings. The death toll was in excess of six thousand, while more than three hundred Bomber Command airmen failed to return in forty-three bombers, twenty-five of them Halifaxes.

During the course of the month, the squadron participated in eleven operations and dispatched 105 Sorties for the loss of two Lancasters and crews.

November 1943

For the eleven nights following Kassel, the crews of the heavy brigade enjoyed a long and, for some, welcome break from operations. November brought with it the long, dark, cloudy nights which enabled Harris to return to his main theme, the destruction of Germany's capital city, and, although the crews were unaware, preparations were already in hand to resume the Berlin offensive. The new month also brought the Hercules-powered Halifax Mk III, which came with a marked improvement in performance over the Mk II and V variants. The first squadrons to benefit would be 4 Group's 466 Squadron RAAF and 6 Group's 433 (Porcupine) Squadron RCAF, and it would be December before the first examples found their way to Graveley for what would prove to be a brief period of service with 35 (Madras Presidency) Squadron.

The next four months would bring the bloodiest, hardest-fought air battles between Bomber Command and the Luftwaffe Nachtjagd and test the hard-pressed crews to the limit of their endurance. In a minute to Churchill on the 3rd, Harris stated that with the participation of the American Eighth Air Force, he could "wreck Berlin from end to end". He estimated that the campaign would cost the two forces between four and five hundred aircraft, but that it would cost Germany the war. This would remove the need for the kind of bloody, expensive and protracted land campaign, which he had personally witnessed during the Great War, and had prompted him to "get into the air" at the earliest opportunity. It should be remembered that this was the first time in the history of air warfare, that the means had existed to prove the theory, that an enemy could be defeated by bombing alone. It is only in the light of more recent experiences, that we have learned of the need, in a conventional conflict at least, to occupy the enemy's territory to secure submission. The Americans, however, were committed to victory on land, where film cameras could capture the glory, and would not accompany Harris to Berlin.

In the meantime, on the 3rd, F/O South was awarded a DFC for his skill, fortitude and presesence of mind during the final Hannover raid, and Düsseldorf was selected to open the month's operational account. No doubt, while the Prime Minister was digesting Harris's epistle, a force of 589 Lancasters and Halifaxes was being prepared for action, 8 Group's contribution amounting to a dozen Mosquitos, eight Halifaxes and nineteen Lancasters. 405 (Vancouver) Squadron briefed the crews of F/L Bennett and P/O Campbell for the main event and twelve others for an 8 Group diversionary raid on Cologne ten miles further south along the Rhine, for which fifty-two Lancasters and ten Mosquitos were detailed. The Cologne-bound element departed Gransden Lodge first between 17.18 and 17.30 with S/L Sattler the senior pilot on duty, some loaded with a cookie and six 1,000-pounders in addition to their marking ordnance and the non-markers with an additional four 500-pounders. They were followed into the air immediately by the Düsseldorf duo and joined up with the bomber stream over the North Sea en-route to the Scheldt, before traversing Belgium to approach the south-western Ruhr through the concentration of fifty to sixty searchlights in the Mönchengladbach-Cologne corridor, some fifteen miles from the target. It was here that the Cologne-bound element peeled off to the south and performed their respective roles from under clear skies and in moonlight from 15,000 to 20,000 feet between 19.35 and 19.41.

Meanwhile, at Düsseldorf, the Bennett and Campbell crews found small patches of cloud below them at 12,000 feet, which drifted across the city along with smoke from the early fires, despite which, the visibility remained generally good, and the Path Finders employed both sky and ground markers to good effect to identify the aiming-point in the city centre. The 405 (Vancouver) Squadron pair bombed from 20,000 feet at 19.46 and 20.04 respectively and observed fires to be developing on both sides of the Rhine with black smoke rising through 6,000 feet as they set course for home. Eighteen aircraft failed to return, and, unusually, eleven were Lancasters and only seven Halifaxes. Post-raid reconnaissance revealed that central and southern districts had sustained widespread damage to industry and housing, but no report came out of Düsseldorf to provide detail. Local sources at Cologne described a highly accurate raid centered around the western bank of the Rhine, where the cathedral was hit a number of times as was the ramp of the Hohenzollern railway bridge.

According to Bill Chorley's Bomber Command Losses, F/O Pringle RCAF was returning to Gransden Lodge, apparently alone, on the 5th after a training flight and was on final approach when JA979 plunged into the ground with fatal consequences for him. The squadron ORB makes no mention of this incident and the idea that a pilot would be alone on a training flight is extremely unlikely. Perhaps the other crew members had baled out, leaving the pilot to attempt a landing, but the lack of a reference in the ORB is suspicious. Minor operations occupied the next week, and the only serious operational activity for 8 Group were forays deep into southern France on the consecutive nights of the 10th and 11th, the first of which was in support of a 5 Group raid on the previously targeted railway yards at Modane, situated in the foothills of the Alps in south-eastern France. A force of 313 Lancasters included a contribution from 8 Group of seventy-five, of which fourteen represented 405 (Vancouver) Squadron, those assigned to marking duties loaded with up to seven 1,000-pounders in addition to the pyrotechnic devices. They departed Gransden Lodge between 21.03 and 21.18 with G/C Fauquier and S/Ls Gowan and Weiser the senior pilots on duty with an outward flight ahead of them of more than 650 miles, which all from Gransden Lodge completed in around four-and-a-quarter hours to be rewarded by the presence of a full moon shining brightly from a cloudless sky. They pinpointed on Lake Bissorte, from where the 5 Group crews carried out a time-and-distance run to the target, which they identified visually and by red and green TIs. The 405 (Vancouver) Squadron crews carried out their respective briefs from 13,000 to 15,500 feet between 00.56 and 01.12 and observed bursts concentrated around the markers and fires appearing to take hold, while a large explosion was observed at 01.13. Returning crews were fairly confident in the quality of their night's efforts and brought back two hundred bombing photos that revealed extensive damage to track and installations within one mile of the aiming point, a success gained at no cost in aircraft and crews.

The following night was devoted to an attack on a similar target at Cannes on the main coastal line between France and Italy, for which twenty-four 8 Group Halifaxes and ten Lancasters were to mark for a 100-strong 4 and 6 Group Halifax main force. While this operation was in progress, elements of 617 Squadron led by W/C Leonard Cheshire attempted and failed to destroy the Antheor Viaduct further west along the coast.

On the 17th, orders were received on 8 Group stations to prepare for an all-8 Group operation against Mannheim, although it is believed that the target was actually the city of Ludwigshafen, Mannheim's twin on the opposite bank of the Rhine, which was home to a number of I G Farben chemicals plants. 405 (Vancouver) Squadron detailed ten Lancasters and loaded each with five 2,000-pounders before sending them on their way from Gransden Lodge between 17.29 and 17.40 with G/C Fauquier and S/Ls Gowan, Sattler and Weiser the senior pilots on duty. S/L Sattler and crew turned back within the hour when both turrets became unserviceable, while the remainder pressed on across France to enter Germany south of Luxembourg. On arrival at the target up to six tenths cloud at 2,500 feet created challenging conditions for visual identification, but it was a blind attack purely on H2s with no TIs and the 405 (Vancouver) Squadron crews carried out their part from 16,000 to 19,000 feet between 20.02 and 20.16, observing little of the outcome. Imposter controllers operating from southern England sent spurious instructions to the enemy night fighter force, persuading many of them to land early, and there were comical exchanges as the opposing parties each insisted that their instructions were the genuine ones. Possibly as a result, only one aircraft was missing from the operation and this was 405 (Vancouver) Squadron's JB226, in which F/Sgt Larson RCAF and his mixed RCAF, RAF and USAAF crew all lost their lives.

Undaunted by the American response to his invitation to join the Berlin party, Harris would return alone, and the rocky road to the "Big City" was re-joined by an all-Lancaster heavy force on the night of the 18/19th, while a predominantly Halifax and Stirling contingent of 395 aircraft acted as a diversion by raiding Mannheim and Ludwigshafen three hundred miles to the south-west. The Berlin-bound crews would benefit from four Mosquitos dropping dummy fighter flares, while other Mosquitos carried out a spoof raid on Frankfurt to protect the Mannheim force. The two forces would cross the enemy coast simultaneously some 250 miles apart to confuse the enemy night-fighter controllers, and the route chosen for the Berlin brigade was via the Frisian Island of Texel to a point north of Hannover, and thence to the target to pass over the centre on an east-north-easterly heading. After bombing they would return south of Berlin and Cologne, before crossing central Belgium to gain the English Channel via the French coast. An innovation for this operation was a shortening of the bomber stream to reduce the time over the target to sixteen minutes. When the first Thousand Bomber raid had taken place in May 1942, with an unprecedented twelve aircraft per minute crossing the aiming-point, there was considered to be a high risk of collisions. The number had since been increased to sixteen per minute, with large raids lasting up to forty-five minutes, but on this night, twenty-seven aircraft per minute were to pass over the aiming-point.

At Gransden Lodge, five crews learned that they and eighteen other Lancaster crews and twenty-one in Halifaxes would be carrying out the marking at Mannheim, while nine had Berlin as their destination. The latter took off first between 17.15 and 17.23 with S/Ls Gowan, Sattler and Weiser the senior pilots on duty and a cookie and up to four 1,000-pounders in each bomb bay. The Mannheim-bound element took to the air between 17.29 and 17.33 *(ORB record badly corrupted)* with no senior pilot on duty and similar bomb loads and headed for the south coast to cross the Channel and enter France a few miles to the east of Abbeville. They continued on across France, driven on by stronger-than-forecast winds, and reached the target a little ahead of schedule to find clear skies and good horizontal visibility, although, haze compromised the vertical view of the city. The early arrival may have upset the plan to a degree, but the blind markers established their position by H2S before delivering their flares and high explosives, and the visual markers experienced little difficulty in identifying the canal, Rhine docks and bridges over the various waterways. The 405 (Vancouver) Squadron crews carried out their assigned tasks from 15,000 to 18,000 feet between 20.39 and 20.51 and had little to report at debriefing, and it was left to local sources to confirm that the northern and north-eastern districts of Mannheim had borne the brunt of the attack, and it was here that most of the destruction occurred, before some of the bombing also spilled into Ludwigshafen. Four industrial premises, including the Daimler-Benz car factory, and 325 other buildings were destroyed at a cost to the Command of twenty-three aircraft.

Meanwhile, the outward flight to Germany's Capital had taken place over a blanket of cloud that covered the whole of northern Germany. Crews were grateful for the red spotfire route marker dropped by the Path Finders north-east of Hannover, which confirmed that they were on track, and described the horizontal visibility as good, despite the absence of a moon. The cloud persisted all the way to the target with tops at 6,000 feet, and the glow of searchlights reflecting in them provided a guide to the crews above as they orbited awaiting the skymarkers. The 405 (Vancouver) Squadron crews carried out their assigned tasks from 18,000 to 21,000 feet between 20.37 and 21.05 *(corrupted record)* and returned home with nothing useful to pass on to the intelligence section at debriefing, most considering the bombing to have been scattered and probably ineffective. S/L Sattler and crew arrived back short of fuel and decided to land at the fighter aerodrome at Friston, where four unsuccessful attempts preceded a fifth, which ended with the Lancaster bouncing a wheel on a nissen hut but managing to touch down safely if a little damaged. Sources in Berlin confirmed that there had been no concentration and catalogued the destruction of 169 houses and a number of industrial units, with many more damaged to some extent. The loss of a relatively modest nine Lancasters was credited partly to the diversion at Mannheim, but the night's overall losses were still high.

On the 19th, 3, 4, 6 and 8 Groups combined to put together a force of 266 aircraft, 170 Halifaxes, eighty-six Stirlings and ten Mosquitos to attack the city of Leverkusen, situated on the eastern bank of the Rhine on the south-western fringe of the Ruhr a few miles north of Cologne. Those reaching the target area found ten-tenths cloud with tops at 10,000 to 12,000 feet, but no Mosquito-laid Oboe TIs because of mass equipment failure, which persuaded the backers-up to withhold their green TIs and employ H2S to drop their high explosives. Bombs were scattered over a wide area to the north of the target, hitting twenty-seven towns, while just a single one landed in Leverkusen.

Harris called for a maximum effort on Berlin on the 22nd, and 764 aircraft were made available, of which ninety Lancasters, twenty-one Halifaxes and eleven Mosquitos were provided by 8 Group. There was excitement at Gransden Lodge as KB700 "Ruhr Express", the first Canadian-built Lancaster was prepared for its first operational sortie along with thirteen others. The seven assigned to marking duties each received a bomb load of a cookie and up to four 1,000-pounders in addition to their pyrotechnics, while those supporting the main force had five 2,000-pounders in their bomb bays as they took off between 16.50 and 17.11 with G/C Fauquier and S/Ls Gowan and Weiser the senior pilots on duty. After climbing out, they adopted an outward route similar to that employed by the all-Lancaster force four nights earlier, which took them from Texel to a point north-west of Hannover, where a slight dogleg to port put them on a due-easterly heading directly to the target. Unlike the previous raid, however, rather than the circuitous return south of Cologne and out over the French coast, they would come home via a reciprocal route. This was based on a forecast of low cloud and fog over Germany, which would inhibit the night-fighter effort, while broken, medium-level cloud over Berlin would facilitate ground marking. An additional bonus was the availability to the Path Finders of five new H2S Mk III sets, while a new record of thirty-four aircraft per minute passing over the aiming-point would be achieved by abandoning the long-standing practice of allocating aircraft types to specific waves. On this night, aircraft of all types would be spread through the bomber stream, and this was bad news for the Stirlings, which, by the very nature of their design, would be below the Lancaster and Halifax elements, and in danger of being hit by friendly bombs. There was massive disappointment when KB700 LQ-Q lost its port-outer engine when just forty miles short of the target and began to lose height. P/O Floren ordered three 2,000-pounders to be jettisoned, but the Lancasters continued to sink, and the remaining ordnance was let go as they turned for home and adopted a direct route that took them over Amsterdam at 4,000 feet, where they survived an uncomfortable passage through heavy flak.

The others pressed on and arrived in the target area to discover that the meteorological forecast had been inaccurate, and that the city was hidden under a blanket of ten-tenths cloud with tops at around 12,000 feet. The blind markers employed H2S to establish their positions before releasing both red TIs and skymarkers, but the TIs disappeared as soon as they hit the cloud and were largely ineffective. This meant that the least reliable Wanganui (skymarking) method would have to be employed, and it was these flares that crews held in their bombsights as they began their bombing runs in the face of intense predicted flak and a mass of searchlights. The aiming point was backed-up with red flares with green stars and also green TIs and the 405 (Vancouver) Squadron crews carried out their assigned duties from 18,000 to 19,000 feet between 19.58 and 20.25. The glow of fires beneath the clouds, and a very large explosion that lit up the sky at 20.10 gave an impression of a successful operation, but a meaningful assessment was impossible. Post-raid reconnaissance and local reports confirmed that this attack on Berlin had been the most effective of the war to date and had caused a swathe of destruction from the city centre through the western residential districts of Tiergarten and Charlottenburg as far as the suburb town of Spandau. A number of firestorm areas were reported, and the catalogue of destruction included three thousand houses and twenty-three industrial premises. Many thousands more sustained varying degrees of damage, costing

175,000 people their homes and an estimated two thousand their lives, and by daylight on the 23rd, the smoke had risen to almost 19,000 feet. Twenty-six aircraft failed to return, eleven of them Lancasters, ten Halifaxes, and five Stirlings, which amounted to a loss-rate among the types respectively of 2.3%, 4.2% and 10.0%.

This proved to be the final straw for Harris as far as the Stirling was concerned, which, because of its short wing design, was restricted to a low service ceiling, and by the configuration of its bomb bay to small calibre bombs. Unlike the Lancaster and Halifax, it lacked development potential and was immediately withdrawn from future operations over Germany, blunting 3 Group's offensive capability until it could fully convert to Lancasters. The Stirling would still have an important role to play on secondary duties, however, bombing over occupied territory, mining, and in 1944, it would replace the Halifax to become the aircraft of choice for the two SOE squadrons, 138 and 161, at Tempsford. Many of those released from Bomber Command service would find their way to 38 Group, where they would give valuable service as transports and glider-tugs for airborne landings.

Having heard preliminary reports of the previous night's success, Harris ordered another immediate attack on Berlin, a decision that would stretch the nerves of the aircrew, who were still in recovery mode. A heavy force of 365 Lancasters and ten Halifaxes was made ready with some difficulty on the 23rd, because such back-to-back long-range operations also put a strain on those bearing the responsibility to get the aircraft off the ground. At Ludford Magna, for example, the armourers would be unable to load all nineteen 101 Squadron Lancasters with the intended weight of bombs, and would have to send them off 2,000lb short. In the Gransden Lodge briefing room, six crews were assigned as backers-up and the others as main force supporters, while out on the dispersals their Lancasters were being loaded with a cookie and up to five 1,000-pounders according to their specific role. They took off between 17.10 and 17.23 with S/Ls Sattler and Weiser the senior pilots on duty, and in a further manifestation of the effects of back-to-back long-range operations, forty-six aircraft returned early, although none from the ranks of 405 (Vancouver) Squadron. Another sign was the dumping of bombs over the North Sea by crews intending to push on to the target but wanting to gain more height. It involved largely those from 1 Group, who were shedding their cookies in protest at their A-O-C's policy of loading each Lancaster to its maximum all-up weight at the expense of altitude. The slogan "H-E-I-G-H-T spells safety" could be found on the walls of most bomber station briefing rooms at the time.

The target was reached by way of the same route adopted on the previous night and was found to be covered by ten-tenths cloud with tops at between 10,000 and 15,000 feet. Guided by the glow of fires still burning beneath the clouds from the night before, the leading Path Finder crews located the town of Rathenow on H2S and carried out a thirty-five-mile timed run to the centre of Berlin. The first red TI was observed at 19.58, then increasing numbers of skymarkers and red and green TIs became evident, which formed a triangle into which the bulk of the bombing fell. The 405 (Vancouver) Squadron crews performed their tasks from 16,000 to 19,000 feet between 19,56 and 20.06 and contributed to another stunning blow against the "Big City". Returning crews described a column of smoke reaching 20,000 feet, and the glow of fires visible again from the Hannover area some 150 miles from the target. Fake broadcasts from England again caused annoyance to the night-fighter force by ordering them to land because of fog over their bases. There were again arguments between the fake and real controllers as each claimed to be the legitimate voice, but despite the confusion, night-fighters still played a major hand in the bringing-down of twenty Lancasters. 405 (Vancouver) Squadron's JB182 went missing without trace with the predominantly RAF crew of F/O Clark RCAF, while JA939 crashed ten miles north-east of Emmen in northern Holland killing F/L Lefroy DFC RCAF and all but one of his experienced crew. The navigator, F/L Cole DFC RAF, was the sole survivor and after capture was taken to the crash site to formally identify his crew mates. Post-raid reconnaissance and local reports confirmed that this operation had destroyed a further two thousand buildings and killed around fifteen hundred people.

While 1, 3 and 5 Groups enjoyed a night off on the 25th, 216 Halifaxes of 4 and 6 Groups were made ready for an operation to Frankfurt, which 8 Group supported with twenty Halifaxes and twenty-six Lancasters. Local reports described a modest amount of housing damage and 3,500 people bombed out of their homes, in return for which, eleven Halifaxes and a single Lancaster failed to return.

The fourth operation in five nights was notified to 4 and 6 Group stations on the 26th, where 142 Halifaxes and six Lancasters were made ready as the main force for a diversionary raid on Stuttgart with fifteen 8 Group Halifaxes and Lancasters to provide the marking. The main event on this night was a raid on Berlin some 320 miles away to the north-east, for which a force of 443 Lancasters and seven Mosquitos was assembled, seventy of the Lancasters provided by 8 Group, fourteen by 405 (Vancouver) Squadron. It is difficult to decipher the bomb loads, but in addition to the marking ordnance there were mixtures of a cookie and 1,000 and 500-pounders according to specific roles as they departed Gransden Lodge between 17.28 and 17.43 with S/Ls Gowan, Sattler and Weiser the senior pilots on duty. The two forces adopted a common route, which involved an outward leg across the French coast and Belgium to a point north of Frankfurt, where they diverged. An indication of the beneficial effects of the two nights off for the Lancaster crews was a massive reduction in early returns compared with the previous Berlin raid. Those reaching the target area found it to be under clear skies, but despite the favourable conditions, the Path Finders overshot the city centre aiming point by six or seven miles and marked an area well to the north-west, which happened to contain many war-industry factories. The 405 (Vancouver) Squadron crews carried out their respective tasks guided by red and green TIs from 18,000 and 21,000 feet between 21.12 and 21.25 and on return spoke of a mass of fires and thick smoke rising to 15,000 feet. Night-fighters took a heavy toll of bombers during the return flight and among twenty-eight missing Lancasters were four representing 8 Group. It was learned later that thirty-eight war-industry factories had been destroyed and many others damaged.

During the course of the month the squadron took part in eight operations and dispatched eighty-eight sorties for the loss of four Lancasters, three crews and a pilot.

December 1943

Berlin would continue to be the dominant theme during December, and as November had ended, so December began with a heavy force of 443 aircraft standing by ready to take off in the late afternoon of the 2nd, all but fifteen of them Lancasters, after the main Halifax element had been withdrawn because of fog over their Yorkshire stations. 8 Group contributed eighty Lancasters, fifteen Halifaxes and eighteen Mosquitos, the twelve-strong 405 (Vancouver) Squadron participants learning at briefing that five of them would act as blind markers, three as backers-up and four to bomb with the main force. The marker Lancasters were loaded with a cookie and four or five 1,000-pounders in addition to their pyrotechnics, while the bombing brigade each received five 2,000-pounders. They took off between 17.11 and 17.27 with S/Ls Gowan, Sattler and Weiser and the newly arrived S/L Millward the senior pilots on duty, the first three-mentioned assigned to the blind marker role, and after climbing out they headed for the east coast to rendezvous over the North Sea with the rest of the force for a straight-in-straight-out route across Holland and northern Germany with no feints or diversions. First, however, the crews had to negotiate a towering front of ice-bearing cloud over the North Sea, which would contribute to a 10% rate of early returns, although there were no 405 (Vancouver) Squadron "boomerangs". They pushed through the challenging conditions and made it to the target area, although mostly south of track after variable winds had thrown them off course and dispersed the bomber stream. They also had to contend with large numbers of enemy night-fighters that harassed the bombers all the way to the target, after the controller had been able correctly to predict it.

The Path Finders were to establish their position at Stendal by H2S, but had strayed some fifteen miles south of track and mistakenly used the town of Genthin as their reference for the run-in. Release-point flares drew the bomber stream to the aiming-point, where good visibility prevailed above a thin layer of two to three-tenths cloud at around 5,000 feet, but up to nine-tenths between 10,000 and 12,000 feet, which the searchlights were able to pierce. The 405 (Vancouver) Squadron crews carried out their assigned tasks from 18,000 to 20,000 feet between 20.08 and 20.25, the main force crews bombing on skymarkers and red and green TIs, and where possible on ground detail like burning streets. Scattered fires were reported and a number of large explosions, some crews claiming the glow to be visible on the horizon from 120 miles into the homeward leg. It was a bad night for the bomber force, which lost forty aircraft, mostly in the target area and on the way home, but there were no empty dispersal pans at Gransden Lodge. Bombing photographs suggested that the raid was only partially successful, causing useful damage in industrial districts in the west and east, but scattering the main weight of bombs over districts and outlying communities to the south.

Having been spared by the weather from experiencing an effective visitation from the Command in October and exploiting the enemy expectation that Berlin would be the target again, Leipzig was the city at the end of the red tape on briefing-room wall-maps from County Durham to Cambridgeshire on the 3rd. Crews were told of its importance as a centre of war production, highlighting the Erla Maschinenwerk aircraft factory, which was producing Messeschmitt BF109s, and the fact that it was ringed on its western side by synthetic oil production plants, which were served by an important railway network distributing much needed supplies across Germany. A force of 527 aircraft was made ready, which included seventy-eight Lancasters and nineteen Halifaxes provided by 8 Group, fourteen of the former belonging to 405 (Vancouver) Squadron. Four of them were assigned to blind marking duties, four as backers-up and six to bomb with the main force, each receiving a cookie, up to five 1,000 pounders and a 500-pounder according to their role.

They took off between 00.18 and 00.49 with S/Ls Gowan, Sattler and Weiser the senior pilots on duty and rendezvoused with the bomber stream over the North Sea before heading towards Berlin as a feint, passing north of Hannover and Braunschweig with ten-tenths cloud beneath them and an hour's journey to Leipzig still ahead of them. Then, as they turned towards the south-east, the Mosquito element continued on to carry out a diversion at Berlin. Night-fighters had already infiltrated the stream at the Dutch coast, but the feint had the desired effect, and few night-fighters were encountered in the target area. However, it is believed that 405 (Vancouver) Squadron's JB222 was approaching the target when shot down to crash near Delitzsch some twenty miles short, with fatal consequences for the predominantly RAF crew of F/O Bowring. Two layers of ten-tenths cloud hung over Leipzig with tops at around 7,000 and 15,000 feet, onto which the primary blind markers delivered red flares with green stars and red TIs, which were added to by the secondary blind markers and backers-up with green TIs. The main force crews bombed on these, observing explosions and a strong glow beneath the clouds, followed by the emergence through the cloud tops of black smoke, which suggested that an accurate and concentrated attack had taken place, particularly as the smoke and glow remained visible for 150 miles into the return journey south-east towards the French frontier. Had many aircraft not then strayed into the Frankfurt defence zone, the losses may have been fewer, but twenty-four aircraft failed to return, fifteen of them Halifaxes. At debriefing the 405 (Vancouver) Squadron participants reported carrying out their assigned tasks from 16,000 to 19,000 feet between 03.57 and 04.09. Local reports confirmed this as a highly successful operation, which had hit residential and industrial areas, and was the most destructive raid visited upon this eastern city during the war. Sadly, for the Command, it would take its revenge in time.

The Command now entered a period of operational inactivity, which would last on Lancaster stations until the 16th and on Halifax stations until the 20th. At Graveley, the first of the new Mk III Halifaxes, HX270, arrived on 35 (Madras Presidency) charge on the 4th, and would be followed by eight more on the 11th. On the 16th, the Lancaster stations were roused to prepare 483 of the type for that night's operation to Berlin, the sixth since the resumption of the campaign, for which 8 Group put up ninety Lancasters along with ten Mosquitos. 405 (Vancouver) Squadron weighed in with thirteen Lancasters, JB374 containing W/C Reg Lane on his first operation since joining the squadron as a flight commander. Lane had completed two tours with 35 (Madras Presidency) Squadron, earning for himself a DSO and DFC, before returning to Canada for a public relations tour in July 1943 and then ferrying KB700 to England. He was posted to the Path Finder Navigation Training Unit, until joining 405 (Vancouver) Squadron in December. The other crews and aircraft on what would turn out to be a sad night for the squadron were those of S/L Gowan in JA976, S/L Sattler in JB484, S/L Weiser in JA974, F/L Allan in JB477, F/L Bennett in JB668, F/O Campbell in JA924, F/O Cloutier in JB188, F/O Drew in JB481, F/O Drimmie in JB280, F/O Fyfe in JB699, F/O McLennan in JB369 and F/S MacKinnon in JB183. Ten Lancaster received a bomb load of a cookie and up to five 1,000-pounders reflecting their marking function, while four were loaded with five 2,000-pounders to deliver as part of the main force. They departed Gransden Lodge between 16.29 and 16.48 and joined up with the bomber stream as it crossed the North Sea on course for the Dutch coast in the region of Castricum-aan-Zee, before heading due east all the way to the target with no deviations. A three-quarter moon would rise during the long return leg over the Baltic and Denmark, but it was hoped that the very early take-off and the expectation of fog to keep the enemy night-fighters on the ground would reduce the risk of interception.

Berlin was obscured by ten-tenths cloud with tops at around 5,000 feet, forcing the blind marker crews to employ red and green skymarkers rather than TIs, the 405 (Vancouver) Squadron participants fulfilling their assigned briefs from 18,500 to 20,000 feet between 19.56 and 20.11.

The return flight over Denmark passed largely without major incident, but the greatest difficulties awaited the 1, 6 and 8 Group crews as they arrived home to find their airfields covered by a blanket of dense fog. With little reserves of fuel to reach distant diversionary aerodromes, they began a frantic search for somewhere to land, stumbling blindly through the murk to catch a glimpse of the ground. For many, this proved fatal, while others gave up any hope of landing and abandoned their aircraft. Twenty-nine Lancasters and a mine-laying Stirling were thus lost, and more than 150 airmen killed in these most tragic of circumstances, and to this number was added the twenty-five Lancasters failing to return from the raid, many of which were accounted for by night-fighters over Holland and Germany while outbound.

It was a bad night for 405 (Vancouver) Squadron, and JB369 was the first of three of its Lancasters to fall foul of the conditions and crash at 23.58 some twenty miles to the north-east of Gransden Lodge near Ely. F/O McLennan RCAF and five of his predominantly RCAF crew persished at the scene, while the rear gunner, W/O Nutting DFM RCAF, survived with cuts and bruises on what was his forty-fifth sortie. He had been found by a local farmer and his nine-year-old son, the latter, Colin Stocker, now the farmer, remaining with him for some hours while his father went for help. W/O Nutting was screened from further operations after this, and the incident is commemorated by a memorial to the crew erected by Mr Stocker close to the crash site. A further fifty-two minutes elapsed before JB477 came to grief some two miles south-east of Graveley, killing three members of the crew and injuring the others, pilot, F/L Allan RCAF, lingering for eleven days in St Hughes Hospital Oxford before succumbing. JB841 came down near Marham in Norfolk at 01.30 with fatal consequences for five of the predominantly RCAF crew, while the pilot, F/O Drew RCAF, survived with injuries and the rear gunner walked away. An analysis and local sources revealed that Berlin's central and eastern districts had sustained considerable damage, mostly to housing and railways, but industrial damage had been insignificant.

Instructions were received on all stations on the 20th to prepare for an operation that night against Frankfurt, for which a force of 390 Lancasters and 257 Halifaxes was assembled. While the main operation was in progress, forty-four Lancasters and ten Mosquitos of 1 and 8 Groups were to carry out a diversion at Mannheim, some forty miles to the south. 8 Group made ready sixty-five Lancasters, twenty-one Halifaxes and three Mosquitos for the main event and sixteen Lancasters and ten Mosquitos for the diversion. At Gransden Lodge six crews were assigned to marking and illuminator duties at Frankfurt with four supporting the main force, the marker Lancasters each receiving a cookie and up to six 1,000-pounders in addition to their pyrotechnics, while the bombing brigade carried a load of six 2,000-pounders. The crews of F/L Bennett, F/O Fyfe and P/O Campbell were Mannheim-bound as they departed Gransden Lodge first between 17.09 and 17.12, each sitting on a cookie and four 1,000-pounder in addition to marker ordnance to create as much attention as possible. They were followed into the air immediately by the main eventers between 17.13 and 17.39 with W/C Lane and S/Ls Gowan, Sattler and Weiser the senior pilots on duty, and after climbing out, set course for Southwold and the North Sea-crossing to the Scheldt estuary, before passing north of Antwerp and flying the length of Belgium to the German frontier north of Luxembourg. The German night-fighter controller had picked up transmissions from the bomber stream as soon as it left the English coast and was able to track it all the way to the target and vector his fighters into position. Many combats took place during the outward flight, and the diversion failed to draw fighters away from the main action.

The problems continued at the primary target, where the forecast clear skies failed to materialize, and the crews were greeted by four to nine-tenths cloud at between 5,000 and 10,000 feet. This allowed some of them to pick out ground features, while others fixed their positions by H2S, if so equipped, and the main force Lancaster crews simply waited for TIs on e.t.a. The Path Finders had prepared a ground-marking plan in expectation of good vertical visibility, and dropped red, green and yellow TIs, while the Germans lit a decoy fire-site five miles to the south-east of the city. Some crews described the marking as late and erratic, and most thought the attack to be scattered in the early stages, becoming more concentrated as it progressed, and many commented on the new cookies detonating with a brighter flash than the old ones. The 405 (Vancouver) Squadron crews carried out their respective tasks from 17,400 to 19,000 feet between 19.29 and 19.45, contributing to a moderately successful raid, which according to some returning crews, left the glow of fires visible for 150 miles into the return journey. An analysis of the operation revealed that any success had been achieved largely as the result of the creep-back from the decoy site falling across the suburbs of Offenbach and Sachsenhausen, situated on the southern bank of the River Main. 466 houses were destroyed and more than nineteen hundred seriously damaged, despite which, the operation fell well short of its aims, and the loss of forty-one aircraft was a high price to pay. The Halifaxes suffered heavily, losing twenty-seven of their number, a loss-rate of 10.5%, compared with the Lancaster's 3.6%. Meanwhile, the Mannheim trio had delivered their attacks out of largely clear skies from 19,000 feet between 19.22 and 19.37 on H2S and largely missed the target.

It was at this time that the Command began to launch operations against flying-bomb storage and launching sites in the Pas-de-Calais region of north-eastern France, one of the ramifications of which would be the virtual independence of 5 Group in the coming spring. Two targets were briefed out on the 22nd, one at Flixecourt and the other at Tilley-le-Haut, both situated between Abbeville and Amiens and described as "constructional works", a euphemism persisting throughout the campaign, which would extend to the end of August 1944. In fact, many of the large sites were, indeed, giant construction projects in which thousands of tons of concrete were employed to build bomb-proof shelters for V-Weapons, the first of which would not actually be deployed against England until June. However, many of the launching sites were very small and were hidden in wooded areas, where the J-shaped buildings, which became known as "ski sites" were well hidden. Two forces totalling fifty-one aircraft were made ready, eleven Lancasters of 617 Squadron, now commanded by W/C Leonard Cheshire, and five Oboe Mosquitos assigned to Flixccourt and twenty-nine Stirlings to Tilley with three Oboe Mosquitos and three 35 (Madras Presidency) Squadron Halifaxes to carry out the marking. Little was observed of the results, but it is believed that the attack by Stirlings was successful, while the 5 Group effort foundered after the Oboe markers failed to ignite and the aiming-point could not be located.

Just two more operations remained before the year ended, and both were to be directed against Germany's capital city, the first, posted on the 23rd, involving a predominantly Lancaster heavy force of 371 aircraft, a figure which included a Path Finder contribution of seventy-seven Lancasters and seven 35 (Madras Presidency) Squadron Halifaxes, plus eight Mosquitos to provide a diversion. 405 (Vancouver) Squadron made ready thirteen Lancasters, loading six with a cookie, three 1,000-pounders and a 500-pounder in addition to their marker ordnance and the remainder with five 2,000-pounders. They departed Gransden Lodge between 00.17 and 00.43 with S/Ls Gowan and Millward the senior pilots on duty and adopted a somewhat circuitous route, which took the bomber stream in a south-easterly direction to the Scheldt estuary, before hugging the Belgian/Dutch frontier to cross into Germany south of Aachen, as if threatening Frankfurt. When a point was reached south of Leipzig, the route turned sharply towards the north and Berlin, while the Mosquito feint threatened Leipzig as the target. The blind primary marker crews picked up Luckenwalde on H2S, some twenty-five miles south-south-west of the target, from where they carried out a timed run. Berlin was enveloped in up to eight-tenths cloud at between 5,000 and 10,000 feet, and skymarkers appeared to be concentrated right over it, with incendiaries seen clearly burning on the ground. The 405 (Vancouver) Squadron participants performed as briefed from 18,500 to 21,000 feet between 03.57 and 04.08 and reported a large number of red and green TIs marking out the aiming-point. There was no hint of failure in the 8 Group ORB, which described well-concentrated fires and at least four large explosions, one described as orange and red and lasting for thirty seconds, and the glow of fires visible from a hundred miles into the return flight. However, the Bomber Command War Diaries claim that a high proportion of H2S equipment failures among the Path Finder element led to scattered and sparse marking, which local reports appeared to confirm, naming the south-eastern suburbs of Köpenick and Treptow as the ones to sustain the most damage. 287 houses and other buildings suffered complete destruction, in return for which, the defences claimed the relatively modest number of sixteen Lancasters.

The fifth wartime Christmas period passed with no operational activity to interfere with the festivities, but the business of war returned on the 29th, when a maximum effort was called for the next assault on Berlin. For the Lancaster operators, this would be the first of three raids on the capital in five nights spanning the turn of the year, and 457 of the type were to be joined by 252 Halifaxes and three Mosquitos to form a force of 712 aircraft. The Path Finder heavy contribution amounted to eighty-three Lancasters and twenty-one 35 (Madras Presidency) Squadron Halifaxes, the crews of which attended briefings to learn of their individual roles. At Gransden Lodge, all fourteen crews were assigned to marking roles, most with a cookie and four 1,000-pounders beneath their feet along with the pyrotechnic ordnance and took off between 17.02 and 17.28 with S/Ls Gowan and Millward again the senior pilots on duty. It was from this juncture that the intolerable strain on the crews of successive long-range flights in difficult weather conditions began to become manifest in some squadrons through the rate of early returns, which on this night reached forty-five or 6.3%.

The bomber stream was routed out over the Dutch Frisian islands pointing directly for Leipzig, and, having reached a point just to the north of that city, was to turn to the north towards Berlin, while Mosquitos carried out spoof raids on Leipzig and Magdeburg. F/Sgt Bonikowsky and crew were two hours out when their starboard-outer engine failed and ended their interest in proceedings. The others reached the target area to find ten-tenths cloud with tops at anywhere between 7,000 and 18,000 feet, and red and green Path Finder release-point flares (Wanganui) hanging over the city. The ground marking TIs disappeared into the cloud tops and could not be seen, leaving the success of the operation in the hands of drifting skymarkers, a proportion of which were delivered by Gransden Lodge crews from 19,000 to 20,000 feet between 19.55 and 20.20. At debriefing, crews reported a considerable red glow beneath the clouds, which remained visible for a hundred miles and gave the impression of a concentrated and successful assault. This was not entirely borne out by local reports, which revealed that the main weight of the raid had fallen onto southern and south-eastern districts, and also into outlying communities to the east. 388 buildings were destroyed, although none of significance, and ten thousand people were bombed out of their homes. Eleven Lancasters and nine Halifaxes failed to return, a loss-rate of 2.4% for the former and 3.5% for the latter. F/Sgt McQuade RCAF was forced to put down JB668 at the emergency landing strip at Woodbridge on the Suffolk coast, after it had been badly damaged by flak over the target and again near Bremen on the way home. A tense crossing of the North Sea ended with a safe landing at 00.01, after which an inspection deemed the Lancaster to be beyond economical repair.

During the course of the month the squadron took part in seven operations and dispatched seventy-nine sorties for the loss of five Lancasters and the better part of four crews. It had been a testing end to a year which had brought major successes and advances in tactics, but it had also been a year of high losses, particularly among the Stirling and Halifax squadrons. While "window" had been an instant success, it had also caused the Luftwaffe to rethink and reorganise, and the night-fighter force which emerged from the ruins of the old system was a leaner, more efficient and altogether more lethal beast than that of before. As far as the crews of Bomber Command were concerned, the New Year offered the same fare as the old one, which none would view with relish. The next three months would see morale at its lowest ebb as the winter campaign ground on in the face of its two powerful enemies, the weather and the Luftwaffe night-fighter force, and they would combine to test the bomber crews to the absolute limit.

W/C A C Clayton
405 Squadron Commanding Officer
December 1942 to April 1943

F/O William Anderson DFC
Badly injured during an attack by a Dornier but he continued to fire and the Dornier subsequently fell blazing to earth.

Target Photo – Le Creusot 19/20th February 1943.

6 Group Meeting 3rd February 1943

U Boot Type VII - U 995
Mainstay of the German Naval Submarine Force – over 700 were built during World War II

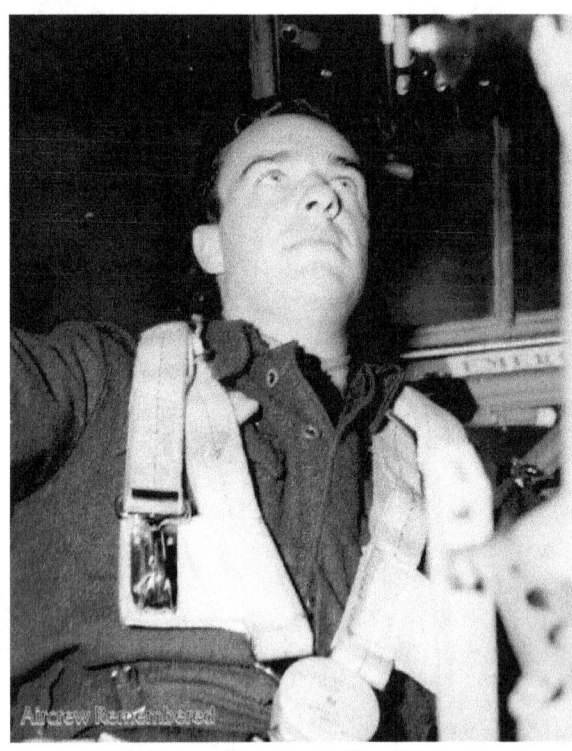

S/L Murray Stanley Fuller Schneider
Homebound - shot down and killed by a night-fighter on 9th October 1943. (Aircrew Remembered)

W/C W Weiser MBE, DFC & Bar

Hamburg docks after repeated attacks by Allied bombing.

Code names for 'Gardening' mining areas (Aircrew Remembered).

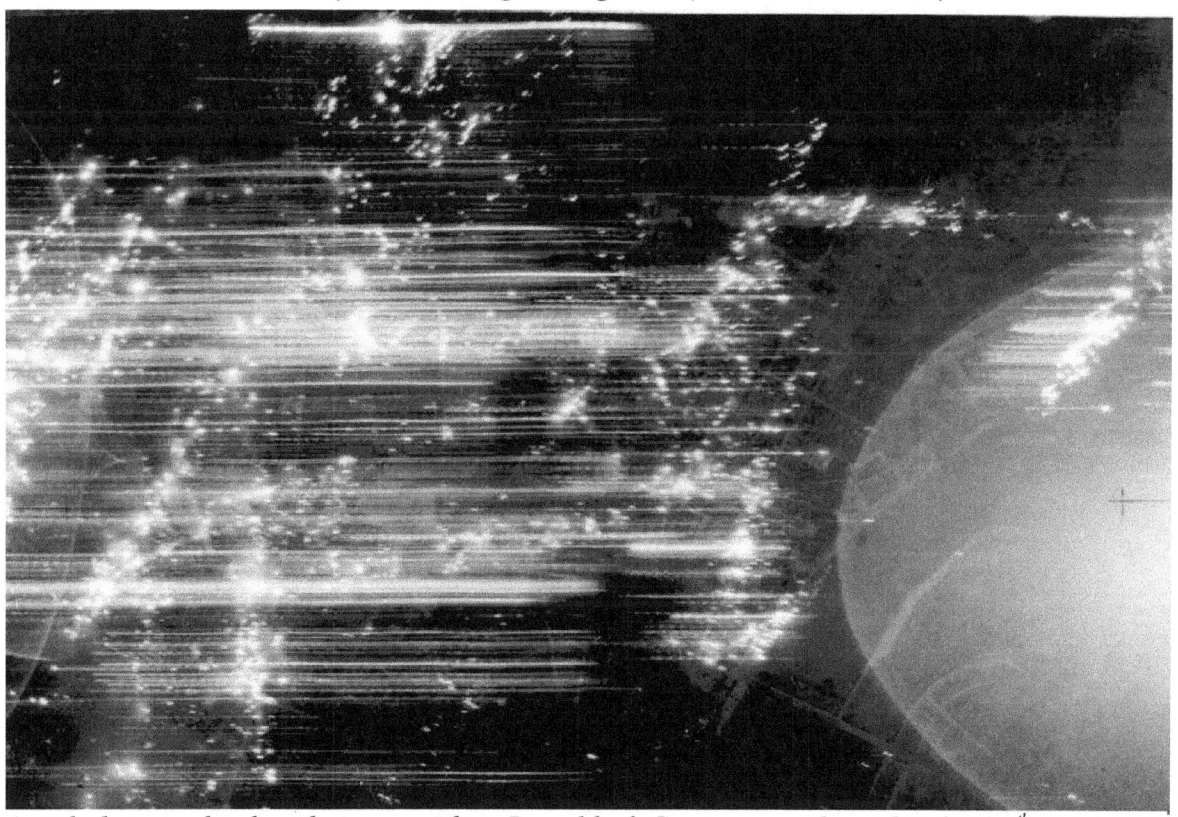
Aerial photograph taken during a raid on Dusseldorf, Germany, on the night of 11/12th June 1943. Sticks of incendiary bombs lie across Karlstadt in the early stages of the attack. The River Rhine and the Oberkasseler brucke can be seen, illuminated by the detonation of a photoflash bomb (lower right).

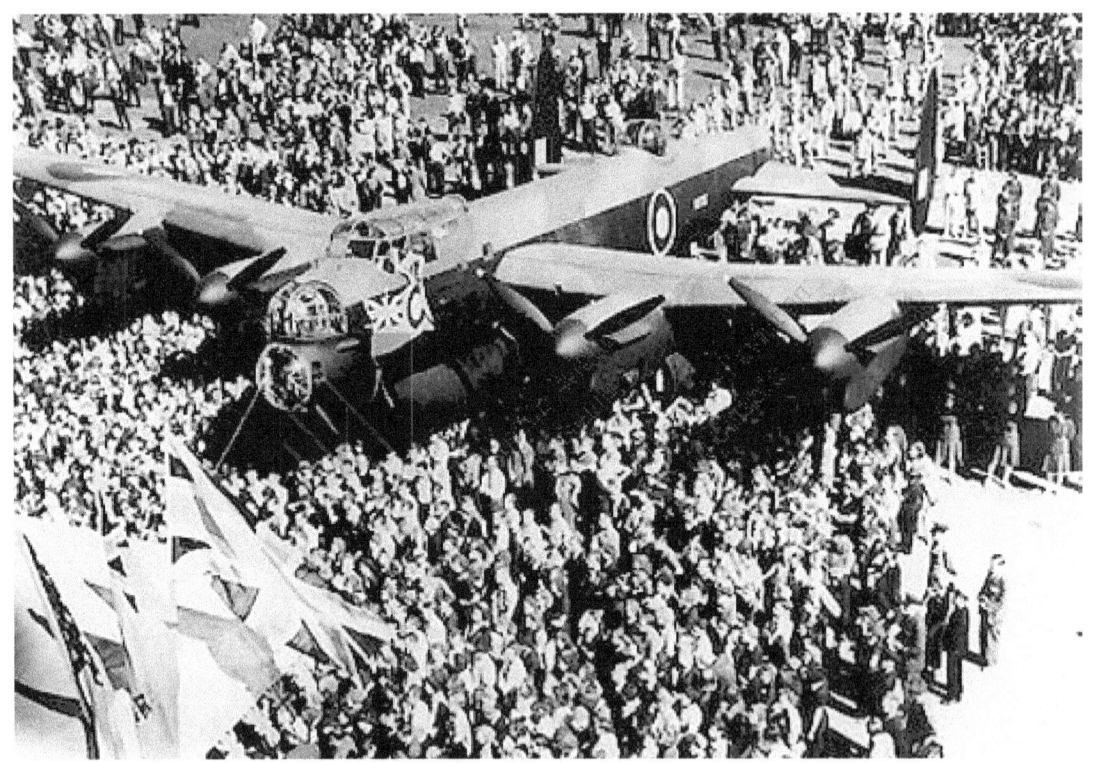

Lancaster KB700. Roll-out of first Canadian-built MkX

1st August 1943 was a proud day for the workers of Victory Aircraft, and indeed for all Canadians, as the first Canadian-built Lancaster rolled off the assembly line.

Lancaster KB700 before departure

Lancaster KB700 about to make its maiden flight at Malton, Canada 1st August 1943.

W/C Reg Lane Crew with Lancaster KB700 shortly after its arrival at Gransden Lodge.

RAF Gransden Lodge 11th June 1943

Bomb Damage to Krupp Factory, Essen.

Photo taken after the second heavy raid on Essen on the night of the 13th March 1943 following the severe and concentrated attacks on the 5th and 6th March and provides ample evidence of the devastation caused to the buildings and the workshops of the Krupps armament works.

This also shows two large sections of the plant battered and, in some case, still burning several hours after the last raiding force had left.

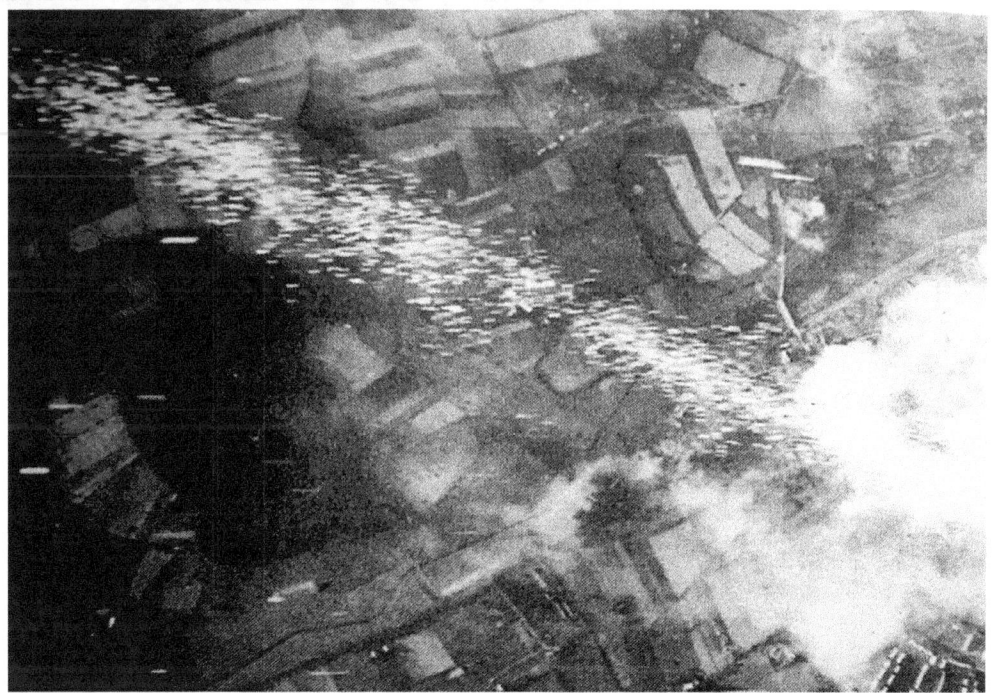

A concentrated mass of 'Window' falls from an RCAF bomber.

Messerschmitt Bf110

Messerschmitt Me262

Junkers Ju88

Pathfinder Force Target Indicator Flares

Dispersal at Gransden Lodge with Lancaster NF349

RAF reconnaissance photograph of V-2 rockets at Peenemünde Test Stands I and VII.

Bomb Damage Peenemünde August 1943.

W/C R.J. Lane
405 Squadron Commanding Officer
January 1944 - August 1944

W/C C Palmer
405 Squadron Commanding Officer
August 1944 – September 1944 (KIA)

King George VI presents a Bar to Air Commodore Fauquier's Distinguished Service Order at RCAF Linton-on-Ouse 1944.

Target Photo – Domberg – 2nd September 1944

Target Photo – Friedrichshafen – 27/28th April 1944.

Remains of Lancaster ND507
The Lancaster crashed on 3rd June 1944 while on an operation to bomb rail yards in northern France. The pilot S/L G E Coldrey, Sgt D A Kelley, P/O N Johnson, F/Sgt J G M Renaud and W/OII L A McRea all died. F/L's G L Court, and J H O'Neill became PoW's.

F/O E Townsend (Pilot)   Sgt D Carrott   F/O W Morrow   F/O E Pomeroy

F/O W P Drew   P/O C J Blyth   W/C C Gray

All died 29th July 1944 when their Lancaster JB707 crashed into Ringkobing Fjord during a Hamburg operation.   *(Aircrew Remembered)*

405 Squadron air and ground crew alongside 'Ruhr Express'

405 Squadron Lancasters on a daylight raid.

S/L Gordon Bennett DSO, DFC and Crew.
S/L Bennett was killed when Lancaster ND526 was shot down on an Aachen operation on 25th May 1944. Six remaining crew members became PoW's while WOII J Frame evaded.

W/C Peter Mains-Smith DSO DFC

S/L G B Elwood DSO, DFC & Bar, Navigator with W/C Fauquier.

Lancaster JB280
Shot down on 2nd January 1944 by a night-fighter with the loss of all crew while on a Berlin operation. F/O T H Donnelly, F/O A J Salaba, F/Sgt W L Clark, SgtB S J West, Sgt R E Watts, Sgt R Zimmer, Sgt L G R Miller.

German E-Boot
On the 14th June 1944, the purpose of a daylight evening raid on Le Havre was to destroy E-Boots threatening the Normandy beachhead. A similar operation took place at Boulogne on the following night.

P/O H A Floren, piloting 405 Squadron 'Ruhr Express'. He was killed on the 14th January 1944 while on a Braunschweig raid.

P/O Harold Floren (third from left) and Crew

Lancaster ND709 or PB451; F/L L L MacKinnon aircrew and ground crew.
Front Row (L-R): Bob Nicholson (fitter); F/L Doug Renton DFC (Nav), G. Connell DFM (W/Op.); F/S John Rennie DFM (MUG); S/L L.L. MacKinnon DSO DFM (Pilot); F/Sgt T. Waters DFM (RG); F/L Ross Baroni DFC (Visual Bomb Aimer); F/O Ed Chappell DFM (FE); F/L Vic Bowden DFC (Set Operator); Sgt McKiney (Ground Crew Chief - 'G-George').

Walcheren Island, Holland. October 1944. Part of the sea wall around Walcheren Island breached by RAF Bomber Command attacks. The flooding was at Ritthern, A village due east of Flushing where several strongpoints were isolated.

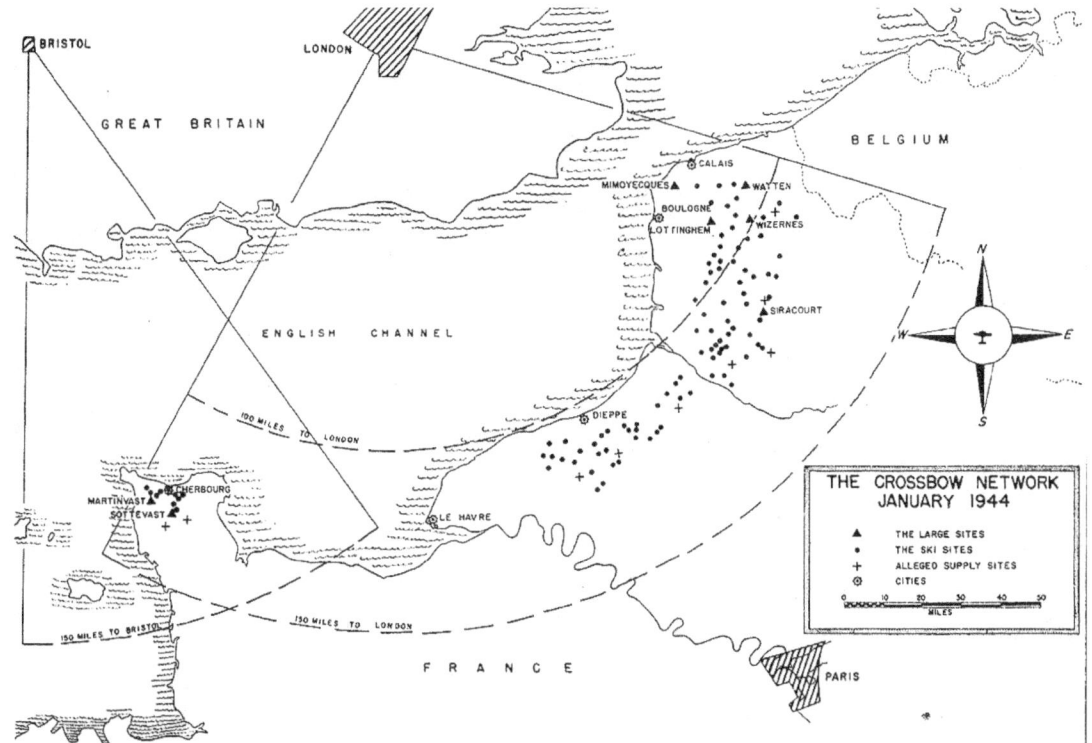

Map showing the two areas where the Germans were setting up their secret "V" weapons to bombard England (right, centre). These are the areas in which the RAF and 8th Air Force heavy bombers concentrated their bombs to destroy the weapons -- part of the pre-invasion plan. Below: Target Photo – Bois de Cassan (not a 405 Squadron photo although they did bomb the target.)

A staged photo taken at Allerton Park showing senior officers from all branches of the armed services planning operations. L – R: AVM C M McEwen, Major A K L Stephenson, Air Commodore C R Slemon and Air Commodore J Fauquier.

RCAF Offices at Allerton Park – 6 Group HQ.

The ruins of Caen 1944
A pair of residents watch a bulldozer clearing away the ruins of destroyed houses, rue de Bayeux, Caen. In the background, the two towers of the Abbaye aux Hommes remain intact.

Target Photos

Left – Bordeaux

Below - Caen marshalling yards bomb bursts 1944

Berlin

Dortmund

Duisburg

Above: Frankfurt. Below: Cap Gris Nez Gun Battery

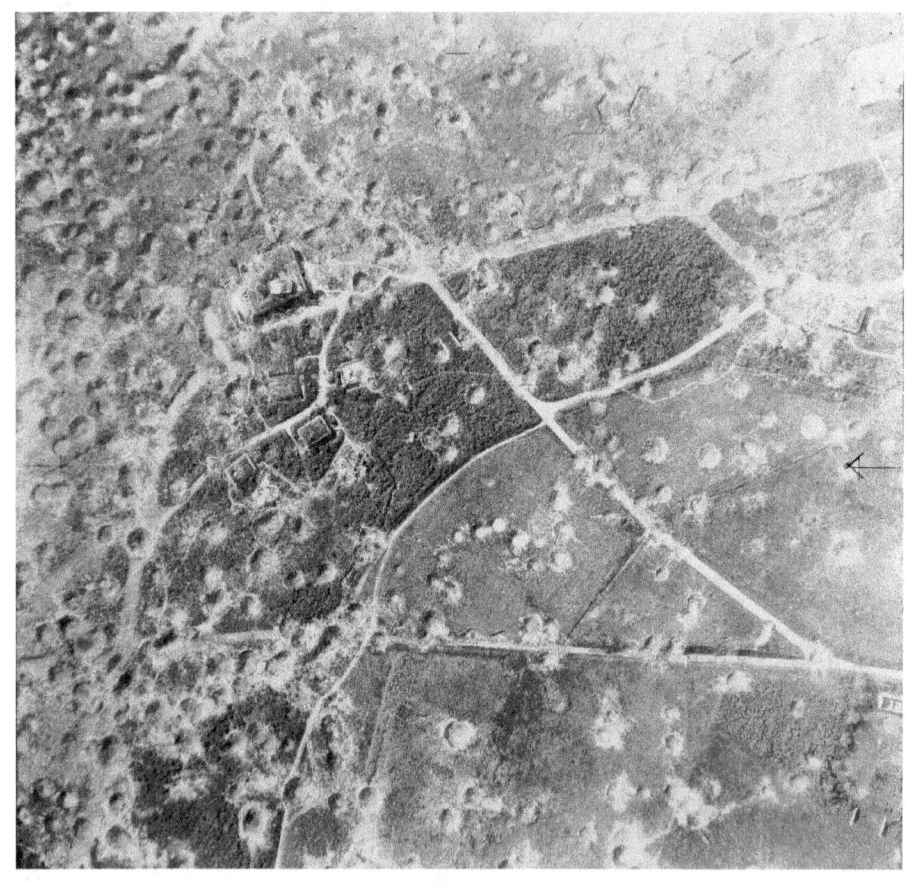

Kassel *Koblenz*

Krupps Factory, Essen

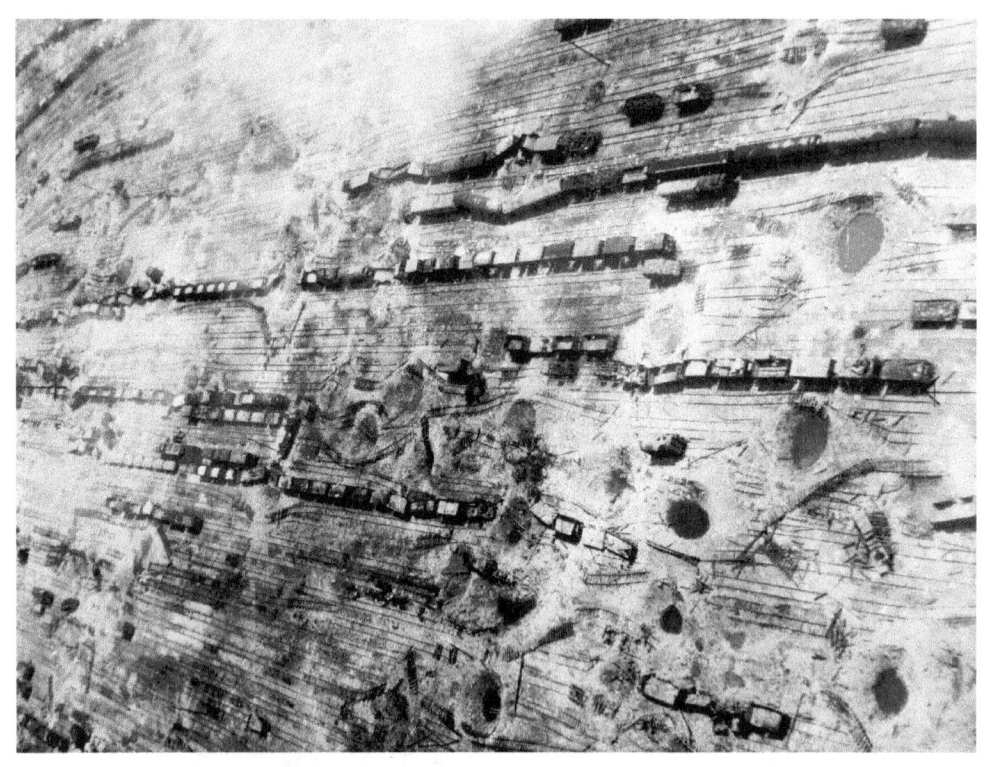

Rail Yards and below: Stuttgart-Nuremburg area

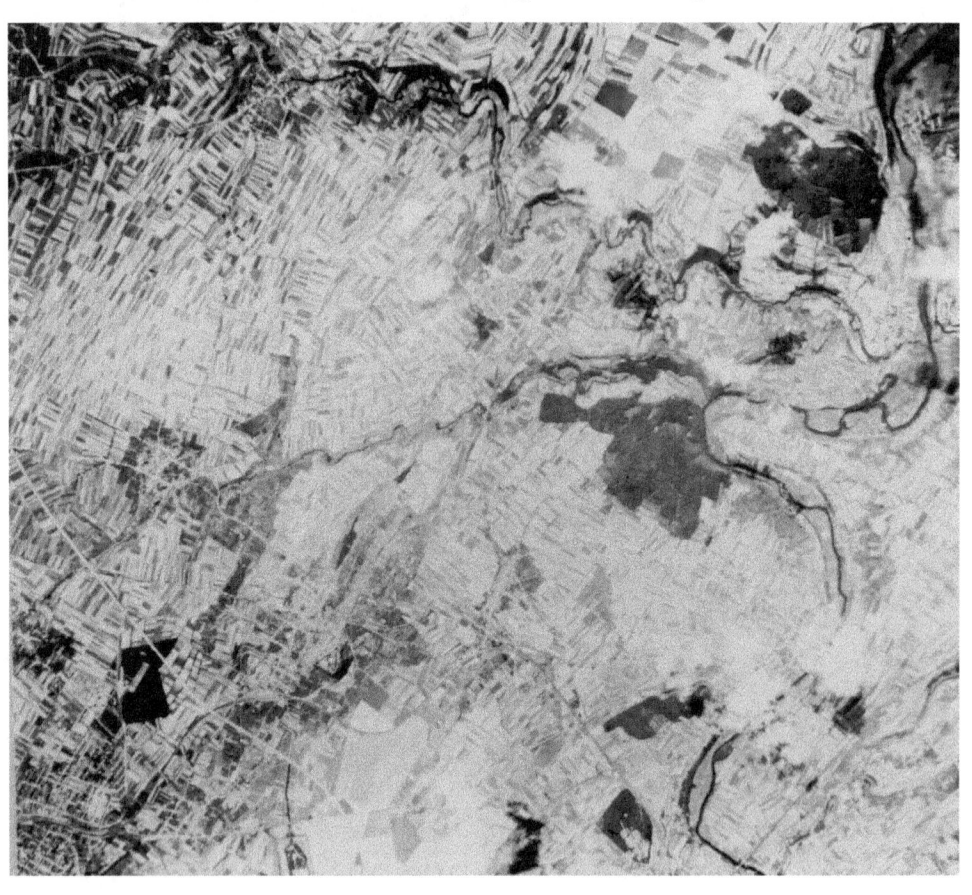

Calais – 26th September 1944

W/C H.A. Morrison
405 Squadron Commanding Officer
September 1944 to October 1944

W/C W F M Newson
405 Squadron Commanding Officer
October 1944 to September 1945

Magdeburg 1945
Attacked by Bomber Command including 405 Squadron on the 16th January 1945.

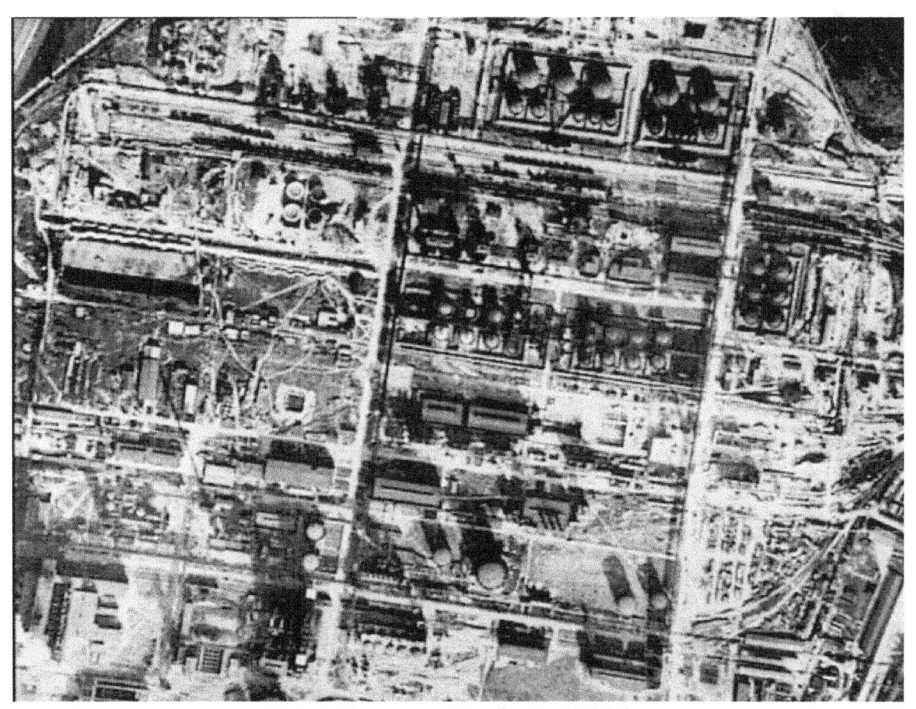

Zeitz, Germany Synthetic Oil Plant
Before the attack on the factory near Leipzig on 16th January 1945....

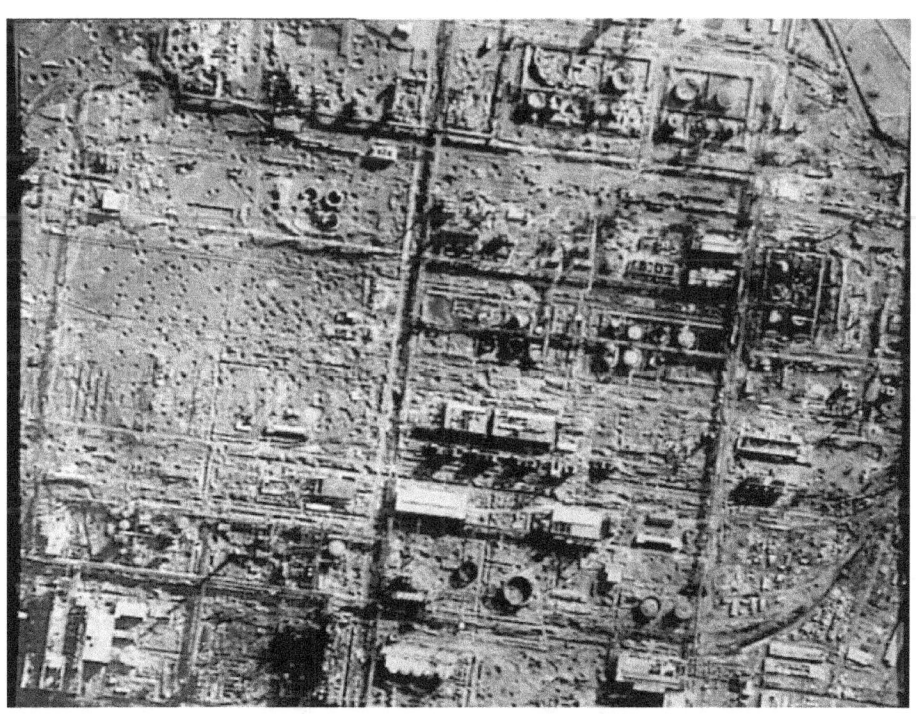

....And after the attack which included 405 Squadron. The plant is a mass of debris amongst a dense concentration of craters. Most of the pipelines are broken, and all the vital parts of the plant have been hit. Large numbers of storage tanks and cooling towers are destroyed or damaged.

Crew of Lancaster ME315. L-R: P/O P Young, P/O C R G Ryan, unknown (not a member of this crew at the time of the incident), S/L C Mussells, F/L Melborn Mellstrom, F/O R T Gale, P/O E L Tempest and F/O Dooley.

On the 10th April 1945, the Lancaster was attacked by an Me163 fighter which, with one burst, shot away rudder, elevator and the rear turret, killing F/L Mellstrom. The H2S set and upper turret were also damaged. An escort of Mustangs moved in to protect the Lancaster until it could reach the front lines. As he had only partial control of the aircraft and the mid-upper gunner was injured, the pilot ordered the crew to bale out.

However, a successful landing was made at Woodbridge and all of the remaining members of the crew returned to their unit.

The Messerschmitt Me163 rocket powered fighter.

Damage to Lancaster ME315 (Photos by kind permission of Aircrew Remembered).

405 Squadron Crew – Gransden Lodge

L-R - F/L Bill Hamblin (MUG), F/O Johnny Ross USAF (RG), F/L Don Vockins – (W/AG), F/O Tom Downey (Nav), F/O Bernard Smoker (2nd Nav), S/L Howie Marcou (Pilot), F/Sgt Eric Bolland (FE), F/O Ron Noice (BA). Shot down in Lancaster PB530 over Dortmund 21st February 1945. By then Hamblin and Vockins had been replaced by Jimmy Werner and Johnny Lewis. All taken into captivity except F/Sgt Bolland who was killed when his parachute failed to open. S/L Marcou was badly wounded.

F/O G E Peaker and Crew

All lost on 19th March 1945 in Lancaster PB451 while on a Witten operation. F/O G E Peaker, F/O E Hayes, F/O R S Butterworth, W/OII R MBaker, F/Sgt E F Perrault, P/O J P H Adam, Sgt A Kirkcaldy Sgt R P Smith. This was the last crew posted missing from 405 Squadron during its tenure as a PFF squadron.

Lancasters of 405 Squadron en route to a target in 1945, as a PFF unit.

The remains of Lancaster KB700 after it was burned out on the ground at Middleton St George in January 1945.

AVM Clifford Michael (Black Mike) McEwen.

AVM McEwen was a First World War fighter pilot with 27 aerial victories and was viewed as an inspirational leader.

As AOC 6 Group, 'Black Mike', led from the front, flying on many operations although strictly forbidden so to do. He would often wear a sergeant's uniform, but word spread, and he was thought of with the greatest respect by his crews, both air and ground. They believed he appreciated and shared their dangers and all would be well as long as he went along with them.

This attitude led to 6 Group crews being viewed as among the very best performing in Bomber Command.

At RAF Middleton St. George, RCAF AVM Clifford Mackay "Black Mike" McEwen, commander of 6 Group (foreground), AVM Arthur "Bomber" Harris (middle) and RCAF Air Marshal G.O. Johnson, AOC RCAF Overseas (background) wave goodbye to the first of 141 Canadian Lancasters departing for Canada. One destined to join Tiger Force was Lancaster KB999, the 300th Canadian-built Lancaster. When it came off the assembly line in Malton, Ontario, Victory Aircraft Corporation production staff dedicated this aircraft to McEwen and had his pennant painted on the nose with the words "Malton Mike". After the end of the war, KB999 was assigned to the RCAF's 405 Vancouver Squadron and flew AVM McEwan back to Canada on 17th June 1945.

The Hague, Netherlands 1945. A rocket launching site near the racecourse in the Duindigt/Hague area after air attacks by RAF Bomber and Fighter Command including 405 Squadron. At (A) can be seen a vertical rocket surrounded by fuelling vehicles. Bomb craters can be seen along the road. The large craters top centre and right of the photograph were made by faulty rocket launchings. Bottom centre of the picture is a large turning loop for the rocket launching convoy.

The gathering of all personnel for V E Day held at RAF Gransden Lodge

January 1944

The change of year was not destined to effect a change in the emphasis of operations, and this was, no doubt, a disappointment, not only to the hard-pressed crews of Bomber Command, but also to the beleaguered residents of Germany's capital city. Proud of their status as Berliners first and Germans second, they were a hardy breed, and just like their counterparts in London during the Blitz of 1940, they would bear their trials with fortitude and humour, and would not buckle under the constant assault from above. They had witnessed the destruction of 25% of their city's living accommodation, and seen evidence of the mounting death toll, and yet banners in the streets proclaimed "You may break our walls", but not out hearts", and the most popular song of the day, Nach Jedem Dezember Kommt Immer Ein Mai, After every December comes always a May, was played endlessly over the airwaves, its sentiments hinting at a change in fortunes with the onset of spring.

Harris allowed the Berliners little time to enjoy New Year, and as New Year's Day dawned, plans were already in hand to continue the onslaught. Before it ended, the first of 421 Lancasters would be taking off and heading eastwards to arrive over the city as the clock showed 03.00 hours on the 2nd. Take-off had actually been delayed because of doubts over the weather, and this meant that insufficient hours of daylight remained to allow the planned outward route over Denmark and the Baltic. Instead, the bomber stream would adopt the previously used almost direct route across Holland and northern Germany, but return as originally planned more circuitously, passing east of Leipzig, before racing across Germany between the Ruhr and Frankfurt and traversing Belgium to reach the Channel near the French port of Boulogne. 8 Group contributed eighty-one Lancasters of which a dozen belonged to 405 (Vancouver) Squadron, four to be occupied by blind marker crews sitting on a cookie and four 500-pounders in addition to their pyrotechnics, two backers-up with marking ordnance and a cookie and six 500-pounders in the bomb bays, and six main force supporters toting a cookie and four 1,000-pounders. They departed Gransden Lodge between 00.08 and 00.37 with S/L Millward the senior pilot on duty and joined up with the bomber stream to cover the four-hundred-mile leg from the Dutch coast to Berlin in under two hours without once catching a glimpse of the ground through the dense cloud. It was no different at the target, which was completely obscured by a layer of ten-tenths cloud with tops in places as high as 19,000 feet. The Path Finders had to employ skymarking (Wanganui), which was somewhat scattered, but the glow of fires, smoke rising through the cloud tops and a huge explosion lighting up the clouds for three seconds at 03.07 suggested an effective raid. The 405 (Vancouver) Squadron crews carried out their assigned tasks from 18,000 to 20,000 feet between 02.56 and 03.11 and ten returned home, F/L Coldrey and crew landing at Gravesend after sustaining heavy damage during co-ordinated attacks by a Ju88 and FW190 shortly after leaving the target. Large holes in the mainplane and elevators and a holed fuel tank guaranteed a tense return flight, during which three hundred gallons of petrol evaporated, but the crew was unhurt and the Ju88 was claimed as damaged.

It had been impossible to assess what was happening on the ground, and it was established, ultimately, that the operation had been a failure, which had scattered bombs across the southern fringes of the city and beyond into wooded and open country, a disappointment compounded by the loss of twenty-eight Lancasters. A sad start to the year for the Canadians saw two empty dispersal pans at Gransden Lodge that should have been occupied by JB280 and JB737, the former having been shot down by the night-fighter of Lt Friedrich Potthast of IV./NJG1 while outbound. The Lancaster crashed at 02.10 in the Drenthe region of northern Holland without survivors from the mixed RCAF/RAF crew of F/O Donnelly DFM RCAF. The long-serving P/O Campbell RCAF and crew were on their way home when they came down in north-eastern France and only the flight engineer and mid-upper gunner survived to fall into enemy hands.

During the course of the 2nd, a heavy force of 362 Lancasters and nine of the new Mk III Hercules-powered Halifaxes was assembled and prepared for a return to Berlin that night. There was snow on the ground, and many of the crews called to briefing were still tired from being late to bed following the almost-eight-hour round trip the night before. Some of these were in a mutinous frame of mind at being on the order of battle again so soon, but their professionalism shone through, and they would fulfil their responsibilities as always. 8 Group provided seventy-four of the Lancasters, nine 35 (Madras Presidency) Squadron Halifaxes and a dozen Mosquitos, while 405 (Vancouver) Squadron managed to put a dozen Lancasters into the air between 23.58 and 00.10 with S/L Millward the senior pilot on duty. Six crews were assigned as either blind markers or visual backers-up and were sitting on a cookie and four 1,000-pounders in addition to their flares and red or green TIs, and the remainder had an extra 1,000-pounder to drop as part of the main force.

The outward route was planned to cross the Dutch coast near Castricum and take the bomber stream to a point south-east of Bremen, followed by a dogleg to the north-east and, finally, a ninety degree change of course to the south-east in the Parchim area to leave a ninety-mile run to the target. The various elements of the force rendezvoused over the North Sea to form the bomber stream, and it was here that they encountered ice-bearing cloud with tops as high as 28,000 feet concealing violent electrical storms. The mood of the crews was reflected by a massive sixty early returns, 15.7% of those dispatched, most provided with a reason to turn back by the conditions, and among these were the crews of F/Sgts Bonikowsky, Borrowes and McQuade. The route changes worked well to throw off the night-fighters, but they would congregate in the target area after the controller correctly identified the capital as the target forty minutes before zero-hour. The blind marker crews employed H2S to establish a fix on Neuruppin and conducted a timed run before releasing their red skymarkers with green stars over the aiming point, which was concealed beneath ten-tenths cloud with tops at 16,000 feet. The 405 (Vancouver) Squadron crews carried out their respective tasks from 17,500 to 20,000 feet between 02.42 and 03.15 employing H2S, skymarkers or the glow of fires as a reference, and reported smoke rising to 20,000 feet as they turned away.

It was not possible to make an accurate assessment of the outcome, and the impression was of an effective attack, when, in fact, it had been another failure. Bombs had been scattered across the city and destroyed just eighty-two houses for the loss of twenty-seven Lancasters, most of which had fallen victim to night-fighters in the target area. 405 (Vancouver) Squadron posted missing the crew of W/O Robinson, who had borrowed ND330 from 83 Squadron for their eighteenth sortie, and all lost their lives when it crashed some twenty miles due north of Braunschweig, almost certainly on their way home when considerably north of their intended track. P/O Wilson and crew almost became another statitistic when hit by flak in the Hannover defence zone on the way home, but they made it back with around fifty holes perforating the fuselage and a navigator with a leg wound to bear witness to their adventure.

Three Berlin trips in five nights was asking a lot of the crews, but there would now be a gap of over two weeks before the "Big City" again appeared as "the target for tonight" for the heavy brigade, while the Mosquitos of 8 Group took over to harass the residents until the final third of the month. This allowed Harris to turn his attention on the 5th upon the Baltic port-city of Stettin, which had not been attacked in numbers since the previous April. It was to be another predominantly Lancaster affair, involving 348 of the type, eighty of them representing 8 Group, along with ten Halifaxes from 35 (Madras Presidency) Squadron. Nine Lancasters at Gransden Lodge received a cookie and a variety of other ordnance commensurate with their blind marking, backing-up and route-marking assignments, while the remaining four were loaded with four 2,000-pounders each as part of the main force. They took off between 23.27 and 00.16 with G/C Fauquier on his forty-third sortie and S/L Millward the senior pilots on duty, and in contrast to the high rate of early returns during the last Berlin operation, there were few on this night and none belonging to 8 Group.

The bomber stream found itself in thick cloud at cruising altitude as it crossed southern Denmark and the Baltic, some crews struggling to find a clear lane even when as high as 23,000 feet. On the plus side, they all benefitted from a Mosquito diversion at Berlin, which kept the night-fighters off the scent. Stettin was found to be partially visible through five-tenths thin cloud with tops at around 10,000 feet, and the visual marker crews were able to identify ground features to establish their positions before releasing their white flares and red TIs. The backers-up employed H2S confirmed by a visual reference, and dropped their red flares with green stars, green TIs and high explosives, upon which the main force crews focused to deliver an accurate and concentrated attack. The 405 (Vancouver) Squadron crews carried out their assigned tasks from 16,500 to 19,500 between 03.39 and 03.55, and at debriefing, would express confidence in the effectiveness of their work, which left the city in flames. Medical staff were on hand as F/L Coldrey and crew landed with a lifeless rear gunner, who had been receiving attention from his crew mates for the final hour of the return flight. After being silent for ten minutes, he had been found unconscious and possibly already deceased, despite his oxygen system functioning normally, and his death would be attributed to natural causes. Fourteen Lancasters and two Halifaxes failed to return from what, indeed, had been an effective operation, which post-raid reconnaissance and local sources confirmed had inflicted heavy damage in central and western districts. A total of 504 houses and twenty industrial buildings had been destroyed, a further 1,148 houses and twenty-nine industrial buildings seriously damaged, and eight ships had been sunk in the harbour.

Following this operation, the crews of the heavy squadrons were rested until mid-month, a situation to which the harshness of the winter may have contributed. When briefings finally took place on the 14th, there was doubtless some relief to see the red tape on the wall maps terminate some way short of Berlin. It led, in fact, to Braunschweig (Brunswick), the historic and culturally significant city situated some thirty-five miles to the east of Hannover. It had not been attacked by the Command in numbers before, and on this night would face a force numbering at take-off 496 Lancasters and two Halifaxes, eighty-nine of the former and both Halifaxes provided by 8 Group. 405 9vancouver) Squadron made ready fourteen of its Lancasters, loading four with a cookie, six 1,000 and four 500-pounders as part of the main force and the rest with a cookie and variety of high explosive and pyrotechnic ordnance for their respective assignments. They departed Gransden Lodge between 16.49 and 17.08 with G/C Fauquier and S/L Sattler the senior pilots on duty and after climbing out, rendezvoused with the the bomber stream during its passage across the North Sea towards Germany's north-western coast. There, it was met by part of the enemy night-fighter response, and the two factions would remain in contact all the way to the target and back.

Complete cloud cover at the target, in places up to around 15,000 feet, meant reliance uon H2S to establish positions and dictated the use of red skymarkers with green stars as the point of aim for the main force element. The 405 (Vancouver) Squadron participants performed their assigned roles from 17,900 to 19,000 feet between 19.07 and 19.34 but were unable to make an assessment of what was happening beneath the clouds. The enemy night-fighters scored consistently and accounted for the majority of the thirty-eight missing Lancasters, many of which came down in the Hannover defence zone, and it was a sobering night for 405 (Vancouver) Squadron, which awaited in vain the return of three experienced crews. There were no survivors from the all-RCAF crew of P/O Floren RCAF in JA974 or the mixed RCAF/RAF crew of F/O Drimmie DFC RCAF in ND423. Of the eight occupants on board ND341, three survived in enemy hands, but F/L Clouteir DFC RCAF and four others lost their lives in the crash on the way home some thirty miles to the south of the target. Local sources confirmed that the attack had almost entirely missed the city, falling mostly onto outlying communities to the south, and was reported as a light raid. This would be a continuing theme for future attacks on this city up to the autumn, as Braunschweig enjoyed something of a charmed life, leading to a belief among the populace that the surrounding villages were being targeted intentionally, in an attempt to drive the residents into the city, before a major operation destroyed it with them in it!

The Path Finders, in particular, had been taking a beating since the turn of the year, with 156 Squadron alone losing fourteen Lancasters and crews in just three operations, four and five on the two Berlin raids, and five again on Braunschweig. This was creating something of a crisis in manpower, particularly with regard to experienced crews, and a number of sideways postings took place between the squadrons to ensure a leavening of experience in each one. Another solution was to take the cream of those emerging from the training units, rather than wait for them to gain experience in a main force squadron.

On Thursday the 20th, orders were received to assemble a maximum effort force for the next round of the Berlin offensive. The main force Halifax squadrons, which had appeared to be in hibernation since late December, were roused from their slumber, and 253 of them joined 495 Lancasters, eighty-eight of them Path Finders and eleven 35 (Madras Presidency) Squadron Halifaxes for the main event, while two small Mosquito elements were made ready to carry out spoof raids on Kiel and Hannover. The Gransden Lodge crews were handed their respective tasks, six as markers and five as part of the main force, the Lancasters of the former receiving a cookie and variety of additional ordnance and the latter five 2,000-pounders each. They took off between 16.15 and 16.28 with S/Ls Bennett and Millward the senior pilots on duty and climbed away into darkening skies, which enabled some crews the rare pleasure of observing other aircraft rising out of the shadows. They turned their snouts towards the North Sea, and, thereafter, the west coast of Schleswig-Holstein at a point opposite Kiel, rendezvousing with the other groups over the North Sea and all the time shedding individual aircraft as a hefty seventy-five crews abandoned their sorties and turned back.

The intact 405 (Vancouver) Squadron element made landfall over the Nordfriesland coast, before turning to the south-east on a more-or-less direct course for Berlin, and soon found themselves being hounded by night-fighters. The enemy controller had fed a proportion of his resources into the bomber stream east of Hamburg, and they would remain in contact until a point between Leipzig and Hannover on the way home, although, curiously, the 5 Group brigade saw nothing of this and would lose just a single Lancaster. The two Mosquito diversions had been completely ignored by the Luftwaffe controller, who knew well in advance that Berlin was to be the target. The Path Finders arrived over the Müritzsee to the north of Berlin with a sixty-mile run-in to the aiming-point, and they found this to be concealed beneath the same ten-tenths cloud that had accompanied them for the entire outward leg. The tops of the cloud lay beneath the bombers at up to 15,000 feet as the blind marker crews delivered their red flares with green stars at 19.32, and the blind backers-up arrived soon afterwards to establish the aiming point for the visual backers-up to maintain. The 405 (Vancouver) Squadron crews performed their assigned roles from 19,000 to 20,300 feet between 19.33 and 19.42 and on return commented on the lack of flak activity over Berlin and the glow of large fires under the cloud and smoke rising through the tops. Thirty-five aircraft failed to return, twenty-two of them Halifaxes, which represented an 8.3% casualty rate compared with 2.6% for the Lancasters. It took a little time for an assessment of the operation to be made because of continuing cloud over north-eastern Germany, by which time four further raids had been carried out. It seems from local reports that the eastern districts had received the heaviest weight of bombs in an eight-mile stretch from Weissesee in the north to Neukölln in the south, although no details of destruction emerged.

When the crews were called to briefing on the 21st, they learned that the city of Magdeburg had been posted to host its first major attack of the war. Situated some fifty miles from Braunschweig and slightly to the south of east, it was on an increasingly familiar route as far as the enemy night-fighter controllers were concerned, and within easy striking distance of the night-fighter assembly beacons. The city had, in fact, been a regular destination for small forces as far back as the summer of 1940, when the Command targeted a ship lift at the eastern end of the Mittelland Canal at its junction with the River Elbe, and the Braunkohle A G Bergius-process synthetic oil refinery (hydrogenation plant), both located in the same Rothensee district to the north of the city centre. On this night, in an attempt to deceive the enemy, a small-scale diversion was planned at Berlin involving twenty-two Lancaster of 5 Group and twelve Mosquitos of 8 Group. A force of 648 aircraft was assembled for the main event, of which seventy-nine Lancasters, twenty-one Halifaxes and three Mosquitos were provided by 8 Group, and at Gransden Lodge the crews received their assignments, eight in marking roles and six to bomb with the main force. They took to the air between 19.48 and 20.07 with W/C Lane and S/Ls Bennett and Millward the senior pilots on duty and a cookie in each bomb bay supplemented by up to three 1,000 and seven 500-pounders and pyrotechnics according to their individual brief. They flew out over the North Sea to a point some one hundred miles off the west coast of Schleswig-Holstein, before turning to the south-east to pass between Hamburg and Hannover. Enemy radar was able to detect H2S transmissions during night-flying tests and equipment checks, and the night-fighter controller was, thereby, always aware of an imminent heavy raid. On this night, the night-fighters were able to infiltrate the bomber stream even before the German coast was crossed, and the recently introduced "Tame Boar" night-fighter system provided a running commentary on the bomber stream's progress, enabling the fighters to latch onto it and remain in contact. The final turning-point was twenty-five miles north-east of the target, from which a timed run and H2S brought the blind markers to the aiming-point along with twenty-seven main force aircraft, the latter having been driven by stronger-than-forecast winds to arrive ahead of schedule. These contained crews anxious to get the job done and vacate the target area as soon as possible, which prompted them to use their own H2S without waiting for the TIs to go down, and together with dummy fires, would be blamed by the Path Finders as the reason for their failure to produce concentrated marking.

The conditions over Magdeburg varied according to the time of arrival, the early birds encountering seven to nine-tenths thin cloud at around 6,000 feet, while those turning up towards the end of the raid found the northern half of the city completely clear with cloud over the southern half only. The 405 (Vancouver) Squadron crews carried out their respective tasks from 17,000 to 20,000 feet between 22.54 and 23.08, and all but one returned to offer their impressions to the intelligence section at debriefing. P/O Wilson RCAF and his mixed RCAF/RAF crew were absent from that process having all lost their lives in the wreckage in the Berlin defence zone of JB188. Returning crews from other groups reported explosions and fires or their glow, and smoke beginning to rise as they turned away. A number reported a flash some twelve minutes after bombing, that lit up the clouds for seven seconds, and two large explosions at 23.15. Fires that initially seemed to be scattered, appeared to become more concentrated as the crews headed for home, and the impression was of a successful operation.

While all of this was in progress, the diversionary force arrived at Berlin, some seventy miles away to the north-east, where the crews encountered a layer of eight to ten-tenths cloud at 10,000 feet. The accuracy of the raid was secondary to drawing off the night-fighters, and the 5 Group ORB expressed the opinion that the diversion had succeeded in the early stages in reducing the impact of the Nachtjagd, although this was not borne out by the figures. In the absence of post-raid reconnaissance and a local report, the outcome at Magdeburg was not confirmed, and it is generally believed now that most of the bombing fell outside of the city boundaries. A record fifty-seven aircraft failed to return, thirty-five of them Halifaxes, and this provided another alarming statistic of a 15.6% loss-rate compared with 5.2% for the Lancasters.

The squadrons were allowed a five-night rest to lick their wounds before the next round of operations began, and in the meantime, on the 22nd, G/C Fauquier bade farewell to the squadron after a nine-month tour of duty and was posted to 6 Group HQ. The citation accompanying the award of a Bar to his DSO reads; *"This officer has commanded the squadron with notable success during the past nine months. He has frequently taken part in sorties against distant and well-defended targets, including several attacks on the German capitol. He is a forceful and gallant leader, whose outstanding ability and unswerving devotion to duty have been reflected in the fine operational work performed by the whole squadron. Group Captain Fauquier has set an example of the highest order."*

Promotion to Air Commodore would follow in time, but he gladly reverted to Group Captain for the honour of commanding 617 Squadron from December 1944 until the end of the bombing war. During this period, he was awarded a second Bar to his DSO. Fauquier was a hard act to follow, but W/C Reg "Shady" Lane was the perfect replacement, created, as he was, from the same mould as his predecessor. He was equally stubborn in resisting a rest from operations and had been around the bomber scene for a considerable time. He was the pilot of one of the 35 (Madras Presidency) Squadron Halifaxes undertaking the type's first operational sorties in March 1941, the occasion on which the then S/L Gilchrist was shot down by an RAF night-fighter. Two nights later he took part in the first Halifax operation over Germany, to attack the Blohm & Voss shipyards at Hamburg. During his spell as a flight commander with 35 (Madras Presidency) Squadron, he shared a half nissen hut with another flight commander, S/L Peter Cribb. W/C Hamish Mahaddie completed two tours with 7 Squadron before becoming Bennett's head of recruitment at 8 Group, gaining in the process the title of "Path Finder Horse Thief". In his book, Hamish – The story of a Path Finder, he recounts a story concerning Lane and Cribb, who apparently, having returned from a night's revelry and not wishing to venture out of bed in the freezing conditions of a typical wartime RAF hut, tried to extinguish the light by taking pot-shots at the bulb with .38 revolvers.

The end of the month was to bring the final concerted effort to destroy Berlin and would involve three trips to the "Big City" in the space of an unprecedented four nights. This hectic round of operations began on the 27th and involved an all-Lancaster heavy force of 515 aircraft. 405 (Vancouver) Squadron detailed fourteen Lancasters, loading the eight assigned to marker crews with a cookie and four 1,000-pounders in addition to their marking ordnance and the remaining six with a cookie and eleven 500-pounders to deliver as part of the main force. They departed Gransden Lodge between 17.44 and 17.58 with S/Ls Bennett and Millward the senior pilots on duty, and after climbing out and joining up with the bomber stream over the North Sea, set course on a complex route that would take them towards the north German coast, before swinging to the south-east to enter enemy territory over the Frisians and northern Holland. Having then feinted towards central Germany, suggesting Leipzig as the target, the force was to turn north-east to a point west of Berlin, from where the final run-in commenced. The long return route would pass to the west of Leipzig before turning due east to miss Frankfurt on its northern side and traverse Belgium to gain the Channel south of Boulogne. Among extensive diversionary measures were an attack on the island of Heligoland by twenty-one 35 (Madras Presidency) Squadron Halifaxes, mining activities off the Dutch coast, and the dispensing of dummy fighter flares and route-markers, all of which would partially succeed in reducing the numbers of enemy night-fighters making contact. It was, therefore, a relatively intact bomber force that approached the target over ten-tenths cloud with tops at 15,000 feet that required the Path Finders to employ sky-marking, and it was red Wanganui flares with green stars that led the main force crews to the aiming-point. The 405 (Vancouver) Squadron crews fulfilled their briefs from 18,000 to 20,000 feet between 20.27 and 20.42 and at debriefing reported the glow of fires and the appearance of a successful raid, but no detailed assessment was forthcoming. Of course, not all would make it back to tell their stories at debriefing, and thirty-three Lancaster dispersal pans stood empty in dawn's early light. Reports from Berlin described bombs falling over a wide area, more so in the south than the north, and damage to fifty industrial premises, a number of them engaged in important war work, while twenty thousand people were bombed out of their homes. A feature of the campaign was the number of outlying communities suffering collateral damage, and on this night, sixty-one such hamlets recorded bombs falling.

Exhausted men fell into their beds with the sound of engines still ringing in their ears, and many of them were back at briefing later in the day to learn that Berlin was again to be their destination that night. A heavy force of 673 aircraft was assembled, consisting of 432 Lancasters and 241 Halifaxes, of which seventy-nine Lancasters and seventeen Halifaxes were provided by 8 Group. Mosquitos bombed Berlin earlier in the evening, in the hope that this would persuade the night-fighter controller that the main force was heading elsewhere. It was a round trip of less than four hours for a Mosquito, and at least one 627 Squadron crew was back at Oakington in time to wish their heavy-weight 7 Squadron colleagues a good flight. In addition, 35 (Madras Presidency) Squadron was to participate in the extensive diversionary operations and send four Halifaxes to support a mining operation in the Forget-me-not garden in Kiel Harbour five hours ahead of the main event. 405 (Vancouver) Squadron loaded fourteen Lancasters with bomb loads similar to those of the previous night and briefed eight crews for a marking role and six to bomb with the main force. They departed Gransden Lodge between 23.56 and 00.09 with S/Ls Bennett and Millward the senior pilots on duty, and after climbing out followed the designated route out over southern Denmark, before turning south-east on a direct course for the target, with an almost reciprocal return and various simultaneous diversionary measures to distract the night-fighter controller. Sixty-six crews turned back early, suggesting some adverse reaction to the back-to-back operations, and among these were those of F/Sgt Bonikowsky and P/O Biden, who were almost two hours out when defeated by severe icing conditions.

The remainder pressed on to the target area, where they encountered the forecast ten-tenths cloud with tops at around 10,000 feet, for which the Path Finders had prepared both a sky and ground marking plan involving red flares with green stars and red TIs backed up with greens. They also met with a hot reception from single and twin-engine fighters, which accounted for twenty-seven aircraft in the Berlin area alone. The 405 (Vancouver) Squadron crews carried out their respective tasks from 18,000 to 20,000 feet between 03.12 and 03.23 and some observed two huge explosions at 03.18 and 03.25, the earlier one described by a 10 Squadron crew as lighting up the sky over a radius of fifty miles. Forty-six aircraft failed to return, twenty-six of them Halifaxes, and those making it back to debriefings and a late breakfast offered the impression of a concentrated and effective attack, which was partly borne-out by local reports of heavy damage in western and southern districts, where 180,000 people were bombed out of their homes. However, as had been the pattern throughout the campaign against Berlin, seventy-seven outlying communities had also been afflicted.

After a night's rest a force of 534 aircraft was made ready on the 30th for the final operation of this concerted effort against Berlin, for which 8 Group made available eighty Lancasters, thirteen Halifaxes and a dozen Mosquitos. At Gransden Lodge seven Lancasters received the standard ordnance for a marking role and the remaining six five 2,000-pounders each to deliver as part of the main force. They took off between 17.05 and 17.23 with S/L Millward the senior pilot on duty and after climbing out, joined with the bomber stream to follow a route similar to that adopted two nights earlier. They remained relatively free of harassment until approaching the target, where they were greeted by ten-tenths cloud at around 8,000 feet, above which, the primary blind markers delivered their red flares with green stars and red TIs. The blind backers-up followed them in and the visual backers-up maintained the aiming point throughout the raid. The 405 (Vancouver) Squadron crews fulfilled their respective briefs from 17,500 to 20,000 between 20.13 and 20.27 and some ninety minutes into the return flight, F/O Biden's Lancaster was hit by flak and attacked three times by a BF110. The gunners responded with vigour until the loss of the port-outer engine and the hydraulics system put both turrets out of action and it was only through violent corkscrewing that the Lancasters was able to shake off the assailant and make it back to a wheels-up landing at Coltishall in Norfolk with three slightly wounded crew members on board. This was one of four Lancasters failing to return to Gransden Lodge, three others now smouldering wrecks on foreign soil and containing the remains of fifteen crewmen. ND493 was outbound at 20,000 feet and some fifty miles north of Berlin when hit by flak and set on fire, and only F/Sgt Bonikowsky RCAF, who was on his twentieth operation, and three of his predominantly RCAF crew were able to save themselves to fall into enemy hands. JA924 was set upon by a night-fighter at 20,000 feet shortly after bombing and spiralled out of control with its port wing ablaze. It was rent by an explosion at 15,000 feet, which flung the pilot, F/L Shackleton, and his wireless operator into space as the sole survivors from this all-RAF crew and both were taken into captivity. ND462 came down some twenty miles east of Magdeburg, also on the way home, and there were no survivors from the predominantly RCAF crew of F/L Roberts RCAF, who were on their eighth sortie with the squadron.

Some returning crews reported passing to the west of Berlin at the end of the raid and observing two huge columns of smoke rising through the cloud tops at 12,000 feet and the glow of fires beneath the cloud, which, according to some, was still visible from a hundred miles into the return flight. Thirty-two Lancasters and a single Halifax failed to make it home, while, in return for these significant losses and according to local reports, central and south-western districts suffered heavy damage and serious areas of fire. Other parts of the city were also hit, while many bomb loads were again scattered liberally onto outlying communities, and at least a thousand people lost their lives. 112 heavy bombers and their crews had been lost to the Command as a result of these three most recent operations, and with the introduction of the enemy's highly efficient Tame Boar night-fighter system based on running commentaries, the advantage had swung firmly back in the defenders' favour.

Two further heavy raids would be directed at Berlin before the end of the winter offensive, one in February and the other in March, but they would be almost in isolation. There is no question that Germany's capital had been sorely afflicted by the three latest operations, but it remained functional and showed no signs of imminent collapse. Berlin was no Hamburg with densely populated, confined housing areas and narrow streets in its old centre, it was a modern city of concrete and steel with wide thoroughfares and open spaces to act as natural firebreaks, to which each new swathe of destruction added, applying the law of diminishing returns. Ultimately, Berlin was just too big, too incombustible and too far away, and this in midwinter conditions and at a time when the Luftwaffe was a much more efficient and lethal adversary than in pre-"window" times.

During the course of the month the squadron participated in nine operations and dispatched 117 sorties for the loss of ten Lancasters and crews and a rear gunner.

February 1944

Bad weather during the first two weeks of February allowed the crews to draw breath and the squadrons to replenish. Harris had intended to maintain the pressure on Berlin and would have launched a further attack had he not been thwarted by the conditions, and as a result the time was filled with training and mining operations. When the Path Finder and main force squadrons next took to the air, it would be for a record-breaking effort to Berlin on the 15th and would also be the penultimate operation of the campaign, and indeed, of the war by Bomber Command's heavy brigade, against Germany's capital city. The force of 891 aircraft represented the largest non-1,000 force to date, and therefore, the greatest-ever to be sent against the "Big City", and it would be the first time that more than five hundred Lancasters and three hundred Halifaxes had operated together. 8 Group contributed seventy-six Lancasters, nineteen Halifaxes and sixteen Mosquitos, and an additional four Halifaxes were prepared at Graveley to join forces with forty-three Stirlings for mining duties in Kiel Bay as part of the diversionary effort. There would also be a raid on Frankfurt-an-Oder, *(not to be confused with Frankfut-am-Main in south central Germany)* a city to the east of Berlin, by a small force of 8 Group Lancasters, while Oboe Mosquitos attacked five night-fighter airfields in Holland.

Thirteen Lancasters were prepared at Gransden Lodge for the main event and three for the diversion at Frankfurt, and it was the latter that took off first between 17.06 and 17.08 with S/L Millward the senior pilot on duty and a cookie, four 1,000-pounders and pyrotechnics in each bomb bay. They were followed immediately into the air over the ensuing fifteen minutes by the Berlin-bound element led by W/C Lane, five loaded with a cookie and either four 1,000-pounders or three 1,000 and three 500-pounders, all in addition to marker ordnance. After rendezvousing with the rest of the bomber stream over the North Sea, they set course for the western coast of Denmark, before crossing Jutland and entering Germany via the Baltic coast between Rostock and Stralsund, with a direct heading, thereafter, for the target. The return route would require the bombers to pass south of Hannover and Bremen and cross Holland to reach the North Sea via Castricum. The gardeners peeled off as they reached the western Baltic, where the coastline was concealed by ten-tenths cloud with tops at around 8,000 feet. The bomber stream had become depleted as it proceeded towards the east, but there were no 405 (Vancouver) Squadron "boomerangs" among the eventual seventy-five early returns. By the time the remainder homed in on the target, they found it lying under ten-tenths cloud at around 10,000 feet, but were able to confirm their positions by H2S, while the main force crews relied on the Path Finders' red release-point flares with green stars and red and green TIs on the ground. The 405 (Vancouver) Squadron crews carried out their assigned tasks from 19,000 to 20,000 feet between 21.11 and 21.27, before returning home to offer their impressions at debriefing.

Meanwhile, the three contributors to the diversion each delivered their cookie, four 1,000-pounders and pyrotechnics from 17,000 to 18,500 feet between 21.15 and 21.20 before returning safely after seven hours aloft. The consensus across the Command was of highly effective and well-concentrated marking at Berlin, followed by accurate bombing, and the burgeoning glow beneath the clouds convinced most that they had taken part in a successful operation. This was borne out by local reports, which confirmed that the 2,642 tons of bombs had caused extensive damage in central and south-western districts but had also spilled out into surrounding communities. A thousand houses and more than five hundred temporary wooden barracks were destroyed, and among important war-industry factories to sustain damage in the Siemensstadt district was the Siemens-Halske electrical engineering and aero-engine plant, which made extensive use of slave labour from nearby concentration camps. The successes were achieved in return for the loss to the Command of forty-three aircraft, twenty-six Lancasters, (4.6%) and seventeen Halifaxes, (5.4%). Perhaps slightly disturbing was the fact that eight of the missing Halifaxes were Mk IIIs, only one fewer than the nine Mk II/Vs.

Despite the recent heavy losses, when orders were received on the 19th to prepare for another major assault that night, this time on Leipzig, the heavy squadrons were able offer 816 aircraft, 561 Lancasters and 255 Halifaxes. 8 Group managed to put up eighty-nine Lancasters, seventeen

Halifaxes and seven Mosquitos, 405 (Vancouver) Squadron briefing fourteen crews, nine as blind markers and backers-up and the remainder to bomb with the main force. They departed Gransden Lodge between 23.48 and 00.18 with S/L Bennett the senior pilot on duty and the marker aircraft a load of a cookie, four 1,000 and two 500-pounders plus marker ordnance, while the bombers had five 2,000-pounders in each bomb bay. After climbing out over the station they joined up with the others heading for the Dutch coast, where a proportion of the Luftwaffe Nachtjagd was waiting for them, while others had been drawn away by the mining diversion off Kiel. Once over enemy terrirory parts of the bomber stream became embroiled in a running battle with night-fighters all the way into eastern Germany. Stronger-than-forecast winds caused many aircraft to arrive at the target early, forcing them to orbit above the ten-tenths low to medium cloud, while they waited for the Path Finders to arrive to mark the target. This kept them in range of the local flak batteries, which accounted for around twenty of them, while four others were lost through collisions. A plentiful supply of markers flares appeared above the clouds from 03.54 to 04.10, but then a two-minute gap allowed the bombing to become scattered, before the arrival of further backers-up replenished the aiming point and kept the main force crews on track. The 405 (Vancouver) Squadron crews carried out their assigned roles from 18,900 to 20,000 feet between 03.56 and 04.12 and observed a considerable glow beneath the cloud, which remained visible for some fifty minutes into the return journey, giving the impression of a successful assault. When all of those aircraft returning home had been accounted for, there was a massive shortfall of seventy-eight, a record loss by a clear twenty-one aircraft. Forty-four Lancasters and thirty-four Halifaxes had failed to return, with a loss-rate of 7.8% and 13.3% respectively, and there were ten absentees for the 8 Group ranks. The Halifax casualties prompted Harris to immediately withdraw the main force Mk II and V variants from further operations over Germany, at a stroke removing a proportion of 4 and 6 Groups' firepower from the front line until they could be re-equipped with the Mk III. In the meantime, the Mk II and V operators would focus their energies for the remainder of the month on gardening duties.

405 (Vancouver) Squadron somehow avoided the carnage, as indeed it would on two further disastrous nights for the Command in late March, and remarkably, despite the horrendous losses and the withdrawal of the older Halifaxes, 598 aircraft were made available on the following night for the first of three heavy raids over a three-week period on Stuttgart. 8 Group contributed eighty Lancasters, sixteen Halifaxes and a dozen Mosquitos, 405 (Vancouver) Squadron detailing thirteen aircraft and briefing eight crews for a marking role and five to bomb with the main force. The Lancasters of the former each received a standard bomb load involving a cookie and 1,000-pounders in addition to their pyrotechnics, while the bombers each had ten 1,000-pounders winched into their bomb bays. They departed Gransden Lodge between 00.26 and 00.39 with S/L Bennett the senior pilot on duty and made their way across the Channel to the French coast, from where the cloud would remain at ten-tenths with tops at 8,000 feet all the way into southern Germany. They benefitted from a North Sea sweep and a diversionary raid on Munich two hours ahead of the main activity, and for once, the night-fighter controller was deceived by the diversionary measures, deploying his forces early and leaving the bomber stream largely unmolested during its time over enemy territory. By the time the target hove into view, the cloud had thinned to five to eight-tenths at around 6,000 feet, and the excellent visibility enabled the crews to draw a bead on the Path Finders' red and green sky-markers and similar-coloured TIs on the ground. The 405 (Vancouver) Squadron crews carried out their assigned tasks from 19,000 to 20,000 feet between 03.56 and 04.14, and on return reported many large fires, the glow from which

remained visible from 250 miles into the return flight. Despite some scattering of bombs, local reports described central districts and those in a quadrant from north-west to north-east suffering extensive damage, and a Bosch factory was one of the important war industry concerns to be hard-hit. In contrast to twenty-four hours earlier, a modest nine aircraft failed to return, and among them was the last Mk II Halifax in Path Finder, and indeed, in Bomber Command service to be lost to a major operation over Germany.

In an attempt to reduce the prohibitive losses of recent weeks, a new tactic was introduced for the next two operations beginning on the 24th, when a force of 734 aircraft was assembled for an operation to the centre of Germany's ball-bearing production, Schweinfurt, situated some sixty miles to the east of Frankfurt in south-central Germany. The plan called for 392 aircraft to depart their stations between 18.00 and 19.00, and to be followed into the air two hours later by 342 others in the hope of catching the night-fighters on the ground refuelling and re-arming as the second wave passed through. While this operation was in progress, extensive diversionary measures would be put in hand that involved more than three hundred other aircraft, including 179 from the training units conducting a North Sea sweep, and 110 Halifaxes and Stirlings mining in northern waters. 8 Group contributed forty-four Lancasters, twenty Halifaxes and six Mosquitos to the first phase, and forty-six Lancaster and five Mosquitos to the second, 405 (Vancouver) Squadron responsible for five Lancasters in the first phase and nine in the second. W/C Lane and S/L Millward were the senior pilots on duty in the first phase, each assigned to visual marking, while the crew of F/O Van Rassel was to act as a blind backer-up, leaving those of F/Os Christison and Jackson to support the main force, each with a bomb load commensurate with their role.

They departed Gransden Lodge between 18.32 and 18.56 and joined up with the bomber stream as it headed south for the Channel crossing to make landfall on the French coast. It followed the course of the Franco/Belgian frontier, harassed by night-fighters, and JB241 was approaching the final turning point some twenty-five miles south-west of Saarbrücken when attacked from below at 20,000 feet. The starboard-inner engine and wing were ablaze as the order to abandon the aircraft was issued and followed almost immediately by an explosion, which catapaulted F/O Jackson DFC RCAF and two of his crew into space and into enemy hands as the only survivors. Some thirty miles further on and five hundred feet lower, ND526 suffered a similar fate, which resulted in F/O Christison RCAF and four of his crew surviving also in enemy hands. It is likely that both had fallen victim to the Nachtjagd's "Schräge Musik" (Jazz) upward-firing cannons, which enable night-fighters to creep up on bombers from below and position themselves to aim at the wing tanks between the engines employing non-tracer ammunition. The others pressed on to the target, some to find clear skies and good visibility, which enabled them to pick out the River Main as they ran in, while others reported three-tenths cloud at 3,000 to 4,000 feet and haze to spoil the vertical visibility. The three remaining 405 (Vancouver) Squadron crews established their positions by H2S and performed their assigned tasks from 16,800 to 19,200 feet between 23.01 and 23.05, leaving red and green TIs for the main force crews to aim at. By this time fires were already established towards the south-western edge of the town and two columns of black smoke were observed to be rising through 5,000 feet as they turned away with an impression of an effective, if somewhat scattered attack.

Meanwhile, the second phase element had taken off from Gransden Lodge between 20.54 and 21.02 with F/Ls Fyfe, McKinnon and Trilsbach the senior pilots on duty, three crews to act as primary blind markers, two as blind backers-up and the rest as main force supporters. They picked up the glow of fires from the earlier raid at a distance of two hundred miles and found the visibility in the target area to be good, despite the rising smoke, and fulfilled their briefs from 17,000 to 19,000 feet between 01.02 and 01.08. All indications afterwards suggested an effective raid, which awaited confirmation from bombing photos and post-raid reconnaissance. Sadly, these revealed that both phases of the operation had suffered from undershooting after some Path Finder backers-up had failed to press on to the aiming-point, and, in that regard, it was a disappointing night. However, an interesting feature was the loss of 50% fewer aircraft from the second wave in comparison with the first, in an overall casualty figure of thirty-three, and this suggested some merit in the tactic.

Since the turn of the year a wind-finder system had been in use, in which selected crews monitored wind speed and direction and passed their findings back to HQ, where the figures were collated and any changes from the briefed conditions re-broadcast to the bomber stream. This had been found to be extremely useful, but, as would be discovered in the ensuing weeks, the system had its limitations.

The main operation on the following night was directed at the beautiful and culturally significant city of Augsburg, situated in Bavaria around thirty miles north-west of Munich. It was home among other war industry factories to the Maschinenfabrik Augsburg Nuremberg (M.A.N) diesel engine works, which had been the target for an epic low-level daylight raid by 44 and 97 Squadron Lancasters in April 1942. On this night, 594 aircraft were divided into two waves, and among them were fifty-seven 8 Group Lancasters and five Mosquitos in the first wave and thirty Lancasters, seventeen Halifaxes and four Mosquitos in the second. The outward routes were different, the first phase beginning the Channel crossing at Eastbourne and crossing the French coast north of Dieppe on an almost direct course to a position south of the target, from where the run-in would commence. The second phase was to skirt England's eastern coast on course for the Scheldt estuary, before flying almost directly to the northern-most point of Lake Constance, then east to the same bombing-run starting point as the first wave. Eleven 405 (Vancouver) Squadron Lancasters were made ready for the first wave and departed Gransden Lodge between 18.47 and 19.03 with S/Ls Bennett and Millward the senior pilots on duty. As target marking became more complex, so the number of roles increased and on this night one crew was to act as a blind marker/illuminator, two as blind backers-up, two as visual backers-up, two as visual markers and four as main force supporters.

The first wave flew out over ten-tenths cloud, but it had dissipated by the time the target drew near, and on arrival, it was possible for crews to gain a visual reference. The 405 (Vancouver) Squadron crews performed their assigned roles from 17,000 to 19,000 feet between 23.39 and 23.51, the marker crews dispensing red and green TIs for the main force element to aim at, and fires were beginning to take hold as they turned away. Meanwhile, the three second-wave crews of F/Ls Fyfe and Trilsbach and F/O Chase had taken off between 21.47 and 21.49, two to act as primary blind markers and one as a blind backer-up and were drawn on for the final one hundred miles by the glow in the sky. They arrived to find visibility still good despite copious amounts of smoke rising through 10,000 feet and carried out their assigned tasks from 18,000 to 19,000 feet between 01.12 and 01.15. As they headed home, there was no doubt in their minds that they had visited an ordeal of almost unprecedented proportions on the hapless occupants of this Bavarian jewel. The loss of twenty-one aircraft seemed to confirm the benefits of splitting the force, and this tactic would remain an important part of Bomber Command planning for the remainder of the war. Post-raid reconnaissance and local sources confirmed a devastatingly destructive operation, in which all facets of the plan had come together in near perfect harmony to spell disaster for this lightly defended treasure trove of culture. Its heart was torn out by blast and fire, which resulted in the destruction of almost three thousand houses along with buildings of outstanding historical significance. There was also some industrial damage, and around ninety-thousand people were bombed out of their homes.

During the course of the month the squadron carried out six operations and dispatched seventy-one sorties for the loss of two Lancasters and crews.

March 1944

March would bring an end to the winter campaign, but a long and bitter month would have to be endured first before any respite came from long-range forays into Germany. The crews had enjoyed a few nights off when the second raid of the series on Stuttgart was posted on the 1st, for which a force of 557 aircraft was made ready. This number included eighty-eight Lancasters, eighteen Halifaxes and thirteen Mosquitos representing 8 Group. At the Gransden Lodge briefing the crews were allotted their tasks for the night, three as primary blind markers, four as blind backers-up, two as visual markers, one as a visual backer-up and six to support the main force, the last-mentioned each carrying five 2,000-pounders. They took off between 23.48 and 00.08 with S/L Bennett the senior pilot on duty and flew out over ten-tenths cloud with tops at between 10,000 and 17,000 feet, which persisted all the way to the target area, where the Path Finders employed a combination of sky and ground-marking. The 405 (Vancouver) Squadron crews carried out their respective tasks from 18,700 to 19,600 feet between 02.57 and 03.14, noting that the marking had become scattered, causing the main force effort to be directed between two main concentrations, largely at red skymarkers with green stars. It was not possible to assess the accuracy of the attack, although a column of smoke had reached 25,000 feet by the end of the raid, and large fires were evident from the glow in the sky visible from up to 150 miles away. The presence of thick cloud all the way there and back made conditions difficult for enemy night-fighters, and a remarkably modest four aircraft failed to return. It was eventually established that the raid had been an outstanding success, which had caused extensive damage in central, western and northern districts, where a number of important war-industry factories, including those belonging to Bosch and Daimler-Benz, had sustained damage.

The above operation proved to be the last for 35 (Madras Presidency) Squadron as a Halifax unit, as it was about to join the rest of the 8 Group heavy brigade as a Lancaster operator, becoming the thirty-seventh operational unit in Bomber Command to equip with the type.

At the end of the first week of the new month, the Halifax brigade, particularly those withdrawn from operations over Germany, fired the opening salvoes of the pre-invasion campaign, the purpose of which was to dismantle by bombing thirty-seven railway centres in France, Belgium and western Germany. It began on the night of the 6/7th at Trappes marshalling yards, situated some ten miles west-south-west of Paris, and continued at Le Mans in north-western France on the following night. For most of the heavy crews, however, there was no employment following

Stuttgart until a return there in mid-month, but in the meantime, matters were afoot at 5 Group, and had been ever since a frustrating series of operations against flying bomb launching and storage sites conducted by 617 Squadron since December had failed to achieve the desired results. The problem had been an inability to achieve pinpoint accuracy with target markers, which was vital to destroy small, precision targets, and Oboe was just not precise enough. Accurate though Oboe undoubtedly was at an urban target, where a margin of error of 400 to 600 yards was as good as pinpoint, precision targets required more. 617 Squadron had obliterated the Oboe markers, only for bombing photos to show that the targets, situated only a matter of yards away, had remained intact. W/C Cheshire and S/L Martin experimented with a dive-bombing technique, which had proved to be successful, but impracticable in a Lancaster, and Cheshire had borrowed a Mosquito for further trials. These were so promising that the 5 Group A-O-C, AVM Cochrane, authorized a number of operations by the squadron against factory targets in France, before taking the idea to Harris. Harris approved, paving the way for 5 Group to become effectively independent of the main bomber force and begin larger-scale trials.

A second attack by 4 and 6 Groups on the Le Mans yards took place on the 13/14th, and this time fifteen locomotives and eight hundred wagons were destroyed, while collateral damage resulted to two nearby factories.

Now that the Mk III Halifax was becoming available in larger numbers, the Command was quickly returning to full strength, and a force of 863 aircraft sat on airfields across the Command waiting to be released against Stuttgart in the early-evening of the 15th. This number included 116 Lancasters and sixteen Mosquitos provided by 8 Group, sixteen of the former made ready at Gransden Lodge, while the crews were allotted their respective roles, two as blind marker/illuminators, two as blind backers-up, one as a visual marker, two as visual backers-up and nine as main force supporters. They took off between 19.30 and 19.45 with pilots of flight lieutenant rank the most senior on duty and rendezvoused with the rest of the force as they passed over Reading on their way to the south coast, and it was an elongated bomber stream that crossed the French coast at 20,000 feet over broken cloud with clear conditions above. The route maintained a course parallel with the frontiers of Belgium, Luxembourg and Germany as if heading for Switzerland, before turning towards the north-east for the run-in to the target. It was during this final leg that the night-fighters managed to infiltrate a section of the stream and score heavily, while adverse winds were responsible for delaying the Path Finders' arrival to open the attack by six minutes. They conducted a timed run from Lake Constance and employed both sky and ground-markers in the face of seven to ten-tenths cloud at between 8,000 and 15,000 feet, the Wanganui flares drifting in the wind over an area to the north-east of the River Neckar, while the TIs landed far apart in the north and south of the city. The 405 (Vancouver) Squadron crews carried out their assigned tasks from 18,500 to 19,500 feet between 23.06 and 23.40, and on their return reported a spread of fires, including two large ones ten miles apart, and smoke rising to bombing altitude. It would be established later that some of the early bombing had been accurate, but that most of the loads had undershot and fallen into open country, a disappointment compounded by the loss, mostly to night-fighters, of thirty-seven aircraft. Among these was ME622, which was attacked by a night-fighter over the target, set on fire and sent crashing to earth with fatal consequences for the long-serving F/L Fyfe RCAF and three members of his predominantly RCAF crew, who had completed at least twenty-five sorties. The navigator, bomb-aimer and rear gunner all survived and were soon in enemy hands.

Many operations had been mounted against Frankfurt during the preceding two years, only a small number of which had been really effective. This state of affairs was about to be rectified, however, and the first of two raids against this south-central powerhouse of industry, the site of the headquarters of the infamous I G Farben company, was posted on the 18th, for which a force of 846 aircraft was made ready. 8 Group would support the operation with 119 Lancasters and seventeen Mosquitos, sixteen of the former made ready at Gransden Lodge, while their crews were assigned to five different roles, one as a blind marker/illuminator, one as a visual marker, three as blind backers-up, two as visual backers-up and nine to support the main force. They took to the air between 19.27 and 19.47 with S/L Bennett the senior pilot on duty and adopted the standard route across France and into Germany in good weather conditions, where they encountered a layer of haze 20,000 feet thick over the target, and, according to most, no more than three-tenths cloud. This allowed the Path Finders to employ the Newhaven ground marking technique, blind marking by H2S with white flares and green TIs, followed by visual backing-up with reds, the 405 (Vancouver) Squadron crews fulfilling their respective briefs from 18,000 to 19,000 feet between 21.54 and 22.16. A large explosion was witnessed at 22.05, and some of the participants in the raid flew home confident that their efforts had been worthwhile. Others, however, reported very peculiar conditions, which prevented the TIs from being seen until directly below, and, even then, they merged into the general kaleidoscope of colours generated by the attack. Post-raid analysis and local reports confirmed that an outstandingly successful raid had taken place, during which, 5 Group alone dropped more than one thousand tons of bombs for the first time at a single target. Local sources calculated that six thousand buildings had been destroyed or seriously damaged in predominantly eastern, central and western districts, and this was in return for the relatively modest loss of twenty-two aircraft.

Frankfurt was named again on the 22nd as the target for that night, for which 8 Group detailed 111 Lancasters and twelve Mosquitos as part of another huge force of 816 aircraft. The fourteen participants from 405 (Vancouver) Squadron were assigned to four different roles, four as blind marker/illuminators, one as a visual marker, two as visual backers-up and seven as main force supporters and departed Gransden Lodge between 18.44 and 19.01 with S/L Millward the senior pilot on duty. After climbing out above their respective stations and forming up into a stream, they adopted an unusual route for a target south of the Ruhr, crossing the enemy coast over Vlieland and Terschelling, before passing to the east of Osnabrück on a direct course due south for the target. They arrived at the target to find five to six-tenths thin, low cloud at around 4,000 feet, before the Path Finder spearhead carried out accurate Paramatta marking (blind marking by H2S). The 405 (Vancouver) Squadron crews carried out their respective tasks from 17,000 to 19,500 feet between 21.44 and 22.01, the main force element aiming their bombs at the release-point flares and red and green TIs marking out the aiming-point. A massive rectangular area of unbroken fire was observed across the centre of the city, the glow from which could be seen for at least a hundred miles into the return flight. F/O Brice's bomb-aimer selected the wrong switches, which prevented the bombs from falling away, and they were eventually released over agricultural terrain close to the Luxembourg frontier. Returning crews reported numerous searchlights lighting up the cloud, and moderate to intense flak that reached up to the bombers' flight level. Local reports confirmed the enormity of the devastation, which was particularly severe in western districts and left this half of the city without electricity, gas and water for an extended period. More than nine hundred people lost their lives and a further 120,000 were bombed out of their homes, at a cost to the Command of twenty-six Lancasters and seven Halifaxes, a loss-rate of 4.2% and 3.8% respectively. It was a bad night for senior officers, 207 and 7 Squadrons losing their commanding officers, while Bardney's station commander, G/C Norman Pleasance, failed to return in a 9 Squadron Lancaster. What was about to happen over the next week and a half, however, would overshadow anything that had gone before, and would certainly not fall within what might be considered acceptable.

It was more than five weeks since the main force had last visited Berlin, and 811 aircraft were made ready on the 24th for what would be the final raid of the war by RAF heavy bombers on the "Big City". 8 Group put up 112 Lancasters and seventeen Mosquitos, of which fifteen of the former were made ready by 405 (Vancouver) Squadron, while their crews were briefed for their respective roles, W/C Lane as Master Bomber, the newly promoted W/C Millward as a visual marker, three as blind markers, two as visual backers-up and six to support the main force. They departed Gransden Lodge between 18.38 and 18.58 and took their respective places in the bomber stream as it traversed the North Sea to the Danish coast near Ringkøbing from where they were to set course for a point on the German Baltic coast near Rostock. When north-east of Berlin they were to turn onto a south-westerly course for the bombing run, and once clear of the defence zone homebound, dogleg to the west and then north-west to pass around Hannover on its southern and western sides, before heading for Holland and an exit via the Castricum coast. The extended outward leg provided a time-on-target of around 22.30, but an unexpected difficulty would be encountered, which would render void all of the meticulous planning. The existence of what we now know as "Jetstream" winds was unknown at the time, and the one blowing from the north with unprecedented strength on this night pushed the bomber stream south of its intended track. Navigators, who were expecting to see the northern tip of Sylt on their H2S screens, were horrified to find the southern end, which meant that they were thirty miles south of track and about to fly over Germany rather than Denmark. The previously mentioned "wind-finder" system had been set up for precisely this eventuality, but the problem on this night was that the wind-finders refused to believe what their instruments were telling them. Winds in excess of one hundred m.p.h had never been encountered before, and fearing that they would be disbelieved, many modified the figures downward. The same thing happened at raid control, where the figures were modified again, so that the information rebroadcast to the bomber stream bore no resemblance to the reality of the situation.

The crews who realised that they had strayed from track set course for the north to try to regain the planned route and avoid the defences that would be met if they turned east over Germany. Many crews would comment on the inaccurate wind information received during the outward journey, and having arrived in the target area, some were convinced that the Path Finders were up to ten minutes late in opening the raid, a fact confirmed to some by the voice of the Master Bomber exhorting them to hurry up. Crews reported a variety of cloud conditions, from three to ten-tenths at between 6,000 and 15,000 feet, but most in the main force were able to pick out the red and green TIs on the ground, and if not, found red Wanganui flares with green stars to guide them to the aiming-point. The 405 (Vancouver) Squadron crews confirmed their positions by H2S before carrying out their assigned tasks from 18,500 to 23,000 feet between 22.22 and 22.42 and observed what appeared to be a scattered attack in the early stages, until fires began to become more concentrated in three distinct areas, and large explosions were witnessed at 22.42 and 22.54. The defences were very active with moderate flak bursting at up to 24,000 feet, and light flak attempting to shoot out the skymarkers, but night-fighter activity was described by the 5 Group

ORB as unusually quiet. There was a shock awaiting the Command as the returning aircraft landed to leave a shortfall of seventy-two, and it would be established later that two-thirds of them had fallen victim to the Ruhr flak batteries after being driven into that region's defence zone by the wind on the way home. Just as at Leipzig 405 (Vancouver) Squadron avoided the carnage and all of its participants returned safely. A post-raid analysis revealed that the wind had also played havoc with the marking and bombing and had pushed the attack towards the south-western districts of the capital, where most of the damage occurred, while 126 outlying communities also received bombs.

It had been an exhausting campaign against Berlin for all concerned, but 405 (Vancouver) Squadron had come through remarkably lightly compared with many of its contemporaries. From 236 sorties to the "Big City", only eleven aircraft had failed to return, while three others had been written off in crashes on return, and one with battle damage too severe to repair. In human terms, seventy-one men had given their lives, and others were languishing in PoW camps in Germany and the occupied countries. From now on, Berlin would be left to the Mosquitos of 8 Group's Light Night Striking Force, which would continue to harass it in increasing numbers until Russian troops arrived in its suburbs in April 1945.

Although Berlin had now been consigned to the past, the winter campaign still had a week to run, and two more major operations for the crews to negotiate. The first of these was posted on the 26th and would bring a return to the old enemy of Essen that night, for which a force of 705 aircraft was made ready. 8 Group contributed sixty-seven of the 476 Lancasters and twenty-two Mosquitos, eight of the former provided by 405 (Vancouver) Squadron, one as a visual backer-up and seven as main force supporters. They departed Gransden Lodge between 19.54 and 20.11 with F/Ls Maine-Smith and Spafford the senior pilots on duty, and after climbing out over the airfield, set course for the Dutch coast to pass north of Haarlem and Amsterdam, before swinging to the south-east on a direct run to the target. There were no early returns as the squadron's remarkable serviceability record continued, and all reached the target to find it under eight to ten-tenths cloud with tops in places as high as 14,000 feet. Oboe performed well and main force crews could see the red TIs as they approached and arrived over the aiming-point to find red and green TIs and Wanganui flares. The 405 (Vancouver) Squadron element carried out their respective tasks from 17,500 to 20,000 feet between 21.59 and 22.10 and gained an impression of a successful raid, and this was based on a considerable glow beneath the clouds as they withdrew. Post-raid reconnaissance soon confirmed another outstandingly destructive operation against this once elusive target, thus continuing the remarkable run of successes here since the introduction of Oboe to main force operations a year earlier. More than seventeen hundred houses were destroyed in the attack, with dozens of war industry factories in the Krupp sector sustaining serious damage, and on a night when the night-fighter controllers were caught off guard by the switch to the Ruhr, the success was gained for the modest loss of nine aircraft.

The period known as the Battle of Berlin, but which was better referred to as the winter campaign, was to be brought to an end on the night of the 30/31st, with a standard maximum-effort raid on Nuremberg. The plan of operation departed from normal practice in only one important respect, and this was to prove critical. It had become standard routine over the winter for 8 Group to plan operations and to employ diversions and feints to confuse the enemy night-fighter controllers. Sometimes they were successful and sometimes not, but with the night-fighter force having clearly gained the upper hand with its "Tame Boar" running commentary system, all possible means had to be adopted to protect the bomber stream. During a conference held early on the 30th, the Lancaster Group A-O-Cs expressed a preference for a 5 Group-inspired route, which would require the bomber stream to fly a long straight leg across Belgium and Germany, to a point about fifty miles north of Nuremberg, from where the final run-in would commence. The Halifax A-O-Cs were less convinced of the benefits, and AVM Bennett, the Path Finder chief, was positively overcome by the potential dangers and predicted a disaster, only to be overruled. A force of 795 aircraft was made ready, of which 110 Lancasters and nine Mosquitos were to be provided by 8 Group, fourteen of the former representing 405 (Vancouver) Squadron. The crews attended briefings to be told of the route, wind conditions and the belief that a layer of cloud would conceal them from enemy night-fighters. However, before take-off, a Meteorological Flight Mosquito crew radioed in to cast doubts upon the weather conditions, which they could see differed markedly from those that had been forecast. This also went unheeded, and from around 21.45 for the next hour or so, the bombers took off for the rendezvous area, and headed into a conspiracy of circumstances, which would inflict upon Bomber Command its heaviest defeat of the war.

Having been assigned to their respective roles, four as blind marker/illuminators, one as a visual marker, three as blind backers-up, one as a visual backer-up and four as main force supporters, the 405 (Vancouver) Squadron element departed Gransden Lodge between 22.19 and 22.33 with S/L Bennett, the newly-arrived S/L Blenkinsop and recently promoted S/L Trilsbach the senior pilots on duty. S/L Blenkinsop had served a tour on Wellingtons with 425 (Allouette) Squadron and had volunteered for a second tour on his return to the UK. It was not long into the flight before they and the other crews began to notice some unusual features in the conditions, which included uncommonly bright moonlight, and a crystal clarity of visibility that allowed them the rare sight of other aircraft in the stream. On most nights, crews would feel themselves to be completely alone in the sky all the way to the target, until bang on schedule, TIs would be seen to fall and other aircraft would make their presence known by the turbulence of their slipstreams as they funnelled towards the aiming-point. Once at cruising altitude on this night, however, they were alarmed to note that the forecast cloud was conspicuous by its absence, and instead, lay beneath them as a white tablecloth, against which they were silhouetted like flies. Condensation trails began to form in the cold, clear air to further advertise their presence to the enemy, and the Jetstream winds, which had so adversely affected the Berlin raid a week earlier, were also present, only this time blowing from the south. As then, the wind-finder system would be unable to cope, and this would have a serious impact on the outcome of the operation. The final insult on this sad night was the route's close proximity to two night-fighter beacons, which the enemy aircraft were orbiting while they awaited their instructions, unaware initially, that they were about to have the cream of Bomber Command handed to them on a plate.

The carnage began over Charleroi in Belgium, and from there to the target, the route was signposted by the burning wreckage on the ground of eighty Bomber Command aircraft. The wind-finder system broke down again, and those crews who either failed to detect the strength of the wind, or simply refused to believe the evidence, were driven up to fifty miles north of their intended track, and, consequently, turned towards Nuremberg from a false position. This led to more than a hundred aircraft bombing at Schweinfurt in error, which combined with the massive losses sustained before the target was reached to reduce considerably the numbers arriving at the primary target. The attack opened at 01.04 with red/yellow flares and TIs, which quickly disappeared into the cloud, and resulted in scattered skymarking at times, while at other times, well-defined clusters were apparent. The entire Gransden Lodge contingent avoided the night-fighters to arrive over Nuremberg having established their positions by H2S and encountered eight to ten-tenths cloud with tops as high as 16,000 feet. They carried out their assigned tasks from 16,000 to 20,000 feet between 01.04 and 01.16, the timings no longer of consequence, and observed the glow of many fires, which, according to some reports, remained visible for 120 miles into the return journey. Ninety-five aircraft failed to return home, eleven of them from Path Finder squadrons, and many others were written off in landing crashes or with battle damage too severe to repair. The shock and disappointment were compounded by the fact that the strong wind had driven the marking beyond the city to the east, and Nuremberg had consequently escaped serious damage.

During the course of the month, the squadron participated in seven operations, and dispatched ninety-seven sorties for the loss of a single Lancaster and crew.

April 1944

The winter campaign had brought the Command to its low point of the war and was the only time when the morale of the crews was in question. What now lay before the hard-pressed men of Bomber Command was in marked contrast to that which had been endured over the seemingly interminable winter months. In place of the long slog to Germany on dark, often dirty nights, shorter range hops to France and Belgium in improving weather conditions would become the order of the day. However, these operations would prove to be equally demanding in their way and would require of the crews a greater commitment to accuracy, to avoid casualties among friendly civilians. Despite this, a decree from on high insisted that such operations were worthy of counting as just one third of a sortie towards the completion of a tour, and until this flawed policy was rescinded, the hint of a mutinous air would pervade the crew rooms. In fact, the length of a tour would take on the characteristic of elastic and fluctuate between thirty-eight and thirty from this point until the end of hostilities. Despite the horrendous losses of the winter campaign, the Command was in remarkably fine fettle to face its new challenge, with 3 Group gradually changing to Lancasters, and the much-improved Hercules powered Halifaxes equipping 4 Group and most of 6 Group. Harris was now in the enviable position of being able to achieve what had eluded his predecessor, namely, to attack multiple targets simultaneously with enough strength to be effective. Such was the hitting-power now at his disposal, he could assign targets to individual groups, to groups in tandem, or to the Command as a whole, as dictated by operational requirements. Although invasion considerations would now take priority over all others, Harris would never entirely shelve his favoured policy of city-busting and would sneak one in whenever an opportunity arose. The mounting of simultaneous operations would place an increasing burden on 8 Group to provide a marking element at each target, and because of the concurrent campaigns during the summer months, it would, inevitably, have to spread its presence more thinly than in the past.

The first eight nights of the new month required little of the heavy brigade, and operations involving them were restricted to gardening forays by the Stirlings and older Halifaxes, while the Mosquitos of 8 Group roamed far and wide. 5 Group alone ventured out in numbers, developing its new low-level marking techniques on the night of the 5/6th against the former Dewoitine aircraft factory at Toulouse in south-western France, which, under a nationalization plan in 1936 involving six aircraft companies, including Lioré et Olivier and Potez, was now operating under the name SNCASE, or Sud Est for short. An outstandingly successful operation ensued, and within hours, Harris had given the go ahead for 5 Group to take on its own target marking force, and become, in effect, an independent entity, a move which would cost the Path Finder Force three of its finest squadrons.

It would be almost two weeks before the necessary moves from 8 Group to 5 Group took place, and in the meantime the pre-invasion campaign got into full swing with the posting of two operations on the 9th. The Lille-Delivrance goods station in north-eastern France was assigned to 239 aircraft from 3, 4, 6 and 8 Groups, while the marshalling yards at Villeneuve-St-Georges, on the southern outskirts of Paris, were to be targeted by 225 aircraft drawn from all groups. 8 Group supported the former with forty Lancasters, including seven from Gransden Lodge, and eleven Mosquitos, and the latter with thirty-six Mosquitos only. The 405 (Vancouver) Squadron crews were all designated as main force supporters and took off between 22.57 and 23.03 with S/L Blenkinsop the senior pilot on duty and a dozen 1,000 and two 500-pounders in each bomb bay. They arrived in the target area within two hours to find three-tenths very thin layer-cloud with tops at around 5,000 feet, through which six Mosquitos dropped red TIs as a reference for the heavy markers force. The 405 (Vancouver) Squadron crews delivered their bomb loads from 15,700 to 16,400 feet between 00.49 and 00.58 and returned safely to pass on their reports to the intelligence section at debriefing. Many crews had witnessed two particularly noteworthy explosions at 00.52 and 00.53, the former accompanied by an uprush of orange flame that reached several thousand feet and lasted for a few seconds before fading to leave a pall of black smoke. Crews arriving towards the end of the attack reported another violent explosion at 01.04, by which time the smoke was passing through 10,000 feet. Local sources confirmed that more than two thousand items of rolling stock had been destroyed, and buildings and installations seriously damaged, but at a collateral cost of 456 French civilian lives.

Meanwhile, excellent weather conditions and clear skies greeted the Paris-bound force as it crossed the French coast at around 14,000 feet, and crews were able to identify the target visually, before aiming at the red and green TIs that had been accurately placed by the Path Finder Mosquitos. Many bomb bursts were observed along with orange explosions, and to those high above, the raid appeared to be highly successful. In fact, many bomb loads had fallen into adjacent residential districts, where four hundred houses had been destroyed or seriously damaged, and ninety-three people killed. In contrast to the huge loss of French lives at the targets, the two operations had cost the Command just a single 35 (Madras Presidency) Squadron Lancaster. The question of collateral damage would remain, but sadly, civilian casualties would prove to be an unavoidable by-product of driving the Germans out of France and the other occupied countries.

On the following day, Monday the 10th, a further five railway yards were posted as the targets for that night, four in France and one in Belgium, and assigned to individual groups. 8 Group detailed forty Lancasters and fifteen Mosquitos to attack the yards at Aulnoye, situated between Cambrai and the Belgian frontier in north-eastern France, and Laon, some thirty-five miles to the south. The plan called for the Mosquito element to mark at both locations, and for the Lancasters to attack Laon as part of an overall force of 148 Lancasters drawn from 3, 6 and 8 Groups. 405 (Vancouver) Squadron made ready seven Lancasters for main force support duties and loaded them with a dozen 1,000 pounders each before sending them on their way between 01.46 and 02.07 with F/Ls

McDonald (not to be confused with S/L McDonald) and Perry the senior pilots on duty. Under clear skies and bright moonlight the attack opened at 03.32 with green TIs followed by reds, which the main force crews seemed to straddle with a display of concentrated bombing, the Gransden Lodge crews carrying out their attacks from 13,500 to 15,500 feet between 03.47 and 03.57. A few fires were beginning to develop as they turned away with smoke drifting across the area and upwards, and post-raid reconnaissance revealed that the marking had been slightly misplaced, causing the bombing to hit the south-eastern corner of the yards only. The Germans would round up local civilians at all targets to repair the damage and get the yards working again before long.

Aachen was a major railway centre with marshalling yards at both the western and eastern ends, Aachen-West and Rothe Erde, but the size of the force assembled for the operation on the night of the 11/12th suggested that it was to be a city-busting exercise also. A main force of 269 Lancasters was drawn from 1, 3 and 5 Groups, while 8 Group contributed seventy-two Lancasters and eleven Mosquitos, ten of the former representing 405 (Vancouver) Squadron. They were all briefed to bomb with the main force and were carrying thirteen 1,000 pounders each as they departed Gransden Lodge between 20.50 and 20.59 with S/L Blenkinsop the senior pilot on duty. The bomber stream climbed to between 18,000 and 20,000 feet by the time it reached the Belgian coast at 3° East and maintained that altitude all the way to the target, where six to ten-tenths thin cloud was encountered with tops at 7,000 to 8,000 feet. Red and green TIs identified the aiming-point, and the 405 (Vancouver) Squadron participants carried out their attacks from 16,500 to 18,500 feet between 22.42 and 22.49, observing many bomb bursts and fires, which suggested that the attack was accurate. The bombers maintained height on the way home until fifty miles from the coast, at which position they began a gentle descent to exit enemy territory at 15,000 feet or above. Reports coming out of Aachen revealed this to be the city's worst experience of the war to date, with extensive damage in central and southern districts, disruption of its transport infrastructure and a death toll of 1,525 people in return for the loss of nine Lancasters. However, post-raid reconnaissance revealed that the railway yards had not been destroyed and would require further attention.

On the 14th, the Command became officially subject to the orders coming from the Supreme Headquarters of the Allied Expeditionary Force (SHAEF), under General Dwight D Eisenhower, and would remain thus shackled until the Allied armies were sweeping towards the German frontier at the end of the summer. On the 18th, 83 and 97 (Straits Settlement) Squadrons were loaned to 5 Group from the Path Finders, on what amounted to a permanent detachment, along with the Mosquito unit, 627 Squadron. The Lancaster units were to become the 5 Group heavy marker force and took up residence at Coningsby, while the Mosquitos would eventually take over the low-level marking role currently performed by 617 Squadron and became co-residents with it at Woodhall Spa. This was a major coup for AVM Cochrane and 5 Group and a bitter blow to AVM Bennett, the Path Finder Air-Officer-Commanding. Relations between Cochrane and Bennett had never been cordial, but this plunged them to new depths. Both were brilliant men, Bennett, an Australian, in particular a man of the greatest intellect, who, despite his total lack of humour, commanded the deepest respect and loyalty from his men. He and Cochrane possessed vastly different opinions on the subject of target marking, Bennett believing that a low-level method exposed the crews to unnecessary danger, while Cochrane insisted that the risks in a fast-flying Mosquito were negligible and would produce greater accuracy. Though 83 and 97 Squadrons were formerly of 5 Group, and at that time, had undoubtedly considered themselves part of the elite, most of the current crop of crews, despite beginning their operational careers in 5 Group, had come to see 8 Group as the pinnacle, and were upset at being removed from what they considered to be an elevated status. Once qualified, they were fiercely proud to wear the Path Finder badge and enjoyed the better prospects of promotion, but happily for them, as the squadrons were only officially on loan to 5 Group, these were privileges that they would retain. Henceforth, 5 Group would be known somewhat disparagingly in 8 Group circles as the "Independent Air Force", or the "Lincolnshire Poachers". To compensate for the loss, two new heavy Path Finder squadrons had already been formed, 635 Squadron at Downham Market in March, and 582 Squadron at Little Staughton on the 1st of April.

The night of the 18/19th was devoted to further attacks on marshalling yards and extensive mining operations in northern waters. At Gransden Lodge, sixteen crews were called to briefing to learn of their part in that night's activities, which in their case, were raids on marshalling yards, locomotive sheds and workshops at Noisy-le-Sec and Tergnier, the former a north-eastern suburb of Paris and the latter situated some ten miles south of St-Quentin, some fifty miles to the north-east. The plan called for eight Oboe Mosquitos and twenty-four 8 Group Lancasters to mark at Tergnier for a main force element of 139 Halifaxes of 4 Group, 405 (Vancouver) Squadron providing three illuminators, two visual markers and three supporters. The Mosquitos were then to carry on towards the south-west to perform similarly at Noisy with twenty-six 8 Group Lancasters and a 6 Group main force of 112 Halifaxes and thirty-five Lancasters, 405 (Vancouver) Squadron providing four illuminators and four visual backers-up. The two elements departed Gransden Lodge together between 21.41 and 21.58 with W/C Lane and S/L Bennett leading those bound for Noisy and S/Ls Blenkinsop, McDonald and Trilsbach the senior pilots on duty for Tergnier. The latter reached their target first to find excellent visibility, identifying the aiming point visually and performing their assigned tasks from 7,000 to 14,000 feet between 23.24 and 23.40. At Noisy-le-Sec, the attack went ahead in similarly good conditions, the 405 (Vancouver) Squadron crews carrying out their assigned tasks from 8,000 to 15,000 feet between 23.50 and 00.01. Post-raid reconnaissance revealed massive damage to installations and more than two hundred delayed action bombs would cause problems for a further week. Although a through line was established, the main area of the yards remained out of action until after the war. Inevitably, however, collateral damage in adjacent residential districts cost 464 French lives. At Tergnier fifty lines were blocked, but much of the bombing fell onto nearby houses and the casualty figure was not made public.

Briefings on 5 Group stations on the 20th informed crews of their part in the first operation to include the three newly transferred squadrons, which was a two-phase attack on railway yards at La Chapelle, situated just to the north of Paris, while the night's main event was to be conducted by a force of 357 Lancasters and twenty-two Mosquitos drawn from 1, 3, 6 and 8 Groups against Cologne. Other operations would be taking place against railway yards at Ottignies, Chambly and Lens, and it was for the last-mentioned that fourteen 405 (Vancouver) Squadron Lancasters were made ready at Gransden Lodge as the 8 Group heavy contribution, following on the heels of seven Oboe Mosquitos ahead of a 6 Group main force of 154 Halifaxes. They took off between 21.52 and 22.14 with W/C Lane acting as Master Bomber and one of four visual markers, among which were also S/Ls Bennett and Blenkinsop, while S/L Trilsbach was one of four illuminators and the remaining six crews were divided between visual backing-up and main force support duties. They reached the target to encounter thick low cloud at between 500 and 1,000 feet and six-tenths thin cloud at 7,000 feet and dispensed their flares before the Oboe Mosquitos arrived five minutes later than planned to release green TIs. W/C Lane was satisfied with the accuracy of the marking and called in the main force element, which performed well to leave the yards, workshops and locomotive sheds severely damaged. The 405 (Vancouver) Squadron crews carried out their assigned tasks from 4,900 to 8,000 feet between 23.34 and 23.57 and returned home satisfied with their night's work.

Although the crews at Cologne could not determine what was happening beneath the cloud, the impression was of an accurate and fairly concentrated attack, which was confirmed by local sources. The main weight of the bombing had fallen to the north and west of the city centre into partially industrial districts, where 192 industrial premises sustained varying degrees of damage, as did 725 dwelling units with commercial premises attached. More than eighteen hundred dwelling units were destroyed and two thousand more damaged, and twelve hundred fires had to be dealt with.

A busy night of operations lay ahead for more than eleven hundred crews on the 22nd, the largest by elements from all but 5 Group against Düsseldorf, for which a force of 596 aircraft was assembled. 5 Group would be testing the efficacy of its low-level marking system at Braunschweig, while 181 aircraft drawn from 3, 4, 6 and 8 Groups attempted to rectify the failure of ten nights earlier at the marshalling yards at Laon. The last mentioned was of interest to seven 405 (Vancouver) Squadron crews, while seven others were briefed for the main event, two as visual backers-up and the rest as main force supporters. Those bound for Laon departed Gransden Lodge first between 22.18 and 22.24 with F/L Perry the senior pilot on duty and each Lancaster carrying twelve 1,000-pounders to deliver with the main force as part of the second wave. The plan called for the northern and southern aiming-points to be marked by Path Finder elements respectively of twenty-seven and twenty-five Lancasters with six Mosquitos and a Master Bomber at each, and this force was well on its way south when the Düsseldorf-bound element took off between 23.11 and 23.26 with S/L Blenkinsop the senior pilot on duty.

Clear skies over north-eastern France enabled the Laon marshalling yards to be identified visually, and the first illuminator crews went in at the northern aiming-point at 6,000 to 12,000 feet between 23.20 and 23.28 to drop hooded flares in advance of yellow TIs, before making a second run to deliver nine 1,000 pounders each. The process was repeated at the southern aiming-point between 23.58 and 00.02, the whole operation taking place under the watchful eyes of the Master Bombers, who were last to drop their high explosives at 00.13. The 405 (Vancouver) Squadron contingent bombed with the main force from 5,000 to 8,000 feet between 00.08 and 00.25 and contributed to a highly successful attack that caused severe damage at a cost to the Command of four Lancasters, three Stirlings and two Halifaxes. F/L Perry and crew returned in a severely damaged Lancaster and with a fatally wounded rear gunner after being taken by surprise by a Ju88, which had approached unseen to fire a single and devastating burst. They reported orbiting the target at 8,000 feet in accordance with the instructions of the Master Bomber and being set upon at 00.05, before making a second pass over the aiming point to bomb at 00.09. A missing 635 Squadron Lancaster contained W/C Cousens, one of the Master Bombers, who lost his life with six others of the eight-man crew. Also missing was 405 (Vancouver) Squadron's JB684, which was accounted for by a night-fighter over France and crashed at Conde-sur-Aisne with fatal consequences for F/Sgt Saltzberry RCAF and his crew. This was the squadron's first failure to return since Stuttgart in mid March.

Meanwhile, Düsseldorf received over two thousand tons of bombs, mostly in its northern districts, where fifty-six large industrial concerns sustained varying degrees of damage and loss of production, more than two thousand houses were destroyed and in excess of a thousand people lost their lives. The 405 (Vancouver) Squadron crews carried out their briefs from 16,000 to 19,000 feet between 01.14 and 01.32 and all returned safely, while the 5 Group effort at Braunschweig was thwarted by communications problems and cloud and failed to achieve its aims.

The busy month of operations continued on the 24th, with briefings for a heavy raid on Karlsruhe in southern Germany and the assembly of a force of 637 aircraft, which included eighty-three Lancasters and nine Mosquitos from 8 Group, fourteen of the former made ready at Gransden Lodge. The 405 (Vancouver) Squadron crews were assigned to five roles, three as blind marker/illuminators, three as blind backers-up, one as a visual marker, two as visual backers-up and five as main force supporters. They took off between 22.00 and 22.20 now with five pilots in the rank of squadron leader after the promotion of F/L Coldrey to join S/Ls Bennett, Blenkinsop, McDonald and Trilsbach, and lost the services of P/O Long and crew to intercom failure when some twenty-five miles out from the Suffolk coast. The others enjoyed a relatively uneventful outward flight across France until 23.40, when they ran into an electrical storm between Liege and Strasbourg that lasted for an hour and affected some H2S sets. Sixty to seventy searchlights were operating as they passed close to Mannheim, and at Karlsruhe they were greeted by moderate flak coming up through the nine to ten-tenths thin cloud that reached up to 18,000 feet. The first illuminator flares were released at 00.35 and were quickly followed by green TIs backed up by reds, the 405 (Vancouver) Squadron crews carrying out their respective tasks from 11,900 to 18,500 feet between 00.35 and 00.48. The main force crews mostly found red and green TIs and red and yellow release-point flares to guide them to the aiming-point, but it proved difficult to assess what was happening beneath the cloud. Local reports confirmed that the strong winds had pushed the attack onto the northern districts of the city and beyond, and nine hundred houses were destroyed or seriously damaged at a cost to the Command of nineteen aircraft.

Three major operations were posted across the Command on the 26th, Essen attracting the largest force of 493 aircraft from all but 5 Group, with 8 Group providing sixty-two Lancasters and eighteen Mosquitos, while 5 Group targeted Schweinfurt. Elsewhere, a main force of 183 Halifaxes of 4 and 6 Groups was to take another swipe at the marshalling yards at Villeneuve-St-Georges in the company of thirty-Lancasters and fifteen Mosquitos of 8 Group, 405 (Vancouver) Squadron supporting both operations with eight crews assigned to Essen and six to Paris. The latter was another two-phase attack with a northern and southern aiming-point serviced by ten Path Finder Lancasters each after Oboe marking by fourteen Mosquitos. This element departed Gransden Lodge first, between 22.19 and 22.24 with S/Ls Bennett and Blenkinsop acting as Master Bomber and Deputy at the northern aiming point, while 35 (Madras Presidency) Squadron's S/L Creswell and F/L Petrie-Andrews performed a similar role at the southern end. They were over the Channel by the time that the Essen-bound crews took to the air between 23.12 and 23.19 with S/L McDonald the senior pilot, and all arrived at Villeneuve-St-Georges in the wake of the first wave to find clear skies and excellent conditions. The Mosquito element was experiencing Oboe equipment problems and only one was able to release a red TI, at around 00.31, which S/L Bennett assessed as being somewhat north of the aiming point. He dropped his own red and green TIs, and although his instructions to the main force went largely unheard, the illuminator flares delivered by four 405 (Vancouver) Squadron crews negated the effects of haze and the aiming point was identified visually. They followed up with their ten 1,000-pounders from 6,000 to 12,000 feet between 00.31 and 00.49.

Meanwhile, some 280 miles to the north-east, the 8 Group element arrived over the Ruhr having lost five Lancasters and four Mosquitos to technical issues, leaving the remainder to find favourable conditions with just patchy cloud and condensation trails to slightly inhibit the view. F/L McDonald and crew ran into intense searchlight activity and were coned by a hundred beams including the blue "master", and despite violent evasive action were unable to escape until dumping their bombs some ten miles north-west of the target. The Oboe Mosquitos opened the attack on time with red TIs at 01.24, and accurate and continuous marking maintained the aiming-point throughout the raid, six of the 405 (Vancouver) Squadron crews performing a main force supporting role and delivering their cookie, six 1,000 and two 500 pounders each from 16,000 to 18,600 feet between 01.28 and 01.32. Most crews found ground detail on which to orient themselves, particularly the River Lippe and parallel canal running east to west on the northern fringe of the Ruhr and confirmed their positions by H2S-fix before bombing. A large yellow explosion was observed at 01.28, an orange one at 01.34 and these were followed by a third one at 01.36. All crews commented on the abundance of searchlights operating in cones of about thirty, and also described thick smoke rising through 10,000 feet from a line of fires across the aiming-point which was beginning to obscure the target. It was clear that a very destructive raid had taken place, achieved at a cost to the Command of a modest seven aircraft, and the only confirmation to emerge locally was a death toll of 313.

The 27th saw a further three operations scheduled, two against railway yards at Aulnoye in France and Montzen in Belgium, and the night's largest effort against the small city of Friedrichshafen, situated on the northern shore of Lake Constance (Bodensee) on the border with Switzerland and close to the Austrian frontier. An all-Lancaster force of 322 aircraft was assembled, the main force element drawn from 1, 3 and 6 Groups with fifty-nine 8 Group Lancasters to provide the marking. At briefings, the crews were told of the importance of Friedrichshafen to the German war effort as a centre of war production, particularly of tank engines and gearboxes. 405 (Vancouver) Squadron was called upon to provide two blind marker/illuminators, one primary visual marker, one blind backer-up and two main force supporters, and they departed Gransden Lodge between 21.29 and 21.34 with S/Ls Bennett and Coldrey the senior pilots on duty. They all reached the target area to find clear skies and established their positions visually on Lake Constance, but it wasn't long before the aiming-point was concealed beneath smoke generated by incendiaries and the resultant fires. A few green TIs were visible through the smoke, and the Gransden Lodge contingent performed their assigned tasks from 15,000 to 18,500 feet between 01.59 and 02.09 before leaving the scene with the impression that the raid was progressing well, with, perhaps, a little scattering to the west.

Meanwhile, 405 (Vancouver) Squadron provided all eight Path Finder Lancasters for an attack on the Montzen marshalling yards, located close to the German frontier fewer than ten miles to the south-west of Aachen. W/C Lane and S/L Blenkinsop had been designated Master Bomber and Deputy and the remaining six crews, including those of S/Ls McDonald and Trilsbach, were to act as illuminators for the main force of 120 Halifaxes and six Lancasters of 4 and 6 Groups. They departed Gransden Lodge between 23.49 and 23.55, the illuminators carrying a bomb load of nine 1,000-pounders each, and all arrived in the target area to find four-tenths thin cloud at 4,000 feet and generally favourable conditions. The marking did not proceed without issues with the TIs falling away from the aiming point, upon which W/C Lane called for S/L Blenkinsop to drop his green TIs, which also slightly missed the mark. W/C Lane then delivered his own green TIs, which S/L Blenkinsop declared to be "bang on", and he was invited to back them up with a white TI before the main force element was called in. The 405 (Vancouver) Squadron contingent fulfilled their briefs from 4,500 to 12,000 feet between 01.24 and 01.43 and as they turned away reported some under and overshooting but a large yellow fire raging in the centre of the yards. On the way home midway between the target and Antwerp, JA976 was attacked by a night-fighter and broke up in the air, flinging clear twenty-four-year-old S/L "Teddy" Blenkinsop DFC RCAF as the sole survivor among the eight occupants. He joined up with a Belgian resistance group but was captured in August, and as punishment for his association with the enemy was denied prisoner of war consideration and was subjected to harsh treatment in the form of slave labour, torture and beatings and ultimately arrived at the infamous Bergen-Belsen camp near Bremen, where he succumbed to heart failure on the 25th of January 1945. He was awarded a Belgian Croix-de-Guerre.

Post-raid reconnaissance and local sources confirmed that the attack on Friedrichshafen had been outstandingly concentrated and had dealt a severe blow to tank production while hitting other industrial premises as well as the town itself. It was not a one-sided affair, however, and having avoided contact with night-fighters on the way to the target, the bombers sustained heavy casualties at their hands in the target area, losing eighteen of their number.

During the course of the month the squadron took part in thirteen operations and dispatched 110 sorties for the loss of two Lancasters and crews and a rear gunner.

May 1944

With the invasion now just five weeks away, the new month would be devoted to attacks on railway targets and coastal defences, in the case of the latter, with the focus on the Pas-de-Calais region of France, to try to reinforce the enemy's mistaken belief that the landings would take place there. The month began with six small to medium-scale raids on the night of the 1/2nd against railway installations and factories in France and Belgium. Three of the operations were by the "Independent Air Force", and 405 (Vancouver) Squadron was not called into action. Briefings took place on 1 and 5 Group stations on the 3rd, for what would become a highly contentious operation that night against a Panzer training camp and transport depot at Mailly-le-Camp, situated some seventy-five miles east of Paris in north-eastern France. The units based there posed a potential threat to Allied forces as the invasion unfolded and needed to be eliminated. The events of the operation proved to be so controversial, that recriminations abound to this day concerning the quality of leadership provided by the 5 Group Master Bomber and marker leader, W/Cs Deane and Cheshire respectively. Despite the problems caused by communications problems, the operation was a major success, which destroyed 80% of the camp's buildings and 102 vehicles, of which thirty-seven were tanks, while over two hundred men were killed. Forty-two Lancasters failed to return, however, two thirds of them from 1 Group, and they were shot down mostly while milling around in the target area under bright moonlight awaiting instructions to bomb. The accusations against W/C Deane and W/C Cheshire were based on an inaccurate understanding of events, but forever soured relations between 1 and 5 Groups.

While the above was in progress, an 8 Group force of eighty-four Lancasters and eight Mosquitos was engaged over a Luftwaffe aerodrome at Montdidier, situated some fifteen miles south-east of Amiens in north-eastern France. 405 (Vancouver) Squadron had briefed two crews as illuminators and a dozen as main force supporters, now referred to in the squadron ORB as "practice bombers" and dispatched them between 22.51 and 23.04 with S/L Bennett the senior pilot on duty. They arrived in the target area to find clear skies and excellent visibility that enable them to identify visually the hangars and runways, over which the first flares appeared at 00.13. They were followed by a red spot fire delivered by an Oboe Mosquito, after which, the Master Bomber released a yellow TI. On reflection, he ordered the bombing to focus on green TIs, which appeared to be right on the aiming-point, and the 405 (Vancouver) Squadron participants delivered a total of eleven four-flare bundles, twelve cookies, sixteen 1,000-pounders and 162 x 500-pounders from 9,000 to 12,000 feet between 00.16 and 00.29. A successful outcome was marred for the squadron by the failure to return of ND881, which had been shot down by a night-fighter during the bombing run and crashed on the northern side of the airfield with no survivors from the predominantly RCAF crew of F/L McDonald RCAF.

The main operation scheduled for the 6th was an attack on the Gassicourt marshalling yards at Mantes-la-Jolie, situated close to the South Bank of the Seine north-west of Paris, for which a force of 149 aircraft was made up of seventy-seven 4 Group Halifaxes and sixty-four 8 Group Lancasters, with eight Mosquitos to provide the initial marking. The 405 (Vancouver) Squadron element of eleven departed Gransden Lodge between 00.54 and 01.04 with the crews of F/L MacKinnon and P/O Borrowes designated as illuminators and the remainder as "practice bombers", each carrying a dozen 1,000-pounders. Five of the Mosquitos aborted, but target identification on a night of bright moonlight was not an issue, and the first flare went down at 02.08. Master Bomber, S/L Creswell of 35 (Madras Presidency) Squadron, was able to pick up the river and the locomotive sheds in the yards visually, and aimed three long-burning yellow TIs and six 1,000 pounders at them from 8,000 feet at 02.09. The TIs were assessed as being west of the aiming-point, and the main force crews were instructed to ignore them and focus instead on a different yellow and a green TI that were burning much closer to the mark. Matters became confused by green TIs falling north of the river and a further red TI to the south, and Deputy Master Bomber, S/L Chidgey, was called in to put a white TI on the aiming-point. This he did satisfactorily, but smoke was now concealing the yards, and the crews were told to bomb a large area of fire, those from Gransden Lodge complying from 8,000 to 10,000 feet between 02.13 and 02.20. Returning crews were confident that the yards had been severely damaged, and this was confirmed to an extent, but many bomb loads had fallen into parts of the old town and other districts to the west, where more than a hundred houses were destroyed, and fifty-four civilians killed. Only three aircraft were lost, but one of these was ND617 of 405 (Vancouver) Squadron, which exploded over the target, killing the predominantly RCAF crew of P/O Borrowes DFC RCAF, who had joined the squadron as a NCO pilot. Four members of his crew were also holders of the DFC and at the time of their deaths had completed more than forty operations.

The railway theme continued on the 8th when marshalling yards at Haine-St-Pierre were posted as the target, at a location believed to be close to the Belgian frontier in north-eastern France. A force of 123 aircraft consisted of a main force of sixty-two Halifaxes and eleven Lancasters of 6 Group and forty-two Lancasters and eight Mosquitos belonging to the path Finders. 405 (Vancouver) Squadron made ready fourteen Lancasters, which departed Gransden Lodge between 02.00 and

02.15 with S/L Trilsbach the senior pilot on duty and one of four designated illuminators, while the remaining ten crews were assigned to bomb with the main force. Four Mosquitos and three Lancasters returned early, leaving the rest of the force to arrive in the target area under clear skies and good enough visibility for a visual identification to be possible. The attack opened on time at 03.19 with Oboe-placed red spotfires closely followed by green TIs, which the Master Bomber, W/C Daniels of 35 (Madras Presidency) Squadron, judged to be some four hundred yards south and south-east of the aiming-point, and he went in at 5,500 feet at 03.21 to release three long-burning yellow TIs and four 1,000 pounders. One of the yellows fell close to a locomotive shed, and within minutes of the main force attack, smoke and dust had risen to 5,000 feet, obscuring the ground. The Gransden Lodge crews carried out their respective tasks from 6,000 to 8,000 feet between 03.23 and 03.28, and all but two returned safely to report a successful operation. The absentee crews were those of P/O Darlow in ND347 and F/L Chase RAAF in ND587 and both were on their way home when crashing within about eight miles of each other on the Belgian side of the frontier with France. The former came down at 03.40 delivering the pilot and two others of the mixed RAF/RCAF crew into enemy hands, while three evaded a similar fate and the rear gunner lost his life. There were no survivors from the latter, which fell victim to the night-fighter of Lt Wilhelm Marstaller of I./NJG4 and crashed at 03.45 a little to the north.

Five railway targets were selected for attention on the night of the 10/11th, and a total of 506 Lancasters, Halifaxes and Mosquitos made ready. The attacks on the marshalling yards at Courtrai (Kortrijk) and Ghent in Belgium and Lens in north-eastern France would benefit from a Path Finder presence of fourteen Lancasters and four Mosquitos each, 405 (Vancouver) Squadron providing the fourteen Lancasters for Ghent. They departed Gransden Lodge between 22.29 and 22.42 with S/Ls Bennett and McDonald the designated Master Bomber and Deputy and the remainder divided equally between illuminator and main force support duties. the former carrying ten 500-pounders and the latter eighteen. The first flares went down from clear skies at 23.38 and lit up the marshalling yards for the Oboe Mosquitos to mark with green TIs two minutes later, after which a constant supply of yellow and white TIs between 23.40 and 23.51 maintained the aiming point. The 405 (Vancouver) Squadron participants performed their assigned roles from 7,000 to 12,000 feet between 23.40 and 23.51 and there was praise for the control exercised by the Master Bomber and Deputy. Most of the bombing was concentrated around the markers, but some collateral damage occurred, and forty-eight Belgian civilians lost their lives.

Marshalling yards at Boulogne and Trouville in France and Hasselt and Louvain in Belgium were handed respectively to 6, 4, 1 and 3 Groups on the 11th, each with Path Finder support, while 5 Group targeted a military camp at Bourg-Leopold in northern Belgium. A force of 135 aircraft for Boulogne included twenty-one Path Finder Lancasters and eight Mosquitos, fourteen of the former provided by 405 (Vancouver) Squadron with F/L MacKinnon and S/L McDonald designated Master Bomber and Deputy and S/L Trilsbach leading the six illuminators and six main force supporters. They departed Gransden Lodge between 22.59 and 23.12 and all reached the target area to find clear skies and a little ground haze, but F/L MacKinnon's bomb sight had become unserviceable and while he remained raid controller, he handed the task of target marking to S/L McDonald. The first illuminator flares went down at 00.24 and a red spotfire was delivered by an Oboe Mosquito right on the aiming point a couple of minutes late at 00.26. The Master Bomber called in the main force and the bombing fell accurately around the markers, which from time to time became obscured by smoke and had to be constantly replenished. The 405 (Vancouver)

Squadron particpants carried out their assigned tasks from 9,500 to 12,000 feet between 00.24 and 00.35, delivering in total forty-eight 1,000-pounders and 118 x 500-pounders in addition to 152 hooded flares. Large explosions were observed at 00.30, 00.33 and 00.38 and black smoke suggested that oil storage tanks had been hit, before the bombing appeared to creep back slightly to the north towards the end of the raid. Sadly, the attack had not been as accurate as at first believed and 128 civilians lost their lives in adjacent residential districts.

The 12th brought a return to Hasselt and Louvain, the latter operation this time to focus on the marshalling yards after the successful destruction of the locomotive works twenty-four hours earlier. 405 (Vancouver) Squadron was not involved, and in keeping with most of the Command's heavy squadrons, would remain operationally idle for the ensuing week.

When operations resumed on the 19th a return to Boulogne was entrusted to a 4 Group main force, while 1 Group was handed Orleans, 5 Group Amiens and 3 Group Le Mans, each with 8 Group providing the marking, while a second 5 Group force took care of its own marking at Tours. At Gransden Lodge six crews were briefed for Le Mans and assigned to illuminator duties as part of an 8 Group contribution of a dozen Lancasters and four Mosquitos marking for a hundred main force Lancasters. Ten other crews were informed that they would be bombing a radar-jamming station near the French coast at Mont de Couple to the east of Cap Gis Nez as part of an all-8 Group force of thirty-nine Lancasters and five Mosquitos. The former element took off first between 22.25 and 22.31 with S/L Trilsbach the senior pilot on duty, and they were followed into the air between 22.53 and 23.02 by the bombing brigade led by F/Ls Lewis, MacKinnon and Perry, each crew sitting on eighteen 500-pounders. The latter arrived at their destination shortly after midnight to find clear skies but haze extending to 11,000 feet and established their positions by H2S in the absence of TIs, seven delivering an attack from 9,800 to 11,000 feet between 00.04 and 00.13, while three others failed to identify the aiming point and withheld their bombs.

Meanwhile, Le Mans was found to be covered by ten-tenths layer cloud between 7,500 and 9,000 feet with clear skies above and good visibility below, and positions were established by H2S during a timed run from Alençon thirty miles to the north. After the flares had been released the master Bomber ordered crews to descend to 8,000 feet to bomb visually, but not all heard the instruction and the dropping of eight 1,000-pounders each by the 405 (Vancouver) element took place from 6,000 to 12,300 feet between 00.17 and 00.35. A large explosion at 00.28 lasted two seconds and lit up the surrounding area, and another at 00.29 sent a column of smoke rising through 9,000 feet. The force was homebound when another large detonation at 00.40 left the reflection of a fire beneath the cloud. At debriefings a number of crews reported observing a Lancaster shot down by flak over the target and losing its port wing. This was almost certainly the 7 Squadron Lancaster containing the Master Bomber, W/C Barron DSO & Bar, DFC, DFM RNZAF, one of 8 Group's most experienced and inspirational captains, who died along with his crew on his eightieth sortie.

For the first time in a year, Duisburg was posted as the target for a heavy raid on the 21st, for which a force of 510 Lancasters was drawn from 1, 3, 5 and 8 Groups. They would be supported by twenty-two Mosquitos, and while this operation was in progress, seventy Lancasters and thirty-seven Halifaxes would undertake gardening duties in the Nectarines and Rosemary gardens around the Frisians and off Heligoland, and in the Forget-me-not, Silverthorn and Quince gardens in the Kattegat and Kiel Bay regions of the Baltic. 8 Group detailed sixty-three Lancasters for the main event, five of them belonging to 405 (Vancouver) squadron, each of which was loaded with a cookie and fourteen SBCs each containing eight 30lb incendiaries for delivery as part of the main force. They departed Gransden Lodge between 22.40 and 22.55 with F/O Smith the senior pilot on duty and had been instructed at briefing to adhere to the plan for the outward route, which involved a few aircraft from 3 Group gaining height as they adopted a north-westerly course as far as Sleaford, so as not to cross into enemy radar cover earlier than necessary. The groups would rendezvous at 18,000 feet over the North Sea at 3° East to cross the enemy coast via the western Frisians at 20,000 feet and climb to 22,000 or 23,000 feet, before increasing speed for the run across the target. They found the Ruhr to be concealed beneath ten-tenths cloud with tops at between 11,000 and 20,000 feet, which would not have been a problem had the Oboe Mosquito element not suffered a 50% rate of equipment failure, leaving eleven to dispense red Wanganui markers with-yellow-stars, which disappeared into the cloud tops almost before they could be seen. A number of crews commented on the data provided by the "windfinder" system to be inaccurate, and this made it a challenge for some to establish their position. A steady stream of marker flares provided an aiming-point for the heavy brigade between 01.04 and 01.18, the 405 (Vancouver) Squadron crews carrying out their attacks from just above the cloud tops at 20,000 to 22,000 feet between 01.10 and 01.15. Returning crews were not enthusiastic about the outcome, and post-raid reconnaissance confirmed that a modest 350 buildings had been destroyed in the southern half of Duisburg and 665 others had been seriously damaged.

Just like Duisburg, Dortmund had not been visited by the heavy brigade for a year when it was posted on the 22nd to face an all-Lancaster heavy force of 361 aircraft drawn from 1, 3, 6 and 8 Groups, while 5 Group targeted Braunschweig. 405 (Vancouver) Squadron briefed two crews as visual recenterers and five main force supporters as part of the 8 Group force of sixty-seven Lancasters and fourteen Mosquitos and sent them on their way from Gransden Lodge between 22.45 and 23.00 with the long-serving American Capt Copenhaver and F/L Perry the senior pilots on duty. They climbed away into heavy cloud and severe icing conditions from 4,000 feet, which persuaded a considerable number of crews to abandon their sorties before reaching enemy territory, and among them was the crew of F/O Keenan, whose port-inner engine failed at the midpoint of the North Sea crossing. Those pressing on were rewarded with improving conditions, and by the time the target hove into view, the cloud had diminished to no more than two-tenths. The attack opened punctually with red and green TIs and red flares with yellow stars, and the 405 (Vancouver) Squadron participants delivered their cookie, six 1,000-pounder and two 500-pounders or six 2,000-pounders from 14,000 to 20,000 feet between 00.44 and 00.51. Many fires were observed, some with oily smoke, and the consensus was of an accurate and effective raid at a cost of eighteen Lancaster. Post-raid reconnaissance revealed that the main weight of the attack had fallen onto predominantly residential districts in the south-east of the city, where six industrial premises and more than eight hundred houses had been destroyed, and almost as many seriously damaged.

While the above operation was in progress, thirteen Lancasters and eight Mosquitos of 8 Group were being prepared for a return to the marshalling yards at Le Mans to mark for a 6 Group main force of 112 Halifaxes. S/L McDonald and F/L MacKinnon were the designated Master Bomber and Deputy, while S/L Trilsbach was the senior pilot on duty among the seven assigned to illuminator duties, and all got away safely from Gransden Lodge between 00.45 and 00.53. They all arrived in the target area to find clear skies and excellent conditions and illumination commenced at 02.23, only for the Deputy Master Bomber to call "dummy run" on his first attempt to mark the aiming point and compel the waiting main force to orbit. There was a further delay when the flares burned out before the main force had a chance to attack, but the bombing eventually got under way and was focused on predominantly yellow TIs, the 405 (Vancouver) squadron crews delivering their eight 1,000-pounders each from 4,000 to 12,100 feet between 02.23 and 02.41. Local sources confirmed extensive damage to the railway yards and the nearby Gnome & Rhone aero-engine factory, and for once civilian casualties were avoided.

The main operation on the 24th involved 442 aircraft in a two-phase attack, ninety minutes apart on marshalling yards at Aachen, Rothe-Erde in the east and Aachen-West. As the most westerly city in Germany, sitting on the frontiers of both Holland and Belgium, it was a major link in the railway network that would be a route for reinforcements to the Normandy battle front. Other operations on this night were directed at coastal batteries in the Pas-de-Calais and war-industry factories in Holland and Belgium. 8 Group committed thirty-five Lancasters and eight Mosquitos to Rothe-Erde in phase 1, and thirty Lancasters and eight Mosquitos to Aachen-West, and it was for the latter that 405 (Vancouver) Squadron made ready seven Lancasters. S/L Bennett was the senior pilot on duty and was to perform the role of visual centerer, while the remaining six crews were assigned as main force supporters and would carry a cookie and sixteen 500-pounders each. They departed Gransden Lodge between 00.24 and 00.30 with S/L Cranswick the senior pilot on duty and undertaking his one-hundredth sortie. They all arrived in the target area to find clear skies, but the vertical visibility was compromised by thick haze as the attack opened with red TIs at 02.21. They were soon backed up with green TIs, and H2S confirmed their accuracy as bombs were delivered by the 1 and 3 Group Lancaster main force in concentrated fashion within close proximity to the aiming-point. The 405 (Vancouver) Squadron crews carried out their assigned tasks from a uniform 16,900 to 17,000 feet between 02.25 and 02.31 and were prevented by the haze and then smoke from making an accurate assessment of the outcome. Night-fighters were very much in evidence in the Antwerp area, and eighteen Halifaxes failed to return from the first phase attack along with one Path Finder Lancaster from 7 Squadron. The night-fighters were probably refuelling as the second phase element passed through, and a more modest six Lancasters were lost in return for a highly destructive raid.

S/L Bennett was another highly experienced Path Finder officer, who had risen from the rank of pilot officer in less than a year and was the holder of the DSO and DFC. By the time of the Aachen operation, he had actually completed his tour, but having undertaken two second dickey operations on his arrival from 408 (Goose) Squadron, was two ahead of his crew. A typically close-knit crew, who had been together since O.T.U., they began operations in June 1943 as "Bennett's Bums", and their captain was determined to see them through to the end of their tour. As they approached the target, ND526 was attacked from below by a night-fighter, which was thrown off by evasive action before serious damage was sustained, and they were able to press on to the target as briefed. On the way home over Holland, and only about twenty minutes from the coast, a second encounter with a night-fighter had more serious consequences, and the pilot ordered the crew to bail out. For F/O Frame in the rear turret, this was more easily said than done as his turret was unserviceable and in the port-starboard configuration, which left him separated from his parachute. He cranked the turret to the fore-and-aft, reached into the fuselage for his chute, clipped it on and hand-cranked himself back into a position to fall free. This was the start of an adventure with the Dutch underground, which would ultimately see him retain his freedom, and return to England on the

24th of September. His first action on return was to make enquiries about his crew, and he learned with great sadness that S/L Bennett almost certainly sacrificed his life to enable his crew to save themselves. He was the only one of the eight men on board to lose his life, while the other six were taken into captivity.

Post-raid reconnaissance and local sources confirmed that both yards had been hit, as were parts of Aachen itself and many adjacent communities, which sustained extensive damage and casualties and left almost fifteen thousand people bombed out of their homes. However, the job was not yet done, and a further attack would be launched in three days' time.

In addition to the return to the Rothe Erde marshalling yards at Aachen on the night of the 27/28th was a second "return" visit, this one to a military camp at Bourg-Leopold in northern Belgium, which had been the target for an attack by 5 Group earlier in the month but had been abandoned because of poor visibility after half of the force had bombed. On this night, a force of 331 aircraft was assembled with a predominantly Halifax main force drawn from 4 and 6 Groups, while 8 Group provided fourteen 35 (Madras Presidency) Squadron Lancasters and eight Mosquitos. Among other operations against railway installations and coastal batteries was an attack on the Luftwaffe aerodrome at Rennes-St-Jacques, situated in the north-western corner of France, for which an all-8 Group force of seventy-eight Lancasters and five Mosquitos was assembled. At Gransden Lodge fifteen Lancasters were made ready, two for the illuminator crews of S/L Trilsbach and F/L MacKinnon and the remainder for main force support duties, each loaded with eighteen 500-pounders. They took off between 23.28 and 23.49 and all arrived at the target to find clear skies and good visibility, which was enhanced by the punctual delivery of illuminator flares. The main force element arrived on time but was forced to wait for up to ten minites until TIs appeared and the Master Bomber issued instructions. Yellow and white TIs fell close to the aiming point and crews were ordered to bomb visually between them, those from 405 (Vancouver) Squadron complying from 11,500 to 14,000 feet between 01.34 and 01.51. They contributed to much damage, and a large explosion suggested that the aerodrome's ammunition dump had been hit.

With the invasion a little more than a week away, the objectives for 181 aircraft on the 28th were a number of coastal batteries, one at Saint-Martin-de-Varreville, situated on the Cherbourg peninsular overlooking what would be Utah beach, the most westerly of the two American landing grounds. The 8 Group ORB provides scant information, probably because of the secrecy surrounding the significance of this target, and mentions only that eight Oboe Mosquitos were dispatched, five of which were abortive. The target battery for fourteen Lancasters each of 35 (Madras Presidency) and 405 (Vancouver) Squadrons was at Mardyck, located just to the west of Dunkerque in the Pas-de-Calais region, believed by the Germans to be the genuine destination for the invasion force. The ORB provides no details, and we know only that the Gransden Lodge crews took off between 23.24 and 23.38 with F/L Perry and Capt Copenhaver the senior pilots on duty and each crew sitting on eighteen 500 pounders. They all arrived in the target area to find clear skies and good visibility, and F/L Perry and crew were the first to carry out an attack, employing Gee in the absence of TIs, and the following seven crews also attacked without the assistance of markers. One crew was observed to jettison some of its load off the coast, while the final five on target aimed at green TIs, the first of which cascaded at 00.40. At debriefing crews reported bombing from 11,000 to 14,000 feet between 00.30 and 00.45, some of those at the head of the stream after making two passes over the aiming point. Inevitably, the lack of TIs initially led to a scattered attack, but the outcome was of secondary importance to the deception purpose of the raid.

The 31st brought briefings across the Command for operations against railway yards, radar-jamming stations and gun batteries, a number of which would be supported by 8 Group. The marshalling yards at Trappes, situated in the Ile-de-France a few miles to the west of Versailles, were to be attacked in two phases by a total of 219 aircraft, and would involve fourteen Lancasters and four Mosquitos at each aiming-point in the east and west. 35 (Madras Presidency) and 405 (Vancouver) Squadrons briefed nine and five crews respectively for the first phase, which was aimed at the eastern end of the yards. A further five and ten crews repectively were briefed to attack the previously targeted radar-jamming station at Mont-de-Couple, situated some three miles inland from the Pas-de-Calais coast at Wissant as part of a 6 and 8 Group force of 111 Lancasters and Halifaxes and four Mosquitos. The Trappes-bound element departed Gransden Lodge first between 22.47 and 22.51, all assigned to illuminator duties with S/L Trilsbach the senior pilot on duty and 35 (Madras Presidency) Squadron's S/Ls Creswell and Chidgey the Master Bomber and Deputy. They were followed into the air by the second element between 22.53 and 23.02 with S/Ls McDonald and Coldrey the Master Bomber and Deputy pairing and the remainder each carrying a cookie and sixteen 500-pounders to drop with the main force.

The Mont-de-Couple force arrived at the French coast to find clear skies, a little haze and a red TI cascading at 23.50, which the Master Bomber assessed as having fallen a hundred yards to the east of the aiming point. This was backed up by green TIs and crews were instructed to undershoot by the requisite distance to compensate for the slight inaccuaracy, the 405 (Vancouver) Squadron participants complying from 8,000 to 13,000 feet between 23.54 and 23.57. At debriefing they reported a concentrated attack that was focused within a radius of two hundred to five hundred yards of the aiming point, and post-raid reconnaissance confirmed that the target had been rendered completely unserviceable, thus removing another small component in the enemy's defences.

Trappes was also found to be under clear skies with a little haze, but with up to five-tenths cloud drifting in at 8,000 feet. The attack opened on time at 00.27 with the release by an Oboe Mosquito of a red TI, which S/L Creswell assessed to be accurate in the light of flares from the illuminators, who would make a second pass to deliver their eight 1,000 pounders each. S/L Creswell backed up the aiming-point with yellow TIs and two 1,000 pounders from 7,000 feet at 00.39, and on return to Gransden Lodge the 405 (Vancouver) Squadron crews reported carrying out their assigned tasks from 11,000 to 12,200 feet between 00.28 and 00.38, many having the engine sheds in their bomb sights. The bombing appeared to cover the assigned area of the yards, and two large explosions were observed towards the end of the attack. The western aiming-point was also dealt with effectively, hopefully to inhibit the movement by rail of enemy troops and equipment to defend the invasion beaches in six days' time.

During the course of the month, the squadron carried out fifteen operations and dispatched 155 sorties for the loss of five Lancasters and crews.

June 1944

June was to be a hectic month which would make great demands on the crews, and the first week was dominated by unsettled weather, which caused concerns for the impending launch of Operation Overlord. The bombing of coastal batteries was to be the priority during the first few days of June leading up to D-Day, but it was a return to the marshalling yards at Trappes that opened 405 (Vancouver) Squadron's account on the 2nd. 8 Group was handed a variety of targets, including coastal batteries at five locations, all in the deception area of the Pas-de-Calais, radar installations at two locations and there would also be a number of Mosquito nuisance raids. The Trappes force consisted of 105 Halifaxes of 4 Group with a sprinkling of 101 Squadron ABC Lancasters and six from Gransden Lodge, the latter taking off between 23.04 and 23.09 with S/Ls Coldrey and Trilsbach the senior pilots on duty and all designated as illuminators. They arrived to find clear skies and excellent visibility, which facilitated a visual identification of the aiming-point and the attack opened with red TIs at 00.44, after which, Master Bomber, W/C Daniels of 35 (Madras Presidency) Squadron, called in his Deputy to mark with a white TI. This fell from 5,000 feet at 00.47 to land some two hundred yards north of the aiming-point and close to the southern edge of a housing estate, and a minute later, W/C Daniels dropped yellow TIs from 7,000 feet that were much nearer to the mark. The main force crews were instructed to bomb on these, while the 405 (Vancouver) Squadron element carried out their assigned tasks to deliver 7" hooded flares and eight 1,000-pounders each from 11,400 to 12,500 feet between 00.43 and 00.51. By this time, smoke had obscured the ground to make an assessment of the outcome something of a challenge, but post-raid reconnaissance revealed that the main weight of bombs had fallen into the eastern half of the yards, creating more unwanted toil for the press-ganged local civilians. At debriefings, crews reported observing eleven aircraft to be shot down during the first leg of the homeward route and among them was ND507, which crashed some nine miles west-south-west of Rambouillet, south-west of Paris. On board was the predominantly RCAF crew of S/L Coldrey RCAF, from which only the navigator and bomb-aimer survived to be taken into captivity. One unidentified crew claimed the destruction of a Ju88 also during this leg of the withdrawal.

On the 4th 259 aircraft from all but 3 Group were prepared for operations against coastal batteries, three to maintain the deception in the Pas-de-Calais and the fourth by 5 Group at Maisy between the American Omaha and Utah beaches overlooking the Normandy coast. 405 (Vancouver) Squadron loaded each of three Lancasters with a 1,000-pounder and sixteen 500-pounders and briefed the crews of S/L Trilsbach and F/Ls Maine-Smith and Yates for duty as blind markers, before sending them on their way from Gransden Lodge between 01.52 and 01.55 bound for the Calais region as part of the 8 Group contribution of thirty-six Lancasters and four Mosquitos. The attack opened with a green TI at 01.26, followed immediately by a red TI dropped from an Oboe Mosquito backed up by others and also by greens from the heavy marker aircraft. The greens were somewhat scattered, but most crews were able to make a visual identification, the 405 (Vancouver) Squadron crews attacking from 10,400 to 11,000 feet between 02.52 and 02.57. The consensus of returning crews was of a successful outcome, but this was of secondary importance to the deception purpose of the raid.

The 5th was D-Day Eve, and, during the course of that night, a record number of 1,211 sorties would be flown against coastal defences and in support and diversionary operations. The weather had been a source of concern for the D-Day planners, and even as Operation Overlord was given the green light, massive uncertainty attended the final decision to go. Sixteen 405 (Vancouver) Squadron crews attended the evening briefing at Gransden Lodge, where, as at every other station, no direct reference was made to the invasion, but unusually, they were given strict altitudes at which to fly and were told not to jettison bombs over the sea. They learned also that they would be among more than a thousand aircraft targeting ten heavy gun batteries along the Normandy coast, and that their specific objective was at Longues, situated between the American Omaha and the British Gold beaches north of Bayeux. Four were designated emergency markers, two as visual backers-up and the remainder as main force supporters and were part of an 8 Group element of sixty-nine Lancasters and five Mosquitos as they took off between 02.56 and 03.11 with S/L McDonald the senior pilot on duty. Despite the target's location fewer than fifteen miles east of Maisy, where the skies were clear, Longues was covered by tenth-tenths thin cloud with tops at around 5,000 feet, through which the glow of red TIs could be seen and bombed by the Gransden Lodge crews from 8,500 to 9,200 feet between 04.19 and 04.28. Any homebound crews looking down through the occasional gaps in the clouds were rewarded by the incredible sight of the greatest armada in history, ploughing its way sedately southwards towards the French coast. A total of five thousand tons of bombs was dropped during the night, and this was a new record. Only seven aircraft failed to return from these operations, and among them was one from 97 (Straits Settlement) Squadron, now on permanent loan to 5 Group. It contained the commanding officer, W/C "Jimmy" Carter, and seven highly experienced crewmen, all but one of them the holder of either a DFC or DFM.

As the beachheads were being established during the course of the 6th, preparations were put in hand to support the ground forces by attacking nine road and railway communications centres through which the enemy could bring reinforcements. 405 (Vancouver) Squadron was ordered to provide the Master Bomber and Deputy pairing for an attack on a "choke point" at Condé-sur-Noireau, a town situated some thirty miles south-south-west of Caen. The crews of S/Ls Trilsbach and McDonald departed Gransden Lodge at 23.53 and arrived at their destination in time to watch three Oboe Mosquitos deliver red and green TIs onto the aiming point, which became obscured by smoke and S/L Trilsbach delayed calling in the main force until he was satisfied of the accuracy of the markers. The bombing began at 01.54, the 405 (Vancouver) Squadron duo dropping their fourteen 500-pounders each from 3,500 and 5,100 feet at 01.51 and 01.55.

Fifteen crews returned to the briefing room at Gransden Lodge on the evening of the 7th, when a dozen of them learned that the targets for a 1, 5 and 8 Group force of 112 aircraft were a six-way road junction at Balleroy, situated between Bayeux and St-Lo, and a tank unit and ammunition dump hidden in the nearby Forêt-de-Cerisy, for which 8 Group was to provide eighty-three Lancasters and ten Mosquitos. The main effort on this night, however, was to be directed at railway targets on the outskirts of Paris at Acheres, Juvisy, Massey-Palaiseau and Versailles, for which 195 Halifaxes, 122 Lancasters and twenty Mosquitos were made ready, the 405 (Vancouver) Squadron crews of S/Ls Trilsbach and McDonald to fulfil the roles of Master Bomber and Deputy and F/L Stronach visual backer-up at the Acheres junction switching station. The two elements took off together between 23.52 and 00.07, those bound for the Forêt-de-Cerisy each carrying eighteen 500-pounders to employ as part of the main force. They all arrived in the target area to find conditions of ten-tenths cloud with a base at 8,000 to 10,000 feet and haze below. The initial Oboe markers appeared to be accurate and on time, but another marker fell simultaneously some five miles to the south-west and attracted some bomb loads. The Master Bomber quickly gained control of the situation and directed the bombing to the correct marker, which was pounded by concentrated bombing. The 405 (Vancouver) Squadron crews carried out their assigned tasks from 4,000 to 7,000 feet between 01.40 and 01.58 and observed large explosions between 01.45 and 01.49, and further evidence of a successful outcome manifested in the form of a dense cloud of black smoke rising through 8,000 feet. Meanwhile, over to the east at Acheres, S/L Trilsbach called the main force crews down to below the cloud base at 7,000 feet, where visibility was good, and the green TIs were seen to be "bang" on the aiming point. The main force bombing was accurate and concentrated, and the 405 (Vancouver) Squadron trio added to the destruction with their ten 500-pounders each from 5,500 to 6,900 feet between 01.18 and 01.22.

The night of the 8/9th was devoted to the disruption of railway communications, for which 483 aircraft were detailed and assigned to five centres, 8 Group providing seventy-five Lancasters and twenty Mosquitos, but none of the former representing 405 (Vancouver) Squadron, which enjoyed a night off. They returned to action on the following night, however, with another raid on the airfield at Rennes, one of four similar targets for the night, all situated south of the beachhead involving a total of 401 aircraft from 1, 4, 6 and 8 Groups. At Gransden Lodge eight Lancasters were loaded with eighteen 500-pounders each as part of the 8 Group contribution of sixty-seven Lancasters and five Mosquitos and would be supporting the main force. They took to the air between 00.35 and 01.04 with F/Ls Perry and Virtue the senior pilots on duty, and all arrived in the target area to find ten-tenths cloud with a base at 7,000 feet and four-tenths below 5,500 feet, through which the first green TIs could be seen burning on the ground at 02.42. The Master Bomber marked the runways with yellow TIs at 02.44 before calling in the main force, those from Gransden Lodge bombing from 5,500 to 8,000 feet between 02.45 and 02.51. F/L Virtue's bomb release failed, and the bombs were jettisoned a mile or so beyond the target.

Four railway objectives were posted as the objectives for more than four hundred aircraft on the 10th, the locomotive sheds at Versailles Matelots assigned to 6 Group with seven 405 (Vancouver) Squadron Lancasters and five Mosquitos representing the Path Finder Force. S/L McDonald and F/L MacKinnon were designated Master Bomber and Deputy, F/L Stronach backer-up, while the four remaining crews fulfilled the role of illuminators. They departed Gransden Lodge between 23.15 and 23.26 and only two of the Mosquitos reached the target after three dropped out with equipment failure. The raid opened with red TIs at 00.33, and they fell close enough to the aiming point to satisfy S/L McDonald, who called in the main force before backing up with his own yellow TIs. A strong night-fighter presence brought about the loss of fifteen Lancasters and three Halifaxes from the four targets, the Versailles force losing three Canadian Halifaxes from the main force and Lancaster ND352 of 405 (Vancouver) Squadron, which crashed at Auneau, some ten miles to the east of Chartres, killing six of the occupants, while F/L Stronach RCAF and one other survived to evade capture.

Four railway targets were earmarked for attention by elements of 1, 3, 4 and 8 Groups on the 11th, among them a bridge at Massy-Palaiseau, situated some seven miles south-west of the centre of Paris, for which 8 Group provided eight 35 (Madras Presidency) Squadron Lancasters and five Mosquitos. Meanwhile, an 8 Group force of fifty-eight Lancasters and three Mosquitos would target a railway junction at Tours in the Loire region of north-west-central France, 405 (Vancouver) Squadron represented by thirteen Lancasters, the crews of which had been briefed to bomb with the main force. They departed Gransden Lodge between 22.00 and 22.12 with S/L

Morrison the senior pilot on duty and eighteen 500-pounders in each bomb bay and reached its target area to encounter up to ten-tenths cloud with a base in places as low as 2,000 feet. There appeared to be some kind of R/T reception issue in the early stages, which prevented the Master Bomber's broadcasts from being received, but an instruction to the main force crews at 00.36 to descend to beneath the cloud base was heard and acted upon by most. The Master Bomber had observed the first red TIs fall from west to east across the target and assessed those to the west to be just south of the aiming-point. The Deputy Master Bomber dropped a yellow TI just north of the aiming-point at 00.39, prompting the Master Bomber to call for the bombing to be aimed between the reds and yellows. He then backed up with his own yellow TIs, while all but two of the Gransden Lodge crews carried out their attacks from 1,000 to 7,400 feet between 00.40 and 00.48 in the face of intense and accurate light flak. The crews of F/Ls Perry and Virtue failed to positively identify the aiming point through the cloud and withheld their bombs and the conditions prevented the others from making an accurate assessment. P/O Melcombe RCAF and his mixed RCAF/RAF crew were absent from debriefing having abandoned ND344 to its fate over France, and only the wireless operator fell into enemy hands. However, the bomb-aimer, F/O Clement RCAF, was reported to have died on the 9th of August while still on the run. (Bomber Command Losses. Vol 5. W R Chorley.)

A new oil campaign began on the night of the 12/13th, prosecuted by 286 Lancasters and seventeen Mosquitos of 1, 3 and 8 Groups, whose target was the Bergius-process Gelsenkirchener Bergwerke plant at Gelsenkirchen, known to the Germans as Gelsenberg A G and to Bomber Command as Nordstern. Such was the accuracy of the attack, that all production of vital aviation fuel was halted for a number of weeks at a cost to the Germans of a thousand tons per day. Meanwhile, 671 aircraft representing 4, 5, 6 and 8 Groups had been prepared to attack six communications targets in France, the marshalling yards at Amiens-St-Roch and Amiens-Longueau in the north-east of the country assigned to 4 Group main forces of ninety-nine and one hundred Halifaxes respectively. S/L McDonald and F/L MacKinnon were the designated Master Bomber and Deputy at the latter and were to be accompanied by five Illuminators led by S/Ls Morrison and Trilsbach, with F/L Perry and crew as backers-up. They departed Gransden Lodge between 22.45 and 22.52 to join up at the target with five Oboe Mosquitos, and all arrived to find clear skies and good visibility having already lost two Mosquitos to equipment failure. The first Oboe red TIs went down a little to the north of the aiming point at 00.04, at which point the illuminators dispensed their flares and S/L McDonald placed his own yellow TIs right on the aiming point to be backed up by F/L MacKinnon. The 405 (Vancouver) Squadron element carried out their assigned tasks from 6,000 to 12,000 feet between 00.04 and 00.19 and the impression passed on at debriefing was of a largely successful outcome. Night-fighters were much in evidence and played their part in bringing down a heavy toll of 4 and 6 Group aircraft, six from Arras, eight from Amiens and nine from Cambrai, and it was during the last-mentioned 6 Group attack at Cambrai that P/O Andrew Mynarski RCAF earned the posthumous award of the Victoria Cross for his heroics in a 419 (Moose) Squadron Lancaster.

The 14th brought the Command's first daylight operation since the departure from Bomber Command of 2 Group twelve months earlier. The target was Le Havre, from where the enemy's E-Boats and other fast, light marine craft were posing a threat to Allied shipping supplying the Normandy beachheads. The two-phase operation was conducted by predominantly 1 and 3 Groups with 617 Squadron representing 5 Group and took place in the evening under the umbrella of a fighter escort. The attack was highly successful, and few craft survived the onslaught. Other operations on this night were directed against railway installations at three locations in France, while elements of 4, 5 and 8 Groups attended to enemy troop and vehicle concentrations, referred to as "choke points" at Aunay-sur-Odon and Évrecy near Caen. A Path Finder presence was required at five locations, in addition to which, the group sent thirty-five Mosquitos to attack the Hydrierwerke-Scholven A G synthetic oil plant situated in the north-western Gelsenkirchen suburb of Buer in the Ruhr. The attack two nights earlier at Cambrai had not destroyed the railway yards and this was one of three similar targets assigned to elements of 4, 6 and 8 Groups. 405 (Vancouver) squadron made ready eight Lancasters, two for the Master Bomber and deputy pairing of F/L MacKinnon and P/O Fisher, five others for an illuminator role and one as a backer-up, all in support of a 6 Group main force of ninety-four Halifaxes from 63 and 64 Bases. Departure from Gransden Lodge was accomplished without incident between 23.33 and 23.46 and all arrived in the target area to encounter ten-tenths cloud with a base at 8,000 feet but good visibility below, which was enhanced by illuminator flares. The Oboe red TIs went down punctually and having been observed to be a little north of the aiming point, F/L MacKinnon dropped four yellow TIs across track about two hundred yards south-west, before calling in P/O Fisher to drop his white TIs, which he did with great accuracy for others to back up with more whites. The 405 (Vancouver) Squadron crews carried out their assigned tasks from 6,300 to 12,000 feet between 00.50 and 00.58 and returned unsure as to the effectiveness of their work.

A force of 297 aircraft from 1, 4, 5, 6 and 8 Groups was assembled later on the 15th to try to do to Boulogne what had been done to Le Havre twenty-four hours earlier. The operation was concluded with equal success, although with substantial collateral damage inflicted upon the town, and while it was in progress, ammunition and fuel dumps and marshalling yards were targeted by other elements. Among four targets requiring a Path Finder presence were the marshalling yards at Lens in north-eastern France, for which 405 (Vancouver) Squadron made ready sixteen Lancasters as part of the 8 Group contribution of seventy-six Lancasters and five Mosquitos. They departed Gransden Lodge between 23.38 and 23.51 with S/Ls Morrison and Trilsbach the senior pilots on duty and each crew sitting on eighteen 500-pounders to deliver as part of the main force. They found the visibility beneath the 7,500-foot cloud base in the target area to be good and most complied with the Master Bomber's instructions at 00.40 to descend into clear air. They carried out their attacks from 5,500 to 9,000 feet between 00.49 and 00.53, aiming at red and yellow TIs, and contributed to an accurate and concentrated attack from which six Lancasters failed to return. Two of them were from Gransden Lodge, and there was just one survivor from among the fourteen crewmen. ND343 contained the all-RCAF crew of W/O Stewart RCAF and received a direct hit from flak over the Pas-de-Calais, which caused it to explode and throw clear the pilot, who arrived safely on the ground to evade capture. JB729 was lost without trace and took with it the predominantly RCAF crew of F/O Keenan RCAF.

Plans were put in hand on the 16th, to launch 829 sorties that night against a number of targets, including four flying-bomb launching sites in the Pas-de-Calais/Hauts-de-France regions of north-eastern France. Just three days earlier, the first V-1 flying bombs had landed on London, and this prompted a response in the form of a second new campaign to open during the month against this revolutionary new menace. The target for seventy Lancasters and five Mosquitos of 8 Group, including eleven of the former provided by 405 (Vancouver) Squadron, was a "constructional works" at Renescure, some four miles east of St-Omer, for which they departed Gransden Lodge between 23.59 and 00.11. All were assigned to bombing duties, for which each carried a load of eighteen 500 pounders, and all had to establish their positions by H2S after arriving at the target to find ten-tenths cloud with tops at between 7,000 and 10,000 feet. The Oboe-laid red TIs left a faint glow for the main force crews to aim at, and all of the 405 (Vancouver) Squadron contingent delivered their attacks from 10,700 to 12,000 feet between 00.55 and 01.04. Returning crews reported a number of explosions, culminating in a large one at 01.06.

Meanwhile, two hundred miles to the east, the oil campaign continued in the hands of 1, 4, 6 and 8 Groups with an attack on the Ruhr-Chemie synthetic oil plant at Sterkrade-Holten, a district of Oberhausen in the Ruhr. 8 Group detailed six Lancasters, three each from 35 (Madras Presidency) and 405 (Vancouver) Squadrons and sixteen Mosquitos, the Gransden Lodge trio taking off between 23.31 and 23.33 with the crews of F/Ls MacKinnon and Perry the senior pilots on duty and each briefed, along with the crew of P/O Fisher, to back up the Oboe TIs visually. On reaching the central Ruhr they encountered ten-tenths cloud with tops at around 14,000 feet, which meant that the TIs soon disappeared from view to leave only a faint glow for the main force crews to aim at. The Path Finder element established their positions by H2s before carrying out their attacks with a cookie and twelve 500-pounders each from 15,300 to 18,000 feet between 01.24 and 01.27. They returned with an expectation that the bombing had been scattered and ineffective, and it was confirmed later that this operation had little impact on oil production. It had been an expensive endeavour for the Command, however, which registered the loss of thirty-one aircraft, twenty-two of them Halifaxes, two-thirds of them having fallen victim to night-fighters.

On the following night 8 Group detailed seven 405 (Vancouver) Squadron Lancasters and five Oboe Mosquitos to support a raid on constructional works at Neuvillle-au-Bois situated a mile-and-a half to the north-east of Oisemont, south of Abbeville. F/L MacKinnon and P/O Fisher were designated Master Bomber and Deputy, while four crews were to act as illuminators and F/L Perry and crew as backers-up. They departed Gransden Lodge between 01.50 and 01.56, each loaded with eight or ten 500-pounders in addition to their pyrotechnics and arrived at the target to find ten-tenths cloud topping out at 7,000 feet. The red Oboe TIs disappeared quickly to leave a faint glow on which F/L MacKinnon released a yellow TI from 11,000 feet at 03.07, which P/O Fisher backed up three minutes later from 9,000 feet. The rest of the squadron participants pitched in with illuminating flares and high explosives from heights up to 11,200 feet between 03.05 and 03.12 and returned with little useful information to pass on at debriefing, which guaranteed another visit to this location.

On each of the ensuing few days, the squadron was notified of operations, only for them to be cancelled later in the day because of unfavourable weather conditions over the Pas-de-Calais. Finally, on the 21st, F/L MacKinnon and P/O Fisher were briefed for the Master Bomber and Deputy roles for a return to Oisemont, one of three sites earmarked for an evening daylight attack by a total of 322 aircraft from 3, 6 and 8 Groups. The Gransden Lodge duo took off at 18.52 and reached the target to find ten-tenths cloud with tops at 4,000 feet. F/L MacKinnon and crew tracked over the target at 17,000 feet with the main force close on their heels, having employed H2S to establish their position for a timed run from Abbeville, and released TIs at 19.56, only to lose them in the cloud. The main force was instructed to orbit while F/L MacKinnon descended to 7,000 feet, but on failing to break into clear air he issued "cauliflower", the order to abandon the operation and headed home, observing a few bomb loads to be dropped on the target by crews employing Gee and H2S.

Later that night, 5 Group embarked on its first involvement in the current oil campaign, when sending two forces to the oil refineries at Wesseling, on the west bank of the Rhine south of Cologne and Scholven/Buer near Gelsenkirchen in the heart of the Ruhr. Those bound for the former were picked up by night-fighters as they made their way across the frontier region of Holland and Belgium, and a bitter battle ensued. By the time the badly mauled survivors reached home, thirty-seven Lancasters had fallen victim to the defences, mostly to night-fighters. Four 5 Group squadrons, 44, 49, 57 and 619, had each lost six aircraft, although one of the 57 Squadron crews was plucked from the sea off Yarmouth without injury.

From this point on daylight operations were to become increasingly common as the summer progressed, while night operations continued unabated. The main focus of attention on the 23rd was on four flying-bomb sites and two marshalling yards in France, seven 405 (Vancouver) Squadron crews attending briefing to learn that their target was a V-Weapon site at Coubronne, situated just a stone's throw to the south-west of Renescure. They were part of an 8 Group force of eighty-one Lancasters and five Mosquitos and departed Gransden Lodge between 00.11 and 00.17 with pilots of flight lieutenant rank leading the way and each crew sitting on twelve 1,000 and two 500-pounders to deliver as part of the main force. 35 (Madras Presidency) Squadron provided the Master Bomber and Deputy pairing of S/L Ingram and P/O Mills, who were confronted in the target area by ten-tenths thin cloud with tops at around 5,000 to 6,000 feet. When the 405 (Vancouver) Squadron participants arrived, they saw plentiful red TIs already cascading into the cloud tops to become a dim glow. S/L Ingram was heard to broadcast "Lucky Strike. Bomb reds if you can see them", at 00.59, and the Gransden Lodge crews complied from 11,000 to 14,500 feet between 01.00 and 01.06. On the way home near Dunkerque, S/L Ingram DFC and crew were shot down and he and his rear gunner lost their lives, while the survivors were taken into captivity.

Three V-Weapon sites occupied the attention of more than three hundred aircraft of 1, 4, 6 and 8 Groups in daylight on the 24th, while a further 739 aircraft from all groups were made ready to target seven others that night. F/L MacKinnon and P/O Fisher were designated Master Bomber and Deputy again for an attack during the afternoon on constructional works at Bonnetot, located between Dieppe and Rouen, and departed Gransden Lodge at 15.57. They arrived at the target to find clear skies and good visibility and approached the aiming point in formation, where F/L MacKinnon released his bombs and TIs from 14,000 feet at 16.58, before sending P/O Fisher on a second run to back up and calling in the main force. After some initial slight undershooting, the aiming point was soon obliterated by explosions, smoke and dust and the operation was declared a success.

Back at Gransden Lodge fourteen crews were being briefed for the evening activities, which in their case was an attack on constructional works at Middel Straete, one of a collection of hamlets bearing the Straete name to the east of Hazebrouck close to France's frontier with Belgium. It was to be an all-8 Group show involving eighty Lancasters from 7, 35, 156, 582 and 635 Squadrons in addition to the 405 (Vancouver) Squadron contingent, with the initial marking to be carried out by five Oboe Mosquitos of 105 and 109 Squadrons. The Gransden gang took off between 00.25 and 00.38 with S/L Morrison the senior pilot on duty and like the rest of the heavy force, eighteen 500 pounders in each bomb bay. They arrived in the target area to find clear skies and haze, and as the main force crews approached, they observed the first red Oboe TIs going down at 01.21, and by the time that they began their bombing runs, the TIs were laid out in a line of half-a-mile or more from south-west to north-east. By using H2S and Gee, crews ascertained that the TIs in the centre were the closest to the aiming-point, and the Gransden Lodge crews carried out their attacks from 12,000 to 14,800 feet between 01.28 and 01.35. However, all markers received some bomb loads, and it was clear that the attack had spread somewhat.

More than seven hundred aircraft were detailed for operations against six flying-bomb sites on the 27th, while two railway yards occupied the attention of other elements. Fifteen 405 (Vancouver) Squadron crews attended briefing, those of F/L MacKinnon and P/O Fisher to learn that they were to act as backers-up to five Oboe Mosquitos marking for a main force at Wizernes, located a short distance to the south-west of St-Omer. The remaining thirteen crews discovered that their target was once more at Neuville-au-Bois near Oisemont, where they would be part of an 8 Group main force of eighty Lancasters supported by five Oboe Mosquitos. The main element departed Gransden Lodge first between 00.15 and 00.28, each crew with eighteen 500-pounders beneath their feet, and on arrival in the target area observed the attack opening punctually with red TIs cascading through up to nine-tenths thin cloud with tops at 7,000 feet. They appeared to be well-concentrated, and the accuracy of their fall was checked by H2S and Gee-fix before the main force was called in, those from Gransden Lodge attacking from 12,100 to 14,500 feet between 01.28 and 01.35. The defenders responded with searchlights and flak, and there was clear evidence of night-fighter activity, despite which, there were no losses from this operation. This force was on its way home by the time that the Wizernes-bound duo took off at 01.55 to arrive in the target area under clear skies and in good visibility. The marking appeared to be scattered and F/L MacKinnon withheld his TIs through uncertainty as to which red TIs represented the most accurate. He and P/O Fisher released their eighteen 500-pounders each from 13,700 and 14,000 feet at 02.47 and 02.48 and returned home uncertain as to the effectiveness of their efforts.

There was a switch to railway targets for twenty-eight Path Finder Lancasters on the 28th, fourteen each from 405 (Vancouver) and 582 Squadrons assigned respectively to Metz in the Grand-Est region of north-eastern France, some forty miles west of Germany's Saarland capital city, Saarbrücken and Blainville located in the Loire Valley to the west of Paris. The Halifax main forces were provided by 6 Group at Metz and 4 Group at Blainville, with F/L MacKinnon and P/O Fisher the designated Master Bomber and deputy at the former, supported by two backers-up and ten illuminators. They departed Gransden Lodge between 22.52 and 23.05 with S/L Morrison the senior pilot on duty and up to seven 1,000-pounders in addition to the pyrotechnic ordnance in each bomb bay. The target area was found to be cloud free and the visibility good as the attack opened at 01.25 with F/L MacKinnon releasing a red TI from 7,500 feet at 01.25 in the light provided by the flare force. The others from the squadron fulfilled their briefs from up to 12,300 feet until 01.35, by which time the aiming point had been well-plastered and the operation was deemed to be successful, as was that at Blainville. However, eighteen Halifaxes were shot down, along with one Lancaster from each operation and the errant Lancaster from the Metz contingent was PA980, which had been attacked by a night-fighter at 12,000 feet when outbound near Reims and was partially abandoned by P/O Smitten RCAF and his predominantly RCAF crew. Both gunners failed to survive, possibly having been killed during the engagement, while the remaining five occupants reached the ground safely and only the navigator fell into enemy hands.

The month ended for 405 (Vancouver) Squadron with participation in a raid by 266 aircraft on a road junction at Villers-Bocage to the south-west of Caen on the evening of the 30th, which provided access for two enemy tank divisions to mount a counterattack at a weak point in the Anglo-American lines. 8 Group contributed twenty-four Lancasters and ten Mosquitos for the operation, which was to be conducted in daylight to boost the chances of accuracy by the 3, 4 and 8 Group main force, including all ten 405 (Vancouver) Squadron Lancasters. Each received a bomb load of either eleven 1,000 and three 500-pounders or eighteen 500-pounders before departing Gransden Lodge between 18.27 and 18.36 with no pilots above flight lieutenant rank on duty. They were greeted in the target area by clear skies and ideal bombing conditions and a Master Bomber exercising the most diligent control, although not all complied with his instructions to descend to a lower height to aid accuracy, the 405 (Vancouver) Squadron contingent bombing from 4,000 to 13,400 feet between 19.58 and 20.05. In the event, the outcome was successful, and the German attack was scrubbed.

During the course of the month the squadron took part in twenty-three operations and dispatched 187 sorties for the loss of six Lancasters and crews.

July 1944

The new month began as June had ended, with flying-bomb sites providing employment for over three hundred aircraft on both the 1st and 2nd. Reconnaissance had revealed that the raids thus far on the "constructional works" at Oisemont/Neuville-au-Bois had failed to completely destroy the site, and another operation was scheduled for the afternoon of the 1st, for which 8 Group put up 405 (Vancouver) Squadron's S/L Trilsbach and P/O Fisher as Master Bomber and Deputy and sent them on their way from Gransden Lodge at 16.33, each with six 1,000-pounders beneath their feet. They were joined at the target by four Oboe Mosquitos, having conducted a timed run from Abbeville by H2S, and both released their loads from 11,500 feet and 12,000 feet respectively at 17.35 through seven-tenths cloud with tops at 5,000 to 6,000 feet. A few seconds later the first red TI was seen to cascade into the cloud and disappear completely, leaving the one hundred 6 Group Halifaxes of the main force to bomb on estimated positions based on Gee and dead-reckoning (DR). The cloud broke a little as the 405 (Vancouver) Squadron pair retreated and some crew members observed a red TI on the edge of a wood, some overshooting to the south and smoke rising through the cloudtops.

Orders were received on the 2nd to return to the site in the early afternoon, which prompted 8 Group to detail seventy-six Lancasters and five Mosquitos, sixteen of the former representing 405 (Vancouver) Squadron. At briefing at Graveley, the 35 (Madras Presidency) Squadron pairing of S/L Cranswick and F/O Forde were designated Master Bomber and Deputy, while at Gransden Lodge S/Ls Morrison and Maine-Smith were the senior pilots on duty and learned that they and the others would be part of the main force, each carrying eleven 1,000 and four 500 pounders. They took off between 12.48 and 13.02, and all reached the target area to encounter seven-tenths drifting cumulus cloud with tops at around 10,000 feet. S/L Cranswick identified the target by the shape of the woods, but any sight of it and the TIs was fleeting, and at 01.59, he ordered the main force crews to bomb on Gee and DR, those from Gransden Lodge complying from 9,000 to 14,200 feet between 13.59 and 14.04.

Three flying-bomb sites were earmarked for attention during the afternoon of the 4th, for which 4 and 6 Group Halifaxes were to provide the main force elements, with F/L Perry and P/O Cadegan performing the roles of Master Bomber and Deputy at Biennais, located between Dieppe to the north and Rouen to the south. They departed Gransden Lodge at 12.43 with six 1,000-pounders and marker ordnance in each bomb bay and flew out under largely clear skies, establishing their position over Dieppe before running into ten-tenths cloud with tops at 12,000 to 15,000 feet. F/L Perry bombed on Gee from 12,000 feet at 13.59, a few seconds before P/O Cadegan followed suit from 15,000 feet, and the 6 Group main force of ninety-nine Halifaxes from 62 and 64 Bases was instructed to deliver its bombs on estimated positions guided also by Gee.

The same 405 (Vancouver) Squadron pair were in action again on the 5th, this time to operate as visual backers-up for an attack on a rocket launching site at Watten, situated a dozen miles south-east of Calais, which was one of four sites earmarked for attention by 542 aircraft, the main force elements drawn from 3, 4 and 6 Groups. Another of the targets was at Wizernes, located two miles south-south-east of St-Omer, for which 405 (Vancouver) squadron made ready ten Lancasters, each to carry eleven 1,000 and four 500-pounders to deliver as part of the main force. They departed Gransden Lodge between 22.21 and 22.29 with the senior pilots of flight lieutenant rank and joined with thirty-two other 8 Group Lancasters as they made their way towards the Channel crossing. They were followed into the air forty-seven minutes later by the Watten-bound duo, which arrived at their destination first, and under clear skies identified ground features including a fork in the river and railway track a mile east-north-east of the aiming point. They backed up the initial red TIs with greens and released their six 1,000-pounders each from 9,000 and 9,500 feet at 00.09 and 00.11 respectively, before leaving the target in the hands of the eighty-strong 3 Group main force. Meanwhile, some nine miles to the north, the 405 (Vancouver) Squadron contingent found equally favourable conditions and joined with the 3 Group main force Lancasters to deliver the contents of their bomb bays onto well-placed red TIs from 8,600 to 13,800 feet between 00.23 and 00.28. The target was well-defended, and a number of aircraft returned to Gransden Lodge bearing the scars of battle.

On the 6th, over five hundred aircraft were engaged on operations against V-Weapons targets, and there was an early start for those detailed to attack a flying-bomb storage site at Siracourt, situated twenty miles inland from Berck-sur-Mer and a V-3 super-gun site at Marquise-Mimoyecques, located some four miles from the French coast at Wissant. Originally planned as one of two sites near Cap Gris Nez, each containing twenty-five barrels angled at fifty degrees and aimed at London, test failures and delays meant that a single three-barrel shaft stretching a hundred metres into the limestone hill, 103 miles from its target, was all that existed at the time. Each fifteen-metre-long smooth-bore barrel, which was designed on the multiple-charge principle to progressively boost the acceleration of the one-ton projectile as it travelled towards the muzzle, was to be capable of pounding London at the rate of hundreds per day without let-up. It was protected by a concrete slab thirty meters wide and five-and-a-half meters thick, which was correctly believed by the designers to be impregnable to conventional bombs. It had been attacked already on a number of occasions without success by the time this latest assault took place under clear skies and in excellent visibility, and it was not until 617 Squadron scored direct hits with 12,000lb Tallboy earthquake bombs later that afternoon that genuine damage could be detected. Provisional reconnaissance revealed four deep craters in the immediate target area, one causing a large corner of the concrete slab to collapse, but the extent of the damage underground would not be apparent to the planners at Bomber Command until after the liberation of France. In fact, the shafts and tunnels had collapsed, entombing workers, and had been rendered unusable and abandoned.

There was still work to occupy both 35 (Madras Presidency) and 405 (Vancouver) Squadrons on this day, and eight crews from each squadron attended briefings to learn of their part in a raid on another constructional works at Coquereaux, situated twenty miles east of Dieppe, for which 6 Group was to provide a main force of forty-eight Halifaxes and twelve Lancasters from 62 Base. A second operation involving members of the Gransden Lodge gang was to be directed at constructional works at Croixdalle, located some fifteen miles to the south-east of Dieppe, for which F/L Perry and P/O Cadegan were the designated Master Bomber and Deputy for a 4 Group main force. The two elements took off together between 19.48 and 20.04 with F/Ls Gosman, Johnston and Weicker the senior pilots on duty among the bombers and each crew sitting on eleven 1,000 and four 500 pounders as part of an 8 Group force of forty-two Lancasters and five Mosquitos, while the Lancasters of the Master Bomber and Deputy pair consisted of six 1,000-pounders in addition to the marker ordnance. Clear skies and good visibility provided ideal conditions at Coquereaux, which was exploited by the main force element when bombing on red TIs from 12,000 to 14,100 feet between 21.30 and 21.35. The bombing was concentrated in the absence of defensive activity, and the site soon became enveloped in smoke, suggesting a successful outcome. A dozen or so miles to the west, the Croixdalle site was covered by ten-tenths cloud at 12,000 feet, but good visibility below enabled F/L Perry and crew to establish their position and observe the first red Oboe TIs to cascade at 21.10 and overshoot the aiming point by a hundred yards. The main force was called in at 21.14 and was instructed to compensate by over or undershooting the TIs, until being told to bomb visually. The main weight of bombs fell in concentrated fashion around the aiming point and a large explosion was observed at 21.17. F/L Perry retained his TIs as they were deemed unnecessary and requested P/O Cadegan to mark the target with yellow TIs at 21.11, while calling the main force crews down to 11,000 feet. The Cadegan crew bombed from 10,600 at 21.13, and the Perry crew from 11,000 feet at 21.19 and headed home confident that the site had been dealt with effectively.

During the course of the 7th, 467 aircraft from 1, 4, 6 and 8 Groups were detailed to carry out the first major operation in support of the Canadian 1st and British 2nd Armies, which were trying to break out of Caen. The original target had been German-fortified villages, but this had been changed to an area of open ground north of Caen, which, ultimately, would prove to be counter-productive by rendering passage through the town difficult because of rubble-blocked streets. 405 (Vancouver) Squadron made ready sixteen Lancasters as part of an 8 Group force of sixty-two Lancasters and ten Mosquitos for aiming-point B, while four Lancasters and ten Mosquitos took care of aiming-point A, with 35 (Madras presidency) squadron's W/C Daniels and S/L Creswell acting as Master Bomber and Deputy at both aiming-points. S/Ls Morrison and Trilsbach were the senior pilots on duty as the 405 (Vancouver) Squadron element departed Gransden Lodge between 20.43 and 20 57, each Lancaster carrying eleven 1,000 and four 500-pounders and arrived at the target to find conditions beneath the 8,000-foot cloud base to be favourable. The red and yellow TIs provided a strong reference for the bomb-aimers above, those in the 405 (Vancouver) Squadron Lancasters releasing their loads in accordance with the Master Bomber's instructions from 7,400 to 9,000 feet between 22.19 and 22.27.

Shortly before noon on the 9th, the crews of S/LTrilsbach and F/L Perry departed Gransden Lodge bound for constructional works at Mont-Candon, located some ten miles to the south-west of Dieppe, where they were to perform the roles of master Bomber and Deputy. This was just one of six flying-bomb launching sites earmarked for attention by a total of 347 aircraft from 3, 4, 6 and 8 Groups. A few minutes later, 35 (Madras presidency) Squadron's F/L Hoover and F/O Forde departed Graveley on their way to perform the duties of Master Bomber and Deputy at Les Catelliers (untraced), where they and five Oboe Mosquitos were 8 Group's only representatives and marking, it is believed, for a 6 Group main force. Forty-five minutes later, seven further Lancasters took off from Graveley to attack a site at L'Hey, located some four miles south-south-east of Dunkerque as part of an 8 Group force of fifty-two Lancasters and five Mosquitos. Included among them were seven Lancasters belonging to 405 (Vancouver) Squadron, which departed Gransden Lodge between 13.00 and 13.06 with F/Ls Gosman, Johnston and Yates and Capt Copenhaver the senior pilots on duty and a bomb load of eleven 1,000 and four 500-pounders in each bomb bay.

The Trilsbach and Perry crews arrived at their target to find eight to nine-tenths cloud with tops at around 5,000 feet and had to establish their positions by H2S and Gee before releasing their six 1,000-pounders and pyrotechnics each from 9,500 and 10,000 feet at 12.57 and 12.58. A red TI was observed to cascade a hundred feet above the clouds and a number of crew members were able to catch a glimpse of the ground through gaps in the cloud without being able to determine detail, and the main force bombing was probably scattered after taking place on estimated positions. Meanwhile, many miles to the north-east at L'Hey, the target lay beneath five to seven-tenths stratus cloud with tops at 5,000 feet and the Master Bomber issued instructions to the main force crews initially to aim their bombs fifty yards to port of the red TIs and then at yellow TIs with a slight undershoot. Those from Gransden Lodge complied from 13,400 to 14,600 between 14.00 and 14.02 and were on their way home before the site became enveloped in smoke, compelling those attacking at the tail end of the raid to employ navigational aids to establish the aiming-point.

Dawn was breaking over the fenlands of Bedfordshire and Camridgeshire on the morning of the 10th as a dozen 405 (Vancouver) Squadron crews departed Gransden Lodge between 04.34 and 04.46 to join sixty-two other 8 Group Lancasters and ten Mosquitos in an attack on a flying bomb storage dump at Nucourt, situated some twenty miles north-west of Paris. They were assigned to bombing duties alongside the 1 and 3 Group Lancaster main force, and each was loaded with eleven 1,000 and four 500-pounders for the purpose. S/L Morrison was the senior pilot on duty as they arrived in the target area to find northern France lying beneath a thin sheet of ten-tenths stratus cloud with tops at 8,000 to 10,000 feet, which masked the red TIs to the extent that the Master Bomber instructed crews to bomb on navigational aids. The 405 (Vancouver) Squadron contingent complied to deliver their attacks from 14,000 to 16,000 feet between 05.59 and 06.09 and returned home safely doubting the effectiveness of their efforts.

The squadron sat out a special and significant operation in the evolution of Path Finder techniques on the 11th, for which a flying bomb site at Gappennes, situated a dozen or so miles inland from Cayeux-sur-Mer, was selected. There would be two attacks, the first by seven Lancasters and a single Mosquito, and the second in two phases by nineteen Lancasters and five Mosquitos, the lead Lancaster for each attack equipped with Oboe in what would be the first "heavy" Oboe operation of the war. The overall lead Lancaster belonged to 582 Squadron, and contained W/C George Grant DSO, DFC & Bar, a veteran pilot and Master Bomber and currently commanding officer of 109 Squadron. In the event, the target was not visible through the ten-tenths cloud, but according to the 8 Group ORB, the Oboe Lancaster performed as intended and the accompanying Lancasters and Mosquito released their bombs on seeing his fall. The second formation ended up with a

Mosquito providing the lead and no assessment was possible in the conditions, but further live trials would follow, and the system would become established as an effective means of attacking vital targets.

The 12th brought operations against flying-bomb sites at Rollez and Thiverny, in which 8 Group marked for 4 and 6 Groups, while 405 (Vancouver) Squadron made ready a dozen of its Lancasters to join with twenty-eight others from the group and six Oboe Mosquitos for an attack on the important marshalling yards at Vaires to the east of Paris. The Gransden Lodge element was to support the 113 Lancasters of the 1 and 3 Group main force, for which eighteen 500-pounders were loaded into each bomb bay. They took off between 18.21 and 18.35 with S/L Morrison the senior pilot on duty and arrived at the target to be confronted by ten-tenths cloud, into which a number of Oboe Mosquitos unloaded red TIs. The Master Bomber caught site of them and backed them up with yellows, before inviting the main force to bomb on the yellows if visible, and if not, to take their bombs home. F/L Gosman and crew bombed the centre of a concentration of TIs from 17,000 feet at 20.00 and were the only crew from the squadron to carry out an attack and one of only three from the main force as a whole.

That night, 230 aircraft from 4, 6 and 8 Groups targeted four flying-bomb launching sites, 6 Group sending forty-nine Halifaxes to Brémont-les-Hauts, twenty miles south-east of Dieppe and forty-two Halifaxes and eight Lancasters to Acquet, located to the north-east of Abbeville. 405 (Vancouver) Squadron provided a Master Bomber and Deputy at each, S/L Trilsbach and F/L Virtue at the former and F/L Perry and P/O Cadegan at the latter. The Bremont-bound pair departed Gransden Lodge first at 22.49 each sitting on six 1,000-pounders in addition to their marker ordnance and arrived at their destination to find five to eight-tenths cloud with tops at 4,000 to 8,000 feet, through which red Oboe markers could be seen on the western edge of a wood around seven hundred yards north of the aiming point. The 405 (Vancouver) Squadron duo fulfilled their briefs from 10,700 and 12,200 feet at 00.03 and 00.06 and observed the main force bombing to be scattered and probably ineffective, when, in fact, it had been accurate and highly destructive. The second pair took off just after midnight and found nine-tenths cloud at 5,000 to 8,000 feet over the target and red TIs delivered by the Oboe Mosquitos but were unable to determine ground detail. They carried out their assigned tasks from 16,000 feet at 01.23 and 01.24 and called in the main force to aim at the centre of the glow of TIs, observing a tendency to undershoot and no assessment was possible.

S/Ls Trilsbach and F/L Perry were on Master Bomber and Deputy duty again on the evening of the 14th, when the target for a fifty-strong 6 Group Halifax main force from 63 Base was a flying-bomb launching site at Anderbelck, located near Verchin, some thirty miles to the south-east of Boulogne. The 405 (Vancouver) Squadron pair departed Gransden Lodge at 00.19 carrying the usual load of six 1,000-pounders and marker ordnance and arrived at the target to find favourable conditions with a little haze and moderately good visibility. The red Oboe TIs appeared to be accurate and were confirmed by H2S before being backed up by greens. S/L Trilsbach ordered the main force element to bomb the centre of the red TIs and carried out his own brief from 12,000 feet at 01.09, while F/L Perry and crew followed up from five hundred feet higher two minutes later. Most of the bombing appeared to be concentrated around the aiming point, but a further operation would be mounted in time.

At lunchtime on the 15th, ten 405 (Vancouver) Squadron crews entered the briefing room at Gransden Lodge to be told that they would be returning to the V-Weapon supply dump at Nucourt later in the afternoon as part of an 8 Group force of forty-seven Lancasters and six Mosquitos. It was to be led by an Oboe Lancaster from 582 Squadron, according to the previously mentioned system first employed at Gapennes on the 11th and was a highly accurate way of delivering large tonnages of bombs onto precision targets in cloudy conditions. When the leader dropped his bombs, the accompanying gaggle did likewise, and the method would be put to good use throughout the remainder of the year, although on this occasion not all would proceed smoothly. The Gransden gang was assigned to the main force and was carrying a load each of eighteen 500 pounders as they took off between 14.46 and 14.57 with pilots of flight lieutenant rank leading the way. They flew out in formations by squadron with 35 (Madras Presidency) Squadron in the lead and ran into thick cloud over the target with tops at 18,000 to 19,000 feet, which caused many aircraft to break formation and throw the original plan into chaos. The Mosquito leader of the second formation released at 16.53, ahead of the first formation, and fourteen Lancasters were able to bomb on his smoke-puffs, while the first formation leader released at 16.59½, leaving the others to bomb from 17,500 to 18,000 feet between 16.59 and 17.02 based on e.t.a., Gee or on observing others. The third formation leader released at 17.04½, and eight Lancasters followed suit, three from 405 (Vancouver) Squadron from 17,100 to 18,500 feet between 17.03 and 17.04, while seven others aborted after becoming cut off by cloud. No results were observed, and it would be up to a Halifax main force to claim good results at this important target later that night.

While the above was in progress, back in Lincolnshire on this Saturday afternoon, the Inter-District RCAF track and field meet was taking place at RAF Digby and was well represented by 405 (Vancouver) Squadron athletes. The versatile leading aircraftsman Newman won the high jump and came second in the 100- and 220-yards sprints, while corporal Morrison won the long jump and hop-step-and-jump, now known as the triple jump.

Sixteen 405 (Vancouver) Squadron crews were called to briefing at midnight on the 17/18th to learn of their part in a tactical support operation to be carried out at dawn by a force of 942 aircraft, of which ninety-five of the Lancasters and twenty-five Mosquitos were to be provided by 8 Group. It was the start of the ground forces' Operation Goodwood, which was Montgomery's plan for a decisive breakout from Caen into wider France as a prelude to the march towards the German frontier. The aiming-points were five enemy-held villages of Colombelles, Mondeville, Sannerville, Cagny and Manneville, all situated to the east of Caen and standing in the path of the advancing British 2nd Army. Five of the Gransden Lodge crews were assigned to what the ORB recorded simply as A2 Caen, which according to the timings would appear to be Mondeville or Caen South, while the remaining eleven crews were to bomb as part of the main force at Cagny. W/C Lane and P/O Fisher were appointed Master Bomber and Deputy for Mondeville, with the crews of F/Ls Perry and Virtue and P/O Cadegan performing the role of backers-up, and departed Gransden Lodge between 04.36 and 04.40, to be followed into the air between 04.51 and 04.59 by the second element with S/L Morrison the senior pilot on duty and eighteen 500-pounders in each bomb bay. The target area lay under clear skies with visibility according to W/C Lane at ten to fifteen miles, and he observed the first Oboe red TIs go down at 06.00 to be backed up P/O Fisher's yellow TIs from 5,000 feet two minutes later. W/C Lane dispensed his yellows from 4,000 feet at 06.15 before following up with six 1,000-pounders five minutes later and the others from the squadron fulfilled their briefs from 7,000 feet between 06.04 and 06.08. At Cagny, the 405

(Vancouver) Squadron participants attacked from 6,500 to 10,000 feet between 06.19 and 06.24 and at debriefings across the Command, crews described a good concentration of bombing and praised the performance of the Master Bombers. Of 6,800 tons of bombs delivered by RAF and USAAF aircraft on these targets, the RAF was responsible for more than 5,000 tons. The operations were a stunning success, which prompted messages of thanks and congratulations from the army commanders, and in the absence of enemy fighters, only six aircraft were lost to flak.

The evening and night brought much further activity involving 1, 6 and 8 Groups at the oil refineries of Wesseling and Scholven/Buer, 3 and 5 Group forces attending to railway junctions at Aulnoye and Revigny respectively, while a small 4 Group contingent attacked the previously targeted flying bomb launching site at Acquet. The last mentioned was supported by the 405 (Vancouver) Squadron crews of F/L Perry and P/O Cadegan as Master Bomber and Deputy, who departed Gransden Lodge at 23.08 with a payload each of six 1,000-pounders and marker ordnance. They arrived at the target to find thin cloud at 2,000 to 3,000 feet and observed the first Mosquito-borne Oboe red TI fall at 00.25 and a second one two minutes later on the edge of a wood. The 405 (Vancouver) Squadron pair carried out their assigned tasks from 12,000 and 13,100 feet at 00.29 and 00.31, but the operation concluded with no fresh damage to report.

The previously attacked flying bomb site at Rollez, situated some thirty miles south-east of Boulogne, was posted as the target on the 19th for a small two-wave raid by sixteen 8 Group Lancasters and four Mosquitos employing the heavy Oboe leader technique. The eight 405 (Vancouver) Squadron participants departed Gransden Lodge between 14.05 and 14.08 with F/Ls Johnston and Weicker the senior pilots on duty and eleven 1,000 and four 500-pounders in each bomb bay. They encountered five-tenths cloud over the target, through which some ground detail, including the aiming point, was identifiable, and the main problem was the slipstream effect on the gaggle, which caused some aircraft to drop a few hundred feet. The bombs were released from 14,400 to 15,000 feet at 16.04, a second after those of the lead Lancaster were observed to go down, and the detonations were concentrated around the aiming point with just a slight spread to the east and south-east.

Back at Gransden Lodge on this day, the award of DSOs was announced to S/L McDonald and navigator S/L Culpin, the latter a frequent member of S/L Trilsbach's crew.

Eight flying-bomb sites were earmarked for attention in daylight on the 20th, all requiring an 8 Group presence to varying degrees, but it was for night operations that eight 405 (Vancouver) Squadron crews were briefed. The target for the backer-up crews of S/L Trilsbach, F/L Virtue and F/Os Cadegan and Fisher was the Kohleöl-Anlage coal liquefaction plant (synthetic oil refinery) in the Welheim district of Bottrop on the northern edge of the Ruhr, while the crews of S/L Maine-Smith, F/L Long and F/Os Herbert and Smith were assigned to illuminator duties for a raid on marshalling yards and a triangular junction at Courtrai (Kortrijk) in Belgium. The former departed Gransden Lodge between 23.37 and 23.40 with a cookie, four 1,000 and eight 500-pounders in each bomb bay, and it was almost two hours later, between 01.50 and 01.57, before the Courtrai-bound element took off with eight 1,000-pounders and twenty-four 7-inch hooded flares beneath their feet. Ten-tenths thin cloud lay over the northern Ruhr as the 405 (Vancouver) Squadron participants carried out their briefs from 17,500 to 17,800 feet between 01.34 and 01.36, while 140 Halifaxes of 4 Group plastered the northern half of the plant. Night-fighters and flak accounted for seven Halifaxes, four belonging to 578 Squadron, which lost two more to a collision at home. The single Lancaster casualty was 405 (Vancouver) squadron's PB174, which crashed outbound at 01.15 at Reutem in eastern Holland, when closing on the German frontier, and took the lives of F/L Virtue RCAF and six others of the predominantly RCAF crew, leaving only the rear gunner to survive and fall into enemy hands. It was the squadron's first loss for three weeks from more than 150 sorties.

Meanwhile, 302 Lancasters and fifteen Mosquitos from 1, 5 and 8 Groups had taken off for northern Belgium, where they were greeted by clear skies and good visibility. The 405 (Vancouver) squadron illuminators dispensed their flares from 10,800 to 12,400 feet between 01.50 and 01.57 and followed up with their bombs to contribute to a devastating outcome at both aiming points at a cost of nine main force Lancasters. Elsewhere, a 3 Group force had been ravaged by night-fighters during a raid on the synthetic oil plant at Moers/Homberg on the western bank of the Rhine opposite Duisburg, and lost twenty Lancasters, seven of them from 75 (New Zealand) Squadron.

A new face had recently arrived at Gransden Lodge to embark on an operational career. The twenty-eight-year-old Somerset-born W/C Stafford P Coulson had spent the war to date as a flying instructor in Canada and was now given a chance to cut his teeth with 405 (Vancouver) Squadron as a prelude to a highly successful tour of operations with a number of Path Finder squadrons. His first sortie was as senior pilot among eight from the squadron detailed for a raid on the previously targeted constructional works at Acquet on the 22nd. This was one of four similar objectives for all-8 Group "Oboe leader" attacks, for which they departed Gransden Lodge between 15.34 and 15.37 with eighteen 500-pounders in each bomb bay. The operation turned into a damp squib when the failure of Oboe forced it to be aborted at 17.17 and all bombs were returned to the dump.

Sixteen 405 (Vancouver) Squadron crews were called to briefing on the evening of the 23rd to be told that, after a two-month break from city busting, Harris had sanctioned a major raid on the naval port of Kiel, for which a force of 629 aircraft was made ready. 8 Group contributed ninety of the Lancasters and nine Mosquitos, the Gransden Lodge element assigned to a variety of roles, one as primary visual marker, four as secondary blind markers, three as visual recenterers and eight to bomb with the main force. They took off between 22.15 and 22.38 with W/C Coulson and S/L Maine-Smith the senior pilots on duty and diverse bomb loads for the marker crews and six 2,000-pounders each for the bombing brigade. After climbing out they headed for the rendezvous point over the North Sea, where they formed up behind an elaborate "Mandrel" jamming screen laid on by 100 Group, before setting course for Denmark's western coast. When they arrived unexpectedly and with complete surprise in Kiel airspace, they rendered the enemy night-fighter controller confused and unable to bring his resources to bear. Kiel was covered by a nine to ten-tenths veil of thin cloud with tops at 5,000 feet, and a skymarking plan was put into action, which enabled the main force to bomb on the glow, first of the flares, and then of fires. The 405 (Vancouver) Squadron crews confirmed their positions by H2S, before carrying out their respective tasks from 17,000 to 19,300 feet between 01.13 and 01.30, the bombing element aiming at the glow of red and green Wanganui markers as they disappeared into cloud. Flak was mostly in barrage form and exploding at 15,000 to 22,000 feet but was not overly troublesome. It was not possible to determine the outcome, but the glow of fires remained visible for a hundred miles into the return journey, which suggested an effective raid. This was confirmed by local reports, which conceded that this had been the town's most destructive raid of the war and had inflicted heavy damage on the port and shipyards and cut off water supplies for three days and gas for three weeks. Many delayed-action bombs had been dropped, and these continued to cause problems for some time.

8 Group divided its forces on the 24th to enable it to support the first of a three-raid series in five nights on the city of Stuttgart, and also a 5 Group attack on an oil refinery and fuel dump at Donges and 6 Group assaults on flying-bomb sites at Ferfay and L'Hey. 8 Group detailed 103 Lancasters for Stuttgart, fourteen of them belonging to 405 (Vancouver) Squadron, the crews of which were assigned to a vartiety of marking tasks, two as secondary blind markers, two as blind marker/illuminators, two as visual recenterers, one as a primary visual marker and seven to bomb with the main force. They were sent on their way from Gransden Lodge between 21.54 and 22.27 with W/C Coulson and S/Ls Trilsbach and Maine-Smith the senior pilots on duty and were well on their way towards the south coast by the time that F/O Cadegan and F/L Johnston took off at 22.53 bound for L'Hey to perform the roles of Master Bomber and Deputy for the fifty-strong 6 Group Halifax main force. They arrived at the target to encounter ten-tenths cloud and a circle of five red TIs delivered by Oboe Mosquitos surrounding the aiming point. The crews of F/O Cadegan and F/L Johnston released their six 1,000-pounders each from 12,000 and 8,600 feet respectively at 23.43 and the former yellow TIs five minutes later. The main force crews were instructed to bomb on the glow and the impression was of a concentrated attack, although this could not be confirmed.

Meanwhile, some three hundred miles to the south, the Stuttgart area, a series of valleys, was found to be covered by nine to ten-tenths cloud with tops at 4,000 to 7,000 feet. Those at the head of the bomber stream dropped red TIs, but they were visible only by their faint glow and the Path Finders switched to the employment of Wanganui flares to mark the aiming-point. It was largely on the position of these skymarkers that the Master Bomber controlled the raid, during which the 405 (Vancouver) Squadron crews carried out their respective tasks from 16,500 to 18,700 feet between 01.38 and 01.56 in accordance with his instructions. They set course for home fairly satisfied with the outcome, although it was impossible to make an accurate assessment. Across the Command, crews reported a glow of fires covering an area of perhaps five square miles, which remained visible for eighty miles into the return journey, and although no specific report came out of Stuttgart for this night, it was established eventually that it had been a successful and destructive raid, gained at a cost of seventeen Lancasters and four Halifaxes.

On the 25th, W/C Lane's former room-mate, the previously mentioned W/C Cribb, took command of 8 Group's 582 Squadron, while ten crews attended briefing at Gransden Lodge to learn of their part in the second Stuttgart operation. They were assigned to a variety of roles, three as secondary blind markers, two as blind marker/illuminators, two as visual centerers, one as primary visual marker and three to bomb with the main force and were part of 8 Group's contribution of ninety Lancasters in an overall force made up of 412 Lancasters and 138 Halifaxes. Take-off from Gransden Lodge began at 21.47 and last but one away at 22.10 with the eight-man crew of F/O Fisher on board was PA972, which failed to leave the ground and ended up on its belly with smashed undercarriage. The crew emerged unscathed, but the Lancaster was deemed to be beyond economical repair, and the squadron element was one visual centerer short as it climbed out with S/Ls Maine-Smith and Trilsbach the senior pilots on duty. Nine early returns reduced The Path

Finder element by almost 10%, leaving the remainder to press on across France and enter Germany via the Strasbourg area accompanied by layers of cloud, which over the target, was at five to ten-tenths with tops in places as high as 20,000 feet. There was haze below the cloud level to create further challenges for the marker force, but the first red TIs were reported to be visible at 01.47 and were backed up with further reds and greens, which appeared to the main force crews to be somewhat scattered. The 405 (Vancouver) Squadron crews carried out their assigned tasks from 16,000 to 18,000 feet between 01.48 and 01.55, but it was impossible to assess the outcome, and there was little optimism at debriefings that a successful operation had taken place. In fact, this was probably the most destructive of the three raids in this current series, but it would be only after the third one that cumulative reports came out of the city to confirm much destruction and heavy casualties.

Also active on this night were the Master Bomber and Deputy pairing of F/O Cadegan and F/L Johnston, who had been assigned to one of three flying bomb sites, each targeted by a dozen Lancasters of 1 Group with five Oboe Mosquitos in attendance to provide the marking. The target for the Gransden Lodge pair was in the Foret-du-Croc, to the north of Paris, for which they took off at 23.15, each carrying six 1,000-pounders in addition to their marker pyrotechnics. F/O Cadegan and crew arrived at the target to find seven-tenths thin cloud at 9,000 feet with haze below and focused on three Oboe red TIs forming a right-angled triangle on the ground. They backed up with green TIs and bombed from 9,000 feet at 00.31 but communications problems may have caused challenges and F/L Johnston reported hearing the Master Bomber only intermittently. He and his crew bombed at 00.33, and the main force remained under instructions to aim for the green TIs until the end of the raid at around 00.40.

The 27th brought daylight attacks on five flying bomb sites for 3 Group main forces with 8 Group Mosquitos and Lancasters to provide the marking and direction. Six 405 (Vancouver) Squadron crews were briefed for a site at Les-Hauts-Boissons and departed Gransden Lodge between 17.09 and 17.11 with W/C Coulson the senior pilot on duty and eighteen 500-pounders in each bomb bay. They encountered three-tenths cloud and good visibility in the target area and approached the aiming point in echelon-starboard formation in pairs in line astern down and released their loads from 15,500 to 15,200 feet at 19.21 on observing the Mosquito leader's to go down. The bombing appeared to be concentrated around the aiming point and smoke was rising skyward as they turned for home.

The night of the 28/29th would prove to be busy, eventful and expensive as the Command prepared for major operations against Stuttgart and Hamburg and a number of smaller undertakings involving a total of 1,126 aircraft. The final raid of the series on Stuttgart was to be by an all-Lancaster heavy force of 494 aircraft drawn from 1, 3, 5 and 8 Groups, of which forty-three Lancasters and two Mosquitos were provided by 8 Group. Meanwhile, the group would also support the annual last-week-of-July attack on Hamburg, 320 miles away to the north, with fifty-three Lancasters and fourteen Mosquitos in company with 187 Halifaxes of 6 Group and fifty-three Lancasters of 1 Group. The operation would take place a year and a day after the devastating firestorm raid of Operation Gomorrah. 405 (Vancouver) Squadron briefed nine crews for Stuttgart and seven for Hamburg, and it was the former element that departed Gransden Lodge first between 22.26 and 22.40 with S/Ls Maine-Smith and Trilsbach the senior pilot on duty with five crews assigned as secondary blind markers, three as visual centerers and one as a primary visual marker.

The sound of their engines had not died away before the Hamburg-bound element took off between 22.44 and 22.50 with W/C Coulson the senior pilot on duty and all carrying six 2,000-pounders to deliver as part of the main force.

The Stuttgart force flew across France in bright moonlight above the cloud layer and exposed themselves to the night-fighter hordes that had infiltrated the bomber stream from 5° East and stayed in contact with it all the way to the target. It was the Luftwaffe's Nachtjagd that would gain the upper hand on this night, but the Gransden Lodge crews must have been in a section of the bomber stream that remained unmolested, as not one reported seeing a night-fighter. A thin layer of up to ten-tenths cloud lay over the city, with tops in places at around 12,000 feet, and the Path Finders initially employed skymarker flares (Wanganui), which quickly disappeared into the cloud tops. Most crews bombed on the basis of their navigational aids, before scattered red and green TIs were seen on the ground in a line from north-west to south-east. The Master Bomber attempted to persuade the main force crews to bomb the glow from a cluster of greens nearest to the aiming-point, and a number of crews descending beneath the cloud base reported green TIs at the southern end of the railway station at 01.56. The 405 (Vancouver) Squadron participants carried out their assigned tasks from 16,000 to 18,000 feet between 01.45 and 01.55, and a large explosion was reported at 01.48. It was impossible to assess the outcome, but most returning crews reported a scattered raid, for which they blamed the weather conditions. Thirty-nine Lancasters failed to return, fourteen of them from 5 Group and only one belonging to the Path Finders.

Mosquitos dispensed "window" ahead of the Hamburg force, which arrived in the target area to find seven to eight-tenths thin cloud with tops at 8,000 to 10,000 feet and clear skies above. The first yellow TIs were observed at 01.05, followed by green/yellow "Wanganui" flares and red TIs two minutes later, before the backers-up added their first green TIs at 01.10, slightly north of the aiming-point. The Master Bomber directed the main force crews to focus on these, and those from 405 (Vancouver) Squadron complied from 18,000 feet between 01.07 and 01.14. The bombing was not concentrated and fell mostly to the west of the city centre into dockland, while a proportion hit areas still in ruins from a year earlier. Night-fighters caught the Hamburg force on the way home, and a further twenty-two aircraft were shot down, bringing the night's casualty figure to sixty-one aircraft. 405 (Vancouver) Squadron's casualty was JB707, which crashed into Ringkøbing Fjord off Jutland's western coast, with fatal consequences for F/O Townsend RCAF and his predominantly RCAF crew. Occupying the rear turret was W/C Charles Gray, who, according to the Path Finder Archive, was thirty-six years of age and was a regular member of the Townsend crew, even though the crew list shows him in the rank of flying officer. He was apparently the same W/C Charles Gray who served as Director of Accounts in the RCAF HQ in Ottawa before remustering for aircrew duties. Although it was difficult to make an accurate assessment of this night's attack on Stuttgart, the series had severely damaged the city, leaving its central districts devastated, with most of its public and cultural buildings in ruins, while 1,171 of its inhabitants had lost their lives.

Briefings took place early on the 30th for operations to assist predominantly American ground forces, which were about to launch an offensive against six German positions in the Villers-Bocage-Caumont region of north-eastern France. 692 aircraft were to be involved, of which seventy-five Lancasters and thirty Mosquitos were provided by 8 Group, fifty-four of the Lancasters assigned to aiming-point E and four to aiming point G. 405 (Vancouver) Squadron was asked to contribute two Lancasters to G and ten to E, the former as backers-up and the latter to drop eighteen 500-pounders each as part of the main force. The crews of F/L Perry and F/O Cadegan departed Gransden Lodge at 06.48 and at the target encountered ten-tenth cloud in a wedge between 2,000 and 6,000 feet, which persuaded the Master Bomber to abandon the operation at 07.58 and send the crews home with their ordnance intact. The second element took off between 06.56 and 07.05 with W/C Coulson the senior pilot on duty, and after joining up with the rest of the force ran into ten-tenths stratus cloud in the target area with a base at 3,000 feet initially and later, 2,000 feet. It proved difficult to establish the location of the aiming-points and only eight of the Gransden Lodge crews had carried out their attacks from 1,200 to 2,000 feet between 08.15 and 08.19, before the Master Bomber called a halt to proceedings, leaving W/C Coulson and F/O Kettlewell with full bomb bays. In fact, fewer than half of the overall number fulfilled their briefs as just two sites were effectively marked by red Oboe TIs and bombed, and four Lancasters failed to return.

During the course of the month the squadron took part in thirty-three operations and dispatched 227 sorties for the remarkably low loss of three Lancasters and two crews.

August 1944

August would bring an end to the flying bomb offensive, and also see a return to major night operations against industrial Germany. Flying bomb sites were to dominate the first half of the month, however, and sites would be targeted in daylight on each of the first six days. It began with the commitment of 777 aircraft to operations against thirteen flying bomb-related sites during the afternoon and evening of the 1st, although there were serious doubts about the weather conditions, which were poor over England. At Gransden Lodge, F/L Perry and F/O Cadegan were designated Master Bomber and Deputy for an attack on "constructional works" at Belle-Croix-les-Bruyeres in Belgium by a 1 Group main force of fifty Lancasters from 13 Base and took off at 19.23 with a bomb load in addition to their marker ordnance of six 1,000-pounders. They exited the English coast at Orfordness over unbroken cloud, which persisted as they crossed the French coast near Calais and was still at ten-tenths with tops at 4,000 feet as they approached the target. On finding no Oboe TIs, F/L Perry was left with no option but to issue the order "Sultana" at 20.24 to send the force home.

Gransden Lodge was not involved when nine flying-bomb-related sites were earmarked for attention at the hands of 394 aircraft in favourable conditions on the 2nd, but held briefings on the 3rd, when more than eleven hundred crews were informed of their part in the day's activities. The target for eight 405 (Vancouver) Squadron crews was recorded in the 8 Group ORB as "constructional works" at L'Isle-Adam situated some fifteen miles north of Paris in the Ile-de-France region, while the squadron ORB referred to it as a "dump". They would be part of an 8 Group force of fifty-seven Lancasters and five Mosquitos and took off between 12.25 and 12.31 with W/C Coulson the senior pilot on duty, each carrying eleven 1,000 and four 500-pounders to deliver as part of the main force. They ran into two to three-tenths cloud in the target area at 10,000 to 12,000 feet, through which the Master Bomber identified the aiming-point at 13.56, assessing the red and yellow TIs to have slightly overshot. He called in the main force to bomb with a corresponding undershoot, until smoke completely enveloped the site, and it became necessary to aim for the centre of that. The 405 (Vancouver) Squadron element carried out their assigned tasks from 13,000 to 15,000 feet between 14.00 and 14.08, before returning to report concentrated bombing and a belief that the operation had achieved its aims. Two Lancasters were bearing the scars from flak hits and F/O Herbert and crew came home on three engines.

Later in the day, the crews of F/Os Cadegan and Fisher and F/L McQuoid attended a briefing to be told that they would be visual backers-up for a raid on a flying-bomb site in the Foret-de-Nieppe, five miles to the east of St-Omer, for which 103 Halifaxes of 4 Group provided the main force. They departed Gransden Lodge between 18.55 and 18.57, each carrying six 1,000-pounders in addition to the pyrotechnic content of their bomb bays, and flew out under clear skies, which prevailed right up to the target, where a large patch of up to seven-tenths cloud spoiled the view. Not all main force crews picked up the instructions of the Master Bomber, one of which was not to bomb if the aiming point could not be identified, but the 405 (Vancouver) Squadron trio heard his instruction at 20.02 to bomb on the yellow TI seen cascading over the aiming point and complied from 14,000 to 15,000 feet between 20.06 and 20.09. Smoke eventually obscured the aiming point and crews were instructed to bomb that, some witnessing a large yellow explosion at 20.10.

Briefings took place on 6 and 8 Group stations during the morning of the 4th to inform 291 crews of their part in operations respectively against the sites at Trossy-St-Maximin and the nearby "constructional works" or dump at L'Isle-Adam. 8 Group detailed nine Lancasters and five Mosquitos for the latter, 405 (Vancouver) Squadron providing five for the Master Bomber and Deputy pairing of the newly promoted S/L Perry and F/O Fisher and one each for the backer-up crew of F/L McQuoid and the supporter crews of S/L Maine-Smith and F/L Long. They departed Gransden Lodge between 11.24 and 11.28, five minutes before the first of their eleven fellow crews took off to join fifty others from the group and five Mosquitos assigned to the Trossy site. They were all safely airborne by 11.42 with W/C Coulson the senior pilot on duty and eleven 1,000 and four 500-pounders in each bomb bay for delivery as part of the main force. Those bound for L'Isle-Adam reached their destination first and on arrival at 12.56, S/L Perry observed Oboe red TIs covering an area that included the aiming point and extended some five hundred yards to the south-west. He aimed yellow TIs through the one to three-tenths cloud and these were backed up by the Deputy before the main force was called in to produce accurate and concentrated bombing that caused explosions and copious amounts of smoke, which soon obscured the TIs and became the focus of later bombing. The 405 (Vancouver) Squadron crews fulfilled their briefs from 14,000 to 15,000 feet between 12.57 and 13.00 and watched mushroom smoke clouds ascending as they turned away.

A dozen or so miles to the north-east the Trossy force encountered three tenths cloud topping out at 13,000 feet with good visibility below and having observed red Oboe TIs at 13.12, the Master Bomber issued instructions to bomb, while the Deputy backed them up with yellows. The Gransden Lodge crews complied from 14,400 to 15,700 feet between 13.13 and 13.18 and reported that the smoke had obscured the aiming-point, leaving those at the tail end to aim for the centre of that.

The 5th dawned bright and clear, and brilliant sunshine glinted off the Perspex of the Lancasters out on their dispersals on 8 Group stations, where Lancasters and Mosquitos were being prepared for operations against flying bomb and oil storage sites, the latter following up on the previous day's efforts, which had been directed at facilities in the Bordeaux region of south-western France. The mighty Gironde estuary narrows as it leads inland towards the south-east, before dividing to become the Garonne River to the west and the Dordogne to the east. Its banks and islands were home to a number of important oil production and storage sites at Pauillac, Blaye, Bec-d'Ambe and Bassens and that part of the Biscay coast was a frequent destination for gardening activities. Bordeaux, a gateway to the Atlantic, was a vitally important port to the enemy, contained U-Boot pens and was heavily defended along the entire length of the waterway. The targets on the 4th had been at Pauillac and Bec-d'Ambes and had been carried out for the first time under the umbrella of an escort of twenty-seven "Serrate" Mosquitos provided by 100 Group. "Serrate" was a radar device that enabled the night-fighter variant of the Mosquito to home in on enemy night-fighters to turn the hunters into the hunted, and it was spectacularly successful.

Twenty-four crews attended briefings in the morning to learn that they would be accompanying 282 Lancasters of 1 and 3 Groups in a return to the Bordeaux region of south-western France to attack the Blaye, Pauillac and Bassens sites. Eight Path Finder Lancasters would attend each, those representing 405 (Vancouver) squadron at Bassens, located on the eastern bank of the Garonne just to the north of Bordeaux itself. S/L Perry was appointed Master Bomber and F/O Fisher Deputy, F/Ls Gosman and Johnston as visual backers up and the remaining four as supporters and departed Gransden Lodge between 14.30 and 14.47 for the long outward flight under the protection of thirty 100 Group Mosquitos. They all arrived in the target area to find layers of cumulonimbus between 2,000 and 18,000 feet with drifting fingers of cloud, upon which S/L Perry initially called "basement 15,000", before being compelled progressively to reduce it to 12,000, then 8,000 and finally 5,000 feet. F/O Fisher dropped yellow TIs from 6,000 feet at 18.55 and immediately ran into cloud, as did S/L Perry following close behind, but the backers-up managed to put their yellows on or near the aiming point and the main force crews were called in at 18.59. Apart from a few stray sticks that fell into the river or on the opposite bank, the site was plastered and soon obscured by smoke, out of which oily explosions were observed. The Gransden Lodge crews carried out their assigned tasks from 3,500 to 6,200 feet between 18.55 and 19.04 and returned confident in the quality of their work, post-raid reconnaissance confirming that all three attacks had been successful.

That evening, the crews of F/Ls Bernand and Weicker, F/O Herbert and P/O Coffey departed Gransden Lodge at 18.00 bound for an "Oboe leader" attack on a flying-bomb site at Noyelles-en-Chaussee, situated a dozen or so miles north-east of Abbeville, each Lancaster loaded with eleven 1,000 and four 500 pounders. At 20.02 the formation ran into ten-tenths ice-bearing cumulonimbus cloud with tops at 30,000 feet and broke up, whereupon three of the 405 (Vancouver) Squadron participants abandoned their sorties and jettisoned their loads. P/O Coffey and crew alone maintained contact with a leader and delivered an attack from 17,400 feet at 20.06 before returning home to make their report.

Gransden Lodge was not called into action on the 6th, when 222 crews from 4, 5 and 8 Groups were briefed for operations against the previously attacked "constructional works" at Bois-de-Cassan and Forêt-de-Nieppe. More than a thousand aircraft were assembled during the course of the 7th to send against five enemy strong points ahead of advancing Allied ground forces. 8 Group committed six Lancasters and two or three Mosquitos to four of the aiming-points, but sixty-six Lancasters and three Mosquitos to "Totalize 5". 405 (Vancouver) Squadron made ready a dozen of its own and briefed two crews as visual backers-up and ten to bomb with the main force. In addition, the crews of F/O Fisher and F/L Johnston were assigned as visual backers-up for aiming point 3 and they departed Gransden Lodge first at 21.44, leaving the second element on the ground until it took off between 22.21 and 22.32 with W/C Palmer leading the squadron into battle for the first time since his arrival as commanding officer-elect and successor to W/C Lane. It will be recalled that W/C Palmer had completed twenty-one sorties with the squadron in 1942 and had earned a commission and a DFC in the process.

The target area was found to be free of cloud, and the first activity occurred at aiming-point 3, where the attack opened at 22.53 with the delivery of yellow TIs, which were followed by green star shells two minutes later. Backing up was continuous and accurate until 23.00, by which time the bombing had obliterated the markers and further backing up led to a degree of undershooting by the main force, persuading the Master Bomber to end proceedings and send the force home. At aiming-point 2 the attack began at 22.55 with yellow TIs followed immediately by red star shells, which the Deputy Master Bomber backed up at 22.57 with a red TI and the Master Bomber a few seconds later. In the early stages, the marking and bombing were very concentrated and accurate, but as smoke began to obscure the area and the Master Bomber's requests for further markers elicited no response, he called a halt and sent the rest of the force home. The first red star shell at aiming point 4 was seen to explode at 23.15 and was followed by others for around five minutes. The Master Bomber corrected misplaced TIs from his Deputy, and the main weight of bombs fell on them, until unheeded requests for further marking persuaded him to end the attack at 23.26. At aiming-point 1 the Master Bomber delivered his green TI accurately after identifying it by yellow TIs confirmed by Gee, and concentrated backing up and bombing led to the same sequence of obliterated markers and the abandonment of the attack before all had emptied their bomb bays.

Yellow TIs opened the attack at aiming-point 5, followed by red star shells, which were confirmed as accurate by Gee-fix. The Master Bomber dropped his red TIs at 23.36, after which, the backers-up maintained the aiming-point, and the main force delivered concentrated and accurate bombing in accordance with instructions. The 405 (Vancouver) Squadron crews performed as briefed from 8,000 to 8,500 feet between 23.39 and 23.49, before returning home confident in the quality of their work, and enthusiastically relating their experiences to the intelligence section at debriefing. In total, 660 aircraft delivered their bombs in these meticulously controlled operations carried out in close proximity to friendly forces.

A fuel storage dump in the Foret-de-Chantilly was the main target during daylight on the 8th, and two similar targets at Aire-sur-Lys and Lucheux, behind enemy lines in north-eastern France, were earmarked for attention that night respectively by main forces from 1 and 3 Groups. 405 (Vancouver) Squadron provided fifteen Lancasters as the 8 Group heavy element at the latter, with S/L Perry and F/O Fisher the designated Master Bomber and Deputy and W/Cs Palmer and the newly-promoted W/C Morrison the senior pilots among ten illuminators and three visual backers-up. They were to be joined at the target by five Oboe Mosquitos to deliver the initial marking and a main force of 3 Group Lancasters and departed Gransden Lodge between 22.08 and 22.22. They flew out in good conditions to cross the French coast at 17,000 feet, before shedding height quickly and passing through a forest of searchlights to find the Oboe marking to be accurate and concentrated around the aiming point. S/L Perry and F/O Fisher backed up with green TIs and the backers-up maintained it with Yellows between 23.48 and 23.52. The 405 (Vancouver) Squadron participants fulfilled their briefs from 9,600 to 14,000 feet between 23.43 and 23.52 and left many fires burning in their wake and columns of smoke rising through 9,000 feet as the bombers turned away. There was little flak, but night-fighters were active, and a 115 Squadron Lancaster was observed to fall in flames as the only failure to return.

The evening of the 9th brought attacks on five flying-bomb sites, for which a total of 311 Lancasters, Halifaxes and Mosquitos were drawn from 1, 3, 6 and 8 Groups, 405 (Vancouver) Squadron providing the Master Bomber and Deputy pairing of S/L Perry and F/L Johnston at Coulonvillers and F/O Fisher and F/L Gosman at Foret-du-Croc. The former took the early shift and departed Gransden Lodge at 19.56 before arriving at their target some seven miles to the north-east of Abbeville to find clear skies and ideal conditions. The red Oboe TIs fell at 21.11, overshooting by around 250 yards to the east, and after S/L Perry and F/L Johnston had delivered their six 1,000-pounders each a minute later from 15,000 feet and 14,600 feet respectively, the 6 Group main force was called in and instructed to compensate accordingly. In the event, the bombing became scattered and mostly overshot the aiming point despite repeated calls to undershoot. They were on their way home by the time that the second pair took off at 22.36 and 22.59 bound for the target to the north of Paris, map-reading their way south across France in perfect conditions. F/O Fisher found five red Oboe TIs in a circle of around two hundred yards diameter and dropped his green TIs among them along with ten 1,000-pounders from 11,000 feet at 23.53, F/L Gosman following up from 12,000 feet two minutes later, before the 6 Group main force element was called in to complete the job. As at Coulonvillers, the bombing became scattered and mostly undershot the aiming point to the frustration of F/O Fisher.

One of the operations on the 9th had been conducted by 617 Squadron against the U-Boot pens at La Pallice on France's Biscay coast and now on the evening of the 10th, 101 Halifaxes and thirty-seven Lancasters from 6 Group's 62 and 64 Bases were to target oil storage facilities in the port, while 5 Group attended to a similar target further south at Bordeaux. Aiming points B and C at La Pallice were briefed out to twenty-one 8 Group crews, ten at Gransden Lodge for the former, with S/L Perry and F/O Fisher the designated Master Bomber and Deputy and W/C Palmer the senior pilot on duty among the six illuminators and two visual backers-up. They departed Gransden Lodge between 20.00 and 20.19 and arrived at the target to be greeted by excellent conditions in which S/L Perry was able to identify the entire area and the precise aiming point. The illumination was effective, and S/L Perry delivered green TIs at 22.54, which fell about 150 yards north-north-east of the aiming point, while a second batch was judged to be slightly south-south-east. The 405 (Vancouver) squadron crews carried out their assigned tasks from 9,800 to 15,200 feet between 22.52 and 23.06 and returned safely to report very little visual evidence of bombing by the main force element and no fires were observed. However, a large oil fire at aiming point C produced volumes of smoke and the operation was deemed to be successful.

Following a day off for Gransden Lodge on the 11th, the crews of S/L Perry, F/O Fisher, F/L Whittall and F/O Kyte were called to briefing to learn of a return to La Pallice, this time to attack the U-Boot pens with a 1 Group main force, while similar targets at Brest and Bordeaux occupied other small forces. The first-two-mentioned were designated Master Bomber and Deputy and the remaining pair as supporters and took off between 11.49 and 11.52 to fly south under the escort of eight Mosquitos of 100 Group. Clear skies and good visibility enabled S/L Perry to identify the aiming point and he called upon F/O Fisher to mark it with green TIs, which were seen to cascade at 14.59 on the northern edge of the site. S/L Perry instructed the main force element to compensate with their bombing and withheld his own TIs, while delivering his two 2,000 and two 1,000-pounders from 14,500 feet. F/O Fisher bombed from 16,000 feet and the two 405 (Vancouver) Squadron supporters dropped their four 2,000 and two 1,000-pounders each from 14,000 and 14,500 feet and the aiming point was soon concealed beneath smoke, which became the aiming point for the tail end of the main force. They turned for home at 15.05, confident that the site had been effectively attacked, but in truth, the pens were impervious to conventional bombs and damage would have been restricted to other site buildings, port installations and access roads. There was, however, a claim that a U-Boot had been hit.

The main operation on this day was an experiment to gauge the ability of main force crews to locate and attack an urban target on the strength of their own H2S equipment in the absence of a Path Finder element. This resulted from the huge volume of operations generated by the four concurrent campaigns, each of which called upon the finite resources of 8 Group, compelling it, in the short term at least, to spread itself more and more thinly. The conclusion of the flying-bomb campaign at the end of the month, together with the end of tactical support for the ground forces, would remove the pressure, and the planned independence of 3 Group through the G-H bombing system from the autumn would solve the problem altogether. In the meantime, however, no one knew what demands might be made of the Command, and it would be useful to see what main force crews could do when left to their own devices. The target was to be Braunschweig, for which a force of 379 aircraft was assembled from all but 8 Group.

It was to be a night of heavy Bomber Command activity at numerous locations involving more than eleven hundred sorties, and a second large operation over Germany would involve 297 aircraft, seventy-six of them 8 Group Lancasters, eleven representing 405 (Vancouver) Squadron. They learned at briefing that their target was the Opel motor factory at Rüsselsheim situated two hundred miles south of Braunschweig, which might help to divide the night-fighter response. The factory had produced motor vehicles up until October 1940 and was a wholly-owned subsidiary of the American General Motors Corporation with a sister plant manufacturing lorries at Brandenburg near Berlin. In 1942, the Rüsselsheim plant was given over to war production and began to manufacture aircraft and tank parts. The Gransden Lodge crews took off between 21.55 and 22.04 with W/C Morrison the senior pilot on duty and designated visual blind marker, while the other crews were assigned as blind marker/illuminators, blind illuminators, blind backers-up and supporters.

They all arrived at the target to find a small amount of thin cloud with haze below, and the attack opened punctually with illuminating flares and green TIs, the former rendered more or less ineffective by the haze. A visual identification of the aiming-point was hindered by the diffused glow from early incendiaries, and green TIs were scattered initially to the north and south until a degree of concentration was eventually achieved. A number of fires developed covering a circular area approximately one-and-a-half miles in diameter, but a detailed assessment was not possible, and the force headed home uncertain as to the outcome and harassed by enemy night-fighters. The Gransden Lodge crews carried out their assigned tasks from 13,000 to 18,500 feet between 00.08 and 00.19 and all arrived home safely to await post-raid reconnaissance to confirm to them that a number of buildings had been damaged within the Opel factory complex, but nothing vital to production, and fires had spread through a wood three miles away and adjacent housing estates to the south-east. There were also many bomb craters in open country, confirming that this target would need further attention. Twenty aircraft failed to return from what was a disappointing endeavour, in addition to twenty-seven missing from the scattered and largely ineffective raid on Braunschweig, and this was a high price to pay for such poor returns.

While the above operations were in progress, a "rush job" called upon the services of 144 crews to attack German troop concentrations and a road junction north of Falaise. 8 Group supported the attack with eleven Lancasters and five Mosquitos, four of the former provided by 405 (Vancouver) Squadron and containing the crews of W/C Coulson, F/Ls Burnand and Johnston and P/O Tite. They departed Gransden Lodge between 00.45 and 00.48 to fulfil the role of illuminators and found a blanket of ten-tenths stratus cloud with tops at 2,000 feet, through which they delivered their twenty-four 7-inch hooded flares and eight 1,000-pounders each from 7,000 and 8,800 feet between 02.09 and 02.17. The bombing appeared to be concentrated around the markers and post-raid reconnaissance confirmed that the area around the junction was heavily cratered and the roads leading from it mostly blocked. 405 (Vancouver) Squadron suffered no losses from its nineteen sorties in the twenty-four-hour period and was enjoying a good first half of the month.

The main activity during the afternoon of the 14th was Operation Tractable, which was launched to support Canadian divisions in the Falaise area and involved 805 aircraft targeting seven enemy troop positions. 8 Group would provide six Lancasters and six Mosquitos at six of the aiming-points and forty-six Lancasters and six Mosquitos at the seventh, A/P 22. At Gransden Lodge 405 (Vancouver) Squadron made ready six Lancasters for A/P 21A and eight for A/P 22, with W/C Morrison and F/O Fisher the designated Master Bomber and Deputy at the former. The remainder of those assigned to A/P 21A were to perform the role of backers-up, while all eight crews bound for A/P 22 were to carry a full bomb load of eighteen 500-pounders. Master Bombers would be on hand to control the bombing at each aiming-point to try to avoid friendly-fire incidents that might arise through the close proximity of the opposing armies. The first element departed Gransden Lodge between 12.44 and 12.50 and was followed into the air between 13.21 and 13.26 by the second with W/C Coulson the senior pilot, and both sections found the target area to be clear of cloud with good visibility that enabled W/C Morrison to identify A/P 21A visually aided by the Mosquito-laid Oboe red TIs burning some three hundred yards to the west. F/O Fisher delivered yellow TIs a hundred yards to the east, and the backers-up and main force crews were ordered to bomb between the two clusters until they disappeared under a blanket of smoke, which then became the new aiming point. The 405 (Vancouver) Squadron crews carried out their respective tasks from 4,800 to 7,900 feet between 13.58 and 14.06 and were back home by 15.20.

Meanwhile, the attack on A/P 22 had proceeded in similar fashion under favourable conditions, but smoke had already drifted across the target area by the time that the 405 (Vancouver) Squadron participants arrived to fulfil their briefs from 7,500 to 8,200 feet between 14.37 and 14.43. Despite the most stringent efforts to avoid friendly-fire incidents, about halfway through the sequence of attacks, some bombs did fall into a quarry occupied by Canadian troops, killing thirteen men, injuring fifty-three others and destroying a large number of vehicles and it is possible that this tragedy occurred during the above-described events. Recriminations abounded thereafter over who was to blame, but it seems to have been a genuine accident brought about as much by events on the ground as in the air, and in truth, this was perhaps one of very few "blue-on-blue" incidents involving Bomber Command. Nevertheless, a number of squadron commanders were apparently "carpeted" for providing insufficiently comprehensive briefings.

The time was now fast approaching, when Harris could claim that he had discharged his obligation to SHAEF and could turn his attention once more upon industrial Germany almost to the exclusion of all else. In preparation for his new night offensive against Germany, he called for operations against enemy night-fighter airfields in Holland and Belgium on the 15th. In response, a list of eight such targets was prepared for attention, those at Eindhoven, Soesterberg, Volkel, Brussels-Melsbroek, St-Trond, Tirlemont-Gossancourt and Le Culot to be targeted in daylight during the course of the morning and early afternoon of the 15th, and Venlo that night, involving, in all, 1004 aircraft. 8 Group provided nine Lancasters for each target, and four and six Mosquitos respectively at Le Culot and Volkel, the latter one of two assigned to elements of 405 (Vancouver) Squadron, while the other was Melsbroek. The crews of P/O Walter and F/O Hannah were the Gransden Lodge representatives at Volkel and took off at 10.20 with a full bomb load of ten 1,000 and four 500-pounders. They arrived over south-eastern Holland to encounter ideal bombing conditions having identified the target when thirty miles distant and fulfilled their briefs from 15,000 and 16,800 feet at 11.56 and 11.59, before returning home to report concentrated bombing that left the target area obscured by smoke and dust.

The Master Bomber for the attack on Melsbroek was S/L Maine-Smith, who was making his debut in the role and was supported by the experienced F/O Fisher as Deputy Master Bomber. They departed Gransden Lodge between 10.38 and 10.46 with the remaining seven crews assigned to backer-up or main force support duties and enjoyed the same perfect conditions as those at Volkel some seventy miles to the north-east. S/L Main-Smith approached the target from the north-west accompanied by two supporters and was informed that F/O Fisher's bomb sight had become unserviceable, and he was unable to mark. S/L Maine-Smith dropped his own red TIs, which fell about fifty yards to the north-east of the aiming point and instructed the main force to compensate accordingly, the 405 (Vancouver) Squadron participants fulfilling their briefs from 15,500 to 17,000 feet between 11.56 and 12.02. The bombing was observed to fall in concentrated fashion across runways and dispersals and only an isolated few sticks fell outside of the aerodrome boundaries. The whole scene disappeared beneath smoke and dust, and it was left to post-raid reconnaissance to confirm the effectiveness of the raid. S/L Maine-Smith landed with flak damage to the starboard wing, which had been picked up over the target.

The new offensive began with simultaneous attacks on Stettin and Kiel on the night of the 16/17th, 8 Group contributing fifty-nine aircraft to the overall all-Lancaster force of 461 assigned to the former and thirty-seven Lancasters and nine Mosquitos to the latter. 405 (Vancouver) Squadron made ready four Lancasters for Stettin and a dozen for Kiel, the former loaded with four 2,000-pounders each, while their crews were briefed for a supporter role. The latter were to perform a variety of marking roles with W/Cs Palmer and Morrison the senior pilots on duty and most had a cookie in the bomb bay in addition to the pyrotechnic ordnance. The Stettin-bound quartet departed Gransden Lodge between 20.59 and 21.02 and was followed into the air by the second element between 21.13 and 21.33, and with around two hundred miles fewer to cover, it was the latter element that arrived at its destination first. Despite thick haze, the Master Bomber was able to identify the target in the light of illuminating flares and observed green TIs to have fallen in a semi-circle on the western half of the town. Reds were also in evidence, but the main force was instructed initially to aim for the greens and only later the reds, and it was estimated that 75% of bomb loads fell within the built-up area, causing extensive damage to the shipyards and dockland. The 405 (Vancouver) Squadron participants carried out their assigned tasks from 16,300 to 18,700 feet between midnight and 00.20 and fires were burning as they retreated westwards across Jutland, with the glow remaining on the horizon for a considerable distance. PB239 failed to return after crashing into the sea off Denmark's western coast and there were no survivors from the predominantly RCAF crew of F/O Fisher DFC RCAF. The loss of such an experienced crew, F/O Fisher with fifty-three sorties to his credit, was a bitter blow to the squadron, and sadly, they would not be the only absentees on this night.

The flight to Stettin took some three-and-a-half hours, and on arrival it was largely hidden to human eye by up to nine-tenths high cloud with a base, according to the Master Bomber's broadcast at 00.52½, at 14,000 feet. There were, however, sufficient breaks to enable them to register clear visibility below, in which the initial flares and green TIs were observed to be a little north and east of the built-up area. This reduced the effectiveness of the illumination but did not prevent the primary visual markers from identifying the aiming-point and dropping a mix of red and green TIs to form a good concentration that the visual recenterers maintained throughout. The main force approached from 12,000 to 20,000 feet and began to bomb the TIs from around 00.56 until 01.21 and reported fires taking hold. The Gransden Lodge crews carried out their assigned tasks from 12,000 to 18,500 feet between 00.54 and 01.02 before three of them returned home safely to make their reports. Absent from debriefing was the all-RCAF crew of P/O Walter, whose PA988 had to be abandoned over Denmark after a fire erupted in the fuselage and starboard wing. The remains of the mid-upper gunner were found in the wreckage, suggesting that he had been fatally wounded during a night-fighter attack, while his colleagues all arrived safely on the ground, the pilot and three others to evade capture, leaving two in enemy hands. Not all returning crews were confident about the outcome of the raid, some suggesting that the bombing had been scattered, when in fact, it had been highly successful and had destroyed fifteen hundred houses, numerous industrial premises, had sunk five ships in the harbour and seriously damaged eight more.

After a day off on the 17th, fifteen crews were called to the Gransden Lodge briefing room on the 18th to learn of two operations for that night, one against the Ruhr-Chemie synthetic oil plant at Sterkrade-Holten in the Ruhr and the other against the much-bombed city of Bremen in north-western Germany. 8 Group was to provide six Lancasters and fourteen Mosquitos for the former and fifty-eight Lancasters and six Mosquitos for the latter in an overall force of 288 aircraft, with 405 (Vancouver) Squadron represented by three and twelve Lancasters respectively. The senior pilots among the Bremen element were W/Cs Morrison and Palmer, who, along with four others were assigned as blind marker/illuminators, leaving six others to be divided equally between blind backing-up and a main force support role. They departed Gransden Lodge between 21.30 and 21.41 and joined the bomber stream as it came together over the North Sea heading for the Dutch coast. At the head of the formation the Mosquitos closed on Bremen to deliver red TIs from clear skies as a beacon to the Lancasters behind, among which the flare force illuminated the aiming-point and enabled most crews to identify it visually and by green TIs backed up by further greens and reds. The 405 (Vancouver) squadron contingent carried out their assigned tasks from 15,000 to 18,600 feet between 00.02 and 00.14, those supporting the main force each unleashing eleven 1,000-pounders. The attack was concentrated and the whole area soon became a sea of flames with explosions and thick black smoke rising to meet the bombers. Mosquito crews returning from Berlin would comment on the glow from Bremen, two hundred miles to the west, as they turned away from the German capital. A reconnaissance Mosquito over Bremen at 01.05 reported an area of intense and unbroken fire covering four by one-and-a-half miles with black smoke rising through 23,000 feet. It was confirmed later that the 1,100 tons of bombs had devastated central and north-western districts, including the docks, destroying 8,635 "dwelling houses", mostly in the form of apartment blocks, and too many industrial units to count, while sinking eighteen ships in the harbour.

The crews of F/Ls Gosman, Johnston and McQuoid had taken off for the Ruhr between 23.00 and 23.02 to perform the role of visual backers-up for a main force of 210 Halifaxes of 4 Group and reached the target to find thin four-tenths cloud but excellent visibility. F/L Gosman's Lancaster was hit by flak during the bombing run, but he and his crew carried on to release the eight 1,000-pounders before taking evasive action and retaining the marker ordnance. The 405 (Vancouver) Squadron participants carried out their tasks from 16,500 to 18,000 feet between 00.53 and 01.00 before returning safely to report TIs on the ground many miles from the aiming point. However, the Master Bomber kept the raid on track and returning crews reported a good concentration of bombing and a large red explosion at 00.56, followed by others, including one with a yellow/orange flash at 01.02. A post-raid analysis concluded that this was a highly effective operation that had caused extensive damage to the plant and must have had a negative effect on production.

During a lull in operations, thereafter, the now Group Captain Reg Lane concluded his third tour of operations on the 23rd and was posted to 6 Group HQ. He was succeeded by W/C Palmer DFC, whose term of office would be brought to a premature conclusion in the not-too-distant future. The renewed assault on Germany began again on the night of the 25/26th, when a record 1,311 sorties were flown on major and support operations. The largest operation involved a main force of 349 Lancasters of 1, 3 and 6 Groups with sixty-three 8 Group Lancasters in an attack on the Opel tank works at Rüsselsheim, which had escaped a telling blow two weeks earlier, while 334 others attended to eight coastal batteries between Brest and the islands to the south of Lorient, which left 5 Group to focus on Darmstadt, a university city to the south of Frankfurt, renowned as a centre of scientific research and development, and one of a few almost virgin targets considered to be worthy of attention. 405 (Vancouver) Squadron briefed sixteen crews, twelve to undertake a variety of marker roles and four as main force supporters and sent them on their way from Gransden Lodge between 20.50 and 21.13 with W/C Morrison and S/L Maine-Smith the senior pilots on duty. They flew out over Selsey Bill and made landfall on the Normandy coast to the east of Caen, patchy cloud giving way to clear skies in the target area with good vertical visibility. The Path Finders opened the attack on time with illuminator flares followed by TIs, which were backed up throughout, and some crews confirmed their positions by H2S before committing themselves to the bombing run. A decoy site some ten miles west-south-west of the target attracted a few bombs in the early stages, but the main weight of the attack fell where intended in the face of little effective opposition from the ground. The 405 (Vancouver) Squadron crews fulfilled their respective briefs from 14,900 to 18,200 feet between 00.52 and 01.09, leaving the main force to aim mostly for red and green TIs and burgeoning fires in the face of numerous searchlights and moderate heavy flak in barrage form. Large explosions were observed at 00.58, 01.02, 01.09 and 01.10 and smoke was seen to be rising through 11,000 feet as the force retreated, leaving a glow from the burning factory visible for eighty miles. Night-fighters were much in evidence and claimed the majority of the fifteen missing Lancasters, in return for which local sources confirmed that parts of the Opel factory had been put out of action for several weeks, although most of the machine tools escaped damage and production was not badly compromised.

On the 26th, W/C Coulson and four of his crew were posted to Graveley to join 35 (Madras Presidency) Squadron, and it would not be long before Coulson began to make a name for himself as a forthright and determined bomber pilot and leader. He would be allowed time to settle in before beginning this next phase of his operational career, and he was not involved in the briefing for that night's operation by 372 Lancasters and ten Mosquitos from 1, 3 and 8 Groups against Kiel. Back at Gransden Lodge thirteen Lancasters were made ready, three crews briefed to fulfil the role of blind illuminators, four as blind markers, one as a primary visual marker and five as main force supporters. They took off between 20.01 and 20.18 with W/C Morrison the senior pilot on duty as part of an 8 Group contribution of eighty-one Lancasters and nine Mosquitos, which was depleted gradually by the early return of 10% of the former. The remainder arrived in the target area at 23.00 to find eight-tenths thin, low stratus cloud with tops at around 4,000 feet, and illuminating flares falling over the town to the west of the estuary. A very effective smoke screen was in operation over the southern part of the town, and only a few red and green TIs were on the ground before the rest of the primary visual marker crews were instructed not to release any more. Those already burning proved to be sufficient, and a good concentration of bombing was achieved south of the aiming-point with a very large explosion observed at 23.10. W/C Morrison and crew failed to identify the aiming point on their first pass and orbited before trying again, only to be thwarted by the smoke screen. The remaining Gransden Lodge crews carried out their assigned tasks from 17,500 to 18,200 feet between 23.00 and 23.13, and all returned safely to report what appeared to be an effective operation. Seventeen Lancasters failed to return, including six Path Finders, three of them from 635 Squadron. A reconnaissance Mosquito flew over Kiel at 25,000 feet at 00.18, and reported a five-mile arc of fire with a large bank of smoke rising through 15,000 feet.

When the crews of F/Os Cadegan, Friedman and McNaughton had settled onto their chairs in the Gransden Lodge briefing room on the morning of the 27th, they learned that they were to take part in a momentous operation against the Gewerkschaft Rheinpreussen A G synthetic oil plant at Moers/Homberg on the West Bank of the Rhine opposite Duisburg on the western edge of the Ruhr. 214 Halifaxes of 4 Group would represent the main force, while thirteen 8 Group Lancasters and fourteen Mosquitos provided the marking. The "momentous" aspect of the operation was the fact that it would be the first by a massed Bomber Command force to take place over Germany in daylight since August 1941, for which the protection of nine squadrons of Spitfires was provided, with a further seven on hand to cover the withdrawal. The 405 (Vancouver) Squadron trio took off between 12.16 and 12.24, the first-mentioned as a backer-up and the others as main force supporters with a bomb load each of a cookie and eight 1,000-pounders. The target area was heavily defended, and when last attacked by the heavy brigade in July, it had exacted a heavy toll of twenty Lancasters, seven from 75 (New Zealand) Squadron alone. The Oboe Mosquitos delivered red TIs accurately onto the aiming-point through the six-tenths cumulus cloud and the Master Bomber called in the main force to aim for them and for the backers-up to maintain it with a supply of green TIs, until bomb bursts and smoke obscured the area. The 405 (Vancouver) squadron participants fulfilled their briefs from 18,000 to 18,500 feet between 13.57 and 14.00, and smoke was rising through 10,000 feet as they turned for home blinded to the outcome by the cloud and smoke.

The final operations against the flying bomb menace took place on the 28th, when twelve sites were attacked by small numbers of aircraft employing the Oboe leader system. 405 (Vancouver) Squadron briefed three Master Bomber and Deputy pairings, F/L Johnston and F/O Kettlewell for L'Hey, S/L Perry and F/L Gosman for Ile-de-Cezembre, and F/O Cadegan and F/L Whittall for Fromental and dispatched them from Gransden Lodge at intervals between 18.40 and 19.41. The attacks were carried out in favourable conditions, the 405 (Vancouver) Squadron participants performing as briefed from 13,100 to 14,000 feet between 19.53 and 19.56 at L'Hey, 10,000 feet at 20.43 at Frometal and 11,000 to 13,000 feet between 21.03 and 21.07 at Ile-de-Cezembre.

While the Kiel operation had taken place on the night of the 26/27th, 5 Group had attacked the distant Baltic port of Königsberg (now Kaliningrad in Russia) situated some 950 miles from its Lincolnshire bases, the most distant target attacked during the war. Successful though this first operation had been, it was deemed necessary to go again on the 29th, while 402 Lancasters of 1, 3 and 8 Groups attended to the Baltic port-city of Stettin 260 miles closer to home. 405 (Vancouver) Squadron briefed sixteen crews, a dozen for a variety of marker roles and four as main force supporters and dispatched them from Gransden Lodge between 21.12 and 21.27 with W/C Palmer the senior pilot on duty and joined up with sixty-six others from the group as they began the North Sea crossing. F/O Ellison and crew turned back at Jutland's western coast after losing their starboard-inner engine and intercom, leaving the others to press on to be greeted at the target by seven to eight-tenths thin cloud at up to 19,000 feet with good visibility below. The attack opened with flares illuminating the aiming-point to provide the markers with a visual reference confirmed by H2S, after which salvoes of red and green TIs fell accurately and invited the main force bomb loads, which fell squarely and in concentrated fashion where intended. The 405 (Vancouver) Squadron crews carried out their assigned tasks from 13,000 to 19,300 feet between 01.51 and 02.05 and by 02.08 the whole area had become a sea of flames. The crew of a reconnaissance Mosquito approaching the target, but still some 250 miles away, reported a huge explosion at 02.09 and later, a large part of the town burning fiercely, with a huge mushroom of smoke ascending through 26,000 feet. The massive level of damage was confirmed, particularly in areas not previously hit, and the catalogue of destruction included more than fifteen hundred houses along with thirty-two industrial premises, a two-thousand-ton ship was sunk, and more than a thousand people lost their lives.

The flying-bomb campaign may have ended on the 28th, but a new one against V-2 rocket storage and launching sites began on the 31st with raids on nine suspected locations in north-eastern France. 601 aircraft were made ready, 8 Group providing four Lancasters and five Mosquitos for the sites at Raimbert, Lumbres North, Lumbres South, Agenville, St Riquier and Pourchinte, all located in the Hauts-de-France region.

During the course of the month, the squadron carried out thirty operations and dispatched 213 sorties for the loss of two Lancasters and crews.

September 1944

The destructive power of the Command was now almost beyond belief with each of its heavy bomber groups capable of laying waste to a German city at one go, and from now until the end of the war, this would be demonstrated in awesome and horrific fashion. Much of the Command's effort during the new month would be directed towards the liberation of the three French ports, Le Havre, Boulogne and Calais, that remained in enemy hands, but operations began for 405 (Vancouver) Squadron on the 1st, when W/C Morrison and F/L Johnston were selected as the Master Bomber and Deputy for a daylight raid on a V-2 rocket store at La Pourchinte, which together with another at Lumbres, a short distance to the north and situated west of St-Omer, were the targets for a main force of ninety-seven 4 Group Halifaxes. The backer-up crew of F/O Cadegan joined the other two in a departure from Gransden Lodge between 07.21 and 07.23 and arrived at the target ninety minutes later to find four-tenths cloud at between 2,000 and 6,000 feet, through which the aiming point could be identified. Mosquito-borne Oboe red TIs were already in evidence and were backed up green TIs delivered by W/C Morrison, by which time F/O Cadegan and crew had bombed from 11,000 feet at 08.42. The crews of W/C Morrison and F/L Johnston followed up with four 1,000 pounders each over the ensuing five minutes from 11,300 and 14,500 feet respectively before heading home to report concentrated bombing.

The 3rd brought action for some Path Finder squadrons in the form of daylight attacks on six Luftwaffe airfields in southern Holland, for which a total of 348 Lancasters, 315 Halifaxes and a dozen Mosquitos was made ready across the Command. 8 Group provided nine Lancasters each for five of the sites and ten Mosquitos divided between two, and all operations were concluded successfully for the loss of a single Halifax from Venlo. Gransden Lodge was not involved in the above, but was called into action on the 5th, when a force of 348 aircraft was assembled to carry out the first operations against enemy strong points around the port of Le Havre. 313 Lancasters from 1, 3 and 8 Groups would be accompanied by thirty Oboe Mosquitos and five Stirlings of 149 Squadron, the last of the type in service with a bomber unit three days ahead of its retirement in favour of Lancasters. Twenty-four of the Lancasters were provided by 8 Group, a Master Bomber and Deputy and two backers-up assigned to each of six aiming points, S/L Perry and W/C Morrison appointed as one of the Master Bomber and Deputy pairings with F/L Johnston and F/O Cadegan as backers-up. They took off between 17.45 and 17.48, and once on their way south, the heavy brigade formed into six waves, and the Master Bombers broadcast time-checks to their sections of the main force and issued the instructions for the bombing height. Ahead, the first waves had reached the target to find excellent conditions with no more than two-tenths cloud topping out at 6,000 feet under a canopy of ten-tenths well above at 18,000 feet. Fortunately, a westerly breeze blew the drifting smoke away, and the harbour and dock installations were clearly visible to the 405 (Vancouver) Squadron quartet in wave 4 as they delivered their marker ordnance and six 1,000 pounders each from 11,500 to 14,200 feet between 18.57 and 19.06 and observed the bombing to be accurate and concentrated. It was estimated that 90% of the bombs fell within the six defined target areas, and the operations were deemed to be a success.

Two operations were briefed out at Gransden Lodge on the 6th, both to be launched in the early evening against the port of Emden and enemy positions around Le Havre. The former, situated on Germany's north-western coast, had been a regular target during the first three years of the war, but had been left in relative peace since June 1942. A force of 105 Halifaxes and seventy-six

Lancasters from 6 and 8 Groups was assembled for the task, forty-two of the Lancasters belonging to Path Finder units, and they would share an escort of Spitfires and US Eighth Air Force Mustangs. The seven crews taking off between 16.18 and 16.24 with F/L Whittall the senior pilot on duty were charged with no target marking responsibilities, and each carried a dozen 1,000 pounders to deliver as part of the main force. They arrived in the target area to find a cloud base at 16,500 feet and good visibility below and the attack opened at 18.24 with red TIs placed accurately on the aiming-point. The Gransden Lodge crews carried out their attacks from 17,000 to 18,000 feet between 18.26 and 18.30, before the aiming-point became obscured beneath brown and black smoke at 18.33. Green TIs were dropped, but soon also disappeared, and remaining crews were instructed to bomb the centre of the smoke. Large explosions were witnessed at 18.28 and 18.34, and the town was left burning fiercely to leave a smoke cloud that remained visible for a hundred miles into the return flight. Few details emerged from local sources, but it is known that the docks area was particularly hard-hit, and shipping sunk.

As the above attack was beginning at Emden at 18.24, 325 miles to the west the Master Bomber and Deputy pairing of W/C Morrison and S/L Perry were departing Gransden Lodge with the visual backer-up crews of F/L Johnston and F/O Cadegan bound for A/P 6 at Le Havre. They were part of an overall force of 344 aircraft assigned to six aiming-points, at which four Path Finder Lancasters and five Oboe Mosquitos would provide the marking. They reached the target to find ten-tenths stratus with a base at around 8,000 feet and W/C Morrison initially gave a "basement" of 10,000 feet, while he flew around at heights from 5,200 down to 3,000 feet assessing the conditions, which he ultimately found to be unacceptable and sent the force home with their bombs. Conditions at the other aiming points were more favourable and the attacks were deemed to be successful.

There was an early start for crews participating in the next round of attacks on five German positions around Le Havre on the 8th, for which 8 Group put up twenty-eight Lancasters and twenty-five Oboe Mosquitos in an overall 1, 3 and 8 Group force of 333 aircraft. The four Stirlings would be the very last to conduct a bombing operation, although the type would remain in Bomber Command service for SOE operations from Tempsford. The Gransden Lodge element consisted of W/C Morrison and S/L Perry as Master Bomber and Deputy and the crews of F/Ls Johnston and Whittall and F/O Cadegan as backers-up, and they took off between 06.57 and 07.01 bound for A/P 13. The weather conditions were not promising as they approached the target area over ten-tenths cumulus with a base at 1,500 feet and topping out at 8,000 feet, but green Oboe TIs were observed through a break in the cloud and assessed to be up to three hundred yards to the east of the aiming point. W/C Morrison ordered the main force to orbit, while he descended into the murk and was at 3,000 feet on his fourth run across the aiming point and still in cloud when hit by three bursts of flak, which severely damaged the starboard wing and started a fierce fire. The Lancaster became uncontrollable, and the order was given to abandon it to its fate, W/C Morrison the last to leave, and all eight occupants arrived safely on the ground, seven of them close to the Allied lines, while PA970 crashed on the shore to the north of the port and the rear gunner fell into enemy hands. Somehow, F/L Johnston and crew were able to identify woods immediately to the south-east of the aiming point and bombed from 4,800 feet at 08.13, leaving the others from the squadron to bring their bombs home. It was a similar story at the other aiming points and only a third of the main force carried out an attack, and even then, more in hope than expectation. The Morrison crew was back home in two to three days, and W/O Kuviak followed them a few days later after being liberated when the German garrison surrendered.

Four aiming-points were earmarked for attention at Le Havre on the morning of the 9th, involving a total of twenty-two 8 Group Lancasters and twenty Oboe Mosquitos marking for 230 Halifaxes of 4 and 6 Groups. Yet again the weather intervened, and the force was sent home with its bombs.

By the 10th the weather over northern France had improved, and a massive effort involving 992 aircraft was mounted by the Command to deal with eight enemy positions during the afternoon and evening. The aiming-points were given the names of a car manufacturers, Buick 1 and 2, Alvis 1, 2, 3 and 4 and Bentley 1 and 2, and 8 Group was to provide forty Lancasters and forty-one Mosquitos to carry out the marking, with a Master Bomber and Deputy and three backers-up at each. 405 (Vancouver) squadron briefed five crews for Alvis 3 with S/L Perry and F/L Johnston the designated Master Bomber and Deputy and the crews of F/L Whittall and F/Os Cadegan and Tite performing the role of visual backers-up. They departed Gransden Lodge between 16.09 and 16.13 and arrived in the target area under clear skies and with excellent visibility and carried out their respective tasks from 9,000 to 10,000 feet between 17.17 and 17.32. The TIs fell at various locations within a few hundred yards of the aiming point and S/L Perry remained on hand to direct the 3 Group main force crews with instructions to over or undershoot accordingly. All operations were concluded successfully, and no aircraft were lost.

The 11th would bring the final attacks on the environs of the port, and involve 218 aircraft drawn from 4, 5, 6 and 8 Groups at two aiming-points with 8 Group contributing five 35 (Madras Presidency) Squadron Lancasters and five Oboe Mosquitos to each, coded Cadillac 1 and Cadillac 2, and an eleventh Lancaster captained by W/C Whetham, who had been designated "Long Stop Master Bomber", to intervene to cancel any misplaced markers.

During the early afternoon, four crews attended briefing at Gransden Lodge to learn of a daunting task facing them a little later, that would require them to present themselves over the heart of the Ruhr in broad daylight. They learned that the targets for 379 aircraft were synthetic oil refineries, the Nordstern (Gelsenberg A G) plant at Gelsenkirchen, the Klöckner Werke A G at Castrop-Rauxel ten miles to the north-east and the Chemischewerke-Essener-Steinkohle A G fifteen miles further to the east at Bergkamen, for which 8 Group committed nineteen Lancasters and ten Mosquitos to the first-two-mentioned and fifteen Lancasters to the last. The crews were no doubt comforted by the news that they would be protected by twenty squadrons of Spitfires and three each of Mustangs and Tempests. The crews of F/Os Dix, Kyte and Woods and P/O McIntyre took off between 16.57 and 16.59 as main force supporters, each with a cookie and sixteen 500-pounders in their bomb bays and joined up with the 6 Group main force of 105 Halifaxes as they made their way out. Nine of the ten Oboe Mosquitos turned back with equipment failure, leaving just one to mark the target, and it was left largely to the Master Bomber to deliver red TIs, which fell some four hundred yards to the north-east of the aiming point. The main force element reached the target area under largely clear skies and complied with the Master Bomber's instructions to bomb four hundred yards to starboard of the red TIs. The 405 (Vancouver) Squadron contingent delivered their attacks from 18,000 to 19,000 feet between 18.42 and 18.47 and contributed to the 354 tons of high explosives that straddled the aiming point and caused a particularly large explosion that emitted a column of thick, black smoke.

That night, 5 Group delivered a crushing blow on the university city of Darmstadt in southern Germany, which destroyed the city centre and neighbouring districts, and set off a firestorm in which more than twelve thousand people perished and seventy thousand were rendered homeless out of a total population of 120,000.

The oil offensive continued on the 12th with briefings on 4, 6 and 8 Group stations for raids on the Hydrierwerke refinery at Scholven-Buer to the north of Gelsenkirchen, the Krupp Treibstoffwerke at Wanne-Eickel to the east and the Hoesch-Benzin plant a dozen miles further east in the Wambel district of Dortmund. 8 Group detailed nineteen Lancasters and fourteen Mosquitos to mark for a 4 Group main force of 134 Halifaxes at Scholven-Buer, nineteen Lancasters and fourteen Mosquitos for the 6 Group target at Wanne-Eickel, both early afternoon attacks, and five Lancasters and eight Mosquitos at Dortmund in the early evening. A dozen 405 (Vancouver) Squadron crews attended briefing, when S/L Perry and F/L Johnston were appointed Master Bomber and Deputy for the Wanne-Eickel raid, with three others as visual backers-up and seven as main force supporters. They departed Gransden Lodge between 12.08 and 12.18 with W/C Palmer the senior pilot on duty and a bombload of a cookie and sixteen 500 pounders in each of the main force support aircraft. Ten Mosquitos and four Lancasters turned back early, and PA981 crashed near Gladbeck-Butendorf on the northern approach to the target at 13.30, probably after being hit by flak, and F/O Sovran RCAF and three others of his predominently RCAF crew fell into enemy hands as the only survivors. The others reached the target to encounter clear skies but an effective smoke screen, into which the Oboe Mosquitos dropped green TIs, while others dispensed "window". At 13.58, F/L Johnston dropped red TIs onto the aiming-point, which were backed up with yellows that quickly disappeared into the smoke. The Gransden Lodge crews carried out their attacks from 15,500 to 16,500 feet between 13.57 and 14.06 in the face of intense predicted and barrage flak, before returning safely to report their impressions. The volume of smoke and many explosions suggested a successful outcome at a cost of three Lancasters and a Halifax.

That night, Frankfurt was posted as the target for a force of 378 Lancasters and nine Mosquitos from 1, 3 and 8 Groups, while a predominantly 5 Group raid took place at Stuttgart, some eighty miles to the south. The nine 405 (Vancouver) Squadron crews had been briefed for blind marker duties, five with additional illuminator responsibilities and F/Ls Burnand, Ellison, Long and Smith were the senior pilots on duty as they departed Gransden Lodge between 19.01 and 19.24. The weather outbound was clear all the way, enabling the crews to map-read their way across France to enter Germany south of Luxembourg, and the first flares went down over Frankfurt at 22.52 to illuminate ground detail. Mixed red and green TIs cascaded as the first main force crews bore down on the aiming-point, and these were backed up promptly and continuously throughout the attack. The 405 (Vancouver) Squadron crews carried out their assigned tasks from 17,000 to 18,500 feet between 22.51 and 23.07, and on return were able to report a pall of smoke rising through 5,000 feet as they turned away, and fires visible a hundred miles and more into the homeward journey. They also reported fires still burning in Darmstadt, where, apparently, most of Frankfurt's fire service was still active. Post-raid reconnaissance established that Frankfurt's western districts had sustained severe damage, where industrial and residential property suffered equally, but this had been achieved at the high cost of seventeen Lancasters, one of them belonging to 8 Group. A similar story of destruction emerged after the Stuttgart crews landed, and local sources would confirm that the northern and western districts had been devastated, in part by a minor firestorm.

Two simultaneous operations were scheduled for 8 Group by daylight on the 13th, the larger one involving twenty-eight Lancasters and ten Mosquitos marking the Nordstern oil refinery at Gelsenkirchen for 102 Halifaxes of 4 Group, while twenty Lancasters were prepared to attack marshalling yards and the town at Osnabrück in company with a main force of ninety-eight 6 Group Halifaxes. 405 (Vancouver) Squadron made ready six Lancasters for main force support duties over the Ruhr and sent them on their way from Gransden Lodge between 16.31 and 16.36 with no senior pilots on duty and a cookie and sixteen 500-pounders in each bomb bay. They arrived at the target to find four to seven-tenths cloud with tops at up to 15,000 feet, and once the raid began, haze and an effective smoke screen combined to create challenging conditions for the Master Bomber, who was was unable to see the red TIs and had to rely on information passed by the Deputy. The order was issued to the main force to aim for any reds they could see, and the Gransden Lodge crews complied from 18,000 to 19,000 feet between 18.27 and 18.29, some observing large explosions but insufficient detail to make an assessment of the outcome.

On the 14th 4 and 6 Groups assembled a main force of 163 Halifaxes and Lancasters and briefed their crews for an attack on the port and town of Wilhelmshaven, while twenty-one 8 Group Lancaster crews learned of their part in proceedings. The seven 405 (Vancouver) Squadron participants departed Gransden Lodge between 16.41 and 16.50 with S/L Gosman the senior pilot on duty and had reached the Waddenzee between the Frisian Island of Vlieland and the Dutch mainland near Harlingen when the entire force was recalled for an undisclosed reason.

A force of 490 aircraft from 1, 4, 6 and 8 Groups was assembled for a raid on Kiel on the 15th, among them fifty-seven Lancasters and seven Mosquitos belonging to 8 Group, a dozen of the former made ready by 405 (Vancouver) Squadron, whose crews were briefed for a variety of illuminating and marking duties. They departed Gransden Lodge between 22.23 and 22.42 with S/L Gosman the senior pilot on duty and flew out in poor weather conditions, which persisted over the North Sea, but had improved in the target area on Schleswig-Holstein's Baltic coast, where clear skies prevailed. Most crews were able to pick out some ground detail, aided by illuminator flares, and the first red and green TIs from the primary visual markers went down onto the aiming-point at 01.10, to be backed up with yellows. A smoke screen was activated, but the TIs remained visible throughout, and fires had gained a hold by the time the force retreated to the west, with the glow from the burning town still visible from Denmark's western coast 120 miles away. On return, the Gransden Lodge crews reported carrying out their assigned tasks from 15,000 to 18,500 feet between 01.06 and 01.22 and expressed confidence in the success of their night's work. Bombing photos were plotted at between two and four miles to the north-east of the planned aiming-point, and two explosions were witnessed at 01.20 and 01.23, which emitted large amounts of smoke. A post-raid analysis based on the bombing photos revealed extensive damage to the old town and port area, and this was confirmed by local reports, which also commented on the number of bombs falling outside of the built-up area. The operation cost 405 (Vancouver) Squadron the predominantly RAF crew of F/L Long RCAF, who all died, when PB527 crashed off the Danish coast. The navigator, F/L Brook, and the bomb-aimer, P/O Edwards, were each decorated with the DFC, and rear gunner F/Sgt Gowdey was just seventeen years old.

The ill-fated Operation Market Garden began on the morning of the 17th, in the wake of attacks on enemy airfields and gun positions by elements of 1, 3 and 8 Groups during the night. Early briefings across the Command on that morning prepared 762 crews for operations against enemy troop positions at seven locations around Boulogne, the next port earmarked to be wrested from enemy control. The raids would be staggered over a four-hour period and benefit from an 8 Group contribution of five Lancasters and five Oboe Mosquito at each aiming-point, the first of which, 1A, would be attacked twice. The sequence of attacks was to begin with 1A and continue with 1B, 1C, 1A again, and then 5, 3, 2 and finally 4, and it was for the second attack on A/P 1A that five 405 (Vancouver) Squadron Lancasters departed Granden Lodge between 08.50 and 08.56 with S/Ls Perry and Gosman the designated Master Bomber and Deputy and the others as backers-up. On arrival at the target the expected green TIs were not visible, but their smoke trails could be traced and bomb craters from the earlier attack were clearly visible. The 405 (Vancouver) Squadron participants carried out their respective roles from 8,500 to 10,500 feet between 09.36 and 09.50 and returned home reasonably satisfied with their morning's work. An analysis confirmed that most of the aiming-points had been dealt with successfully, although some crews had been hampered by drifting smoke. A total of three thousand tons of bombs had proved sufficient to pave the way for Allied ground forces to begin their advance and a week later accept the surrender of the German garrison. This left only Calais of the major French ports still under enemy occupation.

During the previous night, Bomber Command had committed more than 250 Lancasters and Mosquitos to support Operation Market Garden, the ultimately ill-fated "bridge too far" endeavour to cross the Rhine and break into Germany. The targets had been Luftwaffe aerodromes in Holland and flak batteries on Walcheren at the mouth of the Scheldt, and further attacks on the batteries were scheduled for the early evening of the 17th. The crews of S/L Gosman and F/L Whittall attended a briefing to be informed that they were to perform the roles of Master Bomber and Deputy at Biggekerke, one of three aiming points earmarked for attention by 106 Lancasters of 1 Group in company with twenty 8 Group Mosquitos. The 405 (Vancouver) Squadron duo departed Gransden Lodge at 17.15 and arrived at the target under clear skies and in visibility that enabled them to visually identify the canal and villages and deliver their marker and high explosive ordnance from 9,000 to 12,000 feet between 18.12 and 18.14. The bombing appeared to be concentrated around the aiming points, but smoke and dust soon obscured the sites, and it would be left to post-raid reconnaissance to confirm the elimination of the targets.

Bremerhaven wilted under its first heavy raid of the war on the 18/19th at the hands of a 5 Group force of two hundred Lancasters. Accurate low-level marking by the Mosquito element led to the destruction of over 2,600 buildings, as the central and port areas in particular were razed by fire.

The time had now arrived to turn attention upon Calais as the final port still under enemy occupation and 646 crews attended briefings across the Command on the 20th, among them seventy Lancaster and forty Mosquito crews of 8 Group, who would lead attacks on five aiming-points, three of them receiving two visits. At Gransden Lodge, the crews of F/Os Cadegan, Friedman, McDonald and Tite were briefed to perform the role of supporters at aiming point 6A, for which their Lancasters each received a bomb load of eleven 1,000 and four 500-pounders. Aiming-points 6A, 6B and 6C were to face two attacks, which would open at thirty-minute intervals from 16.00 and it was for the second wave on 6A that the 405 (Vancouver) Squadron quartet took off between

16.28 and 16.31, to be followed a minute later by S/Ls Perry and Gosman as Master Bomber and Deputy for the second attack on aiming point 6B, leaving the remaining six squadron participants on the ground until their departure in a supporter role between 16.47 and 16.54. They were greeted at the French coast by clear skies and a little haze, through which the aiming-points could be identified visually by ground features. The first element carried out their assigned tasks from 6,700 to 8,800 feet between 17.18 and 17.26, and the second from 5,000 to 9,400 feet between 17.36 and 17.47, and all returned safely to report accurate and concentrated attacks.

Access to the Belgian port of Antwerp was blocked by heavy gun emplacements on the island of Walcheren at the mouth of the Scheldt and the first of a number of operations was mounted against them by 6 and 8 Groups on the 18th, when adverse weather conditions forced the attempt to be abandoned before any bombing took place. A second try on the 19th was recalled, and it was not until the 23rd that conditions were right for another go when 6 Group provided the main force of thirty-four Halifaxes and three Lancasters for the attack on the Domburg battery. 8 Group provided the services of S/L Gosman and the newly promoted S/L Johnston as Master Bomber and Deputy and F/L Whittall and crew as backers-up. They departed Gransden Lodge between 16.02 and 16.04 and were greeted at the target by three-tenths cloud, through which they were able to visually identify the aiming point and deliver their respective marker and high explosive ordnance from 8,200 to 9,000 feet between 16.57 and 16.59.

That night's activities involved a return to targets in Germany, with the main fare an attack on the Ruhr city of Neuss, situated on the western bank of the Rhine opposite Düsseldorf on the southern edge of the region, for which a force of 549 aircraft was drawn from 1, 3, 4 and 8 Groups. While this was in progress, seventy miles to the north-east, 5 Group would be engaged at two targets, the twin aqueduct section of the Dortmund-Ems Canal near Ladbergen and the nearby Handorf Luftwaffe aerodrome, for which a total of 243 Lancasters and ten Mosquitos was detailed. 8 Group made ready fifteen Lancasters and seventeen Mosquitos for Neuss, but the sensitivity of the Oboe equipment led to the early return of ten Mosquitos, leaving the others to drop their red TIs into the tops of the ten-tenths cloud that lay over the target at up to 10,000 feet. It was not possible to form an impression of what was happening on the ground, and Bomber Command claimed that the main weight of bombs had fallen into the Rhine docks and industrial areas. Local sources reported that 617 houses and fourteen public buildings had been destroyed, and this was achieved at a cost of five Lancasters and two Halifaxes.

The assault on enemy positions around Calais resumed on the 24th, when five aiming-points were briefed out to 188 Lancaster, Halifax and Mosquito crews, who learned that the attacks would follow a sequence beginning at A/P 8, and continuing through 10, 11 and 9 before ending at 12. On 8 Group stations, sixteen Lancaster and twenty-five Mosquito crews were assigned to their targets, 405 (Vancouver) Squadron providing the Master Bomber and Deputy for aiming-point 11 in the form of S/Ls Perry and Johnston, with F/O Kettlewell and crew to back-up. They departed Gransden Lodge between 17.11 and 17.29 and found the target to be concealed beneath ten-tenths low cloud, initially with little defensive response. However, after orbiting out to sea in rain showers and approaching the aiming point at around 1,800 feet, the light flak became intense and accurate and S/L Johnston reported that he had been forced to pull out of his bombing run. S/L Perry also pulled away and the combination of murderous flak and poor bombing conditions persuaded him to abandon the operation, the instruction to the main force Halifaxes transmitted from 18.07 to

18.13, despite which, a number of Halifaxes were observed to continue towards the aiming point. A post-raid analysis revealed that 126 of 163 main force crews had bombed their respective aiming points, mostly on Oboe skymarkers, and of those descending to the cloud base and into the jaws of the light flak batteries, seven Lancasters and a Halifax had been shot down.

The first of 872 aircraft targeting nine aiming-points around Calais on the 25th took off at dawn and would continue until shortly before 09.30. 8 Group detailed fifty-two Lancasters and forty-five Mosquitos, eight of the former made ready at Gransden Lodge, three for aiming point 2B and five for 3A. F/Ls Herbert and O'Connor and F/O Kyte took off for the former between 07.32 and 07.34, each loaded with eleven 1,000 and four 500-pounders to deliver as part of the main force. They arrived at the target to find nine-tenths cloud with tops at around 6,000 feet and were ordered to orbit while the Master Bomber assessed the situation. Some gound features were visible through breaks in the cloud, but the Master Bomber was not comfortable with the conditions and abandoned the operation at 08.24. S/Ls Perry and Gosman departed Gransden Lodge at 09.03 as the designated Master Bomber and Deputy, and they were followed into the air between 09.48 and 09.54 by the crews of W/C Palmer, F/L Whittall and F/O Kettlewell, who had been briefed to perform the role of visual backers-up. Clear skies over the Channel and French coast gave way to nine to ten-tenths low cloud at the target and S/Ls Perry and Gosman went in closely behind another element, which aborted its run and turned for home. S/L Perry instructed the main force to orbit while he assessed the situation, and S/L Gosman reported that he had dropped TIs and four 1,000-pounders from 5,500 feet at 10.51, but believed that they had undershot, and with cloud building, S/L Perry sent the force home. In the event, only a third of the overall force bombed through breaks in the cloud, but it was only a matter of time before the ultimate result was achieved.

Nine separate attacks were briefed out to the crews of 722 aircraft across the Command during the early morning of the 26th, 531 to target four coastal batteries at Cap Gris-Nez, situated some ten miles along the coast to the west of Calais, and 191 to attack enemy positions closer to the port. 8 Group provided five Oboe Mosquitos for each aiming-point, and twelve Lancasters at A/P 7C, four at A/Ps 9, 10 and 8 and five for a second attack on 7C, all at Cap Gris-Nez. The group also detailed four Lancasters for the first crack at A/P 7B, five for the second, six for 7A and five for 7D. 405 (Vancouver) Squadron briefed the crews of F/L Vann, F/O Dix and P/O McIntyre to act as main force supporters at A/P 7C and sent them on their way from Gransden Lodge between 08.51 and 08.57, each with eleven 1,000 and four 500-pounders beneath their feet. They arrived in the target area in company with the 1 Group main force under clear skies with visibility at fifteen miles and delivered their bomb loads mostly onto red TIs from 6,000 to 6,400 feet between 10.05 and 10.11.

They were back home before the second element took off for A/P 7D between 11.41 and 12.01 with S/Ls Perry and Gosman the designated Master Bomber and Deputy, and the crews of W/C Palmer, F/L Whittall and F/O Kettlewell as visual backers-up. They encountered five to six-tenths cloud with a base initially at 3,000 feet, but it began to clear rapidly, and the main force was called in to bomb on red TIs, which soon became obscured by smoke and dust and the "Long Stop" controller called for a brief halt to allow the smoke to clear before the tail end of the main force completed the job. The 405 (Vancouver) Squadron element fulfilled their respective briefs from 2,400 to 3,000 feet between 12.36 and 12.55 and arrived back at base to discover that the crew of W/C Palmer DFC RCAF was not with them. It seems that his Lancaster, PB129, had been brought down by flak to crash in Allied-held territory, and he was killed along with four others of the eight men on board, while two escaped injury and one required hospital treatment. It was W/C Palmer's thirty-eighth sortie, and his loss was a blow to the squadron, which now passed into the hands of W/C Morrison as his successor, but as he was approaching the end of a long tour, his time at the helm would be brief.

Crews were roused early from their beds on the 27th, and, no doubt, expected to be briefed for the next round of attacks on enemy positions around Calais. 341 crews from 1, 3, 4 and 8 Groups, including three belonging to 405 (Vancouver) Squadron, had their expectations fulfilled, while 346 others from 6 and 8 Groups discovered that they would be divided more-or-less equally between the destinations of Bottrop and Sterkrade-Holten, situated within six miles of each other on the northern edge of the Ruhr to the north of Duisburg and Essen. The targets were the Ruhröl A G and Ruhr Benzin synthetic oil plants, for which 8 Group detailed twenty-five Lancasters and eight Oboe Mosquitos and twenty-one Lancasters and seven Mosquitos respectively. 405 (Vancouver) Squadron made ready nine Lancasters for the former, and they departed Gransden Lodge between 07.57 and 08.05 with S/L Gosman and F/L Whittall the designated Master Bomber and Deputy, two crews as backers-up and five to bomb with the main force. They arrived in the target area over what some crews described as ten-tenths thin stratocumulus cloud with tops at 6,000 to 8,000 feet, while others found breaks that provided a glimpse of the ground and a red TI. They established their positions based on DR, H2S or by observing other aircraft, and were instructed by S/L Gosman to bomb by whatever means suited them. F/L Whittall was experiencing problems with his H2S, and his main reference was smoke trails from TIs disappearing into the cloud after picking up a brief glimpse of a canal south of the target. A large explosion was observed at 09.38 and was followed by yellow flames and pitch-black smoke and it was after this that the Gransden Lodge participants carried out their respective tasks from 18,000 to 20,200 feet between 09.27 and 09.31 and were among only a handful from 8 Group to carry out an attack. The mushroom of black smoke had risen to two thousand feet above the cloudtops and was estimated at a mile across. A similar story of challenging conditions emerged from the crews returning from Sterkrade, where the aiming-point had emerged briefly then disappeared and the Master Bomber cancelled then reinstated the attack, before instructing any with bombs still on board to seek out alternative targets.

The final operations to clear the enemy from the Calais area took place on the 28th, and involved 494 aircraft from 1, 3, 6 and 8 Groups targeting four positions around the port and six coastal batteries at Cap Gris-Nez. 8 Group contributed thirty-four Lancasters and fifty Oboe Mosquitos and they flew out under clear skies until some five miles short of the French coast, where they were greeted by nine to ten-tenths cloud with tops at 3,000 feet, which caused some of the attacks to be aborted. 35 (Madras Presidency) Squadron's S/L Leicester took off that evening at 17.15 as the designated Long Stop Master Bomber for the final attacks on enemy positions, for which the 405 (Vancouver) Squadron pair of S/L Gosman and F/L Whittall were to perform the role of Master Bomber and Deputy at A/P 7B at Cap Gris Nez with the crew of F/L Burnand as backers-up, while S/L Perry and F/O Kettlewell were to carry out similar duties at A/P 7C with the crew of F/L Herbert as their backers-up. They departed Gransden Lodge together between 17.47 and 18.04 and the latter section arrived at the target on the heels of the preceeding force, which began to orbit while the Master Bomber and Deputy assessed their options. This meant that S/L Perry had to issue instructions to his main force to orbit also, above the cloud at 8,000 feet, and for F/O

Kettlewell to withhold his TIs. Eventually massed red and green TIs were scattered across a wide area and S/L Perry reluctantly abandoned the operation at 18.45, by which time only F/O Kettlewell and crew had delivered their four 1,000-pounders from 2,700 feet at 18.43. S/L Gosman was unable to identify A/P 7B and also decided to send the main force home with their bombs. Some of the other attacks were successful, and the German garrison surrendered to Canadian ground forces soon afterwards. However, there was much hard work ahead to clear and repair the ports at Le Havre, Boulogne and Calais, and the port of Antwerp also needed to be liberated to speed up the supply of equipment to the front for the push into Germany.

The final operation of the month for 405 (Vancouver) Squadron involved nine crews in a return to Bottrop as part of an 8 Group force of twenty-five Lancasters and ten Mosquitos marking for a 4 Group main force of 101 Halifaxes. 8 Group also put up twenty-one Lancasters and ten Mosquitos to mark for a similarly sized 6 Group main force at Sterkrade-Holten some three miles to the west. The Gransden Lodge element took off between 10.18 and 10.26 with F/Ls McQuoid and Whittall the Master Bomber and Deputy, two crews to act as visual backers-up and five as main force supporters. The target area was found to be covered by nine-to ten-tenths cloud with tops in places as high as 12,000 feet, which persuaded F/L McQuoid to instruct crews at 11.57 to bomb on navigational aids or seek out alternative targets. The 405 (Vancouver) Squadron element remained in close contact as it passed over the aiming point and bombed on estimated positions in the general target area from 18,000 to 20,400 feet between 11.58 and 12.04. Although the main force arrived some five minutes behind schedule, they were in a coherent formation and their bombing should have been concentrated in the right general area.

During the course of the month the squadron carried out twenty-four operations and dispatched 211 sorties for the loss of four Lancasters and three crews.

October 1944

Having now discharged his primary obligation to SHAEF, Harris would now turn his attention once more fully towards industrial Germany, with a particular emphasis on oil production. Following a hectic month in September, the first four days of the new month passed without operational activity for 405 (Vancouver) Squadron. A theme running throughout October would be a campaign against the island of Walcheren in the Scheldt estuary, where heavy gun emplacements were barring the approaches to the much-needed port of Antwerp some forty miles upstream. Attempts to bomb these positions in September had proved unsuccessful, and it was decided to flood the land, both to inundate the batteries and to render the terrain difficult to defend when the ground forces moved in. A force of 252 Lancasters was drawn from 1, 5 and 8 Groups and made ready on the 3rd to attack the seawalls at Westkapelle, the most westerly point of the island. Eight waves of thirty aircraft each took off, accompanied by the Tallboy-carrying Lancasters of 617 Squadron, which would stand off to be called in only if required. A breach was opened by the fifth wave, which was extended by those following behind, and the flood waters had reached the town by the time the last Lancasters turned for home.

While a 5 Group force carried out a scattered attack on Wilhelmshaven on the morning of the 5th, 531 other aircraft of 1, 3 and 8 Groups were being prepared for a two-phase operation that night against Saarbrücken in south-west-central Germany, the first attack on this city for two years. The purpose of the first phase, to be delivered by 184 Lancasters of 3 Group and a sprinkling of 101 Squadron ABC Lancasters, was to hit the marshalling yards to cut enemy rail communications to the advancing American Third Army. The second phase, by 1 Group two hours later, was to be directed at the city, and 8 Group's ninety-six Lancasters and twenty Mosquitos were to be divided equally between the two phases to establish and maintain the aiming-points. 405 (Vancouver) Squadron dispatched sixteen Lancasters from Gransden Lodge as part of the first phase between 17.20 and 17.37 with S/Ls Gosman and Mussells the senior pilots on duty, the last-mentioned, a new addition to the squadron and one of four crews assigned to bomb with the main force, while the remainder were briefed for the usual variety of marking roles from illuminating to blind and visual marking and recentering. They encountered ten-tenths low cloud as they made their way across France, until shortly before the German frontier, when it became thin and broken and had cleared almost completely over the target to leave ground haze to significantly impair the vertical visibility. The Master Bomber and Deputy descended to 10,000 feet in an attempt to identify aiming-point A, the marshalling yards, but the flares were scattered and provided insufficient illumination. Some crews observed red and green TIs, but the majority bombed on H2S, the Gransden Lodge crews mostly carrying out their respective tasks from 13,000 to 19,000 feet between 20.22 and 20.40. F/O Hannah and crew picked up unsatisfactory returns from their H2S equipment during the pass over the aiming point and dropped their hardware on St-Ingbert some six miles to the north-east. There was a suggestion that the Master Bomber and Deputy disagreed as to which markers on the railway yards were accurate, and only 50% of the crews had bombed by the time he broadcast the codeword "Marmalade" to end proceedings at 20.33. The attack on the town proceeded according to plan and caused massive damage, local reports revealing that 5,882 houses had been destroyed, largely in the Altstadt and Malstatt districts, but the relatively modest death toll of 344 people suggested that what was now a front-line city, had been partially evacuated.

Nine crews attended briefing at Gransden Lodge on the morning of the 6th to learn that they were part of two 8 Group elements, both of twenty-three Lancasters and ten Mosquitos, whose job was to mark the Ruhr-Benzin A G and Hydrierwerke-Scholven oil plants at Sterkrade-Holten and Scholven-Buer respectively for a combined 4 Group Halifax force of 254 aircraft. Bound for the former, two as backers-up and seven as main force supporters, they took off between 15.11 and 15.21 with another recent arrival, S/L Marcou, the senior pilot on duty and reached the target under clear skies and in good visibility that enabled them to make a visual identification based on ground features like the Rhine. Red TIs were seen to cascade over the target at 17.11, followed later by yellows, and the 405 (Vancouver) Squadron crews delivered their cookie and four 1,000-pounders of eighteen 500-pounders each from 16,500 to 21,000 feet between 17.11 and 17.17. A number of large explosions were observed, and smoke was rising through 4,000 feet as they turned away.

A second Ruhr campaign opened at Dortmund later on the 6th, for which a 3, 6 and 8 Group force of 523 aircraft was made ready. 5 Group had its own target and prepared 237 Lancasters and seven Mosquitos for what would prove to be the thirty-second and final raid of the war on the city of Bremen. At Gransden Lodge, seven Lancasters were made prepared for Dortmund as part of the 8 Group contribution of thirty-one Lancasters and twenty-eight Mosquitos, and they took off between 17.15 and 17.21 with pilots of flight lieutenant rank leading the way. Three were assigned as blind sky markers, one as a blind marker and three as backers-up and they arrived at the eastern end of the Ruhr to find clear skies and the expected industrial haze. The Oboe Mosquitos delivered

red TIs, starting at 20.20, and these were backed up by green TIs, which fell in concentrated fashion to provide an 800-yard-square carpet for the main force crews to aim at. Six of the 405 (Vancouver) Squadron crews performed as briefed from 17,000 to 19,000 feet between 20.23 and 20.34, before returning to report a number of explosions and fires taking hold. At debriefing, F/L O'Connor and crew reported that their H2S was providing poor returns and while approaching the final turning point, they observed flares well to the north, for which they headed. On e.t.a., the flares were still some distance away, but they continued on until observing the start of an attack astern of their position, but too far away to reach in time. A built-up area appeared on the H2S screen, and this was bombed from 15,300 feet at 20.33 and was plotted later to be Osnabrück. A reconnaissance Mosquito crew brought back confirmation of a devastating attack on Dortmund, which caused massive damage to residential and industrial districts and severely afflicted the transportation system.

Following the failure of Operation Market Garden, the German frontier towns of Cleves (Kleve) and Emmerich were earmarked for attention by daylight on the 7th. Five miles apart and separated by the Rhine, both would suffer massive damage at the hands of large forces from 1, 3, 4 and 8 Groups. 8 Group provided eleven Lancasters and eleven Mosquitos for each, but Gransden Lodge was not required to take part and would remain operationally inactive for the ensuing four days. In the meantime, G/C Newson took full control of 405 (Vancouver) Squadron on the 9th, and thus became the unit's final wartime commander. G/C Newson was an experienced operational pilot, who had been a flight commander with 408 (Goose) Squadron at the start of the first Ruhr campaign back in March 1943, and commanded 431 (Iroquois) Squadron at Croft until the middle of May 1944. After a magnificent operational career, his predecessor, W/C Morrison, was posted to a personnel dispatch centre for repatriation to Canada.

Focus remained on the Scheldt defences at this time, and the gun battery at Fort Frederik Hendrik near Breskens on the East Scheldt was earmarked for attention by elements of 1 and 8 Groups on the 11th, while 115 Lancasters from 5 Group were assigned to others near Flushing on the northern bank of the western Scheldt. At the same time, sixty-one Lancasters and two Mosquitos from 5 Group were to attempt to breach the seawalls at Veere, situated on the eastern side of Walcheren opposite Westkapelle. 405 (Vancouver) Squadron made ready five Lancasters for A/P 2 at the Fort Frederik Hendrik battery, and they departed Gransden Lodge between 15.49 and 15.55 with F/L McQuoid and F/O Kettlewell the Master Bomber and deputy, F/L Whittall in the "Longstop" role and the others as backers-up. A blanket of ten-tenths cloud lay over the Scheldt on their arrival with tops at 3,500 feet, but F/L McQuoid was able to venture under the cloud base and direct the marking and bombing. The 405 (Vancouver) Squadron crews carried out their assigned tasks from 3,600 to 5,000 feet between 16.48 and 16.58 and the main force performed well to deliver most of their bombs on the aiming point. Meanwhile, the attack on A/P 1 was unsuccessful due to the low cloud base and was abandoned.

An early start for nine 35 (Madras Presidency) Squadron crews on the 12th had them in the briefing room while darkness still cloaked Graveley. They were briefed for a return to the Fort Frederik Hendrik coastal battery, which was to be attacked by a 1 Group main force of eighty Lancasters in two waves, fifteen minutes apart. Meanwhile, over at Gransden Lodge the crews of S/L Marcou and F/Os Hartley, Larson and McIntyre were being briefed for an attack on the Krupp Treibstoffwerke oil plant at Wanne-Eickel, where they would join up with twenty-two other 8 Group Lancasters and ten Oboe Mosquitos ahead of a main force of 111 Halifaxes of 6 Group.

They took off between 08.20 and 08.25, each sitting on eleven 1,000 and four 500 pounders to deliver as part of the main force and arrived at the target to find clear skies and the oil plant easily identifiable by ground features. The TIs fell in an arc from north-west to south-east, and smoke from them quickly obscured the ground, forcing the Master Bomber to direct the later bombing towards the centre of the smoke. The 405 (Vancouver) Squadron crews were divided between two aiming points and carried out their attacks on red TIs from 17,000 to 19,000 feet between 10.13 and 10.15 in accordance with the Master Bomber's instructions and observed a direct hit on an oil storage tank at 10.12 that sent thick, black smoke curling skywards. It proved difficult to make an accurate assessment of the outcome, and local sources would claim little damage to the plant, while the GAVEG chemical factory, also engaged in the manufacture of synthetic oil products, was reported as destroyed.

The 14th was the day on which were fired the opening salvoes of Operation Hurricane, a terrifying demonstration to the enemy of the overwhelming superiority of the Allied air forces ranged against it. Bomber Command ordered a maximum effort from all but 5 Group to attack Duisburg, for which 1,013 Lancasters, Halifaxes and Mosquitos answered the call. The American 8th Air Force would also be in business on this day, targeting the Cologne area further south with 1,250 bombers escorted by 749 fighters. 8 Group briefed eighty-seven Lancaster crews for five aiming-points, including one recorded as "special", and twenty Mosquito crews for aiming-points P, S, R and Q. The thirteen 405 (Vancouver) Squadron crews were assigned to four aiming points, six as supporters for the "special" with S/L Marcou the senior pilot among them, four for Q as blind markers, two for P, one as a primary visual marker and the other as a backer-up and F/O Kettlewell as a primary visual marker at R. They took off between 07.08 and 07.36 to join the elongated bomber stream over the North Sea, where they were met by an RAF fighter escort that would shepherd them all the way to the target. The force arrived over the western edge of the Ruhr to find drifting cloud in layers at between 8,000 and 14,000 feet, and the Gransden Lodge participants carried out their assigned tasks from 16,600 to 20,400 feet between 08.43 and 09.09. The Master Bomber at P was unable to identify the aiming-point and instructed the main force crews at 08.42 to bomb the built-up area, only for the cloud to part briefly five minutes later, and for one minute only he was able to redirect them to the aiming-point. Thereafter, between 08.47 and 08.52, he redirected them to the general built-up area, where the bombing appeared to be somewhat scattered. It was a similar story at the other aiming-points, but 4,500 tons of high-explosives and incendiaries fell into the city to cause unimaginable destruction.

A force of 1,005 aircraft was assembled to continue Duisburg's ordeal that night, of which fifteen Lancasters belonged to 405 (Vancouver) Squadron as part of an 8 Group contribution of eighty-nine Lancasters and thirty-eight Mosquitos. The aiming-points for this assault were Q, R and S, and it was for S that ten Gransden Lodge crews were briefed, divided equally between the blind sky marker and backer-up role, while the five assigned to Q were all to bomb with the main force. They took off between 23.16 and 23.48 with no pilots on duty above flight lieutenant rank and arrived in the target area to find the city still burning from the morning raid. They experienced no difficulty in finding somewhere for their hardware, which they delivered according to their assigned roles and aiming-points from 18,000 to 19,000 feet between 01.25 and 01.44. The glow from the tortured city was still visible from the Dutch coast as the bombers reached the safety of the North Sea, and this time five Lancasters and two Halifaxes failed to return. The total weight of high explosives and incendiaries delivered in the two raids by the 2,018 aircraft involved amounted to 9,000 tons, and this massive effort in fewer than twenty-four hours was achieved without a contribution from 5 Group, which took advantage of the activity over the Ruhr to finally devastate the northern city of Braunschweig after a number of unsatisfactory previous attempts during the year.

There was no immediate respite from operations as preparations were put in hand on the 15th to attack Wilhelmshaven that night. Crews would have done their best to catch up on sleep as the work of the day went on around them, and some of those who had landed at dawn were up, briefed and fed in time to join others for an early evening take-off in an overall force of 506 aircraft drawn from all but 5 Group on what would turn out to be the last of fourteen major raids on this naval port during the war. 8 Group contributed eighty-six Lancasters and eight Mosquitos, fifteen of the former provided by 405 (Vancouver) Squadron, which departed Gransden Lodge between 17.28 and 17.43 with S/L Perry the senior pilot on duty. They were assigned to a variety of illuminating and marking roles and flew out under clear skies until the midpoint of the North-Sea crossing, when, according to some, cloud gradually built-up to ten-tenths thin stuff with a base at around 12,000 feet. Typically, there was no agreement as to the conditions, and some crews reported clear skies with haze or cirrus cloud at between 16,000 and 19,000 feet, through which the red and green TIs could be seen and their accuracy confirmed by H2S, while the 8 Group ORB recorded that it was impossible to make out ground features from above 12,000 feet. What may have been spoof green TIs were reported some five miles to the west and north-west of the target, and these attracted some bomb loads. The 405 (Vancouver) Squadron crews carried out their briefed tasks from 13,000 to 18,500 feet between 19.36 and 19.56, the lower heights those of visual markers taking advantage of clearer air. The bombing appeared to be scattered, and this was largely confirmed by local sources, which named only the Rathaus (Town Council HQ) as completely destroyed.

A major step forward in Bomber Command operations came with the virtual independence of 3 Group, beginning on the morning of the 18th after a year of trials with the G-H bombing system. This mirrored to an extent the American method of releasing bombs on observing the leader's fall away, but the RAF system was equally effective at night. The first massed live trial took place against the small city of Bonn, situated some twenty miles to the south-east of Cologne, which had little previous damage to cloud the assessment of the G-H performance. The operation was not entirely successful, but time and practice would lead to a highly effective means of attacking precision targets like oil refineries and marshalling yards in particular, and this would ease the pressure on 8 Group.

There were two major operations on the night of the 19/20th, both over southern Germany, one by 5 Group on Nuremberg, and the other by 565 aircraft of 1, 3, 6 and 8 Groups, on Stuttgart. This was to be a standard city-busting raid to be conducted in two waves, separated by four-and-a-half hours, for which 8 Group detailed forty-eight Lancasters and a dozen Mosquitos to participate in the first wave, and forty-six Lancasters and six Mosquitos for the second. 405 (Vancouver) Squadron made ready sixteen Lancasters for the second wave and sent them on their way from Gransden Lodge between 22.20 and 22.39 with W/C Kenneth Lawson DSO DFC the senior pilot on duty following his recent arrival. Ken Lawson was a highly experienced bomber pilot, who had earned his DFC while flying Wellingtons with 3 Group's 149 Squadron in 1941 as a pilot officer, before being awarded a DSO in July 1943 when serving in the rank of squadron leader with 156 Squadron of the Path Finder Force. On this night he was one of four blind markers, while five others were to act as blind illuminators, four as visual centerers, two as blind sky markers and one as a primary visual marker. They flew out over ten-tenths cloud, which persisted all the way across France and continued to the target, where it topped out at up to around 10,000 feet, through which the glow of fires from the earlier raid provided a reference. The Path Finder crews employed H2S to establish their positions and dropped red and green TIs, which disappeared quickly into the white stuff to leave a faint, reflected glow, forcing the Master Bomber to call for skymarking. The red Wanganui flares with yellow stars fell with a reasonable degree of concentration and continuity, with a few gaps, and the main force focused on them. The 405 (Vancouver) Squadron crews carried out their assigned tasks from 15,000 to 18,500 feet between 00.52 and 01.07 and observed a large explosion at 01.05. No assessment could be made of the outcome, and crews returned to report the clear evidence of fires, while local sources confirmed that the bombing had been scattered across the city and outlying communities and mentioned the important Bosch factory as among industrial concerns to sustain damage.

The Hurricane force had lain dormant since Duisburg, but was roused from its sleep on the 23rd, when Essen was posted as the target that evening for a record 1,055 aircraft carrying 4,538 tons of bombs, more than 90% of which was high explosive, and once again, this massive force would be achieved without the involvement of 5 Group. 8 Group detailed eighty Lancasters and thirty-one Mosquitos, some of the latter to dispense "window", which had been a regular feature of Path Finder tactics for a considerable time. 405 (Vancouver) Squadron dispatched fifteen Lancasters between 16.53 and 17.07 with F/L Ellison performing the dual role of blind skymarker and Master Bomber and the others assigned either to a variety of marking roles and main force support, among which S/L Mussells was the senior pilot. They climbed into scattered cloud and set course via Beachy Head for the French coast for a southerly approach to the target between Cologne and Mönchengladbach. The cloud thickened over the Channel until the tops were at 23,000 feet, but by the time the target hove into view, the cloud had become ten-tenths up to 14,000 feet. The Path Finders had prepared a ground and skymarking plan, and after the Oboe TIs had been swallowed up by the cloud, red skymarker flares were released at 19.28 to be followed by greens three minutes later. The 405 (Vancouver) Squadron crews fulfilled their briefs from 18,000 to 20,500 feet between 19.27 and 19.42 but found it impossible to observe the fall of the bombs. However, an intense glow on the cloud told its own story that there was still plenty of combustible material in the tortured city, and local reports confirmed the destruction of 607 buildings and a further eight hundred seriously damaged along with a death toll of 667 people.

Harris had not yet done with his old enemy and ordered another attack, this time by daylight on the 25th, for which 771 aircraft were made ready, including an 8 Group contribution of thirty-eight Lancasters and a dozen Mosquitos for aiming-point J, the Krupp district, and twenty-five Lancasters for aiming-point G, the general city area. Running parallel with this operation was another taking place some fifteen miles to the west at Moers/Homberg, where the Meerbeck synthetic oil plant was the target for a 6 Group main force of 199 Halifaxes with 405 (Vancouver) Squadron providing sixteen of thirty-two 8 Group Lancasters and twelve Mosquitos. S/L McQuoid and F/O McNaughton were appointed Master Bomber and Deputy, with S/Ls Mussells and Marcou as supporters, nine performing the role of blind skymarkers, two backers-up and one primary visual marker. They departed Gransden Lodge between 13.40 and 13.57 and on arrival at the target were confronted by the forecast ten-tenths cloud, which had been planned for and resulted in skymarking. The first green flares were reported at 15.45, and apart from a two-minute gap soon afterwards, they were continuous throughout the raid. The 405 (Vancouver) Squadron crews carried out their assigned tasks from 17,000 to 19,000 feet between 15.42 and 15.55 but were unable in the conditions to assess the outcome. Meanwhile, at Essen, many bomb bursts and volumes of smoke were evident through the clouds, and it was clear to all that another devastating blow had been visited upon the city, which had by now, lost its status as a major centre of war production. Local reports confirmed the destruction of 1,163 buildings, almost twice the number resulting from the larger attack thirty-six hours earlier, and the death toll was also greater at 820 people.

It was on this day that 142 Squadron was reformed and took up residence at Gransden Lodge as a member of 8 Group's Mosquito Light Night Striking Force. The squadron had begun the war as one of the original Fairey Battle units to be sent to France in September 1939 as part of the Advanced Air Striking Force, and on return to the UK in June 1940 joined the reconstituted 1 Group, converting to Wellingtons in October. Most of the squadron was sent to the Middle East in December 1942, and in early 1943 the home echelon combined with that of 150 Squadron to become 166 Squadron, while the overseas squadron was eventually also disbanded.

On the morning of the 28th, 4 Group made ready a main force of 155 Halifaxes to join forces with eighty-six Lancasters and thirty-six Mosquitos of 8 Group to continue the assault on the defences on the island of Walcheren. Each of the six aiming-points was to be targeted by a section of bombers during a seventy-minute window, and the six 405 (Vancouver) Squadron participants departing Gransden Lodge between 10.14 and 10.18 were assigned to the fourth wave with S/L McQuoid and F/O McNaughton the Master Bomber and Deputy and the others as supporters, each with a bomb load of a cookie and eight 1,000-pounders. They reached the target to encounter largely clear skies and visibility good enough to visually identify the coastal battery aiming-points. F/O McNaughton released his green TIs at 11.13 followed by S/L McQuoid a minute later from 4,500 feet, and they maintained the marking throughout the raid. The 405 (Vancouver) Squadron supporters delivered their payloads from 4,000 to 5,500 feet between 11.14 and 11.22, and when smoke and dust covered the site, the upwind edge became the new aiming point.

The day's offensive activities were not yet over, and preparations for the first of a three-raid mini-campaign against Cologne were already in hand. The last time that the Command had targeted Cologne in such a way was in June/July 1943, when three raids had been mounted over the course of ten nights, resulting in the destruction of 11,000 buildings, 5,500 fatalities and 350,000 people being rendered homeless. This operation was to be conducted in two phases, with one aiming-point in the district of Müllheim, to the north-east of the city centre, and the other in Zollstock to the south-west. A force of 733 aircraft included an 8 Group contribution of twenty-three Lancasters and seven Mosquitos for aiming-point G and thirty-six Lancasters and twelve Mosquitos for aiming-point H. 405 (Vancouver) Squadron briefed two crews for a backing-up role and five to support the main force at aiming point G and sent them on their way from Gransden Lodge between 13.33 and 13.39 with F/L Vann the senior pilot on duty. They were followed into the air between 13.56 and 14.06 by the crews of W/C Lawson and F/Ls Herbert and Smith, who were bound for aiming point H as blind sky markers. They encountered a weather front over the North Sea on their way to making landfall on the French coast in the Dunkerque region but reached the target to find a patch of clear sky over aiming point G and five-tenths cloud over H but excellent visibility. The cathedral and the western end of the Hohenzollern railway bridge were clearly visible as the two

405 (Vancouver) Squadron elements carried out their respective tasks from 17,000 to 20,000 feet between 15.42 and 15.48 and from 18,200 to 18,400 feet between 16.06 and 16.07. A large explosion was reported at 16.04 following a direct hit on a factory, and smoke was rising through 15,000 feet from the various aiming-points as the bombers turned away. Despite reservations about the quality of the bombing of aiming-point H, both aiming-points had been devastated, local reports confirming the destruction of 2,239 blocks of flats and fifteen industrial premises, along with many other buildings of a public nature. Severe damage had also been inflicted upon power stations, transportation and railway and river docks installations.

The main theme on the 29th was the push to wrest Walcheren from the hands of the enemy, and 358 aircraft were drawn from 1, 3, 4 and 8 Groups to target eleven aiming-points on the morning of the 29th. 8 Group put up forty-four Lancasters and thirty-six Mosquitos for six aiming-points, 405 (Vancouver) Squadron contributing F/O Woods and F/L Vann as Master Bomber and Deputy and the crews of P/O Fornberg and F/O Kyte as main force supporters. They departed Gransden Lodge between 11.17 and 11.21 and found clear skies where it mattered over the Scheldt, with high-level cloud above. F/L Vann went in first at 12.27 to drop green TIs and a 1,000-pounder from 5,000 feet to back up the red Oboe TIs, and on his arrival at 12.28 F/O Woods carried out the first of three passes over the target, releasing six green TIs and two 1,000-pounders from 4,000 feet. The supporter crews delivered their eleven 1,000 and four 500 pounders each from 4,000 and 5,000 feet at 12.33 and 12.34, before returning to report an effective operation. The final operations against Walcheren were undertaken by 5 Group on the 30th, when two forces of fifty-one Lancasters and four Mosquitos each were sent against coastal batteries at Westkapelle and Flushing. Ground forces went in on the following day, and a week of heavy fighting preceded the island's capture. Even then, the clearing of mines from the approaches to Antwerp kept the port out of commission for a further three weeks.

A force of 905 aircraft was made ready for another massive assault on Cologne on the 30th, for which 8 Group detailed forty-five Lancasters and thirty-two Mosquitos, eleven of the former fuelled and bombed-up at Gransden Lodge, five for crews acting as blind sky markers and the remainder as main force supporters. They took-off between 18.23 and 18.50 with S/L Marcou and the recently elevated S/L Burnand the senior pilots on duty and climbed away into ten-tenths cloud, which persisted for most of the outward flight, with a full moon shining brightly above. Over the Channel the cloud tops reached 20,000 feet, but this had lowered to 10,000 to 15,000 feet as the target drew near, and main force crews were greeted by red and white marker flares delivered by nine of the Oboe Mosquitos. They drifted in concentrated fashion into the cloud tops, and main force crews confirmed their accuracy by Gee and H2S before carrying out their attacks. The Gransden Lodge crews performed their briefed roles from 18,000 to 19,000 feet between 20.58 and 21.19, and although the ground was obscured, the glow in the clouds suggested a successful outcome. A post-raid analysis suggested a scattered attack, but local reports confirmed heavy damage in south-western suburbs, where housing, communications and utilities were the principal casualties.

A force of 493 aircraft from 1, 3, 4 and 8 Groups was made ready on the 31st to complete the series of raids on Cologne, 8 Group providing forty-one Lancasters and eighteen Mosquitos. 405 (Vancouver) Squadron contributed nine Lancasters, three for blind sky marker crews and six for those assigned to main force support, and they departed Gransden Lodge between 18.26 and 18.45

with W/C Lawson the senior pilot on duty. They were greeted at the target once more by ten-tenths thick cloud with tops at 6,000 to 10,000 feet and the attack opened with red and white flares delivered by Oboe Mosquitos at 20.56, which were backed up in what appeared to be concentrated fashion by greens from the heavy marker element. Crews established their positions by Gee and H2S-fix before carrying out their assigned roles, those from 405 (Vancouver) Squadron attacking from 17,500 to 18,500 feet between 20.58 and 21.11. Returning crews reported concentrated bombing and a large red glow beneath the clouds as they turned for home, and local sources confirmed that the southern districts had received the main weight of bombs. The reporting system was breaking down and precise details were not forthcoming, and it is likely that the city had been largely evacuated by this stage. Most future operations would be directed at the city's numerous and extensive marshalling yards.

W/C Coulson, who had begun his operational career with 405 (Vancouver) Squadron earlier in the year, completed twenty-four sorties as a flight commander with 35 (Madras Presidency) Squadron, and departed Graveley at the end of the month to take command of 582 Squadron at Little Staughton. During the course of the month, the squadron took part in sixteen operations and dispatched 171 sorties without loss.

November 1944

As worthwhile targets became more difficult to find in a country so thoroughly destroyed by bombing, smaller, seemingly irrelevant towns and cities began to find themselves in the bomb sights, particularly if they happened to lie in the path of the retreating enemy forces or on a main railway line. Oil was now the overriding priority, and November's operational activity began on the night of the 1/2nd with an attack on the city area of Oberhausen, which was home to a number of important oil production plants. 8 Group provided twenty-six Lancasters and twelve Mosquitos to mark for a 6 Group main force of 202 Halifaxes and forty-eight Lancasters, but heavy cloud led to scattered bombing and an unsatisfactory outcome.

The Rheinpreussen (Meerbeck) synthetic oil plant at Homberg was the target for a 3 Group G-H raid on the 2nd, while that night, it was Düsseldorf's turn to face a "Hurricane"-size force of 992 aircraft for what would prove to be the final major raid of the war on this much-bombed city. It was one of those rare occasions when the "Lincolnshire Poachers" were invited to operate alongside the other groups, while 8 Group pitched in with eighty Lancasters and thirty-one Mosquitos, sixteen of the former made ready by 405 (Vancouver) Squadron. Seven crews were assigned as blind sky markers, three as backers-up and the rest as main force supporters and departed Gransden Lodge between 16.49 and 17.07 with S/Ls Burnand, Mussells and Marcou the senior pilots on duty. They arrived at the target to encounter clear skies, moonlight and only ground haze to slightly marr the vertical visibility and found that the moonlight nullified the searchlights ringing the city. Of greater concern, however, was the heavy flak bursting at 17,000 to 20,000 feet as they set out on their bombing runs over the suburbs and outer districts towards the aiming-point. The attack opened early with red flares and TIs dropped by eight Oboe Mosquitos at 19.05, which enabled the crews to identify the river, railway tracks and built-up area visually, and the heavy marker element maintained the aiming-point throughout the raid with mostly well-placed green TIs. The 405 (Vancouver) Squadron crews carried out their briefs from 18,000 to 19,000 feet between 19.11 and 19.34, and by 19.20, it was clear that fires were gaining a hold. Smoke was rising through 10,000 feet as the last crews headed for home with the glow from the burning city remaining visible from as far as Charleroi in Belgium, some 115 miles away. It was established later that five thousand houses had been destroyed, along with many important war-industry factories.

Although all of its aircraft returned, 405 (Vancouver) Squadron suffered its first casualty for six weeks after PB413 was hit by flak near Krefeld, and the pilot, F/O Hannah RCAF, sustained serious neck and back wounds. During the confusion, the rear gunner, F/Sgt Perini RCAF, baled out and his fate is not clear. The bomb-aimer, F/L Martin RCAF, took over the controls, and brought the Lancaster back to England, eventually carrying out a forced-landing at Debden airfield in Essex at 22.45. Sadly, F/O Hannah did not recover from his wounds, losing his fight for life on the 27th of January 1945, and he now lies among fallen Canadian comrades in the RCAF Stonefall cemetery on the outskirts of Harrogate.

The continuing campaign against Ruhr cities would be prosecuted by 749 aircraft of 1, 4, 6 and 8 Groups at Bochum on the 4th, while 5 Group renewed its acquaintance with the Dortmund-Ems Canal, which had been repaired following the successful breaching of its banks near Ladbergen in September. 8 Group detailed eighty Lancaster and twenty-nine Mosquitos, six of the latter to dispense "window" ahead of the heavy brigade, and the eight participating 405 (Vancouver) Squadron Lancasters departed Gransden Lodge between 17.55 and 18.01 with S/Ls Mussells and Marcou the senior pilots on duty. They had been designated as backers-up, while the remaining crews were in Lancasters carrying a cookie, six 1,000 and six 500-pounders each to drop as part of the main force. They crossed the North Sea to make landfall on the Dutch coast in the vicinity of The Hague, inviting the attention of the local flak as they passed by, before pressing on for the remaining 130 miles to reach the target, which they found to be under a veil of very thin cloud of up to three-tenths at 5,000 feet. Red Oboe TIs were seen to cascade at 19.26 and were followed over the ensuing minutes by greens to maintain the aiming-point for the duration of the attack. The 405 (Vancouver) Squadron crews carried out their assigned tasks from 17,500 to 18,500 feet between 19.27 and 19.33 and observed a number of large explosions, one throwing flame a thousand feet into the air, and a reconnaissance Mosquito crew reported a circular patch of fire and one particularly intense conflagration visible from one hundred miles away. The success of the operation was confirmed by post-raid reconnaissance and local reports, which confirmed that the city centre and industrial districts had borne the brunt of the attack, with four thousand buildings destroyed or seriously damaged, and almost a thousand people killed. However, the defences demonstrated that they were not yet spent, and brought down twenty-eight aircraft, twenty-three of them Halifaxes.

Bochum's neighbour, Gelsenkirchen, was posted as the target on the 6th, for which a force of 738 aircraft was assembled. In the past, it had been the synthetic oil plants that had drawn the bombers on, but this time part of the force was to attack the built-up area as well as the Nordstern Synthetic oil refinery in the north-western district of Horst. 8 Group detailed sixty-three Lancasters and thirty-one Mosquitos, nine of the former representing 405 (Vancouver) Squadron, which departed Gransden Lodge between 12.16 and 12.34 with F/Ls Payne, Vann and Whittall the senior pilots on duty. Six of the crews had been briefed for a main force support role and three as backers-up, the latter all at aiming point B, and climbed away into cloud that increased to almost ten-tenths at the Dutch coast, but thereafter, began to break up to six to eight-tenths at 9,000 feet. By good fortune, a gap appeared right over the target, which enabled the early arrivals to pick out the distinctive L-shaped docks in the Schalke-Nord district to the north-west of the aiming point. Bombing commenced a few minutes early on red and green TIs, the latter assessed as the more accurate, and the Master Bomber, whose transmissions were weak, directed the crews towards them. However, it wasn't long before thick smoke spread across the area to obscure any sight of the ground, and the Master Bomber directed the crews to focus on the built-up area generally. The Gransden Lodge contingent carried out their respective tasks from 18,000 to 19,500 feet between 13.55 and 13.58 in the face of accurate heavy flak, which inflicted damage on a number of aircraft and was probably responsible for the failure to return of three Lancasters and two Halifaxes. Many explosions were witnessed, and the consensus among the crews at debriefing was of a concentrated attack, although it was impossible to make an accurate assessment. Local reports confirmed that a "catastrophe" had befallen the city, and that more than five hundred people had lost their lives.

According to the 8 Group ORB an attack on the Krupp Treibstoffwerke oil plant at Wanne-Eickel planned for the morning of the 9th was cancelled, while the 405 (Vancouver) Squadron ORB records that ten of its Lancasters departed Gransden Lodge between 08.31 and 08.45 led by W/C Lawson and S/L Hassels. Three crews had been briefed as backers-up and the others as supporters of the 1 Group main force of 226 Lancasters of 1 Group, which means that a further twenty 8 Group Lancasters and twenty-one Mosquitos were involved. They found the target area covered by ten-tenths cloud with tops in places as high as 21,000 feet, into which the Oboe skymarkers disappeared to leave the main force crew reliant upon their navigational equipment in accordance with the Master Bomber's instructions. The 405 (Vancouver) Squadron participants carried out their assigned tasks from 15,000 to 21,000 feet between 10.28 and 10.38 and returned home with no clue as to the outcome. Local sources reported two buildings destroyed and ten fatalities, and one must assume that the ordnance had been spread far and wide in an echo of former, pre-Oboe performances.

Briefings took place on 1, 5 and 8 Group stations on the 11th for operations against the Rhenania-Ossag and Hoesch Benzin synthetic oil plants located respectively in Harburg on the southern bank of the Elbe opposite Hamburg and in the Wambel district of Dortmund in the eastern Ruhr. 8 Group detailed twenty-six Lancaster and nineteen Mosquitos for the latter, 405 (Vancouver) squadron providing seven Lancasters, three for backer-up crews and four for main force supporters. They departed Gransden Lodge between 16.42 and 16.48 with S/Ls Burnand and Marcou the senior pilots on duty and joined with the 186-strong 1 Group main force as they crossed the sea. The 8 Group contingent was depleted by the early return of nine Lancasters and nine Mosquitos, leaving the remainder to be greeted at the target by up to ten-tenths cloud with tops in places at 20,000 feet. Two aiming points were marked out for attention and were attacked by the 405 (Vancouver) Squadron participants either on red TIs glimpsed through a gap in the cloud or on DR and Gee-fix from 18,000 to 19,500 feet between 18.59 and 19.07. The bombing was accurate, and severe damage was inflicted upon the plant, while a nearby aerodrome and housing were also hit.

Another lull in operations for all but the now largely independent 3 Group took the Command through to the 16th, which was devoted to the destruction of the three small towns of Heinsberg, Jülich and Düren, located respectively in an arc from north to east of Aachen, and close to the German lines upon which American ground forces were advancing. A total of 1,188 aircraft was detailed, with 1 and 5 Groups providing the main force of 452 Lancasters for the last-mentioned with thirty-three Lancasters and thirteen Mosquitos of 8 Group, while 4 and 6 Groups were to contribute 254 Halifaxes and forty-five Lancasters between them as the main force at Jülich, with thirty-three Lancasters and seventeen Mosquitos of 8 Group to handle the marking. This left Heinsberg to be the objective for a G-H raid by 182 Lancasters of 3 Group. A dozen 405 (Vancouver) Squadron crews attended briefing to learn that seven of them were to perform the role of backers-up and the remainder main force supporters at Jülich and departed Gransden Lodge between 13.41 and 13.54 with W/C Lawson the senior pilot on duty. They flew to the target over ten-tenths cloud, which cleared to three-tenths stratus above 6,000 feet as they approached the aiming-point, where a red Oboe TI was dropped right onto the aiming-point. The Master Bomber instructed the crews to aim for this and later at greens, before smoke enveloped the town, and the upwind edge of the smoke became the new aiming point. The 405 (Vancouver) squadron crews complied from 13,800 to 16,000 feet between 15.29 and 15.42, and along with most of the main force crews claimed to have hit the target, a claim which could not be confirmed immediately as the majority of photos were unplottable because of the smoke covering the area. It was established soon afterwards that the operation had been a complete success at the cost of a single Halifax that came down without casualties on the edge of Allied territory and four of the nine occupants fell into enemy hands. Post-raid reconnaissance confirmed that the towns had been all-but erased from the map with very heavy casualties, but no report came out of Jülich to provide details. The loss of life proved to be an unnecessary when unfavourable ground conditions prevented the American advance from succeeding.

Briefings took place on 4, 6 and 8 Group stations on the morning of the 18th to inform 479 crews of the details for an attack on the heavily-garrisoned city of Münster, situated some twenty-five miles from the north-eastern edge of the Ruhr. 8 Group contributed fifty Lancasters and eighteen Mosquitos, four of the former prepared by 405 (Vancouver) Squadron, which departed Gransden Lodge between 13.13 and 13.16 with S/L Burnand the senior pilot on duty. Three were to act as blind sky markers and one as a backer-up as they climbed away to rendezvous with the rest of the force during the North Sea crossing, and on arrival at the target they were greeted by a blanket of ten-tenths thick cloud with tops at 8,000 feet. The initial green skymarkers were dropped by three Oboe Mosquitos at 14.58 and red skymarkers soon followed from the heavy marker element, the Gransden Lodge crews fulfilling their briefs from 17,500 to 18,500 feet between 15.00 and 15.13 having confirmed their positions by H2S and Gee fixes. Returning crews reported a compact bomber stream and solid concentrations of markers, but perhaps a scattered attack, the results of which remained hidden beneath the cloud. Little information came out of the city, but what emerged seemed to confirm bombs falling across the built-up area with no points of concentration.

By the time they landed, preparations were already well in hand for a return that evening to the Krupp Treibstoffwerke (fuel works) at Wanne-Eickel. A main force of 253 Lancasters was assembled by 1 Group, while 8 Group contributed thirty-two Lancasters and twenty-four Mosquitos to look after the marking aspect. The twelve-strong 405 (Vancouver) Squadron element was divided equally between backing-up and main force support roles and departed Gransden Lodge between 16.33 and 16.43 with S/Ls Mussells and McQuoid the senior pilots on duty. They climbed away through poor weather conditions of low cloud and mist, which cleared at the French coast, but shortly after crossing the Rhine, a thin layer of stratus slid in at 8,000 feet and remained in place with occasional breaks over the target. Seven of the Mosquitos had laid a "window" screen ahead of the bombers, and four of the Oboe variety delivered red TIs, which were seen to cascade at 18.55 and were followed by others three minutes later and greens at 18.59. Few crews could pick out ground detail, but the red and green TIs were visible through the clouds, and apart from one group of greens, were well placed on the aiming-point. The bombing was focused on the main group of reds and greens, and very soon a large fire developed, which emitted a column of black smoke seemingly from the refinery. The bombers were met by heavy flak in barrage and predicted form as they carried out their attacks, the Gransden Lodge crews crossing the aiming-point at 17,500 to 18,500 feet between 18.56 and 19.06. The consensus among returning crews was of a successful operation, which was confirmed by photo-reconnaissance that revealed fresh damage to the oil plant, and according to local reports, destroyed the nearby Hannibal coal mine.

Briefings took place on some 8 Group stations on the evening of the 20th, when six 405 (Vancouver) Squadron crews learned of their part in an all-8 Group raid on the city of Koblenz by forty-three Lancasters. The purpose of the operation was not made clear, but bridges over the Rhine and Mosel Rivers or the marshalling yards may have been the targets for the Gransden Lodge crews, who were all designated as blind markers and were to carry a dozen 1,000-pounders each in addition to the marker ordnance. They took off between 00.45 and 00.54 with S/L Burnand the senior pilot on duty and reached the target area, situated in central Germany some fifty miles south-east of Cologne, to find ten-tenths cloud with tops at up to 19,000 feet. They established their positions on H2S or Gee and delivered their markers and bombs from 18,000 to 19,500 feet between 02.49 and 03.00, observing a white glow beneath the clouds and gaining the impression of a focused attack. Local sources confirmed damage to communications structures and installations within the city, but also a spreading of the bombing onto outlying communities.

The night of the 21/22nd, would be one of large-scale activity at numerous locations involving 1,345 sorties. Sixteen crews attended briefings at Gransden Lodge during the afternoon to be told of three separate targets earmarked for their attention that evening. Five learned that they were to join thirty-one other 8 Group Lancaster and nine Mosquito crews to mark the railway yards at Aschaffenburg for a 1 Group Lancaster force of 238, while five others were required for a raid by nineteen 8 Group Lancasters on Worms, situated some forty miles to the south-west. A further six crews were informed that they were to be part of an 8 Group contribution of eighteen Lancasters and twenty Mosquitos marking for and supporting a 4 Group Halifax main force in an attack on the Ruhr-Benzin synthetic oil refinery at Sterkrade-Holten in the central Ruhr. The Ruhr-bound sextet took off between 16.00 and 16.19 with F/L Payne the senior pilot on duty and divided equally between backing-up and main force support roles. They were followed into the air by the Worms and Aschaffenburg elements one after the other between 16.22 and 16.31 with S/Ls Marcou and Burnand respectively the senior pilots on duty, the former all main force supporters and the latter with marker roles to perform.

It was shortly after 19.00 when the Aschaffenburg force approached its target some twenty miles south-east of Frankfurt to encounter ten-tenths cloud with tops at 8,000 to 10,000 feet. The Deputy Master Bomber descended to 7,000 feet, but was unable to mark the aiming-point, and the Master Bomber issued instructions for the main force to bomb on navigational aids. A number of red TIs were spotted by some crews, but the remainder complied with the Master Bomber's instructions, and a glow beneath the clouds gave promise of an effective attack. The 405 (Vancouver) Squadron crews carried out their assigned tasks from 16,000 to 16,500 feet between 19.10 and 19.22 and were unable to assess the outcome. Local sources confirmed that fifty bombs had hit the railway yards, while the main weight had fallen into the central and northern districts of the town, destroying five hundred houses and seriously damaging three times that number. Similar conditions at Worms required the Gransden Lodge participants to bomb on H2S from 15,000 to 16,000 feet between 19.28 and 19.32, while some 140 miles to the north-north-west the first red Oboe TIs at Sterkrade were seen cascading through up to five-tenths low cloud at 20.53 and were quickly joined by others to form a good group. These were backed up by greens throughout the attack, during which the Gransden Lodge crews performed their respective tasks from 17,500 to 18,500 feet between 18.59 and 19.03. The bombing appeared to be concentrated around the markers, and a large explosion lasting some fifteen seconds at 21.08 sent a mushroom of cloud to 3,000 feet. A reconnaissance Mosquito crew reported one large fire and others scattered around, but it appeared that no fresh damage to the oil plant could be determined.

There would be no further operations for the majority of the heavy squadrons over the ensuing six days, despite a number being announced only to be scrubbed, while 3 and 5 Groups went about their business independently. The university city of Freiburg, situated in the south-western corner of Germany with the French and Swiss frontiers to west and south, was believed to be inhabited by German troops preparing to resist the approaching American and French forces some thirty-five miles away, and found itself a target on the night of the 27/28th. A force of 341 Lancasters and ten Mosquitos was assembled, 292 of the former belonging to 1 Group and the remainder and ten Mosquitos to 8 Group. 405 (Vancouver) Squadron's seven crews had been designated as blind sky markers and departed Gransden Lodge between 17.16 and 17.22 with W/C Lawson the senior pilot on duty, before climbing into clear skies and setting course to the south-east to exit England at Orfordness on the Suffolk coast. Cloud began to build over the French coast and increased to full cover by the German frontier, but dispersed to five to six-tenths, thin and low over the target. The first flares were released at 19.55, and thanks to mobile Oboe stations operating from the liberated countries, Mosquitos were able to deliver red TIs a minute later, which were soon backed up by greens. The Master Bomber's instructions were loud and clear and directed the 405 (Vancouver) Squadron crews as they delivered their flares and ten 1,000-pounders each from 13,500 to 14,300 feet between 20.04 and 20.14, and once he had instructed the main force crews to aim for the red and green TIs around the aiming-point, 1,900 tons of bombs fell in an orgy of destruction lasting twenty-five minutes. A reconnaissance Mosquito crew reported a city on fire with smoke rising through 8,000 feet, and local sources would confirm the destruction of two thousand houses and severe damage to 450 others. More than two thousand people lost their lives, a further four thousand were injured and almost nine hundred registered as missing in return for the loss of a single Lancaster.

Some forty minutes after the last of the above 405 (Vancouver) Squadron Lancasters had set off for south-western Germany, seven others departed Gransden Lodge for the southern Ruhr as part of an 8 Group force of forty-two Lancasters and fifteen Mosquitos detailed to join forces with 275 Halifaxes and Lancasters of 1 and 6 Groups to attack the Ruhr city of Neuss. They took to the air between 18.04 and 18.10 with S/L Marcou the senior pilot on duty with either a visual centerer or main force support role to perform and headed eastwards above seven-tenths cloud, which had increased to ten-tenths by the time they reached the target with tops below 5,000 feet. The attack opened punctually with red Oboe TIs, which were backed up by green TIs and green and yellow flares from 20.23, and a glow beneath the cloud appeared to be concentrated around what was the intended aiming-point. The Gransden Lodge crews carried out their attacks from 17,500 to 18,500 feet between 20.20 and 20.27, and the flash from numerous explosions gave promise of a successful operation. A reconnaissance Mosquito crew arriving on target at 21.48 reported scattered fires in central and western districts and a good concentration of fires to the east, among which explosions continued. Local sources confirmed the destruction of 145 houses and four industrial premises and severe damage to almost six hundred houses, sixteen industrial and five public buildings.

The squadron was not involved when 8 Group provided thirty-two Lancasters and seventeen Mosquitos to mark for and support a 1 Group main force of 262 Lancasters in an attack on Dortmund. Conditions were unfavourable and in the face of sparse and scattered sky and ground marking, the Master Bomber effectively left the main force to bomb on navigational instruments.

A major raid on Duisburg was scheduled for the last night of the month and a main force of 493 aircraft assembled from 1, 4 and 6 Groups, while 8 Group provided fifty-eight Lancasters and twenty-five Mosquitos, eleven of the former belonging to 405 (Vancouver) Squadron. Five of them were handed a blind sky marker role, four were designated as visual centerers and two as main force supporters and departed Gransden Lodge between 17.29 and 17.40 with S/L Marcou the senior pilot on duty. They were confronted at the target by ten-tenths cloud with tops at 5,000 feet and the attack on aiming point E began at 19.53 with Oboe red TIs, which quickly disappeared into the cloud but left a glow that suggested some degree of concentration. Skymarking commenced at 19.59 and was maintained throughout the attack, during which the two 405 (Vancouver) Squadron crews of F/O McIntyre and P/O Maxwell each delivered their cookie, five 1,000 and six 500-pounders from 18,500 at 19.58. The focus shifted to aiming point F at 20.05, and the remaining Gransden Lodge crews carried out their respective roles from 18,000 to 18,500 feet between 20.06 and 20.11. According to local sources the main weight of bombs fell on residential districts, where 5628 houses were destroyed and more than eight hundred seriously damaged.

During the course of the month the squadron took part in fifteen operations and dispatched 125 sorties for the loss of a pilot and a gunner.

December 1944

December would follow a similar pattern of operations, with the accent remaining on oil and communications, but with city-busting interspersed. The new month began with a heavy attack on the town of Hagen, situated on the south-eastern edge of the Ruhr, ten miles south of Dortmund, which had last been attacked fourteen months earlier and now, on the evening of the 2nd, was about to face five hundred heavy bombers, consisting of a main force from 4 and 6 Groups, with thirty-two Lancasters and twenty-three 8 Group Mosquitos and seven Lancasters of 101 Squadron to provide ABC cover. Sixteen 405 (Vancouver) Squadron crews attended briefing to learn that nine of them would be performing the role of visual centerers and the rest providing main force support. They departed Gransden Lodge between 18.12 and 18.28 with S/Ls McQuoid, Mussells and the recently posted-in Neilly the senior pilots on duty and along with the rest of the force benefitted from a "window" screen provided by six non-marker Mosquitos. The target was found to be concealed by ten-tenths cloud with tops at 15,000 feet and in the absence of any marking, crews established their positions on H2S, those from 405 (Vancouver) Squadron carrying out their assigned tasks from 17,000 to 19,000 feet between 20.57 and 21.09. F/O Wilsher and crew overshot the aiming point after picking up poor H2S returns and bombed a built-up area beyond, which turned out to be Iserlohn, and the consensus at debriefing was of a scattered and possibly ineffective raid, when in fact, it had resulted in a catastrophe for the town, which suffered the destruction of or serious damage to more than sixteen hundred houses and ninety industrial concerns, some of which lost three months production. Among the factories destroyed was one previously mentioned, which was producing accumulator batteries for the new types of U-Boot under construction.

As American forces advanced into the western frontier Eifel region of Germany, attention turned upon the small town of Heimbach, some fifteen miles south-east of Aachen, and upon the nearby Urftsee and its dam. The purpose was to release the water in the reservoir before American forces arrived, and thus prevent the enemy from releasing it strategically to hamper the American advance. It had been targeted by 3 Group on the 3rd and would prove to be elusive and difficult to hit during a number of further attempts over the ensuing days. The operation on the 4th was to be an 8 Group show involving twenty-seven Lancasters and four Mosquitos, the eight of the former belonging to 405 (Vancouver) Squadron departing Gransden Lodge between 12.52 and 12.55 with S/Ls Mussells and Neilly the senior pilots on duty and each Lancaster carrying a cookie and eight 1,000-pounders. They flew out over the Suffolk coast and formed into three sections of nine Lancasters each at 18,000 to 18,500 feet behind Oboe Mosquitos, arriving in the target area over nine-tenths stratocumulus with tops at between 7,000 and 12,000 feet. The first and third sections released their payloads when the Oboe Mosquitos' cookies fell away, those from 405 (Vancouver) Squadron between 15.23 and 15.25, while the second element bombed with the Oboe leader's Lancaster. It was not possible to assess the outcome, but the dam was known to be still intact.

Later in the day, a force of 535 aircraft of 1, 6 and 8 Groups was assembled to send against Karlsruhe in southern Germany, for which 8 Group contributed sixty-four Lancasters and eight Mosquitos, six of the former provided by 405 (Vancouver) Squadron. At briefing four crews were handed a blind marker role, while two were to perform as visual centerers, and they departed Gransden Lodge between 17.21 and 17.26 with W/C Lawson and S/L McQuoid the senior pilots on duty. The weather conditions throughout the operation were generally favourable, with cloud building and decreasing in turns across the Channel and France, and on arrival over the target, the crews found nine to ten-tenths with tops at around 14,000 feet. As they approached, a few crews were able to see red and green TIs through gaps in the clouds, but the majority had to rely on the glow of greens coming through and confirm their accuracy by means of H2S or Gee. It was difficult to assess what was happening because of a scarcity of red TIs, and although the greens were plentiful, they were scattered, but as the cloud drifted towards the east, later arrivals were able to identify the built-up area visually. The 405 (Vancouver) Squadron crews carried out their respective tasks from 18,000 to 18,500 feet between 19.28 and 19.39 and reported fires visible from up to a hundred miles into the homeward flight. It was established ultimately, that severe damage had been inflicted upon the city, particularly in western and southern districts, at a cost of just two aircraft.

This destruction at Karlsruhe paled into insignificance when compared with 5 Group's simultaneous assault on the virgin town of Heilbronn, situated some fifty miles to the east-north-east and north of Stuttgart. It sat astride the River Neckar and had the misfortune to be served by a north-south railway line, but otherwise, was of no genuine strategic importance, and would not have been expecting an attack. The aiming-points were the marshalling yards and the town, and by the time that the force retreated westwards into electrical storms, seven thousand people had died and 82% of the city's built-up area was in the process of being destroyed by what probably amounted to a firestorm. The post-war British Bombing Survey estimated 351 acres of destruction, and a death toll of at least seven thousand people.

On the following night, a force of 497 aircraft was assembled from 1, 4, 6 and 8 Groups to send against the town of Soest, situated just to the north of the Ruhr and five miles from the now famous Möhne Reservoir and its rebuilt dam. It was one of a number of important railway hubs linking the Ruhr with greater Germany, and its marshalling yards were posted as the main target. Gransden Lodge was not called into action, while the forty-seven Lancasters and thirteen Mosquitos of 8 Group that were, contributed to the destruction of a thousand houses and more than fifty other buildings, predominantly in the northern half of the town.

Three major operations were mounted on the night of the 6/7th, against the oil refinery at Leuna (Merseburg) a dozen miles or so west of Leipzig in eastern Germany by 1, 3 and 8 Groups, railway yards at Giessen in west-central Germany by 5 Group, and Osnabrück in the north-west by 4, 6 and 8 Groups. 8 Group contributed seventy-one Lancasters and a dozen Mosquitos to the attack on the I. G. Farbenindustrie A G Merseburg-Leuna refinery, which lay some 250 miles from the Dutch frontier and five hundred miles from the bomber bases of eastern England. 405 (Vancouver) Squadron made ready sixteen Lancasters in an overall heavy force of 475 of the type, which was unusually large for an oil target and reflected the importance of this particular one in the context of the oil offensive. The Gransden Lodge element took to the air between 17.29 and 17.44 with W/C Lawson and S/Ls Mussells and Neilly the senior pilots on duty, fifteen crews assigned to five separate marking roles and one as a main force supporter. They climbed away into unfavourable weather conditions of complete cloud cover over England and patchy cloud over France, which built again as the bomber stream undertook the final leg across Germany. The Path Finders had prepared for "Newhaven" marking (ground), with emergency Wanganui (skymarking) if required, and this proved to be the case as ten-tenths stratocumulus was unexpectedly encountered over the target area with tops at 10,000 feet. On approach, the early arrivals observed TIs cascading into it, but they were not visible by the time the crews came to bomb, and the Path Finders quickly changed to skymarking. Release-point flares were in plentiful supply, their accuracy checked by H2S, and in the absence of instructions from the Master Bomber, they provided the main reference for bombing. The skymarkers were plentiful, continuous and concentrated throughout the raid, which took place in the face of a strong flak defence that, fortunately, was exploding below the bombers' flight level. The Gransden Lodge crews carried out their assigned tasks from 17,000 to 18,500 feet between 20.38 and 20.52 and returned to report large explosions and the glow of fires for around sixty miles into the return journey. Post-raid reconnaissance confirmed much damage to the oil plant, but it would continue to feature on the target list right through to the final month of the bombing war.

The next briefing at Gransden Lodge took place on the 12th, when thirteen crews were provided with the details of that night's operation to Essen by a force of 540 aircraft drawn from 1, 4 and 8 Groups. The 8 Group contribution amounted to eighty-three Lancasters and twenty-eight

Mosquitos, among which the 405 (Vancouver) Squadron participants were designated five, four and four respectively as blind sky markers, visual centerers and main force supporters. They took off between 17.00 and 17.15 with G/C Newson and S/Ls Marcou and Neilly the senior pilots on duty, before climbing away into poor weather conditions with low cloud, which persisted as they passed out over Beachy Head and set course for the French coast on the southerly route to the central Ruhr. While they were heading north over Germany between Cologne and Düsseldorf, the cloud began to clear, but built-up again south of the Ruhr to leave the target completely obscured. The Path Finders were a little late in opening the attack, and a few red TIs were seen to enter the cloud tops at up to 16,000 feet and disappear, whereupon red and yellow release-point flares were dropped at 19.27 to be followed by greens three minutes later. Initially, they appeared to be scattered, but soon became plentiful and concentrated, although some crews would complain that they ignited too high, in the region of 18,000 to 20,000 feet. Generally, however, the marking and bombing were accurate, and many large explosions lit up the clouds, followed by a column of black smoke rising up to 20,000 feet. The Gransden Lodge crews performed their assigned tasks from 18,000 to 19,500 feet between 19.27 and 19.41, before returning with the general opinion that the attack had been scattered and probably ineffective. In fact, it had been very successful, and had caused the destruction of seven hundred houses and inflicted much damage upon industrial buildings, including within the Krupp complex, which was now effectively finished as a producer of war materials.

1 and 6 Groups combined to prepare a main force of 327 Lancasters to send to Ludwigshafen on the evening of the 15th to bomb the city's northern half and the nearby town of Oppau. Both locations contained an important I G Farben factory, which were engaged in the production of synthetic oil and were known to be relying heavily on slave labour. While 405 (Vancouver) Squadron remained at home, 8 Group supported the operation with forty-five Lancasters and fourteen Mosquitos, and contributed to a concentrated attack during which explosions and green and orange smoke were observed, and fires remained visible on the horizon for a hundred miles. The Ludwigshafen I G Farben factory sustained severe damage and fires, and the Oppau plant was put out of action completely, all for the loss of a single Lancaster.

It was on the 16th that German ground forces began a new offensive in the Ardennes, in a short-lived and ultimately doomed attempt to break through the American lines and reach the port of Antwerp in what would become known as the Battle of the Bulge. The inexperienced American forces were taken by surprise and the Germans made startling initial gains, while adverse weather conditions prevented the Allied air forces from blunting their progress.

Another virgin target was the city of Ulm, situated on the Danube to the south-east of Stuttgart and west of Augsburg in southern Germany. It was similar in nature to the recently-bombed Heilbronn, and as a result of the catastrophic raid there, the local Gauleiter had urged the women and children to evacuate the inner city urgently. Plans were put in place to begin evacuation on Monday the 18th, so that Advent could be observed on the Sunday, but something caused a change of plan, and loudspeaker vans toured the city on Sunday urging the population to leave at once in what proved to be a fortuitous move. Unlike Heilbronn, Ulm contained industry, including the important Magirus-Deutz and Kässbohrer lorry factories, and there were also military barracks and depots. A 1 Group main force of 263 Lancasters would benefit from the marking and support of fifty-four Lancasters and thirteen Mosquitos from 8 Group, ten of the Lancasters departing Gransden Lodge between 16.02 and 16.13 with G/C Newson and W/C Lawson the senior pilots on duty. Each crew had been assigned at briefing to one of five marking roles, and all got away safely to encounter cloudy, but fairly good conditions as they headed south to rendezvous with the rest of the bomber stream.

They found the weather deteriorating as they crossed France, and much of the outward flight was spent in cloud, but this cleared at the Rhine to leave excellent visibility, which allowed the crews to map-read their way to the target. Unfortunately, when still some twenty miles short, a layer of thin stratus slid in with tops at 2,000 feet to completely obscure the ground as the Path Finders opened the attack with red TIs at 19.24. These quickly became swallowed up in the cloud or were extinguished by the heavy snow on the ground, but release-point (Wanganui) flares were dropped at the same time, and at 19.31, the Master Bomber, F/L Cook of 35 (Madras Presidency) Squadron, ordered them to be bombed, and he orbited the target from H-3 to H+14, trying to persuade the main force crews to comply and not undershoot on a bunch of errant incendiaries. The 405 (Vancouver) Squadron crews carried out their assigned tasks from 12,000 to 16,000 feet between 19.24 and 19.36 and played their part in an accurate and concentrated raid, which resulted in fierce fires consuming a square kilometre of the city's built-up area. It would be established later that almost 82% of the buildings had sustained damage to some extent, including both lorry factories. There is no question that the evacuation saved many thousands of lives and restricted the civilian death toll to six hundred.

Operations were not yet over for the night of the 17/18th, but it would be well into the early hours of the 18th before a force of 523 aircraft from 4, 6 and 8 Groups departed their stations to attack Duisburg. Thirty-nine Lancasters were provided by 8 Group, including six belonging to 405 (Vancouver) Squadron, along with six Mosquitos for "windowing" and eighteen of the Oboe variety for marking duties. The Gransden Lodge element took off between 03.33 and 03.50 with W/C Rawson and S/L Mussells and three other crews assigned to aiming point G and S/L McQuoid aiming point H. One at each aiming point was to perform the role of visual centerer, while the rest bombed as part of the main force, and they arrived to find the target completely hidden beneath ten-tenths cloud with tops at 6,000 to 8,000 feet. The aiming-points were marked by Oboe Mosquitos, but the TIs disappeared into the cloud to leave a glow as the only reference point for bombing, and most crews confirmed their positions by H2S and Gee before releasing their loads. The 405 (Vancouver) Squadron crews carried out their attacks from 17,000 to 19,000 feet between 06.11 and 06.20 but saw only flashes reflected in the cloud and explosions at 06.12 and 06.16. Despite doubts about the effectiveness of the bombing, 346 houses were destroyed and more than five hundred seriously damaged, and the likelihood is that industry also suffered to some extent.

The dismantling of Germany's railway infrastructure continued with attacks on installations at Trier, Bonn and Cologne on the 19th, the 21st and the night of the 21/22nd and it was for the evening operation against the Nippes marshalling yards to the north of Cologne city centre that a force of 136 aircraft from 4, 6 and 8 Groups was prepared. One of a number of yards on both sides of the Rhine, it was known to be active in supporting the transportation of men and materials to the Ardennes battle front, where the German forces were beginning to run out of steam. 8 Group contributed twenty-one Lancasters and fifteen Mosquitos, eight of the former representing 405 (Vancouver) Squadron, two of which were designated blind sky markers, one a visual centerer and the others main force supporters. They departed Gransden Lodge between 16.04 and 16.12 with

S/L Marcou the senior pilot on duty and arrived in the target area to find ten-tenths low cloud with tops at around 2,000 feet, into which the first red Oboe TIs disappeared at 18.28 to leave a glow that suggested a degree of concentration. Skymarkers were released from 19.36 to 19.40, and a green glow merged with the red to provide a focal point for the main force bombing. The Gransden Lodge crews performed their marking and bombing duties from 17,500 to 18,200 feet between 18.34 and 19.06 after confirming their positions by H2S and Gee but were unable to assess the outcome. Some bombs did hit the yards, destroying forty wagons, a repair workshop and several sections of track, and the city slaughterhouse was also flattened.

Railway yards at Koblenz in south-central Germany and Bingen some thirty-five miles to the south were selected on the 22nd as the targets respectively for 1 and 4 Group main forces numbering 156 Lancasters and ninety Halifaxes, both with Path Finder support. 405 (Vancouver) Squadron provided all fourteen 8 Group Lancasters for the latter, nine of them loaded appropriately for blind sky marking crews and five for visual centerers. They departed Gransden Lodge between 15.46 and 15.59 with W/C Lawson and S/L Marcou the senior pilots on duty and a cookie, five 1,000 and four 500-pounders in each bomb bay along with the requisite marker ordnance. The outward route was covered by ten-tenths cloud until 180 miles from the target, at which point it began gradually to disperse, until only a thin layer of stratus of two to four-tenths remained in the target area. The crews of F/Os Friedman and Woods DFC suffered the frustration of a complete hang-up and while the former were able to release their load manually south-east of the target, the latter were forced to head home with a full bomb bay after a second attempt to release them on the aiming point failed. The others carried out their respective tasks on red and green TIs and Wanganui flares from 16,000 to 18,200 feet between 18.30 and 18.45 and observed the bursts of many cookies on both sides of the River Main. F/O Woods and crew found their undercarriage to be jammed as they prepared to land and were instructed to proceed to the jettison area, where they were able finally to divest themselves of their bomb load. A crash-landing followed near Downham Market, which resulted in terminal damage to PB113, but not to the eight occupants, who walked away apparently unscathed. Absent from debriefing was the all-RCAF crew of F/O Tite DFC, who became the first to go missing since September. PA977 came down somewhere in the Ruhr defence zone with fatal consequences for F/O Tite DFC RCAF and three of his crew, while their colleagues fell into enemy hands.

405 (Vancouver) Squadron was not involved when 8 Group detailed a force of twenty-seven Lancasters and three Mosquitos to attack the marshalling yards in the Gremberg district of Cologne on the eastern side of the Rhine on the 23rd. At briefings, the crews were told to form into three Oboe-led sections for the run across the target, but tragedy struck the formation as it flew out over the Kent coast at South Foreland at 10,000 feet. Two 35 (Madras Presidency) Lancasters collided and crashed into the sea, and although some parachutes were observed, by the time that rescue services arrived on the scene, none of the fourteen men could be saved and only seven bodies were recovered. The remainder of the force continued on in sombre mood and were greeted in the target area by clear skies, good visibility and a defence of the most hostile nature in the form of predicted flak and fighters. The marshalling yards were clearly visible, but the formations broke up ten miles before reaching them as flak shells burst among the Lancasters, and the leader was forced to issue instructions to bomb visually. Five Lancasters of 582 Squadron were shot down, one of them captained by S/L Palmer DFC & Bar, who was the Master Bomber and a member of 109 Squadron, which also lost a Mosquito. Palmer's Lancaster was on fire before reaching the aiming-point and

crashed in the target area killing all but the rear gunner, who fell into enemy hands. S/L Palmer would be awarded a Victoria Cross posthumously in recognition of his valour.

The campaign against railway targets continued without 405 (Vancouver) Squadron on Christmas Eve, when a further attempt was made to cripple the Cologne-Nippes marshalling yards, which had escaped damage at the hands of a 4, 6 and 8 Group force a few days earlier. This time the job was given to a 1 Group main force of eighty-one Lancasters with sixteen Lancasters and five Mosquitos provided by 8 Group as the marker force, and they succeeded in inflicting severe damage on tracks and installations and blew up an ammunition train.

The final wartime Christmas Day was celebrated peacefully on the stations, but the Boxing Day festivities were curtailed for some crews from each Group, when the Command called for attacks on troop positions around St Vith. The weather had prevented air support for the American forces, but the enemy advance had now stalled because of fuel and ammunition shortages and an attempt to withdraw back into Germany was underway in more favourable bombing conditions.

405 (Vancouver) Squadron was not called upon for the above, but it was business as usual for the crews of W/C Rawson, S/L Marcou and F/Os Kettlewell and Vann on the 27th, who were required to support a 1, 3 and 5 Group main force of 186 Lancasters in an attack on the marshalling yards at Rheydt, the town twinned with Mönchengladbach on the western fringe of the Ruhr. 8 Group was to provide fourteen Lancasters and eleven Mosquitos, with 35 (Madras Presidency) squadron's S/L Everett and F/L Roberts designated Master Bomber and Deputy. The Gransden Lodge quartet took off between 12.42 and 13.03, three with marking tasks to perform and one to bomb with the main force and reached the target to find excellent conditions and visibility at fifteen miles. The first red TIs fell some distance north of the aiming point but at 14.58 yellow TIs landed some fifty yards to the north and were backed up by further reds and greens, to which the Master Bomber directed the main force element. The Gransden Lodge crews carried out their respective tasks from 15,500 to 16,500 feet between 14.56 and 15.03 and observed the main weight of bombs to fall in the southern end of the marshalling yards, although some overshot and landed in the town to the east. It was not long before the target area was covered by a mass of fires emitting brown and grey smoke, and the upwind edge of the smoke became the aiming point for the tail end of the attack. Despite some under and overshooting, the consensus was of a successful outcome.

Marshalling yards at Mönchengladbach and Bonn were the targets for forces of moderate size on the 28th, both supported by 8 Group, and it was for the latter that 405 (Vancouver) Squadron made ready sixteen Lancasters as part of an 8 Group effort of twenty-nine Lancasters and sixteen Mosquitos. Six were to mark for a 1 Group main force of 133 Lancasters, while nine others acted as supporters, and departed Gransden Lodge between 16.09 and 16.23 with S/Ls Marcou, Mussells and Neilly the senior pilots on duty. They flew out under clear skies to the south coast and the English Channel, where cloud began to build, and by the time they reached the German frontier it had become ten-tenths with tops at between 2,000 and 8,000 feet with bright moonlight above. Eight non-marker Mosquitos dropped "window" ahead of the bomber stream, before carrying out a second run to drop a cookie each onto the Oboe markers. The initial Oboe TIs went down on time but disappeared into the cloud tops, and only one visual centre dropped greens, before five blind secondary marker crews released red and green skymarker flares in a good concentration. The Master Bomber directed the main force crews to aim for these or the diffused glow of TIs in the cloud, the 405 (Vancouver) Squadron crews carrying out their assigned tasks from 17,500 to 18,500 feet between 18.43 and 18.47. They were unable to assess the results, but Bomber Command claimed major damage to the railway installations, although, apart from the collapse of the Victoria bridge over the main line from Cologne to Koblenz, the damage occurred mainly within the city area, where almost five hundred people lost their lives.

Sixteen 405 (Vancouver) Squadron crews attended briefing on the 29th to learn that they would be heading to the Ruhr later that evening to target the Hydrierwerke synthetic oil refinery at Scholven-Buer in the north-western quarter of Gelsenkirchen. They were part of an 8 Group force of twenty-eight Lancasters and twenty-two Mosquitos marking for and supporting 296 Lancasters of 1 and 6 Groups and departed Gransden Lodge between 15.46 and 16.04 with S/Ls Marcou, Mussells and Neilly the senior pilots on duty. Nine crews were assigned to a number of marking roles and the rest as main force supporters, and all reached the target in the central Ruhr, having enjoyed good weather conditions on the way out. The target was found to be cloud-covered, as the result of which, skymarkers had to be employed and the first Oboe red went down a fraction early at 18.53, followed precisely at Zero-Hour by a good concentration of others to leave their red glow clearly visible through the clouds. The Gransden Lodge participants performed as briefed from 17,000 to 18,500 feet between 18.56 and 19.05, before returning safely to report numerous large explosions, smoke rising to 15,000 feet and fires visible for a hundred miles. A local report detailed three hundred high-explosive bombs hitting the area of the plant, causing fires and inflicting severe damage upon the installations. A further 3,100 bombs fell in other parts of Scholven, causing much residential and industrial destruction, and surface buildings at two coal mines were also hit and severely damaged. The return to Gransden Lodge of PB525 was awaited in vain, and no clue to the fate of F/O Wilsher RCAF and his seven RCAF crew mates has since been uncovered.

The squadron undertook its final operation of the year on the evening of the 30th, when 8 Group committed forty-four Lancasters and twenty-one Mosquitos to support a 4 and 6 Group main force of 356 Halifaxes and forty-eight Lancasters in an attack on Cologne's Kalk-Nord railway yards on the eastern side of the Rhine. The size of the main force suggested that this was an area raid on that part of the city wherein lay important factories including the Klöckner-Humboldt-Deutz works. The nine-strong 405 (Vancouver) Squadron element departed Gransden Lodge between 18.25 and 18.38 with S/Ls Marcou and Mussells the senior pilots on duty, six assigned to a marking role and three as main force supporters. The attack opened at 20.57 with red TIs in a good concentration and they were followed by skymarkers and green TIs. Cloud made precision difficult, but the impression was that the bombing fell largely between the yards and the river, the Gransden Lodge element fulfilling its brief from 18,000 to 18,500 feet between 20.56 and 21.07. Post-raid reconnaissance and local sources confirmed that the yards had been severely damaged, along with two adjacent passenger stations. Two ammunition trains are reported to have blown up, and road communications were also disrupted.

During the course of the month the squadron took part in thirteen operations and dispatched 140 sorties for the loss of three Lancasters and two crews.

All things considered, it had been a good year for 405 (Vancouver) Squadron, particularly so once the winter campaign was over. Its losses were markedly less than two of the founder Pathfinder units, 7 and 156 Squadrons, and matched those of 35 (Madras Presidency) Squadron. As the

German Ardennes offensive faltered, it was clear that the coming year would bring victory, although much remained to be done before the tenacious and courageous enemy forces finally laid down their arms. Some squadrons would sail through the final four months of the bombing war with barely a scratch, while others would sustain heavy casualties. 405 (Vancouver) Squadron was destined to fall somewhere in between.

January 1945

The final year of the war began with a flourish, as the Luftwaffe launched its ill-conceived and ultimately, ill-fated Operation Bodenplatte (Baseplate) at first light on New Year's Day. The intention to destroy the Allied air forces on the ground at the recently liberated airfields in France, Holland and Belgium was only modestly realized, after the entire day fighter strength was committed to low level bombing and strafing attacks into the teeth of the airfield flak defences. The survivors then had to run the gauntlet of Allied fighters to make their escape, and the episode cost the German day fighter force around 250 aircraft and 150 pilots, who were killed, wounded or fell into Allied hands. It was a setback from which the Tagjagd would never fully recover, while the Allies could make good their losses within hours from their enormous stockpiles. The operation also produced some very jittery American anti-aircraft gunners, who, for the remainder of the day and night, would fire at anything that flew, and a number of Bomber Command aircraft would fall victim to "friendly fire" incidents.

The old enemy of Nuremberg was posted on the 2nd as one of two major urban targets for the night and would face a main force of 445 Lancasters drawn from 1, 3 and 6 Groups with a further sixty-nine Lancasters representing 8 Group to provide the marking and bombing support. Meanwhile, 145 miles to the west, twenty-two 8 Group Lancasters would be supporting a simultaneous attack by 351 Halifaxes of 4 and 6 Groups on two I G Farben chemical plants, one in Ludwigshafen and the other close by in Oppau. Both operations would also benefit from Oboe Mosquitos, seven for Nuremberg and twenty-two for Ludwigshafen. 405 (Vancouver) Squadron detailed sixteen Lancasters for Nuremberg and briefed their crews for a variety of marking roles before sending them on their way from Gransden Lodge between 15.48 and 16.06 with G/C Newson, W/C Rawson and S/L Marcou the senior pilots on duty. The two forces were to follow a similar route until dividing shortly before reaching Ludwigshafen, and began the outward flight over six-tenths cloud, which thickened over the Channel and remained at ten-tenths until breaking up from 7°East. The Nuremberg force found the city to be under clear skies with excellent visibility, enhanced both by the contrast between the built-up area and the snow-covered countryside and by the light from illuminating flares that highlighted the River Pegnitz, railway tracks and the built-up area. A tail wind had driven some crews to the target ahead of schedule, and they were forced to orbit until the Path Finders opened the attack, also a minute or two early. The first salvoes of mixed red and green TIs cascaded and fell in a triangular pattern squarely onto the marshalling yards in the centre of the city, and the Master Bomber directed the main force crews to these. The bombing was accurate and concentrated, and the aiming point soon disappeared under smoke, the upwind edge of which became the new aiming-point. The 405 (Vancouver) Squadron crews carried out their assigned tasks from 18,000 to 18,500 feet between 19.20 and 19.44 and all but one returned home to report a highly successful operation.

Absent from debriefing was the crew of W/C Lawson DSO & Bar DFC RAF VR, whose PB477 was now a smouldering wreck on farmland at Rohrau, near Nufringen, twenty miles south-west of Stuttgart, having been shot down while homebound. W/C Lawson and four others lost their lives, while the flight engineer and rear gunner of the mixed RAF, RAAF and RCAF crew survived to fall into enemy hands. W/C Lawson was on his ninety-second sortie, having served tours, it will be recalled, with 149 and 156 Squadrons in 1941 and 1943. Post-raid reconnaissance and local sources confirmed the severity of the destruction at Nuremberg, which reduced to rubble more than 4,600 houses, most of them apartment blocks, along with two thousand medieval houses and four hundred industrial buildings. At least eighteen hundred people lost their lives on the ground, and in return, the defenders claimed five Bomber Command aircraft. The success of the Ludwigshafen operation was confirmed by local reports that five hundred high-explosive bombs had fallen within the confines of the two I G Farben production plants, along with many thousands of incendiaries. This had put an end to all production of synthetic oil, and adjacent industrial buildings, residential property and railway installations had also been destroyed.

Another sad incident on this night was the loss of KB700, the Ruhr Express, which was now with 419 (Moose) Squadron, having begun its operational career with 405 (Vancouver) Squadron back in November 1943. It bounced on landing at Middleton-St-George on return from Nuremberg at the end of its forty-ninth sortie and was consumed by fire after running off the end of the runway.

There was a very late start for 1, 5 and 8 Group crews when they next went to war on the 4/5th, the first wave crews from 5 Group climbing into their aircraft at midnight to take-off at around 01.00 for what would be a controversial operation. The target was the French town of Royan in the Gironde Estuary, where a German garrison was holding out against a siege by Free French forces making for Bordeaux. A French request for assistance found its way to SHAEF, which handed the task to Bomber Command on the basis that the town was occupied only by German soldiers and French collaborators. The second wave crews from 1 and 8 Groups were to follow an hour behind, and almost 350 Lancasters were involved in total, including fourteen from 405 (Vancouver) Squadron. They departed Gransden Lodge between 02.01 and 02.13 with G/C Newson and S/Ls Mussells and Neilly the senior pilots on duty and all assigned to marking roles. It transpired, that two thousand civilians, not collaborators, were still resident in the town, despite an offer from the garrison commander to evacuate them, and they were about to suffer the consequences of their decision to stay. The 405 (Vancouver) Squadron participants carried out their respective tasks from 8,000 to 12,000 feet between 05.23 and 05.35, contributing to more than fifteen hundred tons of high explosive bombs falling on the doomed town and its residents and many hundreds died.

Briefings took place on the 5th for a major assault on the city of Hannover, which was to be conducted in two phases separated by two hours, with 340 Halifaxes from 4 and 6 Groups as the first phase main force and 220 Lancasters of 1 and 6 Groups as the second. 8 Group detailed fifty-nine Lancasters for phase one and thirty-one for phase two with seven Oboe Mosquitos attending each. 405 (Vancouver) Squadron's sixteen participants were all part of the second wave, most briefed to perform a variety of marking roles with just three to bomb with the main force, and they departed Gransden Lodge between 19.15 and 19.32 with W/C Rawson the senior pilot on duty. The route over the North Sea and Holland and as far as 7° East was covered by a layer of up to ten-tenths cloud at between 5,000 and 12,000 feet, but from south of Bremen to the target, clear skies prevailed and the burning city acted as a beacon to draw the bombers on for the last one hundred miles. The Halifax attack had taken place over ten-tenths low cloud with tops at between 2,000 and 5,000 feet, but good H2S returns enabled the Path Finder element to establish its position over the aiming-point in the northern half of the city, and the bombing had been accurate and concentrated. Numerous fires were spread across the city, the glare and smoke from which created challenging conditions for the second phase and most TIs were soon lost to view, but in truth, marking was somewhat superfluous. The 405 (Vancouver) Squadron crews carried out their assigned tasks from 18,000 to 18,500 feet between 21.44 and 21.54, and the main force crews found sufficient red and green TIs to satisfy their needs. This second phase attack added to the destruction inflicted upon Hannover, and once the fires had been extinguished and the dust had settled, the local authorities were able to assess that almost five hundred apartment blocks had been destroyed with their 3,600 individual dwelling units.

Gransden Lodge was not called into action on the 6th for an attack that night by a force of 482 aircraft from 1, 4, 6 and 8 Group stations on an important junction in the enemy's railway system in the town of Hanau-am-Main, situated a short distance to the east of Frankfurt. Forty-eight Lancasters and fourteen Mosquitos were provided by 8 Group, and they contributed to the destruction of 40% of the built-up area and extensive damage to railway installations achieved through a blanket of ten-tenths cloud. A simultaneous 3 Group G-H raid on railway yards at Neuss also achieved its aims, while scattering bombs across adjacent residential districts and causing the destruction of or serious damage to 1,749 houses and nineteen industrial premises.

A major operation against Munich was planned for the 7th, for which a two-wave force of 645 aircraft was drawn from all five of the Lancaster-equipped groups. 5 Group, which was unused to sharing this target, would lead the way with 213 Lancasters and three Mosquitos, leaving the second wave to follow two hours later, the tanks of the heavy brigade containing sufficient fuel for a nine-hour round-trip. 8 Group detailed seventy-one Lancasters and six Mosquitos, fourteen of the former representing 405 (Vancouver) Squadron and departing Gransden Lodge between 19.09 and 19.22 with W/C Rawson and S/Ls Marcou and Neilly the senior pilots on duty. As they climbed away to rendezvous with the rest of the force and set course for the French coast, the 5 Group element was about to cross the Franco-German frontier near Strasbourg with an hour's flight still ahead of it. On arrival at Munich, the spearhead encountered broken medium-level cloud at 14,000 feet, with haze or thin cloud below, by which time, the Master Bomber had made a visual identification of the aiming-point and sent the first two primary blind markers in to deliver their TIs at the same time thirty seconds ahead of the planned opening of the attack. The flare force went in immediately afterwards, and illuminated the city very effectively, allowing ground detail to be identified. Red TIs went down west and east of the River Isar, bracketing the aiming-point, and the Master Bomber ordered the backers up to drop their TIs between the reds, after which, the next batch of flares formed a circle around the aiming point. The main force was then called in, and as they withdrew with empty bomb bays minutes later, they left behind a burning city that would act as a beacon visible to the second phase crews from 130 miles away.

The second phase began well on time with green TIs and red flares with green stars, the former quickly disappearing into the cloud tops and leaving the skymarkers to provide a concentrated reference for the bombing element. Eight of the Gransden Lodge crews had been briefed for marking duties and six as main force supporters, and they carried out their assigned tasks from 18,000 to 18,500 feet between 22.24 and 22.40, some observing five large explosions between

22.27 and 22.41, the last-mentioned resulting in a mushroom of cloud breaking through the cloud tops. F/O Sparling RCAF and his all-RCAF crew lost their lives when PB229 collided on the way home with PB137, a Lancaster of fellow Path Finder unit, 635 Squadron, and crashed some twelve miles south-south-east of the centre of Nuremberg. The other crew also perished, but curiously, only two bodies were recovered and the remaining five are commemorated on the Runnymede Memorial. The other squadron participants returned safely to report a successful night's work, which left substantial damage in central and industrial districts, but as usual at Munich, no local report emerged to provide details. This proved to be the final large-scale attack of the war on Munich, but joint operations led by 5 Group would become an established format for the remainder of the war.

A number of operations were planned against Saarbrücken's marshalling yards and the first took place in daylight on the 13th at the hands of 3 Group employing its G-H system. This was followed up by 274 aircraft from 4, 6 and 8 Groups that night, 8 Group detailing twenty Lancasters and fourteen Mosquitos split equally between aiming-points B and C. The Oboe Mosquitos marked the aiming-points with red TIs, which the heavy marker crews backed up with greens, and the main force Halifax crews delivered their bomb loads accurately into the yards to leave them severely damaged.

On the following day, a 3 Group G-H force of 134 Lancasters was made ready to return to Saarbrücken, and this time, although no mention is made in Bomber Command War Diaries, it seems that they were to be accompanied by nineteen Lancasters and eight Mosquitos of 8 Group. The 405 (Vancouver) Squadron ORB for this period is seriously corrupted, but it seems that nine Lancasters departed Gransden Lodge between 11.52 and 11.58 bound for aiming point A with G/C Newson the senior pilot on duty, three crews assigned to marker roles and six as main force supporters. They arrived in the target area to be greeted by clear skies and favourable conditions and carried out their respective tasks from 17,000 to 18,000 feet between 14.56 and 15.05, and as these yards were not attacked again, it must be assumed that they were put permanently out of action.

That night's operations would generate more than 1,200 sorties, and the main event was an operation against the I G Farbenindustrie synthetic oil refinery situated at Leuna near Merseburg, which was one of many similar sites situated in an arc from north to south to the west of Leipzig. The seven 405 (Vancouver) Squadron participants were part of an 8 Group contribution of fifty-seven Lancasters and six Mosquitos in another of the two-phase operations to be led by 5 Group and followed up by a 306-strong main force of 1 and 6 Group Lancasters three hours later. The 5 Group force numbered 210 Lancasters and nine Mosquitos, which began to depart their stations at around 16.00 for the three-and-a-half-hour outward flight, which would take them via the southerly route to eastern Germany across France. They reached the target area to find clear skies but poor vertical visibility due to a layer of haze, which, in the event, was no hindrance to the primary blind markers, whose job was to establish their position over the aiming-point by means of H2S. They delivered their TIs from 18,000 feet, after which, the first element of the flare force went in. The Master Bomber called for ground marking only, which was carried out by the low-level Mosquito element, and by 20.50 he was satisfied and sent the marker aircraft home.

As the main force crews went in to attack, the 405 (Vancouver) Squadron element was taking off from Gransden Lodge between 19.54 and 20.06 with S/L Neilly the senior pilot on duty. They headed for the Sussex coast in good weather conditions over thin cloud, which would prevail throughout the almost nine-hour round trip and reached the target to encounter ten-tenths thin cloud or smoke, with the glow from the 5 Group raid clearly visible. The illuminating flares went down at 23.54, followed by red and green TIs, and although they could be seen, the ground itself was completely obscured, and the Master Bomber experienced difficulty in identifying the aiming point, eventually instructing the main force to bomb on the red and yellow release-point flares. The Gransden Lodge crews carried out their assigned marking tasks from 18,000 feet between 23.53 and 23.59, and large explosions were reported at 23.59 and 00.18, one of which sent dense clouds of smoke rising through the cloud tops. Many returning crews thought the operation to have been scattered and probably ineffective, when in fact it had been among the most devastating attacks on the synthetic oil industry thus far in the war.

Feverish activity across the Command on the 16th prepared more than twelve hundred aircraft for action, the majority to participate in four major operations that night, three to target oil refineries and the largest to deliver an area attack on the eastern city of Magdeburg, which also contained the Braunkohle Aktien Gesellschaft (production company) Bergius process hydrogenation plant, located in the Rothensee district to the north of the city centre. The independent 3 and 5 Groups were handed the refineries at Wanne-Eickel in the Ruhr and Brüx in Czechoslovakia respectively, leaving 320 Halifaxes of 4 and 6 Groups to take care of Magdeburg and 283 Lancasters of 1 and 6 Groups to ply their trade at Zeitz-Tröglitz, the location of another Braunkohle-Benzin A G plant, situated some twenty miles south-west of Leipzig. 8 Group detailed forty-four Lancasters and seven Mosquitos for Magdeburg and forty-five Lancasters for Zeitz, with 405 (Vancouver) Squadron contributing seven and nine Lancasters respectively, their crews all assigned to a variety of marker roles. They departed Gransden Lodge together between 18.13 and 18.41 with G/C Newson leading the Magdeburg element and S/L Neilly the Zeitz-bound section.

The Halifax brigade set course from the Yorkshire coast to rendezvous with the Path Finder element over the North Sea as they set course to enter Germany via Jade Bay, before passing to the south of Hamburg and reaching the target after an outward flight of almost four hours. The skies were clear and the visibility excellent as the Path Finders illuminated the aiming-point and marked it out with red and green TIs from 21.37, before the Master Bomber called in the main force crews to take advantage of the opportunity. The 405 (Vancouver) Squadron crews performed their marking duties as briefed from 18,000 to 18,500 feet between 21.35 and 21.45, reporting the early bombing to have fallen into the southern districts, before spreading gradually into other parts of the city. By the time of the force's withdrawal, the built-up area appeared to be on fire from end to end and the glow could be seen from a hundred miles into the return flight. It was not a one-sided affair, however, a fact made manifest by seventeen empty dispersals that should have been occupied by Halifaxes.

Meanwhile, some eighty miles to the south, well-placed illumination flares were followed at 22.08 by a mix of red and green TIs, which fell a little to the north and south of the aiming-point. The Master Bomber controlled the situation expertly, and directed the bombing, which became focused where intended and set off a series of sizeable explosions between 22.13 and 22.23, the largest sending a mushroom of black smoke to 10,000 feet and beyond. The Gransden Lodge crews carried out their assigned tasks from 13,000 to 18,500 feet between 22.09 and 22.20 and returned safely to report the oil plant and parts of the town to be ablaze. Among ten missing Lancasters was PB402 containing the eight-man predominantly RCAF crew of F/L Payne RCAF, and there were no survivors of the crash at Pfaffenhaus during the long withdrawal via southern Germany to the French frontier near Strasbourg. Post-raid reconnaissance confirmed the success of the Magdeburg operation, Bomber Command claiming that 44% of the city's built-up area had been destroyed.

Two operations were posted on the 22nd, one by a main force of 260 Lancasters from 1 and 3 Groups with twenty-six Lancasters and sixteen Mosquitos of 8 Group against Thyssen's Vereinigte Stahlwerke coking plant in the Hamborn district to the east of Duisburg city centre, and the other, an area attack fifteen miles to the east on Gelsenkirchen by 152 aircraft of 4, 5 and 8 Groups. It was for the former that thirteen 405 (Vancouver) Squadron Lancasters were prepared, nine for the use of marker crews and four for those bombing with the main force. They departed Gransden Lodge between 17.42 and 17.54 with S/Ls Marcou, Mussells and Neilly the senior pilots on duty and climbed into low cloud that persisted as far as the French coast, after which it gradually diminished to leave the target area clear with moonlight and excellent visibility. Crews were able to confirm visually the accuracy of the Path Finder markers, and apart from one stray red TI in the Ruhrort docks complex, they all fell around the aiming point and attracted the bomb loads. The 405 (Vancouver) Squadron crews carried out their assigned tasks from 17,000 to 19,000 feet between 19.58 and 20.08, the bombing element dispensing five 2,000 and two 1,000-pounders each onto red and green TIs and returned home confident in the quality of their work. They had missed a particularly large explosion at 20.37, which was seen by the last crews to leave the target area, and bombing photos supported the claims of a highly destructive raid. The nearby Thyssen steelworks was also severely damaged after receiving five hundred bombs, and there was much collateral damage in adjacent residential districts. At debriefings on the participating stations, the main force crews were full of praise for the work of the Path Finders.

When eleven crews were called to briefing at Gransden Lodge on the 28th, it was to learn of that night's trip to Stuttgart by 602 aircraft from 1, 4, 6 and 8 Groups divided into two forces separated by three hours, each with its own specific target. The first phase, by 226 aircraft, was to be directed at the marshalling yards in the town of Kornwestheim, situated just beyond the northern boundary of Stuttgart, while the second phase would target the Hirth aero-engine factory at Zuffenhausen, some two miles to the south. 8 Group put up twenty-four Lancasters and thirteen Mosquitos for the first phase and thirty-one Lancasters and fifteen Mosquitos for the second, and it was for the latter that 405 (Vancouver) Squadron loaded six of its aircraft for a marking role and five with eighteen 500-pounders each to deliver as part of the main force. They departed Gransden Lodge between 20.26 and 20.37 with G/C Newson the senior pilot on duty and enjoyed an uneventful outward flight across France to enter Germany north of Strasbourg. They were assisted by Path Finder Mosquitos dispensing "window" ahead of the bomber stream, which, on arrival in the target area, found ten-tenths stratocumulus with tops at up to 12,000 feet and thin stratus between 15,000 and 20,000 feet.

Oboe Mosquitos delivered TIs three to four minutes late, but they disappeared into the cloud as they cascaded and were soon lost to view. Red skymarkers with green stars were plentiful but ignited far too high before drifting in the wind and becoming scattered, which resulted in a lack of concentration and the spraying of bombs across northern Stuttgart. The 405 (Vancouver) Squadron participants fulfilled their respective briefs from 18,000 to 18,500 feet between 23.29 and 23.42, aiming predominantly at skymarkers, and observed large explosions at 23.36 and 23.38 and the glow of fires beneath the cloud. They headed home suspecting that they had failed to deliver an effective blow on the factory and that a decoy fire site and dummy TIs fired into the air by the defenders had also attracted some bomb loads. Their suspicions were partly confirmed by local sources, which did admit to damage to the railway installations and to a number of important war industry factories including the Robert Bosch works. This would prove to be the last of fifty-three major raids on this important industrial city, which now lay largely in ruins. It was a sad end to the month for Gransden Lodge, to which PB650 failed to return after crashing at Deufringen, a dozen miles or so to the south-west of Stuttgart. Pilot, F/O Cummer RCAF, was an American and he was killed along with all but the rear gunner, who was taken into captivity. Following the remarkably low losses incurred during the final quarter of 1944, the relatively expensive month of January reminded everyone that flying in bombers was still an extremely hazardous occupation.

During the course of the month, the squadron took part in ten operations and dispatched 116 sorties for the loss of four Lancasters and crews.

February 1945

The weather at the start of February provided difficult conditions for marking and bombing, and a number of operations would struggle to achieve their aims in the face of thick, low cloud and strong winds. Three major operations were laid on for the night of the 1/2nd, the largest by 382 Lancasters and fourteen Mosquitos of 1, 6 and 8 Groups against Ludwigshafen, while thirty-five miles to the north, 340 aircraft from 4, 6 and 8 Groups attended to the city of Mainz. Further north still, 5 Group's target was the marshalling yards in the town of Siegen, situated some fifty miles east of Cologne. 8 Group would be represented at Ludwigshafen by forty-five Lancasters and fourteen Mosquitos and at Mainz by forty Lancasters and eight Mosquitos, and it was for the former that 405 (Vancouver) Squadron made ready thirteen Lancasters and dispatched them from Gransden Lodge between 16.35 and 16.47 with W/C Rawson and S/Ls Mussells and Neilly the senior pilots on duty. They were assigned to a variety of marking and bombing support roles in an operation to target communications in and through the city to hamper enemy troop movements. The skies were largely clear from the Sussex coast until around 6° East, where cloud began to build and was at nine-tenths with tops at 6,000 feet by the time the spearhead of the bomber stream arrived at the target at the end of a three-hour flight. The Path Finders opened the attack punctually at 19.11 with cascading red TIs backed up by greens and followed by release point flares, and these could be seen by the approaching main force crews until the start of their bombing runs, when the ground became concealed by cloud. They then had to rely on the red and green skymarkers, which resulted in scattered bombing and a degree of undershooting, and small gaps in the cloud revealed incendiary fires on both sides of the Rhine. The 405 (Vancouver) Squadron crews carried out their respective tasks from 17,500 to 18,500 feet between 19.14 and 19.22 and observed large explosions at 19.20, 19.25, 19.36 and 19.42, the last-mentioned by crews fifty miles into their homeward flight. Local sources confirmed that bombs had fallen right across the city and that nine hundred houses had been destroyed or seriously damaged along with the marshalling yards, and a Rhine bridge had been forced to close for repairs.

When briefings took place on the 2nd, they came with the bad news that a tour of operations for main force crews was to be increased again to thirty-six sorties. On 5 Group stations in drizzly

Lincolnshire, 250 crews were told further, that the night's operation was to be against Karlsruhe in southern Germany, and that this was one of three major undertakings involving a total of 1,150 aircraft. Elsewhere, 495 crews from 1, 3, 6 and 8 Groups were informed that Wiesbaden would be their destination and that it would the first time that this city, separated from nearby Mainz to the south by the River Rhine, had been targeted by Bomber Command. The third operation on this night would bring a return to the Ruhr for 277 Halifaxes of 4 and 6 Groups with twenty-seven 8 Group Lancasters and nineteen Mosquitos to provide the marking for an attack on the Krupp Treibstoffwerke synthetic oil plant in the Wanne-Eickel district of Herne. It was for this that 405 (Vancouver) Squadron made ready seven Lancasters and dispatched them from Gransden Lodge between 21.00 and 21.30 with S/Ls McQuoid and Mussells the senior pilots on duty. Four crews had been designated as visual centerers and three as main force supporters and all reached the target area to find ten-tenths cloud with tops at between 4,000 and 8,000 feet, which prevented the visual centerers from delivering their green TIs and left the marking reliant upon red TIs dropped by the Oboe Mosquitos from around 23.10. A red glow beneath the cloud seemed too bright to be a fire and became the focus for many of the main force crews, who took it to be a red TI. The Gransden Lodge contingent fulfilled their briefs from 17,500 to 18,500 feet between 23.15 and 23.21 in the face of intense and accurate flak, and large explosions were noted at 23.15, 23.20 and 23.27. An assessment proved to be impossible, and according to local sources, most of the bombs fell into open ground around a coal mine.

Two Ruhr oil production sites were the focus of attention on the evening of the 3rd, one of them the Prosper coking plant at Welheim, an eastern district of Bottrop, and situated about five miles to the north-east of Duisburg and Oberhausen, and the other was the Hansa benzol plant at Dortmund. The former was assigned to a 1 and 8 Group heavy force of 192 Lancasters, of which 8 Group contributed twenty-eight along with eighteen Mosquitos, while the latter was entrusted to 3 Group and its highly effective G-H bombing system. 405 (Vancouver) Squadron loaded eight of its Lancasters with the appropriate payloads for blind sky marking and visual centering roles and sent them on their way from Gransden Lodge between 16.54 and 17.01 with G/C Newson and W/C Rawson the senior pilots on duty. They adopted one of the familiar routes to the Ruhr and flew out under largely clear skies until a few miles from the target, where a little low cloud began to form at 3,000 feet, but insufficient to interfere with the progress of the raid. The first red TIs appeared punctually at 19.26 and were observed to be both accurate and concentrated, and they were followed by greens which also fell right on the aiming point. The 405 (Vancouver) Squadron crews carried out their respective tasks from 17,500 to 18,000 feet between 19.30 and 19.35 and many main force crews were able to confirm visually the effectiveness of the marking and proceeded to bomb in a very tight pattern. Fires and explosions were evident along with much black smoke and it was clear to most that a successful operation had taken place, albeit in the face of a spirited and accurate flak defence supported by some two hundred searchlights in cones of between ten and twenty beams. Post-raid reconnaissance confirmed that extensive damage had been inflicted upon the plant.

Gransden Lodge was not called upon to provide aircraft on the 4th, when the three main operations were against the Gutehoffnunugshütte Oberhausen A G benzol plant at Osterfeld near Leipzig, the Gelsenkirchener Bergwerke A G (Nordstern) coking plant in the Ruhr and an area attack on the city of Bonn.

The towns of Cleves and Goch are separated by around eight miles and lie east of the Reichswald and to the south of the Rhine, where the British XXX Corps was preparing to advance. 464 aircraft of 4, 6 and 8 Groups were made ready on the 7th to attack the latter, which was part of the enemy's defensive line, while a predominantly 1 Group force dealt with the former. 8 Group detailed forty-seven Lancasters and sixteen Mosquitos, fifteen of the former provided by 405 (Vancouver) Squadron, which departed Gransden Lodge between 19.36 and 19.58 with S/L Marcou the senior pilot on duty and eleven crews assigned to a variety of marking roles. The weather was good as they climbed away over Cambridgeshire and set course for the exit point at Hastings on the Sussex coast via an outward route that was virtually cloud-free until a dozen miles from the target, where it began to build and was at seven to ten-tenths in a band from 5,000 to 7,000 feet when the raid began. This prompted the Master Bomber to bring the main-force crews down to provide them with a view of the red and green TIs on the aiming-point. The first Gransden Lodge blind illuminators arrived on scene at 21.55 and the squadron maintained a presence at between 4,000 and 10,000 feet until 22.08. The Master Bomber broadcast continuously between 22.12 and 22.18, urging the main force crews to bomb the centre of the mixed TIs, before switching at 22.24 to the green TIs. However, as the aiming-point became obscured by smoke and bombs were seen to undershoot by up to two miles, he called a halt to proceedings after only 155 aircraft had bombed. Returning crews reported one violent explosion and a burgeoning red glow beneath the cloud that suggested an effective attack, while a few claimed that they had been unable to pick up the Master Bomber's transmissions. Post-raid reconnaissance revealed much damage to the town, which had been largely evacuated by the civilian population, and most of the 180 known deaths occurred among Russian, Italian and Dutch forced workers.

Three main operations were planned for the night of the 8/9th, two of them targeting oil refineries, one in north-eastern Germany and the other in the Ruhr, both of which required participation by 405 (Vancouver) Squadron. Eleven crews were called to briefing at Gransden Lodge during the afternoon to learn that they were to take part in the third, and what would prove to be the final raid in a series against the Wintershall synthetic oil refinery at Politz, which had begun in December. Situated to the north of Stettin in what is now Poland, it represented a long round-trip of some 1,400 miles, and was to be another two-phase attack led by a 5 Group force of 227 Lancasters and seven Mosquitos and completed two hours later by 241 Lancasters from 1 and 8 Groups. 8 Group's contribution amounted to fifty-seven Lancasters, those representing 405 (Vancouver) Squadron taking off between 19.19 and 19.34 with G/C Newson, W/C Rawson and S/L Marcou the senior pilots on duty and all assigned to marking roles. They approached the target under clear skies and drawn on by six fires resulting from the earlier 5 Group raid, and the attack opened on time with flares illuminating the plant before marking began with red and green TIs from the Deputy Master Bomber at 23.10. These were well-placed on the aiming-point and were soon backed up by others to form an excellent concentration within the boundaries of the site. The marking was maintained throughout the attack, the Gransden Lodge contingent carrying out their assigned tasks from 14,500 to 15,500 feet between 23.08 and 23.17, and the main force exploited the opportunity to deliver a decisive blow against this important contributor to Germany's war effort. The entire area was soon covered by smoke, through which numerous explosions were observed, one of particular violence that lasted seconds and added another column of smoke to the pall that had reached 10,000 feet by the time that the last of the bombers turned for home. The glow remained visible for a hundred miles, and post-raid reconnaissance confirmed that the plant's ability to produce oil had been ended for good. The success cost a dozen Lancasters, one of which reached Sweden, while

ND912 was lost without trace with the predominantly RCAF crew of F/O McIntyre RCAF, whose names are inscribed on the Runnymede Memorial.

The above crews were back on the ground and at debriefing by the time that four others took off between 04.03 and 04.06 as part of an 8 Group contribution of eight Lancasters and twenty Mosquitos to another raid on the Krupp Treibstoffwerke synthetic oil plant at Wanne-Eickel. They were to perform the role of visual centerers for a main force of two hundred Halifaxes of 4 and 6 Groups and arrived in the target area to find five to eight-tenths cloud with tops at 8,000 to 10,000 feet and a base at around 5,000 feet with a large gap right over the target that allowed a clear sight of the concentrated red and green TIs. The 405 (Vancouver) Squadron participants performed as briefed from 18,000 to 18,500 feet between 06.13 and 06.18, while most main force crews confirmed their positions by Gee before bombing the red TIs. They observed what appeared to be an accurate attack, which obliterated the TIs and left a reddish-yellow fire that sent a column of black smoke rising through 10,000 feet. Despite the appearances, however, local sources claimed that the operation was not successful and caused only minor damage to the refinery.

Two major operations were planned for the night of the 13/14th, both involving an 8 Group element, the first of thirty-four Lancasters and eight Mosquitos to mark for a main force of 326 Halifaxes from 4 and 6 Groups against the Braunkohle-Benzin oil plant at Böhlen, situated some seven miles to the south of Leipzig. Six Lancasters departed Gransden Lodge between 18.47 and 18.52, five containing crews, including that of W/C Rawson, assigned to a marking role and one with four 2,000-pounders in the bomb bay to deliver as part of the main force. They headed for the French coast at Dunkerque to track the Franco-Belgian frontier until entering Germany north of Strasbourg and completed the three-and-a-half-hour outward flight to find the target area concealed beneath ten-tenths cloud with tops, according to a number of reports, ranging from 6,000 to 14,000 feet. Most of the illuminators were instructed to withhold their flares, and the main force crews initially to bomb the leading edge of the glow from green TIs and later, the centre. Positions were established by Gee and H2S-fix before bombing took place in accordance with the instructions of the Master Bomber, at least, by those who picked up his broadcasts. The 405 (Vancouver) Squadron crews carried out their assigned marking and bombing tasks from 18,000 feet between 21.55 and 22.05, observing large explosions and assuming from the glow of fires an accurate attack. The retreating crews had to battle through severe icing conditions to reach home, and they were disappointed when a post-raid analysis concluded that the operation had failed to find the mark. This meant that further attempts would be made to destroy the plant over the ensuing weeks.

The second operation on this night was the first round of Operation Thunderclap, the Churchill inspired offensive against Germany's eastern cities, which was devised partly to act in support of the advancing Russian ground forces, and also as a demonstration to Stalin of RAF air power, should he turn against the Allies after the war. The historic and culturally significant city of Dresden was selected to open the offensive in another two-phase affair, with a 5 Group force of 246 Lancasters and nine Mosquitos leading the way, to be followed three hours later by 529 Lancasters of 1, 3, 6 and 8 Groups. It had proved to be a successful policy thus far, with the 5 Group low-level marking system and main force attacks providing a beacon for the second force, and should it be required on this night, 8 Group would provide any necessary marking for phase two from high level.

8 Group detailed sixty-one Lancasters, and ten of these were briefed for five marking roles before departing Gransden Lodge between 22.09 and 22.24 with S/Ls Marcou and Mussells the senior pilots on duty. They made their way to the target, initially in clear skies until 3°East, when large amounts of broken cloud reached 18,000 feet. This dispersed from 12°East to leave clear skies over the target, although a large bank of cloud threatened a short distance away to the east. The fires created by the eight hundred tons of bombs delivered by "The Independent Air Force" were visible twenty minutes from the target, and they were concentrated south of the River Elbe between the marshalling yards and the aiming-point. The smoke prevented the identification of the planned aiming-point despite the use of flares, and this prompted the Master bomber to instruct the blind markers to drop green TIs and for the main force crews to overshoot them by two seconds. Later bombing was directed at red TIs, and, eventually, the centre of the smoke. On return, the 405 (Vancouver) Squadron crews reported carrying out their assigned tasks from 16,500 to 18,500 feet between 01.29 and 01.41 in the face of scant opposition, and in so doing, contributed to a further eighteen hundred tons of bombs, which set off the same chain reaction that had devastated parts of Hamburg in July 1943. A firestorm developed of terrifying proportions, which swept through large parts of the city and inflicted massive casualties on the resident population swelled by an influx of refugees from the eastern front. A modest six Lancasters failed to return, among them the squadron's PB183, from which F/L Frederick RCAF alone of his eight-man all-RCAF crew survived, presumably through being thrown clear as the aircraft exploded, and he was taken into captivity.

On the following morning, three hundred American bombers carried out a separate attack under the umbrella of a fighter escort and completed the destruction. There were claims that RAF aircraft had strafed the streets and open spaces to increase the level of terror, and such accusations abound in the city to this day. In fact, American fighters were responsible, and were trying to add to the general confusion and chaos. Initial propaganda-inspired reports from the Office of the Propaganda Minister, Joseph Goebbels, falsely claimed a death toll of 250,000 people, but an accurate figure of twenty-five thousand has been settled upon since.

The destruction of Dresden has been used in Germany and also by some elements in this country as a weapon with which to condemn Bomber Command and Harris, and label them as war criminals. Curiously, no similar accusations have been levelled at the Americans. It should also be understood that Harris had no interest in attacking Dresden and had to be nagged by Chief-of-the-Air-Staff, Sir Charles Portal, to fulfil Churchill's wishes. Dresden was Germany's seventh largest city, and its largest remaining predominantly intact built-up area, which, according to American sources, contained more than a hundred factories and fifty thousand workers contributing to the war effort. It was also an important railway hub, to the extent that the marshalling yards had been attacked twice in late 1944 by the USAAF. The aircrew simply did the job asked of them, and Dresden was no different from any other attack on a city. The death toll at Hamburg was much higher, and yet there has been no similar outcry. The legacy of this operation served to deny Harris and the men under his Command their due recognition for the massive part they played in the ultimate victory, and only in recent times has a monument been erected in Green Park in London and a campaign clasp awarded, sadly, far too late for the majority. Churchill, with his eyes set on a peacetime election, betrayed Harris and the Command in a typical politically motivated U-turn, in which he accused Harris of bombing solely for the purpose of inflicting terror. In the post-war honours, Harris was the only commander in the field to be omitted.

Round two of Operation Thunderclap was planned for the 14th with Chemnitz as the target for 717 aircraft drawn from 1, 3, 4, 6 and 8 Groups, which would be divided into two waves separated by three-and-a-half hours. 5 Group would also be in the area with 224 Lancasters and eight Mosquitos to target an oil refinery in the small town of Rositz, situated twenty-five miles due south of Leipzig and thirty miles north-west of Chemnitz. 8 Group detailed fifty-nine Lancasters for the first wave and thirty-five for the second, 405 (Vancouver) Squadron supporting both with nine and seven Lancasters respectively. The first wave crews departed Gransden Lodge between 17.40 and 17.48 with W/C Rawson the senior pilot on duty, and all reached the target area to find two thin layers of ten-tenths stratus cloud with tops at 10,000 and 18,000 feet. The blind illuminators opened the attack at 20.52, but as the cloud precluded identification of the aiming-point, the Master Bomber called for skymarking from 20.59 onwards. Salvoes of green/red flares were released by seven aircraft but proved to be scattered over a wide area with no concentration. However, with nothing else to aim at, the main force crews were instructed to bomb on the marker flares, and the widespread evidence of fires confirmed a lack of focus. The 405 (Vancouver) Squadron crews fulfilled their mostly marking briefs from 15,000 to 18,000 feet between 20.52 and 21.07, just as the second wave crews were taking off from Gransden Lodge between 20.50 and 21.00 with F/L McNaughton and S/L Marcou the designated Master Bomber and Deputy and S/L Neilly one of three blind marker/illuminators.

They arrived in eastern Germany to find the same layered cloud, and the attack opened with illuminating flares and green TIs dropped on H2S from 00.25. The TIs disappeared quickly into the cloud, forcing F/L McNaughton to call for skymarking, in response to which four aircraft released green/red flares without achieving concentration. He then instructed the main force crews to aim for the skymarkers until 00.30, at which point, with so few remaining visible, he issued the order to bomb on navigational aids. The Gransden Lodge crews carried out their assigned tasks from 16,000 to 18,500 feet between 00.24 and 00.33 and returned home dissatisfied with the conduct of the raid. Returning crews confirmed that fires appeared to be taking hold across the target area, and the glow was visible for at least an hour into the homeward flight, and some complained of being unable to hear the Master Bomber's transmissions. Post-raid reconnaissance confirmed that many parts of the city had been hit, but much of the effort had been wasted in open country.

While 405 (Vancouver) Squadron remained at home over the ensuing six days, the frontier town of Wesel became the focus of attention for repeated attacks as Allied ground forces prepared to cross the Rhine, and was pummelled four times between the 16th and 19th, three times by 3 Group employing G-H.

The 20th brought preparations for a major assault on the southern half of Dortmund, for which a force of 514 Lancasters was assembled from 1, 3, 6 and 8 Groups. 8 Group detailed forty-eight Lancasters and fourteen Mosquitos, seven of the former departing Gransden Lodge between 22.25 and 22.37 with S/Ls Marcou, Mussells and Neilly the senior pilots on duty. As they climbed away into clear skies, other 8 Group Lancasters and eleven Mosquitos took off from their stations to mark the Rhenania-Ossag oil refinery in the Reisholz district of Düsseldorf for a main force of 156

Halifaxes of 4 Group. At 23.06 the crews of F/L Woods and F/O Hartley departed Gransden Lodge to perform the role of visual centerers for a main force of 112 Halifaxes of 6 Group in an attack on a second Rhenania-Ossag refinery at Monheim, located on the eastern bank of the Rhine a few miles to the south of Düsseldorf and north of Leverkusen. As the bomber streams made their way to their respective targets, the sky filled rapidly with cloud from 5°East and was at eight to ten-tenths over the north-eastern Ruhr and Dortmund, but very low and thin enough for the red Oboe TIs to be clearly visible. At 00.58 the visual centrers released green TIs, and from then onwards the ground marking was well concentrated and maintained and was supplemented by green skymarkers, which, unfortunately, tended to fall short and created a marking creep-back for fourteen miles along the line of approach. The bombing in the early stages was accurate, but as the cloud thickened and the glow through the clouds diminished, it became scattered and much of it fell short. The 405 (Vancouver) Squadron crews performed as briefed from 17,900 to 18,000 feet between 00.59 and 01.10 and all but one returned home to report developing fires but no detail. The absent crew was that of S/L Marcou AFC RCAF, a truly cosmopolitan brotherhood of airmen from Canada, the UK, New Zealand and the United States. They managed to escape from PB530 as it fell from the sky, but the RAF flight engineer failed to survive the descent, while the others fell into enemy hands for a brief period of detainment. The local authorities were beyond the ability to produce an account of the raid by this time, and the next major attack three weeks hence would obliterate all traces of this night and leave the city totally paralysed.

Meanwhile, some thirty miles to the south-west, the Monheim-bound duo found ten-tenths cloud with tops at 5,000 feet and employed Gee to establish their positions before carrying out their assigned tasks from 18,000 feet at 01.41. It was not possible to assess the outcome, but it emerged later that both attacks on the Rhenania-Ossag plants had brought about a complete halt to oil production.

The final heavy raid of the war on the much-bombed city of Duisburg was handed to 362 Lancasters of 1, 6 and 8 Groups on the night of the 21/22nd, for which 8 Group made ready thirty-two Lancasters and eleven Mosquitos, eleven of the former provided by 405 (Vancouver) Squadron. They departed Gransden Lodge between 20.21 and 20.32 with S/L Neilly the senior pilot on duty and all but two crews designated as blind sky markers or visual centerers and two as main force supporters. They climbed away into conditions of little or no cloud, which persisted until shortly before the target, when a band of stratus a thousand feet thick slid over the city at 15,000 feet to cover it completely. The winds outbound were different from those forecast at briefing, and this delayed the arrival of the main force by a few minutes. As they approached, the crews could see the first red TIs cascading at 22.56, but by the time they arrived to bomb, these had disappeared below the cloud, and no more were evident until 23.08. Some considerable difficulty was experienced in identifying the target, and incendiaries were seen to be dropped all the way from Krefeld to Duisburg. By 23.10 the cloud was beginning to break up, and a better concentration was achieved, and had a Master Bomber been present, he might have been able to compensate for the scarcity of the marking. The 405 (Vancouver) Squadron participants performed as briefed from 18,000 to 19,500 feet between 22.59 and 23.16 and returned to report large explosions and the expectation of a successful outcome, which was confirmed by post-raid reconnaissance.

A Halifax main force of 297 aircraft from 4 and 6 Groups was made ready on the morning of the 23rd to send against Essen in the afternoon with an 8 Group contribution of twenty-seven Lancasters and nineteen Mosquitos to provide the marking and other support. 405 (Vancouver) Squadron provided five blind sky markers and five bombers, which departed Gransden Lodge between 13.02 and 13.15 with S/L Neilly the senior pilot on duty. The crews were sitting on either a cookie and twelve 500-pounders or six 2,000-pounders and all reached the target area to encounter ten-tenths cloud in layers between 12,000 and 22,000 feet. The attack opened with seven Oboe Mosquitos releasing red smoke-puffs, which were not picked up by the approaching force, but the green smoke-puffs from the heavy marker aircraft were evident in sufficient numbers to the main force crews running in on H2S, and the bombing appeared to be concentrated. The 405 (Vancouver) Squadron participants carried out their assigned tasks from 18,000 to 20,000 feet between 15.08 and 15.14, but were unable to assess the results, and it was left to local sources to confirm this to have been a highly accurate attack, which delivered three hundred high-explosive bombs and eleven thousand incendiaries onto the Krupp complex, causing massive damage.

The days operations were not yet over, and a force of 366 Lancasters, plus one from the Film Unit, and thirteen Mosquitos was drawn from 1, 6 and 8 Groups to send against the city of Pforzheim, situated in southern Germany between Karlsruhe to the north-west and Stuttgart to the south-east. This would be the first area raid on the city, which was known as a centre for jewellery and watch manufacture but was believed by the Allies to be involved in the production of precision instruments in support of Germany's war effort. 8 Group detailed fifty-three Lancasters and thirteen Mosquitos, six of the former provided by 405 (Vancouver) Squadron, which departed Gransden Lodge between 16.34 and 16.42 with G/C Newson and S/L Mussells the senior pilots on duty. They all got away safely, climbing through ten-tenths low cloud, which persisted until the bombers were over France, where it began to break up, leaving the skies clear and the moon bright as the target drew near. The thin veil of ground haze proved to be no impediment, and the first red Oboe TIs went down at 19.52, to be followed quickly by illuminator flares and salvoes of concentrated reds and greens. The Gransden Lodge crews carried out their assigned tasks from an unusually low 7,500 to 9,500 feet between 19.55 and 20.07, and fires rapidly took hold until the whole town north of the river looked like a sea of flames. By 20.06 the fires were too dazzling for the TIs to be visible, after which, the Master Bomber ordered the smoke to be bombed. The raid lasted twenty-two minutes, during which 1,825 tons of bombs fell into the built-up area, reducing 83% of it to ruins and setting off a firestorm in which 17,600 people lost their lives. This was the highest death toll to result from a single attack on a German city after Hamburg (40,000) and Dresden (25,000). It was during this operation that the final Victoria Cross was earned by a member of RAF Bomber Command. It went posthumously to the Master Bomber from 582 Squadron, Captain Ed Swales of the South African Air Force, who continued to control the attack in a Lancaster severely damaged by a night-fighter, before sacrificing his life to allow his crew to abandon the stricken aircraft.

Gransden Lodge was not called upon on the 24th when 290 Halifaxes from 4 and 6 Groups were made ready for a daylight attack on the Chemwerke-Steinkohle oil refinery in Bergkamen, a community in the north-eastern Ruhr close to the town of Kamen. 8 Group contributed twenty-six Lancasters and twenty-five Mosquitos to provide "windowing", marking and main force support. Local sources reported massive destruction in Kamen, Bergkamen and surrounding villages, but made no mention of the refinery and further operations would be mounted against it over the ensuing days.

8 Group joined forces with 4 and 6 Groups again on the 27th to target the city of Mainz in south-central Germany, for which a force of 311 Halifaxes, 131 Lancasters and eighteen Mosquitos was assembled. 8 Group's contribution amounted to all of the Mosquitos and forty-six Lancasters, among which the crews of F/Ls Forsberg, Kyte and Maxwell represented 405 (Vancouver) Squadron and had been designated as blind sky markers. They departed Gransden Lodge between 14.06 and 14.15 and reached the target after an outward flight of more than three hours to be greeted by ten-tenths cloud as anticipated, before receiving instructions from the Master Bomber to aim for the centre of the plentiful and concentrated green smoke-puff skymarkers. The main force crews complied from an average height of 18,000 feet between 16.38 and 16.46 and were rewarded with the sight of smoke spiralling up through the cloud tops at 9,000 feet as they turned away. On return, the Gransden Lodge crews reported attacking on Gee-fix from 18,000 feet between 16.30 and 16.40 and contributing to the 1,545 tons of bombs that devastated the city and resulted in the destruction of 5,670 buildings. The historic Altstadt was wiped out and more than eleven hundred people lost their lives.

During the course of the month the squadron operated on fifteen occasions and dispatched 129 sorties for the loss of three Lancasters and crews.

March 1945

The new month would see the Command bludgeon its way across Germany, concentrating on oil, rail and road targets, along with the few towns still boasting a built-up area, and it would prove to be a hugely demanding month for Path Finder and main force squadrons alike. The penultimate month of the bombing war began in daylight on the 1st, with the final raid of the many visited upon Mannheim. It was a 1, 6 and 8 Group force of 372 Lancasters and ninety Halifaxes that prepared for take-off that morning, among them fifty-four Lancasters and seventeen Mosquitos representing 8 Group. Ten 405 (Vancouver) Squadron Lancasters departed Gransden Lodge between 12.35 and 12.45 with G/C Newson the senior pilot on duty and F/Ls McNaughton and F/O Dix the designated Master Bomber and Deputy, and after climbing out headed for the south coast over five-tenths cloud to begin the Channel crossing. The cloud built to ten-tenths from the French coast, above which, the main force maintained good formation, but were three or four minutes late arriving at the target. At 14.47 the Master Bomber was heard asking his deputy if he could see the main force, and following a negative response, ordered the marker force to orbit until 15.03, when he called for release-point flares. Blue smoke-puff skymarkers went down accurately and in concentration, and the crews were instructed to aim for the centre of these, the 405 (Vancouver) Squadron element carrying out their assigned marking and bombing tasks from 15,000 to 18,000 feet between 15.05 and 15.12. At debriefing, they were unable to provide an assessment of the results and despite a lack of post-raid reconnaissance or local report, it is known that many bombs fell on neighbouring Ludwigshafen and its surrounds, and much damage occurred.

With Cologne now almost on the front line, it too was earmarked for its final attack of the war on the morning of the 2nd, for which a two-phase operation was planned, the first by 703 aircraft from 1, 4, 6 and 8 Groups and the second, a G-H attack by 155 Lancasters of 3 Group. 8 Group contributed forty-seven Lancasters and twenty-six Mosquitos, nine of the former belonging to 405 (Vancouver) Squadron and departing Gransden Lodge between 07.47 and 08.01 with the recently promoted W/C McQuoid and S/Ls Mussells and Neilly the senior pilots on duty. The crews were allotted three each to blind sky marker, visual centerer and main force support roles as they climbed out and pointed their snouts towards Beachy Head to take their place in the elongated bomber stream before beginning the Channel crossing. All reached the target to find near perfect bombing conditions with a little cloud with tops at around 6,000 feet, and a Master Bomber on hand to tell them where to bomb, although the city's landmarks, the cathedral and nearby main railway station, stood out in the sunshine, almost inviting the bombs to fall. The 405 (Vancouver) Squadron crews carried out their assigned tasks, delivering blue and red smoke-puff TIs and assorted bomb loads from 17,500 to 19,000 feet between 10.01 and 10.16, and many, for a change, were able to see the fall of their bombs. It wasn't long before a mushroom of black smoke began to conceal the ground, and later crews were instructed to bomb the up-wind edge of that. The main concentration of bombing was on the western side of the Rhine, and the western end of the Hohenzollern railway bridge appeared to have been demolished and had collapsed into the Rhine. The second wave by 3 Group was ruined by the failure of a G-H station in England and had to be halted after only fifteen aircraft had bombed. It mattered little, as the damage had been done and the once proud city fell to American forces four days later.

Gransden Lodge was not called into action on the 3rd, when 4 Group detailed 201 Halifaxes for a return to the Bergkamen oil refinery accompanied by twenty-one Lancasters and a dozen Mosquitos from 8 Group to provide the marking. As the bombers approached the English coast homebound, they received warnings of Luftwaffe activity over the bomber stations, which would ultimately be identified as Operation Gisella, a concerted intruder effort by two hundred aircraft. It turned into a highly effective undertaking, which caught the returning bombers at the most vulnerable stage of their flight, the approach to land, and twenty of them were shot down. Post-raid reconnaissance confirmed the success of the Bergkamen operation, and all oil production at the site ceased for the duration of the war.

Preparations for Operation Thunderclap to return to Chemnitz were put in hand on the 5th, and a force of 760 aircraft assembled from all but 5 Group, which itself would be active some thirty-five miles to the north, attacking the oil refinery at Böhlen. 8 Group dispatched ninety-four Lancasters, sixteen of them representing 405 (Vancouver) Squadron, which departed Gransden Lodge between 17.29 and 17.44 with G/C Newson and F/O Dix performing the roles of Master Bomber and Deputy and W/C McQuoid and S/L Neilly the other senior pilots on duty. Those taking off from the more northerly stations, particularly those of 6 Group, climbed into ten-tenths cloud with severe icing conditions, which caused nine of them to crash. Aside from a slight reduction over the Channel and northern France, the complete cloud cover remained in place all the way to the target area, and there were reports of predicted flak around Leipzig, which had probably been stirred-up by the above-mentioned 5 Group operation. The target area was concealed beneath ten-tenths cloud with tops up to 13,000 feet, and crews had to listened out for the Master Bomber's instructions as they lined up for the bombing-run. They observed cascading red and green skymarkers and were told at 21.50 to bomb them with a twelve-second overshoot. When the skymarkers went out at 21.55, they were ordered to bomb the glow in the clouds, before further skymarkers appeared and the original order was repeated. The 405 (Vancouver) Squadron crews carried out their assigned tasks from 15,500 to 17,500 feet between 21.38 and 21.52, but were unable to assess the outcome, reporting only a bright glow beneath the clouds that seemed to cover an area a mile wide. They turned south towards the Czechoslovakian frontier for the homeward flight across southern Germany, where some were pestered by enemy night-fighters, which were probably largely responsible for the failure to return of fourteen Lancasters and eight Halifaxes. It was established eventually that the operation had been a major success, which had destroyed by fire much of the central and southern districts of the city and had also resulted in damage to some important war-industry factories and the destruction of the Siegmar tank-engine works.

The main operation on the 7th was to be undertaken by 526 aircraft of 1, 3, 6 and 8 Groups against the virgin target of Dessau, a city in eastern Germany between Berlin to the north and Leipzig to the south. While this was in progress, 256 Halifaxes and twenty-five Lancasters of 4, 6 and 8 Groups were to target the Deutsche Erdöl oil refinery at Hemmingstedt on the western side of Schleswig-Holstein, while 5 Group went for a similar target at Harburg on the south side of the River Elbe opposite Hamburg. 405 (Vancouver) Squadron briefed twelve crews for a marking role and four to bomb with the main force at Dessau and sent them on their way from Gransden Lodge between 17.30 and 17.46 with W/C Rawson and S/Ls Mussells and Neilly the senior pilots on duty. They climbed through complete cloud-cover, which persisted as the stream traversed the North Sea and Holland, breaking to up to five-tenths at the Ruhr, before building again to eight to ten-tenths over the target with tops at up to 10,000 feet. Night-fighters had infiltrated the bomber stream from the Rhine, and flak intensified in the Braunschweig and Magdeburg defence zones and was the cause of the loss of an engine, which forced F/O Dix and crew to jettison their load and turn back.

As the main force crews approached the city, which since 1925 had been home to the famous Bauhaus architectural school, they observed illuminating flares going down at 21.56, followed by red and green TIs, which proved not to be visible through the cloud. Release point flares soon joined the mix, and they were concentrated at first, but became scattered later as the Master Bomber's instructions suffered from interference after someone in a main force aircraft left a transmitter on. Fortunately, a large break in the clouds at 22.04 provided a clear view of the ground and the many TIs still burning, and the main force crews were able to take advantage. Widespread fires revealed a distinct pattern of streets and many explosions were observed, including one producing a large bluish flash at 22.08. At 22.18, a section of the town burning with white flames suddenly erupted in a terrific red burst and continued to burn red. The Gransden Lodge crews performed their tasks as briefed mostly on H2S from 13,000 to 18,000 feet between 21.53 and 22.10, and within seconds of bombing, F/O Larcon and crew were attacked by three enemy night-fighters. The rear gunner shot down the first one but was then mortally wounded by fire from the second one which also set fire to the turret, before itself being shot down in flames by the mud-upper gunner. The third night-fighter strafed the Lancaster but was ultimately evaded and a return to base completed on three engines. There was praise for the wireless operator, who, before realising that the gunner had died, had forced his way into the burning turret in a vain attempt to either rescue the occupant or help him to bail out.

There was a mention at some debriefings of "scarecrows" over the Ruhr on the way home, but these mythical shells, supposedly created by the enemy to simulate a bomber blowing itself to pieces to demoralise crews, did not exist, even though belief in them was encouraged by the Bomber Command hierarchy. "Scarecrows" were, indeed, some of the missing eighteen

Lancasters blowing up violently. The operation caused extensive damage in the town centre and residential, industrial and railway districts, all of which would have to be completely rebuilt after the war, sadly, in the Eastern Bloc style of concrete architecture.

The pace of operations refused to slacken, and what perhaps should have been a wind-down towards the German capitulation, became one of the most intense operational periods in the entire war. With major operations on five occasions already behind it during the first week of the month, the second week began for 8 Group with orders on the 8th to provide sixty-two Lancasters and ten Mosquitos to mark for 241 Halifaxes of 4 and 6 Groups for an attack on the Blohm & Voss U-Boot yards in Hamburg, where the new Type XXI vessels were under construction. While this operation was in progress, 5 Group would be conducting the last major raid of the war on the already-devastated city of Kassel some 150 miles to the south. 405 (Vancouver) Squadron made ready sixteen Lancasters and dispatched them from Gransden Lodge between 18.02 and 18.16 with W/C McQuoid and S/Ls Mussells and Neilly the senior pilots on duty and they reached the target to find up to nine-tenths thin, drifting low cloud with tops at 6,000 to 8,000 feet, which would eventually conceal the green TIs and force the Path Finders to dispense red and green skymarkers as an alternative. The Gransden Lodge crews carried out their assigned roles from 16,900 to 18,000 feet between 21.23 and 21.36 in accordance with the instructions of the Master Bomber, who directed the bombing towards the middle of three skymarkers. The main force crews complied also from an average of 18,000 feet, and two very large explosions were witnessed at 21.33 and 21.36, and another a minute later that lit up the area for five or six seconds. Returning crews were optimistic that the operation had been successful, but no post-raid reconnaissance took place and local reports were sparse.

An all-time record was set on the 11th, when 1,079 aircraft, the largest Bomber Command force ever to be sent to a single target, was assembled to attack Essen for the last time. 8 Group contributed sixty-six Lancasters and thirty-six Mosquitos, fourteen of the former belonging to 405 (Vancouver) Squadron, which took off from Gransden Lodge between 12.14 and 12.39 with pilots of flight lieutenant rank leading the way, the crews divided equally between marking and main force support roles. Shortly after take-off, F/L Laing and crew, who had been designated as blind sky markers, lost their port-outer engine and proceeded directly to the jettison area to divest themselves of part of their bomb load before continuing on to the target. They and the others arrived in the central Ruhr to find the target covered by ten-tenths cloud with tops at 6,000 feet. This required the Path Finder element to employ skymarkers in the form of blue, and later, red smoke puffs, and the first of these went down at 14.59, to be backed up throughout the course of the raid. The Gransden Lodge crews performed as briefed from 11,800 to 19,000 feet between 14.57 and 15.23, the low height and last bombing time those of the Laing crew, who contributed to the more than 4,600 tons dropped into the already ravaged city and former industrial powerhouse, which during the course of the war had lost more than seven thousand of its inhabitants to Allied bombing. Smoke and dust were emerging through the cloud tops in a tight spiral that had reached 10,000 feet as the last of the bombers retreated, and the city would still be in a state of paralysis when the American ground forces captured it unopposed on the 10th of April.

A little over twenty-four hours later, the short-lived record was surpassed by the departure from their stations in the early afternoon of 1,108 aircraft, which had Dortmund as their destination. This time 8 Group provided sixty-seven Lancasters and thirty-six Mosquitos, seven of the former representing 405 (Vancouver) Squadron, which departed Gransden Lodge between 13.50 and 13.58 carrying the appropriate bomb and pyrotechnic payloads for marking roles and the senior pilots again of flight lieutenant rank. The Ruhr was found to be still under a blanket of ten-tenths cloud with tops at 6,000 feet, conditions for which the Path Finders had prepared a skymarking plan based on green and blue smoke puffs. The first Oboe-aimed greens appeared at 16.26 to be followed a minute later by blues from the blind primary marker aircraft, and the Master Bomber directed the main force crews to aim for the blues. It was not long before brown smoke was observed to be climbing through the clouds to 8,000 feet from the northern end of the city, and there were reports also of a ring of smoke encircling the entire area so dense that it remained visible for 120 miles into the return flight. The Gransden Lodge crews carried out their respective tasks from 18,000 feet between 16.29 and 16.55 and contributed to the delivery of a new record of 4,800 tons of bombs. Photo-reconnaissance revealed that the central and southern districts of the city had received the greatest weight of bombs and had been left in a state of utter chaos with all industry silenced permanently and railway tracks torn up.

Elements of 1 and 8 Groups joined forces on the evening of the 13th, to attack two benzol producers in the Ruhr, the Erin plant at Herne, located between Bochum and Gelsenkirchen, and the Dahlbusch A G plant, south of the Gelsenkirchen city centre. 8 Group detailed sixteen Lancasters and eighteen Mosquitos for each and it was for the former that six 405 (Vancouver) Squadron crews were briefed, while their Lancasters were each receiving a bomb load of a cookie and eight 1,000-pounders to deliver as part of the main force. They departed Gransden Lodge between 17.54 and 18.00 again with no senior pilots on duty and reached the target to find ten-tenths cloud with tops at 10,000 feet and no marking evident. They carried out their attacks on Gee from 18,000 feet between 20.28 and 20.30 and noticed a concentrated pattern of bomb bursts and one large explosion. Meanwhile, five miles to the south-west, clear skies greeted the Dahlbusch force, and the raid culminated with a huge explosion at 20.43 accompanied by a large amount of flame and followed by a mushroom of smoke up rising through 5,000 feet.

Zweibrücken was another new name on a target list, and was a town located to the east of Saarbrücken in south-western Germany through which it was believed enemy forces and equipment were being moved to resist the Allied advance. On the 14th, 8 Group contributed twenty-three Lancasters and eleven Mosquitos to mark for a 6 Group main force of ninety-eight Lancasters and ninety-eight Halifaxes, the job of which was to block passage through the town. 405 (Vancouver) Squadron made ready a dozen Lancasters and briefed G/C Newson and F/L Vann as Master Bomber and Deputy, W/C McQuoid as a supporter and the remainder for marking duties and sent them on their way from Gransden Lodge between 17.37 and 17.49. They arrived in the target area some two-and-a-half hours later to find clear skies and favourable conditions and carried out their respective tasks from 10,000 to 14,000 feet between 20.11 and 20.22. The intention to block the through-passage of all enemy troops and equipment was achieved, and in fact, every public building and 80% of the houses were flattened.

Benzol plants at Bottrop and Castrop-Rauxel in the Ruhr occupied elements of 4, 6 and 8 Groups during the day on the 15th, while Gransden Lodge remained inactive until late in the day, when sixteen crews were called to briefing to learn that their target was to be the Deurag-Nerag oil refinery at Misburg, situated on the north-eastern rim of Hannover. This was one of two major operations taking place that night, the other involving a force of 267 Lancasters, Halifaxes and

Mosquitos of 4, 6 and 8 Groups directed at Hagen on the south-eastern edge of the Ruhr. 1 Group detailed a main force of 212 Lancasters for Misburg, while 8 Group weighed in with forty-six Lancasters and nine Mosquitos, the 405 (Vancouver) Squadron contingent of markers taking off between 17.45 and 18.00 with W/C Rawson and S/L Neilly the senior pilots on duty. Except for the Channel crossing both ways, the operation benefitted from cloudless skies, and this enabled crews to identify the target visually by the light of illuminator flares. The raid began punctually with red TIs, backed up by mixed reds and greens in great concentration right on the aiming-point, and the Master Bomber called in the main force at 21.12. Almost immediately the target was engulfed in flames and smoke was observed to rise through 10,000 feet following an explosion at 21.13. The Gransden Lodge crews fulfilled their respective briefs from 14,500 to 15,000 feet between 21.09 and 21.20, and all but two returned home to report a highly successful operation, characterised by many explosions and fires visible from a hundred miles into the return journey. There was particular praise from the main force crews for the Master Bomber and the Path Finder element generally.

Absent from debriefing were the crews of F/L Parkhurst RCAF and F/O Laing MiD RCAF in PB516 and NE119 respectively, the former having come down in the target area with fatal consequences for the eight predominantly RCAF occupants. The latter had been leaving the target area when abandoned to its fate to crash at 21.25 at Bad Grund, some forty miles south-south-east of Hannover. F/O Laing landed in a tree and was killed after releasing his harness and falling thirty feet to the ground. As local officials, police and Hitler Youth watched their country being smashed from the air and swallowed up by advancing Allied forces, thoughts of vengeance came to the fore, and this was a bad time to fall into enemy hands. There were many incidents around this time of airmen being murdered, and this was the fate befalling three of F/O Laing's crew, the flight engineer, Sgt Morris RAF, the bomb-aimer, F/O Smith RCAF and mid-upper gunner, F/Sgt Marsh RCAF. The remaining three were presumably captured by the military or more honourable factions of the enemy and survived as PoWs.

The focus switched to southern Germany on the following night, with Nuremberg and Würzburg the targets, the former for a 1 Group main force of 231 Lancasters with forty-six Lancasters and sixteen Mosquitos of 8 Group to provide the marking and other support, while the latter was an all-5 Group show involving 225 Lancasters and eleven Mosquitos. 8 Group provided forty-six Lancasters and sixteen Mosquitos, fourteen belonging to 405 (Vancouver) Squadron, which departed Gransden Lodge between 18.05 and 18.20 with W/C McQuoid and S/L Vann the designated Master Bomber and Deputy, ten crews assigned to marking and two to bomb with the main force. They followed the standard route across France to the Strasbourg area and arrived at the target to find largely clear skies with a little drifting cloud and the first Mosquito-borne red Oboe TIs cascading at 21.26. The aiming point was laid bare by illuminating flares and the main force bombing observed to be concentrated as the Gransden Lodge contingent performed as briefed from 16,000 to 18,000 feet between 21.25 and 21.36. Southern and south-eastern districts were the most seriously afflicted, Steinbuhl in particular suffering an ordeal by fire, but the defenders, predominantly the Nachtjagd, fought back to hack down what at this stage of the war was a shocking twenty-four 1 Group Lancasters. As this operation was in progress, some fifty miles to the north-west the historic and minimally industrial city of Würzburg was being subjected to seventeen minutes of carnage, during which more than eleven hundred tons of bombs were dropped with great accuracy, destroying 89% of the built-up area, and killing between four and five thousand people.

Sixteen crews attended briefing at Gransden Lodge on the evening of the 18th to learn of that night's attack on the town of Witten, situated at the eastern end of the Ruhr, which was the home, among other contributors to Germany's war effort, of the Ruhrstahl steelworks and a factory belonging to the Mannesmann company manufacturing steel pipework. All German industry relied heavily on forced workers and at Witten it was those from France and Ukraine housed in the nearby camp in the Schalke district of Gelsenkirchen. 259 Halifaxes of 4 and 6 Group were assembled to act as the main force, while 8 Group detailed forty-five Lancasters and eighteen Mosquitos, the 405 (Vancouver) Squadron element taking off between 01.22 and 01.40 on the 19th, with pilots of flight lieutenant rank leading the way and the squadron divided equally between marking and bombing duties. The factions formed into a bomber stream as they headed for the south coast to cross the Channel and approach the target area over liberated territory, arriving at their destination to find clear skies and the Mosquito-borne red TIs cascading right over the aiming-point. They were backed up by further reds and greens from the heavy marker aircraft, the Gransden Lodge crews carrying out their respective tasks from 17,000 to 18,000 feet between 04.12 and 04.20, while the main force crews performed well to leave fires taking hold as they retreated. PB451 came down somewhere in the target area and took with it to their deaths F/O Peaker RCAF and the other seven occupants, all but one of them also members of the RCAF. On a positive note, this would prove to be the final failure to return of a 405 (Vancouver) Squadron crew. A post-raid analysis revealed that the 1,081 tons of bombs had destroyed 129 acres, or 62% of the built-up area, and that the two factories mentioned above had sustained heavy damage.

Having failed to destroy the Deutsche Erdöl oil refinery at Heide/Hemmingstedt on the night of the 7/8th, 166 Lancasters of 1, 6 and 8 Groups were made ready on the 20th to try again. 8 Group detailed forty-five Lancasters, fifteen of them provided by 405 (Vancouver) Squadron, which had to wait until the early hours of the 21st before departing Gransden Lodge between 02.00 and 02.15 with W/C Rawson and S/Ls Neilly and Vann the senior pilots on duty. Apart from a little patchy cloud, they flew eastwards in clear skies to the target, the main force crews arriving to find red and green TIs already on the way down, but no instructions from the Master Bomber, W/C Le Good of 35 (Madras Presidency) Squadron, until after H-hour. He had noted that the illuminating flares had fallen to the south of the aiming-point but estimated the mixed reds and greens to be accurate, and instructed the main force accordingly at 04.29. Some slightly errant green TIs had fallen a minute earlier and attracted some reds, forcing W/C Le Good to amend his instructions, which were now to bomb the northerly reds and greens. The main force crews, including two of the 405 (Vancouver) Squadron contingent, complied, while the other thirteen from Gransden Lodge carried out their assigned tasks from 10,000 to 15,000 feet between 04.23 and 04.38. The accurate and concentrated attack was punctuated by large explosions between 04.31 and 04.35, accompanied by dense columns of black smoke rising through 8,000 feet, and the plant was put out of action for the remainder of the war.

Gransden Lodge was not called into action on the 21st, when railway yards in north-western Germany at Rheine and Münster were the targets, while it was the Deutsche Vacuum oil refinery that attracted a 1 and 8 Group force to Bremen. The main operation during the afternoon of the 22nd involved elements of 1, 6 and 8 Groups targeting railway yards in Hildesheim, situated some fifteen miles south-east of Hannover, in what was the first and only Bomber Command attack on it of the war. 8 Group contributed thirty-eight Lancasters and eight Mosquitos to the overall force of 227 aircraft, 405 (Vancouver) Squadron chipping in with thirteen Lancasters, which departed Gransden Lodge between 11.51 and 12.01 with S/L Vann and the recently promoted F/L Dix the designated Master Bomber and Deputy and W/C Rawson the senior pilot on duty. F/L Woods and crew lost their port-outer engine as they crossed the North Sea and jettisoned the high explosive contents of the bomb bay while retaining their marking ordnance with the intention of continuing on to the target. However, they were losing too much time and abandoned their sortie with the Dutch coast just ahead, leaving the others to reach the target under largely clear skies. The Oboe red TIs and the reds and greens of the Master Bomber and Deputy fell on the aiming point as a strong reference to the main force crews, who did not disappoint. The 405 (Vancouver) Squadron crews fulfilled their briefs from 12,000 to 15,000 feet between 13.58 and 14.06 and helped to leave the town area 70% destroyed, with the cathedral and most of the historic buildings erased and more than sixteen hundred people killed.

While this operation was in progress, further south on the northern approaches to the Ruhr, the towns of Dorsten, Bocholt and Dülmen were coming under attack by main forces provided by 3, 4 and 6 Groups with 8 Group support for the 6 and 8 Group endeavours.

The focus remained on this part of Germany on the 27th, as the encirclement of the Ruhr by American ground forces required just the capture of the town of Paderborn, situated some thirty-five miles due east of Hamm. 1 Group provided a main force of 225 Lancasters and 8 Group forty-four Lancasters and nine Mosquitos, fourteen of the former representing 405 (Vancouver) Squadron, which departed Gransden Lodge between 15.08 and 15.22 with G/C Newson and S/L Mussells the senior pilots on duty. After climbing out they headed for the Dutch coast under fairly clear skies until the cloud began to build over enemy territory to reach ten-tenths over the target with tops at around 10,000 feet. The Master Bomber was heard calling for skymarkers at 17.25, but the first green smoke-puffs did not appear until 17.28, after which, a steady supply maintained the aiming-point for the next ten minutes. The early arrivals had been forced to orbit, but the crews following behind, who had been preparing to bomb by H2S and Gee, were able now to use the skymarkers as a more reliable reference, while confirming their accuracy by means of navigational aids. The Gransden Lodge crews carried out their marking and bombing roles from 15,000 to 16,500 feet between 17.28 and 17.39 and returned to report a cloud of brown smoke ascending to 2,000 feet above the clouds. The operation was an outstanding success, confirmed by a local report, which stated that three thousand separate fires had occurred, and that the town had been virtually destroyed.

The final operation of the hugely busy penultimate month of offensive activity by the Command ended with a 1, 6 and 8 Group raid on the Blohm & Voss U-Boot yards in the Finkenwerder district of Hamburg, where the new Type XXI vessels were being assembled. A force of 361 Lancasters and a hundred Halifaxes was made ready on the 31st, all of the latter provided by 6 Group, while 8 Group contributed fifty-nine Lancasters and eight Mosquitos. The 405 (Vancouver) Squadron element of fifteen Lancasters included seven for main force support duties each loaded with eighteen 500-pounders, and they departed Gransden Lodge with the others between 06.34 and 06.47 with W/C Rawson and S/Ls Mussells, Neilly and Vann leading the way. They took their respective places as the bomber stream attempted to form up with the main force element headed by 1 Group in squadron-by-squadron line astern formation. However, layer cloud prevented this from happening, and the force was closing on the Dutch coast at 3°East by the time that the cloud broke up sufficiently to allow the forming up to take place. Unfortunately, it built again from 6°East, remaining at ten-tenths for the rest of the flight to the target and when the leading aircraft of the main force were fifteen minutes out, the Master Bomber warned them to look for smoke-puff markers, the first of which appeared at 08.43 in small numbers. It was a further three minutes before they became plentiful, by which time the bombing was well underway in accordance with the frequent instructions and changing aiming points coming through from the Master Bomber. It caused a degree of jostling for position over the target, but most main force crews found red smoke puff markers to aim at and the 405 (Vancouver) Squadron participants carried out their respective tasks from 17,000 to 20,000 feet between 08.43 and 08.55. The Luftwaffe Tagjagd intervened, and eleven aircraft were shot down, the last occasion on which the Command's losses reached double figures from a single target. Most returning crews sensed that the raid had lacked a degree of concentration, but local reports spoke of widespread damage in residential and industrial areas in the south of the city and across the Elbe in Harburg, with energy supplies and communications also hard-hit.

During the course of the month the squadron took part in sixteen operations and dispatched 209 sorties for the loss of three Lancasters and crews.

April 1945

April would be a time to mop up defences, cut off communications and finish off the oil industry, and it began for 1 Group with an operation against what was believed to be a military barracks at Nordhausen, situated 150 miles east of the Ruhr. It was, in fact, a camp for forced workers at the underground secret weapons factory that had been hastily established in caves after the destruction of Peenemünde. Situated in the Harz mountains between Hannover to the north-west and Leipzig to the south-east the site was actually a pair of enormous parallel tunnels under the Kohnstein Hill, which had been developed originally by the BASF Company to mine gypsum between 1917 and 1934. Beginning in late 1943, smaller tunnels had been created as a link between them to form a horizontal ladder effect, and the site turned over to the Mittelwerk GmbH (Gesellschaft mit beschrenkter Haftung, or Limited Company) for the manufacture of V-2 rockets and other secret projects. The "barracks" were part of the Mittelwerk-Dora forced workers camp, where inmates existed under the most horrendous conditions and brutal treatment, while they were starved, worked to death or simply executed by an increasingly desperate regime seeking to change the course of the war. 1 Group provided a main force of 210 Lancasters, and 8 Group a further thirty-seven and eight Mosquitos to conduct the marking. 405 (Vancouver) Squadron made ready a dozen of its own and dispatched them from Gransden Lodge between 13.37 and 13.49 with G/C Newson the senior pilot on duty supported by no fewer than nine pilots of flight lieutenant rank. They had been briefed to perform a variety of marking and bombing tasks, and flew out over moderate cloud, which thickened as the bomber stream progressed eastwards.

By the time the target drew near, there was ten-tenths cloud and the Master Bomber issued instructions to the main force crews to descend to the cloud base at 8,500 feet at 16.02. Four minutes later, as the bombers approached the cloud tops at around 11,000 feet, the Master Bomber rescinded his original order and instructed the crews to climb again, causing confusion and disrupting all semblance of the previously coherent formation. Some futile attempts were made to reform the stream as the Master Bomber called for smoke-puff markers, but these seem to have burst inside the cloud and were not visible. As a last resort, he ordered the crews to "bomb on best navigational aids", to which the main force crews complied mostly from 12,000 to 14,000 feet without being able to assess the outcome. The 405 (Vancouver) Squadron crews did their best to perform as briefed from 11,000 to 15,200 feet between 16.15 and 16.30, while a single 1 Group crew dropped beneath the cloud base to 5,500 feet, and reported two small fires in the town, but no bombing around the aiming point. The target and the nearby town were attacked again twenty-four hours later by 5 Group and sustained severe damage, many friendly foreign nationals losing their lives in the barracks, while those in the tunnels remained safe from bombs, but endured a hellish existence as they were systematically worked to death.

The night of the 4/5th brought a return to the oil offensive at three sites, Leuna and Lützkendorf near Leipzig and Harburg on the southern bank of the Elbe opposite Hamburg. *(Lützkendorf no longer exists on a map of Germany and is now known as either Mücheln or Krumpa)*. 405 (Vancouver) Squadron made ready sixteen Lancasters for Leuna as part of an 8 Group force of thirty-four Lancasters and fifteen Mosquitos, while 3 and 6 Groups provided the main force of 293 Lancasters. The Gransden Lodge crews took to the air between 19.10 and 19.39 with G/C Newson, W/C McQuoid and S/L Vann the senior pilots on duty, each crew having been briefed to perform one of a number of marking functions. The outward route traversed Belgium and passed south of Bonn before crossing central Germany, and on arrival in the target area the spearhead of the bomber stream encountered eight-tenths broken cloud with tops mostly at 3,000 to 5,000 feet. The Path Finders arrived late, but once released at 22.45, their skymarkers were concentrated and maintained the aiming point until 22.55, when even the red and green TIs could be seen on the ground through occasional gaps in the cloud. Both were employed by the main force crews as they bombed from between 17,000 and 21,000 feet, observing bomb bursts, large explosions, small fires and a yellowish glow on the clouds. The Gransden Lodge crews fulfilled their briefs from 15,500 to 18,000 feet between 22.40 and 23.01, and although unable to make a detailed assessment, were persuaded by numerous fires to conclude that the operation had achieved its aims. As they flew back towards the west, they reported that the fires from the 5 Group raid on Nordhausen were still visible.

A force of 440 aircraft from 4, 6 and 8 Groups was assembled on the 8th to send against the Blohm & Voss U-Boot construction yards and naval installations in Hamburg and would follow on the heels of an attack just a few hours earlier by the American 8th Air Force. 8 Group detailed sixty Lancasters and eighteen Mosquitos, ten of the former provided by 405 (Vancouver) Squadron, which departed Gransden Lodge between 19.37 and 19.55 with S/Ls Mussells and Vann the senior pilots on duty and all crews assigned to one of the marking functions. The various elements joined up to form the bomber stream as they traversed the North Sea on course for the western coast of Schleswig-Holstein, intending to approach the target from the north. The Oboe Mosquitos delivered red TIs at 22.24, which were seen to cascade and fall through the ten-tenths, very thin 2,000-to-3,000-foot cloud tops and leave a red glow. Through a small gap in the cloud, the Master Bomber caught a momentary glimpse of red TIs on the ground and having assessed them as being on the aiming-point, ordered them to be backed up with greens before calling in the main force. When these were no longer visible from 22.34, he called for skymarkers and redirected the main force accordingly, the 405 (Vancouver) Squadron crews fulfilling their briefs from 15,700 to

18,000 feet between 22.25 and 22.39. Large explosions were observed at 22.34 and 22.38, but at debriefing not all expressed confidence in the effectiveness of the raid, which had suffered from a degree of undershooting. Post-raid reconnaissance was unable to attribute damage specifically to either the RAF or American attacks, and it is likely that the principal objectives, the shipyards, escaped serious damage during what was the final heavy raid of the war on Germany's second city. Earlier in the day, the length of a tour for a main force crew had been reduced from thirty-six to thirty-three sorties, and those with that number already under their belt, would, no doubt, be celebrating in the local watering holes as the above events were taking place.

Preparations were put in hand on 1, 3 and 8 Group stations on the 9th to prepare 591 Lancasters for a raid that night on the harbour area of Kiel. 8 Group detailed sixty-four Lancasters and nine Mosquitos for aiming-point D and thirty-two Lancasters for aiming-point E, with 405 (Vancouver) Squadron making ready fourteen Lancasters for the former and two for the latter. They departed Gransden Lodge between 19.43 and 19.58 with W/C McQuoid and S/L Vann the designated Master Bomber and Deputy for A/P D and the rest of the squadron, including W/C Rawson and crew, briefed to perform marking roles. They climbed away before setting a similar course to that adopted for Hamburg twenty-four hours earlier and encountered a little cloud before the enemy coast hove into sight. The target itself lay under clear skies with good visibility, and illuminating flares allowed the Master Bombers to identify the outline of the fjord and inner harbour and the two aiming-points. Ground marking commenced at A/P D at 22.25 and at A/P E two minutes later, and both were well-marked with red TIs, backed up by greens, which enabled the main force crews to aim at whichever presented the better target. Eventually, all of the TIs became obscured by smoke, and by the end of the attack the entire area between the aiming-points was on fire, with flames spreading down to the water's edge. A particularly large explosion at 22.35 gave the impression that an ammunition dump had been hit, and other hits on an oil storage depot resulted in thick, black smoke billowing up to a considerable height as the crews turned away. The Gransden Lodge crews carried out their respective tasks from 15,500 to 18,000 feet between 22.23 and 22.36, and photo-reconnaissance confirmed the effectiveness of the operation, revealing the Deutsche Werke U-Boot yards to have sustained severe damage, and the other two shipyards, Krupp-Germania and Howaldtswerke A G Werft, also to have been hit. The pocket battleship Admiral Scheer was seen to have capsized, while the cruisers Admiral Hipper and Emden were badly damaged and adjacent residential districts had suffered also.

The focus of operations on the 10th was upon railway installations in eastern Germany, the Engelsdorf and Mockau marshalling yards in Leipzig for a force of 134 Lancasters, ninety Halifaxes and six Mosquitos by daylight, and a stretch of track linked to the Wahren yards in the same city by seventy-six Lancasters and nineteen Mosquitos of 5 and 8 Groups after dark. A further operation involving 307 Lancasters and eight Mosquitos from 1 and 8 Groups would target the marshalling yards in the town of Plauen, situated close to the frontier with Czechoslovakia thirty miles south-west of Chemnitz. 8 Group detailed eighteen Lancasters and six Mosquitos for the Engelsdorf yards located in the east of the city, six Lancasters for the Mockau yards in the north and sixty-four Lancasters and nine Mosquitos for Plauen. 405 (Vancouver) Squadron briefed four crews for Engelsdorf and dispatched them from Gransden Lodge between 14.41 and 14.44 with primary visual marker, S/L Mussells, the senior pilot on duty and F/L Woods and crew visual centerers, while the crews of F/Ls MacGregor and Hall were to bomb with the main force. The skies over Leipzig were clear and the visibility good as the force arrived, and Master Bomber, 35

(Madras Presidency) Squadron's W/C Le Good, was able to make a visual identification of the aiming-point. The attack began at 17.55 with red Oboe TIs, which were backed up by the Lancasters with other reds. The Gransden Lodge crews fulfilled their briefs from 17,000 to 18,000 feet between 17.58 and 18.02 and observed the main force bombing to be concentrated and accurate. A large explosion occurred at 18.00, and, by the end of the raid, thick, bluish smoke was rising through 10,000 feet.

Immediately after bombing, S/L Mussells and crew were attacked from above and behind by a Me163 Komet rocket-powered fighter, which, with a single burst, shot away the rear turret with its occupant inside, and a rudder and elevators. The mid-upper turret and H2S were also damaged but the short endurance of the fighter prevented a further attack and S/L Mussells nursed the wounded Lancaster back to Allied lines under the protection of a number of Mustang escort fighters. It was decided to press on to the emergency landing strip at Woodbridge on the Suffolk coast, where four members of the crew baled out, and had the mid-upper gunner not been wounded, he and the pilot would have taken to their parachutes also. Despite difficulty in controlling the Lancaster, a safe landing was carried out and all were soon back in the bosom of the squadron.

The above force was on its way home by the time that the nine marker crews briefed for Plauen were taking to the air between 19.00 and 19.16 with the recently posted-in S/L Bennett the senior pilot on duty. The clear skies over south-eastern Germany persisted to welcome the bombers to Plauen, and the red Oboe TIs went down on time to open proceedings. The illumination of the aiming-point was good, and further red TIs landed where intended to be backed up by greens in a tight cluster that satisfied the Master Bomber. The 405 (Vancouver) Squadron crews carried out their briefs from 12,000 to 15,000 feet between 23.07 and 23.14, leaving the main force crews to aim for the TIs, and later the centre of the smoke. A large explosion was observed at 23.11, and by 23.20 the town was completely obscured by smoke rising through 12,000 feet.

Marshalling yards were to feature again on the 11th, when only 4 and 8 Groups would be called upon to combine forces for two operations against targets at Nuremberg and its neighbour, Bayreuth, situated some thirty miles to the north-east. 129 Halifaxes were assigned to the former and one hundred to the latter, and it was for the latter that 8 Group detailed fourteen Lancasters and eight Mosquitos, four of the former provided by 405 (Vancouver) Squadron. They departed Gransden Lodge between 11.58 and 12.01 with G/C Newson and F/O Bogg the designated Master Bomber and Deputy and two crews whose names are undecipherable as blind illuminators, and all reached the target area to be greeted by clear skies and good visibility. The first red TIs fell onto the aiming-point at 14.58 to be backed up by others and the main force crews complied with the instructions of the Master Bomber to deliver an accurate and concentrated attack. The Gransden Lodge crews fulfilled their briefs from 12,000 feet between 14.58 and 15.05 and helped to leave the railway yards enveloped in smoke and extensively damaged, a fact confirmed later by post-raid reconnaissance.

The final major attack on a German city was directed at Potsdam on the night of the 14/15th, and this would be the first incursion into the Berlin defence zone by RAF heavy bombers since March 1944. In the twelve months since then, Mosquitos of 8 Group's Light Night Striking Force (LNSF) had maintained a regular presence over the city, acting as a constant menace, dropping cookies to unsettle the populace and robbing the workers of their sleep. So fast was the "Wooden Wonder", that it was not unknown for a single aircraft to make two trips to Berlin in one night after a change of crew. A force of five hundred Lancasters from 1, 3 and 8 Groups was made ready, of which ninety Lancasters and a dozen Mosquitos represented 8 Group. Fifteen 405 (Vancouver) Squadron Lancasters departed Gransden Lodge between 18.40 and 19.13 with G/C Newson and S/Ls Bennett, Mussells and Neilly the senior pilots on duty, a dozen to undertake marking tasks and three to bomb with the main force. They climbed through cloud, which dispersed over the Channel, built-up again over France, but finally disappeared from the Rhine eastwards to leave the target area under clear skies with excellent visibility. The attack opened with illuminating flares, and the marking commenced six minutes before H-Hour with red TIs, which fell initially a little to the west of the aiming-point. These were soon corrected by other reds planted right on the mark and backed up by greens to leave the main force crews with no doubt about where to direct their bombs. The Master Bomber, W/C Le Good, maintained good control throughout, changing the point of focus as required and keeping the attack firmly on the aiming-point. The Gransden Lodge crews performed as briefed from 17,000 to 18,500 feet between 22.43 and 22.58, and all returned to report many fires and explosions and an afterglow visible for a hundred miles into the return journey. The raid was confirmed as a success, but some bomb loads were found to have spilled into northern and western districts of Berlin.

Distant railway targets awaited two forces on the night of the 16/17th, at Pilsen in Czechoslovakia for 222 Lancasters and eleven Mosquitos of 5 Group, and Schwandorf, situated on the southern bank of the River Naab in northern Bavaria, some thirty-five miles east of Nuremberg, for a main force of 120 Lancasters from 6 Group. 8 Group detailed forty-seven Lancasters and nine Mosquitos to provide the marking at the latter, and 405 (Vancouver) Squadron dispatched its sixteen participants from Gransden Lodge between 00.20 and 00.35 with S/Ls Mussells and Vann the senior pilots on duty. Each had been assigned to marking roles and had a seven-hour round-trip ahead of them as they set course for the passage across France to enter Germany in the Strasbourg region. They reached the target area to find clear skies with haze, and the flare force illuminated the marshalling yards effectively as the first red Oboe TIs cascaded at 03.52. The heavy marker crews followed up with further reds at regular intervals, which were backed up by greens. The 405 (Vancouver) Squadron crews performed as briefed from 8,000 to 15,000 feet between 03.53 and 04.05, reporting four large explosions between 03.55 and 04.04 and a column of black smoke emanating from the aiming-point reaching 8,000 feet by the time that the bombers turned for home.

There was good news for some main force crews to celebrate on the 17th, when the length of a tour was reduced yet again to thirty sorties, releasing many to contemplate a long future. Early briefings across the Command on the 18th informed 969 crews of an assault on the coastal batteries, naval base, airfield and town on the island of Heligoland. 405 (Vancouver) Squadron made ready six Lancasters as part of an 8 Group contribution of fifty-one Lancasters and thirty Mosquitos and sent them on their way from Gransden Lodge between 10.59 and 11.21 with G/C Newson and F/L Dix one of the designated Master Bomber and Deputy pairings and the other four crews to perform as blind sky markers. They flew out to the target under clear skies and in good visibility, Heligoland and its smaller neighbour, Düne, appearing as two tiny dots some thirty miles off Germany's north-western coast. Three aiming-points awaited the bomber, A, B and C, and it is not possible to ascertain for which the Gransden Lodge Master Bomber and Deputy pairing were responsible. The attack at A opened with red Oboe TIs, which were backed up by the Master Bombers with yellows, and it was not long before thick smoke was beginning to drift across the south-eastern corner of the island and obscure the ground. Despite that, aiming-point B remained visible for long enough to be identified, and a massive explosion occurred at 13.26, followed by flame and even more thick, black smoke. Red Oboe TIs marked out the third aiming-point, and each wave of the main force delivered accurate and concentrated bombing, the Gransden Lodge crews carrying out their assigned tasks from 10,000 to 18,000 feet between 13.08 and 13.26, before returning home to report a large column of smoke rising steadily from the south-eastern end, which hid from view what photographs would reveal later to be a surface that resembled a cratered moonscape. Heligoland's ordeal was not yet over, as the following day would bring an onslaught by 617 and 9 Squadrons, the former carrying 10-ton Grand Slams and 6-ton Tallboys and the latter Tallboys. If not already totally evacuated, the island certainly was after this operation.

As the British XXX Corps moved in on the city of Bremen, Bomber Command was asked to bomb enemy strong points in the south-eastern suburbs, where the attack was due to take place in two days' time. A main force of 691 aircraft was drawn from 1, 3 and 6 Groups, while 8 Group put up seventy-six Lancasters and sixteen Mosquitos, nine of the former representing 405 (Vancouver) Squadron, which departed Gransden Lodge between 15.35 and 15.41 with G/C Newson and S/L Mussells the designated Master Bomber and Deputy pairing for aiming point J1. They flew eastwards over cloud, which persisted more or less for the entire outward flight, and as the first wave approached the target at 17.56, the crews could only catch a glimpse of the ground through gaps. The visual marker crews were unable to identify the aiming-points, and the attacks on aiming-points J1, J2 and G were called off at 17.58, 18.13 and 18.49 respectively, and the entire 1 and 6 Group elements sent home with their bombs. 195 aircraft bombed at aiming-point F, before that attack too was abandoned at 19.05.

8 Group was called upon on the 24th to provide seven Lancasters and thirty Mosquitos to carry out an unusual operation that night. They were to deliver leaflets to eight PoW camps, while three 35 (Madras Presidency) Squadron Lancasters dropped medical supplies to the camp at Neubrandenburg in north-eastern Germany.

The final operations of the bombing war were carried out on the 25th, beginning with what was, perhaps, a symbolic attack by a main force of 335 Lancasters of 1 and 5 Groups and twenty-four Lancasters and eight Mosquitos of 8 Group on Hitler's Eaglesnest retreat and the nearby SS barracks at Berchtesgaden in the Bavarian mountains. It required an early start, the nine 405 (Vancouver) Squadron particpants departing Gransden Lodge between 06.00 and 06.12 with G/C Newson and S/L Bennett the senior pilots on duty and among five assigned to marking roles while four others were to bomb with the main force. The vanguard of the bomber stream arrived in the target area on time to find that all was not proceeding according to plan. The deputy Master Bomber had been unable to mark the target, and realising this, the leader of the first wave overshot the final turning point by two-and-a-half minutes, before bringing the force back in a wide orbit. This had the effect of splitting up the formation and aircraft began approaching the aiming-point from a variety of headings. At 09.45 the Master Bomber ordered the crews to bomb visually if they could, but a minute later a red target indicator went down, which appeared to be accurate, and crews selected whatever was best for them. A concentration of bombs was seen to fall across the SS barracks, and it seems that most fell within the confines of the general target area, causing a column of smoke to rise to 10,000 feet. The 405 (Vancouver) Squadron contingent returned safely to report fulfilling their briefs from 15,000 to 18,000 feet between 09.47 and 09.52.

The final offensive operation of the war by 8 Group's heavy brigade was mounted that afternoon against coastal batteries on the Frisian Island of Wangerooge, which controlled the approaches to the ports of Wilhelmshaven and Bremen. A main force of 308 Halifaxes and 130 Lancasters was drawn from 4 and 6 Groups, while 8 Group contributed twenty-eight Lancasters and eight Mosquitos. The four-strong Gransden Lodge element consisting of the blind sky marker crews of F/Ls Larson, Lindsay and Thompson and F/O Maxwell took off between 15.04 and 15.06, each sitting on ten 1,000-pounders and blue smoke-puff markers. On the way out, two Lancasters of 431 (Iroquois) Squadron RCAF collided off Norderney and crashed without survivors, and similarly tragic incidents caused the loss of two 76 Squadron Halifaxes and one each from 408 (Goose) and 426 (Thunderbird) Squadrons RCAF in the target area, with just one survivor among them. The force arrived at the target to find excellent conditions with perhaps three-tenths cloud at 3,500 feet, but not sufficient to inhibit sight of TIs clearly marking out the aiming-point. The Master Bomber instructed the force to overshoot the red TIs, before switching attention to the yellows, and once they became obscured, he focused the bombing on the edge of the smoke. The 405 (Vancouver) Squadron crews carried out their tasks from 12,000 feet between 16.58 and 17.04, the attacks pressed home in the face of a spirited flak response, and while the bombing was observed to be concentrated on the marked area, little damage was inflicted upon the concrete housings. When F/O Maxwell and crew touched down at Gransden Lodge at 18.52, they had the honour to bring down the curtain on the squadron's outstanding contribution to victory.

That night, 5 Group carried out a raid on an oil refinery at Tonsberg in Norway, and then, for all but 100 Group and the 8 Group Mosquito contingent, it was all over. Between the 30th and VE Day on the 8th of May the squadron played its part in the humanitarian Operation Manna, sending a total of thirty backer-up sorties to guide the dropping of food to the starving Dutch people still under enemy occupation, and then it was Operation Exodus, the repatriation of Allied prisoners of war, which would continue well into the summer. The final reckoning of the 405 (Vancouver) Squadron account showed that 758 of its airmen had lost their lives, out of a total casualty figure of 937.

405 (Vancouver) Squadron was earmarked for the Tiger Force for use in the continuing fight against Japan, and in preparation for this it converted fully onto Canadian-built Mk X Lancasters during the course of May. On the 26th, the squadron bade a fond farewell to Gransden Lodge, its home for two years, and resettled at Linton-on-Ouse for a brief period. The training and reorganization for the Pacific theatre was to take place in Canada, and the flight home began on the 16th of June. The sudden end to the war against Japan in August released the squadron from further obligation, and with its duty most honourably and gallantly done, it was disbanded at Greenwood, Nova Scotia on the 5th of September. It is impossible to estimate the contribution of Canada's airmen to the ultimate victory, it can only be recorded, that they served Bomber Command in RAF, RAAF and RCAF squadrons with courage and distinction. After an uncertain start, the Canadian 6 Group finished the war as the equal of any, and 405 (Vancouver) Squadron's magnificent record, both as a main force unit and as Canada's only Path Finder squadron, is unsurpassed. More than 9,900 Canadians gave their lives in Bomber Command service, a figure second only to that sustained by the RAF, and their selfless sacrifice will stand forever as a testament to a great nation.

Roll of Honour

Sgt	Frederick James	ABERY	24.02.44.
W/OII	George Warburton	ACORN	04.12.43.
Sgt	Norman	ACTON	31.05.42.
P/O	Joseph Paul Hector	ADAM	19.03.45.
F/Sgt	Reginald Thomas	ADAMS	30.06.42.
F/O	Roland Ernest Garnault	AGASSIZ	16.06.43.
Sgt	George Edward	AGATE	06.09.43.
F/Sgt	John Drew	AILEY	27.06.42.
P/O	Edward Lloyd	ALBERTS	23.04.44.
P/O	Robert Baker	ALBRIGHT	24.07.42.
W/OII	William Etherington	ALCAZAR	30.06.42.
F/O	James	ALLAN	07.01.45.
F/L	Lawrence	ALLEN	28.04.44.
Sgt	Edward Allison	ANDERSON	01.08.42.
F/Sgt	Floyd Roger Willis	ANDERSON	07.04.43.
P/O	James	ANDERSON	04.12.43.
F/Sgt	Jack	ANDERSON	03.01.44.
Sgt	Jeffcote Louvain	ANGELL	17.06.41.
F/Sgt	David Colin Brodie	ANGUS	18.08.43.
W/OII	Lloyd Dyer	ANNIS	14.01.44.
Sgt	Ronald Frank	ANSELL	27.06.42.
Sgt	Maxwell Warnock	APPERSON	24.07.42.
Sgt	Irving	ARBUCKLE	15.10.42.
ACI	Harry	ARMITAGE	18.09.41.
F/L	John	ARMITT	14.02.45.
F/O	Alexander Thomas	ARMSTRONG	11.06.44.
F/O	Albert Henry	ASHFORD	30.01.44.
Sgt	William Philip	ASHUN	01.04.42.
F/L	John William	ASTBURY	14.01.44.
F/L	Herbert Philipson	ATKINSON	01.05.43.
F/O	Russel James	AYLES	01.10.42.
F/L	David John	BAIN	10.08.42.
W/OII	Ralph Murray	BAKER	19.03.45.
S/L	William Henry	BALDWIN	24.08.43.
P/O	Ross Lloyd	BALTZER	02.06.42.
W/OII	George	BANCESCU	24.05.43.
Sgt	Walter Percy	BEARE	30.06.42.
F/O	Hugh Donald	BEATTIE	14.05.43.
W/OII	Walter Stanley	BEATTY	04.04.43.
Cpl	Joseph Victor Raoul	BEAUDRY	29.11.42.
P/O	William Edward	BEAVO	17.08.43.

Rank	Name	Surname	Date
Sgt	Douglas Glenn	BEBENSEE	14.07.43.
Sgt	John Frederick Peter	BEHN	06.10.42.
F/L	George	BELCHER	04.12.43.
F/Sgt	Charles Harold	BELL	08.11.41.
W/O	James William	BELL	30.06.42.
F/Sgt	Maxwell	BEN-HERTZ	02.10.42.
S/L	Gordon	BENNETT	25.05.44.
W/OII	Thomas Lloyd	BENTLEY	27.04.43.
P/O	George Robert	BERKEY	23.04.44.
Sgt	Henry Roberts	BESSENT	17.12.43.
F/O	Frederick William	BILSON	09.10.43.
S/L	Robert Clare	BISSET	30.11.41.
F/Sgt	Wendell Clifford	BLACK	09.11.42.
Sgt	Douglas Allan	BLACK	10.08.43.
Sgt	William John	BLAKELY	03.01.44.
S/L	Edward Weyman	BLENKINSOP	23.01.45.
P/O	Colin John	BLYTH	29.07.44.
P/O	Joseh Paul Roger	BOILEAU	30.01.44.
F/Sgt	George Eric	BOLLAND	21.02.45.
Sgt	Francis Charles	BOND	01.08.42.
P/O	Robert Alexander	BOOTH	28.04.44.
P/O	Robert Dean	BORROWES	07.05.44.
Sgt	Sidney	BOSWORTH	23.04.44.
F/L	Richard Trent	BOTKIN	09.10.43.
F/O	Clive Arkoll	BOULTON	15.03.45.
F/Sgt	Joseph Raymond Frederick	BOURGEAU	28.12.41.
P/O	Thomas John	BOWLING	18.08.43.
F/O	Norman Harvey	BOWRING	04.12.43.
Sgt	Lawrence Harold	BRADBROOK	30.06.42.
P/O	Allen Catto	BRADLEY	29.11.42.
F/Sgt	James Sydney	BRADLEY	28.04.44.
F/Sgt	Edmund Keith	BRENNAN	30.06.42.
P/O	Alfred Joseph	BRITTS	21.07.44.
F/Sgt	James Morley	BRODDY	10.03.42.
W/OII	Leo Joseph Martin	BRODERICK	06.09.43.
F/L	Robert	BROOK	16.09.44.
F/Sgt	Douglas Harold	BROWN	07.01.45.
Sgt	Thomas	BROWNLESS	03.08.43.
F/L	John Samuel	BRUCE	17.08.44.
P/O	Joseph Aloysius	BRUGGEMAN	16.01.45.
W/OII	Ernest Charles	BRUNET	20.10.43.
Sgt	Alexander Cunningham	BRUNTON	06.09.43.
F/Sgt	James Mathew	BUCKLEY	09.05.44.
Sgt	Francis William	BUNDY	20.10.43.
F/Sgt	Mervyn Kevin	BURKE	24.09.42.

P/O	John Richard Powell	BURKE	01.10.42.
P/O	Michael Adrian	BURNABY	04.05.44.
F/O	Robert Stuart	BUTTERWORTH	19.03.45.
P/O	Thomas McWhirter	CALDERWOOD	10.08.42.
F/L	Maxwell Boyd	CALHOUN	17.08.44.
F/Sgt	Bruce Clarke	CAMERON	02.01.44.
P/O	John Thompson	CAMPBELL	01.10.42.
F/O	Allan Paul	CAMPBELL	02.01.44.
P/O	Richard Alexander	CARNEY	17.08.43.
F/Sgt	Charles Arthur	CARPENTER	01.10.42.
Sgt	Derek Charles	CARROTT	29.07.44.
F/Sgt	Albert Martin	CARTER	01.10.42.
P/O	Joseph William	CARTER	17.08.44.
F/Sgt	Thomas Robert Manard	CATTLE	09.06.42.
Sgt	Robert Joseph	CAVANAUGH	29.11.42.
Sgt	Albert Donald	CHANCE	01.10.42.
Sgt	Ronald George	CHANDOS	18.09.41.
P/O	Joseph Marie Antoine Laurent	CHAREST	30.01.44.
F/L	William McLaurin	CHASE	09.05.44.
P/O	Samuel Stewart	CLARK	29.11.42.
F/O	Clarence Taylor	CLARK	24.11.43.
F/Sgt	Willam Leonard John	CLARK	02.01.44.
F/O	Henry Thomas	CLARKE	24.11.43.
F/Sgt	Joseph Desmond	CLARKE	03.01.44.
F/O	James McVicar	CLEMENT	09.08.44.
P/O	Nicholas Hugh	CLIFFORD	28.04.44.
F/L	William Blaise Burke	CLOUTIER	14.01.44.
S/L	George Edwin	COLDREY	03.06.44.
F/Sgt	James Edward	COLE	28.06.42.
F/O	Kenneth Arthur	COLE	15.03.44.
F/O	Clarence Melville	COLLIER	17.12.43.
Sgt	William	COLLOTON	24.07.42.
F/O	Earl Wellington	CONNOLLY	14.02.45.
Sgt	Hubert William	COOKE	18.08.43.
Sgt	Ben Bales	COPELAND	01.10.42.
P/O	Donald Johnston	COPELAND	09.05.44.
F/Sgt	John	CORMACK	15.04.42.
Sgt	Hubert Leonard	CORNWELL	17.12.43.
Sgt	William	CORRIGAN	17.12.43.
Sgt	Edwin Charles Alfred	COULES	03.09.42.
P/O	Reginald	COX	02.08.41.
F/Sgt	Arthur	COX	08.04.43.
F/O	Vincent	CRAWFORD	12.09.44.
S/L	Nathan	CRAWFORD	02.01.45.
Sgt	Joseph Daniel	CREEDE	27.07.42.

Sgt	Richard Noel Pickwell	CRITCHLOW	24.11.43.
P/O	David Edward	CROCKATT	27.04.43.
Sgt	Morris William	CROFT	20.12.42.
F/Sgt	William James	CROZIER	03.08.43.
F/O	William Michael	CRUMBLEY	16.06.44.
Sgt	John Colvin	CRUMP	24.07.41.
Sgt	Sidney	CUGLEY	24.08.43.
F/O	Franklin Howard	CUMMER	28.01.45.
P/O	Benjamin Robert	CUNLIFFE	16.01.45.
P/O	Francis Leo	CUNNINGHAM	01.10.42.
Sgt	Edward John	CUTTING	03.09.42.
P/O	Joseph Jacques Guy	DAGENAIS	11.06.44.
Sgt	Robert Arthur	DAMMS	05.04.43.
Sgt	Alan	DANBY	27.06.42.
F/Sgt	Ronald Denver	DANIELS	09.05.44.
F/Sgt	Roger Henry Jules	DAOUST	06.01.44.
Sgt	Eric	DARBYSHIRE	03.08.43.
F/L	Henry William Julius	DARE	03.08.43.
Sgt	Thomas	DAVENPORT	21.07.44.
Sgt	John William Thomas	DAVIES	29.08.41.
F/O	Walter Cecil	DAVIES	16.06.43.
F/Sgt	George Albert	DAVIS	04.12.43.
F/O	Harry Denis	DAVY	22.12.44.
F/Sgt	Louis Donald	DAWDY	02.09.42.
Sgt	John Frederick Blair	DAWSON	15.08.41.
Sgt	Lewis Nelson	DEARLOVE	30.06.42.
Sgt	Hubert	DEARNLY	25.07.41.
P/O	James Henry	DEMPSEY	15.03.44.
Sgt	John Cecil	DENNIS	08.04.42.
P/O	James Frederick	DEVITT	22.12.44.
F/Sgt	Winston James	DICKINSON	30.06.42.
P/O	Chester Brockie	DIXON	27.04.43.
F/Sgt	Peter	DMYTRUK	09.12.43.
W/OII	Warren Lee	DOBSON	17.12.43.
P/O	Vernon Fairbank	DODDS	21.07.44.
Sgt	Lloyd Eldon	DODGE	22.10.41.
Sgt	Arthur John	DOLDING	17.11.42.
F/Sgt	Jack Cecil	DONKIN	28.12.41.
F/O	Thomas Henry	DONNELLY	02.01.44.
Sgt	Leslie	DOVASTON	15.03.45.
F/Sgt	Alfred Thomas	DRENNAN	10.09.42.
F/O	Wendell Pierce	DREW	29.07.44.
F/O	Gordon Robert	DRIMMIE	14.01.44.
F/O	Howard Raymond	DRYER	29.12.44.
F/Sgt	Joseph Paul Henri	DUBE	17.11.43.

Rank	Name	Surname	Date
F/L	Eric Cecil	DUKE	02.01.45.
P/O	William Howard	DUNCAN	01.10.42.
P/O	James Barry	DUNNE	02.01.44.
F/O	Robert Keep	DURBRIDGE	10.03.42.
P/O	Gyles Raymond	DYELLE	12.09.44.
F/Sgt	John Henry	DYSON	26.02.42.
F/Sgt	Clarence Gordon	EAGLES	02.09.42.
P/O	Douglas Joseph	EASTHAM	24.02.44.
P/O	Henry Adolphus	ECHIN	30.06.42.
Sgt	Aubrey Harold	EDWARDS	08.04.42.
F/O	John Harvey	EDWARDS	07.04.43.
P/O	Gordon James	EDWARDS	16.09.44.
P/O	Sigurjon	EINARSSON	30.01.44.
F/O	Donald James	ELLIOTT	03.01.44.
P/O	Ronald Oberlin	ELLIS	16.06.44.
P/O	Thomas Henry Navin	EMERSON	14.07.43.
F/O	John Lionel	EMERY	11.06.44.
F/O	Benjamin Hugo	ENNS	29.11.42.
F/O	Roy Stanley	ERICKSON	06.10.42.
Sgt	John Blackburn	ERRINGTON	17.11.43.
Sgt	William Leslie	EVANS	30.11.41.
F/Sgt	John Henry	EVANS	10.08.43.
F/Sgt	George Rhys	EVANS	03.01.44.
F/Sgt	Arthur Colin	EWING	03.09.42.
Sgt	Alan	FAIRLESS	01.10.42.
Sgt	Arthur	FAULKNER	16.06.43.
Sgt	John Albert	FAWKES	24.07.41.
F/L	William Hugh	FETHERSTON	04.04.42.
F/Sgt	William Ewart Nixon	FIELD	27.06.42.
F/O	Thomas Ashton	FILLINGHAM	12.06.43.
F/O	Charles Harold	FISHER	17.08.44.
W/OII	Rowan Charles	FITZGERALD	27.06.42.
P/O	Stanley Herbert	FITZHENRY	02.01.45.
P/O	George Howard	FLEMING	15.08.41.
F/Sgt	Joseph	FLEMING	09.06.42.
Sgt	Charles Harold	FLETCHER	18.09.41.
P/O	Harold Arthur	FLOREN	14.01.44.
F/Sgt	William Joseph	FOLEY	05.04.43.
Sgt	John Edward Thomas	FOOT	30.06.42.
F/Sgt	Joseph Marcel Wencelas	FORTIN	02.06.42.
P/O	Leslie Arthur	FOSTER	28.04.44.
P/O	Allan Martin	FOSTEY	09.02.45.
F/O	Gerald Gordon	FOX	29.12.44.
F/O	Ronald John	FRAAS	08.07.41.
Sgt	Victor Raymond	FRENCH	10.09.42.

F/O	Raymond Alfred	FRENCH	14.02.45.
F/O	Lawrence William Arthur	FREWIN	16.06.43.
P/O	Frederick John Alec	FREY	26.09.44.
Sgt	Michael William	FUGERE	20.12.42.
F/L	Allan Blake	FYFE	15.03.44.
P/O	Bernard Edwin	GALBRAITH	15.03.44.
P/O	Donald Irwin	GALBRAITH	15.03.45.
Sgt	Paul Arthur	GALE	17.01.42.
F/O	Austin Gordon	GAMSBY	16.06.44.
W/OI	Stephen Frederic	GANNON	29.11.42.
Sgt	Albert George Henry	GAPES	15.12.42.
F/L	Raymond	GARDINER	23.11.43.
Sgt	Henry	GARDNER	03.08.43.
F/Sgt	Francis Campbell	GARNETT	10.03.42.
Sgt	James David	GARROW	05.01.42.
P/O	Thomas Donald	GAVIN	02.01.44.
F/Sgt	John Burton	GAYFER	05.01.42.
F/O	Gerald Edward	GEEVES	02.01.45.
F/O	Frederick Arthur George Wilmott	GERTY	02.06.42.
P/O	Edward Emile	GERVAIS	24.09.42.
F/Sgt	Francis Earl	GIBBONS	10.08.42.
Sgt	Robert Charles	GIBSON	30.01.44.
Sgt	Patrick Neil	GILBERT	21.07.44.
F/O	James Frank	GILBEY	14.01.44.
F/Sgt	John Thomas	GILL	09.05.44.
Sgt	Hugh Gordon	GILLESPIE	14.11.42.
F/Sgt	William Edwin	GIMBY	18.08.43.
F/Sgt	Norman	GISLASON	06.10.42.
F/O	Mark	GLUCK	24.05.43.
F/L	Wilfred	GODDARD	26.09.44.
F/Sgt	Robert Edward	GOLDNEY	05.04.43.
W/O	Walter Eric	GOLDSPINK	28.09.43.
Sgt	Wilfred	GOOD	21.01.44.
F/Sgt	Lewis Victor	GOODE	17.06.41.
Sgt	Donald Kenneth	GORDON	28.12.41.
Sgt	Archibald Don	GORDON	07.04.43.
F/O	Fred Merrill	GORDON	14.02.45.
F/Sgt	Raymond Albert Aime	GORIEU	30.06.42.
W/OI	Curtis Albert	GORING	01.09.43.
Sgt	John Edward	GOSS	24.11.43.
Sgt	Henry Patrick	GOVER	10.08.42.
F/Sgt	Alan William	GOWDEY	16.09.44.
Sgt	William Seaman	GRANT	17.09.42.
W/OII	Grant Russell	GRAVES	12.04.42.
F/L	Kenneth MacGregor	GRAY	10.08.43.

W/C	Charles	GRAY	29.07.44.
P/O	Arthur Monson	GREEN	01.10.42.
P/O	Philip Sanson	GREENE	16.06.44.
Sgt	Albert Frank	GREGORY	03.08.43.
P/O	Joseph	GRODECKI	23.04.44.
F/O	Ernest Stuart	GUITON	30.01.44.
Sgt	Thomas Gower	GUNN	30.06.42.
Sgt	Harold William	GUNN	15.12.42.
F/Sgt	Godon Frederick	GURR	17.01.42.
F/Sgt	David George	HACKETT	02.10.42.
F/O	Douglas	HACKETT	30.01.44.
W/O	Ronald William	HAINSWORTH	07.03.45.
P/O	Alan Wardell	HALEY	29.12.44.
W/O	Joseph Walter	HALIKOWSKI	03.04.43.
Sgt	Cyril Roland	HALL	22.10.41.
Sgt	Eric	HALLIWELL	17.12.43.
Sgt	Orlando Delmar Conrad	HAMEL	29.11.42.
F/Sgt	James	HANNA	10.08.43.
F/O	Harold Allan	HANNAH	27.01.45.
F/O	William Albert George	HARDY	01.05.43.
P/O	Lloyd Glen	HARDY	12.09.44.
F/O	Frank Albert	HARMAN	24.08.43.
F/Sgt	William Jessup	HARRELL	30.06.42.
Sgt	Thomas Raymond	HARRIGAN	29.12.44.
F/O	Frank Percival	HARRISON	24.05.43.
F/Sgt	Ralph Eric	HART	14.05.43.
Sgt	Alan Godfrey	HARVET	15.04.42.
Sgt	Sidney Norman	HARVEY	17.06.41.
F/Sgt	Alexander Lawrence Dennis	HASSAN	08.11.41.
Sgt	Aubrey Peter	HATELEY	24.11.43.
F/Sgt	Willard Helvin	HAUGEN	18.08.43.
F/O	John Douglas	HAWKINS	17.08.43.
Sgt	Sydney Buchanan	HAWLEY	14.05.43.
P/O	John Douglas	HAYES	16.06.44.
F/O	Ernest	HAYES	19.03.45.
W/O	Alan	HAZLEHURST	30.01.44.
F/Sgt	Reginald Paul	HEALEY	09.06.42.
F/Sgt	Willam Henry	HEDLEY	20.10.43.
P/O	James	HENDERSON	12.03.43.
Sgt	Charles Orrin	HENDERSON	12.03.43.
Sgt	Douglas	HENNING	31.05.42.
F/Sgt	Robert William	HEXTER	24.07.42.
F/Sgt	Leslie	HEYCOCK	09.06.42.
P/O	Lloyd George	HIGGINSON	09.06.42.
F/Sgt	William Charles	HIGGS	24.11.43.

Rank	Name	Surname	Date
Sgt	Walter Alexander	HILL	10.08.42.
F/L	Lawrence David	HILLIER	03.09.42.
F/Sgt	Charles Edward	HILLMER	30.11.41.
F/O	Alfred	HINSCLIFFE	07.05.44.
P/O	Frederick William	HODGE	22.06.43.
F/Sgt	Adam Kidd	HODGINS	09.11.42.
F/Sgt	Clement Maurice	HOLDER	04.12.43.
Sgt	Reginald Douglas	HOLLAND	09.06.42.
P/O	Francis	HOLLAND	12.03.43.
P/O	George Charles	HOLLAND	04.12.43.
Sgt	Malcolm Keith	HOLLIDAY	16.06.43.
F/Sgt	David Andrew	HOLLIDAY	15.03.45.
Sgt	Roy James	HOLLOBONE	29.08.41.
Sgt	James	HOLMES	28.05.43.
Sgt	Francis	HOOTON	29.11.42.
P/O	John Read	HORN	02.08.41.
Sgt	Elwood Campbell	HOULDNG	14.01.44.
F/Sgt	James Young	HOUSTON	28.05.43.
F/Sgt	Martin Charles	HOWE	01.04.42.
F/Sgt	Moheddeen Abdul Ghias	HOWSAN	01.04.42.
W/OII	John Alfred Nelson	HUCKER	09.10.43.
F/Sgt	Michael	HUDEMA	06.10.42.
P/O	Walter Donald	HUFF	16.06.44.
Sgt	Douglas Miller	HUGHES	29.08.41.
P/O	James John	HUGHES	28.06.42.
Sgt	James	HUNTER	01.08.42.
Sgt	William	HUTCHINSON	03.08.43.
Sgt	Charles Colin	HYNAM	08.11.41.
Sgt	Arnold Wentworth	HYSON	12.08.42.
Sgt	Jack William	IRISH	01.08.42.
Sgt	Eric Leslie	JACKMAN	09.06.42.
F/Sgt	Lawrence Herbert	JACKSON	22.10.41.
F/Sgt	Leonard Douglas	JACKSON	02.06.42.
Sgt	Ronald	JAMES	28.12.41.
F/L	Rodger Bingham	JARVIE	14.01.44.
F/Sgt	Ernest Norman	JEFFERIES	09.06.42.
F/Sgt	Roland Warren	JENNINGS	24.05.43.
F/O	Joseph John Raymond	JOHNSON	21.07.44.
Sgt	William Leo Newton	JOHNSTON	22.10.41.
P/O	Norman	JOHNSTON	03.06.44.
Sgt	Eric Noel	JOLLY	17.08.44.
Sgt	Dewi Edmund	JONES	09.04.42.
Sgt	Malcolm David	JONES	15.04.42.
Sgt	Joseph	JONES	29.11.42.
F/Sgt	Robert John	JONES	07.04.43.

Rank	Name	Surname	Date
P/O	Richard Barron	JONES	15.03.45.
W/OII	William Francis	JORDAN	05.04.43.
Sgt	Kenneth Sidney	JOSLYN	14.01.44.
P/O	Ernest Richard	KAESEMODEL	29.12.44.
F/O	Joseph Anthony	KAUCHARIK	14.02.45.
Sgt	John Hyman	KAUFMAN	24.09.42.
W/O	Joseph Garnet Stewart	KAVANAUGH	23.11.43.
P/O	Solomon	KAY	24.02.44.
S/L	Walter B*ernard*	KEDDY	17.01.42.
F/O	John Ignatius Joseph	KEENAN	16.06.44.
P/O	David Austin	KELLEY	03.06.44.
F/L	Kenneth Donovan	KEMP	17.08.44.
W/OII	Clifford John Vosper	KETTLEY	25.07.43.
F/Sgt	Alan Edward Sidney	KIFF	09.02.45.
Sgt	Ronald Douglas	KILLIN	08.11.41.
Sgt	Henry	KING	10.08.43.
P/O	Leslie Ronald	KING	24.08.43.
Sgt	Alexander	KIRKCALDY	19.03.45.
P/O	William Watson	KIRKPATRICK	12.03.43.
P/O	John Colwell	KITCHEN	01.10.42.
F/Sgt	Charles Albert	KITSON	17.09.42.
F/Sgt	Murray Ralph	KLEISDORFF	27.06.42.
F/Sgt	Alan John	KNIGHT	30.11.41.
F/L	John Kingsley	KNIGHTS	14.02.45.
Sgt	John Albert	KNOX	27.07.42.
F/L	Gordon Winston	KNUPP	09.05.44.
F/Sgt	William Michael	KOSTENUK	29.11.42.
F/Sgt	Peter	KUCHERYK	01.10.42.
F/Sgt	Joseph Wendelin	KUCINSKY	25.06.43.
P/O	Bernard Henry	LABARGE	12.03.43.
P/O	Joseph Harvey Milton	LACELLE	28.06.42.
Sgt	Emanuel George	LACINA	12.03.43.
P/O	Norman Leslie	LAING	27.07.42.
F/L	Leslie Norman	LAING	15.03.45.
F/O	Charles Edwin	LAISHLEY	26.09.44.
F/O	Hyme	LANDAU	17.11.42.
Sgt	Eric Arthur	LANE	14.01.44.
P/O	Andrew Alexander	LANG	01.10.42.
F/Sgt	Guy	LANGFORD	12.08.42.
Sgt	Willis	LANGHORNE	28.12.41.
P/O	Richard Henry	LARSON	17.11.43.
Sgt	William Alexander Benjamin	LAUGHLIN	01.08.42.
F/O	Albert Clayton	LAW	10.07.43.
F/O	William John	LAWRENCE	23.11.43.
W/OII	Allan Keith	LAWRENCE	14.01.44.

F/L	Christopher Daniel	LAWSON	16.06.43.
W/C	Kenneth John	LAWSON	02.01.45.
F/Sgt	Gabriel Emile Joseph	LE BIHAN	28.05.43.
F/Sgt	Osborne Bayfield	LE FURGEY	05.01.42.
P/O	Joseph Louis Philippe	LE PAGE	01.10.42.
P/O	Andrew Owen	LEARMONTH	02.08.41.
F/Sgt	William Desmond	LEAVESLEY	16.09.44.
F/Sgt	Arthur Geoffrey	LEE	15.10.42.
F/L	Henry Keith	LEFROY	23.11.43.
F/Sgt	Nelson	LEFTLY	08.04.42.
P/O	Joseph Henri Thomas Jacques	LEMIEUX	22.06.43.
P/O	John Watt	LENNOX	05.05.43.
W/OII	Nuncie	LEONE	14.01.44.
Sgt	Arthur Bennet	LESLEY	15.08.41.
F/Sgt	Gerald Edwin	LEWIS	15.10.42.
F/L	Harold	LIVERSIDGE	30.06.42.
P/O	Robert Andrew	LIVINGSTON	22.06.43.
F/Sgt	David Kilgour	LLOYD	12.04.42.
P/O	Richard Philip	LOCKE	08.04.42.
F/Sgt	Robert Neville	LONERGAN	10.03.42.
P/O	Stuart Herman	LONG	28.09.43.
F/L	Ronald Walter	LONG	16.09.44.
F/Sgt	John Arthur	LONGLEY	15.10.42.
F/Sgt	Levi	LOWE	15.10.42.
F/O	John Clair	LOWTHER	28.09.43.
F/Sgt	Albert	LUCKHURST	07.07.41.
F/L	Floyd Edward	LUXFORD	03.04.43.
W/C	Gordon Dale	MACALLISTER	26.02.42.
Sgt	John Walter	MACAULAY	27.07.42.
F/Sgt	Robert Gray	MACDONALD	12.03.43.
Sgt	Donald Malcolm	MACFARLANE	15.04.42.
P/O	Donald John	MACFARLANE	29.12.44.
Sgt	William Florence	MACGREGOR	17.06.41.
WO/II	Norman Angus	MACKENZIE	01.09.42.
Sgt	Matthew Walker	MACKENZIE	12.03.43.
P/O	James George	MACKINNON	01.04.42.
F/O	Philip John Ashworth	MAGSON	24.08.43.
F/O	Laurence Herman	MAHLER	09.02.45.
Sgt	Ronald Percy	MANN	30.11.41.
F/O	Peter William	MANNING	17.08.43.
F/Sgt	Walter Sidney	MARCHANT	16.06.44.
F/Sgt	Paul Jones	MARONEY	09.11.42.
F/Sgt	George Frederick	MARR	22.10.41.
ACII	Robert Proctor	MARRIOTT	12.02.42.
P/O	John Robert	MARRIOTT	27.04.43.

F/Sgt	Francis Joseph	MARSH	15.03.45.
Sgt	Harry Alfred	MARSHALL	16.01.45.
Sgt	Robert Tuck	MARTIN	17.06.41.
Sgt	Julian Lee Byron	MARTIN	24.07.41.
W/OI	James	MARTIN	24.05.43.
F/O	Maurice James	MARTIN	09.02.45.
F/Sgt	George Joseph	MASSE	17.01.42.
P/O	Robert Addison	MATHER	30.11.41.
Sgt	James Matthew	MAXON	18.09.41.
W/OII	William James	McALPINE	03.04.43.
W/OI	Edwin Matthew	McARTHUR	01.09.43.
Sgt	William	McCABREY	28.01.45.
F/O	John Warren	McCANN	01.10.42.
F/O	Anthony Gerard	McCARTHY	21.07.44.
Sgt	Francis Anthony	McCLUSKEY	06.10.42.
S/L	John (Jack)	McCORMACK	04.04.42.
F/O	Alexander Purves	McCRACKEN	25.07.43.
P/O	James Robert	McCREA	23.04.44.
P/O	Leslie Asa	McCREA	03.06.44.
F/Sgt	William Granger	McCRON	01.10.42.
F/L	Stanley Clayton	McDONALD	04.05.44.
F/O	Alan James	McEWEN	09.06.42.
Sgt	Allan Garfield	McFEE	30.06.42.
F/Sgt	Edmund Thomas	McGILL	09.06.42.
Sgt	Earl Lewis	McGILLIVRAY	29.11.42.
F/O	George Glover	McGLADREY	14.07.43.
Sgt	Stanley	McGLORY	24.05.43.
F/Sgt	Bernard Arthur	McGRATH	03.09.42.
F/O	Harry Starkey	McINTYRE	18.08.43.
F/O	John Alexander	McINTYRE	04.05.44.
F/O	Hubert Bates	McINTYRE	09.02.45.
W/OII	Gordon Campbell	McKAY	17.08.43.
F/O	Donald Gordon	McKAY	16.01.45.
Sgt	Henry Bruce	McKENZIE	02.08.41.
Sgt	Andrew Fraser	McLEAN	31.05.42.
Sgt	Roy Victor	McLEAN	21.02.43.
W/OII	Cyril Cobb	McLELLAN	02.08.43.
F/O	Burns Alexander	McLENNAN	17.12.43.
Sgt	Graham Alexander	McLEOD	08.11.41.
LAC	Norman Richard	McLEOD	29.03.42.
Sgt	Howard	McQUEEN	03.04.43.
F/Sgt	Ronald Cameron	McRAE	24.05.43.
F/L	Melborn Leslie	MELLSTROM	10.04.45.
F/Sgt	Allan	MENZIES	24.08.43.
Sgt	Sidney	MESSHAM	02.10.42.

F/O	Allan John	MIDDLETON	10.08.43.
F/Sgt	Victor	MIENERT	17.12.43.
Sgt	Malcolm Stephen	MILLER	17.08.43.
F/Sgt	James Arthur	MILLER	24.08.43.
Sgt	Leslie George Robert	MILLER	02.01.44.
P/O	Allan Bernard	MILLER	16.01.45.
P/O	Francis John	MILLER	15.03.45.
F/Sgt	Ralph Elliott	MILLIKEN	29.11.42.
F/Sgt	William Stanley	MILNE	29.11.42.
Sgt	Albert Victor Bolduc	MILOT	16.10.42.
Sgt	Anthony George Lendrum	MITCHELL	24.07.41.
P/O	Keneth Ederic Michael	MITCHELL	03.09.42.
F/L	John Maxfield	MITCHELL	07.05.44.
Sgt	John Patrick	MOLLOY	15.08.41.
F/Sgt	George Raymond	MONTGOMERY	09.06.42.
W/OI	Ralph Joseph	MONTGOMERY	07.05.44.
Sgt	Bernard	MOODY	05.05.43.
Sgt	Robert	MOORE	11.03.43.
F/Sgt	George Edwin	MOORE	29.06.44.
Sgt	Thomas Gwynne	MORGAN	10.08.42.
P/O	Warren Arthur	MORRILL	16.06.44.
P/O	David Gordon	MORRIS	09.06.42.
Sgt	Robert	MORRIS	15.03.45.
F/L	Roy Gordon	MORRISON	14.07.43.
Sgt	Bruce Ralph	MORRISON	21.01.44.
F/O	William Clifford	MORROW	29.07.44.
F/O	Edwin John Barnes	MOSS	24.11.43.
Sgt	Alexander Douglas	MUIR	03.09.42.
W/OI	Edward Warren	MURPHY	02.10.42.
F/Sgt	William Frederick	MURRAY	17.09.42.
F/L	Sidney Leon	MURRELL	22.06.43.
P/O	Philip Arthur	MUSGRAVE	17.08.44.
P/O	Robert Douglas	MUTCH	17.11.43.
P/O	Laurent Joseph Onesime	NADEAU	03.08.42.
P/O	Ross Bell	NAIRN	26.08.44.
F/Sgt	Charles Joseph	NEUBERT	02.10.42.
Sgt	Thomas	NEWTON	30.01.44.
P/O	Arthur Willard	NICHOLS	22.06.43.
W/OII	Thomas Harold	NOLAN	03.01.44.
F/O	Kenneth Albert	NORDHEIMER	17.08.44.
F/O	Henry Eugene	NOVAK	16.01.45.
Sgt	John Fawell	O'BRIEN	01.08.42.
P/O	James Gilmour	O'DELL	23.11.43.
F/Sgt	Frank James	O'DONOHOE	21.02.43.
P/O	Francis Edward	O'HARE	27.04.43.

Rank	Name	Surname	Date
P/O	William Robert	OLIVER	23.04.44.
F/O	Edward Carl	OLSEN	01.10.42.
F/O	Donald Brant	OLSON	14.02.45.
P/O	Grant Murray	O'NEIL	30.01.44.
F/Sgt	Paul Patrick Augustus	ONESON	30.06.42.
F/Sg	John	OTT	24.09.42.
F/Sgt	Thomas Reid	OWENS	24.07.42.
F/Sgt	Raoul Omer Joseph	PAGE	01.04.42.
F/O	Wendell McLean	PALMER	12.03.43.
Sgt	William Reginald	PALMER	30.01.44.
W/C	Charles William	PALMER	26.09.44.
Sgt	Thomas Alan	PARGETER	18.08.43.
Sgt	John Edward	PARK	06.10.42.
Sgt	Benjamin Frederick John	PARKER	21.02.43.
P/O	Andrew Smith	PARKER	14.01.44.
F/L	Keith Edwin	PARKHURST	15.03.45.
F/O	William Earnest	PARSONS	04.05.44.
F/Sgt	Gordon John	PARTRIDGE	17.11.43.
Sgt	Sydney John	PASSEY	03.08.43.
Sgt	Charles Andrew	PATON	17.09.42.
Sgt	Jack Hastings	PAUL	21.01.44.
F/L	Harold Leslie	PAYNE	16.01.45.
Sgt	Reginald Percy	PAYTON	17.08.41.
F/O	Wilfred George F	PEACOCK	26.09.44.
F/O	George Ernest	PEAKER	19.03.45.
F/O	Robert Allen	PEARSON	08.07.44.
1st Lt	James Morris Kenneth	PEDERSEN	17.11.43.
P/O	Stanley	PEEL	01.10.42.
Sgt	Isaac Abraham	PENNER	27.04.43.
F/Sgt	Ernes Francis	PERRAULT	19.03.45.
W/OI	Keith Oliver	PERRY	23.08.43.
F/Sgt	Raymond Floyd	PETERSON	14.01.44.
Sgt	William John	PETHYBRIDGE	09.06.42.
Sgt	Gabriel	PHILLIPS	18.09.41.
F/Sgt	Edmund Cecil	PHILLIPS	26.02.42.
W/OII	Gordon Mclean	PHILLIPS	27.06.42.
P/O	Ross Joseph	PHILLIPS	11.06.44.
F/O	James Murray	PHILLIPS	29.12.44.
F/Sgt	Charles Pearn	PHILP	30.06.42.
F/Sgt	Charles William	PICKERING	10.08.43.
Sgt	Warren Bryan	PICKETT	31.05.42.
F/Sgt	William Stapleton	PIERS	26.02.42.
Sgt	Stanley Thomas	PITT	03.08.43.
W/OII	William Lloyd	PLATT	09.06.42.
Sgt	James Jerome	POCOCK	01.10.42.

F/O	Elwood Cameron	POMEROY	29.07.44.
P/O	Bourneuf Freeman	POTHIER	07.05.44.
F/Sgt	John Victor	POTTER	27.07.42.
Sgt	Robert Bruce	PRENTICE	27.07.42.
Sgt	Charles William	PRICE	25.06.43.
F/Sgt	Clinton Landis	PUDNEY	16.06.43.
P/O	Geoffrey Hiram Standeford	PULLEN	17.06.41.
Sgt	Norman	PYKE	21.01.44.
F/Sgt	Robert Andrew	QUINN	07.01.45.
F/Sgt	John MacCauley	RAE	28.01.45.
W/OII	John	RAIKE	16.09.44.
F/L	David	RAMSAY	28.04.44.
Sgt	John Maxwell	RANKIN	24.09.42.
P/O	John	RANKIN	04.07.43.
P/O	John Robert Francis	RATCLIFFE	03.08.43.
F/Sgt	Graham Sydney	READ	28.09.43.
Sgt	James	REDHEAD	02.01.44.
F/O	John Norman Ralston	REDPATH	20.10.43.
F/Sgt	Percy George Frank	REDSTONE	24.02.44.
Sgt	John Moorby	REED	02.08.41.
F/Sgt	Stanleigh Lowry	REID	02.06.42.
P/O	Joseph Gerard Maurice	RENAUD	03.06.44.
P/O	Alan Joseph	RETTER	16.06.44.
Sgt	James Orville	RICE	03.08.43.
W/OII	Gordon Hubert	RICHARDS	17.11.42.
P/O	Kenneth Craiglaw	RIGBY	03.08.43.
F/Sgt	George William	ROBERTS	03.09.42.
F/Sgt	Frank Duncan	ROBERTS	07.04.43.
F/L	Warren Ainsley	ROBERTS	30.01.44.
P/O	Cyril Edmund	ROBERTS	16.06.44.
Sgt	William Alan	ROBERTSON	05.01.42.
F/Sgt	Ralph Lavis	ROBINSON	22.06.43.
W/O	Arthur William	ROBINSON	03.01.44.
F/L	James Alexander	ROBSON	26.02.42.
F/Sgt	Melvin Peter Frederick	ROBSON	26.02.42.
F/Sgt	Richard Alan	ROLLINS	15.12.42.
Sgt	Maurice Francis Victor	ROOBROECK	17.12.43.
F/Sgt	Norman Wilbur	ROSS	29.11.42.
Sgt	Douglas	ROWBOTHAM	03.08.43.
P/O	Earl Dwyre	ROWE	22.06.43.
Sgt	Sidney Bertram	ROWLAND	28.06.42.
Sgt	James	RYAN	15.12.42.
F/Sgt	Joseph Barney	RYNSKI	22.12.44.
F/O	Alexander Jerry	SALABA	02.01.44.
P/O	Russell Arthur	SALTZBERRY	23.04.44.

F/Sgt	John Wright	SANDERSON	09.04.42.
F/L	Earl Albert	SANDERSON	14.01.44.
P/O	George Edmund	SANKEY	31.05.42.
Sgt	Harry Bertram John	SARGENT	05.04.43.
F/Sgt	Harold Max	SAUNDERS	17.12.43.
F/Sgt	Edwin Robert	SAVAGE	28.01.45.
S/L	Murray Stanley Fuller	SCHNEIDER	09.10.43.
W/OII	Gordon Raymond	SCHNEIDER	17.12.43.
F/O	Arthur Bennett	SCHULTZ	30.01.44.
P/O	Meyer Edsel	SCHWARTZ	24.02.44.
W/OI	William Lawrence	SCOTT	28.06.42.
P/O	Peter John MacIntyre	SCOTT	23.11.43.
P/O	Norman Lester William	SCOTT	07.01.45.
Sgt	Jack Clarence	SCOTTEN	10.09.42.
F/Sgt	Ernest Harold	SELLAR	21.02.43.
P/O	Dudley Thomas	SERVISS	04.05.44.
F/O	Carl John	SHAGENA	21.02.43.
Sgt	George Henry	SHANNON	02.10.42.
Sgt	Jack Wilson	SHARPLES	11.06.44.
Sgt	Robert James Abadore	SHAW	15.12.42.
Sgt	John McDonald	SHAW	29.06.44.
F/Sgt	William	SHELDON	24.09.42.
P/O	John Edward	SHEPHERD	04.05.44.
F/O	Walter Fitzgerald	SHEPPARD	17.12.43.
Sgt	Leslie Roland	SHEWARD	01.10.42.
F/L	Harold Gordon	SHOCKLEY	12.03.43.
W/OII	Lawrence	SIDNEY	30.06.42.
Sgt	Alexander	SIMPSON	30.06.42.
F/L	William	SINCLAIR	09.05.44.
P/O	Stanley John	SLADE	28.09.43.
W/OII	Stewart	SLEETH	27.04.43.
F/Sgt	Henry Maximilian	SLEZAK	27.07.42.
Sgt	Ivan Edward	SMEDLEY	30.01.44.
Sgt	Eric Omer	SMITH	27.06.42.
Sgt	William	SMITH	27.07.42.
F/Sgt	Dennis Frederick	SMITH	14.01.44.
F/L	George John	SMITH	01.05.44.
F/Sgt	Eric George	SMITH	16.06.44.
P/O	Norman Lawrence Lavek	SMITH	16.01.45.
P/O	Gerald Albert	SMITH	28.01.45.
F/O	Donald George	SMITH	15.03.45.
Sgt	Roy Peter	SMITH	19.03.45.
P/O	Michael Sydney	SMYTH	25.07.43.
W/OII	Lloyd Elsworth	SNARR	20.12.42.
P/O	Merlin Kelmer	SOLHEIM	08.11.41.

F/L	Josph Jules Henry Oliver	SOUAILLARD	14.01.44.
F/L	Leslie Garwood	SPARLING	07.01.45.
P/O	Gordon Douglas	SPEARMAN	07.05.44.
F/O	Lloyd George	SPEYER	21.01.44.
F/O	Lawrence William	SPLATT	07.01.45.
P/O	Robert Leslie	SQUIRES	07.05.44.
F/Sgt	Joseph Gordon	St.LOUIS	17.09.42.
F/O	Bruce Anderson	St.LOUIS	28.09.43.
P/O	Armand Leon Joseph	St.PIERRE	09.02.45.
F/O	Douglas Hazen	STAMERS	17.12.43.
F/Sgt	Melville James	STANLEY	29.11.42.
Sgt	Edwin	STANSFIELD	15.08.41.
Sgt	Reginald Ralph	STEVENS	21.01.44.
W/OII	Robert William	STEWART	15.12.42.
F/O	Ernest	STOLLERY	20.12.42.
Sgt	Harold	STONE	02.09.42.
P/O	Thomas Allen	STONE	09.02.45.
F/Sgt	John Lawrence	STORDY	27.04.43.
Sgt	Joshua Ernest	STOTT	15.08.41.
Sgt	Gerald Lee	STRANG	17.12.43.
P/O	Douglas Alfred	STREET	27.07.42.
P/O	George Frederick	STRONG	24.07.42.
Sgt	Walter Irvine	STROTHER	18.09.41.
F/Sgt	Reginald Victor	STUART	07.04.43.
F/Sgt	Arthur Douglas	SWANSBURG	27.07.42.
P/O	Claude Michael	SYLVAH	09.05.44.
Sgt	George Bertram	TATHAM	28.06.42.
Sgt	Cyril	TATTON	24.07.41.
Sgt	George Robert Ian	TAYLOR	29.11.42.
F/Sgt	James Alexander Campbell	TAYLOR	05.04.43.
W/OI	Norman Henry Arthur	TAYLOR	12.06.43.
F/O	Joseph Greig	TAYLOR	09.10.43.
F/L	William	THATCHER	14.01.44.
F/Sgt	Ronald Mason	THOMAS	02.08.41.
Sgt	Douglas Arthur	THOMAS	03.08.43.
Sgt	Norman Watson	THOMPSON	18.09.41.
F/Sgt	John Albert	THOMPSON	02.06.42.
Sgt	Thomas	THOMSON	17.11.43.
F/Sgt	Martin Athur	THORNHILL	11.06.44.
W/OII	William Charles	THURLOW	24.07.42.
Sgt	George Albert	TILLEY	10.03.42.
F/O	Joseph	TITE	22.12.44.
F/Sgt	Gerald Robert	TITUS	27.07.42.
Sgt	Kenneth Richard	TOLLER	12.08.42.
F/O	Marcel Emmett	TOMCZAK	25.07.43.

F/O	Mansell Matthew	TOMLINSON	15.10.42.
Sgt	Cyril Wallace Langford	TONGUE	24.02.44.
P/O	John Walter	TONKYN	23.04.44.
F/O	Elwood Albert	TOWNSEND	29.07.44.
F/O	Temple Daeson	TRIPPE	28.09.43.
P/O	Ronald Victor	TRUEMAN	24.07.41.
Sgt	James Luther	TURNBULL	02.06.42.
Sgt	Benjamin Warren	TURNER	21.02.43.
F/O	Walter Brian	TURNER	28.01.45.
Sgt	Frederick Peter	TURTON	18.09.41.
P/O	William Stone	TYLER	15.04.42.
Sgt	Edwin Florence	UREN	17.11.43.
F/Sgt	Norman Albert	VAN BRUNT	20.12.42.
P/O	Robert Hilary	VAUGHAN	10.08.42.
P/O	Daniel	VERI	07.01.45.
F/Sgt	Aaron Joseph Ronnie	VINEBERG	01.10.42.
F/O	Frederick Harold	VINEY	17.08.43.
F/L	James Denholm	VIRTUE	21.07.44.
P/O	Jack Kenneth	VIVIAN	16.06.44.
F/Sgt	Woodrow Wilcox	WADDELL	09.11.42.
Sgt	John Joseph	WADDELL	14.01.44.
F/Sgt	Ward Ralph	WADDLE	09.11.42.
F/Sgt	Leonard Alfred	WADMAN	31.05.42.
F/Sgt	Gerald Edward	WAGNER	20.12.42.
Sgt	Percy Thomas Walter	WALKER	22.10.41.
Sgt	John William	WALKER	30.01.44.
Sgt	Lionel Robert	WALLACE	07.04.43.
F/Sgt	Cecil Stephen	WALSH	30.06.42.
P/O	Robert	WASHER	20.12.42.
Sgt	Kenneth Storey	WATSON	27.07.42.
F/Sgt	Louis Gilbert	WATSON	15.12.42.
Sgt	Ivor	WATTERS	01.08.42.
P/O	Ernest Miller	WATTS	29.08.41.
Sgt	Ronald Everest	WATTS	02.01.44.
F/O	Glen Mason	WEAVER	04.05.44.
P/O	William Miskimon	WEBB	24.09.42.
F/Sgt	Gerald Arthur	WELSH	31.05.42.
F/L	James Chrystall	WERNHAM	30.03.44.
Sgt	Brian Sidney James	WEST	02.01.44.
Sgt	Albert James	WESTERN	24.07.42.
F/O	Robert George Murray	WHIGHAM	24.07.41.
Sgt	George Arthur	WHITE	30.06.42.
W/OII	John Day	WHITE	03.04.43.
F/Sgt	Edward Kenneth Eddie	WHITE	25.07.43.
F/O	Herbert Asquith	WICKENS	16.06.44.

Sgt	Edwin John	WILLIAMS	28.12.41.
F/Sgt	Lionel Harry	WILLIAMS	02.10.42.
F/O	Frederick Harold	WILSHER	29.12.44.
F/O	George Stephen	WILSON	28.05.43.
P/O	Kenneth Carl	WILSON	21.01.44.
F/Sgt	Thomas Austin	WITHERS	27.07.42.
P/O	Ernest Maurice	WITT	14.07.43.
F/Sgt	Peter	WITYCK	05.01.42.
S/L	Denzil Lloyd	WOLFE	14.07.43.
Sgt	Cyril	WOOD	27.07.42.
Sgt	Albert Joseph	WOOD	25.07.43.
F/O	Kemble Russell	WOOD	20.10.43.
Sgt	Stanley	WOODMAN	01.08.42.
F/O	Hardy Edward	WORT	15.03.45.
Sgt	William	WRIGHT	10.03.42.
F/O	Ralph James	WRIGHT	05.04.43.
Sgt	Ronald Ivor	YORK	16.09.44.
Sgt	Ronald	ZIMMER	02.01.44.

405 (VANCOUVER) SQUADRON

MOTTO **DUCIMUS** (We lead).   Code **LQ**

STATIONS

DRIFFIELD	23.04.41. to 20.06.41.
POCKLINGTON	20.06.41. to 07.08.42.
TOPCLIFFE	07.08.42. to 24.10.42.
BEAULIEU (Coastal Command)	24.10.42. to 01.03.43.
TOPCLIFFE	01.03.43. to 06.03.43.
LEEMING	06.03.43. to 19.04.43.
GRANSDEN LODGE	19.04.43. to 25.05.45.

COMMANDING OFFICERS

SQUADRON LEADER D G TOMLINSON	08.05.41. to 20.05.41.
WING COMMANDER P A GILCHRIST DFC	20.05.41. to 24.07.41.
SQUADRON LEADER W B KEDDY (Temp)	25.07.41. to 16.08.41.
WING COMMANDER R M FENWICK-WILSON	17.08.41. to 16.02.42.
WING COMMANDER G D MacALLISTER	16.02.42. to 27.02.42.
WING COMMANDER J E FAUQUIER DFC	27.02.42. to 06.08.42.
WING COMMANDER L D G FRASER DFC	07.08.42. to 19.11.42.
WING COMMANDER A C P CLAYTON DFC	19.11.42. to 19.04.43.
WING COMMANDER J E FAUQUIER DFC	20.04.43. to 22.01.44.
WING COMMANDER R J LANE DSO DFC	22.01.44. to 22.08.44.
WING COMMANDER C W PALMER DFC	23.08.44. to 26.09.44.
WING COMMANDER H A MORRISON DSO DFC	27.09.44. to 09.10.44.
GROUP CAPTAIN W F M NEWSON DFC	09.10.44. to 05.09.45.

AIRCRAFT

WELLINGTON II	06.05.41. to 04.42.
HALIFAX II	04.42. to 09.43.
LANCASTER I/III/X	08.43. to 09.45.

OPERATIONAL RECORD
ALL GROUPS ALL TYPES

OPERATIONS	SORTIES	AIRCRAFT LOSSES	% LOSSES
452	3852	112	2.9

CATEGORY OF OPERATIONS

BOMBING	MINING	LEAFLET
450	0	2

4 GROUP
ALL TYPES

OPERATIONS	SORTIES	AIRCRAFT LOSSES	% LOSSES
122	918	46	5.0

CATEGORY OF OPERATIONS

BOMBING	MINING	LEAFLET
120	0	2

WELLINGTONS

OPERATIONS	SORTIES	AIRCRAFT LOSSES	% LOSSES
86	522	20	3.8

CATEGORY OF OPERATIONS

BOMBING
86

HALIFAXES

OPERATIONS	SORTIES	AIRCRAFT LOSSES	% LOSSES
36	396	26	6.6

CATEGORY OF OPERATIONS

BOMBING
86

6 GROUP

HALIFAXES

OPERATIONS	SORTIES	AIRCRAFT LOSSES	% LOSSES
13	55	4	7.3

CATEGORY OF OPERATIONS

BOMBING	MINING
13	1

8 GROUP

ALL TYPES

OPERATIONS	SORTIES	AIRCRAFT LOSSES	% LOSSES
317	2879	62	2.1

CATEGORY OF OPERATIONS

BOMBING	MINING	LEAFLET
120	1	2

HALIFAXES

OPERATIONS	SORTIES	AIRCRAFT LOSSES	% LOSSES
29	330	12	3.6

CATEGORY OF OPERATIONS

BOMBING	MINING
120	1

LANCASTERS

OPERATIONS	SORTIES	AIRCRAFT LOSSES	% LOSSES
288	2549	50	2.0

CATEGORY OF OPERATIONS

BOMBING
288

Aircraft Histories

WELLINGTON.   **From April 1941 to April 1942.**

W5368 LQ-K	From 142 Squadron. To 12 Squadron.
W5390 LQ-X	From 21 Operational Training Unit. FTR Dortmund 14/15.4.42.
W5421 LQ-T	To 12 Squadron.
W5427 LQ-N	From 12 Squadron. FTR Dortmund 14/15.4.42.
W5476 LQ-H	FTR Hamburg 30.11/1.12.41.
W5483 LQ-J	FTR Berlin 2/3.8.41.
W5484 LQ-G	To 12 Squadron.
W5487	Destroyed by fire during an enemy air raid on Driffield 4.6.41.
W5488 LQ-D/B	FTR Duisburg 28/29.8.41.
W5489 LQ-A	Destroyed by fire at Pocklington on return from Frankfurt 25.10.41.
W5490 LQ-D	Crashed on approach to Pocklington on return from Dortmund 7.7.41.
W5491	To 104 Squadron.
W5492 LQ-K	Crashed near Pocklington during an air test 18.9.41.
W5493	To 104 Squadron.
W5495 LQ-W	To 12 Squadron.
W5496 LQ-M	FTR Hannover 14/15.8.41.
W5497 LQ-M	Crashed while landing at Pocklington on return from training 18.3.42.
W5498	From 104 Squadron. To 1448 Flight.
W5515 LQ-R/Y	To 305 (Polish) Squadron.
W5516 LQ-D	FTR Kiel 26/27.2.42.
W5518	To 15 Operational Training Unit.
W5521 LQ-P	FTR Berlin 7/8.9.41.
W5522 LQ-Q	FTR Cologne 16/17.6.41.
W5525	To 158 Squadron.
W5527 LQ-F	FTR Hamburg 2/3.8.41.
W5530 LQ-L	To 1443 Flight.
W5531 LQ-U	From 158 Squadron. Crashed in Suffolk on return from Essen 13.4.42.
W5534 LQ-N	FTR Hannover 14/15.7.41.
W5535	Crashed near Pocklington while training 1.9.41.
W5537 LQ-Q/O	FTR Brest 24.7.41.
W5550	To 305 (Polish) Squadron.
W5551 LQ-U	FTR Brest 24.7.41.
W5553 LQ-D	FTR Berlin 7/8.11.41.
W5560 LQ-M	Crash-landed at Lindholme following early return from Wilhelmshaven 22.12.41.
W5561 LQ-J	From 104 Squadron. FTR Emden 28/29.12.41.
W5562	From 158 Squadron. Returned to 158 Squadron.
W5564 LQ-Q	To 158 Squadron.
W5565	To 1443 Flight.
W5572	To 1443 Flight.
W5581 LQ-V	Ditched off Cornwall on return from Brest 24.7.41.

W5589 LQ-F		From 104 Squadron. Crashed while trying to force-land in Yorkshire during an air-test 5.1.42.
W5595		To 104 Squadron.
Z8329 LQ-L		Ditched in the North Sea following early return from Bremen 17.1.42.
Z8344 LQ-F		FTR Stettin 19/20.9.41.
Z8358 LQ-B		From 104 Squadron. FTR Hamburg 8/9.4.42.
Z8375		From 218 Squadron. To 158 Squadron.
Z8412 LQ-P		To 158 Squadron.
Z8414 LQ-U		To 104 Squadron.
Z8418		To 1443 Flight.
Z8419 LQ-V		From 104 Squadron. FTR Le Havre 22/23.10.41.
Z8420		To 158 Squadron.
Z8421 LQ-T		To 15 Operational Training Unit.
Z8428 LQ-N		FTR Essen 10/11.3.42.
Z8431 LQ-J		From 218 Squadron. To 12 Squadron.
Z8437		From 218 Squadron. To 12 Squadron.
Z8439		From 21 Operational Training Unit. To 158 Squadron.
Z8493		To 12 Squadron.
Z8521		To 158 Squadron.
Z8527 LQ-L		FTR Poissy 1/2.4.42.
Z8530 LQ-A		Abandoned over Hampshire on return from Dortmund 15.4.42.
Z8577		To 158 Squadron.
Z8585		To 158 Squadron.
Z8596		To 305 (Polish) Squadron.
Z8597		To 158 Squadron.

HALIFAX. **From April 1942 to September 1943.**

R9363 LQ-Q	From 78 Squadron. Conversion Flight only. To 408 (Goose) Squadron RCAF Conversion Flight.
R9368	From 78 Squadron. Conversion Flight only. To 1659 CU.
R9369	From 78CF. Conversion Flight only. To 1659 Conversion Flight.
R9386	From 78 Squadron. Concersion Flight only. To 1659 Conversion Flight.
R9420	From 78 Squadron. Conversion Flight only. To 1659 Conversion Flight.
R9437	From 78 Squadron. Conversion Flight only. To 1659 Conversion Flight.
R9448	From 35 (Madras Presidency) Squadron. Conversion Flight only. To 1659 Conversion Flight.
R9483	From 35 (Madras Presidency) Squadron. Conversion Flight only. To 1659 Conversion Flight.
W1019	From 35 (Madras Presidency) Squadron. To 419 (Moose) Squadron RCAF.
W1092 LQ-A	To 1659 Conversion Flight.
W1094 LQ-B/F	Crashed on approach to St Eval on return from anti-submarine patrol 26.11.42. (Coastal Command).
W1095 LQ-N	To 1659 Conversion Flight.
W1096 LQ-O	Crashed in Essex 17.11.42. (Coastal Command).

W1097 LQ-P	Crash-landed at Aberporth while training 12.7.42.	
W1109 LQ-S	FTR Düsseldorf 31.7/1.8.42.	
W1110 LQ-C	FTR Bremen 27/28.6.42.	
W1111 LQ-D	FTR Essen 8/9.6.42.	
W1112 LQ-E	To 1659 Conversion Flight.	
W1113 LQ-G	FTR Bremen 29/30.6.42.	
W1145 LQ-S	Abandoned by crew near Binbrook following return from Emden 7.6.42.	
W1152	To Middle East.	
W1173	From 35 (Madras Presidency) Squadron. To 1659 Conversion Flight.	
W1175 LQ-Q	FTR Bremen 27/28.6.42.	
W1186 LQ-P	FTR Hamburg 26/27.7.42.	
W1230 LQ-L	FTR Hamburg 26/27.7.42.	
W1274 LQ-R	FTR Flensburg 23/24.9.42.	
W7703 LQ-Q	Crashed while trying to land at West Malling on return from Aachen 6.10.42	
W7704 LQ-M	To 1659 Conversion Flight via 405 (Vancouver) Squadron Conversion Flight.	
W7707 LQ-K	FTR Cologne 30/31.5.42.	
W7708 LQ-H	FTR Essen 8/9.6.42.	
W7709 LQ-J	FTR Osnabrück 9/10.8.42.	
W7710 LQ-R	FTR Flensburg 1/2.10.42.	
W7713 LQ-T	FTR Essen 1/2.6.42.	
W7714 LQ-K	FTR Bremen 29/30.6.42.	
W7715 LQ-H	FTR Bremen 29/30.6.42.	
W7718 LQ-T	From 10 Squadron. FTR Düsseldorf 31.7/1.8.42.	
W7748 LQ-D	FTR Mainz 11/12.8.42.	
W7763 LQ-C	FTR Osnabrück 6/7.10.42.	
W7768	Crashed on the Isle of Wight on return from Coastal Command patrol 20.12.42.	
W7769 LQ-Q/K	Crashed on approach to Pocklington on return from Duisburg 24.7.42.	
W7770 LQ-E	FTR Essen 16/17.9.42.	
W7780 LQ-Q	FTR Flensburg 1/2.10.42.	
W7802 LQ-T	FTR Flensburg 1/2.10.42.	
W7803 LQ-B	FTR Stuttgart 11/12.3.43.	
W7810	To 1659 Conversion Flight.	
W7853	To 1659 Conversion Flight.	
W7854 LQ-T	FTR Cologne 15/16.10.42.	
W7885	From 35 (Madras Presidency) Squadron. Returned to 35 (Madras Presidency) Squadron.	
BB210	To 1659 Conversion Flight.	
BB212 LQ-P/U	FTR Stuttgart 11/12.3.43.	
BB215	Crashed on landing at Penrhos 11.12.42. (Coastal Command).	
BB216 LQ-D	Crashed in Lincolnshire following early return from Saarbrücken 1.9.42.	
BB250 LQ-E	FTR Stuttgart 11/12.3.43.	
BB334	From 138 Squadron. Returned to 138 Squadron.	
BB367	From Navigation Training Unit. To 1669 Conversion Unit.	

BB369	From Navigation Training Unit. To 1664 Conversion Unit.
BB372	To 35 (Madras presidency) Squadron.
BB373	To 78 Squadron.
BB374	To 1658 Conversion Unit.
DG224 LQ-U	FTR Essen 8/9.6.42.
DG228 LQ-H	FTR Krefeld 2/3.10.42.
DT487 LQ-M	Karlsruhe 2/3.9.42.
DT507	To 1659 Conversion Flight.
DT514	Crashed on landing at Predannock 17.1.43. (Coastal Command).
DT515	To 76 Squadron.
DT551	To 1659 Conversion Flight.
DT553	To 1659 Conversion Flight.
DT560	To 1666 Conversion Unit.
DT562	Struck Off Charge 12.1.43.
DT565	To 1659 Conversion Flight.
DT573	To 1659 Conversion Flight.
DT576 LQ-U	Crashed soon after take-off from Topcliffe on ferry flight 29.11.42.
DT624	Crashed near Beaulieu 15.12.42. (Coastal Command). Repaired. To 1659 Conversion Flight.
DT633	Crashed near Beaulieu 21.2.43. (Coastal Command).
DT695	To 1652 Conversion Unit.
DT699 LQ-G	FTR from mining sortie 6/7.4.43.
DT704 LQ-H	FTR Kiel 4/5.4.43.
DT723 LQ-F	FTR Essen 3/4.4.43.
DT741 LQ-P	FTR Essen 30.4/1.5.43.
DT745 LQ-V	FTR Stuttgart 11/12.3.43.
DT772	To 408 (Goose) Squadron RCAF.
DT802	To 1659 Conversion Flight.
DT808 LQ-V	From 102 (Ceylon) Squadron. FTR Essen 3/4.4.43.
HR723	To 35 (Madras Presidency) Squadron.
HR796	From Navigation Training Unit. To 1667 Conversion Unit.
HR797 LQ-A	FTR Düsseldorf 11/12.6.43.
HR800	From Navigation Training Unit. To 1666 Conversion Unit.
HR804	To 35 (Madras Presidency) Squadron.
HR805	To 10 Squadron.
HR806 LQ-D	Crashed almost immediately after take-off from Gransden Lodge when bound for Düsseldorf 25.5.43.
HR807 LQ-G	FTR Essen 27/28.5.43.
HR808	Crashed on landing at Gransden Lodge while training 18.6.43.
HR809	Crashed on landing at Gransden Lodge while training 2.9.43.
HR810 LQ-X	FTR Mannheim 5/6.9.43.
HR811	To 35 (Madras presidency) Squadron.
HR813 LQ-H	FTR Cologne 3/4.7.43.
HR816 LQ-C	FTR Wuppertal 24/25.6.43.
HR817 LQ-C	FTR Peenemünde 17/18.8.43.
HR832	Crashed in Norfolk during a training flight 16.6.43.

HR833	To 35 (Madras Presidency) Squadron.
HR841	To 35 (Madras Presidency) Squadron.
HR847	To 35 (Madras Presidency) Squadron.
HR849 LQ-E	FTR Hamburg 2/3.8.43.
HR854 LQ-A	FTR Montbeliard 15/16.7.43.
HR856 LQ-W	FTR Turin 16/17.8.43.
HR857	To 35 (Madras Presidency) Squadron.
HR860	To 10 Squadron.
HR864 LQ-M	FTR Essen 25/26.7.43.
HR867	To 102 (Ceylon) Squadron.
HR871 LQ-B	FTR Hamburg 2/3.8.43.
HR872 LQ-K	FTR Mannheim 9/10.8.43.
HR876	To 35 (Madras Presidency) Squadron.
HR905 LQ-G	FTR Aachen 13/14.7.43.
HR910	To 419 (Moose) Squadron RCAF.
HR915 LQ-O	FTR Berlin 31.8/1.9.43.
HR916	To 35 (Madras Presidency) Squadron.
HR917 LQ-G	FTR Hamburg 2/3.8.43.
HR918 LQ-G	FTR Berlin 23/24.8.43.
HR923 LQ-V	FTR Berlin 23/24.8.43.
HR929	To 35 (Madras Presidency) Squadron.
HR984	To 35 (Madras Presidency) Squadron.
HR988	To 428 (Ghost) Squadron RCAF.
HX147	To 35 (Madras Presidency) Squadron.
JB797	To 1658 Conversion Unit.
JB798	To 78 Squadron.
JB875	To 78 Squadron.
JB893	Struck JB906 at Leeming 4.4.43. Repaired. To 408 (Goose) Squadron RCAF.
JB896 LQ-C	FTR Dortmund 23/24.5.43.
JB897 LQ-T	Crash-landed on approach to Wyton on return from Dortmund 5.5.43.
JB899	To 10 Squadron.
JB904 LQ-E	FTR Dortmund 4/5.5.43.
JB905 LQ-G	To 1658 Conversion Unit.
JB906	Struck by JB893 at Leeming 4.4.43 and damaged beyond repair.
JB907	To 78 Squadron.
JB914	Crashed on landing at Leeming during training 13.4.43.
JB916	To 1659 Conversion Flight.
JB917	To 419 Squadron.
JB919	To 77 Squadron.
JB920 LQ-F	FTR Duisburg 26/27.4.43.
JB957 LQ-A	Crash-landed in Huntingdonshire on return from Dortmund 5.5.43.
JB963	To 77 Squadron.
JB966 LQ-D	FTR Bochum 13/14.5.43.
JD123	To 77 Squadron.
JD124 LQ-P	FTR Krefeld 21/22.6.43.

LANCASTER. **From August 1943.**

W4891	From 156 Squadron. To 1 Lancaster Finishing School.
ED842	From 156 Squadron. Training only. To Navigation Training Unit.
ED911	From 97 (Straits Settlement) Squadron. Crash-landed near Gransden Lodge during training 3.9.43.
JA909 LQ-O	From 156 Squadron. To 467 Squadron RAAF.
JA920 LQ-E	From 83 Squadron. Damaged beyond repair in taxying accident at Gransden Lodge after returning from Nuremberg 11.8.43.
JA924 LQ-X/R	From 83 Squadron. FTR Berlin 30/31.1.44.
JA939 LQ-C	FTR Berlin 23/24.11.43.
JA974 LQ-V	From 97 (Straits Settlement) Squadron. FTR Braunschweig 14/15.1.44.
JA976 LQ-E/S	From 97 (Straits Settlement) Squadron. FTR Montzen 27/28.4.44.
JA979	Crashed on approach to Gransden Lodge while training 5.11.43
JA980 LQ-Z	From 7 Squadron. FTR Hannover 8/9.10.43.
JB120 LQ-D	FTR Hannover 27/28.9.43.
JB180 LQ-B	To 83 Squadron.
JB182 LQ-O	From 156 Squadron. FTR Berlin 23/24.11.43.
JB183 LQ-G	From 97 (Straits Settlement) Squadron. To Navigation Training Unit.
JB188 LQ-S	FTR Magdeburg 21/22.1.44.
JB222 LQ-M	FTR Leipzig 3/4.12.43.
JB226 LQ-G	FTR Ludwigshafen 17/18.11.43.
JB230	To 156 Squadron.
JB241 LQ-K	FTR Schweinfurt 24/25.2.44.
JB280 LQ-K	FTR Berlin 1/2.1.44.
JB286 LQ-O/R	To 467 Squadron RAAF.
JB297 LQ-X	To 166 Squadron.
JB307	To 156 Squadron.
JB348 LQ-R	From 97 (Straits Settlement) Squadron. FTR Leipzig 20/21.10.43.
JB369 LQ-O	Crashed in Cambridgeshire on return from Berlin 16.12.43.
JB374 LQ-Z	From Navigation Training Unit. Returned to Navigation Training Unit.
JB410 LQ-D	From 97 (Straits Settlement) Squadron. To 576 Squadron.
JB477 LQ-D	Crashed in Huntingdonshire on return from Berlin 17.12.43.
JB481 LQ-R	Crashed in Norfolk on return from Berlin 17.12.43.
JB482	To 97 (Straits Settlement) Squadron.
JB484 LQ-T/B	To Navigation Training Unit.
JB543	To 7 Squadron.
JB644 LQ-C	To 166 Squadron.
JB668 LQ-T/M/R	FTR Schweinfurt 24/25.2.44.
JB669	From Telecommunications Research Establishment.
JB675	From 7 Squadron. No operations. To 635 Squadron.
JB684 LQ-U	From 7 Squadron. FTR Laon 22/23.4.44.
JB699 LQ-J	From 7 Squadron. To 156 Squadron.
JB707 LQ-O/M	FTR Stuttgart 28/29.7.44.
JB713	From 7 Squadron. No operations. To 635 Squadron.

JB728		To 97 (Straits Settlement) Squadron.
JB729	LQ-E	FTR Lens 15/16.6.44.
JB737	LQ-R	FTR Berlin 1/2.1.44.
KB700	LQ-Q	To 419 (Moose) Squadron RCAF.
KB945	LQ-T	No operations.
KB949	LQ-U	No operations.
KB950	LQ-O	No operations.
KB952	LQ-X	No operations.
KB955	LQ-U	No operations.
KB956	LQ-N	From 408 (Goose) Squadron RCAF. No operations.
KB957	LQ-W	No operations.
KB959	LQ-Y	No operations.
KB961	LQ-A	From 408 (Goose) Squadron RCAF. No operations.
KB964	LQ-B	
KB965	LQ-D	
KB967	LQ-H	No operations.
KB968	LQ-P	No operations.
KB973	LQ-F	No operations.
KB976	LQ-K	No operations.
KB977	LQ-E	No operations.
KB985		No operations.
KB991	LQ-G	No operations.
KB997	LQ-C	No operations.
KB999	LQ-M	From 419 (Moose) Squadron RCAF. No operations.
LM340	LQ-A/H	From 467 Squadron RAAF. To 635 Squadron and back. To 57 Squadron.
LM345	LQ-L	From 156 Squadron. FTR Braunschweig 27/28.9.43.
ME304	LQ-J	To 467 Squadron RAAF.
ME315	LQ-K	From 7 Squadron.
ME370	LQ-K	From 7 Squadron.
ME379	LQ-B	
ME445		From 582 Squadron.
ME622	LQ-H	From Signals Intelligence Unit. FTR Stuttgart 15/16.3.44.
ND330	OL-O	On loan from 83 Squadron. FTR Berlin 2/3.1.44.
ND341	LQ-S	FTR Braunschweig 14/15.1.44.
ND342		To 156 Squadron.
ND343	LQ-H/J	From 97 (Straits Settlement) Squadron. FTR Lens 15/16.6.44.
ND344	LQ-M/V	FTR Tours 11/12.6.44.
ND347	LQ-W	From 7 Squadron. FTR Haine-St-Pierre 8/9.5.44.
ND348		To 156 Squadron.
ND352	LQ-T	FTR Versailles 10/11.6.44.
ND412	LQ-M/P	To 630 Squadron.
ND423	LQ-K	FTR Braunschweig 14/15.1.44.
ND444		To 156 Squadron.
ND462	LQ-J	FTR Berlin 30/31.1.44.
ND464	LQ-V	To 83 Squadron.
ND477		To 156 Squadron.

ND493 LQ-S	FTR Berlin 30/31.1.44.	
ND507 LQ-C	From 83 Squadron. FTR Trappes 2/3.6.44.	
ND524 LQ-G	From 83 Squadron. To 635 Squadron.	
ND526 LQ-M	FTR Aachen 24/25.5.44.	
ND529	To 83 Squadron.	
ND577	To 156 Squadron.	
ND587 LQ-D	FTR Haine-St-Pierre 8/9.5.44.	
ND616 LQ-M/A/D	To Navigation Training Unit.	
ND617 LQ-B	From 97 (Straits Settlement) Squadron. FTR Mantes-la-Jolie 6/7.5.44.	
ND645	To 35 (Madras Presidency) Squadron.	
ND653	To 35 (Madras Presidency) Squadron.	
ND709 LQ-G	From 582 Squadron.	
ND855 LQ-V	From 156 Squadron. To 1667 Conversion Unit.	
ND881 LQ-Q	FTR Montdidier Airfield 3/4.5.44.	
ND912 LQ-X	From 7 Squadron. FTR Politz 8/9.2.45.	
ND916	From 35 (Madras Presidency) Squadron.	
ND974	To 83 Squadron.	
ND980 LQ-W	To 1668 Conversion Unit.	
ND982 LQ-E	To 630 Squadron.	
NE119 LQ-P	From 156 Squadron. FTR Misburg 15/16.3.45.	
NE126	To 7 Squadron.	
NE140	From 582 Squadron. To 1656 Conversion Unit.	
NE180 LQ-C	To 635 Squadron.	
NG437 LQ-M		
PA965 LQ-X/B/D		
PA970 LQ-Y	FTR Le Havre 8.9.44.	
PA972 LQ-D	Crashed on take-off from Gransden Lodge when bound for Stuttgart 25.7.44.	
PA977 LQ-T/A/D	From 635 Squadron. FTR Bingen 22/23.12.44.	
PA980 LQ-E	FTR Metz 28/29.6.44.	
PA981 LQ-K	From 582 Squadron. FTR Wanne-Eickel 12.9.44.	
PA982 LQ-U/V/E	From 156 Squadron. To 7 Squadron.	
PA987	To 635 Squadron.	
PA988 LQ-P	From 35 (Madras Presidency) Squadron. FTR Stettin 16/17.8.44.	
PB113 LQ-J	Crash-landed in Norfolk on return from Bingen 22.12.44.	
PB129 LQ-A	FTR Cap Gris Nez 26.9.44.	
PB174 LQ-P	FTR Bottrop 20/21.7.44.	
PB183 LQ-B/E/C	From 35 (Madras Presidency) Squadron. FTR Dresden 13/14.2.45.	
PB184	To 582 Squadron.	
PB188	To 83 Squadron.	
PB229 LQ-H/X	FTR Munich 7/8.1.45.	
PB233 LQ-O	To 7 Squadron.	
PB239 LQ-D	FTR Kiel 16/17.8.44.	
PB262 LQ-B	Struck Off Charge 12.9.44.	
PB267 LQ-X	From 582 Squadron.	
PB282 LQ-X/Y	From 635 Squadron. To 1656 Conversion Unit.	

PB288 LQ-D	From 35 (Madras Presidency) Squadron.
PB292	To 83 Squadron.
PB402 LQ-D/M	FTR Zeitz 16/17.1.45.
PB413 LQ-K	Force-landed at Debden on return from Düsseldorf 2.11.44.
PB451 LQ-G	From 635 Squadron. FTR Witten 18/19.3.45.
PB452	To 83 Squadron.
PB477 LQ-B	From 635 Squadron. FTR Nuremberg 2/3.1.45.
PB507	To 156 Squadron.
PB511	To 582 Squadron.
PB513 LQ-H/U	From 7 Squadron. To 467 Squadron RAAF.
PB516 LQ-T	From 156 Squadron. FTR Misburg 15/16.3.45.
PB521	To 97 (Straits Settlement) Squadron.
PB525 LQ-P	From 582 Squadron. FTR Scholven-Buer 29/30.12.44.
PB527 LQ-K	From 635 Squadron. FTR Kiel 15/16.9.44.
PB530 LQ-W/Q	From 582 Squadron. FTR Dortmund 20/21.2.45.
PB555 LQ-O	From 635 Squadron.
PB585 LQ-P	From 635 Squadron.
PB614 LQ-V	From 35 (Madras Presidency) Squadron.
PB627 LQ-J	From 635 Squadron.
PB628 LQ-W	From 635 Squadron.
PB650 LQ-U	FTR Stuttgart 28/29.1.45.
PB653 LQ-V	To 467 Squadron RAAF.
PB681 LQ-M	From 582 Squadron. To 1667 Conversion Unit.
PB682 LQ-A	To 106 Squadron via Navigation Training Unit.
SW255 LQ-A	From 35 (Madras Presidency) Squadron.

HEAVIEST SINGLE LOSS 11/12.03.43. Stuttgart. 4 Halifaxes FTR.